France For Dummies
3rd Edition

D0367337

A List of Handy French Words and Phrases

English	French	Pronunciation
Thank you	Merci	mair-*see*
Please	S'il vous plaît	seel voo *play*
Yes/No/and	Oui/Non/et	wee/nohn/ay
Do you speak English?	Parlez-vous anglais?	par-lay-voo ahn-*glay*
I don't understand	Je ne comprends pas	jhuh ne kohm-*prahn* pah
I'm sorry/Excuse me	Pardon	pahr-*dohn*
Good day/Good evening	Bonjour/Bonsoir	bohn-*jhoor*/bohn-*swahr*
My name is . . .	Je m'appelle	jhuh ma-*pell*
Miss	Mademoiselle	mad-mwa-*zel*
Mr.	Monsieur	muh-*syuh*
Mrs.	Madame	ma-*dam*
Where is/are . . . ?	Où est/sont . . . ?	ooh-eh?/ooh-sohn?
. . . the toilets?	les toilettes?	lay twa-*lets*?
. . . the bus station?	la gare routière?	lah gar roo-tee-*air*?
. . . the hospital?	l'hôpital	low-pee-*tahl*?
to the right/to the left	à droite/à gauche	ah drwaht/ah goash
straight ahead	tout droit	too-drwah
a ticket	un billet	uh *bee*-yay
one-way ticket	aller simple	ah-*lay sam*-pluh
round-trip ticket	aller-retour	ah-*lay* ree-*toor*
I want to get off at . . .	Je voudrais descendre à	jhe voo-dray day-son-drah-ah
I would like . . .	Je voudrais	jhe voo-dray
a room	une chambre	ewn *shahm*-bruh
the key	la clé	lah clay
a phonecard	une carte téléphonique	ewn cart tay-lay-fone-*eek*
aspirin	des aspirines	deyz ahs-peer-*eens*
How much does it cost?	C'est combien?	say comb-bee-*ehn*?
Do you take credit cards?	Est-ce que vous acceptez cartes de credit?	es-kuh voo zak-sep-*tay* lay kart duh creh-*dee*?

French Numbers and Ordinals

English	French	Pronunciation
zero	zéro	*zare*-oh
one	un	oon
two	deux	duh
three	trois	twah
four	quatre	*kaht*-ruh
five	cinq	sank
six	six	seess
seven	sept	set
eight	huit	wheat
nine	neuf	nuhf
ten	dix	deess
eleven	onze	ohnz
twelve	douze	dooz
thirteen	treize	trehz
fourteen	quatorze	kah-*torz*
fifteen	quinze	kanz
sixteen	seize	sez
seventeen	dix-sept	deez-*set*
eighteen	dix-huit	deez-*wheat*
nineteen	dix-neuf	deez-*nuhf*
twenty	vingt	vehn
twenty-one	vingt-et-un	vehnt-ay-*oon*
twenty-two	vingt-deux	vehnt-*duh*
thirty	trente	trahnt
forty	quarante	ka-*rahnt*
fifty	cinquante	sang-*kahnt*
sixty	soixante	swa-*sahnt*
seventy	soixante-dix	swa-sahnt-*deess*
eighty	quatre-vingts	kaht-ruh-*vehn*
ninety	quatre-vingt-dix	kaht-ruh-venh-*deess*
one hundred	cent	sahn

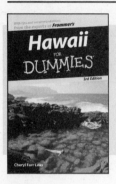
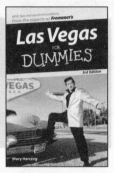

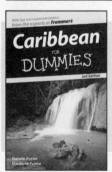
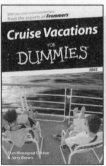

France
FOR
DUMMIES®
3RD EDITION

by Darwin Porter
and Danforth Prince

WILEY

Wiley Publishing, Inc.

France For Dummies®, 3rd Edition

Published by
Wiley Publishing, Inc.
111 River St.
Hoboken, NJ 07030-5774
www.wiley.com

Copyright © 2005 by Wiley Publishing, Inc., Indianapolis, Indiana

Published simultaneously in Canada

For general information on our other products and services, please contact our Customer Care Department within the U.S. at 800-762-2974, outside the U.S. at 317-572-3993, or fax 317-572-4002.

For technical support, please visit www.wiley.com/techsupport.

Wiley also publishes its books in a variety of electronic formats. Some content that appears in print may not be available in electronic books.

Library of Congress Control Number: 2005921458

ISBN-10: 0-7645-7701-8

ISBN-13: 978-07645-7701-7

Manufactured in the United States of America

10 9 8 7 6 5 4 3 2 1

3B/RS/QU/QV/IN

About the Authors

As a team of veteran travel writers, **Darwin Porter and Danforth Prince** have produced numerous titles for Frommers, including best-selling guides to Italy, France, the Caribbean, England, and Germany. Porter, a former bureau chief at *The Miami Herald,* is also a Hollywood biographer, his most recent releases entitled *Katharine the Great,* a close-up of the private life of the late Katharine Hepburn, and *Howard Hughes: Hell's Angel.* Prince was formerly employed by the Paris bureau of *The New York Times,* and is today the president of Blood Moon Productions and other media-related firms.

Publisher's Acknowledgments

We're proud of this book; please send us your comments through our Dummies online registration form located at www.dummies.com/register/. Some of the people who helped bring this book to market include the following:

Editorial

Editors: Tim Gallan, Michael Kelly

Copy Editor: E. Neil Johnson

Cartographer: Roberta Stockwell

Editorial Manager:
Christine Meloy Beck

Editorial Assistant:
Melissa S. Bennet

Senior Photo Editor: Richard Fox

Front Cover Photo: © Studio City/ eStock Photo. Description: Loire: Scenic of Chenonceaux Castle

Back Cover Photo: © Gavriel Jecan/ Corbis. Description: Provence-Alpes-Cote d'Azur: Rows of Lavender growing in field

Cartoons: Rich Tennant (www.the5thwave.com)

Composition Services

Project Coordinator: Kristie Rees

Layout and Graphics:
Lauren Goddard,
Stephanie D. Jumper,
Heather Ryan, Julie Trippetti

Proofreaders: David Faust,
Leeann Harney, TECHBOOKS
Productions Services

Indexer: TECHBOOKS Productions Services

Publishing and Editorial for Consumer Dummies

Diane Graves Steele, Vice President and Publisher, Consumer Dummies

Joyce Pepple, Acquisitions Director, Consumer Dummies

Kristin A. Cocks, Product Development Director, Consumer Dummies

Michael Spring, Vice President and Publisher, Travel

Kelly Regan, Editorial Director, Travel

Publishing for Technology Dummies

Andy Cummings, Vice President and Publisher, Dummies Technology/General User

Composition Services

Gerry Fahey, Vice President of Production Services

Debbie Stailey, Director of Composition Services

Contents at a Glance

Maps at a Glance

● ●

Table of Contents

Chapter 21: The Western Riviera: From St-Tropez to Cannes 429

Part VII: The Part of Tens *475*

Chapter 22: Bon Appétit: Ten Foods You'll Want to Taste While in France 477

Introduction

You're going to *la belle France*. Let us be the first to commend you on your choice. France is a traveler's dream, with so many places to visit, sights to see, and things to do and with so much fabulous food and wine to savor. It's old Europe with cobblestone streets and soaring Gothic cathedrals mixed with new Europe's contemporary art and architecture. The French have mastered — and in some cases invented — the art of living well, and as a visitor you get to discover some of their tricks, such as loitering in sidewalk cafes and lingering over five-course meals.

You probably want to start with Paris, one of the world's most romantic and sophisticated cities. But then you have to make some choices. Will it be the castles of the Loire Valley, the chic towns of the French Riviera, or the historic sites in Normandy? Will you be spending time in the dappled sunshine of Provence or along the rocky coast of Brittany? This book helps you make those choices and nail down all the details for a perfect trip.

About This Book

France For Dummies, 3rd Edition, is a reference book, a critical tool for the first-time traveler, and a useful guide for those who've visited France before. There's no need to read it from front to back — just dive in wherever you want details on hotels, restaurants, sights, or travel tips. It would take a lifetime of travel to see all of France, so this book helps you make choices and narrow down your itinerary. In addition, it gives plenty of insider advice (the kind you'd get from a good friend) about the best places to visit, hotels to stay in, restaurants to try, and some pitfalls to avoid.

We tell you which fancy hotels and restaurants are worth a splurge and which cheap ones will do in a pinch. Planning a trip can be loads of fun, but we think the actual travel part is the best. So this guide is full of hints that help you with the nitty-gritty reality of travel, including some of those unexpected events that can't be planned for ahead of time. Likewise, we don't bog you down with unimportant details or mediocre sights; we give you just the good stuff — really the best of France.

Dummies Post-it® Flags

As you read this book, you may find information that you want to reference as you plan or enjoy your trip — whether a new hotel, a must-see attraction, or a must-try walking tour. To simplify your trip planning, mark these pages with the handy Post-it® Flags included in this book.

Conventions Used in This Book

Because we've designed *France For Dummies,* 3rd Edition, to be read in any order you want, we use some standard listings for hotels, restaurants, and sights. These listings enable you to open the book to any chapter and access the information you need quickly and easily.

Other conventions used in this book include the following:

- ✔ The abbreviations for credit cards: AE (American Express), DC (Diners Club), MC (MasterCard), and V (Visa).

- ✔ Hotels, restaurants, and sometimes attractions are listed in alphabetical order so that moving among the maps, worksheets, and descriptions is easier.

- ✔ Street abbreviations used throughout the book include *rue* (street), *bd.* (boulevard), and *av.* (avenue).

- ✔ The Paris *arrondissement,* or administrative district, is included in each address to give you a better idea of where each place is located. Paris is divided into 20 *arrondissements,* which are indicated by an ordinal number from 1st (in the very center of Paris, abbreviated *1er* in French) to 20th (on the outer edges of the city, abbreviated *20e* in French). They appear after the street address in each citation in this book. For example, "123 bd. St-Germain, 6e," indicates building number 123 on boulevard St-Germain in the 6th *arrondissement.* To get an idea of where each *arrondissement* is located, consult the "Paris Arrondissements" map in Chapter 11.

- ✔ For orientation in the Paris section, we list the nearest subway (or Métro) stop for all destinations (for example, Métro: Pont Marie).

- ✔ All prices in France are provided in euros (€). Be sure to check the exchange rate before you leave for any fluctuation. (A good Web site to check for currency exchange rates is www.oanda.com.) When converting euros to U.S. dollars in this book, we've assumed that one euro equals US$1.20.

All hotels and restaurants in this book are rated with a system of dollar signs to indicate the range of costs for one night in a double-occupancy hotel room or a meal at a restaurant, from "$" (budget) to "$$$$" (splurge). Rates for hotels are based on double occupancy unless otherwise indicated. Restaurant prices include the average price for an appetizer, main course, and dessert. The cost of beverages, particularly wine and beer, is extra. Exact prices are listed in the guide for every establishment, attraction, and activity, but of course, these are subject to change and should be used only as guidelines. Check out the following table to decipher the dollar signs.

Cost	Hotel	Restaurant
$	Less than 100€	Less than 20€
$$	100€–200€	20€–35€
$$$	200€–300€	35€–50€
$$$$	300€ and up	50€ and up

Foolish Assumptions

We've made some assumptions about you and what your needs are as a traveler. Maybe this is your first trip to France. Or maybe you've been to France but don't have much time to spend on trip planning and don't want to wade through a ton of information. Perhaps you've been frustrated with other guidebooks that bore you with background but don't give enough of the helpful information you really need. If any of these apply, then *France For Dummies* is the guide for you.

Dummies Travel guides appeal to a variety of audience segments, including

- ✔ Travelers looking for do's and don'ts from an expert who has visited the destination.
- ✔ Travelers who want "best of" information presented in bite-size pieces.
- ✔ Travelers who don't have much time for travel planning and who don't want to wade through a more comprehensive guidebook, such as Frommer's.
- ✔ Travelers wanting tips on experiencing the "essence" of a destination — the places, events, and/or people that make it unique.
- ✔ Travelers who want to discover a destination's history and culture — presented in an easy-to-understand and -digest format.

How This Book Is Organized

France For Dummies, 3rd Edition, is divided into seven parts. The first two cover everything you need to plan your trip. Part III covers Paris and its environs. Parts IV through VI tackle the top regions of France, with all the best sights. And as with any For Dummies book, Part VII offers the whimsical Part of Tens. You can read these parts independently if you want to zero in on the areas that interest you. Following are brief summaries of each of the parts.

Part 1: Introducing France

The four chapters that comprise Part I introduce France and touch on everything you need to consider before planning a trip. This part leads you to the best in several categories, ranging from the best travel experiences to the best small towns, from the most romantic inns to the best restaurants, from the best castles to the best vineyards. We also present easy-to-digest cultural information, including culinary tidbits, local lingo, and recommended reading and films. You also will find out the pros and cons of each season and region, and we suggest some itineraries that help you see some of France's highlights.

Part 11: Planning Your Trip to France

In Part II, you find the nuts and bolts of trip planning to help you answer questions such as these. How do you develop a realistic budget? How do you find the best flight to France? What's the best way to get around the country? What kind of accommodations should you use in France? We also advise you on how to tie up those frustrating last-minute details that can unnerve the most seasoned traveler.

Part 111: Paris and the Best of the Ile de France

Part III guides you through Paris, this most magical of cities, and its surrounding area. After exploring all the ins and outs of Paris, we take you on day trips to Versailles, Fontainebleau, Chartres, Disneyland Paris, and Giverny.

Part 1V: Tours and the Loire Valley Châteaux

In Part IV, we visit this beautiful region full of history and enchantment. Chapter 14 explores Tours, a lively university town and a good base for exploring the region. Chapter 15 visits eight château towns: Azay-le-Rideau, Chinon, Ussé, Chenonceaux, Chaumont, Blois, Amboise, and Chambord, with tours of the royal residences. Finally, we call on charming Orléans, another good base for exploring the region.

Part V: Normandy and Brittany

Part V is a tour of these authentic regions on the western coast of France. In Normandy, we visit Rouen, a city of half-timbered houses rich in history; Bayeaux, the site of the famous tapestry telling the adventures of

William the Conqueror; the D-day beaches, where Allied forces dared to invade the Nazi-held mainland in 1944; and Mont-St-Michel, Europe's most famous abbey. In Brittany, you'll find Quimper, home of famous pottery; Carnac, site of France's most extensive Neolithic remains; and Nantes, a historic center between Brittany and the Loire Valley.

Part VI: Provence and the Riviera

We cover two of France's best-loved regions in this part. In Provence, we visit the famous towns of Avignon, Arles, and Aix-en-Provence, and the quaint village of St-Rémy. We also take a quick, safe look at Marseille. Along the Riviera, we make quick stops in ten towns: St-Tropez, Cannes, Biot, Antibes, Vence, St-Paul-de-Vence, Nice, St-Jean-Cap-Ferrat, Beaulieu, and deluxe Monaco.

Part VII: The Part of Tens

And no *For Dummies* guide would be complete without The Part of Tens, a quick collection of fun tidbits, including a list of French foods you'll want to try and recommendations for the best gifts to buy in France.

You'll also find two other elements near the back of this book. We've included an *appendix* — your Quick Concierge — containing lots of handy information you may need when traveling in and around France, such as phone numbers and addresses, emergency personnel or area hospitals and pharmacies, lists of local newspapers and magazines, protocol for sending mail or finding taxis, and more. Check out this appendix when searching for answers to lots of little questions that may come up as you travel.

Icons Used in This Book

Throughout this book, you'll notice in the margins little pictures called icons. Consider them signposts or flags to alert you to facts or information of particular interest.

 This icon pegs the best bargains and juiciest money-saving tips. You may find a particularly value-conscious choice of hotel or restaurant, a discount museum or transportation pass, or simply a way to avoid spending more than you have to.

 This icon highlights the best the destination has to offer in all categories — hotels, restaurants, attractions, activities, shopping, and nightlife.

 When you need to be aware of a rip-off, an overrated sight, a dubious deal, or any other trap set for an unsuspecting traveler, this icon alerts you. These hints also offer the lowdown on the quirks, etiquette, and unwritten rules of the area — so you can avoid looking like a tourist and get treated like a local.

This icon, in addition to flagging tips and resources of special interest to families, points out the most child-friendly hotels, restaurants, and attractions. If you need a baby-sitter at your hotel, a welcoming and relaxed atmosphere at a restaurant, or a dazzling sight that delights your child, look for this icon. We include information regarding larger, family-sized rooms at hotels and restaurants that serve meals that go easy on your little one's tummy.

 This icon is a catchall for any special hint, tip, or bit of insider's advice that may help make your trip run more smoothly. Really, the point of a travel guide is to serve as one gigantic "tip," but this icon singles out the nuggets o' knowledge you may not have run across before.

 Sometimes a great hotel, restaurant, or sight may be located in a town or area that we don't have the room to include in this book. We let you in on these secret finds, and you can rest assured, we don't include any spots that aren't truly worth the energy.

Where to Go from Here

To France, of course. And *France For Dummies* takes you there. If you're at the beginning of planning for your trip, you'll want to dig into the first part for tips on when and where to go. If you're ready to start picking hotels, skip right over Part I and jump into the rest of the book. To brush up on your French, flip to the Quick Concierge appendix in the back of this book, where you'll find a glossary.

As the French say, *Bonne continuation.*

Part I
Introducing France

In this part . . .

Planning the perfect trip to France is easy, especially if you answer a few basic questions. Where do I go to find the best France has to offer? When should I go? These opening chapters help you answer these questions so that you can fine-tune plans for your trip. Think about what you're most interested in seeing and experiencing. If it's French culture, you may want your trip to coincide with a festival or celebration. If it's contemporary art, you'll want to hit the Riviera, which has the country's best selection of modern art museums.

Chapter 1 is an overview of the best France has to offer, so you can choose what you like most and focus your trip. Chapter 2 is a cultural catch-all, giving a rundown of the major historical events, the building blocks of local architecture, the native lingo, recommended books and films, and a taste of French cuisine. Chapter 3 outlines the regions and seasons and then gives a list of the country's best annual festivals and events. Those who need help planning an itinerary can check out the four suggestions in Chapter 4.

Chapter 1

Discovering the Best of France

* *

In This Chapter

▶ Savoring France's outstanding travel experiences
▶ Serving up some of the best of France's hotels and restaurants
▶ Finding the best museums in France
▶ Making your way to France's most intriguing castles and cathedrals
▶ Looking for France's premier shopping areas

* *

*F*rance is one of the most popular vacation sites for people traveling abroad. Its reputation for combining sophistication and the art of fine living is unmatched. The country long has been at the heart of European culture, with its elegant language, excellent cuisine, and old-world charm. Traveling through France is like taking a crash course in European history, because you encounter everything from Roman ruins and medieval villages to Gothic cathedrals, Renaissance castles, and early-1900s villas. You can visit vineyards where the world's most prestigious wines are made, or you can travel along the fabled French Riviera, a region long frequented by the rich and famous.

Many travelers to France start with Paris and then, via planes or the French rail system, visit areas such as the Riviera or the Loire Valley. France has such a diversity of sites and regions that many French people spend every vacation exploring their own country. However, as a typical visitor with only one or two weeks of vacation, you'll want to maximize the experience. This chapter offers a handful of essential aspects of France that you won't want to miss on your trip, whether it's a long wee end in Paris or two weeks traveling around the country. You can find more details about the best-of-the-best accommodations, restaurants, and activities that we recommend here — just check out the paragraphs marked with the "Best of the Best" icon in the destination chapters of this book.

The Best Travel Experiences

Although it may be true that any experience in France is a top travel experience, here are a few of our favorites:

- ✔ **Dining out:** The art of dining is serious business in France. Food is as cerebral as it is sensual. Even casual bistros with affordable menus are likely to offer fresh seasonal ingredients in time-tested recipes that may add up to a memorable meal. We offer our favorite restaurants in the destination chapters of this book.

- ✔ **Biking in the countryside:** The country that invented La Tour de France offers thousands of options for bike trips. For a modest charge, trains in France can carry your bicycle to any point. **Euro-Bike & Walking Tours** of DeKalb, Illinois (☎ **800-321-6060;** www.eurobike.com), offers some of the best excursions. The company features both walking and cycling tours of regions, including the Loire Valley and Provence. See Chapters 14 and 18.

- ✔ **Shopping in Parisian boutiques:** The French guard their image as Europe's most stylish people. The citadels of Right Bank chic lie on rue du Faubourg St-Honoré and its extension, rue-St-Honoré. The most glamorous shops sprawl along these streets, stretching east to west from the Palais Royal to the Palais de l'Elysé. Follow in the footsteps of Coco Chanel, Yves Saint Laurent, and Karl Lagerfeld on the shopper's tour of a lifetime. See Chapter 12.

- ✔ **Exploring the Loire Valley:** An excursion to the châteaux dotting this valley's rich fields and forests will familiarize you with the French Renaissance's architectural aesthetics and with the intrigues of the kings and their courts. Nothing conjures up the aristocratic *ancien régime* better than a tour of these legendary landmarks. See Chapter 14.

- ✔ **Climbing to the heights of Mont-St-Michel:** Straddling the tidal flats between Normandy and Brittany, this fortress is the most spectacular in northern Europe. Said to be protected by the archangel Michael, most of the Gothic marvel stands as it did during the 1200s. See Chapter 16.

- ✔ **Paying tribute to fallen heroes on Normandy's D-day beaches:** On June 6, 1944, the largest armada ever assembled departed from England in dense fog and on rough seas. For about a week, the future of the civilized world hung in a bloody and brutal balance between the Nazi and Allied armies. Today you'll find only the sticky sands and wind-torn, gray-green seas of a rather chilly beach. But even if you haven't seen *Saving Private Ryan* or *The Longest Day,* you can picture the struggles of the determined soldiers who paid a terrible price to establish a beachhead on the continent. See Chapter 16.

✔ **Marveling at the Riviera's modern-art museums:** Since the 1890s, when Signac, Bonnard, and Matisse discovered St-Tropez, the French Riviera has drawn artists and their patrons. Experience an unforgettable drive across southern Provence, interspersing museum visits with wonderful meals, people-watching, lounging on the beach, and stops at the area's architectural and artistic marvels. Highlights are Aix-en-Provence (Cézanne's studio), Biot (the Léger Museum), Cagnes-sur-Mer (the Museum of Modern Mediterranean Art), and Cap d'Antibes (the Grimaldi Château's Picasso Museum). Nice, St-Paul-de-Vence, and St-Tropez all have impressive modern-art collections. See Chapters 20 and 21.

The Most Romantic Inns

Traveling to France without the kids? One of these destinations just may end up being the romantic topper to your trip.

✔ **Hotel de l'Abbaye Saint-Germain:** In Paris, this is one of the Left Bank's most charming boutique hotels, built as a convent in the early 18th century and successfully converted. Touches of a sophisticated flair abound and are enhanced by a small garden and a verdant courtyard with fountain and flower beds. Some of the original oak ceiling beams still are in place. See Chapter 11.

✔ **Le Choiseul:** In Amboise in the Loire Valley — in the town where Leonardo da Vinci died — this inn was formed when a trio of buildings from the 1700s were seamlessly blended and joined by Italianate gardens. The modernized guest rooms are luxurious, and the formal dining room, serving a superb cuisine, opens onto views of the Loire River. On the grounds is a garden with flowering terraces. See Chapter 15.

✔ **Hostellerie du Vallon de Valrugues:** In the ancient Provençal town of St-Rémy-de-Provence stands this exquisite hotel, lying in a beautifully landscaped park. Constructed in the 1970s, it evokes a fantasy version of an ancient Roman villa. Beautifully decorated rooms and suites are rented, along with luxurious marble-clad bathrooms. A large heated swimming pool can be enjoyed by all guests, although one private suite has its own pool. See Chapter 18.

✔ **Hotel La Voile d'Or:** In the fishing port of St-Jean-Cap-Ferrat, one of the poshest villages along the French Riviera, this inn, which also is known by its English nickname, the Golden Sail, is installed in a converted 19th-century villa at the yacht harbor, opening onto panoramic views of the water. Guests live in style in the individually decorated bedrooms, enjoying one of the area's most refined cuisines. See Chapter 20.

✔ **La Réserve de Beaulieu:** Between Monaco and Nice, opening onto a beautiful Mediterranean beach, this small **Relais & Châteaux** is an Italianate rose-pink villa from 1881 that was successfully converted, with many of its bedrooms opening onto balconies with panoramic sea views. Individually decorated bedrooms are superdeluxe, with bathrooms to match. The inn also is celebrated for its restaurant, one of Les Grandes Tables du Monde, an organization of the world's top restaurants. See Chapter 20.

✔ **Hotel Byblos:** In chic St-Tropez, at the western fringe of the Riviera, this luxurious hideaway is the choice of visiting celebrities and one of the most exclusive inns west of Cannes. Its owner wanted to create an "antihotel, a place like home." In that, he succeeded, if your home resembles a Middle Eastern palace. On a hill above the harbor, it offers deluxe rooms, each one unique, along with some of the finest nightclubs and dining choices in the west. If Julia Roberts were to appear in St-Tropez, this no doubt would be her hotel. See Chapter 21.

The Best Restaurants

For the finest in haute cuisine, where else do you turn but where cuisine first became haute. Expect no surprises when looking for a five-star meal at one of these restaurants.

✔ **L'Ambroisie:** In the Marais district of Paris (4e), this citadel of haute cuisine opens onto Paris's most beautiful squares, Place des Vosges. One of the most talented chefs of Paris, Bernard Pacaud cooks with vivid flavors and gastronomic skill, reaching a culinary perfection at this 17th-century town house that evokes an Italian *palazzo*. His faithful devotees always are thrilled to find where Monsieur Pacaud's imagination carries him next. See Chapter 11.

✔ **Les Nymphéas:** In the ancient capital of Normandy, the city of Rouen, this grand restaurant bears the name of a painting by Monet *(Water Lilies)*. The setting is a 16th-century half-timbered house near the landmark square in the old town of Rouen. A savory, sophisticated cuisine is served with style and grace, and ingredients are first-rate and often from the Norman countryside. The signature dessert is a warm soufflé flavored with apples and Calvados. See Chapter 16.

✔ **Christian Etienne:** In the once papal city of Avignon, capital of Provence, the city's grandest restaurant is in a stone house whose origins go back to 1180. Near the Palais des Papes, or former papal palace, this citadel of wonderous cuisine always relies on the best produce of any given season. Sometimes the fixed-price menus are theme based, such as many variations on the theme of lobster. See Chapter 18.

✔ **Lou Marquès:** In the Provençal city of Arles, this swank restaurant is part of the deluxe hotel Jules-César. Serving a Provençal cuisine based on market-fresh ingredients, Lou Marquès is part of a Relais & Châteaux. The cuisine features creative twists on long-established recipes. You'll experience delight when you order such dishes as breast of guinea fowl stuffed with olive paste and spit-roasted. See Chapter 18.

✔ **Chantecler:** In Nice, capital of the French Riviera, this posh dining room holds forth at the Hotel Negresco, in the heart of the city. The most prestigious — and the best — restaurant in the city, it serves a top-notch cuisine in refined surroundings, including 16th-century paintings. Top-quality ingredients such as foie gras, black truffles, and giant prawns are used in abundance. See Chapter 20.

✔ **Louis XV:** This golden palace — and one of the best restaurants in the world — is found at the swanky Hotel de Paris at Place du Casino, in the heart of Monte Carlo. Chef Alain Ducasse, "the world's greatest" (at least in his opinion), is the inspiration behind the Provençal and Tuscan cuisine. It's strictly a posh haven *Pour les Groumands* — and rich ones at that. If your dream is of luxury dining and a sublime cuisine, you are more likely to encounter both here, more so than at any other restaurant along the Riviera. See Chapter 20.

The Best Museums

You can find the best of the best museums on and around the banks of the Seine, but you also can expect to find a few nice surprises outside Paris.

✔ **Musée de Louvre:** In Paris (1er), the largest palace in the world houses one of the great treasure troves of art on the planet at its location on Rue de Rivoli. Impressive, even exhausting, there is so much to see here: everything from da Vinci's *Mona Lisa* to the supple statue of *Venus de Milo*. You'll stand in awe at *The Winged Victory* with its cloak rippling in the wind. Get a free map of the Louvre at the information desk to set out on a voyage of artistic discovery. See Chapter 12.

✔ **Musée d'Orsay:** Paris's other great art museum stands in the 7th arrondissement, and it has the greatest collection of Impressionist masterpieces spread across three floors of exhibits. The neoclassical Gare d'Orsay train station was transformed into this unique museum devoted mainly to art from 1848 to 1914. Be prepared to encounter everything from the Symbolists to the Pointillists, from Monet to Manet, and from van Gogh to Renoir. See Chapter 12.

✔ **Centre Georges Pompidou:** Also in Paris is yet a third museum that also is one of the world's greatest depositories of art (in Paris, you quickly get used to saying "the world's greatest"). Open since 1966, this cultural center is called "the most avant-garde building in the world" because of its radical exoskeletal design. Parisians are more likely to refer to the painted pipes and ducts as "the refinery." Even so, its Musée National d'Art Moderne contains one of the world's finest collection of modern art — and there are so many other treasures besides. The location is in the Marais (in both the 3rd and 4th arrondissements) at Place Georges-Pompidou. See Chapter 12.

✔ **Villa Kérylos:** In the exclusive coastal resort of Beaulieu, between Monaco and Nice, this dream house lies at the tip of a rocky promontory jutting into the Mediterranean. The villa is a replica of an ancient Greek residence, and it was designed and built by archaeologist Theodore Reinach, who filled it with treasures from the ancient world, including mosaics, frescoes, and reproductions of Greek works. A special feature is his galleries of antiquities containing, among other delights, copies of famous statues such as the *Venus de Milo* and the *Discus Thrower.* See Chapter 20.

✔ **Musée Picasso:** In the ancient French Riviera town of Antibes, Pablo Picasso came to live, paint and sculpt in the Château Grimaldi (then an art museum) in the autumn of 1946. In gratitude for setting up a studio and residence for him in this town-owned villa, Picasso donated the 181 works he completed during his stay here — not just paintings, but also ceramics and sculpture — to Antibes. The museum was renamed in honor of Picasso upon his death. If you wander its sculpture gardens, you'll be rewarded with a view of the Mediterranean. See Chapter 21.

✔ **Foundation Maeght:** At St-Paul-de-Vence, the most charming of all Riviera hill towns, home to many artists, stands the premier art gallery of the Riviera, lying just outside the walls. In an avant-garde building, it is a showcase for some of the greatest modern art with both a permanent collection — Calder, Chagall, Bonnard, Matisse, and the boys — to changing special exhibitions. See Chapter 21.

The Best Castles & Palaces

From massive — and intimidating, to those who approached them unawares — protective structures to ornate châteaux that housed France's rich and powerful, visiting the country's best castles and palaces offers a studied glimpse into France's history.

✔ **Musée Jacquemart-Andre:** In Paris, in the swank 8th arrondissement district near the Champs-Elysées stands a mansion that's like a jewel box. With its gilt salons and elegant winding staircase, it contains one of the best small collections of 18th-century decorative art in

Paris. A rare collection of French decorative art is exhibited, along with paintings and sculpture from the Dutch and Flemish schools, including *objets d'art* from the Italian Renaissance. You'll see works by Rembrandt, van Dyck, Rubens, Tiepolo, and Carpaccio, and the beat goes on. See Chapter 12.

✔ **Mont-St-Michel:** Massive walls — more than half a mile in circumference — enclose one of the greatest sightseeing attractions and one of the most important Gothic masterpieces of Europe. Mont-St-Michel, lying at a point 324km (201 miles) west of Paris, can be seen for miles around, a rock rising 78m (260 ft.) high. The tides around Mont-St-Michel are notorious, having claimed countless lives. A Benedictine monastery was founded on this spot in 966 by Richard I, Duke of Normandy, although an earlier monastery was located here from A.D. 708. See Chapter 16.

✔ **Château de Versailles:** Just 21km (13 miles) southwest of Paris delivers you to the town of Versailles and a palace in the center of town that, even though unbelievably vast, is as ornately artificial as a jewel box. The kings of France built a whole glittering private world for themselves here until the French Revolution sent many of the inhabitants of this palace to the guillotine. Go on one of the grandest tours of your life, taking in the Hall of Mirrors where the Treaty of Versailles was signed and the apartments where such mistresses as Madame de Pompadour once romped. It's a moving spectacle. See Chapter 13.

✔ **Château de Fontainebleau:** Seven centuries of French royal history spin around this castle in the town of Fontainebleau, 60 km (37 miles) south of Paris. Surrounded by a superb forest, Fontainebleau is more intimate than Versailles and a product of the Renaissance movement in France in the 16th century. Napoléon later added many of the furnishings you'll see. The *Mona Lisa* once hung here. François I, who transformed the site in 1528, purchased the painting from the artist Leonardo da Vinci. See Chapter 13.

✔ **Château de Chambord:** In the little town of Chambord, 191km (118 miles) south of Paris, stands the largest castle in the Loire Valley, created by some 2,000 workers between 1519 and 1545. The building represents the pinnacle of the French Renaissance. Set in a park of more than 5,260 hectares (3,000 acres), it is enclosed by a wall stretching for 32km (20 miles). See Chapter 15.

✔ **Château d'Azay-le-Rideau:** This Renaissance masterpiece dominates a little village of the same name. The castle lies 261km (162 miles) southwest of Paris and has a *faux* defensive medieval look to it. It was occupied by nobles instead of royalty, and construction was ordered in 1515 by Gilles Berthelot, finance minister to François I. Its Renaissance interior is a virtual museum of architecture. See Chapter 15.

The Best Churches & Cathedrals

Any trip to France requires visits to its impressive cathedrals, often more for the views than for their places in French history.

✔ **Cathédrale de Notre-Dame:** In the Ile de la Cité (4e) in the heart of Paris, this fabled cathedral is one of Western civilization's greatest edifices. It is a piece of Gothic architectural perfection — not merely in overall design but in every detail, including the rose window above the main portal. More than any other building in France, Notre-Dame represents the history of a nation. Here, for example, Napoléon took the crown out of the hands of Pope Pius VII and crowned himself. See Chapter 12.

✔ **Sacré-Coeur:** In the 18th arrondissement of Paris, dominating Paris's highest hill, this basilica — once called "a lunatic's confectionary dream" — has outlived its critics and remains an enduring monument on the city's skyline. Built in an oddly oriental neo-Byzantine style, the church, from its white dome, offers the single greatest view of Paris that extends over and far beyond "the mountain of martyrs" (Montmartre). See Chapter 12.

✔ **Sainte-Chapelle:** In the 4th arrondissement of Paris, this church at Palais de Justice is one of the oldest, most beautiful, and oddest in the world. It was constructed in 1246 for the express purpose of housing the relics of the Crucifixion, which had been sent from Constantinople. The relics later were transferred to Notre-Dame. What keeps the chapel on the tourist map are its 15 stained-glass windows, among the greatest ever created. They flood the interior with colored light — deep blue, ruby red, and dark green — and depict more than 1,000 scenes from the Bible. See Chapter 12.

✔ **Cathédrale de Notre-de-Dame-de-Chartres:** This cathedral is one of the world's greatest Gothic cathedrals and one of the finest achievements of the Middle Ages. The cathedral, completed in 1220, is celebrated for its stained-glass windows, which cover an expanse of some 2,508 sq. m (3,000 sq. yds.), the peerless ensemble truly majestic. Most of the glass dates from the 12th and 13th centuries. See Chapter 13.

✔ **Cathédrale Notre-Dame:** Yet another Notre-Dame stands in the city of Rouen, capital of Normandy. It dominates a town known as the "hundred-spired city." Its spirit was captured in a series of paintings by Monet. The cathedral originally was constructed in 1063, but it has seen many building crews through the centuries. It's distinguished by two soaring towers. See Chapter 16.

✔ **Notre-Dame de la Garde:** In Marseille is yet another Notre-Dame that doesn't even compare to the artistic style of the great Gothic churches in the north of France, including Paris. Instead, it holds a bizarre fascination and once was fortified. The style is a kind of Romanesque Byzantine, with domes, multicolored stripes of stone, and plenty of gilt, marble, and mosaics. The views from its terrace are panoramic, and it's worth the trek over to see this curious architectural assemblage. See Chapter 18.

The Best Gardens

The French are quite justifiably proud of their carefully cultivated gardens. Make sure to schedule a few of these favorites into your France itinerary.

- **Jardin des Tuileries:** In Paris, these famous gardens in the 1er arrondissement stretch along the Right Bank of the Seine from the Place de la Concorde to the courtyard of the Louvre. Spread across 29 hectares (63 acres), Paris's most formal gardens are exquisite and laid out as a royal pleasure park back in 1564. The denizens who fought the French Revolution threw open the gardens to the general populace. Filled with statues, fountains, and mathematically trimmed hedges, the Tuileries offer amusement-park entertainment in the summer. See Chapter 12.

- **Jardin du Luxembourg:** In the St-Germain-des-Prés area in the 6th arrondissement on Paris's Left Bank, these once-royal gardens are entered on the corner of boulevard St-Michel and rue des Médicis. A masterpiece of Renaissance landscaping with a jewel of a central pond, the gardens face the Palais de Luxembourg, former abode of Marie de Médici, queen of Henri IV. Throngs of university students are especially fond of these grounds. See Chapter 12.

- **Bois de Boulonge:** Covering some 890 hectares (2,200 acres), this sprawling park and gardens is Paris's favorite outdoor amusement zone. Fabled as a playground since the "Gay Nineties," it borders the northwestern edge of the city. Once a royal forest and hunting ground, it is known today for its race days at Longchamp when you still can admire the best-dressed women in Paris in their finest dresses. Families love the lakes, waterfalls, and discreetly hidden glens. See Chapter 12.

- **The Gardens of Versailles:** Spread across 101 hectares (250 acres), these gardens, former stamping ground of royalty, represent the ultimate in French landscaping perfection. Every tree, shrub, flower, and hedge is disciplined into a frozen ballet pattern and blended with soaring fountains, sparkling little lakes, grandiose steps, and hundreds of marble statues. It's more like a colossal stage setting than a park — even the view of the blue horizon seems embroidered on. It's a Garden of Eden where you expect the birds to sing coloratura soprano. See Chapter 12.

✔ **Monet's Garden at Giverny:** Visitors by the thousands flock to Giverny, 81km (50 miles) northwest of Paris, to see where Claude Monet lived and worked. You can stroll in the garden where he painted his famous water lilies. These gardens usually are at their best in May, June, September, and October. The Japanese bridge, hung with wisteria, leads to a setting of weeping willows and rhododendrons. Monet's studio barge was installed on the pond. See Chapter 13.

✔ **Jardin Exotique:** In the principality of Monaco on the French Riviera, these royal gardens are built on the side of a rock and celebrated for their famous cactus collection. They were begun by Prince Albert I, who was a naturalist and scientist. He spotted some succulents growing in the palace gardens and created this garden from that humble beginning. Of course, the gardens have greatly expanded through the years, with more succulents being added from around the world. One giant cactus is more than a century old. See Chapter 20.

The Best Destinations for Serious Shoppers

France is second to none when it comes to pleasing sophisticated shoppers. Start in the fashion capital of the world (Paris), and work your way around to some of the other shopping destinations in the country.

✔ **Paris:** Not to be ignored is the joy of bringing "something back from Paris," a reminder of your stay. There can be no substitute for memories of strolling along one of the chic boulevards of Paris, browsing in the smart boutiques, and finally purchasing — say, a scarf or handbag. Paris is one of the great shopping meccas of the world, the rival of New York and London. Shopping surrounds you on every street. Right Bank shops are centered in the 1st and 8th arrondissements, and Left Bank shopping uses the hubs of the 6th and 7th arrondissements. See Chapter 12.

✔ **Quimper:** The capital of Brittany is celebrated for its hand-painted pottery, which has been made here since the early 1600s. In your search for *faïence,* you can take a factory tour, explore a museum devoted to pottery, and spend time in local shops hawking this exquisite merchandise. See Chapter 17.

✔ **St-Rémy-de-Provence:** Our favorite town in the province also is a center of home decorating, and antique shops and fabric stores abound in the old town. Walk its narrow streets and shop, shop, and shop, purchasing a wide array of merchandise from antiques to flea-market discoveries, along with *faiences* and fabrics. The town is filled with collectibles, including *santons* (hand-painted clay figurines). See Chapter 18.

- **Aix-en-Provence:** Some of the best markets in all of Provence focus on this town, famous for its fruit and vegetable market, which is open every morning. Even if you don't buy anything (it's likely that you will), you can wander among stall after stall, looking at the products Provence is known for, everything from local cheeses to fresh produce — and most definitely olives and lavender. Seek out some of the specialty stores selling classic Provence sweets such as almond-paste cookies or else craft shops hawking their beautiful handmade baskets. See Chapter 18.

- **Nice:** This city is known throughout Europe for its celebrated flower market, **Marché aux Fleurs,** which is open Tuesday to Saturday beginning at 6 a.m. Chances are, the actual visitor will patronize these markets mainly to sightsee. But Nice also offers plenty of shops where you may want to make more serious purchases, including glassware from Biot, pottery from Vallauris of Picasso fame, and most definitely perfumes from Grasse. See Chapter 20.

- **Cannes:** This posh Riviera resort is known for both its markets and its specialty shops. The biggest market is **Marché Forville,** which you may want to treat as a sightseeing attraction, and dozens of specialty shops will entice you, too. Cannes, attracting yachties, also is known for its high-fashion designer shops, including Chanel and Dior. These pockets of posh lie on or in the vicinity of **La Croisette.** See Chapter 21.

Chapter 2

Digging Deeper into France

● ●

In This Chapter

▶ Getting the lowdown on France's history

▶ Taking a glance at the horizon: France's architecture

▶ Ordering off France's culinary menu

▶ Reading up before you go

● ●

*F*rance is one of the world's most talked-about and most written-about destinations. It's packed with diversions and distractions of every sort: cultural, culinary, sensual, you name it. From its extraordinarily complex and fascinating history to its architectural legacy, from its trend-setting culinary standards to its role in literature and film of today and yesterday, this chapter helps you discover why France has been called *le deuxième pays de tout le monde:* everyone's second country.

History 101: The Main Events

France — influenced by its centuries of monarchies, its fiery Revolution, its native son trying to conquer all of Europe, its role in two world wars, and its countless influential artists, writers, and philosophers — has a culture that is one of the most sophisticated and one of the most traditional of Western nations. This section helps you sort out just who did what to whom and when. Or, if you'd rather peruse a quick-and-dirty dateline of events, look for the nearby sidebar, "Significant dates in France's history."

The area now known as France originally was called **Gaul.** In the first century B.C., it was conquered by the powerful **Romans,** led by Julius Caesar, and was ruled from Rome for 400 years. During that time, the Romans established their colony of **Lutetia** on the Ile de la Cité, an island in the Seine River in the center of what's now Paris. The French language evolved from the Latin of these early invaders. For the next 500 years, the **barbarians,** who were Germanic tribes, invaded Gaul and eventually settled there. One of these tribes, known as the **Franks,** gave its name to France.

Reigning over France

Clovis I (reigned A.D. 481–511) is considered the first king of France, though his influence was strongest in the north of the country. He converted to Catholicism, united territories, and selected Paris as the capital. **Charlemagne** came along a couple hundred years later, reigning (A.D. 768–814) over an area that extended from the Baltic to the Mediterranean seas and included parts of France, Germany, and Italy. Now here was a king the people could rally behind, a great general and bold ruler. The pope in Rome crowned Charlemagne Holy Roman Emperor in 800, giving a spiritual legitimacy to his rule. These times were good for scholarship and the arts.

France and Germany didn't become separated until 843, when Charlemagne's grandsons — Louis, Lothair, Pepin, and Charles — split the kingdom. **Charles the Bald** got France. He and **Louis** united against Lothair by taking the *Oath of Strasbourg,* the first known document written in French and German instead of the usual Latin. Charles, who ruled over a region whose borders resembled the France of today, developed a complex feudal system.

In 1066, William, duc de Normandie, known in history as **William the Conqueror,** began a campaign to conquer England, and the Bayeux Tapestry in Normandy tells the dramatic tale. In 1152, **Eleanor of Aquitaine** stirred things up again between France and England when she divorced the king of France (Louis VII) and married the king of England (Henry II), placing western France under English rule. War between the two countries continued on and off for hundreds of years.

During the Middle Ages, the Catholic church was a powerful force in France. Holy men preached the **Crusades** in the 12th and 13th centuries, inciting armies of men to journey to foreign lands in the name of the church. These so-called **holy armies** set off to conquer lands for the Holy Roman Emperor.

Throughout the next 700 years, five dynasties held the French crown and built the monarchy into one of Europe's most powerful. Of these kings, several stand out for their achievements in bringing about the France of today. An especially long and fruitful reign was that of **Louis IX** (1226–70), called St-Louis. During his reign, Sainte-Chapelle and Cathédrale Notre-Dame were built on the Ile de la Cité in Paris. The arts of tapestry weaving and stone cutting flourished.

Philippe IV (the Fair), who reigned from 1285 to 1314, was instrumental in France gaining its independence from the pope in Rome. Philippe had a French pope elected, **Clement V,** who transferred the papacy to Avignon, where it remained from 1309 to 1378. For a brief period, two popes — one in Rome and one in Avignon — jockeyed for power. Rome eventually won out. In 1348, the Bubonic Plague, called the **Black Death,** wiped out a third of Europe's population. Meanwhile, the **Hundred Years' War** between France and England waged from 1337 to 1453. Things looked bad for the French until 1431, when a peasant girl named **Joan of Arc** led an army to take back Orléans and then accompanied Charles VII to Reims, where he was crowned king. In revenge, the English burned Joan at the stake in Rouen, a town they controlled, in 1431.

François I (1515–47) brought the Italian Renaissance to France by becoming a patron to Leonardo da Vinci and other great Italian artists and architects. Around this time, the Protestant religion was gaining popularity, which led to discrimination by the ruling Catholics against the Protestants. From 1559 to 1598, the Wars of Religion pitted Catholics against the Protestant minority, reaching a climax when **Catherine de Médici,** widow of Henri II, ordered the St. Bartholomew's Day massacre, killing hundreds of Protestants on August 14, 1572. **Henri IV** (1589–1610) earned a place in the history books by signing the Edict of Nantes that guaranteed religious freedom to Protestants. The edict was revoked in 1685.

The sinister Catholic-cardinal-turned-prime-minister, **Cardinal Richelieu,** gained power from 1624 until his death in 1642 and paved the way for the absolute monarchy. **Louis XIV,** who had the longest reign in the history of France (1643–1715), became one of its greatest kings, expanding the kingdom and amassing great wealth. In 1664, he began construction of the Château de Versailles. During his reign, great writers (Pierre Corneille, Molière, and Jean Racine) and architects (François Mansart) were celebrated. During the long reign of his great-grandson, **Louis XV** (1715–74), great thinkers and philosophers like Voltaire, Jean-Jacques Rousseau, Montesquieu, and Denis Diderot voiced their opinions in the period known as the Age of Enlightenment.

Louis XV's grandson, **Louis XVI** (1774–91), married **Marie Antoinette** of Austria in 1770, and their ostentatious manners proved to be the downfall of the French monarchy. From 1776 to 1783, following the maxim "the enemy of my enemy is my friend," France supported the North American colonists' quest for independence from England.

On June 20, 1789, representatives of the National Assembly met in the Versailles tennis court and swore **"The Tennis Court Oath"** to put together a Constitution for France with a legislative government. But impatient for reform, the people of Paris stormed the **Bastille** prison on July 14, 1789. The **Declaration of the Rights of Man** and the **Constitution** were drawn up later that year, and these documents are still cited as models of democratic values. But the mob couldn't be stopped. They arrested Louis XVI in 1791 and put him on trial. He was executed in 1793, the year France was declared a republic, and Marie Antoinette was beheaded later that same year. The dreaded Revolutionary radical Robespierre led this **Reign of Terror,** in which more than a thousand people were beheaded, that finally ended in 1794.

It took the short but powerful Corsican-born general **Napoléon Bonaparte** (reigned 1804–15) to restore order to France after the Revolutionary fervor. In a 1799 coup d'état, Napoléon was named one of three in a ruling consulate, but by 1802, he was made First Consul for life. In 1804, Napoléon crowned himself emperor and his wife, **Joséphine,** empress as the pope looked on. The following year, he was crowned king of Italy. By 1808, having occupied Vienna and Berlin and having invaded Portugal and Spain, Napoléon seemed on his way to conquering Europe and brought great pride to the French. But after his disastrous retreat from Moscow in 1814, he abdicated and was exiled to Elba. Napoléon returned to power the following year and was defeated at Waterloo on June 18, 1815. After that defeat, Napoléon was deported to the island of St. Helena in the South Atlantic and died there in 1821.

The monarchy was restored with **Louis XVIII** (1814–24) and then **Charles X** (1824–30). In 1830, **Louis-Philippe I,** descended from a branch of the Bourbons that had ruled France on and off since the 16th century, was called king of the French, not king of France, under a more liberal constitution, but he was forced out of office in 1847. During these politically tumultuous but fairly prosperous years, Victor Hugo, Stendhal, and Honoré de Balzac wrote great novels. In 1848, Napoléon's nephew, **Louis-Napoléon Bonaparte,** was elected president of the Second Republic. In 1852, he assumed the title of emperor as Napoléon III and, with the help of **Baron Haussmann,** designed Paris's grand boulevards. In July 1870, a dispute over a telegram escalated into France declaring an ultimately unsuccessful war on Prussia. As a result of the military defeats and invasion of France by Prussia, Napoléon III was removed from office. The period of 1875 to 1940 is known as the Third Republic. Meanwhile, on the cultural scene, the artists known as the **Impressionists** scandalized the French Academy and forever changed art. And in 1889 at Paris's Universal Exposition, the **Tour Eiffel** was unveiled. Many Parisians hated it at first, but now it's the universally beloved symbol of Paris.

Creating a nation

World War I (1914–18) was devastating for France. The worldwide economic depression that followed severely weakened the government while Germany gained power under the charismatic and acquisitive **Adolf Hitler.** France declared war on Germany in 1939, following the Nazi invasion of France's ally, Poland. In 1940, the German army invaded France; the French army rapidly collapsed, and the Germans occupied the country. The period called the **Collaboration** is one of France's most shameful. The government was transferred first to Bordeaux and then, under the Nazi-approved President Pétain, to Vichy. French General Charles de Gaulle refused to accept the armistice with Germany and Italy and broadcast a call for resistance from London on June 18, 1940. However, everything changed on June 6, 1944, when thousands of Allied troops from the United States, the United Kingdom, Canada, and exiles from the invaded nations landed on the wind-swept shores of Normandy in the **D-day** invasion. Brilliant Allied military maneuvers led to the eventual surrender of Germany on May 8, 1945.

Significant dates in France's history

✔ **58–51 B.C.:** Julius Caesar conquers Gaul (north-central France).

✔ **2nd century A.D.:** Christianity arrives in Gaul.

✔ **485–511:** Under Clovis I, the Franks defeat the Roman armies.

✔ **768:** Charlemagne (768–814) becomes the Frankish king and establishes the Carolingian dynasty; from Aix-la-Chapelle (Aachen), he rules from northern Italy to Bavaria to Paris.

✔ **814:** Charlemagne dies; his empire breaks up.

✔ **1066:** William of Normandy (the Conqueror) invades England; his conquest is completed by 1087.

✔ **1309:** The papal schism — Philippe the Fair establishes the Avignon papacy, which lasts nearly 70 years; two popes struggle for domination.

✔ **1347–51:** The bubonic plague (Black Death) kills 33 percent of the population.

✔ **1431:** The English burn Joan of Arc at the stake in Rouen for resisting their occupation of France.

✔ **1453:** The French drive the English out of all of France except Calais; the Hundred Years' War ends.

✔ **1789–94:** The French Revolution: The Bastille is stormed on July 14, 1789; the Reign of Terror follows.

✔ **1793:** Louis XVI and Marie Antoinette are guillotined.

✔ **1804:** Napoléon crowns himself emperor in Notre-Dame de Paris.

✔ **1814–15:** Napoléon abdicates after the failure of his Russian campaign; exiled to Elba, he returns. On June 18, 1815, defeated at Waterloo, he's exiled to St. Helena and dies in 1821.

✔ **1870–71:** The Franco-Prussian War: Paris falls; France cedes Alsace-Lorraine but aggressively colonizes North Africa and Southeast Asia.

✔ **1889:** The Eiffel Tower is built for Paris's Universal Exhibition and the Revolution's centennial; architectural critics howl with contempt.

✔ **1914–18:** World War I; French casualties exceed five million.

✔ **1936:** Germans march into the demilitarized Rhineland; France takes no action.

✔ **1939:** France and Britain guarantee to Poland, Romania, and Greece protection from aggressors; Germany invades Poland; France declares war.

✔ **1940:** Paris falls to Germany on June 14; Marshal Pétain's Vichy government collaborates with the Nazis; General de Gaulle forms a government-in-exile in London to direct French resistance fighters.

✓ **1944:** On June 6, the Allies invade the Normandy beaches; other Allied troops invade from the south; Paris is liberated in August.

✓ **1946–54:** War in Indochina; French withdraw from Southeast Asia; North and South Vietnam are created.

✓ **1958:** Charles De Gaulle initiates the Fifth Republic, calling for a France independent from the United States and Europe.

✓ **1968:** Students riot in Paris; de Gaulle resigns.

✓ **1981:** François Mitterrand becomes the first Socialist president since World War II.

✓ **1994:** The Channel Tunnel opens to link France with England.

✓ **1997:** Strict immigration laws are enforced, causing strife for many African and Arab immigrants and dividing the country.

✓ **2000:** France gives legal status to unmarried couples.

✓ **2002:** France switches to the euro, the equivalent of a European dollar.

After the war, the **Fourth Republic** was set up in 1946. Insurrection in France's African and Asian colonies caused huge problems for the government. After suffering great losses, France withdrew from most of its colonies, including Indochina in 1954 and Algeria in 1962. In 1958, General de Gaulle returned to power with the **Fifth Republic.** In May 1968, university students joined with workers in uprisings that paralyzed Paris, spread through the country, and led to de Gaulle's resignation in 1969. Georges Pompidou became president in 1969, followed by Valéry Giscard d'Estaing in 1974. In 1981, the left came to power with the election of **François Mitterrand,** the first Socialist president since World War II. Mitterrand served two terms and bestowed on Paris famous *grands projets* like the Louvre pyramid, Opéra Bastille, and Grand Arche de la Défense.

During the past decade, France has been heavily involved in the development of the **European Union,** the 12 countries that have banded together with a single currency and no trade barriers. In 1993, voters ousted the socialists and installed a conservative government that's headed by **Jacques Chirac** as president. A decade of bombings, strikes, and rising unemployment all faded into the background on December 31, 1999, as **Paris's salute to 2000** with spectacular fireworks over the Tour Eiffel was one of the world's most spectacular celebrations.

In the postmillennium, political headlines in France have centered on its continuing deterioration of relations with its former ally, the United States. The problem centers on Iraq. Most French people bitterly resent the war in Iraq and were extremely critical of George W. Bush during his first four years in office.

On another, more ominous note, attacks against Jews in postmillennium France reached their highest level since World War II. An increase in anti-Semitic acts coincided with heightened tensions in the Middle East. Jewish schools, temples, and cemeteries were attacked.

Building Blocks: Local Architecture

During the heyday of the Roman Empire, only the southernmost region of France was viewed as having any artistic merit in architecture. This region became familiar with the architectural sophistication of the Mediterranean through trade. Provence was quick to adopt the building techniques common in the Roman world, including triumphal arches, massive aqueducts, and mausoleums.

Little remains from the Roman period, roughly from 125 to 450 A.D. Most of the treasure trove you'll see today — engraved weapons and tools, bronzes, statues, and jewelry — is found in museums, no finer collection than that of the **Musée de Cluny** in Paris. For actual Roman ruins and remains, the best town in the south that's covered in this book is the city of **Arles,** with its amphitheater and reconstructed theater, and the **Glanum excavations** outside the charming little Provence town of **St-Rémy-de-Provence.**

Romanesque rigidity

The classical Roman period in time gave way to the coming of an architectural form called **Romanesque** (it wasn't known as that back then). This roughly covers the period from 800 to 1100, its rise coming about because of the growing spiritual power of the church at this time.

The earliest manifestations are thick-walled fortresses that served as refuges during times of invasion. At first these structures were not embellished, relying on load-bearing rounded arches and windows for ornamentation. By the end of the period, around 1100, the facades and interiors of some churches were being covered with sculptures designed to highlight architecture instead of separate works of art.

Many pieces of Romanesque sculpture are solid, rigid, unyielding and lifeless, yet the capitals of the columns often are charming and decorative. Bas-reliefs, especially those depicting the Last Judgment, came into vogue. Reliefs enveloped column capitals and were used to adorn tympanums — arched spaces over doorways or portals. To see the true remains of the Romanesque style, you'd have to go into remote France, beyond the province of this guide. A prime example would be the **Abbey of Fontenay** in Burgundy.

The Gothic cathedral: Awe of the Middle Ages

Of far more interest to the average visitor is the coming of the French Gothic style to all the land. This late medieval period, roughly from 1100 to

1500, still centered on the church, where artisans created stained glass, statues, choir screens, and elaborate, dramatic facades. Gothic figures were more realistic than Romanesque ones but still highly stylized, with exaggerated gestures and features.

The wide Gothic churches and cathedrals included a choir, a circular ambulatory, radiating chapels, pointed arches that carried more weight than rounded ones, clustered (rather than monolithic) columns, cross vaults, and ribbed ceilings. Wide, soaring windows are the most salient Gothic advance. In a Romanesque church the space would have been devoted to thick stone walls. The new Gothic design required the addition of exterior flying buttresses to support the weight of the very heavy roof and ceiling.

In this book, we preview some of the greatest achievements of the Gothic era, none more glorious than the **Cathédrale de Notre-Dame** in Paris with its flying buttresses, rose windows, and gargoyles. For stained glass, **Saint-Chapelle,** near Notre-Dame, is reason enough to fly over. Of course, the 150 glorious stained-glass windows of the **Cathédrale of Chartres** are another great blooming of this art form.

When the 14th-century papal schism encouraged many bishops of Europe to recognize Avignon instead of Rome as the legitimate seat of the papacy, this capital of Provence became a virtual building site. A fortress was required that would also be a palace, and the Gothic **Palais des Papes** fit the bill.

The coming of the Renaissance

The French invasion of Italy in 1494 brought the ideals and aesthetic of the Italian Renaissance to France. This form of art and architecture reached its peak under the reign of François I, a true Renaissance prince who invited not only Cellini but also Leonardo da Vinci to his court at Amboise in the Loire Valley. The Renaissance lasted roughly from 1500 until 1630.

New political and social conditions encouraged aristocratic residences to be filled with sunlight, tapestries, paintings, and music. Adaptations of Gothic architecture, mingled with strong doses of Italian Renaissance, were applied to secular residences more suited to peace than to war. This is particularly evident at **Azay Le Rideau,** one of the loveliest of the Loire châteaux. Begun in 1518, its Italian influences are clearly visible, and it is obvious that this castle was built for pleasure living — not as a fortress to protect its inhabitants.

The artists of the School of Fontainebleau blended late Italian Renaissance style with French elements when redecorating the **Château de Fontainebleau.** Foremost among Renaissance châteaux in France is the **Château de Chambord** in the Loire Valley. Launched in 1519, it is the largest château in the Loire Valley and was the abode of the likes of Henri II and Catherine de Médici along with Louis XIII.

Renaissance architectural features relied on symmetry and a sense of proportion, with steeply pitched roofs often studded with dormer windows projecting from their sloping roofs. Classical capitals such as Doric, Ionic, and Corinthian came back into vogue.

From classicism to decorative rococo (1630–1800)

In the early 17th century, many of Paris's distinctive Italianate baroque domes were created. Louis XIV employed Le Vau, Perrault, both Mansarts, and Bruand for his buildings, plus Le Notre for the rigidly intelligent layouts of his gardens at **Versailles.** Meanwhile, court painters, such as Boucher, depicted allegorical shepherds and cherubs at play, while Georges de la Tour used techniques of light and shadow garnered from Caravaggio during a sojourn in Italy. Châteaux designed in this era included the superexpensive **Vaux-le-Vicomte** and the even more lavish royal residence at **Versailles.**

But by the 18th century, French architects returned to a restrained and dignified form of **classicism.** Public parks in Paris and other leading cities were laid out, sometimes requiring the demolition of acres of twisted medieval sectors. Roman styles of painting, sculpture, and dress became the rage.

From the 1800s to the modern era

The 19th century gave rise to the **First Empire,** with its tasteful neoclassical buildings, which prevailed during the reign of the dictator Napoléon Bonaparte. These buildings were followed by the buildings of the **Second Empire,** during the reign of the vain Napoléon III. Between 1855 and 1869 Napoléon III and his chief architect, Baron Haussmann, demolished much of the crumbling medieval Paris to lay out the wide boulevards that still connect the various monuments in broad, well-proportioned vistas. New building techniques were developed, including the use of iron as the structural support of bridges, viaducts, and buildings — such as the National Library, completed in 1860.

Following the Second Empire, the coming of the **Third Republic** brought the Industrial Age to French architecture. The Paris Exposition in 1878 launched this revolution. But it was the Exposition of 1889 that stunned the world when Alexandre-Gustave Eiffel designed and erected the most frequently slurred building of its day, the Eiffel Tower, for the Paris Exposition that year.

As a direct rebellion against this industrial architecture, the **Art Nouveau** movement came into being with its asymmetrical and curvaceous designs, using stained glass, tiles, wrought iron, and other materials. Art Nouveau was more a decorative movement than an architectural one. French for "New Art," Art Nouveau peaked at the turn of the 20th century, having been launched in the 1880s. One of the most important characteristics of this style is a dynamic, undulating, and flowing curved "whiplash" line of syncopated rhythm. Hyperbolas and parabolas were used in this expression, and conventional moldings sprang to life and just seemed to "grow" into plant-derived forms.

At the dawn of the 20th century, the **Beaux Arts** style of architecture was all the rage, the name coming from the École des Beaux Arts in Paris. Exquisite Beaux Arts buildings with ornate façades were erected throughout Paris, most of the structures at the same height, giving the city an evenly spaced skyline and justifying its claim as the most beautiful city in the world. This new movement added garlands of laurel and olive branches to the gray-white stone of elegant apartment buildings and hotels throughout France.

At the time of the World's Fair in Paris in 1925, **Art Deco** was a movement in decorative arts that also affected architecture. Art Deco quickly modulated into the 1930s *Moderne,* the decade with which the concept is most strongly associated today. It is characterized by the use of such materials as sharkskin and zebraskin, zigzag and stepped forms, bold and sweeping curves (in contrast to the sinuous curves of Art Nouveau), chevron patterns, and sunburst motifs. Art Deco was popular, and in France everything from the interiors of movie houses to ocean liners evoked this style. The enduring edifices of this Art Deco architecture are not found in Paris today but in New York, as exemplified by the Empire State Building and the Chrysler Building.

The latter 20th century was marred by controversy, as the late François Mitterrand launched his *grands projets* to change the face of Paris. A traditionalist like Prince Charles, living across the Channel from France, found much of this new architecture offensive. But the most cutting-edge of French architects had high praise for such works as the controversial **Centre Pompidou,** that modern art museum launched in 1977 with its "guts" showing, including steel supports, plastic tube escalators, and exposed pipes.

A Chinese American architect, I.M. Pei, added **glass pyramids** to the 17th-century courtyard of the Louvre in 1989, drawing screams of protest. That same year Paris opened a curvaceous, dark glass mound called **Opera Bastille.**

Taste of France: Local Cuisine

The French pride themselves on their food and wine, and you'll have a great time eating and drinking in the country. The first thing you may notice is how fresh everything is. Perhaps it's the soil (*le terroir,* as the French call it) that seems to invest all produce with rich flavor. Almost every town holds a daily fruit-and-vegetable market, so chefs throughout France have an abundance of fresh produce at their disposal. And that means you can stop at any market to soak in the atmosphere and gather the fixings for a memorable *pique-nique.*

While in France, you'll learn how to pace yourself through multicourse meals, to look forward to the cheese course, and to never skip dessert. With virtually no turnover of tables in French restaurants, customers are expected to settle in for at least a two-hour meal. Service usually moves at a leisurely pace because the idea is not to rush through the meal but to linger and enjoy the experience.

Each province has its own distinctive cuisine. Of course, the rich and varied restaurants of Paris showcase all of France. Every province of the country is represented by some bistro — often dozens of bistros — serving the foodstuff of each region.

Throughout this book, we provide recommendations on top restaurants and medium-priced places that offer good value so that you can enjoy this most special cuisine. We also highlight the rich and specialized cuisine of specific regions in this book's destination chapters.

Then there's the wine. First made by monks in wineries in the south, French wine is big business, yet it's still essentially controlled by relatively small-time farmers. Most restaurants have a good selection of local vintages on hand, and you may be surprised at how reasonable the prices are compared to what you'd be charged for a similar bottle at a restaurant outside France. House wines, available by the glass and the carafe, tend to be reasonably priced as well.

French cookery achieves palate perfection only when lubricated by wine, which is not considered a luxury or even an addition, but rather an integral part of every meal. Certain rules about wine drinking have been long established in France, but no one except traditionalists seems to follow them anymore. Those "rules" would dictate that if you're having a roast, steak, or game, a good burgundy should be your choice. If it's chicken, lamb, or veal, you'd choose a red from the Bordeaux country, and certainly a full-bodied red with Camembert (a cheese) and a blanc de blanc with oysters. A light rosé can go with almost anything, especially if enjoyed on a summer terrace overlooking a willow-fringed riverbank.

Let your own good taste — and sometimes almost equally important, your pocketbook — determine your choice of wine. Most wine stewards, called *sommeliers,* are there to help you in your choice, and only in the most dishonest of restaurants will they push you toward the most expensive selections. Of course, if you prefer only bottled water or perhaps a beer, then be firm and order either without embarrassment. In fact, bottled water might be a good idea at lunch if you're planning to drive on the roads of France later. Some restaurants include a beverage in their menu rates *(boisson compris),* but that's only in the cheaper places. Nevertheless, some of the most satisfying wines we've drunk in France came from unlabeled house bottles or carafes, called a *vin de la maison.* In general, unless you're a real connoisseur, don't worry about labels and vintages.

When in doubt, you can rarely go wrong with a good burgundy or Bordeaux, but you may want to be more adventurous than that. That's when the sommelier can help you, particularly if you tell him or her your taste in wine (semidry or very dry, for example). State frankly how much you're willing to pay and what you plan to order for your meal. If you're dining with others, you may want to order two or three bottles with an entire dinner, selecting a wine to suit each course. However, the French at even the most informal meals, and especially if there are only two persons dining, select only one wine to go with all their platters, from hors d'oeuvres to cheese. As a rule of thumb, expect to spend about one-third of the restaurant tab for wine.

Word to the Wise: The Local Lingo

You're going to France, so why not try to learn a little of the language? At the very least, try to learn a few numbers, basic greetings, and — above all — the life raft, *Parlez-vous anglais?* (Do you speak English?). As it turns out, many people do speak a passable English and will use it liberally if you demonstrate the basic courtesy of greeting them in their language. *Bonne chance.*

The Cheat Sheet at the front of this book has a list of many of the common words, phrases, and numbers you'll have a chance to use while in France. And the Quick Concierge appendix at the end of this book offers a few more specific phrases to keep in mind while in France. Taking it one step further, you may even want to invest in a copy of *French Phrases For Dummies* (published by Wiley), by Dodi-Katrin Schmidt, Michelle M. Williams, and Dominique Wenzel.

Background Check: Recommended Books and Movies

You can find numerous books on all aspects of French history and society, ranging from the very general, such as the section on France in the *Encyclopedia Americana,* International Edition (Grolier), which presents an illustrated overview of the French people and their way of life, to the specific, such as Judi Culbertson and Tom Randall's *Permanent Parisians: An Illustrated Guide to the Cemeteries of Paris* (Chelsea Green), which depicts the lives of many famous people who are buried in Paris.

✔ **History:** Two books that present French life and society in the 17th century are Warren Lewis's *The Splendid Century* (William Morrow), and Madame de Sévigné's *Selected Letters,* edited by Leonard W. Tancock (Penguin), which contains witty letters to her daughter during the reign of Louis XIV. Simon Schama's *Citizens* (Alfred A. Knopf) is "a magnificent and very electrifyingly new history of the French Revolution" — long, but enjoyable.

Moving into the 20th century, *Pleasure of the Belle Epoque: Entertainment and Festivity in Turn-of-the-Century France,* by Charles Rearick (Yale University Press), depicts public diversions in the changing and troubled times of the Third Republic. *Paris Was Yesterday, 1925-1939* (Harcourt Brace Jovanovich), is a collection of excerpts from Janet Flanner's "Letters from Paris" column of *The New Yorker.* Larry Collins and Dominique Lapierre have written a popular history of the liberation of Paris in 1944 called *Is Paris Burning?* (Warner Books).

Two unusual approaches to French history are Rudolph Chleminski's *The French at Table* (William Morrow), a funny, honest history of why the French know how to eat better than anyone, and *Paris: A Century of Change, 1878–1978,* by Normal Evenson (Yale University Press), a study of the urban development of Paris.

✔ **Autobiography:** You can get a different look at history by reading memoirs of writers' experiences in France. Among the best are *A Moveable Feast* (Collier Books), Ernest Hemingway's recollections of Paris in the 1920s, and Morley Callaghan's *That Summer in Paris: Memories of Tangled Friendships with Hemingway, Fitzgerald and Some Others,* an account of the same period. Another interesting read is *The Autobiography of Alice B. Toklas,* by Gertrude Stein (Vintage Books). It's an account of 30 years in Paris and the biography of Gertrude Stein.

✔ **The arts:** Much of France's beauty is expressed in its art. Three books that approach France from this perspective are *The History of Impressionism,* by John Rewald (Museum of Modern Art), a collection of documents (both writing and quotations by the artists) illuminating this period in the history of art; *The French Through Their Films,* by Robin Buss (Ungar), an exploration of the history and themes of more than 100 films; and *The Studios of Paris: The Capital of Art in the Late Nineteenth Century,* by John Milner (Yale University Press). Milner presents the forces that made Paris one of the most complex centers of the art world in the early modern era.

Nightlife of Paris: The Art of Toulouse-Lautrec, by Patrick O'Connor (Universe), is an enchanting 80-page book with lively anecdotes about the hedonistic luminaries of Belle Epoque Paris, with paintings, sketches, and lithographs by the artist. *Olympia: Paris in the Age of Manet,* by Otto Friedrich (HarperCollins), takes its inspiration from the artwork in the Musée d'Orsay. From here the book takes off on an anecdote-rich chain of historical associations, tracing the rise of the Impressionist school of modern painting but incorporating social commentary too, such as the pattern of prostitution and venereal disease in 19th-century France.

✔ **Fiction:** The *Chanson de Roland,* written between the 11th and 14th centuries, is the earliest and most celebrated of the "songs of heroic exploits." *The Misanthrope* and *Tartuffe* are two masterful satires on the frivolity of the 17th century by the great comic dramatist Molière.

François-Marie Arouet Voltaire's *Candide* is a classic satire attacking both the philosophy of optimism and the abuses of the ancien régime.

A few of the masterpieces of the 19th century are *Madame Bovary,* by Gustave Flaubert (Random House), in which the carefully wrought characters, setting, and plot attest to the genius of Flaubert in presenting the tragedy of Emma Bovary; Victor Hugo's *Les Misérables* (Modern Library), a classic tale of social oppression and human courage set in the era of Napoléon I; and the collection *Selected Stories* by the master of short stories, Guy de Maupassant (New American Library).

Honoré de Balzac's *La comédie humaine* depicts life in France from the fall of Napoleon to 1848. Henry James's *The Ambassadors* and *The American* both take place in Paris. *The Vagabond,* by Colette, evokes the life of a French music-hall performer.

Tropic of Cancer is the semiautobiographical story of Henry Miller's early years in Paris. One of France's leading thinkers, Jean-Paul Sartre, shows individuals struggling against their freedom in *No Exit and Three Other Plays* (Random House).

✔ **Films:** The French are credited with technical inventions that made film possible. French physicists laid the groundwork for the movie camera as early as the mid-19th century. The world's first movie was shown in Paris on December 28, 1895, the creation of the Lumière brothers. Charles Pathé and Leon Gaumont were the first to exploit filmmaking on a grand scale, and by the 1920s the French began to view filmmaking as an art form, infusing it with surreal and Dada themes. French films — good or bad — continue to be made today, although American movies dominate the market.

The biggest worldwide postmillennium hit was *Amelie* (2002), witnessed by millions across the globe. In the film, Amelie is an attractive but introverted woman from a dysfunctional family. In flashbacks we witness scenes from a troubled life. *Affair of the Necklace* (2001) starred Hilary Swank, its plot based on true events integral to the causes of the French Revolution and the beheading of Marie Antoinette. It was filmed on location in France, including the Hall of Mirrors at Versailles. That old classic, still widely shown, *An American in Paris* (1951), stars Gene Kelly at his dancing best. The cinematography captures some of the most enchanting sights of postwar Paris. The latest version of *Moulin Rouge* (2001) starred Nicole Kidman in this pop-culture movie that re-created Paris of the 1890s, with its can-can dancers and Toulouse-Lautrec characters.

Chapter 3

Deciding Where and When to Go

In This Chapter

▶ Exploring France's main areas of interest

▶ Choosing the best season to visit

▶ Finding events that suit your interests

▶ Picking up a few travel tips

This chapter helps you decide which parts of France you want to visit and when to go. We give you the pros and cons of each season so that you can time your trip to make the most of your visit. We also provide a calendar of the most memorable annual events in France — you may want to consider planning your trip to coincide with (or avoid) one of these festivals, sporting events, or celebrations.

Going Everywhere You Want to Be

France For Dummies, 3rd Edition, is a book of highlights, so you won't find a review of all of France's regions (shown in the upcoming map, "The Regions of France"). What follows are short sketches of each of the regions covered in this book to help you choose where you want to go. These locales are the ones with the best and most interesting sites — the blockbusters of France.

Falling in love with Paris: From the Tour Eiffel to Montmartre

France's capital, as you've probably heard, is one of the world's most beautiful, romantic, and exciting cities. **Paris** is so full of things to see and do that you can't possibly cover everything in one trip, even one *long* trip. So don't even try. You may have to limit your sightseeing to the greatest hits — Tour Eiffel, Cathédrale Notre-Dame and Sainte-Chapelle, Musée du Louvre, Musée d'Orsay, and Montmartre and Sacré-Coeur — to leave plenty of time for strolling, shopping, and enjoying cafe life. If you start to become overwhelmed by all the choices, chill out with a boat ride on the Seine or a picnic in the Jardin du Luxembourg. One thing to consider about Paris: Expect rain every day, and you won't be disappointed. (See Chapters 11 and 12 for details on Paris.)

Don't forget the famous sights just outside the city (see Chapter 13), such as Louis XIV's Château de Versailles, the Cathédrale Notre-Dame in Chartres, the Renaissance castle of Fontainebleau, Monet's house at Giverny (with its famous waterlily pond), and even Disneyland Paris.

Exploring the Loire Valley châteaux

The **Loire Valley,** an hour's train ride from Paris, is where France's royalty lived for hundreds of years, and their castles — many of them Renaissance masterpieces — are a thrill to visit. Because more than a dozen famous châteaux are within about 97km (60 miles), this region is easy to explore. You'll even see plenty of people biking from castle to castle. We give you the lowdown on eight "fairytale" castles, including Chambord, the largest, and Chenonceau, the most beautiful (see Chapter 15). Two to four castles in one trip are about right before châteaux fatigue kicks in. We also introduce you to Tours (see Chapter 14) and Orléans (see Chapter 15), cities that bookend the region and are good bases from which to explore the Vallée de la Loire.

Traveling through Normandy and Brittany

Normandy and Brittany, two regions on the west coast, offer a wealth of historic sites and captivating coastal views. **Rouen,** a little less than an hour from Paris by the fast train, is a good place to see the Norman architecture that many people think of as quintessentially *ye olde world:* half-timbered houses on cobblestone pedestrian-only streets. In Rouen, you also find several interesting museums and historic sites, many relating to Joan of Arc, who was burned alive at the stake in the central square. And fans of Impressionism will enjoy seeing the elaborate Cathédrale Notre-Dame in Rouen, which Monet, fascinated by its intricate facade, painted countless times.

Normandy also is the place to view two of France's most famous historic sights (see Chapter 16): the Bayeux Tapestry, in the charming village of Bayeux, and Mont-St-Michel, the most famous of all abbeys set high on a rock just off the coast. (Mont-St-Michel is very popular with visitors, so we give you hints on how to avoid being trampled.) Many sightseers go to Normandy just to see the D-day beaches, where thousands of American, British, and Canadian troops bravely made their way on shore, paving the way for the Allied defeat of the Nazis in World War II. The soldiers' graveyards, white crosses stretching as far as the eye can see, may be the most moving site in the area. The best season to see Normandy is in spring, when apple orchards are in bloom, weather is fairly mild, and fewer visitors are around.

The Regions of France

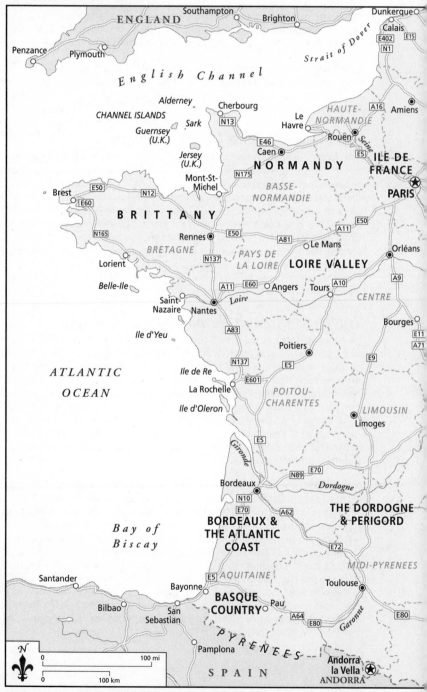

ENGLAND
Southampton
Brighton
Dunkerque
Calais
E402
E15
N1
Penzance
Plymouth
Strait of Dover
English Channel
Alderney
Cherbourg
HAUTE-NORMANDIE
A16
Amiens
CHANNEL ISLANDS
Guernsey (U.K.)
Sark
Le Havre
N13
Rouen
Seine
Jersey (U.K.)
E46
ILE DE FRANCE
E5
Caen
NORMANDY
Brest
E50
N12
Mont-St-Michel
N175
BASSE-NORMANDIE
PARIS
E60
E50
BRITTANY
A11
N165
BRETAGNE
Rennes
E50
A81
Le Mans
E50
Orléans
N137
PAYS DE LA LOIRE
LOIRE VALLEY
A11
Lorient
A11
E60
Angers
Tours
A10
A9
Belle-Ile
Saint-Nazaire
Nantes
Loire
CENTRE
Bourges
Ile d'Yeu
A83
E11
A71
Poitiers
E9
N137
ATLANTIC
OCEAN
Ile de Re
E5
La Rochelle
E601
POITOU-CHARENTES
Ile d'Oleron
LIMOUSIN
Limoges
E5
Gironde
N89
E70
Dordogne
Bordeaux
THE DORDOGNE & PERIGORD
N10
E70
A62
Bay of Biscay
BORDEAUX & THE ATLANTIC COAST
E72
MIDI-PYRENEES
Santander
E5
AQUITAINE
Bayonne
Toulouse
Bilbao
BASQUE COUNTRY
Pau
San Sebastian
A64
E80
Garonne
E80
PYRENEES
N
Pamplona
0   100 mi
0   100 km
Andorra la Vella
ANDORRA
SPAIN

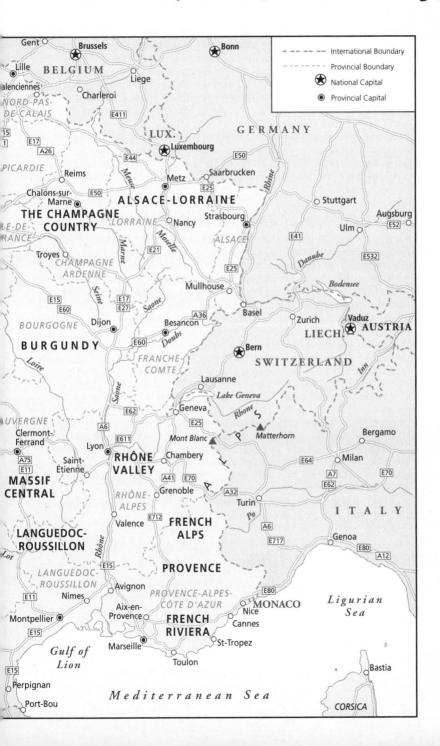

Brittany's rocky coast juts out along France's western edge, and the region is proud of its unique culture and language, which actually is closer to Welsh than French (see Chapter 17). The coast is dotted with fishing villages and pricey resorts. In Brittany, we take you to **Quimper,** home of the famous pottery; **Carnac,** which has thousands of aligned stones dating to Neolithic times; and **Nantes,** a lively city between Brittany and the Loire Valley. Brittany is a more remote region, a little harder to get to, which for some people makes it all the more attractive. Coastal towns in Brittany are popular summer resorts, and if you want to swim in the ocean, you'll need to go during the height of summer when the waters are warm enough. The fall and spring can be desolate but appealing times to see this area — the crowds are few and villages more peaceful.

Seeing the best of Provence and the Riviera

Provence and the Riviera are France's most popular regions. That's because these areas are lovely places to visit, full of interesting sites, a grand cuisine, and people who have a bit of Italian *joie de vivre* mixed in with the classic French hauteur. And of course there's the weather: marvelous sunny days with sea breezes year-round. In **Provence,** you can visit the great French towns of **Avignon,** home of the Palais des Papes; **Arles,** with Roman ruins and memories of the artist Van Gogh; and **Aix-en-Provence,** a beautiful city full of sparkling fountains. You can also explore the quaint village of **St-Rémy,** with more Roman ruins and more memories of Van Gogh. In Chapter 18, we also make a quick tour of **Marseille,** a bustling metropolis and a major transportation hub in the south.

The **Riviera** has so many intriguing and chic resorts that it's hard to choose which one to visit (see Chapters 19, 20, and 21). We guide you through the ten top French towns to visit plus the tiny principality of Monaco. Along the coast from west to east are **St-Tropez, Cannes, Antibes, Nice, St-Jean-Cap-Ferrat, Beaulieu,** and **Monaco.** In the hills are **Biot, Vence,** and **St-Paul-de-Vence.** You can hang out at the most fashionable beaches, stroll through cobblestone villages, see some of France's best modern art museums, and participate in the glamorous nightlife. From the Monte Carlo Casino to the beaches of St-Tropez, this slice of France is a slice of heaven.

Scheduling Your Time

When visiting France, a large country with so many diverse sights, the biggest challenge may be deciding what regions you want to visit. You can't do it all, but you can see and do quite a bit in just a week. Here are some things to keep in mind when planning your trip:

 ✔ **Make choices.** Choose one region or at most two adjoining regions to visit in addition to Paris, unless you're planning a long trip. You'll get a much better feel for the region you visit, and you won't spend so much time en route to places. Good regions to combine are

Normandy and Brittany or Provence and the Riviera. Chapter 4 has some good tips for combining these regions.

✔ **Take the train.** France's train system is exceptionally fast and efficient. The best way to travel to the regions described in this book is to catch a train from Paris and then either rent a car or rely on public transportation to get around. That way, you'll at least avoid driving in and out of Paris, which can be a nightmare. If possible, you also want to avoid driving in and out of other large cities such as Nantes, Rouen, and Nice. The outskirts of these cities aren't at all scenic, and the complex highways and tailgating drivers can make you loony.

In contrast to city driving, you'll find that driving along country roads in France can be a real pleasure. Roads are well marked and often are uncrowded. For more information about riding the rails and other ways to get around France, check out Chapter 7.

✔ **Avoid disappointment and book ahead.** Many people visit France regularly to stay at the top hotels and dine in the top restaurants. If you're planning to splurge on an expensive hotel or a gourmet meal, book well ahead of time. A week or two in advance isn't too early to make a reservation for France's top restaurants. Booking a couple months in advance is a good idea for the best hotels.

✔ **Expect strikes.** France is infamous for its strikes, and the French have a very blasé attitude toward what can be a major inconvenience. The more common strikes usually have to do with transportation. Railroad pullmen on strike means no food or water on long train rides. Air traffic controllers on strike leads to canceled flights into, out of, and around the country. Gas delivery trucks on strike means . . . Well, you get the point. Our advice: Don't cut it close with travel plans. If you absolutely *must* be at a meeting back home on Monday morning, you'd better plan to leave Saturday, not Sunday.

✔ **Enjoy the lifestyle.** One reason French people may not be as annoyed by strikes as other nationalities is their fairly laid-back attitude toward life. To the French, certain pleasures — such as great food, fine wines, and beautiful art — make life worth living. How does that affect you, the visitor? Instead of filling every second of your day running from sight to sight, try to slow down a little and appreciate the details. Spend an afternoon writing postcards in a cafe or strolling through a historic neighborhood. Amble through a village market or visit an unusual monument.

✔ **Adjust to French mealtimes.** The French eat a light continental breakfast, and you can learn to love a scrumptious *pain au chocolat* and *café au lait* first thing in the morning. You'll find that many places are closed between noon and 2 p.m., when millions of French people have a long lunch. Although you can probably find a museum or a shop open during this time, in most of the country, do yourself a favor and have lunch then, too. Although dinner starting after 7:30 p.m. may sound late, that long lunch tides you over until then. The more you fit yourself into the French timetable, the more you'll enjoy your trip and feel like one of the natives.

Revealing the Secrets of the Seasons

As in much of Europe, *high season* in France is summer, and *low season* is winter, leaving the *shoulder seasons* of spring and fall as good times to visit (fewer crowds, decent weather). One exception to this rule is winter on the Riviera, which is popular with retirees. Paris is a rainy city much of the year and quite cold and bleak during winter, but in those dark days of February, the crowds are low and so are the airfares.

The French government has mandated that store sales happen semiannually in January and in late June/early July. The sales *(solders)* last for several weeks; you find the most frenzied activity in the north (Paris and environs) and in the south (the Riviera and environs). Every French person takes a vacation in August, so you find the biggest crowds that month and a number of closings at restaurants, particularly in Paris. Many stores, restaurants, and hotels throughout the country also close for a few weeks in December or January. But one of the best things about a summer visit is that you can bask in daylight that lasts until 10 p.m. Tables 3-1 and 3-2 give you an idea of what the temperature and rainfall are like in Paris and Nice throughout the year.

Table 3-1 Average Temperatures and Precipitation for Paris

	Jan	Feb	Mar	Apr	May	June	July	Aug	Sep	Oct	Nov	Dec
High (°F/°C)	43/ 6	45/ 7	51/ 11	57/ 14	64/ 18	70/ 21	75/ 24	75/ 24	69/ 21	59/ 15	49/ 9	45/ 7
Low (°F/°C)	34/ 1	34/ 1	38/ 3	42/ 6	49/ 9	54/ 12	58/ 14	57/ 14	52/ 11	46/ 8	39/ 4	36/ 2
Rainfall (in./cm.)	2.1/ 5.3	1.8/ 4.6	2.1/ 5.3	1.8/ 4.6	2.5/ 6.4	2.3/ 5.8	2.1/ 5.3	2.0/ 5.1	2.1/ 5.3	2.2/ 5.6	2.2/ 5.6	2.2/ 5.6

Table 3-2 Average Temperatures and Precipitation for Nice

	Jan	Feb	Mar	Apr	May	June	July	Aug	Sep	Oct	Nov	Dec
High (°F/°C)	55/ 13	55/ 13	58/ 14	61/ 16	67/ 19	74/ 23	79/ 26	80/ 27	75/ 24	68/ 20	61/ 16	56/ 13
Low (°F/°C)	42/ 6	43/ 6	46/ 8	49/ 9	56/ 13	62/ 17	67/ 19	68/ 20	63/ 17	56/ 13	48/ 9	43/ 6
Rainfall (in./cm.)	3.0/ 7.6	2.9/ 7.4	2.9/ 7.4	2.5/ 6.4	1.9/ 4.8	1.5/ 3.8	0.7/ 1.8	1.2/ 3.0	2.6/ 6.6	4.4/ 11.2	4.6/ 11.7	3.5/ 8.9

Spring

Cole Porter wrote "I love Paris in the springtime," and with good reason. The parks and gardens of Paris (and those at Versailles, Fontainebleau, and Claude Monet's Giverny) are at their colorful, fragrant best in early May.

- ✔ Spring is off season, so you'll be blessed with short lines for sights and museums.

- ✔ You may also be able to get reservations in the country's top restaurants, which are fully booked come summer.

But keep in mind that April in Paris isn't as temperate as Porter would have you believe.

- ✔ Nearly every Monday in May is a holiday in France, so stores may be closed and other venues affected.

- ✔ Unless you're a racecar fanatic, don't go anywhere near Monaco during the Grand Prix in mid-May. Hotel prices in Monaco and surrounding towns are at their highest and booked well in advance.

- ✔ Count on the weather being very fickle, so pack for warm, cold, wet, dry, and every other eventuality (bring layers, and don't even think about coming without an umbrella).

Summer

High season in France can mean the best of worlds and the worst of worlds. But the best are really great, making summer a fabulous time of year to visit France.

- ✔ Wonderfully long and sultry days are summer's hallmark — we're talking 6 a.m. sunrises and 10 p.m. sunsets — so you're afforded additional hours to wander and discover. Historic sites, museums, and shops keep longer hours and usually are open during lunch, unlike the rest of the year.

- ✔ You can find discounts of 30 percent to 50 percent in most stores during late June and early July, one of the two big months for shopping sales (January is the other).

- ✔ In areas such as Provence and the Riviera, cultural calendars are at their fullest, including Nice's Grand Parade du Jazz and the Festival d'Avignon and Festival d'Aix-en-Provence. (Summer also is the time to attend cultural festivals through the rest of the country. And the great bike race, Le Grand Tour de France, takes place in July.)

- ✔ Although the celebration of Bastille Day (July 14) through most of France means that stores and most attractions are closed, in Paris, festivals are held and panoramic fireworks take place at Tour Eiffel.

If you're concerned about costs and convenience, a summer visit definitely offers greater costs and less convenience.

✔ The influx of visitors during summer means long lines at museums and other attractions throughout the country.

✔ The top restaurants and the best or most affordable hotels may be booked. And airfares reach their peak.

✔ Expect traffic-clogged highways, especially in Provence and the Riviera.

✔ Because most French people take their vacations in August, you'll find tourist areas packed throughout the country.

✔ In Paris, the city's cultural calendar slows down, and some shops and restaurants close for the entire month of August.

Autumn

Fall is a mellow time to visit France, and the days often are clear and crisp.

✔ The wine harvest starts mid- to late September, and by mid-October the country's vineyards are a golden color.

✔ Paris crackles back to life come September, one of the most exciting times of the year, when important art exhibits open along with trendy new restaurants, shops, and cafes.

✔ Airfares drop from their summertime highs.

During the fall months, you may find yourself jostling with a more decidedly business-oriented crowd returning from a late-summer respite.

✔ Finding a hotel at the last minute can be difficult because of the number of business conventions and trade shows happening in Paris and other cities such as Orléans, Tours, Rouen, Nantes, Cannes, and Nice.

✔ Transportation strikes of varying intensities traditionally occur during fall — some may go virtually unnoticed by the average traveler, but others can be a giant hassle.

✔ In some seashore areas, such as Brittany, certain restaurants close for a couple of weeks in October to take a breather from the busy summer.

Winter

Back in the '50s, you didn't go to France in winter unless you had business there. That has changed, and a winter vacation in France can seem almost . . . well, profitable.

🖛 Look for bargain airfares and various discounts. Airlines and tour operators offer unbeatable prices on flights and package tours.

🖛 Lines at museums and other sights mercifully are short.

🖛 Shoppers can save up to 50 percent during the January sales.

Of course, winter weather may be enough to dampen the spirits of some warm-blooded travelers.

🖛 In Paris, winter is gray (sometimes the sun doesn't shine for weeks), dreary, and often bone-chillingly damp.

🖛 Look out for those wind tunnels that lash up and down the grand boulevards in all French cities. (Bring a warm, preferably water-proof, coat.)

🖛 You'll miss the wonderful cafe life that takes place in France in fair weather.

Perusing a Calendar of Events

Running into one of France's great festivals is truly a joy when you're traveling, but unless you plan ahead, you have no guarantee of finding one. The following is a list of the very best special events.

January

The **Monte Carlo Motor Rally** is one of the world's most famous car races. For more details, call ☎ **377-92-16-61-66.** Mid-January; Monaco.

International Ready-to-Wear Fashion Shows (Le Salon International de Prêt-à-porter) take place at the Parc des Expositions, Porte de Versailles and are among the premier fashion shows in a city that practi-cally invented fashion. For more details, call ☎ **01-44-94-70-00** or visit www.pretparis.com. Last week in January (also in late September); Paris.

February

France's biggest Mardi Gras celebration is the renowned **Nice Carnival (Le Carnaval de Nice),** which attracts hundreds of thousands of revel-ers. The highlight of the event is the Mardi Gras parade with dozens of giant floats, but smaller parades occur during the daytime and evenings, as do boat races, concerts, street music and food vendors, masked balls, and fireworks. The Niçoises' love of flowers is celebrated in the Battle of Flowers, when opposing teams throw flowers at each other. For details, call ☎ **08-92-70-74-07** or visit www.nicecarnaval.com. Mid-February to early March; Nice.

March

Tacky and fun, **Foire du Trône** is an annual carnival that features a Ferris wheel, rides and games, hokey souvenirs, and fairground food all set up at the Pelouse de Reuilly in the Bois de Vincennes. For details, call ☎ 01-46-27-52-29. Late March to late May; Paris.

April

One of the most popular athletic events during the year, the **International Marathon of Paris** runs past a variety of the city's most beautiful monuments. The race takes place on a Sunday and attracts enthusiastic crowds. For details, call ☎ 01-41-33-15-68 or visit www.parismarathon.com. Mid-April; Paris.

May

The movie madness that accompanies the **Cannes Film Festival (Festival International du Film)** transforms this city into a media circus, with daily melodramas acted out in cafes, on sidewalks, and in hotel lobbies. Reserve early and make a deposit. Admission to the premieres is by invitation only. Box-office tickets are available for other showings, which play 24 hours a day. Contact the Festival International du Film (FIF), 3 rue Amélie, 75007 Paris ☎ 01-53-59-61-00 (www.festival-cannes.com). Two weeks before the festival, the event's administration moves to the Palais des Festivals, esplanade Georges-Pompidou, 06400 Cannes ☎ 04-93-39-01-01. Third week in May; Cannes.

The **Monaco Grand Prix** is Monaco's biggest event of the year, and with the crowds and noise, you have to really love car racing for this one. Hundreds of racecars speed through Monaco to the fascination of thousands of fans. For details, call ☎ 377-93-15-26-00 or visit www.acm.mc. Late May; Monaco.

Tickets are hard to come by for the **French Open,** a major tennis tournament played in the Stade Roland Garros in the Bois de Boulogne on the western edge of the city. Tickets go on sale two weeks before competition starts. The stadium is at 2 av. Gordon Bennett, 16e. For details, call ☎ 01-47-43-48-00 or visit www.fft.fr/rolandgarros. Begins in late May; Paris.

June

Some 50 concerts are held in churches, auditoriums, and concert halls during the **La Villette Jazz Festival** in the Paris suburb of the same name. Past festivals have included Herbie Hancock, Shirley Horn, and other international artists. Call ☎ 08-03-30-63-06. Late June to early July.

The entire country becomes a concert venue with the **Fête de la Musique,** a celebration of the first day of summer. You can hear everything from classical to hip-hop for free in squares and streets around Paris and other cities. A big rock concert happens in place de la République in

Paris, and a classical concert takes place in the gardens of the Palais Royal. For details, call ☎ **08-36-68-31-12** or 01-49-52-53-35 (Fax: 01-49-52-53-00). June 21; countrywide.

One of the most distinguished aviation events in the world, the **Paris Air Show** takes place in odd-numbered years (2005, 2007) at Le Bourget Airport just outside Paris. You can check out the latest aeronautic technology on display. For details, call ☎ **01-53-23-33-33** or visit www.salon-du-bourget.fr. Mid-June; Paris.

Art exhibits and concerts and the city's most flamboyant parade are part of **Gay Pride** in the gay-friendly Marais neighborhood and in other Paris streets, including boulevard St-Michel. For details, call ☎ **01-53-01-47-01.** Late June; Paris.

July

Les Baroquiales is a cultural festival that spotlights the baroque style, the 17th-century mode of art and architecture that features elaborate ornamentation. Events are presented cooperatively by tourism bureaus with music, theater, and dance concerts joining walking tours and village fairs. Because this annual event is relatively new, you won't find as many crowds or problems with reservations. For details, call ☎ **04-93-04-12-55.** Early July; towns near the French Riviera and Italian border.

The biggest party on **Bastille Day** takes place in Paris. Citywide festivities begin the evening of June 13, with street fairs, pageants, and feasts. Free *bals* (dances) are open to everyone and held in fire stations all over the city. (Some of the best bals are in the fire station on rue du Vieux-Colombier near place St-Sulpice, 6e; rue Sévigné, 4e; and rue Blanche, near place Pigalle, 9e.) On July 14, a big military parade starts at 10 a.m. on the Champs-Elysées; get there early if you hope to see anything. A sound-and-light show with fireworks takes place that night at the Trocadéro. Rather than face the crowds, many people watch the fireworks from the Champs de Mars across the river, from hotel rooms with views, or even from rue Soufflot, in front of the Panthéon. July 14; countrywide.

The most famous bicycle race in the world, **Tour de France** covers more than 2,000 miles throughout France and always ends on the Champs-Elysées in Paris. Spectators need special invitations for a seat in the stands near place de la Concorde, but you can see the cyclists at street level farther up the Champs-Elysées and, depending on the route (which changes each year), elsewhere in the city. Check the newspapers the day before. For details, call ☎ **01-41-33-15-00** or visit www.letour.fr. Month of July; countrywide.

The Orangerie in the Bagatelle gardens on the edge of the Bois de Boulogne is the backdrop for the much-loved **Festival Chopin à Paris,** an annual series of daily piano recitals. For details, call ☎ **01-45-01-51-85.** Early July; Paris.

Inspired by the great American jazz performers, the **Nice Jazz Festival (Grand Parade du Jazz)** is one of the Riviera's biggest annual events. This international jazz festival attracts famous soloists and bands to the spectacular site of the Roman Amphitheater and gardens of Cimiez, the hill north of the city. In the past, performers such as Dizzy Gillespie and Herbie Hancock have brought down the house. For details, call ☎ **04-92-14-46-46** or visit www.nicejazzfest.com. Ten days in early to mid-July; Nice.

As a world-class cultural event, the **Festival d'Avignon** presents works in theater, dance, and music from international troupes. The focus of this prestigious festival usually is on the avant-garde; tickets are pricey. During the same period as the festival, another festival called Festival Off takes place. It's a sort of the off-off-Broadway version with less expensive events and less established performers. For details, call ☎ **04-90-27-66-50** (Fax: 04-90-27-66-83) or visit www.festival-avignon.com. Mid- to late July; Avignon.

Although primarily a music festival with a wide range of styles, from medieval to contemporary, The events of the **Festival d'Aix-en-Provence** are more affordable than the one in the previously described neighboring festival at Avignon. For details, call ☎ **04-42-17-34-34** or visit www.festival-aix.com. Four weeks in July; Aix-en-Provence.

September

Off-limits palaces, churches, and other official buildings throw open their doors to the public for two days during the **Journées Portes Ouvertes.** Long lines can put a damper on your sightseeing, so plan what you want to see and show up early (with a good book, just in case). Get a list and a map of all the open buildings from the Paris Tourist Office, reachable at ☎ **08-36-68-31-12.** Weekend closest to September 15; Paris.

The **Festival d'Automne** is an arts festival around Paris that is recognized throughout Europe for its innovative programming and the high quality of its artists and performers. Obtain programs through the mail so that you can book ahead for events you don't want to miss. For details, call ☎ **01-53-45-17-00.** September 15 to December 31; Paris.

The **International Ready-to-Wear Fashion Shows (Le Salon International de Prêt-à-porter)** at the Parc des Expositions, Porte de Versailles, is one of the premier fashion shows in Paris. For more details, call ☎ **01-44-94-70-00** or visit www.pretparis.com. Late September (also last week in January); Paris.

October

Celebrate the harvest of the wine produced at Montmartre's one remaining vineyard, Clos Montmartre, during the **Fêtes des Vendanges à Montmartre.** You can also watch as the wine is auctioned off at high prices to benefit local charities. (Word of advice: *Don't bid.* The wine isn't very good.) Locals dress in period costumes, and the streets come alive with music. For details, call ☎ **01-46-06-00-32.** First or second Saturday of October; Paris.

Les Voiles de St-Tropez is a regatta for antique wooden sailboats in St-Tropez on the Riviera. It's a tossup whether the most beautiful sight is when all the boats are under full sail in the bay or when they're all docked in the harbor so that you can get a close look at their gleaming hulls. During the weeklong festival, the town is full of youthful sailors from around the world, and evenings are very lively. For details, call ☎ **04-94-97-45-21.** Early October; St-Tropez.

One of the largest contemporary art fairs in the world, the **FIAC (International Contemporary Art Fair)** has stands from more than 150 galleries, half of them foreign. As interesting for browsing as for buying, the fair takes place in Paris Expo-Porte de Versailles. For details, call ☎ **01-41-90-47-47** or visit fiac.reed-oip.fr. Late October; Paris.

November

France's most prestigious wine festival, **Les Trois Glorieuses,** takes place annually in three towns in Burgundy and features wine tastings galore and plenty of street fairs. The biggest event is the wine auction in Beaune, which attracts wine connoisseurs from around the globe. Getting a room in Beaune or nearby villages is difficult during this event. For details, call ☎ **03-80-26-21-30** or visit www.ot-beaune.fr. Third week in November; Clos-de-Vougeot, Beaune, and Meursault, Burgundy.

Lancement des Illuminations des Champs-Elysées, which is the annual lighting of the avenue's Christmas lights, makes for a festive evening, with jazz concerts and an international star who pushes the button that lights up the avenue. For details, call ☎ **08-36-68-31-12** or 01-49-52-53-35 (Fax: 01-49-52-53-00). Late November; Paris.

December

Each year a different foreign city installs a life-sized Christmas manger scene in the plaza in front of the Hôtel de Ville (City Hall) as part of **La Crèche sur le Parvis.** The crèche is open daily from 10 a.m. to 8 p.m. December 1 to January 3; Paris.

Europe's most visible exposition of what's afloat is the **Salon Nautique de Paris (The Boat Fair).** It's of interest to wholesalers, retailers, and individual boat owners. The fair takes place at Parc des Expositions, Porte de Versailles, Paris, 15e. Call ☎ **01-41-90-47-22** or visit www.salonnautiqueparis.com. Second week in December (lasts for ten days); Paris.

In Paris, the **Fête de St-Sylvestre (New Year's Eve)** is celebrated mainly in the Latin Quarter near the Sorbonne with crowds of merrymakers in the streets. Wide streets such as boulevard St-Michel and the Champs-Elysées are filled with pedestrians. December 31; countrywide.

Chapter 4

Four Great France Itineraries

. . . .

In This Chapter

▶ Touring France in one or two weeks
▶ Visiting France with your kids
▶ Taking a tour for art lovers

. . . .

*I*n this chapter, we put together several itineraries to help you plan your trip to France. If you're a first-time or time-pressed traveler with one or two weeks to spend in France, you may find it helpful to have some premier destinations and sights laid out in an easy-to-follow order. Or if you've been to France before, perhaps you'd like to concentrate your upcoming visit on food and wine or great art. You can have an extraordinary taste of the country in just one or two well-planned weeks.

Most of the regions we describe in this book are within a short train ride of Paris. That means you can easily combine a few days in the capital with visits to the highlights of Normandy and the Loire Valley, both only one or two hours away by train. Brittany and Provence are slightly longer trips by train (three to four hours). If you're traveling from Paris to Nice on the Riviera (6½ hours), you may want to take a very early train, so you don't spend the whole day traveling.

 Be flexible while traveling: If you end up loving a town that you were supposed to stay in for just one night, you can change things around and stay for two nights or more. We once ran into a couple in St-Tropez who were scheduled to be traveling all along the Riviera but decided to stay anchored at the resort in St-Tropez for their entire trip.

The following itineraries take you through some wonderful towns and past some major sights (see the map of "Four Great France Itineraries" later in this chapter). The pace may be a bit breathless for some people, so be sure to skip a sight occasionally to have some down time. Of course, you can use any of these itineraries as a jumping-off point to develop a sojourn of your own that matches your personal interests.

Seeing France's Highlights in One Week

Use the following itinerary to make the most of your week in France, but feel free to leave out a sight or two to explore a charming village or to save a day just to relax. One week is far too rushed, of course, but if it's all that you can schedule during this trip, this itinerary at least gives you an introduction to Paris and a chance to see some of the sights of Normandy, a region on the west coast of France not too far from Paris.

✔ Take a flight that arrives in **Paris** as early as possible on **Day One.** Check into your hotel and hit the nearest cafe for a pick-me-up *café au lait* and a *croissant* before sightseeing. Try to see one major and one minor (that is, one that's less time-consuming) attraction your first day in Paris. Major sights include **Musée du Louvre, Tour Eiffel, Musée d'Orsay,** and **Cathédrale Notre-Dame.** Not-so-major attractions include **Arc de Triomphe, Sainte-Chapelle** and the **Conciergerie, Musée National Auguste-Rodin, Centre Pompidou, Jardin des Tuilleries** and **Jardin du Luxembourg,** and **Montmartre** and **Sacré-Coeur.** Buy and send postcards, and wander around to get your bearings. That night, enjoy dinner at the famous brasserie **Bofinger** or one of the many restaurants in the increasingly stylish Marais district.

✔ On **Day Two,** try to see one major and two minor sights. Of course, on the way to these sights, in particular Notre-Dame and Sainte-Chapelle, you'll inevitably have quintessential Paris experiences such as walking along the **quais of the Seine** and visiting the **St-Germain-des-Près neighborhood** on the Left Bank. For more information on the attractions of Paris, refer to Chapter 12.

✔ On **Day Three,** take an early morning train to **Versailles.** You need several hours to tour the palace and the gardens. Return in the afternoon for tea at **Angelina,** shopping at the fancy-food shop **Fauchon,** and a late dinner. (See Chapter 13 for details about exploring Versailles.)

✔ On **Day Four,** take an early train to **Rouen** in Normandy (see Chapter 16), check your bags at the Rouen train station, and walk around the city for a couple of hours, looking at the half-timbered buildings. After lunch, head back to the train station, rent a car (and don't forget to pick up your bags!), and drive to **Bayeux,** where you'll spend the night. On the way, you can stop to explore the beautiful **Abbaye de Jumièges.**

✔ On the morning of **Day Five,** see the **Bayeux Tapestry** and then drive to the **D-day beaches,** stopping at the **American Cemetery** and the **Caen Memorial.** That evening, drive to **Mont-St-Michel** (less than two hours), and stay overnight in the pedestrian village on the rock. If it's summer, you can take an illuminated night tour of the abbey — after most of the other visitors have gone home. See Chapter 16 for more details.

✔ Or you can do the first tour in the morning on **Day 6** before all the buses arrive. Then drive back to Rouen, and catch a train back to Paris and your flight home.

Four Great France Itineraries

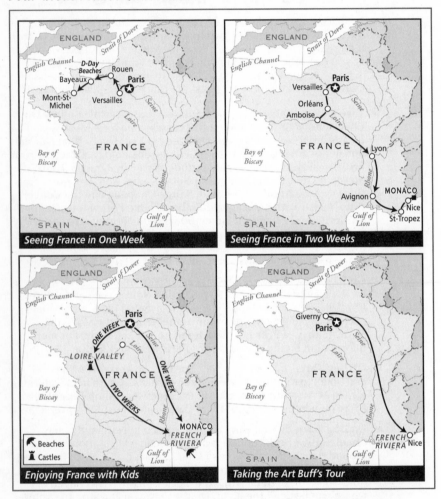

Seeing France in One Week

Seeing France in Two Weeks

Enjoying France with Kids

Taking the Art Buff's Tour

Seeing France's Highlights in Two Weeks

With two weeks to explore France, you have some breathing room — but not that much. If you don't mind the rush, you can also see several regions: Paris (Chapter 12), two Loire Valley castles (Chapter 15), a couple of towns in Provence (Chapter 18), and several towns on the Riviera, including Monaco (Chapter 20).

✔ You can spend **Days One, Two, and Three** in **Paris,** as covered under "Seeing France's Highlights in One Week."

✔ On **Day Four,** leave Paris on an early train to **Orléans** (trip time: 1¼ hours). Rent a car in Orléans, and drive to see the **Château de Chambord,** the largest and most impressive of Loire Valley castles. That afternoon, drive to **Amboise** to stay overnight and visit the **Château d'Amboise** and **Leonardo da Vinci's former residence.** (See Chapter 15 for details on exploring the Loire Valley.)

✔ On **Day Five,** get an early start, and return the rental car in Orléans. You face a choice now: You can take a morning train from Orléans to Paris's **Gare d'Austerlitz** and then catch the Métro or a taxi to the Gare de Lyon, where you'll hop on a TGV (fast train) to **Avignon** (3 hours, 20 minutes). Or you can board a train from Orléans to **Lyon** and change to a train for Avignon. Check into your hotel in Avignon. You should have time to wander through the town to get your bearings, buy some colorful Provençal fabrics, and see one of the smaller sights, such as the **Pont St-Bénézet** (also known as the Bridge of Avignon) or the **Musée du Petit-Palais.** (See Chapter 18 for details on Provence.)

✔ On the morning of **Day Six,** visit the **Palais des Papes.** After lunch, rent a car and drive to **St-Tropez,** where you can wander around the village and people-watch from a cafe along the harbor. Spend the night in St-Tropez. See Chapter 21 for more details.

✔ On **Day Seven,** hit the beach in St-Tropez or visit the **Musée de l'Annonciade,** with its selection of Impressionist paintings — perhaps both. In the afternoon, drive to **Nice** (108km/67 miles). Check into your hotel, wander through the **old town,** stroll on the **promenade des Anglais,** lie on the beach, walk through the **Marché aux Fleurs,** or visit one of the less time-consuming sights, such as the **Palais Lascaris, Musée International d'Art Naïf Anatole-Jakovsky, Musée des Beaux-Arts, Cathédrale Orthodoxe Russe St-Nicholas à Nice, Musée d'Art Moderne et d'Art Contemporain,** or **Musée d'Art et d'Histoire (Palais Masséna).** During the day, stop for a snack of *socca,* a round crêpe made with chickpea flour that's sold steaming hot by street vendors. Have dinner at one of the charming restaurants in Nice's old town. You'll find a number of Italian restaurants and bistros offering traditional Niçoise cuisine, which has Italian influences. You can also take the **Train Touristique de Nice** for a 40-minute sightseeing ride past the major sights. (For detailed information on towns along the Riviera, go to Chapters 20 and 21.)

✔ On **Days Eight and Nine,** explore more of Nice, and head up to the suburb of **Cimiez** to see the **Musée Matisse, Monastère de Cimiez,** and **Roman ruins,** all next to one another, and the **Musée National Message Biblique Marc Chagall,** a short drive away. On **Day Ten,** drive to **Monaco.** On the way, stop in **Beaulieu** for lunch and to see the **Villa Kérylos,** a replica of an ancient Greek residence that overlooks the sea. Arrive in Monaco, check into your hotel, get decked out, have dinner at the **Café de Paris,** and head to the **Monte Carlo Casino** for some glamorous gambling.

✔ On **Day Eleven,** explore Monaco's many sights, such as the changing of the guards in front of the **Palais du Prince** (and the interior, called the **Grands Appartements du Palais);** the **Jardin Exotique,** a cactus garden built into the side of a rock; the **Musée Océanographique,** which includes one of Europe's best aquariums; the **Collection des Voitures Anciennes de S.A.S. le Prince de Monaco,** Prince Rainier's personal antique-car collection; and the **Musée National de Monaco,** with a large antique-doll collection.

✔ On **Day Twelve,** head back toward Avignon to return the rental car, stopping for an overnight on the way in one of three towns: **St-Paul-de-Vence,** a hilltop village of art galleries; **Grasse,** an ancient town and the perfume capital of France; or **Aix-en-Provence,** one of France's most beautiful cities.

✔ After your stay in one of these charming towns, drop off the car in Avignon on **Day Thirteen** and then take the rapid TGV train back to Paris for your return flight home.

Discovering France with Kids in One Week

France offers many attractions that kids enjoy. Perhaps your main concern with having children along is pacing yourself with museum time. Some sights you see may not interest children. Make a deal with them: Promise to take them to where they want to go if they agree to accompany you to what you want to see.

✔ For **Day One,** two of the major attractions of Paris for children and adults alike are **Tour Eiffel** (kids love the elevator) and **Notre-Dame** (be sure to point out the gargoyles at the top). You can work in both of these attractions and perhaps take them on a **boat ride along the Seine.**

✔ For **Day Two,** spend as much time as you can at the **Musée du Louvre.** Your kids may also find objects here to fascinate them. But break up this museum tour by taking advantage of some of the city's parks and gardens with playgrounds for children. Two favorites are **Jardin du Luxembourg,** with a popular playground and puppet shows, and **Jardin des Tuilleries,** with a fountain used for toy boats and, in summer, a *grand toue* (ferris wheel). Take the kids for a stroll along one of the Left Bank neighborhoods at night, stopping in at a bistro patronized by French families. See Chapters 11 and 12 for more details about Paris.

✔ On **Day Three,** head for **Disneyland Paris,** which needs no introduction to most kids. You can spend the night here, of course, or you can return to Paris by fast train that night to avoid the trouble of switching hotels. See Chapter 13 for more details about Disneyland French style.

✔ Because most kids love a beach vacation, and almost everyone appreciates the charms of the **French Riviera,** fly from Paris to the airport at **Nice** for **Day Four.** You can also take the high-speed TGV train south from Paris to Nice. The Riviera, and Nice in particular, have much to entertain you and your brood. Instead of heavy sightseeing the first day, take the kids to the beach in the afternoon. The people-watching alone is likely to leave them wide-eyed (be aware that they'll see plenty of skin; topless bathing is rampant). You can always find plenty of free entertainment along **promenade des Anglais** (the boardwalk) in summer in Nice. Dine that night in a typical family restaurant in the old town. See Chapter 20 for more details.

✔ On **Day Five,** rise early in the morning, and take the fast train linking Nice with the tiny principality of **Monaco.** Kids enjoy the formal changing-of-the-guard ceremony at the palace and the tour of the interior apartments. But the best part of Monaco for kids is the **Musée Océanographique,** one of Europe's best and biggest aquariums, with lots of sharks and other exotic sea creatures. Monaco also has the **Collection des Voitures Anciennes de S.A.S. le Prince de Monaco,** Prince Rainier's personal antique-car collection, and the **Musée National de Monaco,** with a large antique-doll collection. Return to your hotel at Nice for the night.

✔ On **Day Six,** we recommend that you rent a car and drive (carefully, of course) along the **Grande Corniche** of the Riviera. For example, if you head east to **Menton,** near the Italian border, you're treated to one of the most spectacular scenic drives in France. The morning route along the loftiest highway, the Grande Corniche, includes stopovers at **La Turbie** and **Le Vistaero,** the principal towns along this 32km (20-mile) stretch. In the afternoon you can meander much more slowly on the way back by taking the lower road (the same distance), which is called **Corniche Infèrieure.** You'll pass through the ports of **Villefranche, Cap-Ferrat,** and **Beaulieu,** among others. Carry your bathing suits to get in at least two hours of beaching it before your return to Nice that night. See Chapter 20 for more details.

✔ On **Day Seven,** you can leave Nice by plane, flying back to Paris, where you can take a late-afternoon stroll along the **Seine** and its bridges. After a final French family-style meal, plan to return to your destination in the morning.

Taking the Art Buff's Tour

The art lover's tour of France begins, quite naturally, in the city of **Paris.** We probably don't really need to tell you that Paris is one of the great cities for art.

- ✔ You can spend two weeks at the **Musée du Louvre** and still not see everything. But count on spending at least half of **Day One** here. Save the city's other great museum, **Musée d'Orsay,** for another day; the Louvre and d'Orsay are a bit much to tackle on the same day. Instead, visit one of the minor Left Bank museums. We recommend a blissful afternoon spent at the **Musée de Cluny.**

- ✔ On **Day Two,** tackle the **Musée d'Orsay** for its Impressionists. For the afternoon head for the **Musée Picasso.**

- ✔ On **Day Three,** your final look at Paris, visit the **Centre Pompidou** in the morning and explore the **National Auguste-Rodin Museum** in the afternoon. If you have time, check out what's happening at the **Grand Palais,** which usually has a blockbuster art exhibit going on, for which you'll need to reserve a ticket in advance.

  For details on these attractions of Paris, refer to Chapter 12.

- ✔ On **Day Four,** after you've had a taste of the art offerings of Paris, take a day trip to the town of **Giverny** (easily reached by train). Here you can visit **Monet's house and gardens,** where you can ponder the famous lily pond. Return to Paris for one final night. See Chapter 13 for details.

- ✔ On **Day Five,** fly to Nice on the French Riviera or else take a high-speed TGV train south. Because you'll spend most of your day in transit, you may have time on your first day only to see the **museums of Matisse and Chagall** in the suburb of Cimiez. See Chapter 20 for more details.

- ✔ While still based in Nice for **Day Six,** easy day trips west by car rental take you to the **Chapelle du Rosaire,** designed by Matisse in Venice, and the prestigious **Fondation Maeght** in St-Paul-de-Vence. These two towns are the most famous hilltowns of the Riviera. When not exploring the chapel or the foundation, you can wander about on foot, taking in their treasures. See Chapter 20 for more details.

- ✔ On **Day Seven,** hop in your rental car, and head west again. This time you can visit some of France's best modern art collections, spending the morning at **Musée National Fernand-Léger** at Biot followed by **Musée Picasso** at Antibes. Return to Paris for the night and your flight home.

Part II
Planning Your Trip to France

The 5th Wave   By Rich Tennant

"And how shall I book your flight to France — First Class, Coach, or Medieval?"

In this part . . .

*P*art I covers the basics, but this part gets down to specifics: the detailed information you need to book your trip. Chapter 5 covers how to plan a realistic budget, how to cut costs, and how to handle money, among other subjects. Chapter 6 covers the various ways of getting to France and saving some money in the process. Chapter 7 gives you information about getting around France after you arrive. Chapter 8 discusses different styles of accommodations to choose from and how to book a room. Chapter 9 caters to special needs with advice to senior citizens, families, and others. Chapter 10 takes care of details that many people all too often leave until the last minute, including getting a passport, thinking about medical and travel insurance, and packing.

Chapter 5

Managing Your Money

In This Chapter
▶ Developing a workable budget
▶ Cutting costs
▶ Dealing with the local currency and taxes

*S*oit raissonable (be reasonable), the French say, and being reasonable is key to budgeting for a trip to France. Mentally walking through what you'll be spending on your trip from the moment you leave to the minute you get back home is a good way to figure out a budget (don't forget to figure in your transportation to and from the airport). Then add in the flight cost (see Chapter 6 for tips on how to fly to France for less), the price of getting from the airport to your hotel, your hotel rates per day, meals, public transportation costs, admission prices to museums and the theater, other entertainment expenses, and souvenir costs. Afterward, add 15–20 percent for good measure.

Planning Your Budget

Cities rarely are cheap or expensive across the board; Paris tends to be pricey for dining but slightly more affordable for accommodations. Outside Paris, your euro goes further. For example, a four-course dinner in provinces such as Normandy or Brittany costs the same as a two-course dinner in Paris. Prices for historic sites are similar across the country.

This section covers some guidelines for what you're likely to spend while in France. For information about taxes, see the "Taking taxes into account" section later in this chapter.

Table 5-1 gives you a taste of what things cost in Paris, while Table 5-2 shows you the cost of similar items in one of France's provinces — in this case, the Loire Valley.

Table 5-1	What Things Cost in Paris	
Item	*Cost in Euros*	*Cost in US$*
Taxi from Charles de Gaulle Airport to the city center	40€–45€	$48–$54
Taxi from Orly Airport to the city center	25€–30€	$30–$36
Public transportation for an average trip within the city	1.40€	$1.70
Local telephone call	.25€	30¢
Glass of wine	2.80€	$3.35
Coca-Cola (at a cafe)	3.50€	$4.20
Café au lait	4€	$4.80
Roll of ASA 100 color film, 36 exposures	10€	$12
Average hotel room for two	225€	$270
Dinner at a medium-priced restaurant, per person	50€	$60
Admission to the Louvre	8.50€	$10.20
Movie ticket	10€	$12
Concert ticket (at the Théâtre Mogador)	8€–60€	$9.60–$72

Table 5-2	What Things Cost in Chinon, Loire Valley	
Item	*Cost in Euros*	*Cost in US$*
Local telephone call	15€	20¢
Glass of wine	2.50€	$3
Coca-Cola (at a cafe)	2€	$2.40
Café au lait	1.50€	$1.80
Roll of ASA 100 color film, 36 exposures	6.50€	$7.80
Rental car for a weekend	45€–100€	$54–$120
A play in the nearby city of Tours	12€–18€	$14.40–$21.60
Average hotel room for two	35€–75€	$42–$90
Dinner at a medium-priced restaurant, per person	25€–40€	$30–$48
Admission to the castle at Chinon	6€	$7.20

Transportation

The biggest item in your budget probably will be your airline ticket to
France, and that is likely true even with those great deals that pop up in
winter. Every bargain hunter dreams of that one-way $99 fare from the
United States to a European capital such as Paris. And deals like that
occasionally appear. However, the more likely scenario is that you'll get
differing results, which demonstrates the confusion of airline pricing
that can change from one hour to the next. Within a 48-hour period, calls
to Air France produced these results: The cheapest *one-way* fare from
New York to Paris was $650.66. Two hours later, the cheapest *round-trip*
fare from New York to Paris was $498.66. The least expensive fare on the
Internet was $300 NYC/Paris/NYC round trip. Make sure that you check
out the money-saving tips in Chapter 6 before buying your airline tickets.

You have many options for transportation within France. You can get to
almost every town mentioned in this book by public transportation, either
train or bus. If you're traveling long distances by train (say from Paris to
the Riviera), consider buying a France Railpass (see Chapter 7). In Paris,
the Métro has been the model for subways around the world since its
inauguration in 1900. It's one of the best transit systems in terms of price
and efficiency. Getting across town in less than half an hour is no problem, and the cost is lower when you purchase one of several discount
tickets, such as a *carnet* of ten (see Chapter 11 for options and prices).

Renting a car gives you more flexibility than using public transportation,
but it's expensive, mainly because of the high cost of gasoline, or *petrol,*
in Europe. For a medium-sized car holding 15 gallons, expect to pay at
least 55€, or $66, to fill up your tank. Because of uncertainty in the
Middle East and other oil-producing regions, these figures can change
radically overnight. You also must pay to park a car in most French
cities and towns. That said, several regions lend themselves to driving,
including the Loire Valley. And if you want to see some of the smaller
towns on the Riviera, a rental car is the best way.

As for cars in Paris, well, expect your heart to be in your throat the entire
time you drive in the city — unless, of course, you thrive on dealing with
labyrinthine one-way streets, a dearth of parking spaces, hellish traffic,
and the statistically worst drivers in Europe. If you want to rent a car to
see other parts of France or make a day trip outside Paris, do it on your
way out of the city (see Chapter 11 for addresses and phone numbers of
Paris car-rental agencies).

Lodging

Before you start shelling out money for lodging, think about how much
time you'll actually spend in your room. For 60€ to 85€ ($72–$102) in
Paris, and slightly less in the rest of the country, you can rent a clean but
functionally furnished hotel room with a private bathroom and cable TV.
Though these kinds of budget rooms normally are comfortable and have

basic furnishings and décor, they're supplied with thin but serviceable towels and a less-than-stellar array of toiletries (often just a bar of soap). For 120€ ($144) and up — and we do mean up — the upper-tier hotels offer bigger rooms and more services, such as room service and air conditioning.

Hotel rates can vary regionally, from the most popular areas to the least visited. In addition, hotels in virtually all regions covered in this book charge higher rates during summer. The prices are highest in Paris, especially compared with what you can get for the same price in other regions. Expenses also are high on the Riviera, which has some of France's most famous palace hotels. Nevertheless, you can find medium-priced and even cheap hotels in every town in this book, and we give you a wide range of choices. You may want to plan to splurge one or two nights, just to get a feel for how wonderful the service is and how exquisite the accommodations are in France's top hotels.

You can certainly save money by not having breakfast at your hotel, which normally runs 10€ ($12) for a continental breakfast (hot beverage, bread, croissant) at medium-priced hotels. You can get the same food for less by bellying up to the counter at a cafe nearby and thus feel more like a resident.

Dining

Unless you like expensive hotels, expect to pay more for dining in France than for lodging. The French consider dining out one of the finer joys in life, although they pay dearly for it, you still can get a memorable five-course meal with wine at a medium-priced restaurant anywhere in France, except Paris, for about 30€ to 40€ ($36 to $48) per person. In Paris, that amount gets you a decent three-course meal. Paris also has a wide range of cheaper dining options (in addition to the most expensive restaurants in France). For example, you can find restaurants serving satisfying two-course meals for as little as 25€ ($30) and good-tasting ethnic food and sandwich shops that help you save even more money.

The best way to save money on meals in France is by choosing what's called *le menu* or *prix fixe,* a fixed-price meal with two or three choices for each course (first course, main course, dessert). The prix fixe menu often includes a cheese course or a choice between a cheese course and a dessert course. At better restaurants, the prix fixe menu includes two main courses: a fish course and a meat course. At top restaurants, you'll see a very expensive *menu dégustation,* or tasting menu, which includes a selection of the chef's specialties. Choosing a prix fixe menu always is cheaper and a much better value than ordering à la carte.

Alas, *le menu* is less common at restaurants in Paris than it is outside Paris, where you can find at least two and sometimes five or six menus to choose from. If you choose a medium-priced menu (not the cheapest, not the most expensive), you usually get an excellent meal, which often includes chef's specialties and high-quality items such as the catch of the day. Sometimes menus include a glass of wine with one or more courses, and some even feature coffee at the end of the meal.

 If your budget is limited, consider buying a picnic lunch or dinner at a town or village market. You'll be wowed by the selection of fresh produce, breads, meats, and cheeses on display. Purchase a bottle of wine at a grocery store, and you're all set for an idyllic French meal. For this type of meal, a Swiss army knife with corkscrew comes in handy.

 Don't think a cafe is a cheaper alternative to a restaurant. A simple meal of *croque monsieur* and *pommes frites* (a toasted ham-and-cheese sandwich with french fries) accompanied by a beer or soda can set you back 18€ to 22€ ($21.60 to $26.40). You can get a much tastier meal for the same price or less at a restaurant.

Sightseeing

Entry fees at museums and other sights can add up quickly. Refer first to the money-saving advice in the upcoming section, "Cutting Costs — But Not the Fun," and then make a list of must-dos to get a feel for how much money you need to set aside. Many towns in France, including Paris, offer special museum passes that save you money if you plan to see more than two attractions. These passes always are available at tourist offices and sometimes even at the museums or historic sites. Throughout this book, we let you know whether these passes are available. Keep in mind that some sights are free on certain days (such as the first Sunday of every month). You can get this information at the local tourist office.

Shopping

France, especially Paris, is a shopper's mecca, and shopkeepers arrange their wares in windows so enticingly that you'll be tempted to splurge. Shopping is the most flexible part of your budget, and you'll certainly save plenty of money if you skip a few excursions. But France has marvelous things to buy, and in each chapter, we list some special shops in which to look for souvenirs. You can find deals during semiannual sales held in January and July, but remember that a steep 19.6 percent tax (VAT or value-added tax) is added to most goods. If you live outside the European Union, you're usually entitled to get back part of the tax, if you meet certain requirements (see the upcoming "Taking taxes into account" section for more information).

Nightlife

Budget big if you plan to visit clubs and other nightspots. Clubs and bars aren't cheap in France, because cover charges and drinks really add up. But nightlife also is one of the great pleasures of France, particularly in Paris and other larger cities. So don't forgo the spectacles at the Moulin Rouge or Folies Bergère in Paris if you've always wanted to see them. Just know beforehand that they charge a hefty fee for entry and for alcoholic beverages. Plan on seeing the show without dinner, and you'll save some money.

Tipping tips

In restaurants, the tip already is included (*service compris* — the 15 percent is already figured into the bill); however, although technically unnecessary, a small additional tip for satisfactory service (2€/$2.40 per person for a moderately priced meal) still is appropriate. Don't tip a bartender for each round of drinks — instead leave 1.50€ ($1.80) at the end of the night. Hotel service personnel should get 1.50€ ($1.80) per luggage item or service performed, and taxi drivers generally are tipped 10 percent of the fare.

 Some cities have free nightlife, such as street performers and musicians along the beach promenade in Nice. In fact, just wandering around the old cobblestone streets of most French towns in the evening is entertainment enough.

Taking taxes into account

The price of all goods in France includes a 19.6 percent sales tax called the *détaxe,* or value-added tax (VAT). If you live outside the European Union, you can be reimbursed for part of the VAT you paid, but as always, a catch is involved: You have to spend at least 170€ ($204) in the same store *on the same day.* The amount of the refund varies from store to store but generally comes out to about 13 percent of the price you paid on the item. The Paris department stores, Au Printemps and Galeries Lafayette, have special *détaxe* desks where clerks prepare your sales invoices, but small shops don't always have the necessary paperwork.

Cutting Costs — But Not the Fun

The small things are what tend to add up and burst your budget, but if you keep the following common-sense travel tips in mind, you can avoid some of the more common money-wasting traps.

 ✔ **Go during the off season.** If you can travel at nonpeak times (October to March, for example), you'll find hotel prices almost half the price of peak months.

 ✔ **Travel midweek.** If you can travel on a Tuesday, Wednesday, or Thursday, you may find cheaper flights to your destination. When you ask about airfares, see whether you can get a cheaper rate by flying on a different day. For more tips on getting good fares, see Chapter 6.

 ✔ **Try a package tour.** For many destinations, you can book airfare, hotel, ground transportation, and even some sightseeing just by making one call to a travel agent or packager, for a price much less than if you put the trip together yourself. (See Chapter 6 for more on package tours.)

✔ **Always ask for discount rates.** Membership in travel associations, frequent-flier plans, trade unions, seniors organizations, or other groups may qualify you for savings on car rentals, plane tickets, hotel rooms, and even meals. Ask about everything; you may be pleasantly surprised.

✔ **Find out whether your kids can stay in the room with you.** A room with two double beds usually doesn't cost any more than one with a queen-size bed. And many hotels won't charge you the additional person rate if the additional person is pint-size and related to you. Even if you have to pay extra for a rollaway bed, you'll save hundreds by not taking two rooms.

✔ **Try expensive restaurants at lunch rather than dinner.** Lunch tabs usually are a fraction of what dinner costs at top restaurants, and the menu often boasts many of the same specialties.

✔ **Get out of town.** In many places, big savings are just a short drive or taxi ride away. Hotels just outside the city, across the river, or less conveniently located are great bargains. Outlying hotels often have free parking, with lower rates than centrally located hotels that offer amenities you may never use. See Chapter 8 for more about choosing and booking hotels.

✔ **Walk.** A good pair of walking shoes can save you plenty of money in taxi and other local transportation fares. As a bonus, you get to know your destination more intimately, as you explore it at a slower pace.

✔ **Skip the souvenirs.** Your photographs and memories can be the best mementos from your trip. If you're concerned about money, you can do without the T-shirts, key chains, salt-and-pepper shakers, mouse ears, and other trinkets.

Here are some other cost-cutting strategies, specifically related to traveling in France, to keep in mind:

✔ **Take the cheapest way into Paris from the airport.** You can save around 30€ ($36) by taking a train or bus in place of a cab from Charles de Gaulle and about 15€ ($18) from Orly. Both airports are located in Paris.

✔ **Negotiate the room price, especially during the low season.** Ask for a discount if you're a student or older than 60; ask for a discount if you stay a certain number of days.

✔ **Try ethnic neighborhoods in Paris or the larger cities.** In Paris, you can get terrific Chinese food in the 13e arrondissement (neighborhood) between place d'Italie and porte de Choisy; and the 10e, 18e, and 20e offer North African, Turkish, Vietnamese, and Thai cuisines. (For more information about Paris neighborhoods, check out Chapter 11.) Couscous is on the menu at many restaurants and usually is an inexpensive offering. Throughout the book, we list less expensive restaurants and neighborhoods where you can find cheap ethnic meals in larger cities.

✔ **In Paris, use the Métro.** A *carnet* of ten Métro tickets costs 10.50€ ($12.60), a savings of 3.50€ ($4.20) over ten tickets at 1.40€ ($1.70) each. Better yet, if you're in Paris from one to five consecutive days, buy a **Paris Visite pass,** good for unlimited subway and bus travel (see Chapter 11).

✔ **If you plan to visit two or three museums a day in Paris, buy the Carte Musées et Monuments.** The pass costs 18€ ($21.60) for one day, 36€ ($43.20) for three days, and 54€ ($64.80) for five days. Chapter 12 has the details.

Most cities in France have similar museum passes. Check the individual destination chapters in this book for details.

✔ **Take advantage of reduced admission fees at museums.** The discount prices usually apply after 3 p.m. (daily) and all day Sunday.

✔ **For discounts on fashion in Paris, try rue St-Placide in the 6e arrondissement.** Look for stylish, inexpensive clothes at chain boutiques — Monoprix or Prisunic are two common ones — located across the city.

✔ **In Paris, buy half-price theater and other performance tickets.** You can find them at one of the kiosks by the Madeleine, on the lower level of the Châtelet–Les Halles Métro station, or at the Gare Montparnasse.

✔ **Avoid weekends at clubs.** You also can save money by sitting at the bar rather than at a table. Some clubs are cheaper than others, and some are less expensive during the week.

Handling Money

You're the best judge of how much cash you feel comfortable carrying or what alternative form of currency is your favorite; that isn't going to change much during your vacation. True, you'll probably be moving around more and incurring more expenses than you generally do (unless you happen to eat our every meal when you're at home), and you may let your mind slip into vacation gear and not be as vigilant about your safety as when you're in work mode. But those factors aside, the only type of payment that won't be quite as available to you away from home is your personal checkbook.

Understanding the euro

The year 2001 was the last in which local commerce in France was conducted in the famous franc. After January 2002, most countries in the European Union began using the banknotes and coins of the *euro,* the single monetary unit that makes it possible to travel in Europe without continually changing currencies.

Euros come in note denominations of 5, 10, 20, 50, 100, 200, and 500, and coin denominations of 1 euro and 2 euros and 1, 2, 5, 20, and 50 cents. Coins have a common face on one side. The opposite face has a design chosen by the issuing country.

 For more information and pictures of the new currency, check online at the official site of the European Union: www.europa.eu.int.

Converting your dollars

The figures reflected in Table 5-3 were valid at the time of this writing, but they may not be valid by the time of your departure. Nevertheless, the table is useful for giving you an approximate idea of what your dollar (or pound) will likely be worth by the time you arrive in France. For prices in this book, we've converted the euro at $1.20 in U.S. dollars, rounding to the nearest dollar (or euro) for amounts of more than $10 (or euros).

Table 5-3				Estimating Euros			
Euro	**US$**	**UK£**	**CAD$**	**Euro**	**US$**	**UK£**	**CAD$**
1	1.20	0.67	1.63	75	90	50	122
2	2.40	1.34	3.26	100	120	67	163
3	3.60	2.01	4.89	125	150	84	204
4	4.80	2.68	6.52	150	180	101	245
5	6.00	3.35	8.15	175	210	118	285
6	7.20	4.02	9.78	200	240	134	326
7	8.40	4.69	11	225	270	151	367
8	9.60	5.36	13	250	300	168	408
9	11	6.03	15	275	330	184	448
10	12	6.70	16	300	360	201	489
15	18	10	24	350	420	234	571
20	24	13	33	400	480	268	652
25	30	17	41	500	600	335	815
50	60	34	82	1,000	1200	670	1630

Try to get a small amount of euros before you leave, perhaps 100€ or so, to speed your transit in from the airport to your hotel. Check with your bank, or look for an American Express or Thomas Cook travel office in your area. If you're unable to arrive in Paris with euros in hand, however, you can avail yourself of ATMs at the airport.

Using ATMs and carrying cash

The easiest and best way to get cash when you're away from home is from an ATM (automated teller machine). The **Cirrus** (☎ 800-424-7787; www.mastercard.com) and **PLUS** (☎ 800-843-7587; www.visa.com) networks span the globe; look at the back of your bank card to see which network you're on and then call or check online for ATM locations at your destination. Be sure you know your personal identification number (PIN) and your daily withdrawal limit before you leave home. You'll also want to keep in mind that many banks impose a fee every time your card is used at a different bank's ATM, and that fee can be higher for international transactions (up to $5 or more) than for domestic ones (where they're rarely more than $1.50). On top of these fees, the bank from which you withdraw cash may charge its own fee. To compare banks' ATM fees within the United States, use www.bankrate.com. For international withdrawal fees, ask your bank.

Money makes the world go 'round, but dealing with an unfamiliar currency can make your head spin just as fast. When it comes to getting cash in France, you're probably wondering whether you should bring traveler's checks or use ATMs, or how easy it is to pay with a credit card? You find the answers in this section.

Before you leave, check out the ATM locator feature at the Web sites of **Visa** (www.visa.com) and **MasterCard** (www.mastercard.com), where you can identify the locations of cash machines across France. Most of the major banks in France — such as Crédit Lyonnais, Crédit Agricole, Banque Nationale de Paris (BNP), Banque Populaire, Crédit Commercial de France (CCF), and Crédit du Nord — and even some branches of the post office have automatic cash distribution machines. But you won't be able to check your balance or transfer funds, so keep track of your withdrawals while you travel. These banks are in all major cities, and most towns included in this book have at least one major bank. But note that some small villages do not have any major banks.

 In major cities, ATMs are never far away, so you can walk around with 100€ ($120) in your pocket and have enough for eating and most activities. However, before going on a driving tour of the countryside, such as in Brittany or the Loire Valley, which have many small towns and villages, make sure you have a good stock of cash in your wallet.

Charging ahead with credit cards

Credit cards are a safe way to carry money: They also provide a convenient record of all your expenses, and they generally offer relatively good exchange rates. You also can withdraw cash advances from your credit cards at banks or ATMs, provided you know your PIN. If you've forgotten yours or didn't even know you had one, call the number on the back of your credit card, and ask the bank to send it to you. It usually takes five to seven business days, though some banks will provide the number over the phone if you tell them your mother's maiden name or some other personal information.

Keep in mind that when you use your credit card abroad, most banks assess a 2 percent fee above the 1 percent fee charged by Visa, MasterCard, or American Express for currency conversion on credit charges. But credit cards still may be the smart way to go when you factor in things like exorbitant ATM fees and higher traveler's check exchange rates (and service fees)

 Some credit-card companies recommend that you notify them of any impending trip abroad so they don't become suspicious when the card is used numerous times in a foreign location and end up blocking your charges. Even if you don't call your credit-card company in advance, you can always call the card's toll-free emergency number if a charge is refused — a good reason for carrying the phone number with you. But perhaps the most important lesson here is to carry more than one card with you on your trip. For any number of reasons, a card may not work, so having a backup is the smart way to go.

You can use credit cards to buy virtually anything in France, as long as it costs a minimum of 15€ ($18). You can also get cash advances from your Visa and MasterCard at any bank. You'll need a PIN for withdrawing cash with a credit card, and remember, hefty interest fees are charged from the moment you withdraw the money.

 American Express and Diners Club are not widely accepted at small restaurants, shops, and budget hotels in France. And many credit-card companies now tack on additional fees for foreign currency transactions — sometimes up to 4 percent on top of the 1 percent service charge they already take. Worse, according to Lee Dembart, a writer for *The International Herald Tribune,* credit-card companies don't expect you to notice the charge. "Recognizing the additional fee requires that the consumer know what the exchange rate was on the day the charge came through and then do the math," he writes, "steps most people don't take." You can find the official rate for dates in the past at www.oanda.com.

If you don't know how much your credit card charges for currency conversion, ask. If the rate isn't acceptable, consider switching — **MBNA America** (☎ 800-932-2775; www.mbna.com), for example, a Delaware-based credit-card issuer, still charges only 1 percent for currency conversion.

Toting traveler's checks

These days, traveler's checks are less necessary because most cities have 24-hour ATMs that enable you to withdraw small amounts of cash as needed. However, keep in mind that you probably will be charged an ATM withdrawal fee if the bank is not your own. So if you're withdrawing money every day, you may be better off with traveler's checks — provided that you don't mind showing identification every time you want to cash one.

You can get traveler's checks at almost any bank. **American Express** offers denominations of $20, $50, $100, $500, and (for cardholders only) $1,000. You pay a service charge ranging from 1 percent to 4 percent. You can also get American Express traveler's checks over the phone by calling ☎ 800-221-7282; Amex gold and platinum cardholders who use this number are exempt from the 1 percent fee.

Visa offers traveler's checks at Citibank locations nationwide and at several other banks. The service charge ranges between 1.5 percent and 2 percent; checks come in denominations of $20, $50, $100, $500, and $1,000. Call ☎ 800-732-1322 for information. AAA members can obtain Visa traveler's checks without a fee at most AAA offices or by calling ☎ 866-339-3378. **MasterCard** also offers traveler's checks. Call ☎ 800-223-9920 for a location near you.

If you choose to carry traveler's checks, be sure to keep a record of their serial numbers separate from your checks in the event they are stolen or lost. You'll get a refund faster when you know the numbers.

You can exchange traveler's checks for euros at the following banks in Paris: **American Express,** 11 rue Scribe, 9e (☎ 01-47-77-70-00; Métro: Opéra, Chaussée-d'Antin, or Havre-Caumartin; RER: Auber); **Barclays,** 24 bis av. de l'Opéra, 1er (☎ 01-44-86-00-00; Métro: Pyramides), or 96 rue Turenne, 3e (☎ 01-42-77-24-70; Métro: St-Paul); **Citibank,** 125 av. Champs-Elysées, 8e (☎ 01-53-23-33-60; Métro: Champs-Elysées); or **Travelex,** 194 rue de Rivoli, 1er (☎ 01-42-60-37-61; Métro: Tuileries).

Dealing with a Lost or Stolen Wallet

Be sure to contact all of your credit-card companies the minute you discover your wallet has been lost or stolen and file a report at the nearest police precinct. Your credit-card company or insurer may require a police report number or record of the loss. Most credit-card companies have an emergency toll-free number to call whenever your card is lost or stolen; they may be able to wire you a cash advance immediately or deliver an emergency credit card in a day or two.

If you need emergency cash over the weekend, when all banks and American Express offices are closed, you can have money wired to you via **Western Union** (☎ 800-325-6000; www.westernunion.com).

Identity theft or fraud are potential complications of losing your wallet, especially if you've lost your driver's license along with your cash and credit cards. Notify major credit-reporting bureaus immediately; placing a fraud alert on your records may protect you against liability for criminal activity. The three major U.S. credit-reporting agencies are **Equifax** (☎ 800-685-5000; www.equifax.com), **Experian** (☎ 888-397-3742;

www.experian.com), and **TransUnion** (☎ **800-680-7289;** www.trans union.com). Finally, if you've lost all forms of photo ID, call your airline and explain the situation; they may allow you to board the plane if you have a copy of your passport or birth certificate and a copy of the police report you've filed.

Call ☎ **08-36-69-08-80** if you lose or have your **Visa** card stolen. **American Express** card and traveler's check holders can call international collect (☎ **0800-99-00-11** for an AT&T operator; ☎ **0800-99-00-19** for MCI; ☎ **336-393-1111** for money emergencies; or ☎ **01-47-77-72-00** to report lost cards). For **MasterCard,** call ☎ **01-45-67-53-53** or 08-00-90-13-87.

Replacing your bank ATM card can take weeks, usually with a fee. However, larger credit-card companies can replace a card in a day or two at no charge. A bank card has the added disadvantage of enabling a thief to empty out your bank account, if he or she can figure out the PIN.

Chapter 6

Getting to France

● ●

In This Chapter

▶ Flying there — or not
▶ Deciding on a package or escorted tour
▶ Making your own arrangements
▶ Saving money on the Web

● ●

*P*lanning a trip abroad used to be a science so exact that only travel agents, with their numerous contacts and extensive experience, could get you fantastic trips at low prices. These days, the Internet — with its online travel agents; airline, lodging, and car-rental Web sites; and myriad information about your destination — has changed travel planning drastically. You need to decide what kind of travel best suits you — are you an independent traveler, or do you prefer the comfort of a tour group where everything is planned for you? In this chapter, we show you how to get to France simply and easily — regardless of whether you do it yourself or have someone do it for you.

Flying to France

Flying to Paris takes about 7 hours from New York, 9 hours from Chicago, 11 hours from Los Angeles, 8 hours from Atlanta, 8½ hours from Miami, and 7½ hours from Washington, D.C.

The two Paris airports — Orly and Charles de Gaulle — are almost equal in terms of convenience to the city's center, but taxi rides from Orly may take a bit less time than those from de Gaulle. Orly, the older of the two, is 12.8km (8 miles) south of the center, and Charles de Gaulle is 22.5km (14 miles) northeast. Air France's flights from North America fly into de Gaulle (Terminal 2C). U.S.-based airlines fly into both airports.

You also can fly from major U.S. cities to Nice on the Riviera, which takes about an hour longer than flying to Paris and costs about the same. Flights from Paris to Nice are very frequent. Air France flies 30 flights per day. They take 1 hour and 20 minutes and can cost about $111.

Most airlines offer the cheapest fares between November 1 and March 13. Shoulder seasons, offering slightly more expensive fares, are mid-March to mid-June and all of October. From mid-June to September, airfare rates to France are at their highest.

Finding out who flies to France from the United States and Canada

The phone numbers and Web sites that follow are for the major airlines serving Paris. The Web sites offer schedules, flight booking, and package tours, and most have Web pages where you can sign up for e-mail alerts that list weekend deals and other late-breaking bargains.

- ✔ **Air Canada** (☎ 888-247-2262; www.aircanada.ca) flies from Halifax, Montreal, Toronto, and Vancouver.

- ✔ **Air France** (☎ 800-237-2747; www.airfrance.com) flies from Atlanta, Boston, Chicago, Cincinnati, Houston, Los Angeles, Miami, Montreal, Newark, New York City, Philadelphia, San Francisco, Toronto, and Washington, D.C.

- ✔ **American Airlines** (☎ 800-433-7300; www.aa.com) flies from Boston, Chicago, Dallas/Fort Worth, Los Angeles, New York City, and Miami.

- ✔ **British Airways** (☎ 800-247-9297; www.britishairways.com) flies to Paris through London from Atlanta, Baltimore, Boston, Charlotte, Chicago, Cincinnati, Detroit, Houston, Los Angeles, Miami, Orlando, Philadelphia, Phoenix, Newark, New York City, San Diego, San Francisco, Tampa, and Washington, D.C.

- ✔ **Continental Airlines** (☎ 800-525-0280; www.continental.com) flies from Houston and Newark.

- ✔ **Delta Air Lines** (☎ 800-241-4141; www.delta.com) flies from Atlanta, Cincinnati, Nashville, New Orleans, Phoenix, and New York City, and shares flights with Air France from Los Angeles, Philadelphia, and San Francisco.

- ✔ **Iceland Air** (☎ 800-223-5500; www.icelandair.com) flies from Baltimore, Boston, Minneapolis, New York City, and Orlando.

- ✔ **Northwest/KLM** (☎ 800-225-2525; www.nwa.com) flies from Detroit, Memphis, and Minneapolis.

- ✔ **United Airlines** (☎ 800-241-6522; www.ual.com) flies from Chicago, San Francisco, and Washington, D.C.

- ✔ **USAirways** (☎ 800-428-4322; www.usairways.com) flies from Charlotte, Philadelphia, and Pittsburgh.

Finding out who flies to France from the United Kingdom

These airlines serve Paris from the United Kingdom:

- ✔ **Air France** (☎ 0845-0845-111; www.airfrance.com) flies from London and Manchester.

- ✔ **British Airways** (☎ 0880-850-9850; www.britishairways.com) flies from Edinburgh, Glasgow, London, and Manchester.

- ✔ **British Midland** (☎ 0870-6070-555; www.flybmi.com) flies from Leeds, London, and Manchester.

Finding out who flies to France from Australia

Qantas (☎ 13-13-13 anywhere in Australia; www.qantas.com.au) flies from Sydney to Paris.

Getting the Best Deal on Your Airfare

Competition among the major U.S. airlines is unlike that of any other industry. Every airline offers virtually the same product (basically, a coach seat is a coach seat is a . . .), yet prices can vary by hundreds of dollars.

Business travelers who need the flexibility of buying their tickets at the last minute and changing their itineraries at a moment's notice — and who want to get home before the weekend — pay (or at least their companies pay) the premium rate, known as the *full fare*. But if you can book your ticket far in advance, stay over Saturday night, and are willing to travel midweek (Tuesday, Wednesday, or Thursday), you can qualify for the least expensive price — usually a fraction of the full fare. On most flights, the full fare is close to $1,000 or more, but a 7- or 14-day advance-purchase ticket may cost less than half of that amount. Planning ahead obviously pays.

The airlines also periodically boost their sales by lowering prices on their more popular routes. These fares have advance-purchase requirements and date-of-travel restrictions, but you can't beat the prices. As you plan your vacation, keep your eyes open for these sales, which tend to take place during seasons of low travel volume — November to mid-March. You almost never see sale prices during the peak summer vacation months of July and August or around Thanksgiving or Christmas, when many people fly regardless of the fare they must pay.

Consolidators, also known as bucket shops, are great sources for international tickets, although they usually can't beat the Internet on fares within North America. To find one, look in Sunday newspaper travel sections. U.S. travelers can focus on *The New York Times,* the *Los Angeles Times,* and *The Miami Herald.* For less-developed destinations, small travel agents who cater to immigrant communities in large cities often have the best deals.

Bucket shop tickets usually are nonrefundable or rigged with stiff cancellation penalties, often as high as 50 percent to 75 percent of the ticket
price, and some put you on charter airlines with questionable safety
records.

Several reliable consolidators, however, are worldwide and available on
the Internet. **STA Travel** (☎ 800-781-4040; www.statravel.com), the
world's leader in student travel, offers good fares for travelers of all
ages. **ELTExpress** (☎ 516-228-4972; www.eltexpress.com) started in
Europe and has excellent fares worldwide but particularly to that continent. Flights.com also has "local" Web sites in 12 countries. **FlyCheap**
(☎ 800-FLY-CHEAP; 800-359-2432); www.lowestfare.com) is owned by
package-holiday megalith MyTravel and so has especially good access to
fares for sunny destinations. **Air Tickets Direct** (☎ 800-778-3447;
www.airticketsdirect.com) is based in Montreal and leverages the
weaker Canadian dollar for low fares. **Cheap International Flights
Network** (☎ 888-239-6148) offers heavily discounted fares between
New York and Paris.

Booking Your Flight Online

The big three online travel agencies — **Expedia** (www.expedia.com),
Travelocity (www.travelocity.com), and **Orbitz** (www.orbitz.com) —
sell most of the air tickets bought on the Internet. (Canadian travelers
can try www.expedia.ca and www.travelocity.ca, and U.K. residents
can go for expedia.co.uk and opodo.co.uk.) Each has different business deals with the airlines and may offer different fares on the same
flights, so shopping around is wise. Expedia and Travelocity will send
you an **e-mail notification** when a cheap fare becomes available to your
favorite destination. Of the smaller travel agency Web sites, **SideStep**
(www.sidestep.com) receives good reviews from users. It's a browser
add-on that purports to "search 140 sites at once" but in reality beats
competitors' fares only as often as other sites do.

Great **last-minute deals** are available through free weekly e-mail services
provided directly by the airlines. Most of these deals are announced on
Tuesday or Wednesday and must be purchased online. Most are valid
only for travel that weekend, but some can be booked weeks or months
in advance. Sign up for weekly e-mail alerts at airline Web sites or check
megasites that compile comprehensive lists of last-minute specials,
such as **Smarter Living** (smarterliving.com). For last-minute trips,
www.lastminute.com in Europe often has better deals than the major-
label sites.

If you're willing to give up some control over your flight details, use an
opaque fare service such as **Priceline** (www.priceline.com) or **Hotwire**
(www.hotwire.com). Both offer rock-bottom prices in exchange for
travel on a "mystery airline" at a mysterious time of day, often with a
mysterious change of planes en route. The mystery airlines are all major,
well-known carriers — and the possibility of being sent from Philadelphia

to Chicago via Tampa is remote. But, on the other hand, your chances of getting a 6 a.m. or 11 p.m. flight are pretty high. Hotwire tells you flight prices before you buy; Priceline usually has better deals than Hotwire, but you have to play their "name our price" game. *Note:* In 2004, Priceline added nonopaque service to its roster. You now have the option of picking exact flights, times, and airlines from a list of offers — or opting to bid on opaque fares as before.

 Enticing last-minute deals are also available directly from the airlines through a free e-mail service called *E-savers.* Each week, the airline sends you a list of discounted flights, usually leaving the upcoming Friday or Saturday and returning the following Monday or Tuesday. You can sign up for all the major airlines at one time by logging on to **Smarter Living** (www.smarterliving.com), or you can go to each individual airline's Web site. Airline sites also offer schedules, flight booking, and information on late-breaking bargains.

Arriving by Other Means

You can take trains into Paris from any other major city in continental Europe. France is linked to fast train connections from cities in Italy and Germany, and many routes provide night trains. Many passengers take an overnight train for the route from Rome to Paris, for example.

You can also arrive in France by ferry from Italy or England. The ferry service from Italy is out of Genoa. From Dover, England, a ferry lands in Calais, France. But the chunnel train (see below) is so convenient for this route, there's little reason to take the ferry.

If you like driving long distances and have plenty of time, you can drive into France, though the routes around the Alps can be either scary or exhilarating, depending on your disposition.

The **Eurostar** train (☎ **0990-300-003** in London, **01-44-51-06-02** in Paris, and **800-EUROSTAR** in the U.S.; www.eurostar.com) runs through the Channel Tunnel *(chunnel)* and connects London's Waterloo Station with Paris's Gare du Nord and Brussels's Central Station. Both trips take about three hours (you arrive four hours later with the time change). Because the old train-ferry-train route (through Dover and Calais) takes all day and costs almost the same, the Eurostar option is a great deal.

Reserving a seat on the Eurostar always is a good idea. Tour groups and England's frequent bank holidays (three- or four-day weekends) book the train solid, because many Londoners take short vacations to Paris.

 The Eurostar leaves exactly on time, and passengers are not let on less than 15 minutes before departure.

Joining an Escorted Tour

You may be one of the many people who love escorted tours. The tour company takes care of all the details and tells you what to expect at each leg of your journey. You know your costs upfront, and in the case of the tame ones, you don't get many surprises. Escorted tours can take you to the maximum number of sights in the minimum amount of time with the least amount of hassle.

 If you decide to go with an escorted tour, we strongly recommend purchasing travel insurance, especially if the tour operator asks to you pay upfront. But don't buy insurance from the tour operator. If the tour operator doesn't fulfill its obligation to provide you with the vacation you paid for, there's no reason to think that it'll fulfill its insurance obligations either. Get travel insurance through an independent agency.

When choosing an escorted tour, along with finding out whether you have to put down a deposit and when final payment is due, ask a few simple questions before you buy:

- ✔ **What is the cancellation policy?** Can a tour operator cancel the trip if it doesn't get enough people? How late can you cancel if you are unable to go? Do you get a refund if you cancel? Do you get a refund if the operator cancels?

- ✔ **How jampacked is the schedule?** Does the tour schedule try to fit 25 hours into a 24-hour day, or does it give you ample time to relax by the pool or shop? If getting up at 7 a.m. every day and not returning to your hotel until 6 or 7 p.m. sounds like a grind, certain escorted tours may not be for you.

- ✔ **How large is the group?** The smaller the group, the less time you spend waiting for people to get on and off the bus. Tour operators may be evasive about this, because they may not know the exact size of the group until everybody has made reservations, but you should be given a rough estimate.

- ✔ **Is there a minimum group size?** Some tours have a minimum group size and may cancel the tour if they don't book enough people. If a quota exists, find out what it is and how close the tour company is to reaching it. Again, tour operators may be evasive in their answers, but the information may help you select a tour that's sure to happen.

- ✔ **What exactly is included?** Don't assume anything. You may have to pay to get yourself to and from the airport. A box lunch may be included in an excursion, but drinks may be extra. Beer may be included but not wine. How much flexibility do you have? Can you opt out of certain activities, or does the bus leave once a day, with no exceptions? Are all your meals planned in advance? Can you choose your main course at dinner, or does everybody get the same chicken cutlet?

Depending on your recreational passions, we recommend one of the following tour companies:

- **Trafalgar Tours,** 29-76 Northern Blvd., Long Island City, NY 11101 (☎ 800-854-0103; www.trafalgartours.com), offers a 14-day **Best of France** trip starting and ending in Paris, with stops on the Riviera and in Lourdes, Nice, Monaco, and other cities. Most meals and twin-bed accommodations in first-class hotels are part of the package, which is $1,899 per person for the land portion only. Its nine-day, four-city **Treasures of France** tour, also beginning and ending in Paris, has similar meal and accommodation offerings and costs $1,125 per person for the land portion only. Call your travel agent for more information.

- Another good choice is **Globus/Cosmos Tours,** 5301 S. Federal Circle, Littleton, CO 80123 (☎ 800-338-7092; www.globusandcosmos.com). Globus offers first-class escorted coach tours of various regions of France lasting from 7 to 15 days. Cosmos, a budget branch of Globus, offers escorted tours of about the same length. You must book tours through a travel agent, but you can call the 800 number for brochures.

- **Tauck World Discovery,** 10 Norden Place, Norwalk, CT 06855 (☎ 800-788-7885; www.tauck.com), provides superior first-class, fully escorted coach grand tours of France and one-week general tours of specific regions. Its 14-day tour covering the Normandy landing beaches, the Bayeux Tapestry, and Mont-St-Michel, among other places of historic interest, costs $4,150 per person, double occupancy (land only); a 12-day trip beginning in Nice and ending in Paris costs $4,190 per person, double occupancy (land only).

Choosing a Package Tour

For many destinations, package tours can be a smart way to go. In many cases, a package tour that includes airfare, hotel, and transportation to and from the airport costs less than the hotel alone on a tour you book yourself. That's because packages are sold in bulk to tour operators, who resell them to the public. It's kind of like buying your vacation at a buy-in-bulk store — except the tour operator is the one who buys the 1,000-count box of garbage bags and resells them 10 at a time at a cost that undercuts the local supermarket.

Package tours can vary as much as those garbage bags, too. Some offer a better class of hotels than others; others provide the same hotels for lower prices. Some book flights on scheduled airlines; others sell charters. In some packages, your choice of accommodations and travel days may be limited. Some let you choose between escorted vacations and independent vacations; others enable you to add on just a few excursions or escorted day trips (also at discounted prices) without booking an entirely escorted tour.

To find package tours, check out the travel section of your local Sunday newspaper or the ads in the back of national travel magazines such as *Travel & Leisure, National Geographic Traveler,* and *Condé Nast Traveler.* **Liberty Travel** (call ☎ **888-271-1584** to find the store nearest you; www. libertytravel.com) is one of the biggest packagers in the Northeast and usually boasts a full-page ad in Sunday papers.

Another good source of package deals is the airlines themselves. Most major airlines offer air/land packages, including **American Airlines Vacations** (☎ 800-489-4810; www.aavacations.com), **Delta Vacations** (☎ 800-654-6559; www.deltavacations.com), **Continental Airlines Vacations** (☎ 800-301-3800; www.covacations.com), and **United Vacations** (☎ 888-854-3899; www.unitedvacations.com). Several big **online travel agencies** — Expedia, Travelocity, Orbitz, Site59, and Lastminute. com — also do a brisk business in packages. If you're unsure about the pedigree of a smaller packager, check with the Better Business Bureau in the city where the company is based, or go online at www.bbb.org. If a packager won't tell you where it's based, don't fly with it.

Here are some package tour operators with specific French connections:

- ✔ **The French Experience,** 370 Lexington Ave., Room 511, New York, NY 10017 (☎ **800-283-7262** or 212-986-3800; www.frenchexperience. com), offers several fly–drive programs through regions of France (the quoted price includes airfare and a rental car). You can specify the type and price level of hotels you want. The agency arranges the car rental in advance, and the rest is up to you. Some staff can seem unfriendly, but persevere for good deals.

- ✔ The two largest tour operators conducting escorted tours of France and Europe are **Globus/Cosmos Tours** (☎ **800-338-7092;** www. globusandcosmos.com) and **Trafalgar** (☎ **800-854-0103;** www. trafalgartours.com). Both have first-class tours that run about $100 a day and budget tours for about $75 a day. The differences are mainly in hotel location and the number of activities. There's little difference in the companies' services, so choose your tour based on the itinerary and date of departure. Brochures are available at travel agencies, and all tours must be booked through travel agents.

- ✔ **Tauck World Discovery,** 276 Post Rd. W., Westport, CT 06880 (☎ **800-468-2825;** www.tauck.com), provides first-class, escorted coach grand tours of France and one-week general tours of regions in France. Its 14-day tour covering the Normandy landing beaches, the Bayeux Tapestry, and Mont-St-Michel costs $3,790 per person, double occupancy (land only), while a 12-day trip beginning in Nice and ending in Paris is $3,800 to $4,200 per person.

Chapter 7

Getting around France

• •

In This Chapter

▶ Flying to and fro
▶ Catching the train
▶ Renting a car

• •

T his chapter gives you the details you need for traveling within France. Your best bet for getting around the country is via the speedy and efficient train system, especially the super-fast TGV. If you're pressed for time and need to cover a large distance, then opt for a plane. But if you have sufficient time, you can rent a car and tour the countryside.

Normandy and the Loire Valley are within a couple of hours of Paris, so taking the train from the capital makes sense. If you want to explore the countryside, rent a car from a city within the region. Brittany and Provence are three to four hours by train from Paris, so the train still makes sense. However, if you're going all the way south to the Riviera, consider flying.

Traveling by Plane

The French national airline is **Air France** (☎ **800-237-2747** in the United States, 0845-0845-111 in London; www.airfrance.com), which offers domestic flights to every major city in France (though to get to some cities, you have to fly through Paris or Lyon). Although you may consider flying from Paris to Nice, you need to know that flights within France occasionally are delayed or canceled because of strikes. You can take one of 30 flights a day from Paris to the Aéroport Nice–Côte d'Azur, which is an easy shuttle from the center of Nice. The flights take 1 hour and 20 minutes, and the average fare is $300 one way (subject to change). The train to Nice takes 6 hours and 40 minutes. See travel times in Table 7-1.

Table 7-1	Travel Times between the Major Cities			
Cities	*Distance*	*Train Travel Time*	*Driving Time*	*Air Travel Time*
Paris to Tours	241km/150 miles	1 hr.	2 hrs., 45 min.	1 hr., 40 min.
Paris to Rouen	136km/85 miles	1 hr., 10 min.	1 hr., 40 min.	no direct flights
Paris to Nantes	387km/240 miles	2 hrs., 10 min.	4 hrs., 10 min.	1 hr., 5 min.
Nantes to Quimper	234km/145 miles	2 hrs., 30 min.	2 hrs., 30 min.	no flights
Paris to Avignon	710km/441 miles	2 hrs., 40 min.	7 hrs., 15 min.	1 hr.
Avignon to Nice	257km/160 miles	3 hrs., 50 min.	2 hrs., 40 min.	no direct flights
Paris to Nice	966km/600 miles	6 hrs., 40 min.	10 hrs.	1 hr., 20 min.

Taking the Train

Train travel in France is a relative bargain, and the trains are known for being on time. You can go almost anywhere in the country by train — service covers more than 38,000km (about 24,000 miles) of track and about 3,000 stations. The superfast TGVs (pronounced *tay-jay-vay,* meaning Trains à Grand Vitesse), servicing 50 French cities, continually are being improved.

Most trains are clean and comfortable. On all TGVs and some other trains, you have a choice of first- and second-class seating. First class is cleaner and quieter, with slightly larger chairs, and is occupied mainly by businesspeople. Trains traveling long distances have *couchettes* (sleepers), and most contain snack bars. (Always bring bottled water and a snack on a French train. You never know when a strike is going to mean a closed snack bar.)

Make sure that you get on the right *car,* not just the right train. Check your ticket for the *voit* (car) and the *place* (seat). Individual train cars may split from the rest of the train down the line and join a different train headed to a different destination. Making sure that you're on the right car is especially important when taking a night train (if you have a reserved spot, you needn't worry). Each car has its own destination placard, which may also list major stops en route. Always check with the conductor.

If you're at a rail station, and someone at the ticket window tells you that a train you want to take is booked, always ask the conductor. The ticket window computers include bookings for possible no-shows, so a fully reserved train can actually have many seats available.

If you want to bypass Paris entirely or visit the city at the end of your trip, consider taking a train directly from Charles de Gaulle Airport to your destination. You'll find direct trains from the airport to Avignon, Dijon, Marseille, Nantes, and St-Pierre des Corps (just outside Tours), among other cities.

Getting more information

To obtain more information and to buy rail passes before you leave, check out www.raileurope.com, from which you can access rail travel information for travelers from the United States, Canada, and the United Kingdom. Or call one of the following numbers for more information:

- ✔ **In the United States:** Contact **Rail Europe** (☎ 800-4-EURAIL or **800-677-8585;** Fax: 914-682-3712; www.raileurope.com).

- ✔ **In Canada:** Contact **Rail Europe** (☎ 800-361-RAIL or **800-361-7245,** or 905-602-4195; Fax: 905-602-4198).

- ✔ **In the United Kingdom:** Contact **National Rail Enquiries** (☎ 08457-48-49-50;** Fax: 020-7491-9956).

To get train information or to make reservations after you get to Paris, call **SNCF (Societé Nationale des Chemins de Fer, the French National Railroad)** at ☎ **08-36-35-35-39** for English-speaking operators and ☎ **08-36-35-35-35** for French-speaking operators (some of whom may speak a little English). You're charged 0.30€ (35¢) per minute to use this service. You can also go to any local travel agency, of course, and book tickets. A simpler way to reserve tickets is to take advantage of the *billetterie* (ticket machines) in every train station. If you know your PIN, you can use American Express, MasterCard, or Visa to purchase your ticket. You can also find out schedule information on the Web at www.sncf.com.

If you plan on much rail travel, obtain the latest copy of the **Thomas Cook European Timetable of Railroads.** This comprehensive 500-plus-page book is published monthly and documents all Europe's mainline passenger rail services with detail and accuracy. You can purchase the book online at www.thomascooktimetables.com.

Buying French rail passes

Working cooperatively with SNCF, Air Inter Europe, and Avis, **Rail Europe** offers two flexible cost-saving rail passes that can reduce travel costs considerably:

- ✔ The **France Railpass** provides unlimited rail transport throughout France for four days within one month, costing $252 in first class and $218 in second class. You can purchase up to six or more days for an extra $32 per person per day. Children ages 4 to 11 travel for half price.

✔ The **France Rail 'n Drive Pass,** available only for North American travelers, combines good values from both rail travel and Avis car rentals and is best used by arriving at a major rail depot and then renting a car to explore the countryside. The best part is that you don't pay a surcharge for dropping off the vehicle at another location, so you don't have to retrace your steps. The offer includes the France Railpass, along with unlimited mileage on a car rental. The costs are lowest when two or more adults travel together. You can use it during five nonconsecutive days in one month, and it includes three days of travel on the train and two days' use of a rental car. If rental of the least expensive car is combined with first-class rail travel, the price is $249 per person; if rental of the least expensive car is combined with second-class rail travel, the charge is $205 per person. Cars can be upgraded for a supplemental fee. The prices above apply to two people traveling together. Up to six additional rail days can be purchased for $29 per day, and unlimited additional car days can be purchased from $39 per day.

Other passes for France from Rail Europe include the following:

✔ **France Saverpass** offers a discount for two or more people traveling together ($215 first class, $186 second class).

✔ **France Seniorpass** gives a discount to people older than 60 traveling in first class. Prices start at $228 for first-class seating.

✔ **France Youthpass** gives a discount for youth ($189 first class, $164 second class).

Even with a rail pass, you need to make a reservation for TGVs and some other trains. When you make the reservation, you need to specify that you have a rail pass, but remember that only a limited number of seats are available for travelers with passes. If first class is booked, a seat in second class probably will be available. Be aware that on TGVs, you need to pay a 3€ ($3.60) supplement even though you have a rail pass. Pay it at the ticket window before boarding the train. If you wait to pay the supplement to the train conductor, he or she may charge you a small penalty.

Getting around by Bus

The bus system in France, which is separated into about a hundred different small companies, can take you to most out-of-the-way places not reachable by train. The hill towns of the Riviera are particularly well serviced by bus. You can pick up local schedules at tourist offices. Remember that bus service is severely reduced on Sundays. For many routes in France, you pay the driver for the trip. Throughout the book, we provide numbers for bus companies that service individual towns.

As in most countries, French bus stations tend to be a little less safe than train stations, and you need to keep a close watch on your luggage.

Driving around France

Many of France's most luxurious accommodations lie off the beaten track, so you need a rental car (or a taxi) to get there. And nothing beats the flexibility of a rental car for exploring certain regions of France, particularly Brittany and the Loire Valley. Driving times vary depending on traffic near the major cities and how fast you want to go. Paris to Rouen is about 2½ hours, Paris to Nantes is 3½ hours, and Paris to Marseille can be 7½ hours. (The new fast TGV gets you to Marseille in only 3½ hours.)

Understanding the rules of renting a car

Renting a car in France is easy. You need to present a passport, a valid driver's license, and a valid credit card. You also need to meet the minimum age requirements of the company (for Hertz, 21; for Avis, 23; for Budget, 25 — more expensive cars at these companies require at least age 25). Being asked for an International Driver's License is highly unusual in France, but to be safe, you can get one at your nearest AAA office for $10. Here are a few other things to keep in mind before renting your car:

✔ Save the most money by reserving the car before you leave home. Remember, though, that all car-rental bills in France are subject to a 19.6 percent government tax.

✔ Comparison shop using the Internet. As with other aspects of planning your trip, using the Internet can make comparison shopping for a car rental much easier. You can check rates at most of the major agencies' Web sites. Additionally, all major travel sites — **Travelocity** (www.travelocity.com), **Expedia** (www.expedia.com), **Orbitz** (www.orbitz.com), and **Smarter Living** (www.smarterliving.com), for example — have search engines that can dig up discounted car-rental rates. Just enter the car size you want, the pickup and return dates and location, and the server returns a price. You can even make the reservation through any of these sites.

✔ Automatic transmissions are a luxury in Europe, so if you want a car with one, you'll have to pay about double the cost of the rental car.

In addition to the standard rental prices, other optional charges apply to most car rentals (and some not-so-optional charges, such as taxes). The *Collision Damage Waiver* (CDW), which requires you to pay for damage to the car in a collision, is covered by many credit-card companies. Check with your credit-card company before you go so you can avoid paying this hefty fee — as much as $20 a day.

Car rental companies also offer additional *liability insurance* (if you harm others in an accident), *personal accident insurance* (if you harm yourself or your passengers), and *personal effects insurance* (if your luggage is stolen from your car). Your insurance policy on your car at home probably covers most of these unlikely occurrences. However, if your own insurance doesn't cover you for rentals, or if you don't have auto insurance, definitely consider the additional coverage (ask your car rental agent for more information). Unless you're toting around the Hope diamond, and you don't want to leave something like that in your car trunk, you probably can skip the personal effects insurance, but driving around without liability or personal accident coverage never is a good idea. Even if you're a good driver, other people may not be, and liability claims can be complicated.

Here are the contact numbers for the big car-rental companies:

- ✔ **Budget** (☎ **800-527-0700** in the United States and Canada; www. budget.com) maintains about 30 locations in Paris, with its largest branch at 71 bd. Porte Miallot (☎ **01-40-47-00-33**; Métro: Trocadéro). Budget also has offices in Tours, Orléans, Rouen, Nantes, Avignon, Aix, Nice, Marseille, and Cannes, among other cities.

- ✔ **Hertz** (☎ **800-654-3131** in the United States and Canada; www. hertz.com) maintains about 15 locations in Paris, including offices at the city's airports. The main office is 27 rue St-Ferdinand, 17e (☎ **01-45-74-97-39**; Métro: Argentine). Hertz also has offices in most major French towns. If you're in France and want to rent a car for anywhere in France outside of Paris, call ☎ **01-39-38-30-00.**

- ✔ **Avis** (☎ **800-331-1212** in the United States and Canada; www.avis. com) has offices at both Paris airports and an inner-city headquarters at 5 rue Bixio, 7e (☎ **01-44-18-10-50**; Métro: Ecole-Militaire), near the Tour Eiffel. Avis also operates offices in most major French towns.

- ✔ **National,** which is called National Citer in France (☎ 800-CAR-RENT, or **800-227-7368** in the United States and Canada; www.national car.com), is represented in Paris by Europcar, whose largest office is at 165 bis rue de Vaugirard (☎ **01-44-38-61-81**; Métro: St-Sulpre). It has offices at both Paris airports and at about a dozen other locations, including Tours, Nantes, Avignon, Aix-en-Provence, Nice, and Cannes.

Knowing the rules of the road

Using a car, of course, brings the greatest freedom of all, but you have to know French rules of the road. Here are some things to keep in mind as you traverse the cities and countryside:

- ✔ **Seat belts:** Everyone in the car — in both the front and back seats — must wear seat belts.

- ✔ **Kids in the car:** Children ages 11 and younger must ride in the back seat.

✔ **Yield:** Drivers are supposed to yield to the car on their right, except where signs indicate otherwise, such as at traffic circles.

✔ **Speed limits:** If you violate the speed limits, expect a big fine. Those limits are about 130km per hour (80 mph) on expressways, about 100km per hour (60 mph) on major national highways, and 90km per hour (56 mph) on small country roads. In towns, don't exceed 60km per hour (37 mph).

✔ **Defensive driving:** The French are known as the most dangerous drivers in Europe — with even worse reputations than the Italians or Portuguese — because of the speeds at which they drive. As a result, the French have one of the highest per capita death rates by auto in Europe. Expect to be tailgated.

✔ **Gas:** Known as *essence,* gasoline in France is very expensive for drivers used to U.S. prices. At press time, the most widely used type of unleaded gasoline (*super sans plomb*) sold for about 1.12€ ($1.34) per liter, a ratio that works out to a rough equivalent of 4.23€ ($5.07) per gallon. Depending on the size of the tank of your European car, filling it up usually costs between 40€ ($48) and 60€ ($72).

Sometimes you can drive for miles in rural France without coming upon a gas station, so try not to let your tank get dangerously low.

Chapter 8

Booking Your Accommodations

*A*fter you decide where in France you're heading, you need to get down to the nitty-gritty of choosing the type of lodging you want and finding a suitable room at the right price. France tends to charge reasonable hotel rates; many of its hotels offer additional special deals, and this chapter tells you how to find them. Use the money you save on your room for dinners in quality restaurants, spectacular entertainment, or gifts for family and friends (or yourself).

Getting to Know Your Options

Hotels in France have their own set of quirks that you may not be familiar with if you're used to hotels in the United States. Things you may take for granted in U.S. hotels — such as closets, shower curtains, washcloths, and window screens — may not always be there for you in France. Many medium-priced hotels don't have air-conditioning, and their bathrooms usually are quite small. Likewise, many charming French hotels are in ancient buildings and don't have elevators. Sometimes, the stairways are steep, narrow, winding stone passageways. Forewarned is forearmed. Pack light and consider the inconvenience part of the old-world charm.

Because hotel offerings vary greatly, if some particular amenity is very important to you — air-conditioning, elevator, whatever — ask about it when you're reserving your room.

Hotels

Even the most basic hotel rooms in France have telephones and televisions. But only the higher-priced hotels offer satellite televisions that receive English-language stations.

As a rule, basic and medium-priced French hotels offer fewer amenities than their American counterparts, but they're also far cheaper than medium-priced hotels in similar resort areas. For example, a medium-priced hotel room on the Riviera will cost around €125 ($150) per night in season; a medium-priced hotel room on the island of Nantucket in Massachusetts in season will cost around $225. On the high end of the scale, you'd be hard-pressed to find a hotel in the United States that has as much elegance and glamour as some of France's top hotels, mainly because the United States doesn't have 300-year-old palaces and other such grand historic locales.

Fortunately, most towns in France offer a wide range of hotel choices, from unassuming hostelries with small, simple rooms to world-famous palaces with superdeluxe suites. Many travelers want a medium-priced hotel, perhaps with some historic charm, that's in a good location, within walking distance of sights, shopping, and restaurants. So we include those types of places throughout the book, along with inexpensive choices for people who want to save a few euros and expensive places for travelers looking to splurge.

Chain hotels often are concrete block structures on the outskirts of cities. Their bargain rates for standard amenities are popular with business travelers. The big chains are **Mercure** (☎ 800-MERCURE, or 800-637-2873 in the United States and Canada; www.mercure.com), which has medium-priced rooms, and **Formule 1** (☎ 01-69-36-75-29 in France; www.hotel formule1.com), which has inexpensive rooms.

French hotels are government-rated by stars, which always are indicated on the exterior of the building on a plaque and in all brochures for the hotel. The ratings from highest to lowest are four-star deluxe (the best), four-star (excellent), three-star (very nice), two-star (good quality), and one-star (budget). No-star hotels, which don't have the minimum amenities to receive one star, also are available, but you probably want to avoid them, because they often have shared bathrooms in the hallways. Two-star and three-star hotels are the midrange options, and although the quality and comfort of these accommodations can range quite a bit, they always have a clean room with a simple bathroom (sink, toilet, shower and/or tub, and a bar of soap).

All the hotel reviews in this book list the high-season rack rates (the rate the hotel quotes you) and use a specific number of dollar signs to indicate the general price range. Table 8-1 presents the dollar-sign breakdown that we use in this book.

Table 8-1		Key to Hotel Dollar Signs
Dollar Sign(s)	**Price Range**	**What to Expect**
$	Less than 100€ ($120)	These accommodations are relatively simple and inexpensive. Rooms will likely be small, and televisions are not necessarily provided. Parking is not provided but rather catch-as-you-can on the street.
$$	100€–200€ ($120–$240)	A bit classier, these midrange accommodations offer more room, more extras (such as irons, hair dryers, or a microwave), and a more convenient location than the preceding category.
$$$	201€–300€ ($241–$360)	Higher-class still, these accommodations begin to look plush. Think chocolates on your pillow, a classy restaurant, underground parking garages, maybe even expansive views of the water.
$$$$	301€ and up ($361 and up)	These top-rated accommodations come with luxury amenities such as valet parking, on-premise spas, and in-room hot tubs and CD players — but you pay through the nose for 'em.

 Keep in mind that hotel prices can change quite a bit. For example, what was $$$ at press time may be $$$$ when you arrive in France, because the hotel may have completed a renovation and raised its prices. Or the exchange rate, or the value of the euro relative to the dollar, can change in the future.

Relais & Châteaux and Logis de France

Relais & Châteaux is a marketing organization for some of the most deluxe privately owned hotels in France and around the world — France has about 150 of them. To qualify for the organization, hotels must adhere to strict hospitality standards, so you're pretty much guaranteed a grand room at a Relais & Châteaux hotel, usually occupying a historic building such as a former castle, abbey, or mansion. But these hotels are always very pricey, and some insist on half or full board, meaning you have to take one or two meals at the hotel, which also is very expensive but probably very tasty, considering that the restaurants attached to these hotels usually are the best in town.

For an illustrated catalog of these establishments, send $8 to **Relais & Châteaux,** 11 E. 44th St., Suite 707, New York, NY 10017. These booklets are available free at all Relais & Châteaux establishments and online at www.relaischateaux.com. For information or to book a Relais & Châteaux hotel, you can call the hotel directly or the organization head-quarters at ☎ **800-735-2478** or 212-856-0115 (Fax: 212-856-0193).

Establishments with the **Logis de France** designation are usually medium-priced, family-owned hotels that offer good value and standard amenities. You can receive a copy (for $23.95) of a booklet listing these hotels by contacting the **French Government Tourist Office,** 444 Madison Ave., New York, NY 10022 (☎ **212-838-7800**). Or you can contact the **Fédération Nationale des Logis de France,** 83 av. d'Italie, 75013 Paris (☎ **01-45-84-83-84;** www.logis-de-france.fr).

Bed-and-breakfasts

The term for a bed-and-breakfast in France is *gîte* or *chambre d'hôte,* and these accommodations usually are on a farm or in a village home and very inexpensive. Many of them offer a meal of the day, such as lunch or dinner.

At least 6,000 of these accommodations are listed with **La Maison de Gîtes de France et du Tourisme Vert,** 59 rue St-Lazare, 75439 Paris (☎ **01-49-70-75-75;** www.gites-de-france.fr). Sometimes these accommodations are quite nice; you can be in a privately owned castle in the countryside, and madame may let you prepare a meal in her kitchen. In the United States, a good source is **The French Experience,** 370 Lexington Ave., Room 511, New York, NY 10017 (☎ **800-283-7262** or 212-986-3800; Fax: 212-986-3808; www.frenchexperience.com), which also rents furnished houses for as short a period as one week.

Condos, villas, houses, and apartments

For longer-term stays in condos or apartments where you don't mind cooking your own meals and cleaning the house, you can obtain a list of real estate agencies from the **French Government Tourist Office,** 444 Madison Ave., New York, NY 10022 (☎ **212-838-7800**). One of the best French real estate groups is the **Fédération Nationale des Agents Immobiliers,** 129 rue du Faubourg St-Honoré, 75008 Paris (☎ **01-44-20-77-00;** www.fnaim.fr).

If you want to rent an apartment in Paris, the **Barclay International Group,** 6800 Jericho Turnpike, Syosset, NY 11791 (☎ **800-845-6636** or 516-364-0064; Fax: 516-364-4468; www.barclayweb.com), can give you access to about 3,000 apartments and villas scattered throughout Paris (plus 39 other cities in France), ranging from modest modern units to the most stylish. Units rent for one night to six months and start at around $80 per night, double occupancy. You pay through Barclay in advance of your trip for these units.

At Home Abroad, 405 E. 56th St., Suite 6H, New York, NY 10022-2466 (☎ **212-421-9165;** Fax: 212-533-0095; www.athomeabroadinc.com), specializes in villas on the Riviera and in the Provençal hill towns. Rentals are usually for two weeks. For no fee, At Home Abroad sends you photographs of the properties and a newsletter.

Renting a private residence may help you save money on your food costs. Breakfast at a medium-priced hotel normally runs 10€ ($12) for a continental breakfast (hot beverage, bread, croissant). Instead, make use of whatever kitchen facilities your rental may have to prepare the occasional meal. Or do what the locals do and search the neighborhood for a nearby cafe.

Finding the Best Room at the Best Rate

The **rack rate** is the maximum rate that a hotel charges for a room. It's the rate you get if you walk in off the street and ask for a room for the night. You sometimes see these rates printed on the fire/emergency exit diagrams posted on the back of the door to your room.

Hotels are happy to charge you the rack rate, but you almost always can do better. Perhaps the best way to avoid paying the rack rate is surprisingly simple: Just ask for a cheaper or discounted rate. You may be pleasantly surprised.

Searching for the best rates

In all but the smallest accommodations, the rate you pay for a room depends on many factors — chief among them is how you make your reservation. A travel agent may be able to negotiate a better price with certain hotels than you can get by yourself. (That's because the hotel often gives the agent a discount in exchange for steering his or her business toward that hotel.)

 Reserving a room through the hotel's toll-free number may also result in a lower rate than calling the hotel directly. On the other hand, the central reservations number may not know about discount rates at specific locations. For example, local franchises may offer a special group rate for a wedding or family reunion, but they may neglect to tell the central booking line. Your best bet is to call both the local number and the toll-free number and see which one gives you a better deal.

Room rates (even rack rates) change with the season as occupancy rates rise and fall. But even within a given season, room prices are subject to change without notice, so the rates quoted in this book may be different from the actual rate you receive when you make your reservation. Be sure to mention membership in any travel associations, seniors organizations, frequent flyer programs, any other corporate rewards programs you can think of — or your Uncle Joe's Elks lodge in which you're an honorary inductee, for that matter — when you call to book. You never know when the affiliation may be worth a few dollars off your room rate.

Throughout France, as in many tourist centers worldwide, hotels routinely overbook, so booking by credit card doesn't automatically hold your room if you arrive later than expected or after 6 p.m. The hotel clerk always asks when you expect to arrive, and the hotel usually holds the room until that time. Always pad your expected arrival by a few hours to be safe. But all bets are off after 7 p.m., and the hotel is likely to give away your room to someone off the street unless you call and specifically ask them to hold it. A credit-card number does, however, hold a room better than just your word over the telephone that you will show up. If you've made a reservation very far in advance, confirm within 24 hours of your expected arrival. If you're experiencing a major delay, alert the hotel as soon as you can.

Keeping your lodging costs down

 Bartering for a cheaper room isn't the norm in France's budget hotels. Most establishments are small and privately owned; they post their rates in the reception area and may not be willing to negotiate. To be fair, they may not be able to afford to let rooms go for less.

Here's some advice to keep in mind when trying to save money on a room:

✔ Don't forget that your travel agent may be able to negotiate a better price at top hotels than you can get by yourself.

✔ Always ask whether the hotel offers any weekend specials, which typically require you to stay two nights (either Friday and Saturday or Saturday and Sunday). In Paris, you can find this kind of deal from September to March at almost all price levels.

✔ *Forfaits* (*fohr*-feh) are discounts that require you to stay a certain number of nights — perhaps a minimum of three or five nights. Sometimes something else is thrown in (such as a bottle of champagne) to sweeten the deal. If you're going to be in a city for more than three days, always ask about a *forfait* and then pick the hotel with the best deal.

✔ Visit Paris during the summer low season. That's no typo. Room rates in Paris tend to be lower in July and August, which, though big tourist months, are considered low season by Paris hoteliers. November and December also are low season, while October is heavy with conventioneers, making it difficult to find a room.

✔ Visit regions outside of Paris during the shoulder seasons of spring and fall when prices can be considerably lower, particularly along the Riviera.

✔ In hotels outside of Paris, the best room in a medium-priced hotel usually is much better than the worst room at a high-priced hotel, and it's usually cheaper. Ask for the price of the best room, the room with the best views, or the quietest room.

✔ Don't forget about package deals (see Chapter 6) that include air-fare, hotel, and transportation to and from the airport.

✔ Look on the Internet for deals (see the following section, "Surfing the Web for hotel deals").

✔ If you're a risk taker, stop in at the **Office de Tourisme de Paris,** 18 rue de Dunkerque, 10e (☎ **08-92-68-30-00**), during July and August or November and December — slow seasons for Paris hotels. At these times, hotels with unsold rooms often sell to the tourist office at reduced rates, and you can stay in a three-star hotel at a two-star price. During the summer slow season, however, you have to wait in a long line and are not guaranteed a room.

Surfing the Web for hotel deals

Shopping online for hotels generally is done one of two ways: by booking through the hotel's own Web site or through an independent booking agency (or a fare-service agency such as Priceline). These Internet hotel agencies have multiplied in mind-boggling numbers of late, competing for the business of millions of consumers surfing for accommodations around the world. This competitiveness can be a boon to consumers who have the patience and time to shop and compare the online sites for good deals — but shop they must, for prices can vary considerably from one site to the next. And keep in mind that hotels at the top of a site's listing may be there for no other reason than that they paid money to get the placement.

Of the big three sites, **Expedia** offers a long list of special deals and virtual tours or photos of available rooms so you can see what you're paying for (a feature that helps counter the claims that the best rooms are often held back from bargain-booking Web sites). **Travelocity** posts unvarnished customer reviews and ranks its properties according to the AAA rating system. **Orbitz** features a handy tool that enables you to search for specific amenities in which you may be interested. Also reliable are **Hotels.com** and **Quikbook.com.** An excellent free program, **TravelAxe** (www.travelaxe.net), can help you search multiple hotel sites all at once — even ones you may never have heard of — and conveniently lists the total price of the room, including taxes and service charges. Another booking site, **Travelweb** (www.travelweb.com), is partly owned by the hotels it represents (including the Hilton, Hyatt, and Starwood chains) and therefore is plugged directly into the hotels' reservations systems — unlike independent online agencies that have to fax or e-mail reservation requests to the hotel (a good portion of which get misplaced in the shuffle). More than once, travelers have arrived at their hotels only to be told that they have no reservations. To be fair, many of the major sites are undergoing improvements in service and ease of use — none of which can be bad news for consumers. Expedia, for exam-ple, soon will be able to plug directly into the reservations systems of many hotel chains. In the meantime, **getting a confirmation number** and **making a printout** of any online booking transactions are good ideas.

In the opaque Web site category, **Priceline** and **Hotwire** are even better for hotels than for airfares. With both, you're allowed to pick the neighborhood and quality level of your hotel before offering up your money. Priceline's hotel product covers Europe, but it's much better at getting five-star lodging for three-star prices than at finding anything at the bottom of the scale. On the downside, many hotels stick Priceline guests in their least desirable rooms. Be sure to go to the BiddingforTravel Web site (www.biddingfortravel.com) before bidding on a hotel room on Priceline; it features a fairly up-to-date list of hotels that Priceline uses in major cities. For both Priceline and Hotwire, you pay upfront, and the fee is nonrefundable. *Note:* Some hotels do not provide loyalty program credits or points or other frequent-stay amenities when you book a room through opaque online services.

Reserving the best room

After making your reservation, asking one or two more pointed questions can go a long way toward ensuring that you get the best room in the house. Always ask for a corner room. They're usually larger, quieter, and have more windows and light than standard rooms, and they don't always cost more. Likewise, ask whether the hotel is renovating; if it is, request a room away from the renovation work. Inquire, too, about the location of the restaurants, bars, and discos in the hotel — all sources of annoying noise. And if you aren't happy with your room when you arrive, talk to the front desk. If the hotel has another room, it should be happy to accommodate you, within reason.

Chapter 9

Catering to Special Travel Needs or Interests

- -

In This Chapter

▶ Visiting France with children
▶ Getting discounts for seniors
▶ Locating wheelchair-accessible attractions and accommodations
▶ Identifying resources for gay and lesbian travelers
▶ Traveling solo

- -

*W*hether it's the food, the history, the stunning art and architecture, or that inimitable French *joie de vivre* (joy of living), France ranks among the most visited of all tourist destinations, and more resources than ever make it available — and enjoyable — to all. This chapter covers the how-to guides, tour companies for travelers with disabilities, and English-speaking baby sitters that are only some of the ways travelers with special needs are making the most of France these days.

Traveling with the Brood: Advice for Families

France has a very family-oriented culture, so feel free to bring your kids along. They'll undoubtedly be wide-eyed at the cultural differences and interested in the unusual historic sights. However, you may want to reconsider taking younger children to the fanciest hotels and restaurants unless your kids are very well behaved. Some of these establishments have a somewhat inhospitable reaction to screaming tots. Throughout the book, the Kid Friendly icon lets you know which hotels and restaurants are best for kids. Your best indication for kid-friendly restaurants is whether they have *enfant* (child) menus posted outside. Many historic sights and museums are free or half-price for kids.

Paris, the City of Light, is full of attractions worthy of your children's attention, and the kids can only benefit from the experience. Parks and playgrounds and kid-specific sights and museums abound, along with interesting boat rides and bike tours. Paris also is safer than most big cities.

Teenagers are fascinated by the beach scene on the Riviera or by any other beach scene in France. In addition, older children may enjoy some of the more spectacular attractions like the Palais des Papes in Avignon and the Château de Chambord in the Loire Valley. Teens also seem to love France's cafe society, where you can find a central spot to sit and people-watch for hours on end.

Getting kids ready for France

If you plan your trip well in advance, your kids may get a kick out of learning the language from one of the many French-language books and videotapes on the market. Stories such as Ludwig Bemelmans's *Madeline* series, Albert Lamorisse's *The Red Balloon,* and Kay Thompson's *Eloise in Paris* are great for kids younger than 8. You can order them from the **Librairie de France,** 610 Fifth Ave., New York, NY 10020 (☎ **212-581-8810;** Fax: 212-265-1094; www.librairiedefrance.com). Older teens may appreciate Ernest Hemingway's *A Moveable Feast,* Victor Hugo's *Les Misérables,* Rose Tremain's *The Way I Found Her,* and Peter Mayle's books about Provence.

Preview museums and other sights that you want to visit by checking out their Web sites (start with the sidebar "Going online to introduce your kids to France" elsewhere in this chapter). Children younger than 18 are admitted free to France's national museums but not necessarily to Paris's city museums. (No consistent rule exists to help you distinguish between a national and a city museum — unless "Nationale" is part of the museum's name — though national museums tend to close on Tuesdays and Paris city museums tend to close on Mondays.) If you stay long enough, consider a day trip to Disneyland Paris, easily accessible by public transportation (see Chapter 13 for more about Disneyland Paris).

If your children are younger than 12 and you're traveling by rail through France, check out the **Carte Enfant Plus.** Available at any SNCF (French National Railroads) station, it offers a 50 percent discount for the child and up to four adult travel companions. The card costs 55€ ($66) and is good for a month, but only a limited number of seats are available, and discounts aren't offered for periods of peak travel or during holidays. Reserve in advance.

Although the French love kids and welcome them just about everywhere, they do expect them to be well mannered. Proper behavior is expected, especially in restaurants and museums. French children are taught at an early age to behave appropriately in these settings, and French adults expect the same from your kids.

Going online to introduce your kids to France

Checking out some of the following Web sites with your children is a good way to introduce them to the sights they'll find in Paris and the rest of France:

✔ **Avignon and Provence:** www.avignon-et-provence.com

✔ **Brittany:** www.brittany-guide.com

✔ **Châteaux in the Loire Valley:** www.chateauxandcountry.com

✔ **Cité des Sciences et de l'Industrie:** www.cite-sciences.fr

✔ **Disneyland Paris:** www.disneylandparis.com

✔ **The French Riviera:** www.provencebeyond.com

✔ **Les Catacombes:** www.multimania.com/houze

✔ **Musée du Louvre:** www.louvre.fr

✔ **Musée d'Orsay:** www.musee-orsay.fr

✔ **Tour Eiffel:** www.tour-eiffel.fr

Bringing along baby

You can arrange ahead of time for such necessities as a crib, bottle warmer, and, if you're driving, a car seat (small children are prohibited from riding in the front seat). Find out whether the place where you're staying stocks baby food; if not, take some with you for your first day and then plan to buy some. Plenty of choices are available. Transportation in Paris isn't as stroller-friendly as it is in the United States. Be prepared to lift your child out of the stroller to board buses and climb up and down stairs and/or walk long distances in some Métro stations. The upside to being in Paris is that you and your child can stroll in some of the world's prettiest parks and gardens.

Locating some helpful resources

If you need a baby sitter in Paris, contact the English-speaking caregivers **Allo Maman Poule?** (7 villa Murat, 16e; ☎ **01-45-20-97-97**). Specify when calling that you need a sitter who speaks English. If you need a baby sitter anywhere in France besides Paris, check with the local office of tourism for recommendations.

For more information on baby-sitting, refer to this book's appendix. For passport information for children, see Chapter 10.

The books *Family Travel* (Lanier Publishing International) and *How to Take Great Trips with Your Kids* (The Harvard Common Press) are full of good general advice that can apply to travel anywhere. Another reliable tome with a worldwide focus is *Adventuring with Children* (Foghorn Press).

You can also check out *Family Travel Times,* published six times a year by Travel with Your Children, 40 Fifth Ave., 7th Floor, New York, NY 10011 (☎ 888-822-4FTT or 212-477-5524; www.familytraveltimes.com). It includes a weekly call-in service for subscribers. Subscriptions are $39 a year. A free publication list and a sample issue are available upon request.

Familyhostel (☎ 800-733-9753; www.learn.unh.edu/familyhostel) takes the whole family, including kids ages 8 to 15, on moderately priced international learning vacations. Lectures, field trips, and sightseeing are guided by a team of academics.

You can find good family-oriented vacation advice on the Internet from sites like the **Family Travel Forum** (www.familytravelforum.com), a comprehensive site that offers customized trip planning; **Family Travel Network** (www.familytravelnetwork.com), an award-winning site that offers travel features, deals, and tips; **Traveling Internationally with Your Kids** (www.travelwithyourkids.com), a comprehensive site that offers customized trip planning; and **Family Travel Files** (www.thefamily travelfiles.com), which offers an online magazine and a directory of off-the-beaten-path tours and tour operators for families.

Making Age Work for You: Advice for Seniors

While in France, always carry a form of ID that shows your date of birth, mention that you're a senior when you first make your travel reservations, and don't be shy about asking for senior discounts. People older than 60 qualify for reduced admission to theaters, museums, and other attractions and for other travel bargains, such as the 45€ ($54) **Carte Senior,** which entitles holders to an unlimited number of train rides and reductions of 25 percent to 50 percent on train trips (except during holidays and periods of peak travel). The Carte Senior also offers some discounts on entrance to museums and historic sites. It's valid for one year, and you can buy one at any SNCF station anywhere in France. Be prepared to show an ID or a passport as proof of age when you buy the card.

Members of **AARP** (formerly the American Association of Retired Persons), 601 E St. NW, Washington, DC 20049 (☎ 888-687-2277 or 202-434-2277; www.aarp.org), get discounts on hotels, airfares, and car rentals. AARP offers members a wide range of benefits, including *AARP: The Magazine* and a monthly newsletter. Anyone older than 50 can join.

Many reliable agencies and organizations target the 50-plus market. **Elderhostel** (☎ 877-426-8056; www.elderhostel.org) arranges study programs for those ages 55 and older (and a spouse or companion of any age) in more than 80 countries around the world, including France. Most courses last two to four weeks abroad, and many include airfare, accommodations in university dormitories or modest inns, meals, and tuition. **ElderTreks** (☎ **800-741-7956;** www.eldertreks.com) offers small-group tours to off-the-beaten-path or adventure-travel locations, restricted to travelers 50 and older. **INTRAV** (☎ **800-456-8100;** www.intrav.com) is a high-end tour operator that caters to the mature, discerning traveler, not specifically seniors, with trips around the world.

Recommended publications offering travel resources and discounts for seniors include: the quarterly magazine *Travel 50 & Beyond* (www.travel50andbeyond.com); *Travel Unlimited: Uncommon Adventures for the Mature Traveler* (Avalon); *101 Tips for Mature Travelers,* available from Grand Circle Travel (☎ **800-959-0405;** www.gct.com); *The 50+ Traveler's Guidebook* (St. Martin's Press); and *Unbelievably Good Deals and Great Adventures That You Absolutely Can't Get Unless You're Over 50* (McGraw-Hill), by Joann Rattner Heilman.

Accessing France: Advice for Travelers with Disabilities

Alas, features that make French towns so beautiful — uneven cobblestone streets, quaint buildings with high doorsills from the Middle Ages, and sidewalks narrower than a wagon in some areas — also make using a walker or a wheelchair a nightmare. According to French law, newer hotels with three stars or more are required to have at least one wheelchair-accessible guest room. (See Chapter 8 for more about the French government's hotel ratings.) However, most of the country's budget hotels, exempt from the law, occupy older buildings with winding staircases and/or elevators smaller than phone booths and are generally not good choices for travelers with disabilities. On the brighter side, many hotels have at least one ground-floor room, which may suffice. In addition, the tourist office in the town you're visiting will be able to give you information about hotels with facilities for people with disabilities.

In Paris, the public transportation system isn't the most accessible to folks with mobility problems. Few Métro stations have elevators, and most feature long tunnels, some with wheelchair-unfriendly moving sidewalks and staircases. Escalators often lead to a flight of stairs, and many times when you climb up a flight of stairs, you're faced with another set of stairs leading down. Wheelchair lifts currently are not standard equipment on city buses; nor do buses "kneel" closer to the curb to make the first step lower.

But don't let these inconveniences change your mind about visiting France.

French resources for travelers with disabilities

Before your trip, contact the **French Government Tourist Office,** 444 Madison Ave., New York, NY 10022 (☎ **212-838-7800**) for the publication (with an English glossary) *Touristes Quand Même.* It provides an overview of facilities for persons with disabilities in the French transportation system and at monuments and museums in Paris and the provinces. You can also obtain a list of hotels in France that meet the needs of travelers with disabilities by writing to **L'Association des Paralysés de France,** 17 bd. Auguste-Blanqui, 75013 Paris (☎ **01-40-78-69-00**).

You can contact the **Groupement pour l'Insertion des Personnes Handicapées Physiques** (Help for the Physically Handicapped), Paris Office, 98 rue de la Porte Jaune, 92210 St-Cloud (☎ **01-41-83-15-15**), and Les Compagnons du Voyage of the **RATP** (☎ **08-92-68-77-14;** www.ratp. fr) for help in planning itineraries using public transportation.

In Paris, the modern line 14 of the Métro is wheelchair accessible, as are the stations Nanterre-Université, Vincennes, Noisiel, St-Maur–Créteil, Torcy, Auber, Cité-Universitaire, St-Germain-en-Laye, Charles-de-Gaulle–Etoile, Nanterre-Ville, and several others. Bus No. 91, which links the Bastille with Montparnasse, is wheelchair accessible, and so are new buses on order. Some high-speed and intercity trains are equipped for wheelchair access, and a special space is available in first class (at the price of a second-class ticket) for wheelchairs, though you must reserve well in advance.

Other resources for travelers with disabilities

A good English-language guide for travelers with disabilities is *Access in France,* which you can obtain by calling ☎ **020-7250-3222,** visiting www.radar.org.uk, or writing to **RADAR,** Unit 12, City Forum, 250 City Road, London EC1V 8AF. It costs approximately $18.

More options and resources for travelers with disabilities are available than ever before. Check out *A World of Options,* a 658-page book of resources for travelers with disabilities, which covers everything from biking trips to scuba outfitters around the world. The book costs $35 for members and $45 for nonmembers and can be ordered from **Mobility International USA,** P.O. Box 10767, Eugene, OR, 97440 (☎ **541-343-1284,** voice and TYY; www.miusa.org).

Many travel agencies feature customized tours and itineraries for travelers with disabilities. **Flying Wheels Travel** (☎ **507-451-5005;** www.flyingwheelstravel.com) offers escorted tours and cruises that emphasize sports and private tours in minivans with lifts. **Access-Able Travel Source** (☎ **303-232-2979;** www.access-able.com) provides extensive access information and advice for traveling around the world with disabilities.

Organizations that offer assistance to travelers with disabilities include the **MossRehab** (www.mossresourcenet.org), which provides a library of accessible-travel resources online; **SATH (Society for Accessible Travel and Hospitality)** (☎ 212-447-7284; www.sath.org; annual membership fees: $45 adults, $30 seniors and students), which offers a wealth of travel resources for all types of disabilities and informed recommendations on destinations, access guides, travel agents, tour operators, vehicle rentals, and companion services; and the **American Foundation for the Blind** (AFB) (☎ 800-232-5463; www.afb.org), a referral resource for the blind or visually impaired that includes that includes information on traveling with Seeing Eye dogs.

For more information specifically targeted to travelers with disabilities, the community Web site **iCan** (www.icanonline.net/channels/travel/index.cfm) has destination guides and several regular columns on accessible travel. Also check out the quarterly magazine **Emerging Horizons** ($14.95 per year, $19.95 outside the United States; www.emerginghorizons.com); **Twin Peaks Press** (☎ 360-694-2462), offering travel-related books for travelers with special needs; and *Open World Magazine,* published by SATH (subscription: $18 per year, $35 outside the United States).

Following the Rainbow: Advice for Gay and Lesbian Travelers

France is one of the world's most tolerant countries toward gays and lesbians, with no laws discriminating against them. In fact, many French cities — including Paris, Nice, and St-Tropez — are meccas for gay travelers. In Paris, where famous gay people such as Oscar Wilde, James Baldwin, Alice B. Toklas, and Gertrude Stein once lived, same-sex couples are treated with polite indifference by everyone from hotel clerks to waiters.

In Paris, the gay center is the **Marais neighborhood,** stretching from the Hôtel de Ville to place de la Bastille. The biggest concentration of gay bookstores, cafes, bars, and clothing boutiques is here, and so is the best source of information on Parisian gay and lesbian life, the **Centre Gai et Lesbien** (3 rue Keller, 11e; ☎ 01-43-57-21-47; Métro: Bastille). The center's staff coordinates the activities and meetings of gay people around the world. Centre Gai et Lesbien is open daily from 2 to 8 p.m.

Another helpful source in Paris is **La Maison des Femmes** (163 rue Charenton, 12e; ☎ 01-43-43-41-13; Métro: Charonne), which has a cafe and a feminist library for lesbians and bisexual women. It holds meetings on everything from sexism to working rights and sponsors informal dinners and get-togethers. Call Monday to Friday, 9 a.m. to noon or 3 to 5 p.m., for more information.

In Paris, gay magazines that focus mainly on cultural events include *Illico* (free in gay bars, about 2€/$2.40 at newsstands) and *e.m@le* (available free at bars and bookstores). *Lesbia* is a magazine that caters to lesbians, of course. You can find these magazines and others at Paris's largest and best-stocked gay bookstore, **Les Mots à la Bouche** (6 rue Ste-Croix-la-Bretonnerie, 4e; ☎ **01-42-78-88-30;** Métro: Hôtel-de-Ville). Open Monday to Saturday 11 a.m. to 11 p.m. and Sunday, 2 to 8 p.m., the store carries both French- and English-language publications.

Most large cities in France have gay bars, and we've listed those in the nightlife sections of the appropriate chapters.

For advice on HIV issues, call **F.A.C.T.S.** (☎ **01-44-93-16-69**) Monday, Wednesday, and Friday 7 to 9 p.m. The acronym stands for Free Aids Counseling Treatment and Support, and the English-speaking staff provides counseling, information, and doctor referrals.

The International Gay and Lesbian Travel Association (IGLTA) (☎ **800-448-8550** or 954-776-2626; www.iglta.org) is the trade association for the gay and lesbian travel industry and offers an online directory of gay- and lesbian-friendly travel businesses.

Many agencies offer tours and travel itineraries specifically for gay and lesbian travelers. **Above and Beyond Tours** (☎ **800-397-2681;** www.abovebeyondtours.com) is the exclusive gay and lesbian tour operator for United Airlines. **Now, Voyager** (☎ **800-255-6951;** www.nowvoyager.com) is a well-known San Francisco–based gay-owned and operated travel service. **Olivia Cruises & Resorts** (☎ **800-631-6277** or 510-655-0364; www.olivia.com) charters entire resorts and ships for exclusive lesbian vacations and offers smaller group experiences for gay and lesbian travelers.

The following travel guides are available at most travel bookstores and gay and lesbian bookstores, or you can order them from **Giovanni's Room** bookstore, 1145 Pine St., Philadelphia, PA 19107 (☎ **215-923-2960;** www.giovannisroom.com); *Frommer's Gay & Lesbian Europe,* an excellent travel resource (www.frommers.com); *Out and About* (☎ **800-929-2268** or 415-644-8044; www.outandabout.com), which offers guidebooks and a newsletter ($35/year; 10 issues) packed with solid information on the global gay and lesbian scene; *Spartacus International Gay Guide* (Bruno Gmünder Verlag; www.spartacusworld.com) and *Odysseus,* both good, annual English-language guidebooks focused on gay men; the *Damron* guides (www.damron.com), with separate, annual books for gay men and lesbians; and *Gay Travel A to Z: The World of Gay & Lesbian Travel Options at Your Fingertips* by Marianne Ferrari (Ferrari Publications; Box 35575, Phoenix, AZ 85069), a very good gay and lesbian guidebook series.

Exploring Your Special Interests

Whether biking or barging, a host of options is available for special-interest vacations in France. Exploring these options is a good idea if you're journeying with a large group — say, a family reunion — because organizers take care of all the complex details and itineraries. People who like to travel with lots of luggage may also enjoy these tours, because they often help you transport your suitcases from one spot to the next.

Cruising on a barge

Before the advent of railways, many of the crops, building supplies, raw materials, and finished products of France were barged through a series of rivers, canals, and estuaries. These passageways are now accessible for unique travel cruises. On all these trips, you sleep on the barge and are served first-rate meals.

- ✔ **French Country Waterways, Ltd.,** P.O. Box 2195, Duxbury, MA 02331 ☎ **800-222-1236** or 781-934-2454; www.fcwl.com), leads one-week tours from $3,195 to $4,795, double occupancy.

- ✔ **World Waterways**, 494 8th Ave., 22 Floor, New York, NY 10001 (☎ **800-833-2620** or 212-594-8787; www.worldwaterways.com), operates one-week cruises starting at $1,295 per person.

- ✔ **Le Boat**, 45 Whitney Rd., Suite C-5, Mahway, NJ 07430 (☎ **800-992-0291** or 201-560-1941; Fax: 201-560-1945; www.leboat.com), focuses on regions of France not covered by many other barge operators. The company's luxury crafts fit through the narrow canals and locks of Camarque, Languedoc, and Provence. Each six-night tour has ten passengers in five cabins outfitted with mahogany and brass, plus meals prepared by a Cordon Bleu chef. Prices are highly variable; six nights in Loire begin at $2,790 per person, rising to $3,590 in summer.

Biking

Backroads, 801 Cedar St., Berkeley, CA 94710 (☎ **800-462-2848** or 510-527-1555; Fax: 510-527-1444; www.backroads.com), runs bike tours of Brittany and Normandy, the Loire Valley, and Provence. Per-person rates are $2,898 for six days or $3,798 for nine days.

Bike Riders, P.O. Box 130254, Boston, MA 02113 (☎ **800-473-7040;** www.bikeriderstours.com), runs seven-day biking tours of Provence starting at $3,180. Participants can bike 15 to 35 miles per day on gently rolling terrain, stay at Relais & Châteaux hotels, and dine at several highly regarded restaurants.

Picking up the language

Alliance Française, 101 bd. Raspail, 75270 Paris (☎ 800-6-FRANCE, or **800-637-2623,** in the United States or 01-42-84-90-00; Fax: 01-42-84-91-01; www.alliancefr.org), is a state-approved nonprofit organization with a network of 1,100 establishments in 138 countries, offering French-language courses to some 350,000 students. The international school in Paris is open all year; one-month courses range 376€ to 800€ ($451.20 to $960).

Learning to cook

At the **Ritz-Escoffier Ecole de Gastronomie Français,** 15 pl. Vendôme, 75001 Paris (☎ 01-43-16-30-50; www.ritzparis.com), you can attend a public demonstration of some of the sophisticated culinary techniques that have made France and its chefs famous. They're conducted every Monday and Thursday from 3 to 5:30 p.m. and cost 55€ ($66) each. Advance reservations are recommended, and no previous culinary experience is necessary. Classes are conducted in a mixture of English and French, often with a French chef whose words are translated progressively as he or she prepares a complicated meal (a starter, a main course, and a dessert) from beginning to end. The school also conducts classes aimed at both amateur and professional chefs that last between 1 and 12 weeks each.

Chapter 10

Taking Care of Remaining Details

· ·

In This Chapter

▶ Obtaining a passport

▶ Deciding on insurance

▶ Staying healthy abroad

▶ Staying in touch

▶ Dealing with airport security

· ·

*S*ometimes planning a trip abroad seems to last longer than the actual trip itself. Although this chapter can't go out and do everything for you, it does gives you advice to help organize those innumerable loose ends and last-minute details that can frustrate even the most seasoned traveler.

Traveling to France with a valid passport is the first requirement — that and your ticket if you're flying or arriving by boat. But you also need to know about such all-important items as travel and medical insurance, which become important only when you really need them.

Finally, we offer tips about staying connected by cellphone or e-mail, and some words of advice about keeping up with the latest airport security measures.

Getting a Passport

A valid passport is the only legal form of identification accepted around the world. You can't cross an international border without it. Getting a passport is easy, but the process takes some time. For an up-to-date country-by-country listing of passport requirements around the world, go to the "Foreign Entry Requirements" Web page of the U.S. State Department at travel.state.gov/visa/americans1.html.

Applying for a U.S. passport

If you're applying for a first-time passport, follow these steps:

1. **Complete a *passport application* in person at a U.S. passport office; a federal, state, or probate court; or a major post office.**

   To find your regional passport office, either check the **U.S. State Department** Web site, `travel.state.gov`, or call the **National Passport Information Center** (☎ 877-487-2778) for automated information.

2. **Present a *certified birth certificate* as proof of citizenship.**

   Bringing along your driver's license, state or military ID, or Social Security card also is a good idea.

3. **Submit *two identical passport-sized photos,* measuring 2-x-2-inches in size.**

   You often find businesses that take these photos near a passport office. *Note:* You can't use a strip from a photo-vending machine because the pictures aren't identical.

4. **Pay a *fee.***

   For people 16 and older, a passport is valid for ten years and costs $85. For those 15 and younger, a passport is valid for five years and costs $70.

Make sure that you allow plenty of time before your trip to apply for a passport; processing normally takes three weeks, but it can take longer during busy periods (especially spring).

If you have a passport in your current name and issued within the past 15 years (and you were older than 16 when it was issued), you can renew the passport by mail for $55. Whether you're applying in person or by mail, you can download passport applications from the U.S. State Department Web site at `travel.state.gov`. For general information, call the **National Passport Agency** (☎ 202-647-0518). To find your regional passport office, either check the U.S. State Department Web site or call the **National Passport Information Center** toll-free number (☎ 877-487-2778) for automated information.

Traveling with minors

Having plenty of documentation always is wise when traveling with children in today's world. Keep up to date on details of the changing entry requirements for children traveling abroad by going to the U.S. State Department Web site: `travel.state.gov/visa/americans1.html`.

To prevent international child abduction, governments in the European Union (EU) have initiated procedures at entry and exit points. They often (but not always) include requiring documentary evidence of your relationship with your children and permission for the child's travel from any parent or legal guardian who isn't present. Having such documentation on hand, even if not required, facilitates entries and exits. All children must have their own passports. To obtain a passport, the child **must** be present — that is, in person — at the center issuing the passport. Both parents must be present as well if the child is younger than 14. If one or both parents cannot be present, then a notarized statement from the absent parent or parents is required.

For more information about passport requirements for your children, call the **National Passport Information Center** (☎ 877-487-2778) Monday to Friday 8 a.m. to 8 p.m. eastern standard time.

Applying for other passports

The following list offers more information for citizens of Australia, Canada, New Zealand, and the United Kingdom:

- ✔ **Australians** can visit a local post office or passport office, call the **Australia Passport Information Service** (☎ 131-232 toll-free from Australia), or log on to www.passports.gov.au for details on how and where to apply.

- ✔ **Canadians** can pick up applications at passport offices throughout Canada, post offices, or the central **Passport Office, Department of Foreign Affairs and International Trade,** Ottawa, ON K1A 0G3 (☎ 800-567-6868; www.ppt.gc.ca). Applications must be accompanied by two identical passport-sized photographs and proof of Canadian citizenship. Processing takes five to ten days when you apply in person or about three weeks by mail.

- ✔ **New Zealanders** can pick up a passport application at any New Zealand Passports Office or download one from its Web site. For information, contact the **Passports Office** (☎ 0800-225-050 in New Zealand or 04-474-8100; www.passports.govt.nz).

- ✔ **United Kingdom** residents can pick up applications for a standard ten-year passport (five-year passport for children younger than 16) at passport offices or travel agencies. For information, contact the **United Kingdom Passport Service** (☎ 0870-521-0410; www.ukpa.gov.uk).

Dealing with a lost passport

Always pack a photocopy of the inside photo page of your passport separate from your wallet or purse. In the event your passport is lost or stolen, the photocopy can help speed up the replacement process. When traveling in a group, never let one person carry all the passports. If the passports are stolen, obtaining new ones can be much more difficult, because at least one person in a group needs to be able to prove his or her identity so the others can be identified.

If you're a U.S. citizen and either lose your passport or have it stolen in Paris, go to the Consulate of the **American Embassy** at 2 rue St-Florentin, 1er (☎ **01-43-12-22-22;** Métro: Concorde). Canadians in the same circumstances need to visit the Consulate of the **Canadian Embassy,** 35 av. Montaigne, 8e (☎ **01-44-43-29-00;** Métro: Franklin-D-Roosevelt or Alma-Marceau). Australians need to go to the **Australian Embassy** at 4 rue Jean-Rey, 15e (☎ **01-40-59-33-00;** Métro: Bir-Hakeim). New Zealanders need to visit the **New Zealand Embassy,** 7 rue Léonard-de-Vinci, 16e (☎ **01-45-01-43-43,** ext. 280; Métro: Victor-Hugo). If you have your passport stolen anywhere else in France outside of Paris, contact local police (the phone number for police anywhere in France is ☎ **17**), who will direct you on how to get a new passport.

Playing It Safe with Travel and Medical Insurance

Three kinds of travel insurance are available: trip-cancellation insurance, medical insurance, and lost-luggage insurance. The cost of travel insurance varies widely, depending on the cost and length of your trip, your age and health, and the type of trip you're taking, but expect to pay between 5 percent and 8 percent of the vacation itself. Here is our advice on all three:

✔ **Trip-cancellation insurance** helps you get your money back if you have to back out of a trip, if you have to go home early, or if your travel supplier goes bankrupt. Allowed reasons for cancellation can range from sickness to natural disasters to a State Department declaration that your destination unsafe for travel. (Insurers usually won't cover vague fears, though, as many travelers discovered when they tried to cancel their trips after the terrorist attacks of September 11, 2001, because they were wary of flying.)

A good resource is **"Travel Guard Alerts,"** a list of companies considered high risk by Travel Guard Group (www.travelguard.com). Protect yourself further by paying for the insurance with a credit card — by law, consumers can get their money back on goods and services not received if they report the loss within 60 days after the charge is listed on their credit card statement.

Note: Many tour operators include insurance in the cost of the trip or can arrange insurance policies through a partnering provider, a convenient and often cost-effective way for the traveler to obtain insurance. Make sure the tour company is a reputable one, however. Some experts suggest that you avoid buying insurance from the tour or cruise company you're traveling with, saying it's better to buy from a third-party insurer than to put all your money in one place.

✔ For travel overseas, most **medical insurance** health plans (including Medicare and Medicaid) don't provide coverage, and the ones
that do often require you to pay for services upfront, reimbursing
you only after you return home. Even if your plan covers overseas
treatment, most out-of-country hospitals make you pay your bills
upfront and send you a refund only after you've returned home and
filed the necessary paperwork with your insurance company. As a
safety net, you may want to buy travel medical insurance, particularly
if you're traveling to a remote or high-risk area where emergency
evacuation is a possible scenario. If you require additional medical
insurance, try **MEDEX Assistance** (☎ 888-MEDEX-00; www.medex
assist.com) or **Travel Assistance International** (☎ 800-821-2828;
www.travelassistance.com; or **Worldwide Assistance Services,
Inc.**, at ☎ 800-777-8710; www.worldwideassistance.com).

✔ **Lost luggage insurance** is not necessary for most travelers. On
international flights (including U.S. portions of international trips),
baggage coverage is limited to approximately $9.07 per pound, up
to approximately $635 per checked bag. If you plan to check items
that are more valuable than this standard liability, find out whether
your valuables are covered by your homeowner's policy, get baggage
insurance as part of your comprehensive travel-insurance package,
or buy Travel Guard's BagTrak product. Don't buy insurance at the
airport, because it's usually overpriced. Be sure to take any valuables
or irreplaceable items with you in your carry-on luggage, because
many valuables (including books, money, and electronics) aren't
covered by airline policies.

If your luggage is lost, immediately file a lost-luggage claim at the
airport, detailing its contents. For most airlines, you must report
delayed, damaged, or lost baggage within four hours of arrival.
Airlines are required to deliver luggage — once it's found — directly
to your house or destination free of charge.

For more information, contact one of the following recommended insur-
ers: **Access America** (☎ 866-807-3982; www.accessamerica.com), **Travel
Guard Group** (☎ 800-826-4919; www.travelguard.com), **Travel Insured
International** (☎ 800-243-3174; www.travelinsured.com), and **Travelex
Insurance Services** (☎ 888-457-4602; www.travelex-insurance.com).

Staying Healthy When You Travel

Getting sick will ruin your vacation, so we *strongly* advise against it
(of course, last time we checked, the bugs weren't listening to us any
more than they probably listen to you).

For travel abroad, you may have to pay all medical costs upfront and be
reimbursed later. For information about purchasing additional medical
insurance for your trip, see the previous section.

Avoiding "economy-class syndrome"

Deep vein thrombosis — or "economy-class syndrome" as it's known in the world of flying — is a blood clot that develops in a deep vein. It's a potentially deadly condition that can be caused by sitting in cramped conditions — such as an airplane cabin — for too long. During a flight (especially a long-haul flight), get up, walk around, and stretch your legs every 60 to 90 minutes to keep your blood flowing. Other preventive measures include frequent flexing of the legs while sitting, drinking lots of water, and avoiding alcohol and sleeping pills. If you have a history of deep vein thrombosis, heart disease, or another condition that puts you at high risk, some experts recommend wearing compression stockings or taking anticoagulants when you fly; always ask your physician about the best course for you. Symptoms of deep vein thrombosis include leg pain or swelling, or even shortness of breath.

Talk to your doctor before leaving on a trip if you have any serious and/ or chronic illnesses. For conditions such as epilepsy, diabetes, or heart problems, wear a **MedicAlert identification tag** (☎ 800-825-3785; www. medicalert.org), which immediately alerts doctors to your condition and gives them access to your records through Medic Alert's 24-hour hot-line. Contact the **International Association for Medical Assistance to Travelers (IAMAT)** (☎ 716-754-4883 or, in Canada, 519-836-0102; www. iamat.org) for tips on travel and health concerns in the countries you're visiting and lists of local, English-speaking doctors. The United States **Centers for Disease Control and Prevention** (☎ 800-311-3435; www.cdc.gov) provides up-to-date information on health hazards by region or country and offers tips on food safety.

The French government pays 70 percent of the cost of doctor visits, and its national health insurance covers 99 percent of France's population. Visitors needing medical care in France find that doctors almost always see them the day of the appointment, and patient fees are relatively inexpensive. Patients almost always have to pay upfront unless they're citizens of European Union countries with reciprocal medical arrange-ments. Usually, U.S. health insurance companies reimburse most of the cost of treating illnesses in foreign countries, so be sure to keep all receipts.

One benefit that U.S. citizens will notice in France is that without the HMOs to keep an eye on costs, doctors are focused on the patient's com-fort rather then the bottom line. For example, injuries for which a U.S. doctor wouldn't check you into the hospital at all may mean five days in a French hospital. Socialized medicine in France also means much less paperwork. As long as you have medical insurance in the United States that covers you abroad, you don't have to worry about treatment in France. The medical establishment is of high quality, with care for patients the number-one concern.

If you do get sick, ask the concierge at your hotel to recommend a local doctor — even his or her own doctor, if necessary. In Paris, you can also call **SOS Help** (☎ **01-46-21-46-46;** www.soshelpline.org) between 3 and 11 p.m. for help in English and to ask for an English-speaking doctor. The **Centre Médical Europe** (44 rue d'Amsterdam, 9e; ☎ **01-42-81-93-33;** www.centre-medical-europe.com) is another good option. A host of specialists are located here, and foreigners pay only 20€ ($24) for a consultation.

Staying Connected by Cellphone

If you don't bring your cellphone with you, you can rent one for your stay in France. Located at the major Paris airports as well as at 2 av. de la Porte de Saint Cloud, 75015, **Call'Phone** (☎ **01-40-71-72-54**) offers rentals and is open daily 6 a.m. to 6 p.m. There is no charge for the rental of the phone, but a minimum of five minutes of local calls per day will be billed.

For the rest of you who plan to bring your cellphones with you, the rest of this section is for you. The three letters that define much of the world's **wireless capabilities** are GSM (Global System for Mobiles), a big, seamless network that makes for easy cross-border cellphone use throughout Europe and dozens of other countries worldwide. In the United States, T-Mobile, AT&T Wireless, and Cingular use this quasiuniversal system; in Canada, Microcell and some Rogers customers are GSM, and all Europeans and most Australians use GSM.

If your cellphone is on a GSM system, and you have a world-capable multi-band phone (such as many Sony Ericsson, Motorola, or Samsung models), you can make and receive calls across civilized areas on much of the globe, from Andorra to Uganda. Just call your wireless operator and ask for "international roaming" to be activated on your account. Unfortunately, per-minute charges can be high — usually $1 to $1.50 in France.

That's why buying an *unlocked* world phone from the get-go is so important. Many cellphone operators sell *locked* phones that restrict you from using any other removable computer memory phone chip (called a **SIM card**) other than the ones they supply. Having an unlocked phone enables you to install a cheap, prepaid SIM card (found at a local retailer) in your destination country. (Show your phone to the salesperson; not all phones work on all networks.) You'll get a local phone number — and much, much lower calling rates. Getting an already locked phone unlocked can be a complicated process, but it can be done; just call your cellular operator and say you'll be going abroad for several months and want to use the phone with a local provider.

For many, **renting** a phone is a good idea. (Even world-phone owners have to rent new phones whenever they're traveling to non-GSM regions.) Although you can rent a phone from any number of overseas sites, including kiosks at airports and at car-rental agencies, we suggest renting the phone before you leave home. That way you can give loved ones and busi-ness associates your new number, make sure the phone works, and take the phone wherever you go, which is especially helpful for overseas trips through several countries where local phone-rental agencies often bill in local currency and may not let you take the phone to another country.

Phone rental isn't cheap. You'll usually pay $40 to $50 per week, plus air-time fees of at least a dollar a minute. If you're traveling to France, though, local rental companies often offer free incoming calls within their home country, which can save you big bucks. The bottom line: Shop around.

Two good wireless rental companies are **InTouch USA** (☎ **800-872-7626;** www.intouchglobal.com) and **RoadPost** (☎ **888-290-1606** or 905-272-5665; www.roadpost.com). Give them your itinerary, and they'll tell you what wireless products you need. InTouch also will advise you for free on whether your existing phone will work overseas; simply call ☎ **703-222-7161** between 9 a.m. and 4 p.m. EST, or go to intouchglobal.com/travel.htm.

Accessing the Internet Away from Home

Travelers have any number of ways to check their e-mail and access the Internet on the road. Of course, using your own laptop — or even a PDA (personal digital assistant) or electronic organizer with a modem — gives you the most flexibility. But even if you don't have a computer, you still can access your e-mail and even your office computer from cybercafes.

It's hard nowadays to find a city that *doesn't* have a few cybercafes. Although no definitive directory exists for cybercafes — these are independent businesses, after all — two places to start looking are www.cybercaptive.com and www.cybercafe.com. The latter site, for example, lists some 150 cybercafes in France alone.

Aside from formal cybercafes, most **youth hostels** nowadays have at least one computer you can get to the Internet on. And most **public libraries** across the world offer Internet access free or for a small charge. Avoid **hotel business centers** unless you're willing to pay exorbitant rates.

Most major airports have **Internet kiosks** scattered throughout their gates. These kiosks, which you'll also see in shopping malls, hotel lob-bies, and tourist information offices around the world, give you basic Web access for a per-minute fee that's usually higher than cybercafe prices. The clunkiness and high price of these kiosks mean they should be avoided whenever possible.

To retrieve your e-mail, ask your **Internet Service Provider (ISP)** whether it has a Web-based interface tied to your existing e-mail account. If your ISP doesn't have such an interface, you can use the free **mail2web** service (www.mail2web.com) to view and reply to your home e-mail. For more flexibility, you may want to open a free, Web-based e-mail account with **Yahoo! Mail** (mail.yahoo.com). (Microsoft's Hotmail is another popular option, but Hotmail has severe spam problems.) Your home ISP may be able to forward your e-mail to the Web-based account automatically.

If you need to access files on your office computer, look into a service called **GoToMyPC** (www.gotomypc.com). The service provides a Web-based interface for you to access and manipulate a distant PC from anywhere — even a cybercafe — provided your "target" PC is on and has an always-on connection to the Internet (such as with Road Runner cable). The service offers top-quality security, but if you're worried about hackers, use your own laptop rather than a cybercafe computer to access the GoToMyPC system.

In addition, major ISPs have **local access numbers** around the world, enabling you to go online simply by placing a local call. Check your ISP's Web site or call its toll-free number, and ask how you can use your current account away from home and how much it will cost. If you're traveling outside the reach of your ISP, the **iPass** network has dial-up numbers in most of the world's countries. You'll have to sign up with an iPass provider, which then tells you how to set up your computer for your destination(s). For a list of iPass providers, go to www.ipass.com and click "Individuals Buy Now." One solid provider is **i2roam** (☎ **866-811-6209** or 920-233-5863; www.i2roam.com).

Wherever you go, bring a **connection kit** of the right power and phone adapters, a spare phone cord, and a spare Ethernet network cable — or find out whether your hotel supplies them to guests.

In general, the electricity in France is 200 volts AC (60 cycles), though you'll encounter 110 and 115 volts in some older establishments. Adapters are needed to fit sockets. Asking at your hotel before plugging in any electrical appliance is always a good idea.

Keeping Up with Airline Security Measures

With the federalization of airport security, security procedures at U.S. airports are more stable and consistent than ever. Generally, you'll be fine if you arrive at the airport **two hours** before your international flight; if you show up late, tell an airline employee, and she'll probably whisk you to the front of the line.

Bring a **current, government-issued photo ID** such as a driver's license or passport. Keep your ID at the ready to show at check-in, the security checkpoint, and sometimes even the gate. (Children younger than 18 don't need government-issued photo IDs for domestic flights, but they do for international flights to most countries.)

In 2003, the TSA phased out **gate check-in** at all U.S. airports. And **e-tickets** have made paper tickets nearly obsolete. Passengers with e-tickets can beat the ticket-counter lines by using airport **electronic kiosks** or even **online check-in** from your home computer. Online check-in involves logging on to your airlines' Web site, accessing your reservation, and printing out your boarding pass — and the airline may even offer you bonus miles to do so. If you're using a kiosk at the airport, bring the credit card you used to book the ticket or your frequent-flier card. Print out your boarding pass from the kiosk and simply proceed to the security checkpoint with your pass and a photo ID. If you're checking bags or looking to snag an exit-row seat, you'll be able to do so using most airline kiosks. Even the smaller airlines are employing the kiosk system, but always call your airline to make sure these alternatives are available. **Curbside check-in** also is a good way to avoid lines, although a few airlines still ban curbside check-in; call before you go.

Security checkpoint lines are getting shorter, but some doozies remain. If you have trouble standing for long periods of time, tell an airline employee; the airline will provide a wheelchair. Speed up security by **not wearing metal objects** such as big belt buckles. If you've got metallic body parts, a note from your doctor can prevent a long chat with the security screeners. Keep in mind that only **ticketed passengers** are allowed past security, except for folks escorting children or passengers with disabilities.

Federalization has stabilized **what you can carry on** and **what you can't.** The general rule is that sharp things are out, nail clippers are okay, and food and beverages must be passed through the X-ray machine — but that security screeners can't make you drink from your coffee cup. Bring food in your carry-on rather than checking it, as explosive-detection machines used on checked luggage have been known to mistake food (especially chocolate, for some reason) for bombs. Travelers in the United States are allowed one carry-on bag, plus a "personal item" such as a purse, briefcase, or laptop bag. Carry-on hoarders can stuff all sorts of things into a laptop bag; as long as it has a laptop in it, it's still considered a personal item. The Transportation Security Administration (TSA) has issued a list of restricted items; check its Web site (www.tsa.gov/public/index.jsp) for details.

Airport screeners may decide that your checked luggage needs to be searched by hand. You can now purchase luggage locks that enable screeners to open and relock a checked bag if hand-searching is necessary. Look for Travel Sentry certified locks at luggage or travel shops and Brookstone stores (you can buy them online at www.brookstone.com). Approved by the TSA, these locks can be opened by luggage inspectors with a special code or key. For more information about the locks, visit www.travelsentry.org. If you use something other than TSA-approved locks, your lock will be cut off your suitcase whenever a TSA agent needs to hand-search your luggage.

Part III

Paris and the Best of the Ile de France

The 5th Wave   By Rich Tennant

WHILE IN PARIS, DAVE VISITS THE MUSÉE d'ORSAY — FAMOUS FOR ITS IMPRESSIONISTS

Now I do for you the actor, James Cagney. You dirty rat...

In this part . . .

*A*re you a stranger to Paris? Or has it been a long time since you last visited? Then (re)introduce yourself to the city and whet your appetite for finding out more about it. In Chapter 11, you get an overview of Paris and (re)discover why it's such a great place to visit. In Chapter 12, you find out about the top sites and how much time to devote to them, including where to go to see theater, opera, ballet, and concerts and where to carouse until the following morning. In Chapter 13, you can choose one of five great side trips to the Ile de France (the area surrounding Paris): magnificent Versailles; impressive Fontainebleau; one of the world's greatest Gothic masterpieces, the Cathédrale de Chartres; Disneyland, France's top attraction (at least in terms of attendance numbers); and Giverny, the vibrant gardens and home of impressionist painter Claude Monet.

Chapter 11

Settling into Paris, City of Light

. . . .

In This Chapter

▶ Getting to Paris and finding your bearings
▶ Traveling around Paris
▶ Choosing where to stay and where to dine
▶ Savoring a beverage at the best cafes

. . . .

*A*fter you finish this chapter, you'll be walking around like a *vrai Parisien/enne* (true Parisian) in no time. You can find out about the different ways to get to Paris and, when there, how to get around the city's most happening neighborhoods by bus, Métro, taxi, bike, and on foot. Don't worry about where you'll sleep or what you'll eat — that's all taken care of here with descriptions of some of the best centrally located and reasonably priced hotels and restaurants in Paris. Discover where you can eat when you're in a hurry or just don't have room for a big meal. And finally, we tell you about our picks for cafes, where you can sit back, read the paper, write your postcards, or best of all, watch the people — while lingering over a coffee or a glass of wine.

Getting There by Plane

Finding transportation to Paris isn't difficult. As France's capital, the major auto routes converge here, trains arrive here from all parts of France and Europe — even from England — and the city is served by two airports, Aéroport Charles-de-Gaulle and Aéroport d'Orly. This section covers getting to Paris by plane.

Getting oriented at CDG

Most visitors to Paris land at **Aéroport Charles-de-Gaulle** (☎ **01-48-62-22-80**), the larger, busier, and more modern airport, commonly known as CDG and sometimes called Roissy–Charles-de-Gaulle, 14½ miles (23.3 km) northeast of downtown Paris. Nearly all direct flights from North America arrive at CDG, which is laid out in an orderly fashion — an example of

French efficiency where lines tend to move quickly. The airport is well signposted and is a fairly easy adjustment as your entrance into France.

Bi-level **Terminal 1 (Aérogare 1)** is the older and smaller of CDG's two terminals and is used by foreign airlines; narrow escalators and moving sidewalks connect its podlike glass terminals. The bright and spacious **Terminal 2 (Aérogare 2)** is used by Air France, domestic and intra-European airlines, and some foreign airlines, including Air Canada. It's divided into halls A through F. A free **shuttle bus** *(navette)* connects the two terminals. Signs in French and English direct you to customs, baggage claim, and transportation to the city. Staff at information desks (☎ **01-48-62-22-80**) also are on hand to answer questions in both terminals.

If you didn't arrive with some euros, you'll have a chance to acquire some at ATMs in the various terminals.

Navigating your way through passport control and customs

Don't anticipate any great problems when you pass through passport control or customs. France is a fairly welcoming country, and unless you arouse undue suspicion, you'll pass rather smoothly through the receiving lines. You may — or may not — be required to open your luggage for a customs inspection.

Most items brought into France for your personal use (firearms and drugs excluded, of course) pass through without challenge. In other words, two tubes of toothpaste are okay. A half-million dollars in diamonds and rubies may arouse suspicion.

If you're traveling to France from another country, remember that goods and gifts purchased *duty free,* which means that you need not pay tax in the country of *purchase,* are not necessarily duty free in France. However, unless a traveler is bringing in large amounts of goods and gifts, fellow members of European Union countries travel rather freely between member nations.

Before getting in a passport or custom control line, have all necessary documents handy, including a valid passport, which you need for entering France. You must also produce a visa and work permits, if you fall into that category, when demanded. Most travelers pass through the lines without challenge. In these days of increased terrorism alerts, however, you may be challenged to find out whether you're entering France legally.

Getting from CDG to your hotel

You can get to and from the airport in several different ways, and they're all easy.

✔ **By taxi:** The easiest way — but certainly not the cheapest — to your hotel from the airport is by taxi. A cab into town from CDG takes from 50 minutes (subject to traffic) and costs about 40€ to 45€ ($48–$54) from 7 a.m. to 8 p.m., about 40 percent more at other times. Taxis are required to turn the meter on and charge the price indicated plus .90€ ($1.10) for each piece of luggage stowed in the trunk. If your French is poor or nonexistent, write down the name and full address of your hotel for your driver. The five-digit postal code is the most important morsel of information, because it lets the driver know the *arrondissement* (municipal district) to which to drive you. Check the meter before you pay — rip-offs of arriving tourists are not uncommon. If you feel that you may have been overcharged, demand a receipt (which drivers are obligated to provide), and contact the Paris Préfecture of Police (☎ **01-53-73-53-73** or 01-53-71-53-71). Taxi stands at **Terminal 1** are at Exit 18, arrivals level; in **Terminals 2A and 2C,** at Exit 6; in **Terminals 2B and 2D,** at Exit 8; and in **Terminal 2F,** at Exit 11, arrivals level.

✔ **By shuttle:** If you don't want to schlep your bags through Paris's streets and Métro, an airport shuttle is the way to go. Though more expensive than airport buses and trains, shuttles are cheaper and roomier than a taxi. And you can reserve in advance and pay by credit card. **World Shuttle,** 13 rue Voltaire 94400 Vitry-sur-Seine (☎ **01-46-80-14-67** or 06-83-85-23-45; Fax: 01-46-80-20-57), costs 23€ ($28) for one person, 14€ ($17) per person for a party of two or more, and 90€ ($108) for parties of seven or eight from Charles-de-Gaulle and Orly.

PariShuttle, 128 bis av Paris, 94800 Villejuif (☎ **01-53-39-18-18;** Fax: 01-53-39-13-13; www.parishuttle.com), offers a similar service. As you wait for your bags, call PariShuttle's toll-free number to confirm pickup. You are picked up in a minivan at Orly or Charles-de-Gaulle and taken to your hotel for 25€ ($30) for one person, 18€ ($22) per person for parties of two to five, and 15€ ($18) per person for six to eight people. Book and pay ten days in advance. World Shuttle and PariShuttle both accept Visa and MasterCard.

✔ **By train:** If you're not overloaded with baggage and want to keep down your expenses, a good option is to take the **RER** suburban commuter train to the Métro. RER (Réseau Express Régional) **Line B** stops near Terminals 1 and 2. Easy, cheap, and convenient, you can ride the train to and from the airport daily from 5 a.m. to midnight. A free shuttle bus connects Terminal 1 to the RER train station. If you land in **Terminal 1,** exit the terminal on the arrivals level where you see shuttle-bus signs marked "RER." If you land in **Terminal 2A,** the free shuttle bus is located at Exit 6; in **Terminal 2C,** it's at Exit 6; in **Terminal 2B,** the shuttle bus is at Exit 7; and in **Terminal 2D,** the shuttle is at Exit 7. In **Terminal 2F,** the shuttle bus is at Exit 2.06 on the arrivals level. You can also take a walkway to the RER station. Ask an airport employee or look for the round RER logo. (RER is pronounced *air-uh-air* in French.)

Buy the **RER plus Métro** ticket at the RER ticket counter for 7.60€ ($9.10), and hang on to your ticket in case of ticket inspection. (You can be fined if you can't produce your ticket for an inspector.) You need your ticket later to get off the RER system and into the Métro. From the airport station, trains depart about every 15 minutes for the half-hour trip into town, stopping on the **Right Bank** at Gare du Nord and Châtelet–Les Halles, and on the **Left Bank** at St-Michel, Luxembourg, Port-Royal, and Denfert-Rochereau, before heading south out of the city.

✔ **By bus:** A bus is better than the RER if you're heading into Paris during off-peak driving hours or your hotel is located near one of the drop-off points. If your hotel is located on the **Right Bank,** in the **8e, 16e,** or **17e** arrondissement, take **Air France coach Line 2,** which stops at rue Gouvion Saint-Cyr at Porte Maillot before ending up at 1 av. Carnot at place Charles de Gaulle–Étoile, the name for the huge traffic roundabout at the Arc de Triomphe. The bus costs 11.50€ ($14) one way and runs every 15 minutes from the airport from 7 a.m. to 11 p.m. and 6 a.m. to 11 p.m. back to the airport. You needn't have flown Air France to use the service, and tickets are available on the bus. The trip takes about 40 minutes to get from the airport into the city and vice versa in light traffic, such as on weekend mornings. During weekday morning rush hour, however, the same trip can take twice as long. From **Terminal 1,** pick up the coach at Exit 36, arrivals level; from **Terminals 2A and 2C,** Exit 5; from **Terminals 2B and 2D,** Exit 6; and from **Terminal 2F,** Exit 0.07, arrivals level.

If your hotel is located on the **Right Bank** near the **Bastille (11e** or **12e)** or on the **Left Bank** in **Montparnasse (14e),** take the **Air France Line 4** coach, which stops at bd. Diderot in front of the Gare de Lyon before ending up on rue du Commandant Mouchotte near the Gare de Montparnasse. The bus costs 11.50€ ($14) one way and runs every 30 minutes from 7 a.m. to 9:30 p.m. to and from the airport. It takes about 50 minutes to get from the airport into the city in light traffic. Catch this coach from **Terminal 1** at Exit 34, arrivals level; **Terminals 2A and 2C** at Exit 1; from **Terminals 2B and 2D** at Exit 2; and from **Terminal 2F** at Exit 0.07, arrivals level.

Take the **Roissybus** if your hotel is on the **Right Bank** near the **Opéra** (2e or 9e). It costs 8€ ($9.60) and leaves every 15 minutes from the airport between 6 a.m. and 11 p.m. and to the airport between 5:45 a.m. to 11 p.m. The drop-off point is on rue Scribe, a block from the **Opéra Garnier** near American Express. You can get to your destination in 45 to 50 minutes in regular traffic. Buy your tickets in the small office next to where the bus is parked. Pick up this coach from **Terminal 1,** Exit 10, arrivals level; **Terminals 2A and 2C,** Exit 9 from Terminal 2A; **Terminals 2B and 2D,** Exit 12 from Terminal 2D; and from **Terminal 2F,** Exit 0.08, arrivals level.

Getting oriented at Orly

Intra-France and continental flights make the most use of **Aéroport d'Orly** (☎ 01-49-75-15-15), 8½ miles (14 km) south of the city, although overseas flights also land here. Orly airport has two terminals — **Ouest** (West) and **Sud** (South) — and the terminals are easy to navigate. French domestic flights land at Orly Ouest, and intra-European and intercontinental flights land at Orly Sud. Shuttle buses connect these terminals, and other shuttles connect them to Charles-de-Gaulle every 30 minutes or so. You can pick up city maps and other visitor essentials at a nearby tourist information desk. You also can find ATMs in Orly's terminals.

Getting from Orly to your hotel

Orly offers a number of transportation options to get you from the airport to your hotel.

✔ **By Jetbus:** The cheapest trip into town is on the **Jetbus.** You take this bus from Orly to Métro station Villejuif–Louis Aragon in south Paris (**13e**). It costs 5.15€ ($6.20) for the 15-minute ride. Beginning at 6:30 a.m., the bus leaves every 15 minutes from **Orly Sud,** Exit H, platform 2, and from Exit C, arrivals level, in **Orly Ouest.** The bus departs Paris for Orly from 6:15 a.m. to 10:15 p.m. An **Orly bus** also operates from 6 a.m. to 11:35 p.m. from Exit J, arrivals level, at **Orly Ouest** and from Exit H, platform 4, at **Orly Sud** to the Left Bank's Denfert–Rochereau station. It costs 5.70€ ($6.85) for the 25-minute journey. It departs Paris for Orly from 5:35 a.m. to 11 p.m.

✔ **By taxi:** A taxi from Orly into Paris costs about 25€ to € ($30–$36), depending on traffic, and takes anywhere from 25 minutes to an hour. The taxi stand at Orly Sud is just outside Exit L, and at Orly Ouest, it's at Exit I. The same advice as when taking a taxi from Charles-de-Gaulle holds true here: Write down the full name and address of your hotel for the driver. And remember that cabs charge .90€ ($1.10) for each piece of luggage that's put in the trunk.

✔ **By bus:** Take the **Air France coach Line 1** if your hotel is located on the **Left Bank** near Les Invalides (**7e**). Buses leave **Orly Sud** at Exit K, platform 6, and **Orly Ouest** at Exit D, arrivals level, every 12 to 15 minutes. The trip takes 15 minutes and costs 7.50€ ($9). You can request that the bus stop at Montparnasse–Duroc (**14e**).

✔ **By train:** You can also take the **RER C line,** which is a bit of a hassle. You catch a free shuttle bus from Exit G, platform 1, at **Orly Sud** and Exit F on the arrivals level at **Orly Ouest** to the **Rungis** station, where RER C trains leave every 15 minutes for **Gare d'Austerlitz (13e).** A one-way fare is 5.25€ ($6.30), and the trip into the city takes 30 minutes, making various stops along the Seine on the **Left Bank.**

If you're staying on the **Right Bank,** you can take the **RER B line** to **Châtelet** Métro station. From **Orly Sud,** it departs from Exit K near the baggage-claim area; from **Orly Ouest,** it leaves from Exit D on the departures level. You connect at the **Antony** RER station, where you board the RER B train to Paris. Hold on to the ticket, because you'll need it to get into the Métro/RER system. A trip to the **Châtelet** station on the Right Bank takes about 30 minutes and costs 7.50€ ($9).

Getting There by Land or Sea

If flying is not your cup of tea — or it's simply not convenient for you — you can also get to Paris by train, bus, car, or even hovercraft.

Arriving by train

If you're already in Europe, you may want to go to Paris by train, especially if you have a Eurailpass. For information, call France's national train company **SNCF** (Societé National des Chemin de Fer; ☎ **08-92-35-35-35** [.35€/minute or 40¢/minute]; www.sncf.com), or go to a travel agent or one of the information booths at the stations.

If you come from northern Germany, Belgium, or London, you'll likely arrive at the **Gare du Nord.** Trains from Normandy come into the **Gare St-Lazare** in northwest Paris. Trains from the west (Brittany, Chartres, Versailles, or Bordeaux) head to the **Gare de Montparnasse;** those from the southwest (the Loire Valley, or Pyrénées, Spain) to the **Gare d'Austerlitz.** Trains from the south and southeast (the Riviera, Lyon, Italy, or Geneva) arrive at the **Gare de Lyon;** from Alsace and eastern France, Luxembourg, southern Germany, and Zurich, it's the **Gare de l'Est.**

Arriving by bus

Buses connect Paris to most major cities in Europe. One of the biggest intra-European bus companies is **Eurolines.** It doesn't have North American offices, so travelers must make bus transportation arrangements after arriving in Europe. In Great Britain, contact **Eurolines** (☎ **0990-143-219**). In Paris, the contact is **Eurolines** (28 av. du Général-de-Gaulle, 93170 Bagnolet; Fax ☎ **01-49-72-51-61** [.46€/minute or 55¢/minute]). International buses pull into Paris's **Gare Routière Internationale** at av. Charles-de-Gaulle in the suburb of Bagnolet, just across the *périphérique* (ring road) from the Gallieni Métro station.

Arriving by ferry and tunnel

About a dozen companies run hydrofoil, ferry, and hovercraft across the English Channel, or *La Manche* ("the sleeve"), as the French say. Services operate daily and most carry cars. Hovercraft and hydrofoils make the trip in 40 minutes; the shortest ferry route between Dover and Calais is about 1½ hours. The major routes are between Dover and Calais, and Folkestone and Boulogne (about 12 trips a day). Depending on weather conditions, prices and timetables can vary. Making a reservation always is important, because ferries are crowded.

For information stateside, call **BritRail** (☎ 866-BRITRAIL; www.brit rail.com) or **Britain Bound Travel** (☎ 800-805-8210). In Britain, contact **Hoverspeed** (☎ 0870-240-8070; www.hoverspeed.co.uk). Special fares are offered, but they change frequently. A good travel agent in London can help you sort out the maze of ferry schedules, find a suitable option, and book your ticket.

The Channel Tunnel (Chunnel) opened in 1994, and the popularity of its **Eurostar** train service to Paris and Amsterdam has had the happy effect of driving down prices on all cross-channel transport. This remarkable engineering feat means that if you take your car aboard **Le Shuttle** in Britain, you can be driving in France an hour later. You can purchase tickets in advance or at the tollbooth. For further information and reservations in the United Kingdom and the United States, call **BritRail** or **Britain Bound Travel** (see preceding paragraph for numbers); in Australia, call **GSA: Rail Plus** (☎ 61-3-9642-8644).

Arriving by car

If you drive, remember that the *périphérique* circles Paris — and its exits aren't numbered. The major highways are the **A1** from the north (Great Britain and Belgium); the **A13** from Normandy and other points in northwest France; the **A109** from Spain and the southwest; the **A7** from the Alps, the Riviera, and Italy; and the **A4** from eastern France. Avoid rush hours (weekdays 7:30 to 9:30 a.m. and 5:30 to 7:30 p.m.) and the days before long weekends and holidays.

Orienting Yourself in Paris

You've arrived at your hotel, checked in, and maybe unpacked a little. Taking a nap prolongs your jet lag, so go out and act like a Parisian — have a cup of coffee at a cafe and then get ready to explore. *Note:* Those little shots of espresso you get in Paris cafes have less caffeine than a cup of coffee American-style, so ask for a cafe Americain or, even better, a cup of tea (*thé,* pronounced *tay*).

The Seine River divides Paris into two halves: the **Right Bank** *(Rive Droite)* on the north side of the river and the **Left Bank** *(Rive Gauche)* on the south side. The larger Right Bank is where the city's business sector, stately monuments, and the high-fashion industry are located. The Left Bank has publishing houses, universities, and a bohemian reputation because students, philosophers, and creative types have been congregating there for centuries. Two of the city's tallest monuments are on the Left Bank — the Tour Montparnasse (that lonely tall black building hovering on the edge of the city) and the Tour Eiffel. Sacré-Coeur, the white wedding cake of a basilica on the hill overlooking Paris, is on the

Right Bank, and so are Notre-Dame and St-Chapelle, though technically they are on neither bank, but rather on an island in the Seine.

The city is divided into 20 numbered *arrondissements* (pronounced *ah-rohn-DEEZ-mahn*). And although visitors tend to think of Paris in terms of neighborhood names, Parisians think of the city in terms of arrondissement numbers. For example, ask a homeowner where he works and he's more likely to say "in the 5th" or, in native-speak, *le cinquième,* and not "in the Latin Quarter" or "*le quartier Latin.*" The layout of these districts follows a distinct pattern. The first (abbreviated *1er* for *premiere*) arrondissement is dead-center Paris, comprising the area around the Louvre. From here, the rest of the districts spiral outward and clockwise, in ascending order. The lower the arrondissement number, the more central the location. To get a better idea, consult the "Paris Arrondissements" map in this chapter.

Arrondissement numbers are key to locating an address in Paris. We list addresses the way they appear in Paris, with the arrondissement number following the specific street address (for instance, 29 rue de Rivoli, 4e, is in the 4th arrondissement). Arrondissement numbers are on street signs and indicated in the last two digits of the postal code; for instance, an address with the postal code 75007 is in the 7th arrondissement. When you know the arrondissement in which an address is located, finding that spot is much easier. Numbers on buildings running parallel to the Seine usually follow the course of the river east to west. On north–south streets, numbering begins at the river.

Paris by arrondissement

This section runs you quickly through Paris. Neighborhoods are listed first by arrondissement and then by neighborhood name. Only the best-known arrondissements — meaning the ones that you're most likely to stay in or visit — are mentioned.

On the Right Bank

Your tour of Right Bank arrondissements starts with the central one: the **1er arrondissement.**

✔ One of the world's greatest art museums (some say *the* greatest), Musée du Louvre, lures visitors to Paris to the **1er arrondissement (Musée du Louvre/Palais-Royal/Les Halles)**. You can see many of the city's elegant addresses along the rue de Rivoli and arched arcades under which all kinds of touristy junk is sold. Walk through the **Jardin des Tuileries,** the most formal garden of Paris, or take in the classic beauty of the **place Vendôme,** opulent, wealthy, and home of the Hôtel Ritz. Browse the arcaded shops, and view the striped columns and seasonal art on display in the garden of the **Palais Royal,** once home to Cardinal Richelieu. The sketchy **Forum des Halles,** an above- and below-ground shopping and entertainment center, also is here. This arrondissement tends to be crowded, and hotels are higher priced during Paris high tourist season (in early fall) because the area is so convenient.

✔ Often overlooked, the drab **2e arrondissement (La Bourse)** houses the **Bourse** (stock exchange) and pretty 19th-century covered shopping passageways. The district, between the **Grands Boulevards** and **rue Etienne Marcel,** is home to the **Sentier,** where the garment trade is located and wholesale fashion outlets abound. Sex shops and prostitutes line parts of **rue St-Denis.**

✔ The **3e arrondissement (Le Marais)** is one of Paris's hippest neighborhoods and hosts one of the city's most popular attractions, the **Musée Picasso,** and one of its most interesting museums, **Musée Carnavalet.** Paris's old Jewish neighborhood is here around **rue des Rosiers,** and **rue Vieille-du-Temple** is home to numerous gay bars and boutiques.

✔ Aristocratic town houses, courtyards, antiques shops, flower markets, the **Palais de Justice, Cathédrale Notre-Dame, Sainte-Chapelle,** the **Centre Georges Pompidou,** and the **place des Vosges** — they're all here on the two islands of the **4e arrondissement (Ile de la Cité/Ile St-Louis/Centre Pompidou).** The islands located in the middle of the Seine compose one of the prettiest, and most crowded, of Paris's arrondissements. The area around the Centre Pompidou is one of Paris's more eclectic; you see everyone from pierced and goth-style art students to chic Parisians sipping coffee at Café Beaubourg to visitors buying football shirts from one of the many souvenir stores.

✔ The **8e arrondissement (Champs-Elysées/Madeleine)** is the heart of the Right Bank, and its showcase is the **Champs-Elysées.** The fashion houses, the most elegant hotels, expensive restaurants and shops, and the most fashionably attired Parisians are here. The Champs stretches from the **Arc de Triomphe** to the city's oldest monument, the Egyptian obelisk on **place de la Concorde.**

✔ Everything from the **Quartier de l'Opéra** to the strip joints of **Pigalle** falls within the **9e arrondissement (Opéra Garnier/Pigalle),** which was radically altered by Baron Haussmann's 19th-century redevelopment projects; his *Grands Boulevards* radiate through the district. You'll probably pay a visit to the 9e to shop at its infamous department stores, **Au Printemps** and **Galeries Lafayette.** Try to visit the swanky **Opéra Garnier** (Paris Opera House), which has been beautifully restored.

✔ In the movie *Amélie,* the young heroine Amélie likes to skip stones on the Canal St-Martin, located here in the **10e arrondissement (Gare du Nord/Gare de l'Est).** Although most of this arrondissement is dreary (**Gare du Nord** and **Gare de l'Est** are two of the city's four main train stations), the canal's **quai de Valmy** and **quai de Jemmapes** are scenic, tree-lined promenades. The classic movie *Hôtel du Nord* was filmed here.

Paris Arrondissements

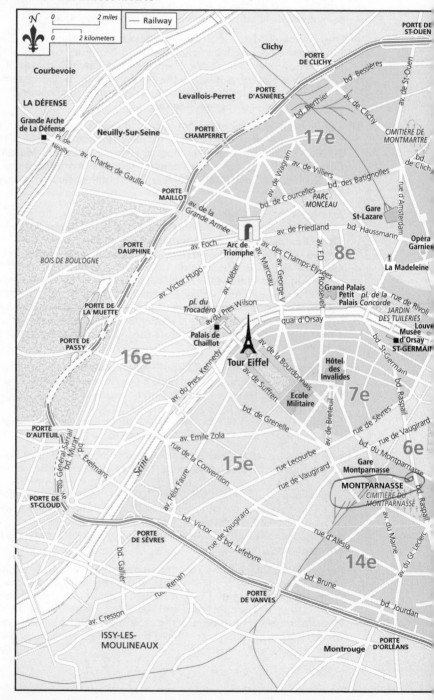

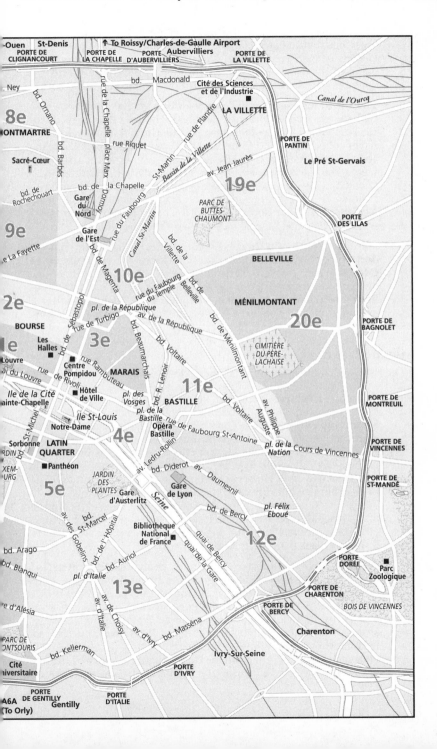

✔ The **11e arrondissement (Bastille)** has few landmarks or famous museums, but the area is a mecca for young Parisians looking for casual, inexpensive nightlife. Always crowded on weekends and in summer, the overflow retires to the steps of the **Opéra Bastille,** where in-line skaters and skateboarders abound and teens flirt.

✔ The **16e arrondissement (Trocadero/Bois de Boulogne)** is where the moneyed live. Highlights include the **Bois de Boulogne, Jardin du Trocadéro, Musée de Balzac, Musée Guimet** (famous for its Asian collections), and **Cimetière de Passy,** resting place of Manet, Talleyrand, Giraudoux, and Debussy. One of the largest arrondissements, the 16e is known today for its exclusivity, its BCBG residents *(Bon Chic Bon Genre),* its upscale rents, and some rather posh (and, to some, rather smug) residential boulevards. The arrondissement also embraces what some consider the best place in Paris from which to view the Tour Eiffel, **place du Trocadéro.**

✔ **Montmartre, Moulin Rouge, Basilica of Sacré-Coeur,** and **place du Tertre** are only some of the attractions in the **18e arrondissement (Montmartre).** Take a walk through the winding old streets here, and you feel transported into another era. The city's most famous flea market, **Marché aux Puces de la Porte de St-Ouen,** on the arrondissement's outskirts, is another landmark, as is the **Bateau-Lavoir,** where Picasso had his studio.

On the Left Bank

The following are neighborhoods you're likely to visit on the Left Bank:

✔ Bookstores, schools, churches, night clubs, student dives, Roman ruins, publishing houses, and expensive boutiques characterize the **5e arrondissement (Latin Quarter),** called "Latin" because students and professors at the **Sorbonne,** located here, once spoke Latin. Stroll along **quai de Montebello,** inspecting the inventories of the *bouquinistes* (booksellers), and wander the shops in the old streets of **rue de la Huchette** and **rue de la Harpe** — but don't eat here; other neighborhoods in the 5e offer much better places. The 5e also stretches down to the **Panthéon** and to the steep cobble-stoned **rue Mouffetard** behind it, where you can visit one of the city's best produce markets, eat at a variety of ethnic restaurants, or raise a glass in *très* cool Café Contrescarpe.

✔ The art school that turned away Rodin, **École des Beaux-Arts,** is in the **6e arrondissement (St-Germain-des-Près/Luxembourg),** and so are some of the chicest designers around. But the secret of the district is in its narrow streets and hidden squares. Everywhere you turn in the district, you encounter famous historical and literary associations. For instance, the restaurant **Brasserie Lipp,** located here, is where Hemingway lovingly recalls eating potato salad in *A Moveable Feast,* and the **Café les Deux Magots** is depicted in *The Sun Also Rises.* The 6e takes in the **rue de Fleurus,** where Gertrude

Stein lived with Alice B. Toklas, and down the street is the wonderful **Jardin du Luxembourg,** Parisians' most loved park. (*Note:* Try to find the Statue of Liberty here.)

✔ The city's most famous symbol, **Tour Eiffel,** dominates the **7e arrondissement (Tour Eiffel).** Part of the **St-Germain** neighborhood is here, too. The **Hôtel des Invalides,** which contains both **Napoléon's Tomb** and the **Musée de l'Armée,** is also in the 7e, as are **Musée Rodin** and **Musée d'Orsay,** the world's premier showcase of 19th-century French art and culture. The Left Bank's only department store, **Le Bon Marché,** is here, and so are streets selling beautiful shoes, clothing, and objects for the home.

✔ Although high-rise buildings dominate much of the **13e arrondissement (Chinatown/Butte-aux-Cailles),** a nightlife scene is emerging on the dance barges along the **quai Tolbiac** (where the **Bibliothèque François Mitterand** sits) and in the cozy network of winding streets making up the **Butte-aux-Cailles** (literally, "hill of pebbles") neighborhood. The 13e also is a lively hub for Paris's Asian community, with Vietnamese and Chinese restaurants along **av. d'Ivry** and **av. de Choisy** next to stores selling items from France's former colonies in Southeast Asia. The Chinese New Year Parade takes place here in late January or February.

✔ The **14e arrondissement (Montparnasse)** is the former stomping ground of the "lost generation": writers Gertrude Stein, Ernest Hemingway, Edna St. Vincent Millay, Ford Madox Ford, and other expatriates gathered here in the 1920s. After World War II, it ceased to be the center of intellectual life in Paris, but the memory lingers in its cafes. Some of the world's most famous literary cafes — including **La Rotonde, Le Select, La Dôme,** and **La Coupole —** are in the northern end of this large arrondissement, near the Rodin statue of Balzac at the junction of boulevard Montparnasse and boulevard Raspail. Some of the literary giants (most notably Jean-Paul Sartre and Simone de Beauvoir) are buried nearby, in the **Cimitière du Montparnasse.** At its southern end, the 14e contains pleasant residential neighborhoods filled with well-designed apartment buildings, many built between 1910 and 1940.

Finding information after you arrive

The prime source of information is at Opéra-Grans Magasins, 11 rue Scribe, 9e (☎ **08-92-68-30-00;** www.paris-touristoffice.com; Métro: Opéra). The office is open Monday to Saturday 9 a.m. to 6:30 p.m. Smaller information offices are found at: Gare de Lyon, 20 bd. Diderot, 12e, open Monday to Saturday 8 a.m. to 6 p.m., Métro: Gare de Lyon; Gare du Nord, 18 rue de Dunkerque, 10e, open daily 12:30 p.m. to 8 p.m., Métro: Gare du Nord; Montmartre Tourist Office, 21 place du Tertre, 18e, open daily 10 a.m. to 7 p.m., Métro: Abbesses; and Espace du Tourisme d'Ile-de-France, Carrousel du Louvre-Place de la Pyramide Inversée 99, 1er, open daily 10 a.m. to 7 p.m., Métro: Palais Royal/Musée du Louvre. For yet another branch, go to the Office de Tourisme de Paris, 25 rue des

Pyramides, 1er, open daily 10 a.m. to 7 p.m. (Sunday 11 a.m. to 7 p.m. November to April), Métro: Pyramides. For more information, call the number listed earlier. At the main and auxiliary offices, you can reserve concert, theater, or cabaret tickets without an extra fee.

Getting around Paris

Paris is one of the prettiest cities in the world for strolling, and getting around on foot is the best way to really appreciate the city's character. The best walking neighborhoods are **St-Germain-des-Prés** on the Left Bank and the **Marais** on the Right Bank, both of which are filled with romantic little courtyards, offbeat boutiques, and congenial cafes and watering holes. The **quais of the Seine** and its bridges also are lovely, especially at sunset, when the sun fills the sky with a pink glow that's reflected on the water. And try not to miss the pretty **Canal St-Martin** with its arched bridges and locks in the 10e, featured in the movies *Amélie* and *Hôtel du Nord*.

By Métro and RER

Open from 5:45 a.m. to 12:45 a.m., the **Métropolitain** (the Métro) is an efficient, quick, cheap, and safe way to get around — pretty spry for a 105-year-old. Don't be afraid to use it. The only times you may want to avoid it are the hours between 6 and 8 p.m. and 7 to 10 a.m.; in other words, rush hour. Operated by the RATP (Régie Autonome des Transports Parisiens), as are city buses, the Métro has a total of 16 lines and more than 360 stations, making it likely that one is near your destination. The Métro is connected to the suburban commuter train, the **Réseau Express Régional (RER)**, which connects downtown Paris with its airports and suburbs.

Boarding the Métro

Navigating the Métro is easy, and you'll be a pro in no time. Here's what you do:

1. **Using this book, figure out what station is the closest to where you are.**

   For example, if you want to go to the Louvre and are in your hotel in the Latin Quarter — the Familia — check the listing in this book for your hotel. It gives the nearest Métro station, your starting point, as Jussieu. Look at the Métro map on the inside front cover of this book for the line that the Jussieu station is on. (Each end of the lines on the Métro map is marked with the number of the line.) The Jussieu station is on Line 7.

2. **Look for your destination station — for example, the Louvre.**

   You see find these two stops for the Louvre: the Palais Royal-Musée du Louvre station on Line 7 and the Louvre Rivoli station on Line 14. Choose the Palais-Royal Musée du Louvre station, and you won't have to change trains.

3. **Walk to the Métro station; you will recognize it either by an elegant Art Nouveau gateway reading "MÉTROPOLITAIN" or by a big yellow *M* sign.**

Unless otherwise marked, all Métro stations have a ticket booth, where you purchase from an attendant either a single ticket (1.40€/$1.70) or, the better deal, a group of ten tickets called a *carnet* (10.50€/$13). Most stations also have machines where you can purchase tickets.

4. **When you get beyond the ticket booths, you enter the Métro system through a turnstile with two ticket slots. Insert your ticket into the nearer slot with the magnetic strip facing down.**

The ticket pops out of the second slot. Remove it, and then either walk through a set of rubberized doors that briskly open on each side or push through a turnstile. Keep your ticket with you until you exit the station. At any point while you're in the Métro, an inspector may ask to see your ticket. If you fail to produce it, you are subject to a steep fine. When you ride the RER, you must keep your ticket because you have to insert it in a turnstile when you exit the station.

After you're past the Métro's entrance, you need to make sure that you take the train in the right direction. Look at your subway map, and trace the line past your destination to its end. The name of the station at the end of the line is the name of the subway train on which you'll be traveling; in the case of Line 7, the train is *La Courneuve.* Follow the signs directing you to the platform where this train stops. To get back to your hotel from the Louvre, you take the train marked *Villejuif Louis Aragon* and exit at the Jussieu station.

Transferring Métro lines

Suppose, however, that the Métro line nearest to you doesn't go directly to your destination. For example, you want to go to the Arc de Triomphe from Jussieu, and the stop is Charles de Gaulle–Étoile. Find the Charles de Gaulle–Étoile stop on the Métro map. You see that Charles de Gaulle–Étoile can be reached by Line 6 or Line 1. But you are on Line 7. You have to change trains, an action that is called a *correspondance,* or transfer.

On your map are blank white circles where a number of lines intersect, indicating where the transfer stations are, where you change subway trains. To figure out where you need to change trains to get on Line 1 or Line 6, use the map to see where Line 7 and Line 1 or Line 7 and Line 6 intersect. Line 7 and Line 6 intersect at Stalingrad, opposite from where you want to go. But Line 7 and Line 1 intersect at Concorde, very close to Charles de Gaulle–Étoile. To make sure you go in the right direction on Line 1, look on your map for the name of the station at the very end past Charles de Gaulle–Étoile. It is *Grande Arche de La Défense,* and your train will be marked with this name.

You get out at Concorde and look for the bright orange *Correspondance* sign above the platform and the white sign that shows the number 1 in a circle. This number refers to the line you want, so go in the direction the sign indicates. You eventually come to two stairwells leading to the platforms. The stairwells are marked by navy blue signs that indicate the direction of the train. The signs also list all the stops the train makes. Make sure you choose the stairwell leading to the train going in the direction of Grande Arche de La Défense. Then board the train and exit at Charles de Gaulle–Étoile. Blue signs reading *"sortie"* mark all exits.

The distances between platforms at the *correspondance* stations can be very long. You may climb stairs and walk a short distance, only to descend stairs to walk some more. Châtelet is particularly long. Some lines are connected by moving sidewalks that seem to do nothing but make a very long walk only a little less long. People with limited mobility may want to take the bus or a cab.

The Métro connects with the suburban commuter train, the RER, at several stations in the city. The RER operates on a zone fare system, but Métro tickets are valid on it within the city. You probably won't go past the first two zones, unless you visit Disneyland on the A4 or Versailles on the C5. When you ride the RER, it is important to keep your ticket, because you will need to insert it into a turnstile to leave the station.

The doors on most Métro cars do not open automatically. You must lift a door handle or press a button.

By bus

The bus system is convenient and can be an inexpensive way to sightsee without wearing out your feet. Most Parisian buses run from 6:30 a.m. to 8:30 p.m.; a few run until 12:30 a.m. Each bus shelter has a route map, which you want to check carefully. Because of the number of one-way streets, the bus is likely to make different stops depending on its direction. Main stops are written on the sides of the buses, with the endpoints shown on the front above the driver.

Métro tickets are valid for bus travel, and although you can buy single tickets from the conductor, you can't buy *carnets* on the bus. Board at the front of the bus. If you have a single-trip ticket, insert it into the slot in the small machine right behind the driver; the machine punches your ticket and pops it back out. If you have a pass, show it to the driver. To get off at the next stop, press one of the red buttons on the safety poles; the *arrêt demandé* (stop requested) sign lights up above the driver.

The downside of taking the bus is that it often gets mired in heavy Parisian traffic, so we don't recommend it if you're in a hurry. And, like the Métro, it's better to avoid riding the bus during rush hours when it seems *le monde* (the world) is sharing the bus with you.

Bus routes that are great for sightseeing include **Bus 69** (Tour Eiffel, Hôtel des Invalides, Musée du Louvre, Hôtel de Ville, place des Vosges, Bastille, and Cimetière du Père-Lachaise), **Bus 80** (department stores on bd. Haussmann, Champs-Elysées, av. Montaigne haute-couture shopping, and Tour Eiffel), and **Bus 96** (St-Germain-des-Prés, Musée de Cluny, Hôtel de Ville, and place des Vosges).

By taxi

When it comes to hiring a taxi in Paris, you have three options. We rank them here in order of how successful they are.

- ✔ **Call:** The best way to find a cab is by phoning **Taxis Bleus** (☎ 08-25-16-10-10), **Alpha Taxis** (☎ 01-45-85-85-85), or **G7** (☎ 01-47-39-47-39). Keep in mind, however, that taking a taxi is more expensive because the meter starts running as soon as the driver commences his journey to get you. The flag drops at 4.25€ ($5.10), and from 7 a.m. to 7 p.m., you pay 1€ ($1.20) per kilometer. You can hail regular cabs on the street when their signs read "LIBRE." If you lose possessions in a taxi, contact the taxi company itself. Or else write to **Service des Taxis de la Préfecture de Police**, 36 rue des Morillons, 75015 Paris (☎ 01-55-76-20-00; Métro: Convention).

- ✔ **Stand in line:** You can also wait at a taxi stand; they're denoted by blue *Taxi* signs. Depending on the time of day, however, a long line of people may be waiting ahead of you for a limited number of cabs that stop.

- ✔ **Whistle:** Finally, you can hail a cab, as long as you're not within 60 meters (200 feet) of a taxi stand. Look for a taxi with its white light illuminated, meaning the taxi is available. An orange light means the cab is occupied or on the way to a pickup. You may get a cab driver who refuses to take you to your destination; by law, he or she can refuse you only during his or her last half-hour at work. But be prepared for the selective vision of drivers. Seeing a free taxi or two pass you by isn't unusual.

By car

Streets are narrow; parking is next to impossible; and nerve, skill, ruthlessness, and a knowledgeable copilot are required whenever you insist on driving in Paris. We *strongly* recommend that you do not. (If you must drive in Paris, do it in August, when traffic is lighter.) If you do decide to drive, these tips may make your experience a bit more . . . er, pleasant:

- ✔ Get an excellent street map, and ride with another person. Traffic moves so lightning-fast that you don't have time to think at intersections.

- ✔ For the most part, you must pay to park in Paris. Depending on the neighborhood, expect to pay 1.50€ to 2.50€ ($1.80 to $3) an hour for a maximum of two hours. Place coins in the nearest meter, which issues you a ticket to place on your dashboard. You can also buy parking cards at the nearest *tabac kiosk* for meters that accept only cards. Parking is free on Sundays, holidays, and for the entire month of August.

✔ Drivers and passengers must wear seat belts. Children younger than 12 must ride in the back seat. You are supposed to yield to a car on the right unless signs indicate otherwise, as at traffic circles.

✔ If you want to rent a car to explore the Ile de France or travel on from Paris, try **Avis**, Gare d'Austerlitz, 13e (☎ **01-45-84-22-10**; www.avis.com); **Hertz France**, Gare de l'Est, 10e (☎ **01-42-05-50-43**; www.hertz.com); or **National**, Gare de Lyon, 12e (☎ **01-40-04-90-04**; www.nationalcar.com). A Ford Focus here costs about 120€ ($144) per day with all taxes and related costs. Chapter 7 offers more about renting a car in France.

✔ Watch for *gendarmes* (police officers), who lack patience and who consistently contradict the traffic lights. Horn blowing is frowned upon except in emergencies. Flash your headlights instead.

By bicycle

City planners have been trying to encourage more cycling by setting aside about 99km (62 miles) of bicycle lanes throughout Paris. The main routes run north–south, from the Bassin de La Villette along the Canal St-Martin through the Left Bank, and east–west, from Château de Vincennes to the Bois de Boulogne and its miles of bike lanes. For more information and a bike map, pick up the **Plan Vert** from the tourist office. In addition, the banks of the Seine are closed to cars and opened to pedestrians and cyclists each Sunday from March through November from 10 a.m. to 5 p.m. Although bicycling may not make much of a dent in the air quality, it is a fun and healthy way to spend a Sunday afternoon.

To rent a bicycle, contact **Paris À Vélo C'est Sympa!**, 22 rue Alphonse Baudin, 11e (☎ **01-48-87-60-01**; Métro: Richard de Noir). The price is 12.50€ ($15) a day, 9.50€ ($11) for a half-day, and 24€ ($29) weekends. A 250€ ($300) deposit on a credit card is required.

Where to Stay in Paris

If this visit to Paris is your first, your expectations about what a hotel room should look like probably are based on what is available in your own country. Rooms here, however, tend to be smaller than you may expect, even in expensive places (unless you opt for a modern chain hotel or such palaces as the Ritz). Parisian doubles almost never are big enough to hold two queen-size beds, and the space around the bed probably won't be big enough to put more than a desk and perhaps a chest of drawers. Welcome to Europe; the story is the same in London, Rome, and most other continental capitals where buildings date back two, three, or sometimes four centuries, when dimensions — and people — were smaller.

What to do when every room seems full

What if you've browsed the list of hotels, chosen the ones you think will suit you, and everything is booked? Don't despair; the staff at one of the branches of the **Office de Tourisme de Paris** (25 Rue des Pyramides, 1er; ☎ **08-92-68-30-30;** Fax: 01-49-52-53-00; www.paris-touristoffice.com; Métro: Pyramides) can make a hotel reservation for you. Keep in mind, however, that you need to arrive in person at the office or at one of its branches. This office is open daily 10 a.m. to 7 p.m. (Sunday 11 a.m. to 7 p.m., November through April). For a fee, the staff will make an accommodations reservation for you on the same day you want a room.

Parisian hotels also vary widely in plumbing arrangements. Some units come with only a sink; others are equipped with a toilet and either a shower or tub. Private bathrooms with tubs often have handheld shower devices; pay attention to where you aim — shower curtains are a rarity. Good news, though: The trend is upward these days; many small-hotel renovations are putting a small shower, toilet, and sink in each room.

As for acoustics, they tend to be unpredictable in old Parisian hotels. Your quarreling neighbors may be as annoying as street noise, so bring earplugs or ask for a room at the rear of the hotel. Also, most budget hotels in Paris do not have air-conditioning, but fortunately, their solid stone walls tend to keep out the summer heat.

In compiling this list of hotels, we first considered the average traveler's wish list. And for most of you, that's location. Thus, the first criterion, though ruthless, was simple: If the hotel isn't located in the first eight arrondissements, it isn't recommended in this book. To be sure of the location of hotels you may consider, see the "Paris Accommodations" map.

Prices for recommended hotels are designated with dollar signs — the more you see, the more expensive the hotel. Check the Introduction to this book for how the dollar-sign system works.

Castex Hôtel
$$ Le Marais (4e)

A popular budget classic, the Castex is near *everything* in the Marais. A renovation in 2004 elevated it to a government-rated three-star status, which means its prices rose considerably, although they still are affordable. New improvements, for example, include a TV for every room. Each large room has a writing table or a desk and chair; some have views overlooking the courtyard. The staff is friendly and accommodating. Reserve at least a month in advance.

Paris Accommodations

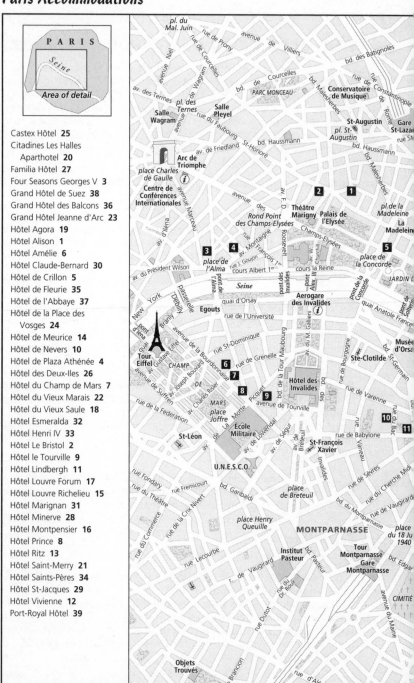

Castex Hôtel **25**
Citadines Les Halles
    Aparthotel **20**
Familia Hôtel **27**
Four Seasons Georges V **3**
Grand Hôtel de Suez **38**
Grand Hôtel des Balcons **36**
Grand Hôtel Jeanne d'Arc **23**
Hôtel Agora **19**
Hôtel Alison **1**
Hôtel Amélie **6**
Hôtel Claude-Bernard **30**
Hôtel de Crillon **5**
Hôtel de Fleurie **35**
Hôtel de l'Abbaye **37**
Hôtel de la Place des
    Vosges **24**
Hôtel de Meurice **14**
Hôtel de Nevers **10**
Hôtel de Plaza Athénée **4**
Hôtel des Deux-Iles **26**
Hôtel du Champ de Mars **7**
Hôtel du Vieux Marais **22**
Hôtel du Vieux Saule **18**
Hôtel Esmeralda **32**
Hôtel Henri IV **33**
Hôtel Le Bristol **2**
Hôtel le Tourville **9**
Hôtel Lindbergh **11**
Hôtel Louvre Forum **17**
Hôtel Louvre Richelieu **15**
Hôtel Marignan **31**
Hôtel Minerve **28**
Hôtel Montpensier **16**
Hôtel Prince **8**
Hôtel Ritz **13**
Hôtel Saint-Merry **21**
Hôtel Saints-Pères **34**
Hôtel St-Jacques **29**
Hôtel Vivienne **12**
Port-Royal Hôtel **39**

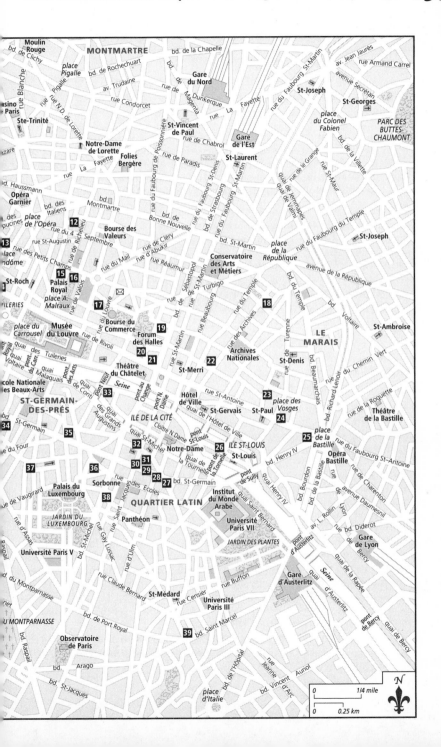

See map p. 134. 5 rue Castex. ☎ *01-42-72-31-52. Fax: 01-42-72-57-91.* www.castex-paris-hotel.com. *Métro: Bastille or Sully-Morland. Rack rates: 120€–140€ ($144–$168) double. AE, DC, MC, V.*

Citadines Les Halles Aparthotel
$$–$$$ Louvre (1er)

Staying in one of the Citadines apartment hotels is like living in your own Paris apartment. Studios and one-bedrooms have fully equipped kitchenettes, and services may include a 24-hour reception desk, satellite TV, air-conditioning, housekeeping, baby-equipment rental, and a laundromat. Les Halles is sketchy at night, so if you're a single traveler, this hotel may not be the best bet.

Citadines has 17 locations in Paris; other central locations include 18 rue Favart (☎ **01-40-15-14-00;** Fax: 01-40-15-14-50); 129–131 bd. Haussmann (☎ **01-56-88-61-00;** Fax: 01-45-63-46-64); and 8 rue de Richelieu, one block north of the Musée du Louvre (☎ **01-55-35-28-00;** Fax: 01-55-35-29-99).

See map p. 134. 4 rue des Innocents (91.4 m/300 feet from the Forum des Halles). ☎ *01-40-39-26-50. Fax: 01-45-08-40-65.* www.citadines.com. *Métro: Les Halles. Rack rates: 145€–169€ ($174–$203) per night for 1–6 days, 129€–144€ ($155–$173) for 7–29 days, 2-person studio; 215€–253€ ($258–$304) for 1–6 days, 195€–225€ ($234–$270) for 7–29 days, 4-person (1-bedroom) apt. AE, MC, V.*

Familia Hôtel
$–$$ Latin Quarter (5e)

You can tell that this hotel is a labor of love for the owners, the Gaucherons; they've made it the prettiest it can be. Flowers spill out of window boxes, and the stone walls in some of the bedrooms have been painstakingly restored or have had *toile de jouy* wallpaper added. In other rooms, artists from l'École des Beaux-Arts have painted sepia-toned murals of Parisian scenes. The cozy lobby exudes the atmosphere of a tiny castle with rich tapestries, a winding staircase, and frescoed walls. Some rooms have balconies (numbers 21, 22, 23, 51, 52, and 53) with views of the Latin Quarter. From the fifth and sixth floors, you can see Notre-Dame. Bathrooms are small but modern and tiled. All rooms have cable TV and hair dryers. Staff understand what it's like to travel with children and try to provide kid-friendly services (such as bottle heating) and larger rooms for the weary traveler who requests ahead. Take note that most rooms in the hotel are on the small side, and the least expensive doubles in the corners are tiny. And with no air-conditioning, it can get hot in Paris heat waves. Jardin des Plantes is down the street, and the Seine is across the street from the garden's front entrance.

See map p. 134. 11 rue des Écoles. ☎ *01-43-54-55-27. Fax: 01-43-29-61-77* www.hotel-paris-familia.com. *Métro: Jussieu. Rack rates: 81€–111€ ($97–$133) double. Breakfast 6€ ($7.20). AE, DC, MC, V.*

Grand Hôtel des Balcons
$$ St-Germain-des-Prés (6e)

Denise and Pierre Corroyer are proud of their gracious and comfortable hotel with its balconied rooms, modern light-oak furnishings, bright fabrics, 19th-century stained-glass windows, and Art Nouveau furnishings. Although most rooms and their wrought-iron balconies are small, clever use of space has allowed for large closets and full-length mirrors. Bathrooms are also small but well designed and come equipped with a clothesline. The higher-priced doubles, triples, and quads are big and luxurious; some have double-sink bathrooms. Free tea and coffee are available in the lounge, and if you'll be celebrating your birthday while in Paris, the breakfast buffet (which includes sausage and eggs) is free. The Théâtre de l'Odéon is only steps away.

See map p. 134. 3 rue Casimir-Delavigne. ☎ *01-46-34-78-50. Fax: 01-46-34-06-27.* www.balcons.com. *Métro: Odéon, RER: Luxembourg. Rack rates: 120€–150€ ($144–$180) double. Buffet breakfast 10€ ($12). AE, DC, MC, V.*

Grand Hôtel de Suez
$–$$ Latin Quarter (5e)

Guests return for the hotel's many good-sized, quiet rooms at a budget price. Beds are firm, storage space is ample, and the modern bathrooms have hair dryers. But don't even think of opening the windows to the street-side balconies — the Boulevard St-Michel is as noisy as a carnival. Bathrooms have either a shower or bath. The hotel is in a good location near Musée de Cluny, Jardin du Luxembourg, and the Panthéon. The Seine and Notre-Dame are a ten-minute walk away.

See map p. 134. 31 bd. St-Michel. ☎ *01-53-10-34-00. Fax: 01-40-51-79-44.* www.hotel desuez.fr. *Métro: St-Michel. Rack rates: 80€–105€ ($96–$126) double. Breakfast 4€ ($4.80). AE, DC, MC, V.*

Grand Hôtel Jeanne d'Arc
$ Le Marais (4e)

Reserve well in advance for this budget hotel that's on an attractive little street just off place St-Catherine. It's in an 18th-century building, and contemporary artists have brightly handpainted the walls of the breakfast and sitting rooms. The decent-sized rooms have big windows, card-key access, large bathrooms, direct-dial telephones, satellite TV, and bedside tables, but storage space is a bit cramped. If a view is important, make sure you request one, because some rooms don't have views. The hotel is in the center of the Marais, and it can be a little noisy, but you're near Musée Picasso, place des Vosges, and the Bastille, and the atmospheric Au Bistro de la Place cafe is in the square next door.

See map p. 134. 3 rue de Jarente. ☎ *01-48-87-62-11. Fax: 01-48-87-37-31.* www.hotel jeannedarc.com. *Métro: St-Paul or Bastille. Rack rates: 80€–95€ ($96–$114) double. Breakfast 6€ ($7.20). MC, V.*

Hôtel Agora
$–$$ Louvre (1er)

This government-rated two-star hotel on a busy pedestrian street near Les Halles has a traditional French air after you take the small elevator or climb the curved staircase to its eclectic lobby (the ugly entryway disguises a good find). Rooms have antique furniture, marble mantlepieces, floral prints, and old-fashioned wallpapers. The windows are double-glazed, thankfully, which helps muffle the outside noise. Fifth-floor rooms have balconies with views of the impressive St-Eustache church. European film crews often stay here because of the location and reasonable prices.

See map p. 134. 7 rue de la Cossonnerie. ☎ **01-42-33-46-02.** *Fax: 01-42-33-80-99. Métro: Châtelet. Rack rates: 80€–131€ ($96–$157) double. Breakfast 8€ ($9.60). AE, MC, V.*

Hôtel Alison
$$ Madeleine (8e)

Located between the Madeleine and the Palais de l'Elysée and near the Champs-Elysées and rue Faubourg St-Honoré, this hotel has a sleek, upscale ambience perfectly in tune with the classy neighborhood. The large, well-appointed rooms are furnished in a modern style, with black furniture and light walls. The rooms have plenty of storage, a safe, trouser presses, and double-glazed windows. Hair dryers and Roger & Gallet toiletries grace gleaming, tiled bathrooms with wall-mounted showers. You can relax in the plush lobby or enjoy a drink in the hotel bar.

See map p. 134. 21 rue de Surène. ☎ **01-42-65-54-00.** *Fax: 01-42-65-08-17. Métro: Madeleine or Concorde. Rack rates: 110€–140€ ($132–$168) double. Breakfast 8€ ($9.60). AE, DC, MC, V.*

Hôtel Amélie
$ Tour Eiffel (7e)

The pretty Hôtel Amélie has flower pots brimming with bouquets at each window. The interior is more modest, with small renovated rooms and tiny closets, but the white-tiled bathrooms offer hair dryers and good-quality toiletries. Despite the central location, the atmosphere is peaceful, almost serene. The hotel has no elevator.

See map p. 134. 5 rue Amélie. ☎ **01-45-51-74-75.** *Fax: 01-45-56-93-55. Métro: La Tour-Maubourg. Rack rates: 74€–92€ ($89–$110) double with shower; 80€–100€ ($96–$120) double with bath. Breakfast: 7€ ($8.40); free for stays in August after four nights. AE, MC, V.*

Hôtel Claude-Bernard
$$ Latin Quarter (5e)

Evident from the moment you enter the lobby, the government-rated three-star Hôtel Claude-Bernard keeps very high standards. The spacious rooms have tasteful wallpaper, sleek bathrooms, decorative balconies with flowers, and often a charming piece of antique furniture, such as a writing desk. Some particularly attractive suites have couches and armchairs. A sauna is available for guests' use, and all rooms have air-conditioning.

See map p. 134. 43 rue des Écoles. ☎ *01-43-26-32-52. Fax: 01-43-26-80-56.* www. hotelclaudebernard.com. *Métro: St-Michel. Rack rates: 118€ –149€ ($142–$179) double 198€ –249€ ($238–$299) suite for 1–4 persons. Continental breakfast 7.90€ ($9.50). AE, DC, MC, V.*

Hôtel de Fleurie
$$–$$$ St-Germain-des-Prés (6e)

Just off place Odéon on a pretty side street, the Fleurie has many comforts, including air-conditioning, marble bathrooms with heated towel racks, quality toiletries, Oriental carpets, and fresh flowers. The rooms are on the small side, but all are furnished in a modern or classic style. Book at least eight weeks in advance for one of the *chambres familiales* — connecting rooms with two large beds that are ideal for families. Rooms have dataports, or you can check your e-mail on the hotel computer in the lobby for .30€ (35¢) per minute.

See map p. 134. 32–34 rue Grégoire-de-Tours. ☎ *01-53-73-70-00. Fax: 01-53-73-70-20. Métro: Odéon. Rack rates: 165€ –185€ ($198–$222) double with queen-size bed; 240€ –265€ ($288–$318) deluxe rooms (large room with twin beds or king-size beds); 290€ –325€ ($348–$390) chambre familiale (family suite). Breakfast 10€ ($12), 5€ ($6) children younger than 12. AE, DC, MC, V.*

Hôtel de l'Abbaye
$$$ St-Germain-des-Prés (6e)

This former convent is one of the Left Bank's most delightful and cozy hotels — a popular stop for travelers who have a taste for chic surroundings on a budget. You enter through a courtyard and check in at the reception desk, which is in the convent's original vault. Some of the rooms have their original oak ceiling beams, and all are air-conditioned and have 19th-century–style furnishings and damask upholstery. The standard rooms are a good size for Paris, and the duplex suites are spacious. Some first-floor rooms open out onto a vine-covered terrace. Rooftop suites have terraces. In summer, you can have breakfast — included in the price of your room — in the flower-filled courtyard; in winter, you can lounge in front of the lobby fireplace.

See map p. 134. 10 rue Cassette. ☎ *01-45-44-38-11. Fax: 01-45-48-07-86.* www. Hotel-Abbaye.com. *Métro: St-Sulpice. Rack rates: 211€ ($253) double; 296€ –393€ ($355–$472) suites; 430€ –449€ ($516–$539) duplex suite. Breakfast included. AE, V.*

Hôtel de la Place des Vosges
$$ Le Marais (4e)

King Henri IV once kept his horses here, but you'd never know this hotel was a former stable by its plush, antiques-filled lobby. Many of the small but well-maintained rooms have beamed ceilings, and the bathrooms are tiled. Most beds are firm, but storage space is lacking. All rooms have TVs (suspended by a chain from the ceiling), desks, and hair dryers. The larger top-floor room has a pretty view over the Right Bank, but the elevator stops a floor down, a consideration if you have a lot of luggage. The entrance to the place des Vosges is only steps away.

See map p. 134. 12 rue de Birague. ☎ *01-42-72-60-46. Fax: 01-42-72-02-64. Métro: Bastille. Rack rates: 120€–140€ ($144–$168) double; 205€–250€ ($246–$300) top-floor room. Breakfast 7€ ($8.40). MC, V.*

Hôtel de Nevers
$ St-Germain-des-Prés (6e)

Tucked away in the St-Germain-des-Près premier shopping area, this renovated 17th-century house provides simple rooms at reasonable prices. Enter the charming wood-beamed lobby, thick with North African rugs and amber-toned wall coverings, where friendly staff check you in. You then are escorted up a quaint, tapestry-adorned winding staircase (no elevator) to a very clean room with wooden bureaus and wood-framed mirrors. Bathrooms are spotless and well maintained, if not brand new. Although you must pay in cash, you can save your credit cards for more shopping in the nearby stores.

See map p. 134. 83 rue du Bac. ☎ *01-45-44-61-30. Fax: 01-42-22-29-47. Métro: Rue du Bac. Rack rates: 83€ ($100) double with shower; 93€ ($112) twin beds with bathroom; 93€ ($112) double with bathroom and terrace. Continental breakfast 6€ ($7.20); 20€ ($24) for extra bed. MC, V for making reservations, cash or traveler's checks only for payment.*

Hôtel des Deux-Îles
$$ Ile St-Louis (4e)

With only 17 double rooms, this charming hotel is intimate and superbly located on the Ile St-Louis (practically in Notre-Dame's backyard). Rooms have exposed oak ceiling beams and provincial upholstery, and the lobby is a warm and cozy gem with fresh flowers and bamboo furniture. Off the lobby is a garden that some rooms overlook and a basement breakfast room with a fireplace. Though they have amenities including bathrooms, hair dryers, satellite TV, and air-conditioning, rooms run from tiny to small, so if you have a large amount of luggage, you may want to look elsewhere. Paris' best ice cream shop, Berthillon, is just around the corner. You can find the ice cream in nearby brasseries, too.

See map p. 134. 59 rue St-Louis-en-l'Ile. ☎ *01-43-26-13-35. Fax: 01-43-29-60-25. Métro: Pont Marie. Rack rates: 158€ ($190) double. Breakfast 10€ ($12). AE, DC, MC, V.*

Hôtel du Champ de Mars
$ Tour Eiffel (7e)

A country house tucked away on a colorful street near Tour Eiffel, the Champ de Mars is a bargain that's hard to beat. Its 20 rooms have flowing curtains, fabric-covered headboards, throw pillows, and cushioned high-backed seats. Bathrooms are in mint condition with hair dryers, large towels, and good lighting, and those with tubs have wall-mounted showers. A cozy breakfast room is in the remodeled basement. Reserve at least four months in advance. In the summer, the best two rooms are on the ground floor and open onto the leafy courtyard; they stay cool despite the lack of air-conditioning. A Franprix grocery store is two doors down.

See map p. 134. 7 rue du Champ de Mars. ☎ **01-45-51-52-30.** _Fax: 01-45-51-64-36._ www.hotel-du-Champ-de-mars.com. _Métro: École-Militaire. RER: Pont de l'Alma. Rack rates: 76€–80€ ($91–$115) double. Breakfast 6.50€ ($7.80). AE, MC, V._

Hôtel du Vieux Marais
$$ Le Marais (4e)

This hotel has undergone a total renovation and now has a sparkling, elegant lobby, air-conditioned rooms, a lighted garden, new wardrobes, and tiled bathrooms with a Mexican-inspired design. Rooms are average size and spotless, and have _faux_-leather upholstery; some overlook the garden. The service is impeccable, and the staff is friendly and helpful. The Centre Pompidou modern art museum is a two-minute walk away, and all the shops and restaurants of the Marais are within walking distance. If you have enough time, visit the nearby Musée Picasso, Musée Carnavalet, and place des Vosges.

See map p. 134. 8 rue du Plâtre. ☎ **01-42-78-47-22.** _Fax: 01-42-78-34-32. Métro: Hôtel-de-Ville. Rack rates: 107€–137€ ($128–$164) double. Breakfast 9€ ($10.80). MC, V._

Hôtel du Vieux Saule
$$ Le Marais/Bastille (3e)

This hotel in the Marais near place de la République not only offers air-conditioning but also a free sauna. The cheerful, small rooms have tiled bathrooms, hair dryers, safes, double-glazed windows, luggage racks, satellite TV, trouser presses, and even small irons and ironing boards. The rooms on the fifth floor tend to be bigger. Breakfast is a buffet served in the original 16th-century cozy vaulted cellar accessed by a winding staircase (no elevator).

See map p. 134. 6 rue de Picardie. ☎ **01-42-72-01-14.** _Fax: 01-40-27-88-21._ www.hotelvieuxsaule.com. _Métro: République. Rack rates: 121€–136€ ($145–$163) double; 151€–166€ ($181–$199) deluxe double. Buffet breakfast 9€ ($11). AE, DC, MC, V._

Hôtel Esmeralda
$ Latin Quarter (5e)

This 19-room hotel is a favorite of many travelers, and you may have to book at least two months in advance. The Esmeralda is funky and ramshackle, with an old, winding wooden staircase and outstanding views of Notre-Dame and the Seine from its front rooms. Shabby-chic velvet coverings and antique furniture create a homelike warmth that almost makes up for the disappointingly dark rear rooms. The front rooms with a view have modern bathrooms with tubs, and some are exceptionally large, making them perfect for travelers with children. The location — in the center of everything, and just steps away from the Shakespeare and Company bookstore — couldn't be better for parents accompanying little ones who tend to tire quickly.

See map p. 134. 4 rue St-Julien-le-Pauvre. ☎ **01-43-54-19-20**. *Fax: 01-40-51-00-68. Métro: St-Michel. 19 units. Rack rates: 85€–95€ ($102–$114) double. Breakfast 6€ ($7.20). No credit cards.*

Hôtel Henri IV
$ Louvre (1er)

This hotel is old, with no elevator. Only five rooms have showers or baths, only two have toilets, and none has a phone. But this is one of Europe's most famous budget hotels, and it is nearly always full. It occupies a dramatic location on place Dauphine — the northernmost tip of Ile de la Cité, across the river from St-Germain and the Louvre and a few steps from Pont-Neuf. The 17th-century building houses cozy rooms that are past their prime, though many find them romantically evocative (others think they are just run-down). Each room has a sink, but guests share the spotless toilets and showers on each of the five floors. Manager François Balitrand is a wealth of knowledge about the hotel and place Dauphine. Book far in advance.

See map p. 134. 25 place Dauphine. ☎ **01-43-54-44-53**. *Métro: Pont-Neuf or Châtelet. Rack rates: 44€ ($53) double with shower but no toilet; 68€ ($82) double with toilet and bath or shower. Rates include breakfast. No credit cards.*

Hôtel le Tourville
$$–$$$ Tour Eiffel (7e)

This splendid restored mansion just steps behind Les Invalides can be addictive. You get almost all the amenities of a pricier hotel — Roger & Gallet toiletries, hair dryers, air-conditioning, chic décor with antiques — for prices that still are manageable. Rooms are decorated in soft yellows, pink, or "sand," with crisp white damask upholsteries, antique bureaus and lamps, fabulously mismatched old mirrors, and marble bathrooms. Rooms also have satellite TV, hair dryers, and 24-hour room service. You may want to ask for one of the four wonderful rooms with walk-out terraces covered in vines or a junior suite with whirlpool bath. The staff is kind and helpful. The grocery store a few doors down is open until 10 p.m.; a tabac is right next door.

See map p. 134. 16 av. de Tourville. ☎ **01-47-05-62-62**. *Fax: 01-47-05-43-90. Métro: École-Militaire. Rack rates: 165€ ($198) standard double; 215€ ($258) "superior" double; 240€ ($288) double with private terrace; 310€ ($372) junior suite. Breakfast 12€ ($14). AE, DC.*

Hôtel Lindbergh
$$ St-Germain-des-Prés (7e)

Aviation-themed photos add a tasteful touch to the décor at this welcoming hotel named for the American aviator. The rooms range from simple and charming, with colorful bedspreads and matching bathrooms, to refined and elegant, with classic touches — graceful floor-length curtains, fabric headboards, and color-coordinated cushioned seats. The hotel is at the edge of the St-Germain-des-Près shopping district, and the Musée Rodin is within walking distance.

See map p. 134. 5 rue Chomel. ☎ *01-45-48-35-53. Fax: 01-45-49-31-48.* www.hotel lindbergh.com. *Métro: Sévres-Babylone. Rack rates: 108€ ($130) double with shower; 108€–112€ ($130–$134) double with shower and bath; 146€–156€ ($175–$187) larger double accommodating 1–4 persons. Breakfast 8€ ($9.60). AE, MC, V.*

Hôtel Louvre Forum
$ Louvre (1er)

For a truly central, reasonably priced hotel just steps from the Louvre, it's difficult to beat this comfortable modern hotel. The brightly colored rooms have tiled bathrooms (with hair dryers) and furniture including writing tables, lamps, chairs, and a small armoire with hanging space and shelves. (Rooms on the lower floors are a bit cramped.) Service is a bit chilly, but it's a small price for such a great location. The hotel is only a short walk from the elegant Palais Royal, once the garden of Cardinal Richelieu and the young Louis XIV.

See map p. 134. 25 rue du Bouloi. ☎ *01-42-36-54-19. Fax: 01-42-33-66-31. Métro: Louvre-Rivoli. Rack rates: 85€ ($102) double with shower; 95€ ($114) double with full bath. Continental breakfast 9€ ($11). AE, DC, MC, V.*

Hôtel Louvre Richelieu
$ Louvre (1er)

The rooms in this hotel are a good size, and the location is terrific — halfway between the Louvre and the Opéra. Enter through a corridor with restored stone walls; the pleasant reception area and lobby are on the second floor. The two-bed double rooms are dark, but spacious, and have high ceilings. Each room has a writing table, a small closet, and a luggage rack. The lack of an elevator here means you may want to pack light. Reserve at least two weeks in advance for summer.

See map p. 134. 51 rue de Richelieu. ☎ *01-42-97-46-20. Fax: 01-47-03-94-13* www. louvre-richelieu.com. *Métro: Palais-Royal–Musée du Louvre, Pyramides. Rack rates: 72€ ($86) double with toilet; 84€ ($101) double with bathroom. Breakfast 6€ ($7.20). MC, V.*

The big splurge

If you want only the best, plushest hotels Paris has to offer, look no further. These hotels give you more than a room — they give you an experience. Service is impeccable, décor features quality to the last antique knick-knack, and rooms are enormous compared to the typical European standard. The hotel's restaurant may be overseen by a renowned chef, and the fare often is excellent and pricey. Usually a spa, fitness center, and/or pool is available for guests. These hotels do everything with more style than their less-expensive counterparts, which is why they play host to many celebrities.

- ✔ **Four Seasons Georges V:** 31 av. George V, 8e; ☎ **01-49-52-70-00;** Fax: 01-49-52-70-10; www.fourseasons.com/paris; Métro: George V.

- ✔ **Hôtel de Crillon:** 10 place de la Concorde, 8e; ☎ **01-44-71-15-00;** Fax: 01-44-71-15-03; www.crillon.com; Métro: Concorde.

- ✔ **Hôtel de Meurice:** 228 rue de Rivoli, 1e; ☎ **01-44-58-10-10;** Fax: 01-44-58-10-15; www.meuricehotel.com; Métro: Tuileries.

- ✔ **Hôtel de Plaza Athénée:** 25 av. Montaigne, 8e; ☎ **01-53-67-66-65;** Fax: 01-53-67-66-66; www.plaza-athenee-paris.com; Métro: Alma Marceau.

- ✔ **Hôtel Le Bristol:** 112 rue du Faubourg St-Honoré, 8e; ☎ **01-53-43-43-00;** Fax: 01-53-43-43-01. www.lebristolparis.com; Métro: Miromesnil.

- ✔ **Hôtel Ritz:** 15 place Vendôme, 1e; ☎ **01-43-16-30-30;** Fax: 01-43-16-36-69; www.ritzparis.com; Métro: Opéra.

Hôtel Marignan
$ Latin Quarter (5e)

It's plain and unassuming on the outside, but owners Paul and Linda Keniger have invested much time and energy in renovating this hotel. They have retained much of the building's architectural detailing, such as the stucco ceiling moldings, while tiling bathrooms and adding new beds. They welcome families, don't mind if you bring your own food into the dining room, and make the kitchen available during the low season. You also have a washer–dryer and iron at your disposal. Signs in English recommend neighborhoods to visit and tours to take, and you can always ask one of the Kenigers for recommendations. The hotel is very close to the Sorbonne, and its good rates attract students. Rooms fill up quickly in July and August, so if you plan to travel then, book well in advance.

See map p. 134. 13 rue du Sommerard. ☎ 01-43-54-63-81. Fax: 01-43-25-16-69. Métro: Maubert-Mutualité or St-Michel. Rack rates: 55€ ($66) double with shower in hall; 78€–88€ ($94–$106) double with shower in room. Breakfast 3€ ($3.60). No credit cards.

Hôtel Minerve
$–$$ Latin Quarter (5e)

The owners of the Familia Hôtel (reviewed earlier in this section), Eric and Sylvie Gaucheron, have purchased and renovated the Hôtel Minerve next door. More upscale than the Familia, rooms also are larger and have wood-beamed ceilings, exposed stone walls, carved mahogany wood furnishings, and expensive wallpapers. Pretty handpainted sepia frescos can be found in several of the rooms, and ten rooms have large balconies with a table and chairs overlooking the street. The same welcome mat is rolled out for kids.

See map p. 134. 13 rue des Ecoles. ☎ *01-43-26-26-04. Fax: 01-44-07-01-96.* www. hotel-paris-minerve.com. *Métro: Cardinal Lemoine or Jussieu. Rack rates: 96€ ($115) double with shower; 112€–128€ ($134–$154) double with shower and tub. Breakfast 8€ ($9.60). AE, MC, V.*

Hôtel Montpensier
$ Louvre (1er)

Supposedly the former residence of Mademoiselle de Montpensier, cousin of Louis XIV, this hotel's high ceilings and windows, stained-glass ceiling in the lounge, and grand staircase create a sense of faded grandeur. Many rooms on the first two floors, which date from the 17th century, are either drab or have a faded elegance (depending on your point of view), while rooms on the fifth floor (an elevator is available) have attractive slanted ceilings and good views over the rooftops. Most rooms are comfortably outfitted with easy chairs, ample closet space, and modern bathrooms with hair dryers — but no shower curtains in rooms with tubs. Reserve at least a month in advance for July. Prices are attractive for its location, just two blocks from the Jardin du Palais Royal and down the street from the Louvre and the Jardin des Tuileries.

See map p. 134. 12 rue Richelieu. ☎ *01-42-96-28-50. Fax: 01-42-86-02-70.* www. hotel-paris-montpensier.com. *Métro: Palais-Royal–Musée du Louvre. Rack rates: 78€ ($94) double with toilet and sink; 92€ ($110) double with bathroom. Breakfast 7€ ($8.40). AE, MC, V.*

Hôtel Prince
$ Tour Eiffel (7e)

Just a ten-minute walk from the Tour Eiffel, the Prince is a good value for the location. Its rooms are modern and soundproofed and have exposed brick walls, matching curtains and bedspreads, and big bathrooms with fluffy towels. Though they vary in size, all units are pleasant, comfortable, and well kept with double-glazed windows, luggage racks, TVs, mini-fridges, and ample closets; some have hair dryers and safes. A ground-floor room is available with facilities for travelers with disabilities. If you're too worn out from sightseeing to stagger out the door to the two downstairs cafes (not part of the hotel), the hotel manager will arrange for a local restaurant to deliver a meal.

See map p. 134. 66 av. Bosquet. ☎ *01-47-05-40-90. Fax: 01-47-53-06-62.* www.hotel-paris-prince.com. *Métro: École-Militaire. Rack rates: 83€ ($100) double with shower; 81€–107€ ($97–$128) double with tub. Buffet breakfast 7.50€ ($9). AE, DC, MC, V.*

Hôtel Saint-Merry
$$–$$$ Le Marais (4e)

This hotel will bring out the "goth" in you. Formerly the 17th-century presbytery of the Church of Saint-Merri, it retains a medieval, and eccentric, atmosphere. Beds have wood screens for headboards, except for Room No. 9, where the bed has flying buttresses on either side. If you prefer sunny rooms, this place is not for you; the rooms are dark, with beamed ceilings, stone walls, wrought-iron chandeliers, sconces, and candelabra. Fabrics are sumptuous; rugs are Oriental; and bathrooms are pleasantly modern and fully tiled, and come equipped with hair dryers. Higher prices are for larger rooms with views. TVs are in suites only.

See map p. 134. 78 rue de la Verrerie. ☎ *01-42-78-14-15. Fax: 01-40-29-06-82. Métro: Hôtel-de-Ville or Châtelet. Rack rates: 160€–230€ ($192–$276) double; 300€–377€ ($360–$452) suite. In-room breakfast 11€ ($13). AE, V.*

Hôtel Saints-Pères
$$ St-Germain-des-Prés (6e)

The late poet Edna St. Vincent Millay loved the garden filled with camellias, and travelers make this romantic hotel one of the Left Bank's most popular. Designed in the 17th century by Louis XIV's architect, the hotel is furnished with antiques, old paintings, tapestries, and gilt mirrors, but its 39 rooms have modern amenities such as TVs and minibars. The most requested room is the *chambre à la fresque,* which has a 17th-century painted ceiling. Breakfast is served in the garden in good weather. The hotel is a stone's throw from Brasserie Lipp, Café de Flore, and the Deux-Magots.

See map p. 134. 65 rue des St-Pères. ☎ *01-45-44-50-00. Fax: 01-45-44-90-83. Métro: St-Germain-des-Près or Sèvres-Babylone. Rack rates: 120€ ($144) double; 290€ ($348) suite. Breakfast 12€ ($14). AE, DC, MC, V.*

Hôtel St-Jacques
$$ Latin Quarter (5e)

This hotel has an old-Paris feel that is accentuated with traditional furniture and fabric-covered walls, as well as with stenciling on the walls, *trompe l'oeil* painting (a clever technique in which architectural elements are "added" to a room by painting them in to appear real) around the doors, and murals. Modern comforts include generally spacious rooms, an elevator, immaculate tiled bathrooms with hair dryers and toiletries, double-glazed windows, and ample closet space. Though they aren't accessed by the elevator, the rooms on the top floor are less expensive and have great views. The hotel is in a good location near the Sorbonne,

Panthéon, and the Musée de Cluny, and not far from bd. St-Germain, rue Mouffetard, and the Arènes de Lutèce.

See map p. 134. 35 rue des Écoles (at rue des Carmes). ☎ *01-44-07-45-45. Fax: 01-43-25-65-50. Métro: Maubert-Mutualité. Rack rates: 112€ ($134) double. Breakfast 7.50€–9€ ($9–$11). AE, DC, MC, V.*

Hôtel Vivienne
$ Louvre/Opéra (2e)

Hôtel Vivienne is well located between the Louvre and the Opéra and offers comfortable, if not the most luxurious, rooms at a good price. Rooms and bathrooms vary in size from adequate to huge, and all are in good shape. Some rooms have adjoining doors, perfect for families; others have small terraces. The renovated bathrooms have hair dryers and wall-mounted showers in the tubs, and some rooms have views of the Tour Eiffel. Children younger than 10 stay free.

See map p. 134. 40 rue Vivienne. ☎ *01-42-33-13-26. Fax: 01-40-41-98-19. Métro: Bourse, Richelieu-Drouot, Grands Boulevards. Rack rates: 79€ ($95) double. Breakfast 7€ ($8.40). MC, V.*

Port-Royal Hôtel
$ Latin Quarter (5e)

The rates of a budget motel but the look of a high-class hotel make this a frugal traveler's dream. Halls are freshly painted, the elevator is supersized, and all the units are decorated with flowery pastel wallpaper. The front rooms have double-glazed windows for peace and quiet, and many rooms have decorative fireplaces. A breakfast/TV room and a small courtyard for outside dining are located on the premises. The hotel has been run by the same family for more than 60 years. Note that credit cards aren't accepted, but a Credit Lyonnais bank with an outdoor ATM is a few doors down.

See map p. 134. 8 bd. Port-Royal. ☎ *01-43-31-70-06. Fax: 01-43-31-33-67. Métro: Gobelins. Rack rates: 48€–51€ ($58–$61) double with sink; 73€–87€ ($88–$104) double with bathroom. Shower 2.50€ ($3). Continental breakfast 5€ ($6). No credit cards.*

Where to Dine in Paris

One of the best things about visiting Paris is finding out what a high-quality French meal tastes like. You're going to want to experience a true French lunch or dinner that stretches blissfully over several courses, and you can do just that at the establishments listed in this chapter. They have all the ingredients of a first-rate dining spot — fantastic cooking, reasonable prices, and great atmosphere — and create the kind of experience that lingers on in your memory long after the last dishes are cleared away. We also list cafes, tearooms, wine bars, and sandwich shops for when you're in the mood for just a light bite.

Paris Dining

Au Bascou **23**
Au Bistro de la Place **44**
Au Bon Accueil **7**
Au Pied de Cochon **22**
Au Poulbot Gourmet **10**
Auberge de Jarente **26**
Bofinger **46**
Brasserie Balzar **37**
Brasserie Ile St-Louis **43**
Café Beaubourg **25**
Café de Flore **30**
Café de L'Industrie **47**
Café de la Place **51**
Café des Deux Moulins **1**
Café les Deux-Magots **33**
Café Mabillon **32**
Café Marly **18**
Carré des Feuillants **16**
Caveau du Palais **29**
Cercle Ledoyen **5**
ChantAirelle **39**
Chardenoux **49**
Chez Casimir **13**
Chez Marie **11**
Chez Michel **12**
Fouquet's **2**
Jo Goldenberg **27**
L'Ambroisie **45**
L'Atelier de Joël Robuchon **17**
L'Ébauchoir **50**
L'Eté en Pente Douce **19**
La Bastide Odéon **36**
La Chaise au Plafond **28**
La Chope **40**
La Cigale **9**
La Coupole **52**
La Palette **34**
La Petite Chaise **8**
La Poule au Pot **21**
La Tour de Monthéry **20**
Le Cinq **3**
Le Grenier de Notre-Dame **41**
Le Père Claude **6**
Les Comptoirs du Charbon **24**
Pause Café **48**
Restaurant du Palais-Royal **15**
Restaurant Perraudin **38**
Rotisserie En Face **35**
16 Haussmann **14**
Spoon Food & Wine **4**
Vagenende **31**
Vivario **42**

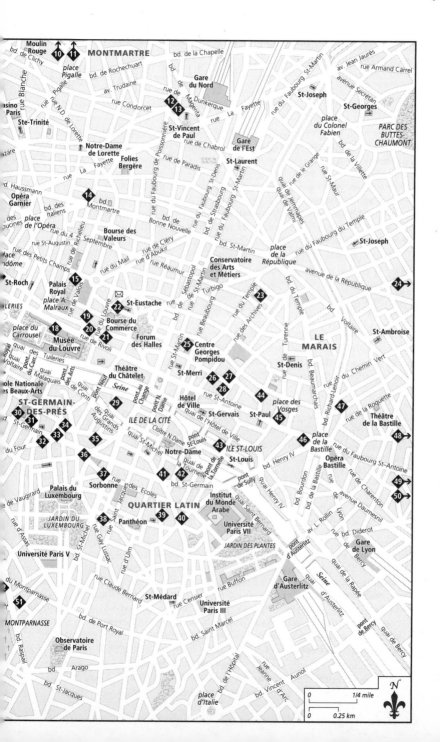

The list here concentrates on moderately priced establishments from homelike neighborhood favorites to chic "in" spots. Also included are some bargain eateries and a few of the city's most sumptuous restaurants where haute cuisine is an art form. For an idea of where these restaurants are located, check out the nearby "Paris Dining" map.

Restaurants are listed alphabetically for easy reference, followed by price range, neighborhood, and type of cuisine. Price ranges reflect the cost of a three-course meal for one person ordered a la carte featuring an appetizer, main dish, dessert, and coffee. (See the Introduction of this book for more about price ranges.)

Don't make price your only criteria for choosing a restaurant. Most establishments offer fixed-price menus (also called *formules* or *prix fixe*) that can bring the cost down one whole price category. Also, if you're eager to try a place that's above your budget, visit it at lunch, when meals are cheaper.

The top restaurants

Au Bascou
$–$$ **Le Marais (3e)   BASQUE/SOUTHWEST**

Specializing in dishes from the Basque country, the corner of southwestern France that borders with Spain, the popular Au Bascou offers excellent meals. Start with *piperade,* a savory concoction of sautéed peppers and onions on salad leaves topped with ham; then try superb seasonal fish or *agneau de lait des Pyrénées rôti* (roasted milk-fed lamb). Finish with *gâteau Basque,* a cake made of ground almonds and jam. A bottle of Basque's Irrouleguy, a smooth red wine, makes a fine accompaniment to meals, and the service is friendly without being condescending.

See map p. 148. 38 rue Réaumur. ☎ *01-42-72-69-25. Reservations recommended. Métro: Arts et Métiers. Main courses: 15€ ($18). AE, MC, V. Open: Mon–Fri noon to 2 p.m. and 8–10:30 p.m.*

Auberge de Jarente
$$$ **Le Marais (4e)   BASQUE**

When you've had enough of cream sauces, come here for the taste of southwest France, where cooks use olive oil, tomatoes, and all kinds of peppers. The prix fixe menu may include starters such as *les chipirons au piment d'Espelette* (squid with a type of hot Basque pepper) or *la soupe des poissons* (fish soup) and for a main course, Basque-influenced dishes like redfish with coriander and garlic or duck breast with oyster mushrooms and sautéed apples. Choose from smooth Basque wines such as *irouleguy, tursan,* and *madiran.* The rustic décor includes a cavelike cozy downstairs, and service is efficient.

See map p. 148. 7 rue de Jarente. ☎ *01-42-77-49-35. Reservations recommended. Métro: Bastille or St-Paul. Prix fixe: 18€ –28.75€ ($22–$35). AE, V. Open: Tue–Sat noon to 2:30 p.m. and 7:30–10:30 p.m. Closed three weeks in August.*

Au Bon Accueil
$–$$$$ Tour Eiffel (7e)   MODERN BISTRO

The menu here changes daily according to what owner Jacques Lacipière finds in the markets. If you're ordering from the prix fixe menu, you may start with *filets de sardines mi-cuites à l'huile et romarin méli mélo de legumes provencaux* (sardines lightly grilled in oil with a blend of vegetables from Provence) followed by *steak de thon poélé et son caviar d'aubergine aux olives* (seared tuna steak with eggplant "caviar" and olives). Perfectly prepared main dishes include scallops with asparagus and whole lobster from Brittany roasted in herbs and tomatoes. Luscious desserts feature fig tart and crème brûlée made with walnuts. The place is nearly always full, so reserve in advance.

See map p. 148. 14 rue de Monttessuy. ☎ *01-47-05-46-11. Reservations strongly recommended. Métro: Alma Marceau. Main courses: 25€–32€ ($30–$38); three-course prix fixe 31€ ($37). MC, V. Open: Mon–Fri noon to 2:30 p.m. and 7:30–10:30 p.m.*

Au Pied de Cochon
$–$$$ Les Halles (1er)   CLASSIC FRENCH

This welcoming gardenia-bedecked restaurant on a side street in Les Halles opened in 1946 and is a vibrant part of the history of this old market neighborhood. With marble, murals, elaborate sconces, chandeliers, and lots of foreign visitors, the restaurant provides great fun at manageable prices. You can have a plate of a half-dozen oysters or onion soup to start. Follow with grilled salmon or an *entrecôte maître d'hôtel* (rib steak in rich red-wine sauce) or their specialty and namesake, *pied de cochon* (pigs feet). Or, if you're daring — and hungry — have the 44€ ($53) *plateau rouge:* half a Canadian lobster, langoustines, shrimp, crab, and other redfish served on a towering pile of shaved ice. Finish with mouth-watering *profiteroles* (cream puffs).

See map p. 148. 6 rue Coquillière. ☎ *01-40-13-77-00. Reservations recommended. Métro: Châtelet–Les Halles. Main courses: 16€–30€ ($19–$36). AE, DC, V. Open: Daily 24 hours.*

Au Poulbot Gourmet
$$$ Montmartre (18e)   CLASSIC FRENCH

Photos of old Montmartre and original drawings by illustrator Francisque Poulbot adorn the walls, and chic burgundy leather banquettes usually are filled with a local crowd savoring moderately priced classic cuisine. Chef Jean-Paul Langevin brings tremendous finesse to the preparation and presentation of dishes such as *noisette d'agneau* (lamb slices), served with delicate splashes of mashed potatoes and spinach, and *marmite de poissons,* assorted fresh fish in a light saffron sauce. As an appetizer, the *oeufs pochés* (poached eggs) with smoked salmon is a standout. For dessert, try the *charlotte glacée,* a ringed concoction made with ladyfingers and ice cream.

See map p. 148. 39 rue Lamarck. ☎ *01-46-06-86-00. Reservations recommended. Métro: Lamarck-Caulincourt. Three-course prix fixe: 35€ ($42). MC, V. Open: Mon–Sat noon to 1:30 p.m. and 7:30–10 p.m.; Sun noon to 1:30 p.m. Oct–May only.*

Bofinger

$$ Le Marais (4e)   ALSATIAN/BRASSERIE

Bofinger is one of Paris's best-loved restaurants, with its dark wood, gleaming brass, bright lights, curved and painted glass ceiling, and waiters with long white aprons delivering good food. It's owned by the Flo brasserie chain, which means that you'll see similar menus in the chain's other restaurants that include Julien and Brasserie Flo. The downstairs dining room is ornately decorated with Art Nouveau flourishes and a glass-domed ceiling. Upstairs is cozier, with wood paneling and separate rooms for smokers. The menu features many Alsatian specialties, such as *choucroute* (sauerkraut with smoked ham), oysters, and foie gras, for which the restaurant is renowned. Best of all, the prices actually are quite moderate for Paris.

See map p. 148. 5–7 rue de la Bastille. ☎ *01-42-72-87-82. Reservations strongly recommended. Métro: Bastille. Main courses: 15€–35€ ($18–$42); lunch and dinner prix fixe menu, including a half-bottle of wine: 31.90€ ($38). AE, MC, V. Open: Mon–Fri noon to 3 p.m. and 6:30–1 a.m.; Sat–Sun noon to 1 a.m.*

Brasserie Balzar

$–$$ Latin Quarter (5e)   ALSATIAN/BRASSERIE

Brasserie Balzar has played host to some of France's most famous intellectuals, including Jean-Paul Sartre, and always is full of bohemians, even during off hours. The brasserie was the center of a controversy a few years ago when a group of regulars, including Adam Gopnik of *The New Yorker,* fought to keep a chain from buying it but ultimately failed. Nothing apparently has changed, however. People still stop here for coffee and pastries between lunch and dinner, and drop in for drinks in the evening. Regulars go for *poulet rôti avec frites* (roast chicken with French fries) or *choucroute garni,* but you can also get a good veal liver *(foie de veau), steak au poivre,* and a few fresh fish dishes. Portions are copious. For dessert, try the *gâteau au chocolate amère* (bittersweet chocolate cake).

See map p. 148. 49 rue des Écoles. ☎ *01-43-54-13-67. Reservations recommended. Métro: Cluny-Sorbonne. Main courses: 13€–22€ ($16–$26). AE, MC, V. Open: Daily noon to midnight.*

Brasserie Île St-Louis

$–$$ Ile St-Louis (1er)   ALSATIAN/BRASSERIE

It's loud and bustling, and one of our favorite places for comfort food. It's also the last remaining independent brasserie in Paris, owned by the same family for more than 60 years. Once the favorite haunt of writer James Jones *(The Thin Red Line),* who kept a mug, or *chope,* at the bar, its location is situated directly off the footbridge from Ile de la Cité to Ile St-Louis, with an unparalleled view of the eastern tip of Ile de la Cité (including the back of Notre-Dame). The food is quintessentially Alsatian — choucroute with heaps of tender, biting sauerkraut and meaty slices of ham, or the hearty cassoulet, laden with rich beans and tender pieces of lamb and pork, or ham shank atop a bed of lentils.

See map p. 148. 55 quai de Bourbon. ☎ *01-43-54-02-59. Reservations recommended. Métro: Pont Marie. Main courses: 16.50€–26€ ($20–$31) lunch and dinner. V. Open: Thurs–Tues noon to midnight.*

Carré des Feuillants
$$$$ Place Vendôme (1er)   MODERN FRENCH

This establishment is a bastion of perfection, an enclave of haute gastronomy between the place Vendôme and the Tuileries. When chef Alain Dutournier turned this 17th-century convent into a restaurant, it was an overnight success. The interior is like an early-1900s bourgeois house with several salons opening onto a sky-lit courtyard across from a glass-enclosed kitchen. You'll find a sophisticated reinterpretation of cuisine from France's southwest, using seasonally fresh ingredients and lots of know-how. The best examples are roasted veal kidneys cooked in their own fat and grilled wood pigeon with chutney and polenta. Lighter dishes are scallops wrapped in parsley-infused puff pastry served with cabbage and truffles, and mullet-studded risotto with lettuce. For dessert, try the pistachio cream cake with candied tangerines.

See map p. 148. 14 rue de Castiglione (near place Vendôme and the Tuileries). ☎ *01-42-86-82-82. Reservations required far in advance. Métro: Tuileries, Concorde, Opéra, or Madeleine. Main courses: 54€–62€ ($65–$74); prix fixe lunch 140€ ($168). AE, DC, MC, V. Open: Mon–Fri noon to 2 p.m. and 7:30–10 p.m.*

Caveau du Palais
$–$$ Louvre/ Ile de la Cité (1er)   CLASSIC FRENCH

Located in the heart of the charming, tree-lined place Dauphine, a secluded little park nestled at the tip of Ile de la Cité, is this pretty little restaurant serving excellent food at reasonable prices. Try the house's special *côte de boeuf,* grilled giant ribs prepared for two. The *confit de canard et pommes Sarladaise,* duck served with crispy potato bits sauteed in *foie gras* drippings, is another enticing dish. Have a look at the original art on the walls; the owners display the work of up-and-coming artists.

See map p. 148. 19 place Dauphine. ☎ *01-43-26-04-28. Reservations recommended. Métro: Pont Neuf. Main courses: 19€–25€ ($23–$30). AE, DC, MC, V. Open: Daily noon to 2:30 p.m. and 7–10:30 p.m.*

Cercle Ledoyen
$$$$ Champs-Elysées (8e)   CLASSIC FRENCH

Cercle Ledoyen is a haven of greenery and gourmet pleasures off the noisy Champs-Elysées. It's also pricey, but oh, is it worth it. Ledoyen's chef,

Christian Le Squer of Brittany, offers light, classic cooking. The menu varies but may feature a successful seafood entree such as langoustines with vinaigrette sauce. Other dishes that are a model of excellence include braised turbot with a truffle butter sauce and roasted sweetbreads with a mushroom sauce and fresh herbs. Desserts, such as pear tart, are wonderful, too. If the restaurant looks familiar, Robert Altman shot scenes from his film *Prêt-à-Porter* here.

See map p. 148. 1 av. Dutuit. ☎ *01-53-05-10-02. Reservations required. Métro: Champs-Elysées Clemenceau. Main courses: 57€–88€ ($68–$106). AE, DC, MC, V. Open: Tues–Fri 12:30–2:30 p.m. and 8–10 p.m.*

ChantAirelle
$–$$ Latin Quarter (5e) AUVERGNE

This charming little place has a backyard garden that children will love, while parents will appreciate the atmosphere that literally reeks of the Auvergne, the rugged south-central region of France. (Tiny bottles of essential oils made from native plants give you the smell of the region.) An old church door and a tiny fountain have been incorporated into the décor, and a sound system plays bird songs and church bells. Order an appetizer — maybe some of the famous *charcuterie* or cold sliced meats — only if you're ravenous; the delicious peasant food is presented in enormous portions. Main courses such as *yssingeaux,* cabbage stuffed with beef, mushrooms, and sausage and wrapped in layered pastry, or *potée* (a tureen filled with pork, cabbage, potatoes, turnips, and leeks in broth) are substantial. Although most dishes use ham or pork, vegetarians can enjoy the *croustade forestière* of assorted mushrooms and eggs poached with Fourme d'Ambert cheese. The best Auvergne wine is the Chateaugay, a fine fruity red.

See map p. 148. 17 rue Laplace. ☎ *01-46-33-18-59.* www.chantairelle.com. *Reservations recommended. Métro: Maubert-Mutualité. Main courses: 13.50€–20.80€ ($16–$25). MC, V. Open: Mon–Fri noon to 2 p.m.; Mon–Sat 7–10:30 p.m.*

Chardenoux
$–$$ Bastille (11e) CLASSIC BISTRO

This small, charming place is at the top of the list of Parisians' favorite bistros. From the etched plate-glass windows to the swirling stucco decorations on the walls and ceiling and the lacy curtains in the windows, its turn-of-the-20th-century décor is the very essence of old Paris. (It has been appointed a Monument Historique.) Service is friendly and English-speaking, too. A variety of French regional dishes appears on the menu — try the *oeufs en meurette,* a Burgundian dish of poached eggs in a sauce of red wine and bacon, or the *boeuf en daube,* braised beef Provençal style. Desserts are pure comfort food, especially the fruit tarts and the nougat in raspberry sauce.

See map p. 148. 1 rue Jules-Valles. ☎ *01-43-71-49-52. Reservations strongly recommended. Métro: Charonne. Main courses: 15€–24€ ($18–$29). AE, MC, V. Open: Mon–Fri noon to 2 p.m.; Mon–Sat 8–11:30 p.m.*

Chez Casimir

$ Gare du Nord (10e) CLASSIC FRENCH

The trip is worth it from almost anywhere to experience this hidden delight near the Gare du Nord, far from the more touristy sides of Paris. Chef Frederique Saffrey works magic in his kitchen, cooking with ingredients he finds at the market that morning or the night before. Start with the refreshing cucumber soup with melon chunks and slices of parmesan cheese served with toasted bread (take as much as you want from the pot placed on your table); then have *filet de rascasse avec des spaghetti de courgettes* — scorpionfish filet served with spaghetti-style cooked zucchini, fresh-cut tomatoes, and a touch of vinegar — or leg of lamb cooked on the bone with aromatic juices and fresh peas. For dessert, indulge in homemade pastry topped with raspberries and vanilla cream or *pain perdu* (French toast) and cherries cooked with honey. The wine list is highly affordable, with prices starting at 8€ ($9.60) for a half bottle.

See map p. 148. 6 rue de Belzunce. ☎ **01-48-78-28-80.** *Reservations recommended. Métro: Gare du Nord. Main courses: 13€–14€ ($16–$17). MC, V. Open: Mon–Fri noon to 2 p.m. and 7 p.m.–1 a.m.; Sat 7 p.m.–1 a.m.*

Chez Marie

$–$$ Montmartre (18e) CLASSIC FRENCH

At the base of the steps heading to the Place de Tertre, you can find some of the cheapest eats in this neighborhood, which is not exactly known for bargain dining. Food is hearty; the owners are charming and friendly; and they welcome children in their humbly decorated cozy dining room with wood benches, red and white picnic tablecloths, and wallpaper in the style of Toulouse Lautrec. Stick to the basics, such as lamb and *frites* (French fries) or duck *confit* (duck cooked and preserved in its own fat), and you are guaranteed to leave full and content, with money in your wallet.

See map p. 148. 27 rue Gabrielle. ☎ **01-42-62-06-26.** *Reservations not needed. Métro: Abbesses. Main courses: 7€–13€ ($8.40–$16); three-course menus (include apéritif): 9.50€–18.50€ ($11–$22). AE, DC, MC, V. Open: Daily noon to 2:30 p.m. and 6–11:30 p.m..*

Chez Michel

$$$ Gare du Nord (10e) BRETON

Crowds of Parisians come here for excellent, unusual food at very fair prices. Chef Thierry Breton, the chef at the Presidential Palace during François Mitterand's tenure, puts old-fashioned Breton dishes on his menu; look for succulent scallops, handpicked by scuba divers, that are served with truffles in the winter. The menu may include *crème d'homard Bréton* (cream of lobster soup) or a side of homestyle farm-raised pig roasted in butter. For the cheaper menu, sit in the cellar at wooden tables and eat all the shellfish, pâtés, and salads you can fit into your stomach — which is sure to be stretched by the end of the night. Choose from more than 100 different wines at retail cost — a truly dizzying experience.

See map p. 148. 10 rue Belzunce. ☎ *01-44-53-06-20. Reservations recommended. Métro: Gare du Nord. Prix fixe: 30€ ($36); menu dégustation homard (lobster menu; reserve two days in advance) 60€ ($72). MC, V. Open: Tues–Sat noon to 2 p.m. and 7 p.m. to midnight. Closed last week of June and first two weeks of July.*

Jo Goldenberg
$ Le Marais (4e)   CENTRAL EUROPEAN

The atmosphere here is convivial, the long red banquettes surrounded by photographs of famous patrons, including former French President Mitterand, and original paintings by up-and-coming artists. Eastern specialties abound, including poulet paprika, goulash, bagels, and Wiener schnitzel, as well as typical deli offerings such as pastrami and corned beef — allegedly invented right here by Goldenberg senior in the 1920s. Adding to the festive air are the Gypsy musicians who begin playing around 9 p.m.

See map p. 148. 7 rue des Rosiers. ☎ *01-48-87-20-16. Reservations not needed. Métro: St-Paul. Main courses: 13€–18€ ($16–$22). AE, MC, V. Daily 9 a.m. to midnight.*

La Bastide Odéon
$$–$$$ St-Germain-des-Près (6e)   PROVENÇAL

After an evening stroll in the Jardin du Luxembourg, head across the street for some savory Provençal cooking in a lovely dining room. The menu changes regularly, but Chef Gilles Ajuelos's dynamic creations include cold omelet stuffed with eggplant and basil in a red-pepper sauce, or leek and goat cheese terrine with balsamic caramel, and as dessert, roasted pear and ricotta with gingerbread and cottage cheese ice cream. You can also savor an iced tomato soup with grappa (a strong, colorless brandy) or olives from the chef's *cuisine du marché* (from the market).

See map p. 148. 7 rue Corneille. ☎ *01-43-26-03-65. Reservations recommended. Métro: Odéon. Main courses: 19€ ($23). AE, MC, V. Open: Tues–Sat noon to 2 p.m. and 7:30–10:30 p.m. Closed for 2 weeks in Aug.*

La Cigale
$ Tour Eiffel (7e)   CLASSIC BISTRO

La Cigale serves feathery soufflés (among other specialties) to a sophisticated and high-spirited clientele in an intimate space of soft lighting and cozy tables. The food is simply some of the best you can get in Paris for these prices. The delicate soufflés are beaten high; brim with camembert, sautéed spinach, or tarragon cream; and melt in your mouth. And that's before dessert, which offers — you got it — soufflés of heavenly lemon and sinful chocolate. If you're not in the mood for a soufflé, other tempting entrees include a rump roast and succulent lamb chops.

See map p. 148. 4 Impasse Recaimier. ☎ *01-45-48-86-58. Reservations recommended. Métro: Sèvres-Babylone. Main courses: 40€–50€ ($48–$60). MC, DC, V. Open: Mon–Sat noon to 2 p.m. and 7:30–11 p.m.*

Dining zones

If you're short on time or money, the following streets have many restaurants with fast service at low prices:

✔ **Avenue d'Ivry** and **Avenue de Choisy,** 13e: Far off the tourist track, the Vietnamese, Chinese, and Thai restaurants along these wide avenues cater to the local Southeast Asian population. Prices are cheap, quality is high, and you can eat like the locals.

✔ **Bd. de Belleville,** 11e: This is the street of *couscouseries* (couscous restaurants) that are reasonably priced and satisfactory, if not outstanding. Middle Eastern snacks, pastries, and a glass of mint tea make an exotic and inexpensive meal.

✔ **Bd. du Montparnasse,** 14e: In one block (between rue Vavin and bd. Raspail), you'll find four cafes that have literary associations — La Coupole, Le Dôme, Le Select, and La Rotonde — as well as high- and moderately-priced seafood restaurants, crêperies, sandwich shops, and ethnic specialties.

✔ **Métro Belleville,** 11e: The streets radiating out from this station are the northern headquarters for Asian cuisine. You can usually slurp down noodle soup at any hour of the day and well into the night.

✔ **Rue des Rosiers,** in the Marais (3e): People have been known to trudge across town for the huge pita-bread sandwiches sold on this street. Stuffed with falafel, eggplant, and salad, and then topped with your choice of sauce, this must be the best 5€ ($6) meal in town.

✔ **Rue du Montparnasse,** 14e: The street between bd. Edgar Quinet and bd. du Montparnasse is a Crêperie Row of inexpensive Breton eateries. Whether the *crêpes* are sugared up with syrups and jam or stuffed with vegetables and meat (these are often called *galettes*), they make a tasty light meal for less than 10€ ($12).

✔ **Rue Sainte-Anne,** 9e: Sushi is expensive in Paris, but because this street lies in the same neighborhood as many Japanese businesses, you find the freshest fish and most authentic Japanese dishes at moderate prices.

L'Ambroisie
$$$$ Le Marais (4e)   HAUTE CUISINE

This is the place to take someone you want to *really* impress. Chef Bernard Pacaud has achieved international renown in this gorgeous 17th-century mansion on the place des Vosges. His food is just exquisite. Specialties may include fricassée of lobster in wine sauce, roasted free-range chicken with black truffles, and an award-winning *tarte fine,* a chocolate pie with bitter chocolate and mocha ice cream. The restaurant has two high-ceilinged Renaissance-inspired salons, a cozy back room, and terrace dining in the summer; it calls out for marriage proposals, anniversaries, and other special and romantic events.

See map p. 148. 9 place des Vosges. ☎ *01-42-78-51-45. Métro: St. Paul. Reserve at least four weeks ahead. Jacket and tie advised. No prix fixe menu; expect to spend at least 200€–220€ ($240–$264) per person per meal. AE, MC, V. Open: Tues–Sat noon to 1:30 p.m. and 8–9:30 p.m. Closed two weeks in Feb and three weeks in Aug.*

La Petite Chaise
$$ St-Germain-des-Prés (7e)   CLASSIC FRENCH

Originally built in the mid-17th century, this small gem is allegedly the oldest restaurant in Paris. The entranceway, adorned with a smoky antique mirror from the early 18th century, leads to a softly illuminated, cozy dining room reminiscent of an old country inn. Start with *escargots bourguignon* or the homemade *foie gras de canard maison*. As a main dish, the *magret de canard pomme et miel* (duck breast cooked with apples and honey) melts away your appetite. A piece of chocolate cake with English cream tops off your meal with the elegance the nobility used to enjoy in their visits to the restaurant 300 years ago. The old maxim holds true: The best things in life never change.

See map p. 148. 36 rue de Grenelle. ☎ *01-42-22-13-35. Reservations required. Métro: Sèvres-Babylone. Main courses (with a half-bottle of wine): 24€–29€ ($29–$35). MC, V. Open: Daily noon to 2 p.m. and 7–10:45 p.m.*

La Poule au Pot
$$–$$$ Les Halles (1er)   CLASSIC BISTRO

Poule au pot, an old French recipe of chicken stewed with broth and vegetables, has been served here since 1935 with much success, if the celebrity names in the *livre d'or* (a gold book filled with the names of visiting stars) mean anything. When Les Halles was still Paris's marketplace, its workers would come here to share a bowl of *poule au pot*. After the market's demise, visits from such celebrities as Maurice Chevalier, Miou Miou, the Rolling Stones, and Prince kept this Parisian bistro on the map. The atmosphere created by the long zinc bar, *pots* of wine, red leather banquettes, wood paneling, and waiters in long aprons will transport you back to another French era. How can the menu serve anything other than traditional French fare? Begin with *foie gras maison* (house goose liver pâté) or *œufs cocotte à la crème* (eggs baked with cream); then try the *rognons de veau à la graine de moutarde* (veal kidneys cooked with mustard grains) or the succulent house *poule au pot* (27€/$32) with a tureen of the broth on the side. Finish with a velvety crème brûlée.

See map p. 148. 9 rue Vauvilliers. ☎ *01-42-36-32-96. Reservations not needed. Métro: Châtelet-Les Halles. Main courses: 20€–33€ ($24–$40). MC, V. Open: Tues–Sat 7 p.m.–5 a.m.*

L'Atelier de Joël Robuchon
$$$$ **Tour Eiffel (7e)**   MODERN FRENCH

Upon his retirement in the mid–'90s, Joël Robuchon was hailed as the greatest chef in France. His mashed potatoes alone were a masterpiece — acclaimed as the world's greatest. Well, he's back. But not quite as grandly as before. His new restaurant is in a government-rated four-star hotel and serves all day and into the early morning. Robuchon has hired and trained a team of master chefs. The restaurant has a sleek red-and-black-lacquered finish and is dimly lit. Each dish is masterfully prepared but not as elaborate as those memorable dishes from the golden age of 1996. Seated at a dining bar wrapped around the open kitchen, you can enjoy, among other delights, sushi, which can be consumed with a basket of sourdough bread or a crusty baguette. The menu is ever changing, but you may start with a pumpkin-and-cauliflower soup with smoky bacon or a divine chicken-liver terrine. Among the sublime main courses is caramelized quail glazed with a shallot-perfumed sauce or a buttery and tender platter of langoustines in a pastry pâté. Duckling comes both roasted and braised, and is flavored with spices such as ginger, nutmet, and cinnamon. The fish and shellfish are shipped fresh from Brittany.

See map p. 148. In the Hôtel Pont Royal, 5–7 rue de Montalembert. ☎ *01-42-22-56-56. Reservations required. Métro: Rue du Bac. Main courses: 16€–50€ ($19–$60); prix fixe menu: 80€ ($96). AE, DC, MC, V. Open: Mon–Fri 11 a.m.–2 a.m.*

La Tour de Montlhéry
$–$$ **Les Halles (1er)**   CLASSIC FRENCH

Barrels of wine, a zinc bar, and a homelike dining room with hams and sausages dangling from the beams make this a true Parisian restaurant. It's also a meat lover's place. The less expensive items on the menu tend to be dishes such as tripe Calvados and stuffed cabbage and kidneys. Other typical dishes are grilled lamb chops and, for those who want to try truly authentic, reputably delicious French fare, *cervelles d'agneau* (sautéed lamb's brain). *Bon courage.*

See map p. 148. 5 rue des Prouvaires. ☎ *01-42-36-21-82. Reservations required. Métro: Châtelet–Les Halles. Main courses: 16€–26€ ($19–$31). V. Open: Mon–Fri 24 hours. Closed July 15–Aug 15.*

L'Ébauchoir
$–$$ **Bastille (12e)**   BISTRO

Tucked into a part of the Bastille often overlooked by visitors, this restaurant is well worth the trek. A mural pays homage to the working-class roots of the neighborhood, and the space is just large enough to render dining here a bit noisy. Friendly waiters rush to show diners seated at the first-come, first-served tables the day's offerings written on a tall chalkboard, and once you've sampled lunch or dinner, you find the decibel level is more than made up for — the food is superb. Diners may be offered appetizers of warm *foie gras* or stuffed ravioli followed by mouth-watering red label filet of bass with a saffron cream or steak in a red-wine Bordelaise sauce. For dessert, the *mille feuille* (a flaky multilayered pastry) is divine. On one visit, the waiter recommended mountain honey they had received that day from an *apiculteur* (beekeeper) to accompany dessert.

See map p. 148. 45 rue de Citeaux. ☎ 01-43-42-49-31. Reservations not needed. Métro: Faidherbe-Chaligny. Main courses: 14€–22€ ($17–$26). MC, V. Open: Thurs–Sat noon to 2:30 p.m. and 8–11 p.m.; Mon noon to 2:30 p.m.

Le Cinq
$$$$ Champs-Elysées (8e)   HAUTE CUISINE

Chef Philippe Legendre has earned high praise for this heavenly bastion of elegance. Every element is in place, from the stately yet serene dining room with its high ceilings and overstuffed chairs to the Limoges porcelain and Riedel stemware created for the restaurant and the perfect waitstaff. The sumptuous and inventive cuisine includes *crème de cresson de source glacée au caviar Sevruga* (chilled watercress cream with Sevruga caviar); *blanc manger au caviar d'Aquitaine, avocat mariné à l'huile de noisette* (sole mousse with French caviar and avocado marinated in hazelnut oil); and for dessert, the delightful *autour de la fraise,* a whimsical assortment of strawberry confections ranging from strawberry tiramisu to sorbet of strawberry and green tomato. Dining here is truly a special experience.

See map p. 148. 31 av. George V. ☎ 01-49-52-71-54. Métro: George V. Reservations required. Gourmet tasting menu: 230€ ($276); main courses: 50€–110€ ($60–$132). AE, MC, V. Open: Daily 6:30–10:30 p.m.

Le Grenier de Notre-Dame
$ Latin Quarter (5e)   VEGETARIAN

Le Grenier is GREEN, from the walls and tablecloths to the outdoor patio under a balcony of hanging plants, as if to prove that yes, this is a vegetarian restaurant. Food is good; especially recommended is the *cassoulet végétarien*, with white beans, onions, tomatoes, and soy sausage. The couscous and the cauliflower *au gratin* are also tempting. Le Grenier has a well-deserved reputation for desserts, such as *tarte de tofu.* The wine list includes a variety of organic offerings.

See map p. 148. 18 rue de la Bûcherie. ☎ 01-43-29-98-29. Reservations not accepted. Métro: Maubert-Mutualité. Three-course menu: 14.50€ ($17); main courses: 12€–14.50€ ($14–$17). MC, V. Open: Mon–Thurs noon to 11 p.m.; Fri–Sun 11:30 p.m.

Le Père Claude
$$ Tour Eiffel (15e)   CLASSIC BISTRO

The rotisserie behind the bar signals that the house specialty here is roasted meat, and that's an understatement; Le Père Claude is known for its enormous portions of red-meat dishes. Starters include warm sausage with pistachio and apples or *terrine de gibier et foie gras de canard* (game terrine with duck liver). The *panaché de viandes* is an assortment of perfectly roasted meat served with a comforting heap of mashed potatoes. Make sure you specify how you want the beef cooked, or it will be served the way the French like it — *bleue,* or very, very rare. Seafood lovers won't be disappointed in the mussel soup with saffron or the *assiette de pecheur aux pates fraiches* (fisherman's plate with fresh terrine). French President Jacques Chirac and boxing promoter Don King have been spotted (separately) chowing down here, but it's usually home to families and, to a lesser extent, visitors with big appetites. After dinner, you can stroll up the avenue de la Motte-Picquet and take in a view of the illuminated Tour Eiffel.

See map p. 148. 51 av. de la Motte-Picquet. ☎ *01-47-34-03-05. Reservations required. Métro: La-Motte-Picquet–Grenelle. Main courses: 18€–30€ ($22–$36). AE, MC, V. Daily 11:30 a.m.–2:30 p.m. and 7 p.m. to midnight.*

Restaurant du Palais-Royal
$$–$$$ Louvre (1er)   CLASSIC FRENCH

The elegant arcade that encircles the gardens inside the Palais-Royal also surrounds this restaurant, making it one of the most romantic locations in Paris. Sit at the terrace on warm, sun-filled days, and begin your meal with starters such as marinated leeks in a beet-juice vinaigrette or scallop salad. Main dishes vary with the season but may include grilled tuna steak with a Basque relish, or filet mignon and frites. The desserts are sumptuous, and the good house red wine is served Lyonnaise-style in thick-bottomed bottles. The dining room shines in tones of gold, silver, and warm red, in case dining outside just isn't an option.

See map p. 148. 43 rue Valois. ☎ *01-40-20-00-27. Reservations required. Métro: Palais-Royal–Musée du Louvre. Main courses: 24€–46€ ($29–$55). AE, DC, MC, V. Open: Mon–Fri 12:15–2:15 p.m. and Mon–Sat 7:15–9:30 p.m. Closed from the end of Dec to the end of Jan.*

Restaurant Perraudin
$–$$ Latin Quarter (5e)   CLASSIC BISTRO

People say that Hemingway went to the Closerie des Lilas when rich, and Perraudin was his favorite spot when broke. Professors and students from the nearby Sorbonne, as well as families and tourists, also enjoy this historic bistro, with its red-checked tablecloths and lace lampshades, jolly atmosphere, and staff that welcomes kids. A bargain lunch menu offers a choice of three appetizers, two main courses, and cheese or dessert. You may start with tomatoes and mozzarella or *flammekueche* (square, thin-crusted pizzas topped with cream, herbs, or cheese); then have ham with endive or roast beef, followed by tarte tatin. Classic dishes such as duck confit and *gigot d'agneau* (leg of lamb) with *gratin Dauphinois* (cheese-topped potatoes) are on the à la carte menu. Arrive early for a table, because reservations aren't accepted here.

See map p. 148. 157 rue St-Jacques. ☎ *01-46-33-15-75. Reservations not accepted. Métro: Luxembourg. Main courses: around 6€ ($7.20); three-course gastronomic menu: 28€ ($34). MC, V. Mon–Fri noon to 2:30 and 7:30–10 p.m.*

Rotisserie En Face
$$$ St-Germain-des-Près (6e)   MODERN BISTRO

This baby bistro is across the street *(en face)* from Jacques Cagna's first huge Parisian success, Restaurant Jacques Cagna. It's the first of four bistros he subsequently opened. The décor is cozy and subdued, yet a bit eclectic — the focus of the room is the figurine of a woman in a striped bathing suit, arm slung companionably over a fish. Cagna's modern approach to hearty bistro dishes draws crowds of publishing people for lunch and the local elegant set for dinner. Everything's delicious and may even warrant a return trip before you go back home. Freshly baked warm bread accompanies starters such as the *quenelles de brochet, sauce Nantua aux crustacés* (poached pike dumplings filled with mousse in a creamy crustacean sauce), or a dozen wild Burgundy snails, and main courses of *cuisse de lapin à la sauge et légumes grillés à l'huile d'olive* (spit-roasted rabbit leg served with gravy and vegetables grilled in olive oil) or *aïoli de morue fraîche, bulots, laitue de mer et légumes de saison à la vapeur* (codfish filet with sea snails, braised seaweed, steamed vegetables, and garlic mayonnaise). Finish up with a caramel and walnut ice cream cake, or raspberry and red-currant flan.

See map p. 148. 2 rue Christine. ☎ *01-43-26-40-98. Reservations required. Métro: Odéon. Three-course menu: 40€ ($48). AE, DC, MC, V. Open: Mon–Fri noon to 2:30 p.m.; Mon–Sat 7–1 p.m.*

16 Haussmann
$$$ Opéra (9e)   CLASSIC FRENCH

Bold concoctions are the hallmarks of this restaurant. *Oeufs coques à la crème d'épices et caramel de xérés* (soft-boiled eggs in sherry cream sauce with spices) is a good dish to start off your meal, and the cod roasted with truffle oil and basil is a delicious main course. Even with a tureen of salmon spread as an hors d'oeuvre, the two-course menu may not satisfy a large appetite, so plan on sampling one of the luscious desserts. A good selection of wines is available by the glass.

See map p. 148. In the Hôtel Ambassador, 16 bd. Haussmann. ☎ *01-48-00-06-38. Reservations recommended. Métro: Chausée d'Antin or Richelieu-Drouot. Two-course menu: 30€ ($36); three-course menu: 38€ ($46). AE, DC, MC, V. Open: Mon–Fri noon to 2:30 p.m. and 7–10:30 p.m.; Sat 7–10:30 p.m. Closed 3 weeks in Aug.*

Spoon Food & Wine
$$–$$$ Champs-Elysées (8e)   MODERN BISTRO

Chef Alain Ducasse has reinvented the joy of eating out in this restaurant designed to celebrate dining "freedom." A variety of international dishes is presented through a menu of mixing and matching; the customer chooses the condiment, side dishes, and vegetables from the menu, which is shown in columns numbered 1, 2, and 3. For example, say you decide you want fish. Choose the type of fish you want from Column 1 (pan-seared tuna and pan-seared scallops are among the choices), then decide which sauce you want from Column 2 (spicy citrus and satay are among sauces listed). Column 3 lists the side dishes, such as Thai rice or caramelized chicory. It's an interesting concept that doesn't always work, but it's a lot of fun all the same. Spoon has one of the most international wine lists in Paris, with 120 from South Africa, Argentina, and New Zealand. Desserts are delicious; the only odity is bubble gum ice cream. Opt for the oozing warm chocolate "pizza"; it's simply heaven.

See map p. 148. 14 rue de Marignan. ☎ *01-40-76-34-44.* www.spoon.tm.fr. *Reservations required one month in advance. Métro: Franklin-D-Roosevelt. Main courses: 22.50€–40€ ($27–$48). AE, MC, V. Open: Mon–Fri noon.–2:00 p.m. and 7–10:30 p.m.*

Vagenende
$–$$ St-Germain-des-Prés (6e)   ALSATIAN/BRASSERIE

M. Chartier, of the 9e arrondissement restaurant of the same name, founded Vagenende in 1904 as a *bouillon* (a workers' canteen or soup kitchen). The restaurant evolved into a brasserie that is now classified as a Monument Historique. The Art Nouveau décor is authentic — mirrors, frescoes, and swirling floral patterns abound within walls of dark wood, making this the place to live out your Belle Époque fantasy. Lace curtains, globe lights, and spacious booths enhance the classic atmosphere. The dishes are equally classic: You may choose to start out with a half-dozen Fine des Claires oysters or soup of rockfish served with red-pepper mayonnaise. Main courses include *confit de canard* (duck confit), suckling pig with carmelized onions and Indian spices, or *pavé de morue sauce vierge* (cod with lemon-flavored sauce). Finish up with a vanilla and bourbon-flavored crème brûlée.

See map p. 148. 142 bd. St-Germain. ☎ *01-43-26-68-18. Reservations recommended. Métro: Odéon. Main courses: 16€–23€ ($19–$28); prix fixe: 23€ ($28). AE, DC, MC, V. Open: Daily noon to 1 a.m. Closed Aug.*

Vivario
$–$$ Latin Quarter (5e)   CORSICAN

You'll want to see Corsica after you eat at Vivario, an excellent spot to sample the hearty flavors of the Belle Isle, Napoléon's birthplace. Many of the products used in Vivario's dishes come straight from sunny Corsica to the dim, cavelike restaurant, with ceiling beams and stone walls. To start, opt for the rich traditional Corsican soup, teeming with beans, vegetables, and generous pieces of dried prosciutto. Or try the charcuterie plate, served with a Mason jar of spicy cornichons. Follow with *cabri rôti à la Corse* (roast goat) or eggplant with cheese and spicy tomato sauce. Chewy whole-wheat baguettes accompany the meal, which may end with a selection of Corsican cheeses or the Corsican dessert *fiadone*, a cheesecake made with mild *bruccio*, the island's famous, pungent cheese.

See map p. 148. 6 rue Cochin. ☎ *01-43-25-08-19. Reservations recommended. Métro: Maubert-Mutualité. Main courses: 15€ ($18). AE, MC, V. Open: Mon–Sat 7:30 p.m.–1 a.m.*

Taking an afternoon break in Parisian tea salons (salons de thés)

If you're tired of all those short blasts of French coffee, tea's your alternative. Paris tea salons have a wide range of blends, steeped to perfection in refined and often elegant settings. The pastry selections in these places are usually excellent, but save your full meals for a restaurant — tea salons tend to be expensive.

- ✔ **Angelina:** 226 rue de Rivoli, 1er; ☎ **01-42-60-82-00.** Open daily 9 a.m. to 5:45 p.m. (lunch served noon to 3 p.m.). Métro: Concorde or Tuileries.

- ✔ **A Priori Thé:** 35–37 Galerie Vivienne (enter at 6 rue Vivienne, 4 rue des Petits-Champs, or 5 rue de la Banque), 2e; ☎ **01-42-97-48-75.** Open Monday to Friday 9 a.m. to 6 p.m.; Saturday 9 a.m. to 6:30 p.m.; Sunday noon to 6:30 p.m. Métro: Bourse, Palais-Royal–Musée du Louvre, or Pyramides.

- ✔ **La Formi Ailée:** 8 rue du Fouarre, 5e; ☎ **01-43-29-40-99.** Open daily noon to midnight. Métro: Maubert-Mutualité.

- ✔ **Marais Plus:** 20 rue des Francs-Bourgeois, 3e; ☎ **01-48-87-01-40.** Open daily 11 a.m. to 7 p.m. Métro: St-Paul.

- ✔ **Mariage Frères:** 13 rue Grands Augustins, 6e; ☎ **01-40-51-82-50.** Open daily noon to 7 p.m. Métro: Hôtel-de-Ville.

- ✔ **Salon de Thé de la Mosquée de Paris:** 39 rue Geoffroy-St-Hilaire, 5e; ☎ **01-43-31-18-14.** Open daily 9 a.m. to midnight. Métro: Monge.

- ✔ **Tea Caddy:** 14 rue St-Julien-le-Pauvre, 5e; ☎ **01-43-54-15-56.** Open daily noon to 7 p.m. Métro: St-Michel.

Experiencing the Parisian cafe

Here are some of Paris's best places to read the paper, write postcards, people-watch, soak up the city's atmosphere, and relax with a cup of coffee, glass of wine or beer, or grab a sandwich, salad, or a traditional French specialty such as *pot-au-feu* (beef boiled with vegetables). Cafes generally are open from about 8 a.m. until 1 a.m.

Au Bistro de la Place

This square on the place du Marché Sainte-Catherine is a pedestrian zone on the site of an 18th-century market, and this bistro is prettiest of all on the outdoor terrace here. The food also is the best here; you may find fresh vegetable soup served hot or cold or fresh goat cheese marinated in olive oil with salad. If you don't come here for a meal, visit during off-peak hours to enjoy a leisurely drink or pastry on the terrace.

See map p. 148. 2 place du Marché Sainte-Catherine, 4e. ☎ 01-42-78-21-32. Métro: St-Paul.

Café Beaubourg

This hip, but dark, bi-level cafe is cool and elegant, with large circular columns that soar to an illuminated ceiling. The walls are filled with books, and a small wooden bridge spans the upper part of the cafe and leads to quieter, artistically designed tables. The bathrooms are attractions in themselves; they have the serenity of Zen gardens. Simple food may include a smooth gazpacho, salmon club sandwich, or goat cheese salad. The outside terrace is in a strategic spot overlooking the Centre Pompidou, and you'll become a main attraction yourself as passersby cast curious glances at the people chic enough to eat here.

See map p. 148. 100 Rue St. Martin, 4e. ☎ *01-48-87-63-96. Métro: Rambuteau or Hôtel-de-Ville.*

Café de Flore

In the heart of St-Germain-des-Prés, this cafe is still going strong, even though the famous writers have moved on — and you now pay high prices. Sartre is said to have written *Les Chemins de la Liberté (The Roads to Freedom)* at his table here, and he and Simone de Beauvoir saw people by appointment here. Other regulars included André Malraux and Guillaume Apollinaire. Paris's leading intellectual bookstore, La Hune, is right next door.

See map p. 148. 172 bd. St-Germain, 6e. ☎ *01-45-48-55-26. Métro: St-Germain-des-Prés.*

Café de la Place

This old-fashioned cafe overlooking small, tree-lined place Edgar Quinet has become a popular spot for young neighborhood residents. Browse the menu of inexpensive bistro specialties, or opt for a simple sandwich and a glass of wine. If you're lucky, you'll see a *brocante* (like a garage sale) or crafts fair in the square. Café de la Place also is a good place to stop before any trips from the Gare du Montparnasse, which is around the corner and just down the street.

See map p. 148. 23 rue d'Odessa, 14e. ☎ *01-42-18-01-55. Métro: Edgar-Quinet.*

Café de L'Industrie

This popular bar and cafe is young, friendly, and casual. Plants, wooden floors, and wooden Venetian blinds lend the two spacious rooms a vaguely colonial flavor. Hip Bastille denizens drift in and out all day, and after 9:30 p.m., the place is mobbed. Bartenders specialize in rum drinks.

See map p. 148. 16 rue St-Sabin, 11e. ☎ *01-47-00-13-53. Métro: Bastille.*

Café des Deux Moulins

Amélie was a quirky low-budget film that was nominated for five Oscars and was seen by more than 25 million people around the world following its release in 2001. The film was set in Montmartre, and the cafe featured in the film has developed into a mandatory stopping-off place for the constantly arriving "cult of *Amélie*." In the film, Amélie worked as a waitress at the Café des Deux Moulins. The musty atmosphere, with its 1950s décor, mustard-colored ceiling, and lace curtains, has been preserved, even the wall lamps and unisex toilet. The menu is much the same as it has always been — escalopes of veal in a cream sauce, beef filets, calf's liver, green frisée salad with bacon bits and warm goat cheese, and pig's brains with lentils. The kitchen serves hamburgers, but with an egg on top. The classic dish is a demi-Camembert with a glass of Côtes du Rhône.

See map p. 148. 15 rue Lepic, 18e. ☎ *01-42-54-90-50. Métro: Blance.*

Café les Deux-Magots

Like its neighbor, Café de Flore, les Deux-Magots was a hangout for Sartre and Simone de Beauvoir. The intellectuals met here in the 1950s, and Sartre wrote at his table every morning. With prices that start at 4€ ($4.80) for coffee and 2.20€ ($2.65) for a croissant, the cafe is an expensive place for literary-intellectual pilgrims, but an idyllic spot to watch the nightly promenade on the boulevard St-Germain. Service can be snippy.

See map p. 148. 6 place St-Germain-des-Prés, 6e. ☎ *01-45-48-55-25. Métro: St-Germain-des-Prés.*

Café Mabillon

Welcome the dawn at Café Mabillon, which stays open all night. During the day, contemporary rock music draws a young, hip crowd to relax on the outdoor terrace or in the ultramodern interior. At night, the music changes to techno, and the bordello-red banquettes fill with a wide assortment of night owls. As dawn approaches, the sound drops to a level just loud enough to keep you from dozing off in your seat.

See map p. 148. 164 bd. St-Germain-des-Prés, 6e. ☎ *01-43-26-62-93. Métro: Mabillon.*

Café Marly

This stunning cafe at the Musée du Louvre has a gorgeous view of the glass pyramid that is the museum's main entrance. With high ceilings, warmly painted pastel walls, and luxurious red sofa chairs, the rooms could house the museum's latest art collection. Don't let the elegant ambience intimidate you; there's good food to be had. Choose from the carefully selected wine list, sit on the balcony, and enjoy the exquisite lighting on the pyramid and surrounding 18th-century facades. After 8 p.m., seating is for dinner only.

See map p. 148. 93 rue de Rivoli, cour Napoléon du Louvre, 1er. ☎ *01-49-26-06-60. Métro: Palais-Royal–Musée du Louvre.*

Fouquet's

Not far from the Arc de Triomphe, the early-20th-century Fouquet's is a Champs-Elysées institution. Patrons have included James Joyce, Charlie

Chaplin, Marlene Dietrich, Winston Churchill, and Franklin D. Roosevelt. You pay dearly for the glitzy associations and nostalgia, however.
See map p. 148. 99 av. des Champs-Elysées, 8e. ☎ *01-47-23-50-00. Métro: George V.*

La Chaise au Plafond

Tucked away on a pedestrians-only side street in the heart of the Marais, this friendly, stylish place is a perfect spot for a time-out after visiting the Musée Picasso. It serves enormous salads, imaginative sandwiches, and thick tarts. A weekend brunch (about 17€/$20) is served, but the tiny cafe tables aren't designed to hold the assortment of dishes, so you may feel squeezed.
See map p. 148. 10 rue Trésor, 4e. ☎ *01-42-76-03-22. Métro: Hôtel-de-Ville.*

La Chope

This cafe is worth a stop for its location on top of rue Mouffetard, right on place de la Contrescarpe. The square centers on four lilac trees and a fountain. It can get rowdy at night.
See map p. 148. 9 rue Mouffetard, 5e. ☎ *01-43-54-06-81. Métro: Cardinal Lemoine.*

La Coupole

La Coupole has been packing them in since Henry Miller came here for his morning porridge. The cavernous interior is always jammed and bristling with energy. Japanese businesspeople, French yuppies, models, tourists, and neighborhood regulars keep the frenzied waiters running until 2 a.m. You won't know which is more interesting, the scene on the street or the parade that passes through the revolving doors. The food is good, too, but prices are high.
See map p. 148. 102 bd. Montparnasse, 14e. ☎ *01-43-20-14-20. Métro: Vavin.*

La Palette

Students from the nearby École des Beaux-Arts, artists, and gallery owners linger and watch the life of the Left Bank flow by. The interior is decorated with colorful murals, and a palette hangs over the bar. The fare is open-faced sandwiches and salads at reasonable prices. Service can be snippy.
See map p. 148. 43 rue de Seine, 6e. ☎ *01-43-26-68-15. Métro: Mabillon.*

Les Comptoirs du Charbon

In the heart of the trendy rue Oberkampf, this turn-of-the-20th-century dance hall is one of the hottest spots in Paris for people who like people and don't mind being crowded. The stunning Art Nouveau interior has high ceilings, hanging lamps, and walls covered with mirrors, wood, and handpainted murals — which you can barely perceive through the bustle and haze. During the day or early evening you can relax, hang out, chat, or read a newspaper. After about 9 p.m., the music gets louder, the long wood bar and banquettes fill up, and you are lucky to get in, let alone get a seat.

See map p. 148. 109 rue Oberkampf, 11e. ☎ *01-43-57-55-13. Métro: Parmentier. MC, V.*

L'Eté en Pente Douce

To escape the shoulder-to-shoulder tourists on place du Tertre, head down the eastern steps under Sacré-Coeur to this popular cafe situated in a leafy square. The terrace here faces the stairs and iron lamps painted by Utrillo, and someone is always performing for the captive audience. The interior is brightly decorated with mosaics, unusual *objets d'art*, and a lovely painted ceiling. Between lunch and dinner, the restaurant serves a tempting array of pastries and sandwiches.

See map p. 148. 23 rue Muller, 18e. ☎ *01-42-64-02-67. Métro: Chateau-Rouge.*

Pause Café

Featured in the French hit movie comedy, *Chacun Cherche Son Chat (Each Looks for Her Cat)*, this cafe has become one of Paris's hottest. Its hip clientele are denizens of the club scene (flyers inside give dates for upcoming events) or cool residents of the neighborhood. A groovy distressed interior features paintings of big-eyed worried women, while outdoors is made tropical with cloth-and-bamboo umbrellas and potted palms. You can get a tasty 8€ ($9.60) quiche of the day or bowl of gazpacho soup made with fresh ingredients for 5€ ($6), as well as beer and drinks.

See map p. 148. 41 rue de Charonne, 11e. ☎ *01-48-06-80-33. Métro: Lédru-Rollin.*

Wine bars

With good selections of wines by the glass and tasty light meals served all day in pleasant surroundings, the Paris wine bar is often a cozy and sophisticated alternative to the cafe.

À la Cloche des Halles

This tiny bar and cafe is crowded at lunchtime with people dining on plates of ham or quiche, accompanied by a bottle of wine. It's convivial and fun, but noisy and crowded. If you can't find a seat, you can usually stand at the bar and eat. Look closely at the exterior for the bell that once tolled the opening and closing of the vast food market for which this neighborhood was named.

28 rue Coquillière, 1er. ☎ *01-42-36-93-89. Métro: Les Halles or Palais-Royal–Musée du Louvre. Mon–Fri 8 a.m.–9 p.m.; Sat 10 a.m.–6 p.m.*

Aux Négociants

The photographer Robert Doisneau came here often (his picture is on the wall), but today a discerning crowd of regulars keeps this tiny, unpretentious wine bar near Montmartre humming. The excellent pâtés and terrines are homemade and served with fresh, chewy bread.

27 rue Lambert, 18e. ☎ *01-46-06-15-11. Métro: Château-Rouge or Lamarck-Caulincourt. Mon–Fri noon to 2 p.m.; Tues–Fri 6:30–10:30 p.m.*

Bistro du Peintre

Painters, actors, and night crawlers hang out here nightly. The zinc bar, wood paneling, large terrace, and superb Belle Époque style would make this wine bar a highlight even if the wine selection were not so reasonably priced.

116 av. Ledru-Rollin, 11e. ☎ *01-47-00-34-39. Métro: Ledru-Rollin. Daily 7 a.m. to midnight.*

Clown Bar

You may just stand shoulder to shoulder with a real clown from the nearby Cirque d'Hiver. The bar is decorated with a mélange of circus posters and circus-themed ceramic tiles. The wine list features an extensive selection of French offerings.

114 rue Amelot, 11e. ☎ *01-43-55-87-35. Métro: Filles du Calvaire. Mon–Sat noon to 2:30 p.m. and 7 p.m.–1 a.m., Sun 7 p.m.–1 a.m.*

La Tartine

This is the wine bar that time forgot — pure unsophisticated prewar Paris, from the nicotine-browned walls and frosted globe chandeliers to the worn wood furniture. The ambience is funky and working-class, but a broad segment of society savors glasses of wine at the bar or lingers over a newspaper and a *tartine* (open-face sandwich) in the high-ceilinged room. This is one of the few wine bars in Paris open on Sunday.

24 rue de Rivoli, 4e. ☎ *01-42-72-76-85. Métro: St-Paul. Tues–Sat 7 a.m.–11:30 p.m.; Sun–Mon 10 a.m.–10 p.m.*

Le Griffonnier

A first-rate kitchen is here, and so is a terrific wine cellar. Sample bistro specialties such as *confit de canard maison,* or try a hearty plate of charcuterie, terrines, and cheese, usually from the Auvergne region of central France, and ask your waiter to recommend the wine. Hot meals are served only at lunchtime and Thursday evenings.

8 rue des Saussaies, 8e. ☎ *01-42-65-17-17. Métro: Champs-Elysées–Clemenceau. Mon–Fri 7:30 a.m.–9 p.m. Closed on major holidays.*

Le Sancerre

This quiet place is great for relaxing with a light meal or glass of wine after visiting the Tour Eiffel. Loire wines are the specialty, including, of course,

Sancerre. Le Sancerre serves typically French items, such as omelettes of all varieties with a side of fried potatoes, and duck-liver terrine. The more adventurous can sample the ubiquitous *andouillette*, sausage that is decidedly an acquired taste.

22 av. Rapp, 7e. ☎ *01-45-51-75-91. Métro: Alma Marceau. Mon–Fri 8 a.m.–10 p.m.; Sat 8:30 a.m.–4:30 p.m.*

Mélac

Owner Jacques Mélac has an excellent selection of wine from nearly all the regions of France, which he dispenses to a lively crowd of regulars. He's happy to give you recommendations. Usually a hot *plat du jour* is available for lunch, but you can feast on a selection of first-rate pâtés, terrines, charcuterie, and cheeses all day.

42 rue Léon Frot, 11e. ☎ *01-43-70-59-27. Métro: Charonne. Mon–Sat 9 a.m.–3 p.m. and 7:30–10:00 p.m.*

Taverne Henri IV

Although on the expensive side, the wine and food are excellent at this authentic, old-fashioned bar where regulars, mostly male, read the newspaper, discuss the news of the day, and smoke nonstop. The variety of wines by the glass can accompany open-faced sandwiches (including warm goat cheese), pâtés, and such cheeses as Cantal and Auvergne blue.

13 place du Pont Neuf, 1er. ☎ *01-43-54-27-90. Métro: Pont-Neuf. Mon–Fri noon to 10 p.m.; Sat noon to 4 p.m.*

Willi's Wine Bar

Willi's has become a Paris institution since it opened in 1980. You can sample 250 different varieties of wine while sitting at the polished oak bar or have dinner in the high-ceilinged oak beamed dining room from a full menu of main courses costing just 25€ to 35€ ($30 to $42). Each year, the owners commission an image relating to wine from an artist, and the colorful paintings are available for sale as prints for between 38€ to 200€ ($46 to $240).

13 rue des Petits-Champs, 1er. ☎ *01-42-61-05-09. Métro: Bourse or Pyramides. Mon–Sat noon to 2:30 p.m. and 7–11 p.m.; bar open Mon–Sat noon to midnight.*

Chapter 12

Exploring Paris

● ●

In This Chapter

▶ Checking out the top attractions in Paris
▶ Taking a guided tour of Paris
▶ Finding the best places to shop
▶ Experiencing Paris's nightlife

● ●

*I*n this chapter, we review fewer than 20 of the best of Paris's many attractions, but that's still probably more than you'll be able to visit in a single trip. But you can make use of two multiattraction passes that are designed especially with busy visitors in mind, though only one of them is a good deal.

If you plan to visit two or three museums a day, purchase the **Carte Musées et Monuments,** on sale at most major museums and Métro stations. It provides for free entry to 70 attractions and monuments in and around Paris, including the Musée du Louvre and the Musée d'Orsay. (*Note:* The Tour Eiffel does not accept it.) The pass costs 18€ ($22) for one day, 36€ ($43) for three days, and 54€ ($65) for five days. Another benefit? When using the pass, you don't have to stand in line at attractions, a distinct plus on a hot day in the Louvre's courtyard.

The not-so-good deal is the **Paris Visite** card, available at most Métro stations and good for unlimited travel for one, two, three, or five days. Although it has discounts for some museums and monuments, unless they are sights you want to see (a brochure lists discounted sights), the card turns out to be quite expensive. Costs for a **Paris Visite** card range from 8.50€ ($10) for one day to 26.65€ ($32) for five days.

The Top Attractions: From the Arc to the Tour

In addition to the top attractions listed here (and shown on the "Paris's Top Attractions" map), make time for a cruise on the Seine River. For details, check out the "Cruising the Seine" section later in this chapter.

Paris's Top Attractions

Arc de Triomphe **1**
Basilique du Sacré-Coeur **10**
Cathédrale de Notre-Dame **16**
Centre Georges Pompidou **12**
Champs-Elysées **3**
Cimitière du Père-Lachaise **13**
Hôtel des Invalides
  (Napoléon's Tomb) **5**
Jardin and Palais du
  Luxembourg **8**
Jardin des Tuileries **9**
Jardin du Palais-Royal **13**
Musée d'Orsay **7**
Musée du Louvre **11**
Musée Jacquemart-André **2**
Musée Nationale d'Auguste
  Rodin **6**
Musée Picasso **14**
Panthéon **19**
Parc Zoologique de Paris **20**
Place des Vosges **15**
Sainte-Chapelle and
  Conciergerie **17**
Tour Eiffel **4**

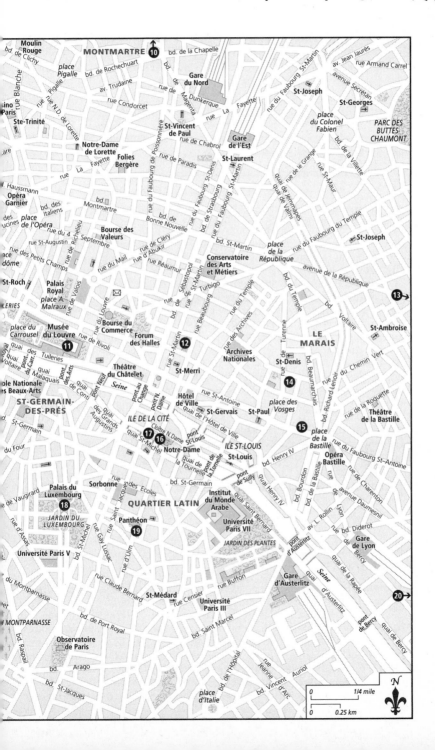

Avoiding traffic around the Arc de Triomphe

After you arrive at the Arc, you don't want to tangle with the traffic that zips around the circle. To reach the stairs and elevators that climb the Arc, take the underpass using the white Métro entrances. Don't try to cross on surface streets. Attempting to dodge the warp-speed traffic zooming around the circle will likely get you seriously hurt.

Arc de Triomphe
Champs-Elysées (8e)

Arc de Triomphe is the largest triumphal arch in the world, commissioned by Napoléon to honor his army and its 128 victorious battles. Although the Arc has witnessed the agony of defeat, as in 1871 when Paris was seized by the Prussians during the Franco-Prussian War, and in 1940, when Nazi armies marched through the arch and down the Champs-Elysées, it better symbolizes the thrill of victory. De Gaulle striding through the Arc to symbolize Paris's liberation in 1944 is one of the country's most cherished memories. The racers in the Tour de France ride up the Champs and around the Arc on the race's last day. Today the Arc houses the Tomb of the Unknown Soldier, which was dedicated in 1921 to honor the 1.5 million French soldiers who died during World War I; every evening at 6:30 the flame is symbolically relit. The panoramic view, however, is the real draw for visitors. From the top, 49 meters (162 ft.) up, you can see in a straight line the Champs-Elysées, the obelisk in the place de la Concorde, and the Louvre. That big cube at the far end is the Grande Arche de la Défense in St-Denis, built to be the modern equivalent to this Arc. Allow an hour to visit, an hour and a half in high summer.

See map p. 172. Place Charles-de-Gaulle, 8e. ☎ *01-55-37-73-77. www.monum.fr. Métro: Charles de Gaulle–Étoile. Bus: 22, 30, 31, 52, 73, 92. Admission: 7€ ($8.40) adults, 4.50€ ($5.40) ages 18–25, free for children younger than 18. Open: Daily Apr–Sept 10 a.m.–11 p.m.; Oct–Mar 10 a.m.–10:30 p.m. Closed major holidays.*

Basilique du Sacré-Coeur
Montmartre (18e)

The white Byzantine–Romanesque church dominating Paris's highest hill — the one that you can see from all across the city — is Basilique du Sacré-Coeur, built between 1876, after France's defeat in the Franco-Prussian War, to 1919. The best reason to come here is for the city-spanning views from its dome — visibility is nearly 50 kilometers (about 30 miles) across the rooftops of Paris on a clear day. The climb from church floor to dome, however, is on a flight of nail-bitingly steep corkscrew steps. A better idea, and one that kids enjoy, is to conserve your pre-Dome climbing energy by taking the elevator up from the Anvers Métro station, walking the short distance from rue Steinkerque and turning left onto rue Tardieu, where a *funiculaire* (kind of a cable car) whisks you from the base of the Montmartre butte right up to the outside of the church. The church's interior is not as striking as its exterior and is, in fact, vaguely depressing.

On the other side of Sacré-Coeur is the **place du Tertre,** where Vincent van Gogh once lived; he used it as a scene for one of his paintings. The place is usually swamped by tourists and quick-sketch artists in the spring and summer. Following any street downhill from place du Tertre leads to the quiet side of Montmartre. The steps in front of the church come alive around dusk, when street musicians entertain the crowd gathered to watch the city's lights come on. Be alert: pickpockets are all around Montmartre.

See map p. 172. 35 rue du Chevalier-de-la-Barre. ☎ *01-53-41-89-00.* www.sacre-coeur-montmartre.com. *Métro: Abbesses. Take elevator to surface and follow signs to funiculaire, which runs to the church (fare: 1 Métro ticket). Bus: The only bus that goes to the top of the hill is the local Montmartrobus. Admission: To basilica, free; to dome, 5€ ($6) adults. Open: Basilica daily 6 a.m.–11 p.m. Dome and crypt daily 9:30 a.m.–6:30 p.m.*

Cathédrale de Notre-Dame
Ile de la Cité (4e)

Crusaders prayed here before leaving for the holy wars. Napoléon crowned himself emperor on site and then crowned his wife, Josephine, empress. When Paris was liberated during World War II, General de Gaulle rushed to this cathedral to give thanks.

Construction of Notre-Dame started in 1163, when Pope Alexander III laid the cornerstone, and was completed in the 14th century. Built in an age of illiteracy, the cathedral windows tell the stories of the Bible in its portals, paintings, and stained glass. Angry citizens pillaged Notre-Dame during the French Revolution, mistaking religious statues above the portals on the west front for representations of kings and beheading them.

Nearly 100 years later, when Notre-Dame had been turned into a barn, writer Victor Hugo and other artists called attention to Notre-Dame's dangerous state of disrepair, and architect Viollet-le-Duc began the much-needed restoration. He designed Notre-Dame's spire, a new feature, and Baron Haussmann (Napoléon III's urban planner) evicted the residents of the houses that cluttered the cathedral's vicinity and tore down the houses for better views of the cathedral.

Before entering, walk around to the east end of the church to appreciate the spectacular flying buttresses. On a sunny morning catch the giant rose windows — which retain some of their 13th-century stained glass — in all their glory. The highlight for kids is undoubtedly climbing the 387 narrow and winding steps to the top of one of the towers for a fabulously Quasimodo view of the gargoyles and of Paris. *Word of advice:* If you plan to visit the tower, go early in the morning. Lines stretch down the square in front of the cathedral in the summer.

See map p. 172. 6 place du Parvis Notre-Dame. ☎ *01-42-34-56-10.* www.monum.fr. *Métro: Cité or St-Michel. RER: St-Michel. Bus: 21, 38, 85, 96. Admission: To church, free; to tower, 6.10€ ($7.30) adults, 4.10€ ($4.90) ages 18–25 and seniors, younger than 18 free. Free guided visits (for groups only) in English noon Wed, Thurs. Open: Cathedral daily 8 a.m.–6:45 p.m. (closed Sat 12:30–2 p.m.); treasury Mon–Sat 9:30 a.m.–5:30 p.m. Six masses celebrated on Sun, four on weekdays, one on Sat.*

Centre Georges Pompidou
Le Marais (3e, 4e)

Since its opening in 1966, the Centre National d'Art et de Culture Georges Pompidou was so surprisingly popular that more visitors than ever expected, about 160 million, caused the building to begin crumbling. It closed for three years starting in 1997 and underwent a renovation that cost more than $100 million. Its reopening on January 1, 2000, was planned to coincide with the new century. The renovation didn't change at all the brightly colored escalators, elevators, air-conditioning, and tubular passages resembling a giant gerbil habitat that run along the building's outside, but the inside is more of a spacious haven in which to view, touch, or listen to modern art and artists. The newer of Paris's two modern art museums, the Centre Georges Pompidou includes two floors of work from the Musée National d'Art Moderne, France's national collection of modern art. The Centre Pompidou also houses a cinema and a huge public library; spaces for modern dance and music; temporary exhibits that often include video and computer works; and nearly 150 drawings, paintings, and other works by Romanian sculptor Constantin Brancusi in the Brancusi Atelier, a small building near the museum's entrance.

British architect Richard Rogers and Italian architect Renzo Piano designed the building in the late 1960s as part of a redevelopment plan for the Beaubourg neighborhood. The nearby Igor Stravinsky fountain (with no admission charge) has fun sculptures by Tinguely and Niki de Saint Phalle that include red lips spitting water, a mermaid squirting water from "strategic" body parts, and a twirling grinning skull.

You must purchase a ticket to the Centre Pompidou to take in the rooftop panorama, but if visiting the museum just doesn't appeal, consider stopping at the Pompidou's ultrahip top-floor Restaurant Georges. For the same price as an adult's full-package admission (10€/$12), you can relax with a glass of wine and enjoy the view from indoors.

See map p. 172. Place Georges-Pompidou. ☎ *01-44-78-12-33.* www.centre pompidou.fr. *Métro: Rambuteau, Hôtel-de-Ville, or Châtelet–Les Halles. Bus: 21, 29, 38, 47, 58, 69, 70, 72, 74, 75, 76, 81, 85, 86. A one-day package to all exhibits, the Brancusi Atelier, and the Musée National d'Art Moderne is 10€ ($12) adults, 8€ ($9.60) ages 18–25, free for children younger than 18; admission to exhibits only is 7€ ($8.40) adults, 5€ ($6) ages 13–25, free for children younger than 13. All admissions free the first Sun of the month. Open: Wed–Mon 11 a.m.–9 p.m.*

Notre-Dame de Paris

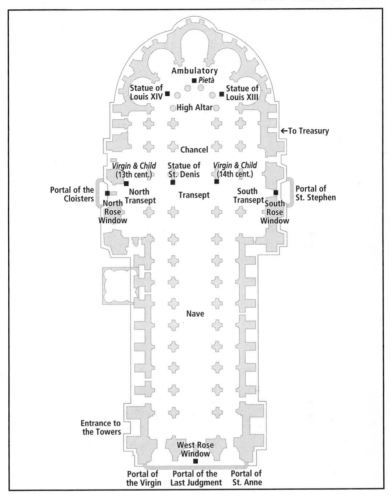

Ambulatory
■ *Pietà*
Statue of ■ ○ ○ ○ ● Statue of
Louis XIV   Louis XIII
○High Altar○

←To Treasury

Chancel

Virgin & Child   Statue of   *Virgin & Child*
(13th cent.)   St. Denis   (14th cent.)

Portal of the   North   South   Portal of
Cloisters   North Transept   Transept   Transept South   St. Stephen
North   South
Rose   Rose
Window   Window

Nave

Entrance to
the Towers

West Rose
Window
■

Portal of   Portal of the   Portal of
the Virgin   Last Judgment   St. Anne

Champs-Elysées
Champs-Elysées (8e)

If you were in Paris when the French won the World and Euro Cup soccer championships (1998 and 2000, respectively), you understand what the Champs-Elysées means to the French. As close to a million singing, flag-waving Parisians spilled into the avenue, it was said the country hadn't experienced such group euphoria since the days following the Liberation of Paris by the Allies in 1944. The Champs also overlooked the city's biggest New Year's party; in 2000, crowds of people gathered here to watch astonishing fireworks and cheer the new century. The Champs is the avenue where the military march on Bastille Day, and the Tour de France ends here. The scene on France's most famous street is liveliest at night, with people lining up for the numerous cinemas (see English-language-films here by looking for *v.o.* [for *version originale*] on schedules and movie posters) and floodlights illuminating the Arc de Triomphe and place de la Concorde. Restaurants consist mainly of standard chain cafes (Chez Clément, Hippo) and American-style fast food (McDonald's), though good restaurants abound on the streets surrounding the avenue (see Chapter 11). You can shop at reasonably priced stores, such as Zara, and the very *luxe* (Louis Vuitton), and at the kind of chain stores you'd see in any American mall (the Disney Store, Quiksilver). Many of the stores are open on Sunday. Allow an hour and a half to walk from top to bottom, longer if you want to shop, eat, or dawdle.

See map p. 172. Champs-Elysées (8e). Métro: Concorde, Champs-Elysées Clémenceau, Franklin-D-Roosevelt, George V, Charles de Gaulle–Étoile. Bus: Many lines cross it, but only 73 travels its entire length.

Cimitière du Père-Lachaise
Montmartre and Beyond (20e)

Cresting a high hill overlooking Paris, the world's most visited cemetery is more outdoor museum than place of mourning. No wonder Parisians have always come here to stroll and reflect; with its winding, cobbled streets, park benches, and street signs, the 44½ hectare (110-acre) Père Lachaise is a mini-city unto itself. Many visitors leave flowers or notes scrawled on Métro tickets for their favorite celebrity residents, who include Isadora Duncan, Edith Piaf, Oscar Wilde, Chopin, Jim Morrison, Modigliani, Molière, Pissarro, Proust, Sarah Bernhardt, and Gertrude Stein. If you're interested in nothing else, go for the striking and often poignant statuary: the boy who seems to sit up in bed as if he'd heard a noise; the young woman who's frozen, mid-dance, as if turned to stone without warning. You can obtain a free map from the gatekeeper at the main entrance, but a better map is sold outside the entrance for 3€ ($3.60). Allow at least two hours to visit.

See map p. 172. 16 rue du Repos. Main entrance on bd. du Ménilmontant. Métro: Père-Lachaise. Bus: 60, 69, 102. Admission: free. Open: Mar 16–Nov 5 Mon–Fri 8 a.m.–6 p.m., Sat 8:30 a.m.–6 p.m., Sun 9 a.m.–6 p.m.; Nov 6–Mar 15 Mon–Fri 8 a.m.–5:30 p.m., Sat 8:30 a.m.–5:30 p.m., Sun 9 a.m.–5:30 p.m.

Hôtel des Invalides (Napoléon's Tomb)
Tour Eiffel and Invalides (7e)

Invalides was built by Louis XIV, who liked war and waged many, as a hospital and home for veteran officers and soldiers. It still has offices for departments of the French armed forces, and part of it still is a hospital. The best way to get the sense of awe that the Hôtel des Invalides inspires is to walk to it by crossing the Alexander III bridge. The dome of **Église du Dôme** (gilded with 12 kilograms/27 lbs. of real gold) is one of the high points of classical art, rising 107 meters (351 ft.) from the ground. Sixteen green copper cannons point outward in a powerful display.

Enemy flags captured during the military campaigns of the 19th and 20th centuries hang from the rafters in two impressive rows at the **Église de St-Louis,** known as the Church of the Soldiers, but most visitors come to see the **Tomb of Napoléon,** where the emperor is buried in six coffins, one inside the other, under the great dome. The first coffin is iron, the second is mahogany, the third and fourth are lead, the fifth is ebony, and the outermost is oak. The emperor's remains were transferred here 20 years after his death in 1820 on the island of St. Helena, where he was exiled following his defeat at Waterloo.

Musée de l'Armée — admission is included when you buy your ticket for Napoléon's tomb — is one of the world's greatest military museums. It features thousands of weapons from prehistory to World War II, such as spearheads, arrowheads, maces, cannons, and guns, in addition to battle flags, booty, suits of armor, and uniforms from all around the world. The De Gaulle wing tells the story of World War II on touch screens, with videos, a decoding machine, and other artifacts. Set aside two hours for a complete visit or a half-hour to see the tomb.

See map p. 172. Esplanade des Invalides. ☎ *01-44-42-37-72. Métro: Latour-Maubourg, Invalides, or Varenne. Bus: 63, 83, 93. Admission: 7€ ($8.40) adults, 5€ ($6) children 12–17, free for children younger than 18. Open: Daily Oct–Mar 10 a.m.–5 p.m.; Apr–Sept 10 a.m. 6 p.m. Tomb of Napoléon open until 6:45 p.m. June–Sept. Closed major holidays.*

Jardin and Palais du Luxembourg
St-Germain-des-Prés (6e)

Not far from the Sorbonne (a branch of the Université de Paris) and just south of the Latin Quarter is the 6th arrondissement's **Jardin du Luxembourg,** one of Paris's most beloved parks. Children love it for its playground, toy-boat pond, pony rides, and puppet theater. Besides pools, fountains, and statues of queens and poets, the park has tennis and *boules* courts (*boule* means *ball;* in this game, players compete to see who can roll their small steel ball closest to a larger steel ball that lies farther down the court). The park was commissioned by King Henri IV's queen, Marie de Médici, who also had the **Palais du Luxembourg** built at the northern edge of the park. The Palais resembles the Palazzo Pitti in Florence, where Marie had spent her childhood and for which she was homesick. When the queen was banished in 1630, the palace was abandoned until the Revolution, when it was used as a prison. It is now the seat of the French Senate and is not open to the public. Orchards in the park's southwest corner contain 360 varieties of apples, 270 kinds of pears, and various grapevines. Members of the French Senate get to eat the fruit, but leftovers go to a soup kitchen. Walk north, and you come across a bevy of beehives behind a low fence. A beekeeping (apiculture) course is taught here weekends. Try to find the Statue of Liberty tucked away nearby.

See map p. 172. Main entrance at the corner of bd. St-Michel and rue des Médicis. ☎ *01-43-29-12-78. Métro: Odéon. RER: Luxembourg, Port-Royal. Bus: 38, 82, 84, 85, 89. Admission: free. Open: Daily dawn to dusk.*

Jardin des Tuileries
Louvre (1er)

The Tuileries are a great place to rest your feet and catch some rays on conveniently placed wrought-iron chairs surrounding the garden's fountains. In keeping with the French style of parks, trees are planted according to orderly design, and the sandy paths are arrow straight. Spread out across 25 hectares (63 acres), the city's most formal gardens originally ran between the Louvre and the Palais des Tuileries, which was burned down during the 1871 Paris Commune. You can get a light snack at one of the outdoor cafes. During the summer, a carnival features an enormous Ferris wheel (with panoramic views of the city), a log flume, a funhouse, arcade-style games, snacks, and machine-made soft ice cream (but the best is the homemade ice cream sold from a stand beyond the Arc de Triomphe du Carrousel at the entrance to the Tuileries). Come for a stroll before or after visiting the Louvre.

See map p. 172. Entrances on rue de Rivoli and place de la Concorde. Métro: Concorde or Tuileries. Bus: 42, 69, 72, 73, 94. Admission: free. Free guided visits of the gardens (in French) Sun, Wed, Fri 3 p.m. Open: Daily 8 a.m. to dusk.

Jardin du Palais-Royal
Louvre (1er)

In 1630, Cardinal Richelieu ordered the Royal Palace built as his personal residence, complete with grounds landscaped by the royal gardener. Today the palace is no longer open to the public, but its statue-filled gardens,

---

The scoop on Paris ice cream

Rhubarb, plum, cassis, honey nut . . . if Paris doesn't have the best ice cream in the world, it must run a close second. Such flavors, such creaminess. Ask for a *cornet seule* (single-scoop cone) or *cornet double* (double-scoop) — even the cone is delicious. Prices range from 1.20€ ($1.45) for a single to 3€ ($3.60) for a double-scoop cone. Most places open daily around 10:30 a.m. and close around 8 p.m. Remember, though, that sitting down to order ice cream is always more expensive; it can be twice as much as ordering your cone to go. The best ice cream is at **Berthillon** (31 rue St-Louis-en-l'Ile, 4e; ☎ 01-43-54-31-61; Métro: Cité). Though Berthillon closes from July 15 through the first week in September, a note on the door directs customers to other nearby shops that sell its ice cream. The following also put soft-serve to shame:

✔ **Dammam's:** 20 rue Cardinal Lemoine, 5e; ☎ 01-46-33-61-30; Métro: Cardinal Lemoine.

✔ **La Butte Glacée:** 14 rue Norvins, 18e; ☎ 01-42-23-91-58; Métro: Abbesses.

✔ **Le Bac à Glaces:** 109 rue du Bac, 7e; ☎ 01-45-48-87-65; Métro: Rue du Bac.

✔ **Octave:** 138 rue Mouffetard, 5e; ☎ 01-45-35-20-56; Métro: Sonvier Daubanton.

including the controversial prison-striped columns built in 1986 (which make a great photo op), remain one of the most restful places in the city. The square is also ringed by restaurants, art galleries, and specialty boutiques, and is home to the Comédie Française.

See map p. 172. Entrances on rue de Rivoli and place de la Concorde. Métro: Concorde or Tuileries. Bus: 42, 69, 72, 73, 94. Admission: free. Open: Daily 7:30 a.m. to dusk.

Musée d'Orsay
Tour Eiffel and Invalides (7e)

Most visitors to Paris go to the Louvre because they feel they have to; they go to the Musée d'Orsay because they want to. It's a wonder. Take a moment at the top of the central staircase to envision where the trains once pulled into this former train station under the curved roof. Then enjoy the Musée d'Orsay's real claim to fame — its unsurpassed collection of Impressionist masterpieces. The museum has three floors of exhibits. On the ground floor are Ingres's *La Source,* Millet's *L'Angelus,* the Barbizon school, Manet's *Olympia,* and other works of early Impressionism. Impressionism continues on the top level, with Renoir's *Le Moulin de la Galette,* Manet's *Déjeuner sur l'Herbe,* Degas's *Racing at Longchamps,* Monet's cathedrals, van Gogh's *Self-Portrait,* and Whistler's *Portrait of the Artist's Mother.* You also find works by Gauguin and the Pont-Aven school, Toulouse-Lautrec, Pissarro, Cézanne, and Seurat. Symbolism, naturalism, and Art Nouveau are represented on the middle level; the international Art Nouveau exhibit includes furniture, *objets d'art,* and Koloman Moser's *Paradise,* a beautiful design for stained glass. Give yourself three hours, including a lunch break in the museum's gorgeous, turn-of-the-20th-century Musée d'Orsay restaurant on the middle level. For less expensive and quicker light bites, try the Café des Hauteurs on the fifth floor (with a view of the Seine through its clock window) or the snack bar on the mezzanine.

See map p. 172. 62 rue de Lille/1 rue Bellechasse. ☎ *01-40-49-48-14 or 01-40-49-48-48 for information desk.* www.musee-orsay.fr. *Métro: Solférino. RER: Musée-d'Orsay. Bus: 24, 63, 68, 69, 73, 83, 94, 94. Admission: 7€ ($8.40) adults; 5€ ($6) ages 18–24 and seniors and on Sun; free for children younger than 18. Free the first Sun of every month. (Note: Admission may cost more to include major temporary exhibits.) Open: Tues–Wed and Fri–Sat 10 a.m.–6 p.m.; Thurs 10 a.m.–9:45 p.m.; Sun 9 a.m.–6 p.m. From mid-June through the end of Sept, the museum opens at 9 a.m.*

Musée du Louvre
Louvre (1er)

The huge Louvre palace evolved over several centuries, first opening as a museum in 1793; with more than 30,000 treasures, it would take you a month of visits to see it all. A visit to the Louvre doesn't have to be overwhelming. In fact, three simple steps can help you have an enjoyable Louvre experience: 1. Decide what you want to see before you go, and see it first. 2. Pick up a free map of the Louvre at the information desk under the pyramid, or purchase a guide. The Louvre bookstore in the Carrousel de Louvre sells many comprehensive guides and maps in English; you can also get brochures for "visitors in a hurry" or a guidebook, "The Louvre, First Visit." 3. Take a guided tour. You can try the 90-minute tour by a museum guide (☎ 01-40-20-52-63) that covers the most popular works and gives you a quick orientation to the museum's layout. If you prefer to set your own pace, you can rent a four-hour "audiotour" (5€/$6) at the entrance to any of the wings.

The Louvre is organized in three wings — Sully, Denon, and Richelieu — over four floors exhibiting art and antiquities from Oriental, Islamic, Egyptian, Greek, Etruscan, Roman, Oceanic, European, and North and South American civilizations, as well as sculpture, *objets d'art*, paintings, prints, drawings, and the moats and dungeon of the medieval Louvre fortress.

If you're in a hurry but want to do the Louvre on your own, take a quick "best of the Louvre" tour. Start with Leonardo da Vinci's *Mona Lisa* (Denon wing, first floor). On the same floor nearby are two more of the Louvre's most famous French paintings: Géricault's *The Raft of Medusa* and Delacroix's *Liberty Guiding the People*. Next, visit the *Winged Victory* and Michelangelo's *Slaves* (both Denon wing, ground floor) before seeing *The Venus de Milo* (Sully wing, ground floor). After that, let your own interests guide you. Consider that only Florence's Uffizi Gallery rivals the Denon wing for its Italian Renaissance collection, which includes Raphael's *Portrait of Balthazar Castiglione* and Titian's *Man with a Glove*. The revamped Egyptian-antiquities department is the largest exhibition of Egyptian antiquities outside Cairo.

See map p. 172. Rue de Rivoli. ☎ 01-40-20-50-50 for recorded message, 01-40-20-53-17 for information desk. www.louvre.fr. Métro: Palais-Royal–Musée du Louvre. Admission: 8.50€ ($9.60) adults; 6€ ($7.20) after 6 p.m. and on Sun; free first Sun of month, Bastille Day (July 14), and for children younger than 18. Tours in English (call 01-40-20-51-77 for hours) 14.50€ ($17). Open: Mon (certain rooms only) and Wed 9 a.m.–9:45 p.m.; Thurs–Sun 9 a.m.–6 p.m. Closed Tues.

Musée Jacquemart-André
Champs-Elysées (8e)

The combination of an outstanding art collection and a gorgeous 19th-century mansion makes this museum one of the jewels of Paris and a paradise for Renaissance art fans. It's worth visiting as much for a glimpse of how filthy-rich Parisians lived in the 19th century as for its Italian and Flemish masterpieces by Bellini, Botticelli, Carpaccio, Uccello, Rubens, Rembrandt, and van Eyck. Edouard André, the heir of a prominent banking family, and his wife, Nélie Jacquemart, a well-known portraitist, commissioned architect Henri Parent to build their "house" and then set about filling it with French, Flemish, and Italian paintings, furniture, and tapestries. Highlights of the collection include Rembrandt's *Docteur Tholinx,* Van Dyck's *Time Cutting the Wings of Love,* a fresco by Jean Baptiste Tiepolo, Fragonard's naturalistic *Portrait d'un Vieillard,* and a portrait of *Catherine Skavronskaia* by Elisabeth Vigée-Lebrun, one of Marie Antoinette's favorite artists. As you wander the ornate gilt-ridden rooms, pause in the "winter garden," a tour de force of marble and mirrors flanking an unusual double

The Louvre

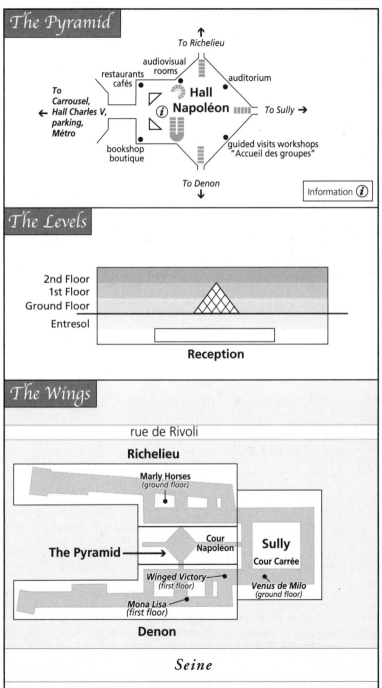

Some Louvre tips

The main entrance to the Louvre is through I.M. Pei's glass pyramid in the courtyard; pregnant women, visitors with children in strollers, and travelers with disabilities have priority. You'll almost always find a long, slow line here, and you can get in faster at one of the Louvre's other entrances: at 99 rue de Rivoli, where you take an escalator downstairs through the Carrousel du Louvre passage filled with stores; through the Jardins du Carrousel entrance near the Arc de Triomphe du Carrousel off the courtyard; or the Porte des Lions entrance between the Jardins du Carrousel and the quai des Tuileries.

If you already have tickets or have the Carte Musées et Monuments, you can use the special entrance at the **passage Richelieu** between rue de Rivoli and the courtyard.

Order tickets by phone from FNAC ☎ **08-92-68-46-94** (0.34€/40¢ per minute), and pick them up at any FNAC store (except FNAC photo shops). A 1.60€ ($1.90) commission is charged by FNAC. A nearby branch is at Forum des Halles, 1 rue Pierre Lescure. You can also buy Louvre tickets at Le Printemps, Galeries Lafayette, Le Bon Marché, and BHV; ask at the information desks in these stores.

staircase. Take advantage of the free audio narrative that guides you through the mansion. Allow an hour for your visit, and then take a break in what was Madame Jacquemart's lofty-ceilinged dining room, now a tearoom serving light lunches and snacks.

See map p. 172. 158 bd. Haussmann, 8e. ☎ *01-45-62-11-59.* www.musee-jacquemart-andre.com/jandre/home_en.htm. *Métro: Miromesnil. Bus: 22, 52, 83, 93. Admission: 8.50€ ($10) adults; 6.50€ ($7.80) students and children younger than 18. Open: Daily (including Christmas) 10 a.m.–6 p.m.*

Musée Nationale d'Auguste Rodin
Tour Eiffel and Invalides (7e)

Auguste Rodin, regarded by many as the greatest sculptor of all time, lived and worked here from 1908 until his death in 1917. His legendary sensuality, which outraged 19th-century critics, is expressed here in this collection that includes all of his greatest works. *The Kiss* immortalizes in white marble the passion of doomed 13th-century lovers Paolo Malatesta and Francesca da Rimini. In the courtyard, *Burghers of Calais* is a harrowing commemoration of the siege of Calais in 1347, after which the triumphant Edward III of England kept the town's six richest burghers as servants. Also in the courtyard is *The Thinker*. The *Gates of Hell* is a portrayal of Dante's *Inferno*. Intended for the Musée des Arts Decoratifs, the massive bronze doors were not completed until seven years after Rodin's death. The museum is in the 18th-century Hôtel Biron, which was a convent before it became a residence for artists and writers. Matisse, Jean Cocteau, and the poet Rainer Maria Rilke lived and worked in the mansion before Rodin moved here at the height of his popularity. Spend at least 90 minutes in the museum. If you don't have a lot of time or money, pay the 1€ ($1.20) admission to visit just the gardens, where Rodin's works stand among 2,000 rosebushes. Allow at least an hour to visit the garden, longer if you want to break for coffee in the garden cafe.

See map p. 172. Hôtel Biron, 77 rue de Varenne, 7e. ☎ *01-44-18-61-10.* www.musee-rodin.fr. *Métro: Varenne. Bus: 69, 82, 87, 92. Admission: 5€ ($6) adults; 3€ ($3.60) ages 18–24 and seniors and on Sun; 1€ ($1.20) for garden only; free for children younger than 18. Open: Apr–Sept Tues–Sun 9:30 a.m.–5:45 p.m.; Oct–Mar Tues–Sun 9:30 a.m.–4:45 p.m. Garden closes at 6:45 p.m. in summer, 5 p.m. in winter, last admittance one hour before.*

Musée Picasso
Le Marais (3e)

You can pay a visit to the Musée Picasso on each trip to Paris and see something different each time (the works are rotated). The museum was created in 1973 by Picasso's heirs, who donated his personal art collection to the state in lieu of paying outrageous inheritance taxes after his death. The spectacular collection includes more than 200 paintings, almost 160 sculptures, 88 ceramics, and more than 3,000 prints and drawings — every phase of Picasso's prolific 75-year career is represented. Works can be viewed chronologically; budget at least a few hours here, if not more. The museum also displays works by other artists collected by Picasso, including Corot, Cézanne, Braque, Rousseau, Matisse, and Renoir. The 17th-century Hôtel Salé housing it all (the name *Salé* means *salty;* the former owner was a salt-tax collector) has a gorgeous carved stairway and is worth a visit in its own right.

See map p. 172. Hôtel Salé, 5 rue de Thorigny. ☎ *01-42-71-25-21. Métro: Chemin-Vert, St-Paul, or Filles du Calvaire. Bus: 29, 96. Admission: 5.50€ ($6.60) adults; 4€ ($4.80) ages 18–25 and on Sun; free for children younger than 18. Free the first Sun of each month. Open: Apr–Sept Wed–Mon 9:30 a.m.–6 p.m.; Oct–Mar Wed–Mon 9:30 a.m.–5:30 p.m.*

Panthéon
Latin Quarter (5e)

The Panthéon is to France what Westminster Abbey is to England: a final resting place for many of the nation's greatest citizens. Inside the domed church's barrel-vaulted crypt are the tombs of Voltaire, Rousseau, Hugo, Braille, and Zola. André Malraux was the last to be entombed here in 1996. Louis XV originally built the Panthéon as a church in thanksgiving to St-Geneviève after his recovery from gout. Construction started in 1755, but after the French Revolution, the church was renamed the Panthéon, in remembrance of ancient Rome's Pantheon, and rededicated as a burying ground for France's heroes. All Christian elements were removed, and windows were blocked. From 1806–84, officials turned the Panthéon back into a church two more times before finally declaring it what it currently is today. You can't miss the Panthéon at night; it's lit from the inside with eerie blue lights that give it the appearance of a UFO — or a trendy disco.

See map p. 172. Place du Panthéon. ☎ *01-44-32-18-00.* www.monum.fr. *Métro: Maubert-Mutualité. Bus: 21, 27, 83, 84, 85, 89. Admission: 7€ ($8.40) adults; 4.50€ ($5.40) ages 18–25; free for children younger than 18. Open: Daily Apr–Sept 10 a.m.– 5:45 p.m.; Oct–Mar 10 a.m.–5:15 p.m.*

Place des Vosges
Le Marais (4e)

The most beautiful square in Paris sits right in the middle of Le Marais — a symmetrical block of 36 rose-colored townhouses, nine on each side, with handsome slate roofs and dormer windows. At ground level is a lovely arcaded walkway that's now home to galleries, cafes, antiques dealers, and smart boutiques. In the early 17th century, Henri IV transformed this area into the most prestigious neighborhood in France, putting his royal palace here, and the square quickly became the center of courtly parades and festivities. After the Revolution, it became place de l'Indivisibilité and later place des Vosges, in honor of the first *département* in France that completely paid its taxes. Victor Hugo lived at no. 6 for 16 years. Allow 30 minutes to walk all the way around the square under the arcades and for a brief stroll in the park.

See map p. 172. Métro: St-Paul. Bus: 69, 76, 96.

Sainte-Chapelle
Ile de la Cité (4e)

If you save Sainte-Chapelle for a sunny day, its 15 perfect stained-glass windows soaring 15 meters (50 ft.) high to a star-studded vaulted ceiling will take your breath away. You may think you've stepped into a kaleidoscope by mistake. Louis IX, the only French king to become a saint, had Sainte-Chapelle ("Holy Chapel") built as a shrine to house relics of the crucifixion, including the Crown of Thorns that Louis bought from the Emperor of Constantinople. Building Sainte-Chapelle certainly cost less than the outrageously expensive Crown of Thorns, which was said to have been acquired at the Crucifixion and now resides in the vault at Notre-Dame.

Built between 1246 and 1248, Sainte-Chapelle has two chapels, one on top of the other. Palace servants used the *chapelle basse* (lower chapel), ornamented with fleur-de-lis designs. The *chapelle haute* (upper chapel, accessed by 30 winding steps) is one of the highest achievements of Gothic art. If you spend the time (which can take hours or even a day), you would see that the 1,134 scenes in the stained glass of the 15 windows trace the Biblical story from the Garden of Eden to the Apocalypse. The first window to the right represents the story of the Crown of Thorns; St. Louis is shown several times. Some evenings, when the upper chapel becomes a venue for classical-music concerts, the effect of its chandelier lights dancing off the windows is magical.

See map p. 172. 4 bd. du Palais, Palais de Justice. ☎ *01-53-40-60-97.* www.monum. fr. *Métro: Cité or St-Michel. RER: St-Michel. Bus: 21, 27, 38, 85, 96. Admission: 6.10€ ($7.30) adults; 4.10€ ($4.90) 18–25; free for children younger than 18. Open: Daily Apr–Sept 9:30 a.m.–6 p.m. and Oct–Mar 9 a.m.–5 p.m. Closed major holidays.*

Amélie's Montmartre

This Right Bank neighborhood (18e) is for anyone who loved the 2001 film *The Fabulous Destiny of Amélie Poulain* (or simply *Amélie* in North America). The film's heroine, Amélie, lived here and worked in an actual Montmartre bar, Les Deux Moulins, located at 15 rue Lépic. You can get to Montmartre by taking the Métro to the Anvers or Abbesses stop, the entrance of which is graced by a fabulous Art Nouveau Métro sign. You can either walk to the top of the *butte* (hill) or take the *funiculaire* up, but we suggest that you walk from the Anvers Métro station the short distance from rue Steinkerque and turn left onto rue Tardieu, where the *funiculaire* whisks you from the base of the Montmartre butte right up to the outside of Sacré-Coeur. After visiting Sacré-Coeur and the touristy, but fun, place du Tertre, a square with overpriced restaurants and artists clamoring to sketch your portrait, wander down the hill and stumble across Paris from another era — surprisingly unspoiled lanes, quiet squares, ivy-clad shuttered houses with gardens, and even Paris's only vineyard. Together, they create a sense of the rustic village it once was.

Tour Eiffel
Tour Eiffel and Invalides (7e)

Did you know the Tour Eiffel has its own post office? Anything you mail from here is postmarked with a Tour Eiffel stamp. Did you know the tower is lit up at night by 336 projectors with bulbs ranging from 150 to 1,000 watts? We could fill an entire page with trivia about Paris's most famous symbol. (Did you know that it weighs 7,000 tons, soars 321 meters [1,056 ft.], and is held together with 2.5 million rivets?) But what you really want to know are the practicalities: *Do I have to climb stairs? Do elevators go to the top? Are there bathrooms? Are there snacks? Can I ascend in a wheelchair?*

The tower has three levels that are all accessible by elevator. No elevator goes directly from ground level to the top; you must change elevators at the second level. Though you can take stairs from the ground to the first and second levels, you cannot take stairs from the second level to the top. Most likely you'll wait in a specially roped-off line for elevators on the first and second levels. In high season, the wait can sometimes be as long an hour — for each line. Bathrooms are on each level, and snack bars and souvenir stands are on the first and second levels. Wheelchair access is available for the second level but not to the top.

Gustave Eiffel beat 699 others in a contest to design what was supposed to be a temporary monument for the Exposition Universelle (World's Fair) in 1889. His designs for the tower spanned 5,016 sq.m (6,000 sq. yds.) of paper. Praised by some and damned by others, the tower created as much controversy in its time as I.M. Pei's pyramid at the Louvre did 100 years later. Upon completion, the Tour Eiffel was the tallest human-built structure in the world, and the Prince of Wales (later Edward VII) and his family were invited to ascend it first. People have climbed it, bungee-jumped from it, and cycled down the tower's steps. In 1989, the tower's centennial was celebrated with 89 minutes of music and fireworks, and in the 1990s it counted down the days and then the minutes until the Millennium. Word of advice: Six million people visit the Tour Eiffel each year. To avoid *loonnnggg* lines, go early in the morning or during the off season. If that isn't possible, allow at least two hours for your visit: one hour to line up for tickets and another just to access the elevators on levels one and two. Food is available at the Altitude 95 restaurant on the first floor, which is simply gorgeous but overpriced for the quality of its meals. A first-floor snack bar and a second-floor cafeteria also do not offer the best values. The best food at the tower is also its most expensive, without a doubt — the Jules Verne, one of Paris's most celebrated restaurants, is on the Tour Eiffel's second level. If you can get a reservation here, you'll have spectacular views, exquisite food, and a private entrance to the tower. Since 1999, double sweeping beacons have preceded the tower's illumination each night. If you have the patience for it, the Tour Eiffel at night is recommended. Its lights frame the lacy steelwork in a way that daylight doesn't, while beneath you the city twinkles and the Seine reflects it all.

You won't be able to avoid pesky (and illegal) vendors trying to cajole you into buying everything from tower keychains to postcards to mechanical butterflies; they constantly approach tourists standing in line for the Tour Eiffel admission tickets. Be very attentive — some of these vendors work in tandem with pickpockets who will rip you off while you're busy looking at the displays. As for the quality of the merchandise, it's pretty bad; buy your souvenirs from shops and licensed vendors.

See map p. 172. Parc du Champs de Mars (7e). ☎ *01-44-11-23-23.* www.toureiffel.fr. *Métro: Trocadéro, Bir-Hakeim, or École-Militaire. RER: Champs-de-Mars. Bus: 42, 69, 82, 87. Admission: 10.70€ ($13) adults, 5.90€ ($7.10) ages 3–11 to highest level (1,060 ft.); 7.50€ ($9) adults, 4.10€ ($4.90) ages 3–11 to 2nd level (380 ft.); 4.10€ ($4.90) adults, 2.30€ ($2.75) ages 3–11 for elevator to 1st level (188 ft.); 3.80€ ($4.55) adults, 3€ ($3.60) ages 3–11 for stairs to 1st and 2nd levels. Children younger than 3 are free. Open: Daily Sept 1–June 13, 9:30 a.m.–11 p.m.; June 14–Aug 31, 9 a.m. to midnight. Fall and winter, stairs close at 6:30 p.m.*

Enjoying Paris's Parks and Gardens

Parisians love their green spaces, and Paris has many to visit, from parks for flowers and plants to parks for admiring views. The beauty and serenity of planted gardens, splashing fountains, and arrow-straight paths are relaxing, and your kids will love the puppet shows and pony rides (Jardin de Luxembourg, Bois de Boulogne, Bois de Vincennes). Most parks are open daily until sunset unless otherwise noted.

The legendary **Bois de Boulogne** in western Paris (16e) once was a royal forest and hunting ground. Napoléon III donated it to the city, and Baron Haussmann transformed it, using London's Hyde Park as his model. Today the Bois is not just for picnickers. Its 890 hectares (2,200 acres) offer jogging paths, horseback riding, cycling (rentals are available), and boating on two lakes. The **Longchamp** and **Auteuil** racecourses are here, and so is the beautiful **Pré Catalan,** a garden containing many of the herbs and plants mentioned in Shakespeare's plays. The rose gardens at the **Parc de la Bagatelle** are gorgeous, and the thematic gardens reveal the art of gardening through the centuries. A water-lily pond pays homage to a certain famous painter (think Monet). The château here, which you can view only from the outside, was built by Comte d'Artois in 1775, after he made a bet with his sister-in-law, Marie Antoinette, that he could do it in fewer than 90 days. It took 66 days. Under Napoléon, it was used as a hunting lodge. Take the Métro to Porte Maillot.

The **Bois de Vincennes,** 12e (☎ 01-47-74-41-00; Métro: Porte Dorée or Chateau de Vincennes), houses the spectacular **Parc Floral de Paris,** which has a butterfly garden, library, miniature golf, and the **Parc Zoologique de Paris.** You can rent bikes (☎ 01-47-47-76-50) here and ride around the extensive grounds or row a rented canoe around a winding pond. You can even rent "quadricycles" — bicycles built for four (10€/$12).

The Bois de Boulogne's **Jardin d'Acclimatation** (☎ 01-40-67-90-82) has an amusement park loved by Parisian children. To get there, take Métro Line 1 to Les Sablons, and exit on rue d'Orléans; the entrance is about 15 meters (50 ft.) away. Or take bus No. 43, 73, 82, or 174, or the open-air "Petit Train," from the Bois de Boulogne's Porte Maillot entrance: 5€ ($6) round-trip adults, 5€ ($6) round-trip children and students. Admission to the Jardin d'Acclimation is 2.50€ ($3) adults and children ages 3 and older, free for children younger than 3. Open daily 10 a.m. to 6 p.m. (until 7 p.m. June to September).

Parc de Belleville, 20e, topped by the **Maison de l'Air,** a museum with displays devoted to the air that we breathe, is a superb place to visit with children. Enjoy fountains, a children's play area, an open-air theater with many concerts during the summer, and rock formations and grottoes that evoke the days when the hill was a strategic point to fight enemies such as Attila the Hun. The park also is an idyllic place to watch the sun set across western Paris. Access the park by taking the rue Piat off rue de Belleville and enter through an iron gate spelling out the words *Villa Ottoz.* A curved path leads you to tree-lined promenades (more than 500 trees are here), with the first of the magnificent Left Bank views peeping through the spaces between pretty houses. Beds of roses and other seasonal flowers line walks, and views of the city's Left Bank become more pronounced the higher up the terraced pathways you go. Take the Métro to Pyrénées, and then walk down rue de Belleville and turn left onto rue Piat, where arched iron gates lead into the park. You can also take the Métro to Courrones, cross bd. de Belleville, and turn left onto rue Julien Lacroix, where you find another entrance.

Seeing Paris by Guided Tour

If you're a newcomer to the wonders of Paris, an orientation tour can help you understand the city's geography. But even if you've been coming to Paris for ten years or more, one of the various tours can introduce you to sides of the city you never knew existed. Being lucky enough to be shown around by guides whose enthusiasm makes the city come to life can be the high point of your entire trip.

Cruising the Seine

One of the most romantic and beautiful ways to see Paris is by one of the sightseeing boats that cruise up and down the Seine. Don't, however, take one of the overpriced dinner or lunch cruises — they cost between 85€ ($102) and 125€ ($150) per person. Instead, opt for an evening cruise. With its dramatically lit monuments and romantic bridges, Paris is breathtaking at night.

Three companies offer evening (and daytime) tours that are all similar and cost about the same. Vedettes boats are smaller and more intimate, and not all of them are covered. Commentary is live with Vedettes Pont Neuf and Bateaux-Parisiens, taped on Bateaux-Mouches.

✔ **Bateaux-Mouches,** pont de l'Alma, Right Bank, 8e (☎ **01-42-25-96-10** or 01-42-76-99-99; www.bateaux-mouches.fr; Métro: Alma Marceau). Departures: Every 30 minutes 10 a.m. to 8 p.m., every 20 minutes 8 to 11 p.m., March to mid-November; 11 a.m. and 2:30, 4, 6, and 9 p.m., November to March. Rates: 7€ ($8.40) for adults, 4€ ($4.80) for children 4 to 12 and adults older than 65; children younger than 4 ride free.

✔ **Bateaux-Parisiens,** port de la Bourdonnais, Left Bank, 7e (☎ **01-44-11-33-44;** www.bateauxparisiens.com; Métro: Bir-Hakeim). Departures: From Easter to Halloween every half-hour from 10 a.m. to 11 p.m.; every hour November 1 to Easter from 10 a.m. to 1 p.m. and 5 to 8 p.m., every half-hour from 1 to 5 p.m. and 8 to 10 p.m. Rates: 9.50€ ($11), adults, 4.50€ ($5.40) children 3 to 12; free for children younger than 3.

✔ **Vedettes Pont Neuf,** square du Vert-Galant (next to pont Neuf), 1er (☎ **01-46-33-98-38;** www.vedettesdupontneuf.com; Métro: Pont-Neuf). Departures: Every half-hour March through October 10:30 a.m. to 10:30 p.m.; every 45 minutes November through February 10:30 a.m. to noon and 2 to 10 p.m., Saturdays and Sundays every half-hour from 10 a.m. to 10:30 p.m. Rates: 10€ ($12) adults, 5€ ($6) children 12 and younger.

For a boat ride without commentary, take one of the **Batobus** shuttles (☎ **01-44-11-33-99;** www.batobus.com) that stop at Trocadéro, Musée d'Orsay, Louvre, Notre-Dame, and Hôtel de Ville. A ticket costs 7.50€ ($9) adults or 3.50€ ($4.20) children younger than 12. You can also purchase a one-day pass, costing 11€ ($13) for adults or 5€ ($6) for children, that enables you to get on and off shuttles as you wish.

Motoring around by bus

The biggest bus tour company has been **Cityrama** (4 place des Pyramides, 1er; ☎ 01-44-55-61-00; www.cityrama.fr; Métro: Palais-Royal–Musée du Louvre). A 90-minute orientation tour costs 15€ ($18) adults, 7.50€ ($9) kids younger than 12. A variety of partial-day and full-day tours also are available, with fares ranging from 39€ ($47) adults, 19.50€ ($23) children, to 92€ ($110) adults, 46€ ($55) children. Tours to Versailles (starting at 37€/$44 adults, 18.50€/$22 children) and to Chartres (53€/$64 adults, 26.50€/$32 children) are a better bargain because they take the hassle out of visiting these monuments. Nighttime illumination tours include a Seine boat cruise and start at 30€ ($36) adults, 15€ ($18) children younger than 12.

Paris l'OpenTour (☎ 01-42-66-56-56; www.paris-opentour.com), from Paris's public transportation system, the RATP, has bright yellow-and-green convertible double-decker buses that take you to three different areas. You listen to recorded commentary in English through a set of headphones that are given to you when you get on the bus. The Paris Grand Tour covers Paris's most central sights, minus the islands; the Montmartre tour goes to the Montmartre *funiculaire* and points north; and the Bastille–Bercy tour goes east. The OpenTour makes its stops at regular city bus stops marked with the OpenTour logo. You can board at any of these stops and buy the pass right on the bus. The pass is also on sale at the Paris Tourist Office, at L'OpenTour kiosks near the Malesherbes (8e) and Anvers (9e) bus stops, at the RATP office at place de la Madeleine (8e), at the Montmartre tourist office (21 place du Tertre), at some hotels, and at the main Batobus docks on the Seine. A two-day pass costs 28€ ($34) adults, 12€ ($14) children 4 to 11, and 21€ ($25) for holders of the Paris Visite pass, and you can get on or off the bus as many times as you want, which, in our opinion, makes this the more worthwhile tour. The buses run daily every 25 minutes throughout the year from around 9:30 a.m. to 6 p.m.

RATP (☎ 08-92-68-77-14; www.ratp.fr) also runs the **Balabus,** a fleet of orange-and-white buses that operate only on Sundays and holidays, noon to 8 p.m. from April to September. Routes run between the Gare de Lyon and the Grand Arche de La Défense, in both directions, and cost you just one Métro ticket. The bus has a "Bb" symbol across its side and on bus stops along its route.

Walking the city streets

If you plan to spend more than a month in Paris, we strongly advise you contact **WICE** (20 bd. Du Montparnasse, 15e; ☎ 01-45-66-75-50; fax 01-40-65-96-53; www.wice-paris.org; Métro: Duroc or Falguière). Originally established as the Women's Institute for Continuing Education, but now open to both men and women, WICE offers more than 50 educational courses on how foreigners can cope with life in France and how they can deepen their understanding of French art, architecture, and literature. Membership in the organization costs 65€ ($78), but the benefits, in our opinion, for anyone spending considerable time in France are enormous. Expect an ongoing roster of art openings; book-club meetings; language, oil painting, and watercolor classes; use of an on-site French and English library; and availability of some of the most interesting walking tours in Paris. Priced at 18€ ($22) each and lasting about 90 minutes, recent walking tours have included "The Senate," "The Paris Commune of 1871," and such outlying attractions as Fontainebleau and Versailles. Paris residents who are members of WICE love these tours, so try to reserve a spot in advance. (Unfortunately, the organization's Web site isn't equipped to handle online payments, so you'll have to fax or phone WICE with a valid credit card or pay in person with cash.) If you visit the organization in person, know in advance that the entrance is accessible through the building's central courtyard.

Paris Walks (☎ **01-48-09-21-40;** www.paris-walks.com) was founded by Peter and Oriel Caine and has become a popular English-language outfit whose guided walks cost 10€ ($12) adults, 7€ ($8.40) students younger than 25, and 5€ ($6) children. Specific tours concentrate on a single neighborhood (such as "The Village of Montmartre" or "The Historic Marais"), a particular theme (such as "Hemingway's Paris"), or a single sight (such as "Les Invalides" or "The Paris Sewers"). Call for the designated meeting place.

Moveable Feast (☎ **06-66-92-34-12**) offers offbeat two-hour guided walks, such as "Paris is a Woman," which takes visitors to the haunts and former residences of some of Paris's most famous women (Colette, Josephine Baker, Sarah Bernhardt, Janet Flanner, Gertrude Stein, and Coco Chanel). "The Belly of Paris" takes aspiring gourmands to Les Halles (called "the Belly of Paris" by writer Émile Zola), where they explore restaurants, markets, and the culinary history of Paris. Another itinerary includes sites from "Medieval Paris." Tours are 12€ ($14) adults, 10€ ($12) students and seniors. Call to reserve a place and find out starting points.

Paris à Pied (☎ **800-594-9535** in the United States, 01-46-27-11-56 or 06-64-77-11-56 in Paris; www.parisapied.com) has three-hour tours geared to first-time visitors. The Minneapolis-based company offers tours that cost $45 and are limited to eight people. Tours include "The Heart of Old Paris," "The Latin Quarter," "Montmartre," and "The Marais."

Cycling around Paris

For cyclists, **Paris à Vélo C'est Sympa** (☎ **01-48-87-60-01;** www.parisvelosympa.com; Métro: Richard Le Noir; meeting place: 22 Rue Alphonse Baudin) has three-hour Heart of Paris tours at 10 a.m., Friday to Monday from April to October and on Saturday and Sunday at 10 a.m. November to March. Reservations are required, and most tours are in French (call or stop in for times of English-speaking tours). The company also has night *(nocturne)* bike tours Saturday at 8:30 p.m., May to September. Other tours include "Paris Contrasts," "Unusual Paris," and "Paris at Dawn." Prices for all tours are 32.50€ ($39) adults, 28€ ($34) ages 12 to 26, 18€ ($22) ages 10 and 11. Children younger than 10 are not permitted.

Fat Tire Bike Tours, 24 rue Edgar Faure, 15e (☎ **01-56-58-10-54;** www.fattirebiketoursparis.com), has friendly guides to take you on day or night bike tours of the city lasting three to four hours and costing 24€ ($29) day, 28€ ($34) night, 48€ ($58) both tours. Reservations are not accepted; look for the yellow sign in front of the *Pilier Sud* (South Pillar) of the Tour Eiffel. Day tours are at 11 a.m. and 3:30 p.m., May 15 to July 31, 11 a.m. only March 1 to May 14 and August 1 to November 30. Night tours are beautiful (especially the ride past the Grand Pyramid through the courtyard at the Louvre) and start at 7 p.m. daily from April through October; during the month of March and the first two weeks of November, tours run Sunday, Tuesday, and Thursday at 7 p.m.

Suggested One-, Two-, and Three-Day Sightseeing Itineraries

Paris has so much to see and do that first- and even second-time visitors to the city can feel overwhelmed just trying to figure out where to begin. If you're short on time or have young children with you, you want to maximize your opportunities to see the best Paris has to offer in the most efficient way possible. The following itineraries can help you figure out where to start and what to do. But please feel free to branch out and explore those interesting alleyways and pretty green spaces you encounter all around you. That's what's so much fun about Paris — it reveals itself in all kinds of ways, making the trips of each independent visitor different and special.

If you have one day

On **Day One,** start early by having coffee and croissants at a cafe. Then begin at the true center of Paris: **Notre-Dame,** on the **Ile de la Cité.** The cathedral is a great starting point for any tour, and it's also Paris's starting point: You are at *Kilometre Zéro,* from which all distances in France are measured. From there, take a short walk to the island's other Gothic masterpiece, **St-Chapelle,** in the **Palais de Justice.** Afterward, cross the Seine to the **Musée du Louvre.** Select just a few rooms in a particular collection for your first visit — this is one of the world's largest and finest museums, and it would take months to see everything. Take a well-deserved lunch break in the museum's comfortable **Café Marly** (see Chapter 11).

From the museum, stroll through the beautiful **Jardin des Tuileries** to the **place de la Concorde,** with its Egyptian obelisk and fountains. Walk up the **Champs-Elysées** to the **Arc de Triomphe,** and browse the stores (**FNAC** and **Virgin Megastore** are good places to buy music, and they each have a cafe on the premises for a break; **Zara** is good for the latest fashion at low prices). Walk south on avenue Marceau or take bus 92 to Alma Marceau, and board the **Bateaux-Mouches** for a **Seine boat ride.** After you disembark, have dinner at the friendly and reasonably priced **L'Assiette Lyonnaise,** 21 rue Marbeuf, 8e (☎ **01-47-20-94-80**). From Pont L'Alma walk down av. George V to rue Marbeuf and make a right. L'Assiette Lyonnaise is on your right.

If you have two days

On the first day, follow the itinerary for one day but spend a longer time at the Louvre. Explore the **Left Bank** on **Day Two.** Take the Métro to La Motte-Picquet-Grenelle, and stop into **Monoprix** just across the street for cheap picnic food. Walk northwest along av. de Suffren until you reach the **École Militaire.** Facing the École Militaire is the **Champs de Mars,** where you can spread out to have a picnic before visiting the **Tour Eiffel.** After you climb the tower, visit the **Église du Dôme** (which contains the **Tomb of Napoléon**) on the other side of the École Militaire. Admission also includes entrance to the **Musée de l'Armée.** Across bd. des Invalides is the beautiful **Musée Nationale d'Auguste Rodin,** where you can enjoy a slow walk around the beautiful gardens before gazing at the artwork inside. Then walk north along bd. des Invalides to the Seine, and head east for quai Anatole France (this is a long walk) and the **Musée d'Orsay** (you can also hop on the Métro at Varenne, at the corner of bd. des Invalides and Varenne, change to RER Line C, and get off at Musée d'Orsay) to spend a few hours with the Impressionist masters. Afterward, walk over to the Métro's **Assemblée Nationale** station at the intersection of bd. St-Germain and rue de Lille. Take the Métro two stops to rue du Bac, and exit onto bd. St-Germain, making sure to walk in the direction traffic is heading, all the while browsing in upscale shops and art galleries. At pl. St-Germain-des-Près, look for one of the famous cafes, **Café de Flore** or **Les Deux Magots** (see Chapter 11), and have a drink. When you've finished, take rue Bonaparte (which intersects St-Germain-des-Près) to Parisians' favorite park, **Jardin du Luxembourg.** Stroll through the park, and exit at the bd. St-Michel gates. Walk down bd. St-Michel toward the river. You will be in the **Latin Quarter.** The **Panthéon** is at the top of the hill on rue Soufflot. Many inexpensive and good restaurants are behind the Panthéon on rue Mouffetard.

If you have three days

On **Day Three,** get up early and take the Métro to St-Paul, in the heart of the **Marais.** Walk over to Paris's oldest square, the aristocratic **place des Vosges,** bordered by 17th-century townhouses. Then head over to rue Thorigny for the **Musée Picasso.** Try to be here when it opens at 9:30, and allow two hours for your visit. Afterward, follow rue du Vieille Temple to rue des Rosiers, and pick up lunch from **Jo Goldenberg** (see Chapter 11). Browse the stores here and on rue des Francs Bourgeois, which turns into rue Rambuteau. Follow rue Rambuteau to rue Beaubourg, where you'll face the back of **Centre Georges Pompidou.** Spend two hours exploring it. Afterward, jump on the Métro and head for **Cimitière Père Lachaise.** Spend the afternoon searching out Père Lachaise's famous residents with the 3€ ($3.60) map (it's the best one) sold outside the gates on bd. de Ménilmontant. Afterward, take the Métro's Line 2 to the Anvers station. Walk down rue Tardieu to the base of **Sacré-Coeur.** Take the *funiculaire* (one Métro ticket) to the top, and spend 15 to 20 minutes inside Sacré-Coeur before climbing to its dome. After climbing down, head behind the church to **place du Tertre,** which still looks like an old-fashioned Parisian square, despite artists begging to paint your picture (some can be quite persuasive, but they're too expensive, and it's better to just politely tell them "*non, merci*"). Even though the cafes are picturesque — and more expensive — save your appetite for **Au Poulbot Gourmet** (see Chapter 11); follow rue Lamarck down the hill to the restaurant.

Shopping the Local Stores

Every first-time visitor to Paris needs to set aside a little time for shopping — it's simply some of the best in the world. Even the window shopping is good; you'll notice that the tiniest *pâtissier* (pastry shop) will have exquisite, enticing goods arranged just so in windows beckoning you inside (window shopping in French is aptly translated to *faire du leche-vitrines,* or *window licking*). Paris is truly a shopper's heaven, from the toniest *haute-couture* shop to the hidden *depot-vente* (resale shop) selling last year's Yves St-Laurent at greatly reduced prices. Even non-shoppers will find something: the eye-popping hardware store in the basement of BHV, the inexpensive furnishings at Conforama, and the mouth-watering *epicerie* (grocer) at Le Bon Marché. This section gives you an overview of the Parisian shopping scene, with hints about where to find the bargains, the best shopping neighborhoods, and even how to get some of your money back.

Taking a look at the shopping scene

The cost of shopping in Paris doesn't have to be jaw-droppingly expensive. If you plan to spend only at couturiers, then yes, you will be paying top price. But Paris has many stores selling clothing and goods at prices comparable to what you'd pay in North America. And you can find items cheaper in Paris than they are in your hometown: some French and European brands of perfume and cosmetics, shoes, clothing from French-based companies such as Petit Bateau and Lacoste, French-made porcelain, cookware, and glassware. Obviously, you'll pay more for any name imported from the United States, such as Donna Karan and Calvin Klein, and for any souvenirs in areas heavily frequented by tourists. Keep the following tips in mind for happy hunting:

✔ **Remember the VAT.** A 19.6 percent value-added tax (VAT) has been tacked onto the price of most products, which means that most things cost less at home. (For details on getting a VAT refund, see the following section "Getting a refund on the VAT.")

✔ **Practice selective shopping.** Appliances, paper products, housewares, computer supplies, electronics, and CDs/DVDs are notoriously expensive in France, though the cost of computers is beginning to come down. To recognize a bargain, it helps to check out the prices of French products before your trip.

✔ **Christmas (shopping) in July (and January).** Probably the best time to find a bargain in Paris is during the government-mandated twice-annual sales *(soldes)* in January and July, when merchandise gets marked down 30 percent to 50 percent or more. (Parisians line up outside their favorite stores the first days of these sales.) If you can brave the crowds, you just may find the perfect designer outfit at a fraction of the retail price.

✔ **Save Sundays for sightseeing.** Store hours are Monday through Saturday from 9 or 9:30 a.m. (sometimes 10 a.m.) to 7 p.m., later on Thursday evenings, without a break for lunch. Some smaller stores are closed on Monday or Monday mornings and break for lunch for one to three hours beginning at around 1 p.m., but this is becoming increasingly rare. Small stores also may be closed for all or part of August and on some days around Christmas and Easter. Sunday shopping is gradually making inroads in Paris but is limited mostly to tourist areas. Try the Carrousel du Louvre at the Louvre, rue de Rivoli across from the Louvre, rue des Francs-Bourgeois in the Marais, and the Champs-Elysées.

✔ **Be on your best behavior.** Politeness is imperative when you shop in Paris. Always greet the salespeople with *"Bonjour, madame"* or *"Bonjour, monsieur"* when you arrive. Whether you've bought anything or not, say, *"Merci, au revoir,"* (Thank you, goodbye) when you're leaving.

Getting a refund on the VAT

If you spend more than 175€ ($210) in a single store, you're entitled to a refund on the value-added tax (VAT), also referred to in France as TVA. The discount, however, is not automatic. Food, wine, and tobacco don't count, and the refund is granted only on purchases you take *with you* out of the country — not on merchandise you ship home.

To apply, you must show the store clerk your passport to prove your eligibility. You are given an export sales document (in triplicate — two pink sheets and a green one), which you must sign, and usually an envelope addressed to the store. Or if you are shopping in a store participating in the Europe Tax-Free Shopping program (indicated by the TAX-FREE sticker in the store's windows), you get a Tax-Free Shopping Cheque showing the amount of refund owed to you when you leave the country. Bring all documents to the airport's *détaxe* booth, where a customs official will stamp them. To get an immediate cash refund, you pay a fee of 4.60€ ($5.50). Otherwise, enclose the appropriate document (the pink one) in the store envelope the clerk provided when you bought your merchandise, and mail it from the airport. The wait for a refund is anywhere from one to three months. (Our recommendation? Pay the 4.60€/$5.50 and be done with it.)

Travelers leaving from Charles-de-Gaulle Airport may visit the *détaxe* refund point in Terminal 1 on the departure level between Gates 14 and 16; in Terminal 2 Hall B between doors 6 and 7 near the baggage claim area or in Hall A between doors 5 and 6; and in Terminal T9 near the departure gates. In Orly, the *détaxe* booth is in Orly West between Halls 3 and 4 on the departure level. If you are claiming a tax refund, try to arrive at the airport as early as possible; because you must show everything you're declaring to a customs official, you may have to wait in line. Plus after you've finished with *détaxe,* you'll have to stand in line again to check your luggage.

If you're traveling by train, go to the *détaxe* area in the station before boarding because you can't get your refund documents processed on the train. Give the three sheets to the Customs official, who stamps them and returns a pink and a green copy to you. Keep the green copy, and mail the pink copy to the store.

Your reimbursement is either mailed as a check (in euros) or credited to your credit-card account. If you don't receive your tax refund in four months, write to the store, giving the date of purchase and the location where the forms were given to Customs officials. Include a photocopy of your green refund sheet. Department stores that cater to foreign visitors, such as Au Printemps and Galeries Lafayette, have special *détaxe* areas where clerks prepare your invoices for you.

Visiting the great shopping neighborhoods

The shopping in Paris is among the finest in the world, and you don't need *beaucoup* bucks to afford it. You'll latch on to great finds for every taste and dollar amount. Read this section to get a significant head start on where to go to begin the hunt.

The land of luxe: The 8e

When people around the world need a luxury shopping fix, they go to Paris, and all you have to do is head for the 8e to find out why. Nearly every French designer is based on two streets — **avenue Montaigne** (Métro: Alma-Marceau, Franklin-D-Roosevelt) and **rue du Faubourg St-Honoré** (Métro: Concorde), where prices of more than 1,000€ ($1,200) are normal and snooty sales clerks are *de rigueur.* But you can still have a good time window-shopping here, even if you don't have a platinum card.

Although these streets boast some of the same big designer names, they are completely different in temperament. Avenue Montaigne is wide, graceful, lined with chestnut trees, and undeniably hip, attracting the likes of **Plein Sud** at No. 2 and **Dolce & Gabbana** at No. 22 (☎ **01-47-20-42-43** and 01-42-25-68-78, respectively) and **Prada** at No. 10 (☎ **01-53-23-99-40**). Other designers on this street include **Céline,** 36 av. Montaigne (☎ **01-56-89-07-92**); **Chanel,** 42 av. Montaigne (☎ **01-47-23-74-12**); **Christian Dior,** 30 av. Montaigne (☎ **01-40-73-54-44**); **Escada,** 53 av. Montaigne (☎ **01-42-89-83-45**); **Ferragamo,** 45 av. Montaigne (☎ **01-47-23-36-37**); **Christian Lacroix,** 73 rue du Faubourg St-Honoré (☎ **01-42-68-79-04**, respectively); **Balmain,** 49 av. Montaigne (☎ **01-47-23-37-62**); **Ungaro,** 2 av. Montaigne (☎ **01-53-57-00-00**); and **Valentino,** 17 av. Montaigne (☎ **01-47-23-64-61**).

Rue du Faubourg St-Honoré is jammed with shoppers walking along the small, narrow sidewalks. **Gucci** is located at No. 23 and at 60 av. Montaigne (☎ **01-42-96-83-27**), **Hermès** (pronounced "air-*mess*") at No. 24 (☎ **01-40-17-47-17**), and **Yves St-Laurent** at No. 38 (☎ **01-42-65-74-59**). Begin at the rue Royale intersection, and head west. Other designer stores you will run across here include **Ferragamo,** 50 rue du Faubourg St-Honoré (☎ **01-43-12-96-96**); **Gianni Versace,** 62 rue du Faubourg St-Honoré (☎ **01-47-42-88-02**); **La Perla,** 20 rue du Faubourg St-Honoré (☎ **01-43-12-33-60**); **Chloé,** 54 rue du Faubourg St-Honoré (☎ **01-44-94-33-00**); **Sonia Rykiel,** 70 rue du Faubourg St-Honoré (☎ **01-42-65-20-81**); and **Missoni,** 1 rue du Faubourg St-Honoré, (☎ **01-44-51-96-96**).

Arty and individual: The 3e and 4e

The Marais (3e, 4e) is an ancient neighborhood crammed with magnificent Renaissance mansions, artists' studios, secret courtyards, and some of the most original shops in the city. You'll find 15 museums in the Marais alone, so divide your time between culture and commercialism, and when you're hungry, **Jo Goldenberg,** another Marais institution (see Chapter 11), should fill you up nicely.

Rue des Francs-Bourgeois (Métro: St-Paul or Rambuteau) is the highlight of the area, full of small shops selling everything from fashion to jewels. **Rue des Rosiers** (Métro: St-Paul), a fashion destination in its own right, boasts white-hot designers standing shoulder to shoulder with Jewish delis. Everything is really close in the Marais, so don't be afraid to ramble down the tiniest lane whenever whim dictates. Part of the fun of this neighborhood is that it's such a mixed (shopping) bag.

Marais highlights include **Paule Ka,** 20 rue Mahler (☎ **01-40-29-96-03**), for the sort of 1960s clothing made famous by Grace Kelly, Jackie Onassis, and Audrey Hepburn; **Autour du Monde Home,** 8 rue des Francs-Bourgeois (☎ **01-42-77-06-08**), a clothing/housewares store with everything from relaxed and sporty cotton dresses to delicate linen sheets and inventive tableware; and **Issey Miyake,** 3 pl. des Vosges (☎ **01-48-87-01-86**), for loose, structured clothing that screams *artiste*. Fans of the hot brand **Camper,** 9 rue des Francs-Bourgeois (☎ **01-48-87-09-09**), can buy their comfortable men's and women's shoes made in Spain. Also check out **Zadig et Voltaire**, 42 rue des Francs-Bourgeois (☎ **01-42-72-15-20**), for casual clothes with a flair from new and established European designers.

BCBG bourgeois chic: The 6e

Be part of the BCBG (*Bon Chic Bon Genre* is what the French call stylish young professionals with old family money) who call this area home, and shop amid art and antiques galleries, high-end designer clothing shops, decently priced shoe and accessories stores, and sophisticated and trendy boutiques. You won't go thirsty with famed literary hangouts such as Café de Flore and Les Deux Magots nearby. You may not even go broke — all price ranges are represented here.

Louis Vuitton has a huge store behind Les Deux Magots on 6 place St-Germain (☎ 01-45-49-62-32), and Christian Dior is nearby at 16 rue de l'Abbaye (☎ 01-56-24-90-53). You'll pay designer prices at Emporio Armani, 149 bd. St-Germain (☎ 01-53-63-33-50); Céline, 58 rue de Rennes (☎ 01-45-48-58-55); Christian Lacroix, 2 place St-Sulpice (☎ 01-46-33-48-95); or Prada, 5 rue de Grenelle (☎ 01-45-48-53-14). For stores carrying items easier on the pocketbook, we recommend Stefanel, 54 rue de Rennes (☎ 01-45-44-06-07) and Comptoir des Cotonniers, 59 Ter rue Bonaparte (☎ 01-43-26-07-56); APC Surplus, 45 rue Madame (☎ 01-45-48-43-71); and Tara Jarmon, 18 rue du Four, Bonaparte (☎ 01-46-33-26-60).

It was bound to happen — Gap and other chain stores have taken up residence in the Marché St-Germain, a modern shopping mall that's a bit out of place in a neighborhood known for bookstores and upscale boutiques. Visit if you need air-conditioning; otherwise, don't waste your time. Prices are higher, and styles are the same as at home.

Young and branché: The 2e

Branché is a high compliment among Paris's younger set; it means plugged in, or hip, and the 2e is where you head if you are. The area sells a mix of high-fashion and discount, with Jean-Paul Gaultier in the pretty Galerie Vivienne on one end and Kookaï Le Stock on the other. The cheapest shopping is in the Sentier area, around the Sentier Métro stop, which is Paris's garment district, overlapping parts of the 3e and 1er. Prostitutes frequent the area later in the day and evening. The best, but not the cheapest, shops are found within a square formed on the south by rue Rambuteau, on the west by rue du Louvre, on the north by rue Réamur, and on the east by rue St-Martin. This is where you can find hip secondhand clothes, funky clubwear, and "stock" boutiques selling last season's designs at a discount.

For last year's unsold stock of women's and teen's clothing visit Et Vous Stock, 15 rue de Turbigo, 2e (☎ 01-40-13-04-12), and Kookaï Le Stock, 82 rue Réamur, 2e (☎ 01-45-08-93-69). Kiliwatch, 64 rue Tiquetonne, 2e (☎ 01-42-21-17-37), sells the cool looks of up-and-coming designers mixed in with vintage clothing. Kokon To Zai, 48 rue Tiquetonne, 2e (☎ 01-42-36-92-41), sells funky designerwear in a small store that dazzles with mirrors and neon. Le Shop, 3 rue d'Argout, 2e (☎ 01-40-28-95-94), sells two floors of clubwear, as well as skateboards and CDs — all to tunes spun by a DJ. Those with a more sophisticated palate can go to Barbara Bui, 23 rue Etienne-Marcel, 1er (☎ 01-40-26-43-65), for elegant, contemporary fashion (she also has a trendy cafe two doors down). For sophistication with an edge, head to Jean-Paul Gaultier, 6 rue Vivienne (☎ 01-42-86-05-05). Other stores include Agnès b., 6 rue du Jour (☎ 01-45-08-56-56), timelessly chic with lots of black clothes for men and women, and Les Petites Pierlot, 3 rue Montmartre, 1er (☎ 01-40-28-45-55), for casual wear that includes the striped sailor sweater, a French wardrobe basic.

Sampling the city's department stores

Two of Paris's major department stores, Au Printemps and Galeries Lafayette, offer visitors a 10 percent discount coupon, good in most departments. If your hotel or travel agent doesn't give you one of these coupons (they're sometimes attached to a city map), you can ask for it at the stores' welcome desks; the clerks speak English.

If you're at **Le Bon Marché** (24 rue de Sèvres, 7e; ☎ 01-44-39-80-00; Métro: Sèvres-Babylone) during the sales, you can find tons of deals at Paris's only Left Bank department store. Elegant, but small enough to be manageable, much of this store's merchandise is exquisite and includes designers such as Vivienne Westwood, Burberry, and Yohji Yamamoto. The third floor is particularly renowned for its large shoe selection and grand lingerie department (where dressing rooms have phones to summon your salesperson). But it isn't cheap. Make sure to visit the huge supermarket (it's in a separate building next door), where you can find nearly any kind of food. A cafe and cafeteria accompany a small antiques market on the second floor.

Au Printemps (64 bd. Haussmann, 9e; ☎ 01-42-82-50-00; Métro: Havre-Caumartin) is one of Paris's largest department stores, and a recent renovation costing millions of euros has made it into one of Paris's best. Merchandise is sold in three different buildings: Printemps de l'Homme (menswear), Printemps de la Maison (furniture and accessories), and Printemps de la Mode (women and children's fashion). Designers include Dolce & Gabbana and Burberry. Fashion shows are staged under the 1920s glass dome at 10 a.m. every Tuesday year-round.

Near the Marais, **BHV** (*Bazar de l'Hôtel de Ville,* 52 rue de Rivoli, 1er; ☎ 01-42-74-90-00; Métro: Hôtel de Ville) sells the usual clothing, cosmetics, luggage, and leatherware at decent prices, but it's really worth a visit for its giant basement-level hardware store with everything you need to fix up your home and a cafe (decorated like a tool shed) serving light bites.

Galeries Lafayette (40 bd. Haussmann, 9e; ☎ 01-42-82-34-56; Métro: Opéra or Chaussée-d'Antin) gets downright crowded, and if you visit during the sales, you'll be thoroughly fatigued. Fortunately, choices for refreshment abound from Ladurée tea salon to burgers to the self-serve Lafayette Café on the sixth floor, which also has panoramic views of Paris. Merchandise here is good quality, and excellent deals can be had during the sales: Look for women's clothing from Comptoir des Cotoniers and Agnès B and for the gourmet grocery store, Lafayette Gourmet, in the men's store.

Right now, probably the best thing about **La Samaritaine** (19 rue de la Monnaie, 1er; ☎ 01-40-41-20-20; Métro: Pont-Neuf or Châtelet–Les Halles), besides the fact that its prices are slightly lower than Galeries Lafayette and Au Printemps, is its views. Look for signs in its main building to the *panorama,* a free observation point with a view of Paris that includes the Tour Eiffel. (Take the stairs to the roof if you have lots of energy; otherwise, wait for the elevator.) Located between the Louvre and the Pont Neuf, La Samaritaine is housed in four buildings with Art Nouveau touches and has an Art Deco facade on quai du Louvre. The fifth floor of store No. 2 has a good, inexpensive restaurant. LVMH (Louis Vuitton Moet Hennessy) is the owner.

Clothing is low-priced and stylish at **Monoprix** (various locations; ☎ 01-44-61-08-00), and the stores also are good for accessories, low-priced cosmetics, lingerie, and housewares. Many locations also have large grocery stores.

For the most part, **Tati** (4 bd. Rochechouart, 18e; ☎ 01-55-29-50-00; Métro: Barbés-Rochechouart) is tacky. But you never know what you may find here if you dig; the occasional gem awaits those who are persistent. Other branches are located at 172 rue du Temple, 3e (☎ 01-42-71-41-77); 49 Bis rue Réaumer, 3e (☎ 01-53-01-24-90); and 30 av. d'Intalie, 13e (☎ 01-53-80-97-70).

Checking out the city's flea and flower markets

The prettiest of the markets is the **Marché aux Fleurs** (4e; Métro: Cité), the flower market on place Louis-Lépine on Ile de la Cité. Visit Monday to Saturday to enjoy the flowers, even if you don't buy anything. On Sunday, the market becomes the **Marché aux Oiseaux,** selling birds and more unusual creatures, including hedgehogs, skunks, raccoons, ferrets, mice, guinea pigs, and rabbits. If you don't mind seeing creatures in cages, it can be quite interesting.

An option for Saturday, Sunday, or Monday (open 9 a.m.–8 p.m.), the huge **Marché aux Puces de la Porte de St-Ouen,** 18e (Métro: Porte-de-Clignancourt), is said to be the largest flea market in the world. It features several thousand stalls, carts, shops, and vendors selling everything from vintage clothing to antique chandeliers, paintings, furniture, and toys. It's a real shopping adventure, and you need to arrive early to snag the deals — if you can find any. The best times for bargains are at opening time and just before closing.

 Don't pay the ticketed price or the price the vendor first quotes you; always haggle. You can usually get at least 10 percent off. Most flea markets accept cash only, and you don't have to pay any VAT on your purchases.

 You'll see stalls selling cheap junk starting at the underpass just past the Clignancourt Métro stop. Watch out for pickpockets, and don't stop here. Turn left onto rue des Rosiers, the market's main street.

Visitors to Paris usually choose the Clignancourt market over the convivial market at **Porte de Vanves,** 14e (Métro: Porte de Vanves), a gem waiting to be discovered. Probably the smallest of the fleas, and a bit more upscale (so are its prices), it's a good place to browse among friendly dealers. Open Saturday and Sunday 8:30 a.m. to 1 p.m.

What to look for and where to find it

From antiques to wine (okay, so not quite A to Z), here are some great stores representing both economy and first-class shopping in Paris.

Antiques

Le Louvre des Antiquaires (2 place du Palais-Royal, 1er; ☎ 01-42-97-29-86; Métro: Palais-Royal–Musée du Louvre) is an enormous mall filled with all kinds of shops selling everything from Jean Cocteau sketches to silver cutlery. Items are pricey, but some good deals exist here. A cafe and toilets are located on the second floor.

Le Village St-Paul (23–27 rue St-Paul, 4e; no phone; Métro: St-Paul), a secluded 17th-century village has been turned into an indoor–outdoor arts and antiques fair with shops that display paintings, antiques, and other items both inside and in the courtyard. It's easy to walk past the entrances, so look for the signs just inside the narrow passageways between the houses on rue St-Paul, rue Jardins St-Paul, and rue Charlemagne. Keep in mind that this is a very popular destination on the weekend. Closed Tuesday and Wednesday.

Books

Booksellers hawking posters, postcards, and used books from green wooden boxes on some of the Seine's quais are worth a browse (*bouquinistes:* Quai de Montebello, Quai St-Michel, and various other Left and Right Bank quais). Many of these merchants come from a long line of booksellers dating to the time of Henri IV in the 17th century.

Gibert Joseph (26, 30 bd. St-Michel, 6e; ☎ 01-44-41-88-88; Métro: Odéon or Cluny-Sorbonne) is *the* Parisian students' bookstore, selling new and secondhand books, records, videos, and stationery on several floors and in several branches on bd. St-Michel.

Librarie La Hune (170 bd. St-Germain, 6e; ☎ 01-45-48-35-85; Métro: St-Germain) is sandwiched between cafes Les Deux Magots and de Flore. This bookstore has been a center for Left Bank intellectuals since 1945, when Sartre was among its clients. Most books are in French. It's open until midnight every night but Sunday.

Shakespeare and Company (37 rue de la Bûcherie, 5e; ☎ 01-43-26-96-50; Métro or RER: St-Michel) isn't the original with the same name (that's in Manhattan), but English-speaking residents of Paris still gather in this wonderfully dark and cluttered store, named after Sylvia Beach's legendary literary lair. The store has a selection of new books, but the majority of them are used. Poetry readings take place on Sundays.

Quality fiction in English is the highlight of the **Village Voice** (6 rue Princesse, 6e; ☎ 01-46-33-36-47; Métro: Mabillon or St-Germain), a small two-level store in St-Germain-des-Prés, along with an excellent selection of poetry, plays, nonfiction, and literary magazines. Owner Odile Hellier has played host to free poetry and prose readings with authors and poets since 1982.

Children's clothing

Du Pareil au Même (168 bd. St-Germain, 6e; ☎ 01-46-33-87-85) is the store to buy clothes for every child on your list — apparel is practical, *très mignons* (very cute), and reasonably priced. Other branches include 1 rue St-Denis, 1er (☎ 01-42-36-07-57), and 14 rue St-Placide, 6e (☎ 01-45-44-04-40).

When BCBG women (see "BCBG bourgeois chic: The 6e," earlier in this chapter) have kids, **Jacadi** (256 bd. St-Germain, 7e; ☎ 01-42-84-30-40) is where they buy their very proper children's clothes. Many branches are located all across the city, including 17 bd. Poissonière, 2e (☎ 01-42-36-69-91).

Part of a French chain with a dozen stores in Paris, **Natalys** (92 av. des Champs-Elysées, 8e; ☎ 01-43-59-17-65; Métro: Franklin-D-Roosevelt) sells children's wear, maternity wear, and related products. Other branches include 69 rue de Clichy, 9e (☎ 01-48-74-07-44) and 47 rue de Sèvres, 6e (☎ 01-45-48-77-12).

Tartine et Chocolat (105 rue du Faubourg St-Honoré, 8e; ☎ 01-45-62-44-04; Métro: St. Philippe du Roule) has typically French, precious, and pricey clothes. Another branch is located at 266 bd. St-Germain, 7e (☎ 01-45-56-10-45).

Crystal and glassware

Baccarat's (30 Rue de Paradis, 10e; ☎ 01-40-22-11-00; Métro: Château-d'Eau, Poissonnière, or Gare-de-l'Est) crystal has been world-renowned since the 18th century. This store is also a museum, so even if its prices are too high, feel free to browse the collections that include perfume bottles, 19th- and 20th-century glassware, and coats of arms.

Lumicristal (22 Bis rue de Paradis, 10e; ☎ 01-47-70-27-97; Métro: Château-d'Eau, Poissonnière, or Gare-de-l'Est) discounts crystal by Daum, Limoges, and Baccarat.

La Maison Ivre (38 rue Jacob, 6e; ☎ 01-42-60-01-85; Métro: St-Germain-des-Prés) carries an excellent selection of handmade pottery from all across France, with an emphasis on Provençal and southern French ceramics. You can find splendid pieces of ovenware, bowls, platters, plates, pitchers, mugs, and vases here.

Housewares

Find bright and affordable kitchen implements, such as magnetized salt-shakers, pepper shakers, and wine openers that look a tad, well, *human,* at **Alessi** (14 rue du Faubourg St-Honoré, 8e; ☎ 01-42-66-14-61; Métro: Madéleine or Concorde). You'll also find some cutlery, dishes, and linens.

Cedre Rouge (116 rue du Bac, 6e; ☎ 01-42-84-84-00; Métro: Sèvres-Babylone or Rue du Bac) sells that urban rustic look made with natural materials for apartment, country home, and garden. It isn't cheap, but you'll find some unusual gifts (such as tiny snail candleholders). Finds include Tuscan pottery, Irish linen tablecloths and napkins, Murano glass, teak and wicker furniture, and beeswax candles.

Conforama (2 rue de Pont-Neuf, 1er; ☎ 01-42-33-78-58; Métro: Pont Neuf) is a giant seller of everything for your home at reasonable prices: furniture, appliances, garden tools and accessories, and everyday china and glass.

Cooks love **Déhillerin** (18–20 rue Coquillière, 1er; ☎ 01-42-36-53-13; Métro: Les Halles), with its discounted prices for high-quality copper cookware, glasses, dishes, china, gadgets, utensils, pots, and kitchen appliances.

Verrerie des Halles (15 rue du Louvre, 1er; ☎ 01-42-36-80-60; Métro: Louvre-Rivoli) sells china and glassware made for restaurants at discount prices.

Jewelry and collectibles

Biche de Bère (16 rue des Innocents, 1er; ☎ 01-40-41-02-13; Métro: Châtelet) has chunky and unusual jewelry in sterling silver and gold plate.

Bijoux Burma (50 rue François, 1er, 8e; ☎ 01-47-23-70-93; Métro: Franklin-D-Roosevelt) has some of the best costume jewelry in the city, the secret weapon of many a Parisian woman. It also has a branch at 8 bd. Des Capucines (☎ 01-42-66-27-09).

Eric et Lydie (7 passage du Grand Cerf, 2e; ☎ 01-40-26-52-59; Métro: Etienne-Marcel), in the arty Passage du Grand Cerf, contains unusual, beautiful, and reasonably priced costume jewelry, hair ornaments, and other accessories.

Monic (5 rue des Francs-Bourgeois, 4e; ☎ 01-42-72-39-15; Métro: St-Paul) in the Marais — open Sunday afternoons — sells a wide range of affordable costume jewelry and designer creations.

Pylones (57 rue de St-Louis-en-l'Ile, 4e; ☎ 01-46-34-05-02; Métro: Pont-Marie) offers collectibles from *The Simpsons,* children's umbrellas that stand on their own, bicycle bells shaped like ladybugs, and a variety of other unusual gift items. It's a fun place to browse. It's at 7 rue Tardieu, 18e (☎ 01-46-06-37-00).

Why? (41 rue des Francs-Bourgeois, 4e; ☎ 01-44-61-72-75; Métro: St. Paul) is for the teenager-at-heart, with inflatable chairs, dirty cards and jokes, Tintin figurines, notebooks, and T-shirts.

Men's clothing

With quality shirts in nearly every color imaginable, **Façonnable** (9 rue du Faubourg St-Honoré, 8e; ☎ 01-47-42-72-60; Métro: Madeleine) also sells casual pants, jackets, suits, and other men's furnishings (all a bit on the conservative side). Another branch is located at 174 bd. St-Germain, 6e (☎ 01-40-49-02-47).

Although **Loft Design** (56 rue de Rennes, 6e; ☎ 01-45-44-88-99) sells women's clothing, this shop is worth a visit for the menswear, which is reasonably priced and fashion-forward, especially the thick cotton sweaters and casual trousers.

Madelios (23 bd. de la Madeleine, 1er; ☎ 01-53-45-00-00) offers one-stop shopping for men, selling everything from overcoats to lighters. If companions get bored waiting, the store is part of a small mall that has some pleasant shops for browsing.

Specialty foods

Fauchon (26 place Madeleine, 8e; ☎ 01-47-42-60-11; Métro: Madeleine) is a large gourmet store stocked with pink-labeled cans of coffee, caviar, foie gras, biscuits, wines, oils, candy, pastries, and on and on. It isn't necessarily a good value, but visiting is worth it if only for the store's long history. Its tea salon is next door.

Hediard (21 place Madeleine, 8e; ☎ 01-43-12-88-88; Métro: Madeleine), with branches all across the city, is Fauchon's rival; it sells most of the same products, though slightly cheaper than Fauchon, and has good hot and cold prepared food.

La Grande Epicerie de Paris (at Le Bon Marché, 38 rue de Sèvres, 7e; ☎ 01-44-39-81-00; Métro: Sèvres-Babylone), although not cheap, is one of the best luxury supermarkets in Paris. Look for gourmet gifts, such as olive oils, homemade chocolates, or wine. It makes for one-stop picnic shopping, too, with a wide array of prepared foods and cheeses.

Each candy at **La Maison du Chocolat** (225 rue du Faubourg St-Honoré, 8e; ☎ 01-42-27-39-44; Métro: Ternes) is made from a blend of as many as six kinds of South American and African chocolate, flavored with just about everything imaginable. We feel guilty even referring to it as candy. All the merchandise is made on the premises. If the smell doesn't lure you in, the windows will.

La Maison du Miel (24 rue Vignon, 9e; ☎ 01-47-42-26-70; Métro: Madeleine or Havre-Caumartin) sells varieties of honey you never dreamed possible (pine tree, for example), identified according to the flower to which the bees were exposed.

Toys and games

For more than 150 years, **Au Nain Bleu** (408 rue St-Honoré, 8e; ☎ 01-42-60-39-01; Métro: Concorde or Madeleine) has been selling toy soldiers, stuffed animals, games, and puppets. More modern toys also are on hand, including airplanes and model cars.

In addition to the books, videos, and music for children, **FNAC Junior** (19 rue Vavin, 6e; ☎ 01-42-82-80-24; Métro: Vavin) has story hours and activities for its young guests.

Floor 4 of the **Galeries Lafayette** main store (40 bd. Haussman, 9e; ☎ 01-56-24-03-46; Métro: Havre-Caumartin, Chaussée-d'Antin-La Fayette, Opéra, Trinité) is devoted to toys and children's clothing. And you'll find a play area that your kids will love.

Wines

At **Le Jardin des Vignes** (91 rue de Turenne, 3e; ☎ 01-42-77-05-00; Métro: St-Sébastien-Froissart), bottles of rare wines, champagne, and cognac are sold at reasonable prices. The friendly owners are really excited about wine and also offer tastings.

Legrand Filles et Fils (1 rue de la Banque, 2e; ☎ 01-42-60-07-12; Métro: Bourse) stocks fine wines, brandies, chocolates, coffees, and oenophile paraphernalia, and conducts wine tastings one night a week.

Les Caves Augé (116 bd. Haussmann, 8e; ☎ 01-45-22-16-97; Métro: St-Augustin), the oldest wine shop in Paris, has a sommelier on site.

The flagship store of the **Nicolas** chain (31 place de la Madeleine, 8e; ☎ 01-42-68-00-16; Métro: Madeleine), with more than 250 branches in and around Paris, offers good prices for bottles you may not be able to find in the United States.

Women's clothing

1-2-3 (146 rue de Rivoli, 1er; ☎ 01-40-20-97-01; Métro: Louvre-Rivoli) sells stylish women's suits, blouses, and sweaters, most in synthetics, and accessories at moderate prices. Other branches include 30 av. Italie, 13e (☎ 01-45-80-02-88).

Cacharel (64 rue Bonaparte, 6e; ☎ 01-40-46-00-45) is known for its beautiful and reasonably priced women's, children's, and men's clothes, some in pretty Liberty of London flower-printed fabrics.

Colette (213 rue St-Honoré, 1er; ☎ 01-55-35-33-90; Métro: Tuileries) has some of the city's most cutting-edge fashion in *très* artistic displays.

Corinne Sarrut (4 rue de Prè aux Clercs, 6e; ☎ 01-42-61-71-60; Métro: St. Germain) designed the charming outfits with nipped-in waists and swingy skirts worn by Audrey Tautou in the film *Amélie*.

Merchandise is mostly made from synthetic or synthetic blend fabrics at **Etam** (9 bd. St Michel, 5e; ☎ 01-43-54-79-20; Métro: St-Michel), but the fashions are recent, and the stores are *everywhere*. The Etam lingerie store at 47 rue de Sèvres, 6e (☎ 01-45-48-21-33), has some pretty and affordable nightclothes and underwear.

You can find some nice young and modern styles at **La City** (37 rue Chaussée d'Antin, 9e; ☎ 01-48-74-41-00; Métro: Chaussée d'Antin), and though everything is synthetic, the prices are reasonable. Other branches are located at 18 rue St-Antoine, 4e (☎ 01-42-78-95-55), and 5 Bis rue St-Placide, 6e (☎ 01-42-84-32-84).

Shoe Bizz (42 rue Dragon, 6e; ☎ 01-45-44-91-70; Métro: St. Germain) carries the latest fashions for your feet at budget-friendly prices. Another branch is at 48 rue de Beaubourg, 3e (☎ 01-48-87-12-73).

Young adult clothing

Brightly painted **Antoine et Lili** (95 quai Valmy, 10e; ☎ 01-40-37-41-55; Métro: Gare de l'Est) is a good place to stop if you're strolling the quays of the Canal St-Martin; it sells fun bohemian-style clothes and accessories and decorations. A garden and a small "canteen" are also here. Another branch is at 7 rue d'Albioni, 16e (☎ 01-45-27-95-00).

Cop-Copine (80 rue Rambuteau, 1er; ☎ 01-40-28-03-72; Métro: Les Halles; RER: Châtelet-Les Halles) sells cutting-edge and flattering fashion. Its youthful clothes look good on everyone.

H & M (120 rue de Rivoli, 1er; ☎ 01-55-34-96-86; Métro: Hôtel-de-Ville, Louvre-Rivoli), the Swedish "IKEA of fashion," has a large selection of up-to-the-minute men's and women's fashions at low prices.

Mango (82 rue de Rivoli, 1er; ☎ 01-44-59-80-37; Métro: Hôtel-de-Ville, Louvre-Rivoli), with stores all across Paris, is popular with young Parisian women for its inexpensive, fashion-conscious, body-hugging clothes.

Zara (128 rue de Rivoli, 1er; ☎ 01-44-82-64-00; Métro: Hôtel-de-Ville, Louvre-Rivoli) offers well-made copies of today's hottest styles for women, men, and children at extremely low prices. Locations are all over the place, including 2 rue Halévy, 9e (☎ 01-44-71-90-90 and 01-44-71-90-93), and 44 av. Champs-Elysées (☎ 01-45-61-52-81).

Living It Up after Dark

Paris may not be a city that never sleeps, but it's just as fabulous after the sun sets as it is during the day. Take your pick of French-language, English-language, and avant-garde theater productions or ballet, opera, and symphony. But keep in mind that events can sell out quickly.

The Ménilmontant neighborhood is still a haven for barhoppers, though residents complain that it's getting too trendy. Clubs have also opened up in barges on the Seine. You can always check out the overpriced can-can cabaret spectacles at venues such as the Moulin Rouge, the Lido, and the Crazy Horse — though Parisians wouldn't be caught dead at 'em, they still draw plenty of healthy business from visitors.

For those desiring culture, Paris's performing arts scene is world class. The Paris theater scene has nearly always been dynamic, with plenty of experimentation. If your French is rusty, however, you may want to consider alternatives to French-language productions — such as ballet or one of the many avant-garde productions in which language is secondary — or not spoken at all.

The performing arts

Several local publications available at newsstands provide up-to-the-minute listings of performances and other evening entertainment. *Pariscope: Une Semaine de Paris* (.40€/50¢) is a weekly guide with thorough listings of movies, plays, ballet, art exhibits, clubs, and more, including an English-language insert with selected listings. *L'Officiel des Spectacles* (.35€/40¢) is another weekly guide in French. *Paris Nuit* (3.05€/$3.65) is a French monthly containing good articles and listings.

You can pick up the free music monthlies, *La Terrasse* and *Cadences,* outside concert venues. The *Paris Free Voice* is a free monthly publication that spotlights events of interest to English-speakers, including poetry readings, plays, and literary evenings at English-language bookstores and libraries. You can find it at cybercafes and English-language bookstores.

Classical and organ concerts

More than a dozen Parisian churches regularly schedule inexpensive or free **organ recitals** and concerts. Among them are **Notre-Dame** (☎ 01-42-34-56-10; Métro: Cité); **St-Eustache,** 1 rue Montmartre, 1er (☎ 01-42-33-77-87; Métro: Châtelet); **St-Sulpice,** place St-Sulpice (☎ 01-46-33-21-78; Métro: St-Sulpice), which has an amazing eight-columned pipe organ; **St-Germain-des-Prés,** place St-Germain-des-Prés (☎ 01-43-25-41-71; Métro: St-Germain-des-Prés); the **Madeleine,** place de la Madeleine (☎ 01-47-42-13-09; Métro: Madeleine); and **St-Louis en l'Ile,** 19 rue St-Louis-en-l'Ile (☎ 01-44-62-00-55; Métro: Pont-Marie). In a less magnificent setting, the Sunday concerts at 6 p.m. at the **American Church,** 65 quai d'Orsay (☎ 01-45-56-09-50; Métro: Invalides), are friendly and inviting. For reservations or questions about any of these concerts and venues, contact **La Toison d'Art** (☎ 01-44-62-00-55).

Maison de la Radio, 116 av. du President Kennedy, 16e (☎ 01-56-40-15-16; Métro: Kennedy-Radio France), offers free tickets to recordings of some concerts. Tickets are available on the spot an hour before the recording starts. The **Conservatoire National Superieur de Musique** at the Cité de la Musique, 209 av. Jean Jaurés, 19e (☎ 01-40-40-45-45; Métro: Porte de Pantin), also stages free concerts and ballets performed by students at the conservatory.

The **Théâtre Mogador,** 25 rue de Mogador, 9e (☎ **01-56-35-12-00;** Métro: Trinité, Chausée d'Antin, St-Lazare) is the home of the Orchestre de Paris. The orchestra, directed by Christoph Eschenbach, is scheduled to perform, during the 2005 season, works that include Schumann's *Concerto for Piano and Orchestra,* Mendelssohn's *Mer Calme (Calm Seas),* Beethoven's *Symphony #6,* and Mussorgsky's *Pictures at an Exhibition.* Tickets range from 8€ to 60€ ($9.60 to $72); chamber music concerts cost 11€ ($13).

Opera and ballet

At **Châtelet, Théâtre Musical de Paris,** 1 place du Châtelet, 1e (☎ **01-40-28-28-00;** www.chatelet-theatre.com; Métro: Châtelet), tickets for opera and ballet range from 11€ to 114€ ($13–$137); tickets for concerts and recitals are 10€ to 76€ ($12–$91). The box office is open daily 10 a.m. to 7 p.m. Expect to pay a 2€ ($2.40) charge for phone and Internet reservations.

You can see the national opera and ballet troupes perform at both the radiant **Palais Garnier,** place de l'Opéra, 9e (☎ **01-40-01-25-99** [.34€/ minute or 40¢/minute] for reservations; Fax: 01-40-01-25-60; www.opera-de-paris.fr; Métro: Opéra; RER: Auber), and the ultramodern **Opéra National de Bastille.** The Palais Garnier conducts more ballet performances, and the Opéra Bastille puts on more opera. Tickets are priced from 10€ ($12) for seats that have little or no visibility to 114€ ($137). Reserve by phone up to four weeks in advance, and buy at the ticket windows for same-day and performances up to 14 days in advance. A 3€ ($3.60) surcharge is added for reservations made online and by phone. The box office is open Monday to Saturday 10 a.m. to 6:30 p.m.

The **Opéra National de la Bastille,** 120 rue de Lyon (☎ **01-40-01-17-89;** Fax: 01-40-01-25-60; www.opera-de-paris.fr; Métro: Bastille), offers first-class comfort and splendid acoustics at each level of the auditorium, though Parisians still think the building is a badly designed eyesore. The opera house is located at the place de la Bastille; at night, young adults crowd the steps, showing off skateboard moves, talking on cellphones, and flirting. Tickets cost 10€ ($12) for limited- or no-visibility seats to 114€ ($137). Reserve by phone up to four weeks in advance, and buy at the ticket windows for same-day and performances up to 14 days in advance. Expect a 3€ ($3.60) surcharge for reservations made online and by phone. The box office is open Monday to Saturday 11 a.m. to 6:30 p.m.

Opéra-Comique, place Boieldieu, 2e (☎ **08-25-00-00-58** for reservations; Fax: 01-49-26-05-93; www.opera-comique.com; Métro: Richelieu Drouot), offers wonderful musical theater in the Salle Favart, a more intimate venue (the auditorium is so small you can hear people whispering on stage) than its opera-hall counterparts. Jerome Savary is the musical director. Expect such highly entertaining shows as *La Vie Parisienne,* a musical about Offenbach's life in Paris, and *La Toujours Belle et La Toute Petite Bete,* based lightly on *The Beauty and the Beast.* Tickets are priced from 14€ to 122€ ($17–$146), depending on the performance. The box office is open Monday to Saturday 9 a.m. to 9 p.m.

Theater

The theaters listed here are "national theaters," supported by the government, but many private ones also exist. For full listings, consult *Pariscope.*

A good mix of modern and classic tragedies and comedies comes alive in performances in the **Salle Richelieu** of the **Comédie Française,** 2 rue de Richelieu, 1er (☎ **01-44-58-15-15;** Fax: 01-44-58-15-00; www.comedie-francaise.fr; Métro: Palais-Royal–Musée du Louvre). If you don't understand very advanced French, chances are you won't enjoy the performances. Tickets are 10€ to 44€ ($12–$53); 9€ to 20€ ($11–$24) ages 27 and younger. Last-minute seats for ages 27 and younger are on sale one hour before the start of the performance and cost 10€ ($12). Reduced-visibility seats are 4.50€ ($5.40). To make a reservation up to 14 days in advance, phone daily from 11 a.m. to 6 p.m. To order tickets 15 days to 2 months in advance, fax your order or purchase online; no phone reservations are accepted.

In 1996, the Comédie Française took over the **Théâtre du Vieux Colombier,** 21 rue Vieux-Colombier, 6e (☎ **01-44-39-87-00** or 01-44-39-87-01; Fax: 01-44-39-87-19; www.comedie-francaise.fr; Métro: St-Sulpice), an intimate 300-seat venue where mostly modern works are performed. Tickets cost 27€ ($32) adults, 8€ ($9.60) Saturday; 13€ ($16) ages 27 and younger, 6€ ($7.20) Saturday; and 20€ ($24) seniors, 6€ ($7.20) Saturday. To make a reservation up to 14 days in advance, call Tuesday to Saturday 11 a.m. to 6 p.m. or Sunday and Monday 1 to 6 p.m. To order tickets 15 days to 2 months in advance, fax your order or purchase online; no phone reservations are accepted.

Comédie Francaise also has a workshop in the Carrousel du Louvre, **Studio Théâtre** (☎ **01-44-58-98-58;** www.comedie-francaise.fr; Métro: Palais Royal–Musée du Louvre/Louvre-Rivoli), where actors perform one-hour plays and readings. Video projections of plays and films also are shown here. Tickets are sold at the ticket window one hour before the performance and cost 16€ ($19) adults, 12€ ($14) seniors, and 8€ ($9.60) ages 27 and younger.

For popular, contemporary plays, the **Théâtre National de Chaillot,** 1 place du Trocadéro, 16e (☎ **01-53-65-30-00;** www.theatre-chaillot.fr; Métro: Trocadéro), is your place. Part of the Art Deco Palais de Chaillot, the theater is located directly across the Seine from the Tour Eiffel. Tickets are 26€ ($31) adults, 20€ ($24) seniors, and 12€ ($14) ages 26 and younger.

Théâtre National de la Colline, 15 rue Malte-Brun, 20e (☎ **01-44-62-52-52;** www.colline.fr; Métro: Gambetta), has modern drama from around the world, and its Petit Théâtre, located upstairs, has short plays and offerings from international theater's less famous and up-and-coming playwrights. Arrive early to have a glass of wine and admire the view from the Café de la Colline in the lobby. Tickets cost 26€ ($31) adults, 21€ ($25) seniors, and 13€ ($16) younger than 30. On Tuesdays, adults and seniors pay 18€ ($22).

Cabaret

When seeing a Parisian cabaret show, have dinner somewhere else and save yourself some cash. For the money you'd spend at the cabaret, you can have a fabulous meal at one of the pricier suggestions in Chapter 11. Be aware that none of the cabaret shows is suitable for children and that every other member of the audience may be from another country — these are some of the least "Parisian" experiences you can have while still being in Paris.

The sexiest acts are at **Crazy Horse Paris,** 12 av. George V, 8e (☎ **01-47-23-32-32;** www.lecrazyhorseparis.com; Métro: Alma Marceau). Dancers, who have names such as Chica Boum, Pussy Duty-Free, and Zany Zizanie, appear on swing seats or slithering and writhing in cages — you get the picture. Cover and two drinks cost from 90€ to 110€ ($108–$132), with additional drinks from 20€ ($24). Two shows nightly at 8:30 and 11 p.m., with an additional show from April through June on Saturdays at 10:15 p.m.

At the **Lido,** 116 av. des Champs-Elysées, 8e (☎ **01-40-76-56-10;** www.lido.fr; Métro: George V), award-winning chef Paul Bocuse designed the above-average menu, but it's still not worth the money to dine here. Its revue, *C'est Magique,* offers "flying" dancers and an ascending stage that periodically delivers feathered women, fountains, an ice rink, high-tech laser lighting, and video projections. Other acts include a magician who performs rabbit tricks. The show, with a half-bottle of champagne, is 100€ ($120) Friday and Saturday, and 80€ ($96) Sunday to Thursday. Dinner with a half-bottle of champagne is 140€ to 200€ ($168–$240). Two shows nightly at 10 p.m. and midnight.

English-language shows

Summer is a good time to catch English-language shows in Paris. Your options include the following:

✔ **Théâtre de Nesle,** 8 rue de Nesle, 6e (☎ **01-46-34-61-04;** Métro: St-Michel) or the **Théâtre des Déchargeurs,** 3 rue des Déchargeurs, 1er (☎ **01-42-36-00-02;** Métro: Châtelet) sometimes stage English-language plays.

✔ For comedy in English, try **Laughing Matters,** in the historic Hôtel du Nord, 102 quai de Jemmapes, 10e (☎ **01-53-19-98-98;** www.anythingmatters.com; Métro: Jacques Bonsergent). This company is thriving; the lineups always are terrific, featuring award-winning comics from the United States, the United Kingdom, Ireland, and Australia. Shows start at 8:30 p.m.; admission costs 20€ and 22€ ($24 and $26) at the door.

The most famous of the cabarets is the **Moulin Rouge,** place Blanche, Montmartre, 18e (☎ **01-53-09-82-82;** www.moulinrouge.fr; Métro: place-Blanche). The place has been packing in crowds since 1889, and singers such as Edith Piaf, Yves Montand, and Charles Aznavour made their reputations here. Even Frank Sinatra performed here. The show, *Féerie,* features comedy, animals, and magic acts, with the requisite scantily clad women bumping and grinding around the stage. A bar seat and two drinks cost 95€ ($114) for the 9 p.m. show, 85€ ($102) for the 11 p.m. show. Dinner is available at the 7 p.m. show and costs 125€ to 135€ ($150–$162); you must arrive for dinner by 7 p.m.

Gustav Eiffel designed the building of the **Paradis Latin,** 28 rue Cardinal-Lemoine, 5e (☎ **01-43-25-28-28;** www.paradislatin.fr; Métro: Cardinal-Lemoine), the club that's the most French of the cabarets. A genial master encourages audience participation during a show that's less gimmick-filled than the others. To save money, forego dinner for the lower-priced Champagne Revue, which includes a half bottle of bubbly and costs 80€ ($96); dinner-plus-show packages range from 114€ to 200€ ($137–$240). Performances are Wednesday to Monday, with a 9:30 p.m. showtime.

Jazz

Today, the Paris jazz scene still is vibrant, as new generations develop a taste for the sound. Look through the current *Pariscope* for the artists you admire. If you don't care who's playing, and you're just out for a night of good music, you can stop by any of the following clubs.

A noisy crowd of foreigners and locals appreciates **Caveau de la Hûchette,** 5 rue de la Hûchette, 5e (☎ **01-43-26-65-05;** Métro or RER: St-Michel), for a rollicking good time. Cover is 10.50€ ($13) Sunday to Thursday, and Friday and Saturday before 9 p.m., 13€ ($16) for Friday and Saturday between 9 p.m. and 1 a.m. Music starts at 9:30 p.m. **Baiser Salé,** 58 rue des Lombards, 1er (☎ **01-42-33-37-71;** Métro: Châtelet), is a small space that gets crowded with fans of fusion jazz, funk, and Caribbean. Cover Tuesday and Thursday to Sunday varies from 8€ to 16€ ($9.60–$19). On Monday nights, admission is free. The club is open daily from 6 p.m. to 6 a.m.

The crowd is casual and down to earth and the jazz is some of France's most interesting at **Duc des Lombards,** 42 rue des Lombards, 1er (☎ **01-42-33-22-88;** Métro: Châtelet–Les Halles). Cover is 19€ to 25€ ($23–$30). You can dine and drink at **Le Petit Journal Saint-Michel,** 71 bd. St-Michel, 5e (☎ **01-43-26-28-59;** Métro: Cluny-La-Sorbonne, RER: Luxembourg), with its warm, relaxed, and French atmosphere. Recent jazz acts included the Paris Swing Orchestra. Cover is 16€ to 19€ ($19–$23), or you can do dinner plus a show for 42€ to 47€ ($50–$56).

New Morning, 7–9 rue des Petites-Ecuries, 10e (☎ **01-45-23-56-39;** Métro: Château-d'Eau), is one of Paris's best jazz clubs, and the best artists from around the world perform here. Cover is from 22€ to 25€ ($26–$30), depending on the act. With its medieval look and vaulted ceilings, **Slow Club,** 130 rue de Rivoli, 1er (☎ **01-42-33-84-30;** Métro: Châtelet–Les Halles), is a dungeon filled with dancers and fans of big American and European artists who perform swing, Dixieland, and classic jazz. Cover is 13€ ($16). Anything goes at **Les 7 Lézards,** 10 rue des Rosiers, 4e (☎ **01-48-87-08-97;** www.7lezards.com; Métro: St-Paul), the more experimental, the better. Depending on the performer, entry ranges from 12€ to 16€ ($14–$19). This is the place where jazz musicians go to wind down.

Classy cocktails

If you're looking for a quiet, romantic place to unwind with a drink — or if you're on the prowl for where the hip, hot, cutting-edge folks hang out — these places should fit the bill. Most bars and lounges in Paris open daily at 9 p.m., but no one arrives until after midnight. They generally close around 4 a.m.

At **Alcazar,** 62 rue Mazarine, 6e (☎ **01-53-10-19-99;** Métro: Odéon), elements of traditional brasserie style, such as banquettes and mirrors, are slicked up and mixed with innovations such as a glassed-in kitchen theatrically installed along the left wall. The comfortable upstairs bar is ideal for a view over the downstairs restaurant, once one of Paris's hottest eateries.

The atmosphere at the **China Club,** 50 rue de Charenton, 12e (☎ **01-43-43-82-02;** Métro: Bastille), is one of hushed elegance. The Colonial-decorated restaurant just a few steps from the Bastille is a popular nighttime attraction. If you hate cigars, avoid the trendy upstairs *fumoir* (smoking room). All cocktails are well made (8€/$9.60), but the Chinese food is overpriced.

It isn't hip, it isn't even new, but **Harry's New York Bar,** 5 rue Daunou, 2e (☎ **01-42-61-71-14;** Métro: Opéra), definitely serves a classy cocktail. In fact, it's one of Europe's most famous bars and is as popular today as it was in the time of that notorious Lost Generation of writers who really knew how to ring up a bar tab. The Bloody Mary was said to have been invented here, and the selection of whiskeys is amazing. Visit the downstairs if only to look at the 1930s Piano Bar, resembling the inside of a cozy yacht. It isn't cheap, of course — the lowest-priced alcohol (beer) is 6.60€ ($7.90) a glass.

Beautiful people dressed in black come to **La Fabrique,** 53 rue du Faubourg St-Antoine, 11e (☎ **01-43-07-67-07;** Métro: Bastille), a sleek dark bar and restaurant, to drink at the minimalist bar and eat the delicious Alsatian specialty, *Flammekueche* — large, square, thin-crusted pizzas topped with cream, herbs, and toppings of your choice, including salmon, ham, and goat cheese. Although the bar is open until around 5 a.m., depending on the crowds, food is served only until midnight. Be ready to stand in line on the weekends, and look out for private parties when the restaurant is closed to the public.

At **The Lizard Lounge,** 18 rue du Bourg-Tibourg, 4e (☎ 01-42-72-81-34; Métro: Hôtel-de-Ville), the music is loud, but the heavy-gauge steel balcony overlooking the main bar offers a chance for quieter conversation. This stylish but easygoing bar is a pleasant place to hang out with an arty, international crowd. You also can come early in the evening for a reasonably priced light meal prepared in the open kitchen. Wednesday to Saturday, a DJ spins dance music in the basement.

The huge downstairs restaurant at **Man Ray,** 34 rue Marbeuf, 8e (☎ 01-56-88-36-36; Métro: Franklin-D-Roosevelt), is dominated by statues of two winged Asian goddesses who appear concerned — possibly about the food. But don't visit for dinner; have a drink at the upstairs bar while listening to jazz. Take note that as the restaurant winds down around 11 p.m., the music takes on a harder edge, and a sleek international crowd stands shoulder to shoulder along the curving bar. American artist and photographer Man Ray's photos adorn several walls. Celebrity owners include Sean Penn, Johnny Depp, and John Malkovich. Drinks start at 10€ ($12).

Dance clubs

Paris clubs change their programming from night to night. The current fad is the international DJ spinning his or her own mix of house music. If you don't like house, try one of the *bal musettes* (dances); music is usually by a local band. The barges along the Seine in the 13e attract a good mix and play everything from house to blues, and you can have a good, though often crowded, time right on the river. Check the TimeOut section in *Pariscope* magazine (in English) for barge-concert schedules. Salsa, the hottest trend a few years back, is still going strong. Whether you like dancing to techno, house, salsa, world, classic rock, or swing, you'll find it somewhere in Paris (and legions of Parisians eager to dance with you).

To club on a budget, go out during the week, when cover charges may be (officially or unofficially) waived. Yes, it's sexist, but women often get in free, especially if they're dressed in something slinky, low-cut, or short (or all three). Black clothes are *de rigueur* for men and women, and the later you go — or earlier in the morning, as the case may be — the more fashionable.

Many nightclubs accept reservations, so if you're worried about getting past the bouncers, give your club of choice a call.

The Irish light ship (a boat that lights the path for other ships) **Batofar,** 11 quai François Mauriac, 13e (☎ 01-56-29-10-00; Métro: Bibliothèque François Mitterand or Quai de la Gare), has concerts Monday to Sunday, and the party can go on all night. With reasonably priced drinks (3€–10€/ $3.60–$12) and a 20-something clientele, it can get crowded, but it's still a lot of sweaty fun. Music can be anything from drum-and-bass to British pop. Hours vary (check listings in *Pariscope*), but things usually start around 7 p.m. Cover ranges from 6€ to 12€ ($7.20–$14) depending on the band or DJ for the night. A small snack bar is onboard.

You can catch a monthly *bal* (dance) and have a ball at **Elysée Montmartre,** 72 bd. De Rochechouart, 18e (☎ **01-44-92-45-36;** Métro: Anvers), a club that serves the dual function of disco and major concert hall. Illustrious past acts included Björk, U2, and the Red Hot Chili Peppers. Dance music is usually house; the monthly *bals* usually have live local bands. Check *Pariscope* for events and prices. Dances are open 11 p.m. to 5 a.m. Cover charges vary from 15€ to 20€ ($18–$24) for dancing and more for concerts.

One of the best things about **Le Wax,** 15 rue Daval, 11e (☎ **01-40-21-16-16;** Métro: Bastille), is the price — free. You have to really like house music; the club is the premier place for DJs who spin it all night long. Decor is very *Clockwork Orange,* with plastic bubbles on the walls, yellow plastic couches, and lots of crimson and orange. Open 6 p.m. to 2 a.m. Tuesday to Thursday; 6 p.m. to 5 a.m. Friday to Saturday.

La Coupole, 102 bd. du Montparnasse, 14e (☎ **01-43-27-56-00;** Métro: Montparnasse-Bienvenüe), has a basement dance hall — a retro venue with plush banquettes and old-fashioned sounds that's a big draw for out-of-towners. Come on Friday for house; Tuesdays are salsa nights, with dance classes starting at 9:30 p.m. for 10€ ($12) (including a drink). Regular cover is 18€ ($22) on Friday and Saturday from midnight to 5 a.m. and on Tuesday from 9:30 p.m. to 3 a.m.

At **La Java,** 105 rue du Faubourg-du-Temple, 10e (☎ **01-42-02-20-52;** Métro: Belleville), a diverse crowd comes to dance without restraint to mostly Cuban and Brazilian music, played by a live band on Friday and Saturday nights. If you have a taste for something fun, funky, and very authentic, and you like Latin music, this charming old dance hall may be your great night out. Salsa classes are scheduled Thursday nights. Cover Thursday is 10€ ($12); on Friday and Saturday, the cover is 15€ ($18). Open 11 p.m. to dawn.

The huge tri-level **La Locomotive,** 90 bd. de Clichy, 18e (☎ **01-53-41-88-88;** Métro: place-Clichy), is popular with American students and is especially busy on Sundays. People dance to rock and techno, though occasionally metal concerts are staged. La Locomotive is a very big place, and in the *sous-sol* (basement, the coolest of the three levels), you can even see the remnants of an old railway line (hence the name). The Bar Americain looks more Roman, with fake statuary and columns crowned by lions. Beers and Evian start at a high 9€ ($11) during the week, 10€ ($12) on weekends. Cover Sunday to Thursday is 14€ ($17) with one drink; cover on Friday and Saturday night is 20€ ($24) with one drink. Women get in free on Sunday until 1 a.m. Open 11 p.m. to 5 a.m.

Queen, 102 av. des Champs-Elysées, 8e (☎ **01-53-89-08-89;** Métro: George V), is one of the hottest clubs in town, with nightly crowds so thick you can find it difficult to get a drink. Clientele is about two-thirds gay. To get past the strict drag queens at the door, it helps to have a beautiful face and body or at least the ability to disguise your faults with great clothes. Women usually get in only with male friends. Cover (including one drink, with or without alcohol) is 10€ ($12) Sunday to Thursday, 20€ ($24) on Friday and Saturday. Open daily midnight to 7 a.m., 8 a.m. on weekends.

Fast Facts

American Express

The big Paris office, 11 rue Scribe, 9e (☎ 01-47-14-50-00; Métro: Opéra Chaussée-d'Antin or Havre-Caumartin; RER: Auber), is open weekdays 9 a.m. to 6:30 p.m. The bank is open 9 a.m. to 5 p.m. on Saturday, but the mail pickup window is closed.

ATM Locators

ATMs are widely available, with banks on many Paris corners. Before you leave home, ask your bank to print out a list of ATMs that accept your bankcard or MasterCard or Visa cards. Or check out the following sites: www.visaeu.com or www.mastercard.com.

Business Hours

The **grands magasins** (department stores) generally are open Monday to Saturday 9:30 a.m. to 7 p.m.; smaller shops close for lunch and reopen around 2 p.m., but this is rarer than it used to be. Many stores stay open until 7 p.m. in summer; others are closed on Monday, especially in the morning. Large offices remain open all day, but some close for lunch. **Banks** are normally open weekdays 9 a.m. to noon and 1 or 1:30 to 4:30 p.m. Some banks also open on Saturday morning.

Currency Exchange

Banks and *bureaux de change* (exchange offices) almost always offer better exchange rates than hotels, restaurants,

and shops, which should be used only in emergencies. For good rates, without fees or commissions, and quick service, try the **Comptoir de Change Opéra**, 9 rue Scribe, 9e (☎ 01-47-42-20-96; Métro: Opéra; RER: Auber). It is open weekdays 9 a.m. to 6 p.m., Saturday 9:30 a.m. to 4 p.m. The *bureaux de change* at all train stations (except Gare de Montparnasse) are open daily; those at 63 av. des Champs-Elysées, 8e (Métro: Franklin-D-Roosevelt), and 140 av. des Champs-Elysées, 8e (Métro: Charles de Gaulle–Étoile), keep long hours. Despite disadvantageous exchange rates and long lines, many people prefer to exchange money at American Express (see the listing earlier in this section).

Dentists

You can call your consulate and ask the duty officer to recommend a dentist. For dental emergencies, call **SOS Urgences Stomatologique Dentaire** (☎ 01-43-36-36-00) daily from 8:30 a.m. to midnight.

Doctors

Call your consulate and ask the duty officer to recommend a doctor, or call **SOS Médecins** (☎ 01-43-37-77-77), a 24-hour service. Most doctors and dentists speak some English. You can also call for an appointment at the **Centre Médicale Europe**, 44 rue d'Amsterdam (☎ 01-42-81-93-33). Consultations cost about 20€, and specialists are available.

Embassies/Consulates

If you have a passport, immigration, legal, or other problem, contact your consulate. Call before you go: They often keep strange hours and observe both French and home-country holidays. Here's where to find them: **Australia,** 4 rue Jean-Rey, 15e (☎ 01-40-59-33-00; Métro: Bir-Hakeim); **Canada,** 35 av. Montaigne, 8e (☎ 01-44-43-29-00; Métro: Franklin-D-Roosevelt or Alma Marceau); **New Zealand,** 7 ter rue Léonard-de-Vinci, 16e (☎ 01-45-00-24-11; Métro: Victor-Hugo); **Consulate of Great Britain,** 35 rue Faubourg-St-Honoré, 8e (☎ 01-44-51-31-00; Métro: Madeleine); **Embassy of Ireland,** 4 rue Rude, 16e (☎ 01-45-00-20-87); and **United States,** 2 rue St-Florentin, 1er (☎ 01-43-12-22-22; Métro: Concorde).

Emergencies

Call ☎ **17** for the police. To report a fire, dial ☎ **18.** For an ambulance, call ☎ **15.** The main police station, 7 bd. du Palais, 4e (☎ **01-53-71-53-71;** Métro: Cité), is open 24 hours a day.

Hospitals

Two hospitals with English-speaking staff are the **American Hospital of Paris,** 63 bd. Victor-Hugo, Neuilly-sur-Seine (☎ 01-46-41-25-25), just west of Paris proper (Métro: Les Sablons or Levallois-Perret), and the **Hôpital Franco-Brittanique,** 3 rue Barbes Levallois-Perret (☎ 01-46-39-22-22), just north of Neuilly, across the city line northwest of Paris (Métro: Anatole-France). The American Hospital charges about $677 a day for a room, not including doctor's fees. The emergency department charges more than $100 for a visit, not including tests and X-rays.

Information

Before you go: French Government Tourist Office (www.francetourism.com), 444 Madison Ave., 16th floor, New York, NY 10022-6903. This office does not provide information over the phone. When you arrive: Office de Tourisme de Paris, 11 rue Scribe, 9e (☎ 08-92-68-31-12; 0.34€/min. [40¢/min.]; www.paris-tourist office.com).

Internet Access

Cybercafe de Paris, 11 and 15 rue des Halles, 1er (☎ 01-42-21-11-11; Métro: Châtelet), charges 4€ to 7€ ($4.80–$8.40) per hour for internet access.

Laundry & Dry Cleaning

The more expensive your hotel, the more it will cost to get your laundry or dry cleaning done there. Instead, find a laundry near you by consulting the Yellow Pages under *Laveries pour particuliers.* Take as many coins as you can. Washing and drying 6 kilos (13¼ lbs.) usually costs about 4€ to 5.50€ ($4.80–$6.60). Dry cleaning is *nettoyage à sec;* look for shop signs with the word *pressing,* and don't expect to have your clothes back within an hour; you may be able to get them back the next day if you ask nicely. The dry cleaning chain **5 à Sec** has stores all across Paris.

Mail

Large post offices are normally open weekdays 8 a.m. to 7 p.m., Saturday 8 a.m. to noon; small post offices may have shorter hours. Many post offices (PTT) are scattered around the city; ask anybody for the nearest one. Airmail letters and postcards to the United States cost .90€ ($1.10); within Europe 0.50€ (60¢); and to Australia or New Zealand, .90€ ($1.10).The city's main post office is at 52 rue du Louvre, 75001 Paris (☎ 01-40-28-76-00; Métro: Louvre-Rivoli). It's open 24 hours a day for urgent mail, telegrams, and telephone calls. It handles *Poste Restante* mail: sent to you in care of the post office and stored until you pick it up; be prepared to show your passport and pay 0.60€ (70¢) for each letter you receive. If you don't want to use *Poste Restante*, you can receive mail in care of American Express. Holders of American Express cards or traveler's checks get this service free; others have to pay a fee.

Maps

Maps printed by the department stores usually are available free at hotels, and they're good for those visiting Paris for only a few days and hitting only the major attractions. But if you plan to really explore the city, the best maps are those of the *Plan de Paris par Arrondissement*, pocket-sized books with maps and a street index. They're extremely practical, and prices start at around 10€ ($12). You can find them in Paris bookstores, **Monoprix,** and some of the bigger newsstands. Most Parisians carry a copy because they, too, get lost at times.

Police

Dial ☎ 17 in emergencies; otherwise, call ☎ **01-53-71-53-71.**

Restrooms

Public restrooms are plentiful, but you usually have to pay for them. Every cafe has a restroom, but it is supposed to be for customers only. The best plan is to ask to use the telephone; it's usually next to the toilette. For a 2€ ($2.40) coin, you can use the street-side toilets, which are automatically flushed out and cleaned after every use. Some Métro stations have serviced restrooms; you are expected to tip the attendant 0.50€ (60¢).

Safety

Paris is relatively safe; your biggest risks are pickpockets and purse snatchers, so be particularly attentive on the Métro and on crowded buses (especially in the confusion of getting on and off), in museum lines, popular shopping areas, and around tourist attractions. Popular pickpocketing tactics include: someone asking you for directions or bumping into you while an accomplice takes your wallet or bands of children surrounding and distracting you and then making off with purchases and/or your wallet. Women should be on guard in crowded tourist areas and on the Métro against overly friendly men who seem to have made a specialty out of bothering unsuspecting female tourists. Tricks include asking your name and nationality, and then taking advantage of your politeness by sticking like a burr to you for the rest of the day. They're usually more harassing than harmful, but if you're too nice, you may be stuck spending time with someone with whom you prefer not to. A simple "leave me alone" (*laissez-moi tranquille* ["lay-say mwa tran-keel"]) usually works.

Taxis

Taxis Bleues (☎ 08-25-16-10-10), **Alpha Taxis** (☎ 01-45-85-85-85), or **G7** (☎ 01-47-39-47-39). Be aware that the meter starts running as soon as you call a cab, so they're more expensive than regular cabs. You can hail taxis in the street (look for a taxi with a white light on; an orange light means it's occupied), but most drivers will not pick you up if you are in the general vicinity of a taxi stand (look for the blue "taxi" sign).

Telephone/Telex/Fax

Most public phone booths take only telephone debit cards called *télécartes,* which can be bought at post offices and at *tabacs* (cafes and kiosks that sell tobacco products). You insert the card into the phone and make your call; the cost is automatically deducted from the "value" of the card recorded on its magnetized strip. The *télécarte* comes in 50- and 120-unit denominations, costing about 10€ and 15€ ($12 and $18), respectively, and can be used only in a phone booth. Cashiers will almost always try to sell you a card from France Télécom, the French phone company, but cards exist that give you more talk time for the same amount of money. Instead of inserting the card into a public phone, you dial a free number and tap in a code. The cards come with directions, some in English, and can be used from public and private phones, unlike France Télécom's card. Look for *tabacs* that have advertisements for Delta Multimedia or Kertel, or ask for a *télécarte international avec un code.*

For placing international calls from France, dial 00 and then the country code (for the United States and Canada, 1; for Britain, 44; for Ireland, 353; for Australia, 61; for New Zealand, 64), the area or city code, and the local number (for example, to call New York, you'd dial 00 + 1 + 212 + 000-0000). To place a collect call to North America, dial 00-33-11, and an English-speaking operator will assist you. Dial 00-00-11 for an American AT&T operator; MCI 0800-99-00-19; Sprint 0800-99-00-87. For calling from Paris to anywhere else in France (called *province*), the country is

divided into five zones with prefixes 01, 02, 03, 04, and 05; check a phone directory for the code of the city you're calling.

If you're calling France from the United States, dial the international prefix, 011; then the country code for France, 33; followed by the city code and the local number, but leave off the initial zero (for example, 011 + 33 + 1-00-00-00-00). Avoid making phone calls from your hotel room; many hotels charge at least 0.29€ (35¢) for local calls, and the markup on international calls can be staggering.

Trains

The telephone number for reservations on France's national railroads (SNCF) is ☎ **08-92-35-35-35** (0.46€/min. or 55¢/min.). Open 7 a.m. to 10 p.m. daily. Remember, you must validate your train ticket in the orange ticket *composteur* on the platform or pay a fine.

Water

Tap water in Paris is perfectly safe, but if you're prone to stomach problems, you may prefer to drink mineral water.

Weather Updates

Try europe.cnn.com/WEATHER.

Chapter 13

Traveling Beyond Paris: Five Great Day Trips

*J*ust as you're getting used to Paris, it's time to leave. Don't worry; it's just for the day. You'll probably be back in time to have a nightcap in a cafe. The sights in this chapter are the most widely visited attractions in the Ile de France, the suburbs, and countryside surrounding Paris, as shown in the map "The Ile de France." If you have more time, you may want to visit the home of painter Claude Monet at Giverny, with its spectacular gardens and famous lily pond. Although it's technically in the Normandy region, a visit to Monet's house is only an hour from Paris by car.

Appreciating the Château de Versailles

When you first set eyes on the royal château of Versailles (☎ 01-30-83-78-00; www.chateauversailles.fr), you won't know where to look first. "Incredible" doesn't do it justice, especially when you realize it attests to the power that royalty had and the one king — Louis XIV — who truly believed he deserved it. Louis hired the best to build Versailles: Louis Le Vau and Jules Hardouin-Mansart, France's premier architects; André Le Nôtre, designer of the Jardin des Tuileries; and Charles Le Brun, head of the Royal Academy of Painting and Sculpture; for the interior. Construction got under way in 1661.

In 1682, Louis XIV transferred the court to Versailles to live with him to prevent plots against him (because his citizens' taxes paid for Versailles, he was a little paranoid). Historians estimate that anywhere from 3,000

The Ile de France

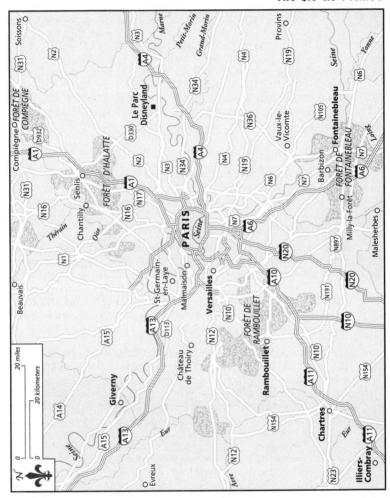

to 10,000 people, including servants, lived at Versailles, and court etiquette grew to be absurd (including the occasional power struggles between attendants over who ranked high enough to dress Marie Antoinette while the young queen waited, shivering). When you see all this over-the-top magnificence and try to estimate the cost, you may understand better the anger of the revolutionaries a century later.

Louis enjoyed an incredibly long reign — 72 years. When he died in 1715, he was succeeded by his great-grandson, Louis XV, who continued the outrageous pomp and ceremony and made interior renovations and redecorations until lack of funds forced him to stop. His son and daughter-in-law, Louis XVI and Marie Antoinette, had simpler tastes and made no major changes at Versailles. But by then, it was too late. On October 6, 1789, a mob marched on the palace and forced the royal couple to return to Paris. Versailles ceased to be a royal residence.

Louis-Philippe, who reigned from 1830 to 1848 and succeeded Louis XVIII, prevented the château's destruction by donating his own money to convert it into a museum dedicated to the glory of France. John D. Rockefeller also contributed to the restoration of Versailles, and the work from that contribution continues to this day.

Seeing the sights

More than 3 million tourists visit Versailles each year, so arrive early; you'll want to have as much of a head start as possible to make sure you cover the grounds (shown in the nearby "Versailles" map).

Highlights of the castle and gardens

Kings used the six Louis XIV–style **Grands Appartements** for ceremonial events, and lived with their families in the **Petits Appartements.** Louis stashed his mistresses, Mme. du Barry and Mme. de Pompadour, in his second-floor apartment (which can be visited only with a guide). Attempts have been made to restore the original decor of the queen's bedchamber, which Marie Antoinette renovated with a huge four-poster bed and silks in patterns of lilacs and peacock feathers.

The **Salons of War and Peace** flank the château's most famous room, the 72-meter (236-ft.) long **Hall of Mirrors,** which Hardouin-Mansart began work on in 1678. Le Brun later added 17 large windows and corresponding mirrors. The ceiling paintings represent the accomplishments of Louis XIV's governance. Jacques-Ange Gabriel designed the **library,** with its delicately carved panels. The **Clock Room** has Passement's astronomical clock, which took 20 years to make; it's encased in gilded bronze.

Gabriel also designed the **Royal Opéra** for Louis XV. Try to imagine it as it used to be — floor coverings of bearskin, lit by 3,000 powerful candles. Hardouin-Mansart built the gold-and-white **Royal Chapel** between 1699 and 1710. After his father's death, Louis XVI, with his wife, Marie Antoinette, prayed for guidance here, feeling they were too young to run the country.

After you've seen the château, plan to spend at least an hour strolling through the **Formal Gardens,** spread across 101 hectares (250 acres). Le Nôtre created a Garden of Eden, using ornamental lakes and canals, geometrically designed flowerbeds, and avenues bordered with statuary. Louis XV, imagining he was in Venice, used to take gondola rides with his "favorite" of the moment on the mile-long Grand Canal.

Versailles

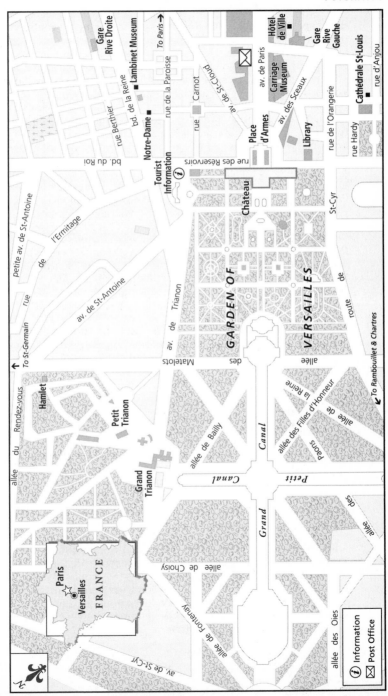

Gare Rive Droite
Lambinet Museum
To Paris →
rue Berthier
bd. de la Reine
Notre-Dame
rue de la Paroisse
Carnot
rue
av. de St-Cloud
Hôtel de Ville
Gare Rive Gauche
Cathédrale St-Louis
rue d'Anjou
av. de Paris
Carriage Museum
av. des Sceaux
rue de l'Orangerie
rue Hardy
Place d'Armes
Library
Tourist Information
rue des Réservoirs
bd. du Roi
Château
St-Cyr
Petite av. de St-Antoine
de l'Ermitage
de
rue
av. de St-Antoine
To St-Germain
GARDEN OF
av. de Trianon
Matelots
des
VERSAILLES
allée
de
route
To Rambouillet & Chartres
Hamlet
Petit Trianon
la Reine
allée de
allée des Filles d'Honneur
Paons
Rendez-vous
du
allée
Grand Trianon
allée de Bailly
Canal
Petit
Canal
Grand
des
allée
Paris
Versailles
FRANCE
allée de Choisy
allée de Fontenay
av. de St-Cyr
allée des Oies
i Information
⊠ Post Office

The underrated treasures

Because of the crowds and long lines, most guests are content to visit only the château and gardens, but you can see much more at Versailles if you've got the stamina. The most important of the remaining sights are the **Grand Trianon** and the **Petit Trianon,** both opulent love nests constructed for the mistresses of kings. A long walk across the park takes you to the pink-and-white-marble Grand Trianon, designed in 1687 by Hardouin-Mansart for Louis XIV. It has traditionally served as a residence for the country's important guests, though de Gaulle wanted to turn it into a weekend retreat for himself. Napoléon I spent a night here, and U.S. President Richard Nixon slept in the room where Mme. de Pompadour (an important mistress of Louis XV) died. Gabriel, designer of the place de la Concorde, built the Petit Trianon in 1768 for Louis XV; Louis used it for his trysts with Mme. du Barry, his mistress after Mme. de Pompadour. Marie Antoinette adopted the Petit Trianon as her favorite residence, where she could escape the constraints of palace life.

Behind the Petit Trianon is the **Hamlet,** a collection of small thatched farmhouses and a water mill where Marie Antoinette could pretend she was back at her family's country retreat in Austria. Nearby the Hamlet is the **Temple of Love,** built in 1775 by Richard Mique, Marie Antoinette's favorite architect. In the center of its Corinthian colonnade is a reproduction of Bouchardon's *Cupid Making a Bow out of the Club of Hercules.*

Near the stables is the entrance to the **Carriage Museum,** which houses coaches from the 18th and 19th centuries. Among them is one used at the coronation of Charles X and another used at the wedding of Napoléon I and Marie-Louise. One sleigh rests on tortoise-shell runners. A ticket to the Petit Trianon also admits you to this museum.

The particulars

From May 2 to September 30, the palace is open Tuesday to Sunday 9 a.m. to 6:30 p.m.; from April to October, the Grand Trianon and Petit Trianon are open daily from noon to 6:30 p.m. The rest of the year, the palace is open Tuesday to Sunday 9 a.m. to 5:30 p.m.; the Grand Trianon and Petit Trianon are open November to March daily noon to 5:30 p.m. The park and the gardens are open every day except in bad weather from 7 a.m. in summer, 8 a.m. in winter, until sunset (between 5:30 p.m. and 9:30 p.m. depending on the season).

Admission to the palace is 7.50€ ($9) adults; 5.30€ ($6.35) for ages 18 to 24 and older than 60, free for those younger than 18. Combined admission to the Grand and Petit Trianons is 5€ ($6) adults, 3€ ($3.60) 18 to 24 and seniors; younger than 18 are admitted free. Admission to the gardens is 3€ ($3.60) adults; free for children younger than 18. Admission to the Coach museum is 2€ ($2.40); children younger than 18 free. Admission to Jeu de Paume is free.

One-hour audio tours of the King's Chambers are 11.50€ ($14) adults, 8€ ($9.60) ages 10 to 17. Lecturer-led one-hour tours of the palace are 11.50€ ($14) adults, 8€ ($9.60) ages 10 to 17; 1½-hour tours are 13.50€ ($16) adults, 9.50€ ($11) ages 10 to 17; two-hour tours are 15.50€ ($19) adults, 10.80€ ($13) ages 10 to 17. All tours are free for children younger than 10.

Getting to Versailles

To reach to the château from Paris **by car,** head west on the A13 highway from Porte d'Auteuil toward Rouen. Take the Versailles-Château exit, 22½km (14 miles) from Paris. Park in the visitors' parking lot at place d'Armes for 4.50€ ($5.40) Monday to Friday, 5.50€ ($6.60) weekends. The drive takes about a half-hour, but it can take more than an hour in traffic.

Cityrama, 4 place des Pyramides, 1er (☎ 01-44-55-61-00; www.cityrama. fr), has different **bus** trips to Versailles ranging from 36€ ($43) adults and 18€ ($22) children to 76€ ($91) adults and 38€ ($46) children. **Paris Vision,** 214 rue de Rivoli, 1er (☎ 01-42-60-30-01; www.parisvision.com), offers bus excursions starting from 36€ to 60€ ($43–$72); half-price for ages 4 to 11.

Dining locally

The town of Versailles has no shortage of places where you can break for lunch, but after you're on the palace grounds, you may find it infinitely more convenient to just stay put; otherwise, you have to hike back into town and back out to the palace again. In the château, you can eat at a cafeteria just off the Cour de la Chapelle. In the Formal Gardens, an informal restaurant, **La Flotille,** is on Petite Venise. (To get here from the château, walk directly back through the gardens to where the canal starts. Petite Venise and the restaurant are to your right.) Finally, several **snack bars** are located in the Gardens near the Quinconce du Midi and the Grand Trianon.

Château de Fontainebleau: Napoléon's Lair

Fontainebleau (☎ 01-60-71-50-70) contains more than 700 years of royal history, from the enthronement of Louis VII in 1137 to the fall of the Second Empire in 1873. What this place is most famous for, however, is Napoléon's farewell to his Imperial Guard, which he delivered on the grand curved stairway before leaving for exile. If you get tired of the palace's splendor, you can walk around the beautiful gardens and then rent bikes to ride in the nearly 17,000 hectares (42,000 acres) of the kings' old hunting grounds, the Forêt de Fontainebleau. For a preview of the grounds, check out the "Fontainebleau" map in this section.

Seeing the sights

In 1528, François I transformed a run-down royal palace into Fontaine-bleau for his mistress, and his successor, Henri II, left a beautiful memorial to the woman he loved, a **ballroom** decorated with the intertwined initials of his mistress, Diane de Poitiers, and himself. The *Mona Lisa* once hung here; François I bought the painting from da Vinci himself. Stucco-framed paintings now hanging in the **Gallery of François I** include *The Rape of Europa* and depict mythological and allegorical scenes related to the king's life.

Make sure to see the racy ceiling paintings above the **Louis XV Staircase.** Originally painted for the bedroom of a duchess, the stairway's architect simply ripped out her floor and used her bedroom ceiling to cover the stairway. One fresco depicts the queen of the Amazons climbing into Alexander the Great's bed.

When Louis XIV ascended the throne, Fontainebleau was largely neglected because of his preoccupation with Versailles, but it found renewed glory under Napoléon I. You can walk around much of the palace on your own, but most of the Napoleonic rooms are accessible only on guided tours, which are in French. Napoleon had two bedchambers; mirrors adorn either side of his bed in the grander chamber (look for his symbol, a bee), while a small bed is housed in the aptly named **Small Bedchamber.** A red-and-gold throne with the initial N is displayed in the **Throne Room.** You can also see Napoléon's **offices,** where the emperor signed his abdication, though the document exhibited is only a copy.

After a visit to the palace, wander through the gardens, paying special attention to the bucolic carp pond with its fearless swans. If you'd like to promenade in the forest, a detailed map of its paths is available from the **Office de Tourisme** (4 rue Royale, near the palace; ☎ 01-60-74-99-99). You can also rent bikes nearby from **A la Petite Reine** (32 rue des Sablons; ☎ 01-60-74-57-57) for 13€ ($16) a day, 16€ ($19) on weekends with a credit-card deposit. **Tour Denencourt,** about 5km (3 miles) north of the palace, makes a pleasant ride and has a pretty view (ask at the bike shop for directions).

The Château de Fontainebleau is open Wednesday to Monday 9:30 a.m. to 6 p.m. June to September; 9:30 a.m. to 5 p.m. October to May. Admission to the Grands Appartements is 5.50€ ($6.60) adults, 4€ ($4.80) ages 18 to 26 and older than 60, and for all on Sunday. Children younger than 18 are free.

Getting to Fontainebleau

By train, the Montargie line to Fontainebleau Avon station departs hourly from the Gare de Lyon in Paris. The trip takes 35 to 60 minutes and costs 7.40€ ($8.90). Fontainebleau Avon station is just outside the

Fontainebleau

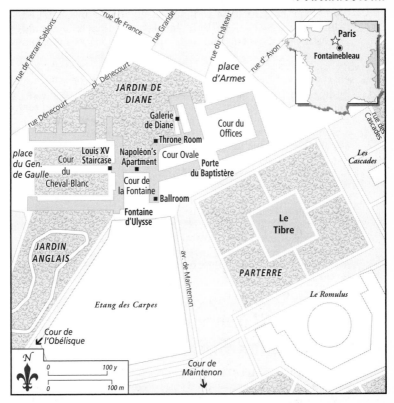

town in Avon, a suburb of Paris. From the station, the town bus (direction Château) makes the 3-kilometer (2-mile) trip to the château every 10 to 15 minutes on weekdays, every 30 minutes on Saturdays and Sundays.

If you're **driving,** take the A6 south of Paris, first in the direction of Nantes/Bordeaux/Aéroport Orly/Rungis/Évry/Lyon for about 9km (5½ miles) and then continuing south toward Évry/Lyon/Chilly Mazarin for about 35km (22 miles). Follow the N37 exit toward Fontainebleau/Montargis Par Fontainebleau/Milly-La-Forêt in the direction of Fontainebleau for 7km (5 miles), and then take the N7 in the direction of Fontainebleau for 6km (4 miles) and exit at Fontainebleau.

Cityrama, 4 place des Pyramides, 1er (☎ 01-44-55-61-00; www.cityrama.fr), has **bus tours** combining both Fontainebleau and Barbizon (see the next section) for 57€ ($68) adults, 28.50€ ($34) children ages 4 to 11.

Dining locally

If you're arriving by train and plan to visit only Fontainebleau, consider bringing a picnic from Paris. In fine weather, the château's gardens and a nearby forest beckon. But if you have a car, save your appetite for Barbizon.

On the western edge of France's finest forest lies the village of Barbizon, home to a number of noted landscape artists — Corot, Millet, Rousseau, and Daumier. The colorful town offers a lively mix of good restaurants, boutiques, and antiques shops — the perfect place to while away an afternoon. For lunch, try the **Hôtellerie du Bas-Breau,** 22 rue Grande (☎ **01-60-66-40-05;** www.bas-breau.com). The 50€ ($60) prix fixe lunch and 71€ ($85) dinner feature such hearty homestyle dishes as duckling in wild-cherry sauce or braised lamb with thyme. The restaurant is open daily noon to 2:30 p.m. and 7 to 9:30 p.m.

If you stay in Fontainebleau for lunch, try **Le Table des Maréchaux,** 9 rue Grande (☎ **01-60-39-50-50**); its 33€ to 55€ ($40–$66) prix fixe lunch and dinner served daily may include starters of smoked salmon in a creamy mustard sauce or gazpacho with grilled almonds and pine nuts, main courses of grilled duck breast with regional spices or tuna sautéed in herbs. In warm weather, diners can eat on the outdoor terrace.

Cathedral at Chartres: Checking Out the Stained Glass

Cathédrale de Notre-Dame-de-Chartres (☎ **02-37-21-56-33**), one of the world's greatest Gothic cathedrals and one of the finest creations of the Middle Ages, comes second in importance to a majority of its visitors. Instead, a small scrap of material — said to be worn by the Virgin Mary when she gave birth to Jesus — draws the masses.

Seeing the cathedral

The cathedral that you see today (see the map "Notre-Dame de Chartres") dates principally from the 13th century, when it was built with the combined efforts and contributions of kings, princes, church officials, and pilgrims from all across Europe. This Notre-Dame was among the first to use flying buttresses.

Take one of Malcolm Miller's excellent guided tours of Chartres Cathedral (☎ **02-37-28-15-58**) at a cost of 10€ ($12) adults, 5€ ($6) students. He gives fascinating tours at noon and 2:45 p.m. daily (except Sunday) from Easter through November; he's sometimes available in winter as well.

Notre-Dame de Chartres

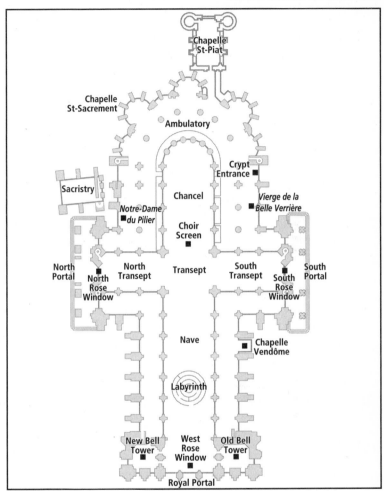

A good time to visit the cathedral is on Sunday afternoons, when free organ concerts (4:45 to 5:45 p.m.) and the filtered light coming in from the western windows make the church come wonderfully alive.

Begin at the beginning — with the **entryway.** People say that Rodin sat for hours on the edge of the sidewalk, contemplating the portal, spellbound by its sculptured bodies draped in long, flowing robes, with amazingly lifelike faces. Before entering, walk around to both the north and south portals, which date from the 13th century. The bays depict such biblical scenes as the expulsion of Adam and Eve from the Garden of Eden and episodes from the life of the Virgin.

Next, just inside, are the **Clocher Vieux** (Old Tower), with its 106-meter (350-ft.) steeple dating from the 12th century, and the **Clocher Neuf** (New Tower). Originally built in 1134, the new tower's current elaborate ornamental tower was added between 1507 and 1513 following one of the many fires that swept through the cathedral.

You can climb to the top of the Clocher Neuf, but make sure your shoes aren't slippery — parts of the tower are without a railing and are quite steep and narrow.

The cathedral also is known for its celebrated **choir screen.** Don't let the term fool you; this is a carved wood structure that took nearly 200 years to complete. The niches, 40 in all, contain statues illustrating scenes from the life of Mary. The screen is in the middle of the cathedral toward the back. **Sancta Camisia,** the holy relic that some people believe Mary wore during the birth of Jesus, is behind the choir screen in a chapel to the left of the church's treasury.

Few of the rushed visitors ever notice the choir screen; they're transfixed by the **stained-glass windows.** Bring a pair of binoculars to better focus on the panes covering more than 2,500 sq. m (more than 3,000 sq. yds.). The glass is unequaled anywhere in the world and is truly mystical. It was spared in both world wars because of a decision to remove it — piece by piece.

Most of the stained glass dates from the 12th and 13th centuries. Many visitors find it difficult to single out one panel or window of particular merit; however, the oldest is the 12th-century **Notre Dame de la belle verrière** (Our Lady of the Beautiful Window, sometimes called the Blue Virgin) on the south side. Its colors are such a vibrant, startling blue, many find it hard to believe that the window is 1,000 years old.

Look down in the **nave** — the widest in France — at the 13th-century labyrinth. It was designed for pilgrims to navigate on their hands and knees as a form of penance, all 304m (1,000 ft.) of it. These days, much of it is covered with fold-up chairs for Mass.

The cathedral is open daily April to September 8:30 a.m. to 8 p.m.; October to March 9 a.m. to 7 p.m. Ask at the Chartres tourist office (☎ 02-37-18-26-26) outside the cathedral for information about tours in English and a schedule of Masses that are open to the public. From April to September, the North Tower is open Monday to Saturday 9:30 to noon and daily 2 to 5:30 p.m.; October to March, Monday to Saturday 10 to noon and daily 2 to 4:30 p.m. Admission to the tower is 4.60€ ($5.50) for adults, 3.10€ ($3.70) for 18 to 25; children younger than 18 are free.

Other diversions

If you have extra time at Chartres, spend it by exploring the medieval cobbled streets of **Old Town.** At the foot of the cathedral are lanes with gabled and turreted houses and humped bridges spanning the Eure River. One house, on rue Chantault, dates back nine centuries.

Stop at the **Musée des Beaux-Arts de Chartres,** 29 Cloître Notre-Dame (☎ 02-37-36-41-39) to see paintings by old masters such as Watteau, Brosamer, and Zurbarán. The museum is open every day except Tuesday and Sunday morning, 10 a.m. to noon and 2 to 8 p.m. Admission is 3.80€ ($4.55).

Getting to Chartres

To reach Chartres **by train,** pick up one of the hourly SNCF trains (☎ 08-92-35-35-35; www.sncf.com) from Paris's Gare Montparnasse to the town of Chartres. A round-trip ticket costs about 24.20€ ($29); the trip takes an hour.

By car, take the A10/A11 highway from Porte d'Orléans and follow the signs to Le Mans and Chartres. The drive takes about 75 minutes.

Cityrama, 4 place des Pyramides, 1er (☎ 01-44-55-61-00; www.cityrama. fr), offers 5-hour **tour bus** excursions leaving from Paris every Tuesday, Thursday, and Saturday for 51€ ($61) adult, 25.50€ ($31) child. **Paris Vision,** 214 rue de Rivoli 1er (☎ 01-42-60-30-01; www.parisvision.com), also has a tour that departs the same days for the same amount.

Dining locally

You can find plenty of restaurants, cafes, and snack bars around the town, but the finest dining is at **La Vieille Maison,** 5 rue au Lait (☎ 02-37-34-10-67). Even if the cuisine weren't superb, the 14th-century building that contains it could be visited for its historic value. But the cuisine is also superb. The menu changes four or five times a year, reflecting the seasons of Ile de France and its produce. The best specialties are foie gras of duckling, roasted crayfish with Indian spices, and supreme of turbot with baby vegetables. Dessert raves go to a thin apple-and-fig tart with walnut-flavored ice cream. Main courses cost 45€ to 65€ ($54–$78), with prix fixe menus going for 29€ to 46€ ($35–$55). Hours are Tuesday to Sunday noon to 2:15 p.m. and Tuesday to Saturday 7 to 9:15 p.m.

Disneyland Paris: A Welcome from Mickey

Disneyland Paris (☎ 01-60-30-60-30; www.disneylandparis.com) opened in 1992 to much resistance and controversy. In the 21st century, it's France's top attraction, with more than 50 million visitors a year — 40 percent of them French, and half of those Parisian. Set on a little more than 2,000 hectares (5,000 acres, or about one-fifth the size of Paris) in the suburb of Marne-la-Vallée, the park incorporates elements of its Disney predecessors, adding a European flair. Allow a full day to see the park.

Exploring the theme parks

Disneyland Paris resort now has two theme parks: the Disneyland Park and the newer Walt Disney Studios Park. **Disneyland Park** is a total vacation destination, clustering together five "lands" of entertainment (Main Street, U.S.A; Frontierland; Adventureland; Fantasyland; and Discoveryland); six massive and well-designed hotels; a campground; a nightlife center (Le Festival Disney); swimming pools, tennis courts, and a 27-hole golf course; and dozens of restaurants, shows, and shops.

Walt Disney Studios Park is a movie studio come to life, where children can participate in the process. The entrance (the Front Lot) resembles the Hollywood Disney studios, water tower, gates and all. You can visit a film studio that resembles a street; as they walk around the park, kids can become a part of the filming of impromptu comedy sketches and get to see themselves on screen later in the day. In the Animation Courtyard, cartoon characters come to life via black light and mirrors, and children can play at being animators at interactive displays. The French Disney Channel has its studios here, in the Production Courtyard; children get to see how a TV studio really works and may be asked to be extras.

For sustenance, the En Coulisse restaurant serves the kind of food kids like and Americans are known for — hamburgers, pizza, salads, and ice cream. Other choices include an international buffet, Rendez-Vous des Stars, and the Backlot Express Restaurant, serving sandwiches and other quick fare. Food kiosks selling popcorn, ice cream, hot dogs, and so on are located throughout the park.

If your kids are younger than 7, they'd be best suited for Main Street, U.S.A., Fantasyland, Sleeping Beauty's Castle, and the afternoon parade. Children ages 7 through 12 will enjoy Frontierland, the Phantom Manor ghost house, the Big Thunder Mountain roller coaster, Adventureland, the Indiana Jones and the Temple of Doom roller coaster, and the Pirates of the Caribbean ride. Teens will like Discoveryland, the Space Mountain roller coaster, and the Star Tours simulated spacecraft ride.

Admission to the park for one day is 40€ ($48) for visitors older than 11; 30€ ($36) for children ages 3 to 11; children younger than 3 enter free (all this is, of course, subject to change). Admission for a three-day "Hopper" pass good for unlimited access to both parks is 109€ ($131) adults, 84€ ($101) children. Entrance to Le Festival Disney (the consortium of shops, dance clubs, and restaurants) is free; a cover charge is usually in order for the dance clubs.

Disneyland Paris is open from the middle of June to the middle of September daily from 9 a.m. to 11 p.m.; off-season hours vary but are generally Monday to Friday 10 a.m. to 8 p.m., and Saturday and Sunday 9 a.m. to 8 p.m. Hours vary with the weather and season, so call ☎ **01-60-30-60-30** before setting out.

A guide for visitors in wheelchairs gives important information about access to rides and other attractions all across the park. You can pick up a copy at City Hall in the Disneyland park or call to get a copy sent to you (☎ **01-60-30-60-30**).

Avoid waiting in long lines with the free Fast Pass. You present the pass at the ride you want, are given a time frame of when to come back, and get to board the ride first when you return. Ask for it at the ticket booth or City Hall.

Getting to Disneyland Paris

To reach Disneyland Paris **by train,** take the RER Line A from the center of Paris (Invalides, Nation, or Châtelet–Les Halles) to Marne-la-Vallée/ Chessy, a 35-minute ride. Trains run every 10 to 20 minutes, depending on the time of day. The station is at the entrance to the park.

Avoid lines at the resort by buying Disneyland passes at all RER A stations except Marne-la-Vallée and at Métro stations including Charles de Gaulle–Étoile, Franklin D. Roosevelt, Gare de Lyon, Porte Maillot, Esplanade de la Défense, Anvers, Père Lachaise, Place de Clichy, Gallieni, Havre-Caumartin, Villiers, Alésia, Barbès-Rochechouart, Châtelet, Denfert-Rochereau, and Gare de l'Est. The pass is good for either Disneyland Park or Walt Disney Studios but not both.

Shuttle buses connect the resort's hotels (except the Davy Crockett Ranch) with Orly Airport (every 45 minutes daily between 9 a.m. and 7 p.m.) and Roissy–Charles-de-Gaulle (every 45 minutes daily between 8 a.m. and 8 p.m.). One-way transport to the park from either airport costs 14€ ($17) adults, 9€ ($11) ages 3 to 11. Within the park, a free shuttle bus connects the various hotels with the theme park, stopping every 6 to 15 minutes, depending on the time of year. Service begins an hour before the park opens and stops an hour after closing.

By car, take the A4 highway east and exit at Park Euro Disney. Guest parking at any of the thousands of spaces costs 8€ ($9.60). A series of moving sidewalks speeds up pedestrian transit from the parking areas to the theme-park entrance.

Spending the night

If you want to stay at Disneyland overnight or for a few days, you need to book well in advance. Plenty of hotels are available at different price levels, and you can explore the options and book accommodations on the park's Web site at www.disneylandparis.com.

Giverny: Monet's Gardens

Monet moved to Giverny (☎ **02-32-51-28-21** for Fondation Claude Monet, which runs the museum; www.fondation-monet.com) in 1883, and the water lilies beneath the Japanese bridge in the garden, as well as the flower garden, became his regular subjects until his death in 1926. In 1966, the Monet family donated Giverny to the Académie des Beaux-Arts in Paris, perhaps the most prestigious fine-arts school in France, which subsequently opened the site to the public. Giverny has since become one of the most popular attractions in France, but even the crowds can't completely overwhelm the magic.

Even before you arrive at Giverny, you likely already have some idea of what you're going to see. The gardens are usually at their best in May, June, September, and October. Should you yearn to have them almost to yourself, plan to be at the gates when they open. Try to spend at least a half-day at Giverny, longer if you plan to eat lunch and visit the American Museum.

The gardens are open April to November, Tuesday to Sunday 9:30 a.m. to 6 p.m., including Easter Monday and Whit Monday (51 days after Easter). Admission to the house and gardens is 5.50€ ($6.60) adults, 4€ ($4.80) students, 3€ ($3.60) children 7 to 12; admission to the gardens only is 4€ ($4.80) and to the house only is 1.50€ ($1.80).

Getting to Giverny

To reach Giverny **by train,** pick up an SCNF train (☎ **08-92-35-35-35;** www.sncf.com) at the Gare St-Lazare in Paris; one leaves approximately every hour for the 45-minute trip to Vernon, the town nearest the Monet gardens. The round-trip fare is about 22€ ($27). From the station, buses make the 5-kilometer (3-mile) trip to the museum for 2€ ($2.40), or you can go on foot — the route along the Seine makes for a scenic walk.

By car, take Autoroute A13 from the Porte d'Auteuil to Bonnières and then D201 to Giverny. The whole trip takes about an hour.

Cityrama, 4 place des Pyramides, 1er (☎ **01-44-55-61-00;** www.cityrama. fr), has two tour-bus trips to Giverny: Tuesday to Saturday, a five-hour trip at 60€ ($72) adult, 30€ ($36) children; and Sunday or Wednesday, an all-day Giverny–Auvers-sur-Oise trip at 100€ ($120) adult, 90€ ($108) children that includes lunch at the American Museum. **Paris Vision,** 214 rue de Rivoli, 1er (☎ **01-42-60-30-01;** www.parisvision.com), offers two trips: a Versailles–Giverny all-day trip on Tuesday and Friday, including lunch at the **Moulin de Fourges,** for 108€ ($130) adult, 75€ ($90) children younger than 4; and Sunday, a trip with lunch for 112€ ($134) adult, 78.40€ ($94) children.

Giverny: It isn't just for Monet anymore

It's estimated that at one point, more than 50 American artists lived in Giverny with their families, and you can see much of their work at the **Musée d'Art Américain Giverny** (☎ 02-32-51-94-65; giverny.org/museums/american/), a little more than 90 meters (100 yds.) from Monet's house and gardens. Some say Monet's influence was responsible for the influx of American artists into the village of Giverny in the late 1880s. Others claim that Monet had little contact with the Americans and that it was Giverny's beauty that captured the hearts of painters such as John Singer Sargent and William Metcalf, who began spending summers there. The museum is open April to November, including Easter Monday and Whit Monday (51 days after Easter), Tuesday to Sunday 10 a.m. to 6 p.m. Admission is 5.50€ ($6.60) adults, 4€ ($4.80) students and seniors, 3€ ($3.60) children ages 12 to 18 and free for ages younger than 12. Admission also is free the first Sunday of every month.

Dining locally

Your entry ticket is no longer valid once you leave Monet's home, so think ahead about whether you want to eat lunch before or after your visit. Most people arrive in early afternoon, so crowds are slightly lighter in the mornings.

The square directly across from Monet's house and the street adjacent to it have many little cafes and crêperies. But if you're in the mood for more substantial fare, walk back to town and treat yourself to **Le Relais Normand,** 11 place d'Evreux (☎ **02-32-21-16-12**), an old Norman manor house with fireplace and terrace. The chef's signature dishes — and they're worthy of the acclaim — are filet of monkfish with a smooth saffron sauce, or, for a touch of decadence, tournedos Rosini (tender filet of beef with foie gras). Prix fixe menus range from 21€ to 27€ ($25 to $32). The restaurant is open Monday to Saturday noon to 2 p.m. and 7 to 9 p.m.

Part IV
Tours and the Loire Valley Châteaux

The 5th Wave By Rich Tennant

"Now THAT was a great meal! Beautiful presentation, an imaginative use of ingredients, and a sauce with nuance and depth. The French really know how to make a 'Happy Meal'."

In this part . . .

The Loire Valley is France's most romantic region, where some two dozen of the most impressive châteaux in Europe are contained within a 113km (70-mile) radius. In Chapter 14, we take you to Tours, the valley's principal city and the traditional place to base yourself for an exploration of the castles. The other good base city is Orléans, covered in Chapter 15 along with the eight most impressive châteaux. The Loire Valley is where the kings and nobles of France chose to live for several centuries, and each castle has witnessed its share of bliss and bloodshed. You can visit two or three castles in one day or spend a week exploring the region and visiting a dozen or more. This area dazzles with examples of the flowering of Renaissance architecture in France, and the images of fierce medieval battlements set against soaring Renaissance turrets and towers will stay with you for years to come.

Chapter 14

Tours: Gateway to Châteaux Country

*W*riter Honoré de Balzac once proclaimed that **Tours,** 232km (144 miles) southwest of Paris, was "laughing, loving, fresh, flowered, and perfumed better than all the other cities of the world." We can't vouch for the perfumed part, but we can say that the city feels especially lively, perhaps because of the 32,000 students who call it home along with the 135,000 other residents. Above all, Tours is the ideal base for an exploration of the Loire Valley's châteaux (see Chapter 15).

At the junction of the Loire and Cher rivers, Tours is the capital of the Touraine region, which was France's political and religious capital for 80 years during the 15th and 16th centuries. As a result, the region near Tours is a showcase of royal and noble residences built during the Renaissance. Writers such as François Rabelais, Balzac, and Réné Descartes lived here, and artists from Leonardo da Vinci to Alexander Calder have drawn inspiration from the area.

Getting There

Tours is an hour from Paris by **TGV,** the fast train, departing from Gare Montparnasse. About six trains per day make the trip, costing 26.50€ ($32) each way. Contact the national train company, **SNCF,** at ☎ **08-92-35-35-35** (www.sncf.com) for schedules and reservations. Trains arrive in Tours at the splendid *beaux-arts* **Gare S.N.C.F.,** 3 rue Edouard-Vaillant. A suburban train station is at St-Pierre-des-Corps, 5km (3.1 miles) from Tours, where you may need to change trains.

The **bus** station, **Gare Routière,** is on place du Général-Leclerc. For bus schedules (an information kiosk is on rue de la Dolve in Tours), call

☎ **02-47-66-70-70.** The **Aéroport de Tours** is 6km (3.7 miles) northeast of the city; for information, call ☎ **02-47-49-37-00.** Direct flights are available to Tours from Lyon but not from Paris. If you're **driving** from Paris, you can take A10 southwest to Tours; it's about a 2¼-hour trip.

Getting Information and Getting Around

You exit the **train station** at Tours onto wide place du Général-Leclerc, planted with lilac trees. Across the street is a modern conference center, and next door, on the right, is the **tourist office** (78–82 rue Bernard-Palissy; ☎ **02-47-70-37-37;** www.ligeris.com), with maps, details on guided tours of the city and nearby châteaux, and other useful information. In addition, the office's staff can book a hotel room for you. From mid-April to mid-October, the office is open Monday to Saturday 8:30 a.m. to 7 p.m. and Sunday 10 a.m. to 12:30 p.m. and 2:30 to 5 p.m. From mid-October to mid-April, hours are Monday to Saturday 9 a.m. to 12:30 p.m. and 1:30 to 6 p.m., Sunday 10 a.m. to 1 p.m.

Walking from one end of central Tours to the other is an easy walk (see the nearby "Tours" map), and most of the good hotels are about a ten-minute walk from the train station. For taxi service, call **Allo Taxi** at ☎ **02-47-20-30-40.** Several car rental offices are in or near the train station, including **Avis** (inside the station; ☎ **02-47-20-53-27**), open Monday to Friday 8 a.m. to 12:30 p.m. and 1:30 to 6:30 p.m., and Saturday 9 a.m. to noon and 2 to 6 p.m.; and **Hertz** (57 rue Marcel-Tribut; ☎ **02-47-75-50-00**), open Monday to Saturday 8 a.m. to noon and 2 to 7 p.m. You can rent a bike at **Vélomania** (109 rue Colbert; ☎ **02-47-05-10-11**) for 14.50€ ($17) per day. The shop is open Monday 3:30 to 7:30 p.m., Tuesday to Friday 10:30 a.m. to 1:30 p.m. and 3:30 to 7:30 p.m., Saturday 10:30 a.m. to 7:30 p.m., and Sunday 6 to 7:30 p.m. (for return of bikes).

Spending the Night

If you want to experience life on a 17th-century country estate, think about staying and/or dining at the government-rated three-star **Château de Beaulieu** (67 rue de Beaulieu; ☎ **02-47-53-20-26;** Fax: 02-47-53-84-20) in Joue-les-Tours, 7.2km (4½ miles) southwest of Tours. Another upscale restaurant/hotel choice is the **Château Belmont** (see "Dining Locally" later in this chapter).

Best Western Le Central
$–$$ Tours

Although it occupies an early-1900s building, the Best Western is fully modern — the interior was gutted and refurbished with panache. This full-service hotel has 38 rooms, decorated with tasteful reproductions and offering several amenities, and a good location near the center of town. In good weather, breakfast is served in the extensive gardens.

Tours

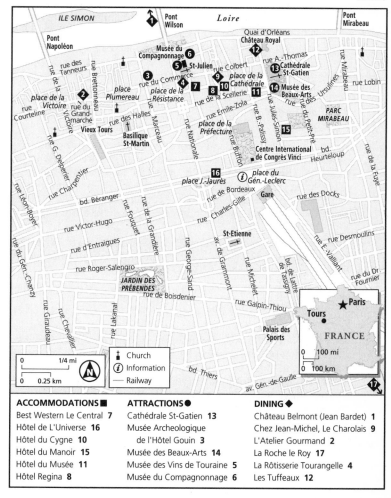

ACCOMMODATIONS ■	ATTRACTIONS ●	DINING ◆
Best Western Le Central **7**	Cathédrale St-Gatien **13**	Château Belmont (Jean Bardet) **1**
Hôtel de L'Universe **16**	Musée Archeologique	Chez Jean-Michel, Le Charolais **9**
Hôtel du Cygne **10**	de l'Hôtel Gouin **3**	L'Atelier Gourmand **2**
Hôtel du Manoir **15**	Musée des Beaux-Arts **14**	La Roche le Roy **17**
Hôtel du Musée **11**	Musée des Vins de Touraine **5**	La Rôtisserie Tourangelle **4**
Hôtel Regina **8**	Musée du Compagnonnage **6**	Les Tuffeaux **12**

See map p. 241. 21 rue Berthelot. ☎ *02-47-05-46-44. Fax: 02-47-66-10-26.* www.best
western.com. *Parking: 8.50€ ($10). Rack rates: 91€–132€ ($109–$158) double.
Breakfast: 11€ ($13). AE, DC, MC, V.*

Hôtel de l'Universe
$$–$$$ Tours

This 85-room hotel was erected in 1853, making it the oldest in town. It has
been upgraded to government-rated four-star status, with its midsize
rooms redecorated and made more upscale. The bathrooms, with shower

and tub, have also been renewed. On weekdays, the hotel fills with business travelers; on weekends, it plays host to many area brides and grooms. Amenities at this air-conditioned hotel are limited to the basics, such as room or laundry service.

See map p. 241. 5 bd. Heurteloup. ☎ *02-47-05-37-12. Fax: 02-47-61-51-80.* www. hotel-univers.fr. *Parking: 10€ ($12). Rack rates: 185€–255€ ($222–$306) double. Breakfast: 17€ ($20). AE, DC, MC, V.*

Hôtel du Cygne
$ Tours

You pass through a mosaic-floored courtyard to enter the Cygne, an 18-room, four-floor hotel (no elevator) well run by Christian and Nicole Langlois. This hotel, one of the oldest in Tours, is located in a landmark 18th-century building on a quiet side street near the center of town. While all rooms are decorated in a simple contemporary style, accommodations on the lower floors are much larger — and a bit more expensive — than those above.

See map p. 241. 6 rue du Cygne. ☎ *02-47-66-66-41. Fax: 02-47-66-05-13. E-mail:* hotelcygne.tours@wanadoo.fr. *Parking: 7€ ($8.40). Rack rates: 47€–60€ ($56–$72) double. Breakfast: 6.50€ ($7.80). MC, V.*

Hôtel du Manoir
$ Tours

This 20-room hotel is in a residential neighborhood two blocks from the train station, but you may prefer to be a little closer to the center of town. Although the exterior is an attractive 19th-century town house that you enter through a beautiful courtyard, the interior is somewhat dowdy. Most of the generic small rooms come with tiny French balconies; units facing the street get lots of sunlight but can be noisy. The Manoir is run by the same management as the Hôtel du Musée (see following listing), a more historically interesting property.

See map p. 241. 2 rue Traversière. ☎ *02-47-05-37-37. Fax: 02-47-05-16-00. E-mail:* manoir37@aol.com. *Rack rates: 46€–56€ ($55–$67) double. Breakfast: 7€ ($8.40). AE, DC, MC, V.*

Hôtel du Musée
$ Tours

This 22-room hotel is imbued with old-world style, from the gracious welcome to the high-ceilinged rooms decorated with antiques. The Musée gets our vote for the most charming medium-priced hotel in Tours, with its winding stone staircase and tapestried walls. Though it's a good ten-minute walk from the train station, the hotel is close to the cathedral, museums, and the medieval section of town.

See map p. 241. 2 place François-Sicard. ☎ *02-47-66-63-81. Fax: 02-47-20-10-42. Rack rates: 42€–50€ ($50–$60) double. Breakfast: 6€ ($7.20). MC, V.*

Hôtel Regina
$ Tours

Annie and Gérard Lachaize run the best budget hotel in Tours, and it's close to the center of town, between rue Colbert and rue de la Scellerie, near antiques shops, restaurants, and museums. The 20 rooms, which vary in size, are simple and homey — not to say homelike — and are well maintained and often quite sunny. Some rooms contain showers and toilets, but most require you to use the bathrooms in the halls.

See map p. 241. 2 rue Pimbert. ☎ *02-47-05-25-36. Fax: 02-47-66-08-72. Rack rates: 24€–32€ ($29–$38) double. Breakfast: 4.60€ ($5.50). MC, V.*

Dining Locally

A number of gastronomic specialties of the Loire Valley go particularly well with the region's wines. While exploring, look for menu items such as *rillons* or *rillettes* (cooked pork chunks), *geline* (traditional free-range chicken), *coq au vin* (chicken stewed in wine), writer François Rabelais's favorite *fouaces* (traditionally prepared bread rolls), and *poires tapées* (dried pears steeped in wine). A special cheese of the region is Ste-Maure-de-Touraine. Local wines to taste include Vouvray, Montlouis-sur-Loire, Amboise, Azay-le-Rideau, Chinon, Bourgueil, and St-Nicholas-de-Bourgueil.

Château Belmont (Jean Bardet)
$$$$ Tours   FRENCH

Occupying an elegant Napoléon III mansion outside the town center in a parklike setting, this restaurant serves the cuisine of chef Jean Bardet. The grand home also is a select hotel (160€ to 310€/$192 to $372 double). Because Bardet is one of France's most famous chefs, he is closely watched and analyzed; critics can't find much to fault here besides the stuffy service endemic to fancy French restaurants. Bardet's dramatic menus feature liberal doses of foie gras and truffles, and vegetables and herbs from his own gardens. One favorite of his is a lobster dish prepared with Vouvray wine and spiced fresh ginger.

See map p. 241. 57 rue Groison. ☎ *02-47-41-41-11.* www.jeanbardet.com. *Reservations required far in advance. Main courses: 45€–90€ ($54–$108); prix fixe: 90€–150€ ($108–$180). AE, DC, MC, V. Open: Daily noon to 2 p.m. and 7:30–9:30 p.m. Closed Sun nights and Mon all day Jan–Apr and Nov–Dec; closed Mon lunch Apr–Nov.*

Chez Jean-Michel, Le Charolais
$$ Tours   FRENCH

This restaurant in the antiques quarter specializes in matching local cuisine, such as *coq au vin* and *matelote d'anguille* (stewed eel), with fine Loire Valley wines (the owner is a former sommelier, so he knows his vintages). This is one of those small, well-priced restaurants where you may end up having one of your trip's most memorable meals; the management is clearly keeping an eye on the details while turning out sophisticated fare.

See map p. 241. 123 rue Colbert. ☎ *02-47-20-80-20. Reservations recommended. Prix fixe: 26€ ($31). MC, V. Open: Mon–Fri noon to 2 p.m. and 7:30–10 p.m.*

La Roche le Roy
$$$ St-Avertin   FRENCH

One of the hottest chefs in town, Alain Couturier, blends new and old techniques in a gabled 15th-century manor south of the town center. Couturier's repertoire includes scalloped foie gras with lentils, cod with saffron cream sauce, pan-fried scallops with truffle vinaigrette, and matelote of eel with Chinon or Bourgeuil wine. His masterpiece is suprême of pigeon with "roughly textured" sauce. For dessert, try a slice of warm orange-flavored chocolate served with coffee-flavored sherbet.

To find La Roche le Roy, take av. Grammont south (following signs to St-Avertin-Vierzon) from the center of town. The road crosses a bridge but doesn't change names. The restaurant is beside the road on the southern periphery of Tours.

See map p. 241. 55 rte St-Avertin. ☎ *02-47-27-22-00. Reservations recommended. Main courses: 22€–32€ ($26–$38); prix fixe: 29€ ($35) lunch, 44€–63€ ($53–$76) dinner. AE, MC, V. Open: Tues–Sat noon to 1:45 p.m. and 7:30–9:30 p.m. Closed 1 week in Feb, 3 weeks in Aug.*

La Rôtisserie Tourangelle
$$ Tours   FRENCH

This restaurant has been a local favorite since shortly after World War II. In the commercial heart of Tours, it has two dining rooms and an outdoor terrace for warm-weather dining. The ever-changing menu may include homemade foie gras and whitefish caught in the Loire served with *beurre blanc* (white butter). Regional ingredients mix well with the local wines, as exemplified by pikeperch with sabayon and *magret de fillet de canard* (duckling) served with a "jam" of red Chinon wine. Other well-prepared menu items include a small filet of fried foie gras served with baked apples and grapes soaked in Calvados; and strips of beef cooked in port, served with fried cèpes (flap mushrooms). In summer, strawberry parfait with raspberry coulis is a perfect finish.

See map p. 241. 23 rue du Commerce Tours. ☎ *02-47-05-71-21. Reservations required. Main courses: 15€–18€ ($18–$22); prie fixe: 16€–45€ ($19–$54). Open: Sun and Tues–Fri 12:15–1:30 p.m., Tues–Sat 7:15–9:30 p.m.*

L'Atelier Gourmand
$$ Tours   FRENCH

You may have trouble getting a seat at this popular spot near bustling place Plumereau; this well-run restaurant offers creative gourmet cuisine at reasonable prices. You can't go wrong sticking with the prix fixe menus featuring Loire Valley classics such as *rillettes* (pork) or *andouille* sausage dishes as a first course and fresh salmon from the Loire as a main course. In good weather, try for a seat on the terrace.

See map p. 241. 37 rue Etienne-Marcel. ☎ *02-47-38-59-87. Reservations recommended. Main courses: 13€–16€ ($16–$19); prix fixe: 18€ ($22). MC, V. Open: Mon–Sat 7:30–9:30 p.m., Tues–Fri noon to 2 p.m.*

Les Tuffeaux
$$ Tours   FRENCH

This small restaurant, two blocks north of the cathedral, offers some intriguing gourmet choices and a romantic dining room with Asian rugs on the tiled floors, lace curtains, beamed ceilings, and stone walls. Chef/owner Gildas Marsollier has created extensive menus offering good value with plenty of little extras, including a little plate of sweets in addition to dessert. Popular dishes are the diced artichoke and green beans with red mullet, the sautéed crayfish in sweet peppers, and the duckling filet with tomato purée and savory tiny beans.

See map p. 241. 19 rue Lavoisier. ☎ *02-47-47-19-89. Main courses: 18.50€–20€ ($22–$24); prix fixe: 22€–38.50€ ($26–$46). AE, DC, MC, V. Open: Daily noon to 1:30 p.m. and 7:30–9:30 p.m. Closed Sun, Mon, and Wed lunch.*

Exploring Tours

You may notice right away that Tours is a college town, with a hip young populace strolling the avenues and hanging out in cafes and bars with names such as Mr. Cool, Route 66 Café, and Le Fly.

Seeing Tours by shoe leather

For a short walking tour of the town, begin in front of **Cathédrale St-Gatien.** Continue north on rue Lavoisier and make a left on rue Colbert, where you pass old cafes and shops, and 15th- and 16th-century homes. Two blocks up on your right is the passageway **Coeur Navre,** which was used to lead the condemned to the place of public execution. Fans of antiquarian books and antiques will enjoy **rue de la Scellerie,** a block south of rue Colbert; this antiques quarter also is home to the **Grand Théâtre,** built in 1869. Continue west on rue de la Scellerie to wide **rue Nationale,** a main boulevard containing every shop you could want, including major department stores such as La Samaritaine and Au Printemps. Turn left on rue Nationale and walk south. In one block, rue Nationale becomes a pedestrian-only street with boutiques and outdoor cafes. In a few more short blocks, you reach the base of rue Nationale and the heart of town, **place Jean-Jaurès,** where you can see the imposing 19th-century façades of the law courts and town hall. Retrace your steps back up rue Nationale to rue du Commerce and take a left. In several blocks, you reach the restored medieval district, **place Plumereau,** called "place Plume" by locals. This area is characterized by cobblestone pedestrian streets surrounded by half-timbered buildings. You can find

---

Market-hopping around Tours

You can find more than 30 regularly occuring markets in Tours. Here are the most animated:

✔ The **gourmet market** takes place the first Friday of every month from 4 to 10 p.m. at place de la Résistance.

✔ The **flower market** takes place Wednesday and Saturday 9 a.m. to 6 p.m. on boulevard Béranger.

✔ The **antiques/flea market** is open Wednesday and Saturday 7 a.m. to 5 p.m. at place de la Victoire.

✔ The **craft market** takes place on Saturday 9 a.m. to 6 p.m. at place des Halles.

✔ **Traditional food markets** take place Tuesday to Sunday mornings at different spots in the city; ask the tourist office for details.

✔ The covered market, **Les Halles et Grand Marché,** with a huge selection of fresh meat, cheese, and produce from the region, is open at place Gaston-Pailhou Tuesday to Saturday 6 a.m. to 7 p.m. and Sunday 6 a.m. to 1 p.m.

---

a host of fine boutiques and small shops on **rue du Grand-Marché,** just south of place Plume. Rue du Grand-Marché leads to **place de la Victoire,** the location of an antiques/flea market.

Between April and November, the tourist office also choreographs guided walking tours of the old town in French and English. Each departs from the tourist office, usually at either 10 a.m. or 2:30 p.m., according to a frequently changing schedule that varies randomly; each lasts about two hours. Advance reservations are important. The cost is 5.50€ ($6.60) for adults and 4.50€ ($5.40) for children younger than 12. For reservations and a schedule of the day's departure times, contact the tourist office (see "Getting Information and Getting Around," earlier in this chapter).

Seeing Tours by diesel power or by horsepower

One of the best ways to obtain a commentary-filled overview of Tours, its monuments, and its layout involves participating in a 50-minute ride aboard a **simulated train** through the streets of the city. Running on diesel-powered rubber wheels and resembling the kind of choo-choo promoted in *The Little Engine That Could,* it operates between July and September, daily at 10 and 11 a.m., and again every hour on the hour between 2 and 6 p.m., for a per-person price of 5€ ($6) for adults and 2.50€ ($3) for children younger than 12 (no discounts for students). Rides last about 50 minutes and incorporate the city's historic core and exterior views of its cathedral. The "train" departs from and returns to a spot directly in front of the city's tourist office. You can purchase your tickets either at the tourist office or directly aboard the train.

An alternative way of seeing the city that's a bit more old-fashioned and a bit more kitsch is aboard one of the **horse-drawn carriages** *(les Calèches)* operated by the local outfit known as **Fil Bleu** (☎ **02-47-66-70-70**). Each is a wagonlike affair, suitable for up to ten passengers, pulled through the city's medieval neighborhoods by a pair of slow-moving workhorses. No commentary is associated with these excursions, which cost 1€ ($1.20) per person (no discount for students or children). Carriages depart between May and September only, every Sunday at 3, 4, and 5 p.m., and Tuesday to Saturday at 10 and 11 a.m. and 3, 4, and 5 p.m. (no tours on Monday).

In July and August, you can take a **horse-and-buggy tour** through the ancient city center. For details, contact **Touraine en Roulotte** at ☎ **02-47-55-04-06.**

Experiencing the top sights

In this section are the best sights, but you can find a half a dozen other attractions in Tours. If you're interested in seeing everything, you'll find it cost effective to stop at the tourist office to purchase the 7€ ($8.40) **Carte Multi-visites,** which gets you into several sights (Musée des Beaux-Arts, Musée St-Martin, Musée du Compagnonnage, Musée d'Histoire Naturelle, Musée des Vins de Touraine, and Centre de Création Contemporaine) and a guided city tour. Call ☎ **02-47-70-37-37** for details.

Cathédrale St-Gatien
Tours

Soaring up to a clerestory and three rose windows, this flamboyant Gothic cathedral took 300 years to construct, beginning in 1236. Before entering the cathedral, take note of the gorgeous stained-glass windows, which have been compared to those of Paris's Sainte-Chapelle (see Chapter 12). An explanation of the images represented on the windows is given in several languages, including English; this explanation can be found on the right as you enter. A sculpted tomb containing the children of Charles VIII and Anne de Bretagne (Anne of Brittany) is in the chapel, and in the church's northeast corner is a remarkable spiral staircase similar to one at the Château de Blois (see Chapter 15). The cloisters were built from 1442 to 1524, and you can visit with or without a guide. During August and September, free classical music concerts are performed on Sundays at 5 p.m.

See map p. 241. Place de la Cathédrale. ☎ *02-47-70-21-00. Admission: Free. Open: Daily 9 a.m.–6 p.m.*

Musée des Beaux-Arts
Tours

Next to the Cathédrale St-Gatien, the Museum of Fine Arts is housed in a beautiful gated mansion (the former Palais des Archevêques), with formal gardens. Inside, you can find 18th- and 19th-century paintings depicting the Loire Valley region, and a good selection of 16th- and 17th-century Dutch and French pictures. You don't want to miss the 17th-century painted wood chimney and the circa-1600 iron-and-bronze alarm clock. The third floor offers modern art, including a Calder mobile. The ground floor features a medieval collection, two paintings (behind glass) by Mantegna (*Christ in the Garden of Olives* and *Resurrection*) and an unattributed *Flight to Egypt* thought to be painted by Rembrandt.

See map p. 241. 18 place François-Sicard. ☎ *02-47-05-68-73. Admission: 4€ ($4.80) adults, 2€ ($2.40) students and seniors, free for children younger than 13. Open: Wed–Mon 9 a.m.–12:45 p.m. and 2–6 p.m. Closed Jan 1, May 1, July 14, Nov 1 and 11, and Dec 25.*

Finding other cool things to see

In case the top sights aren't enough, here are some more things to see in Tours:

- ✔ While wandering up rue Nationale toward the river, you can stop in at the **Musée des Vins de Touraine,** housed in the vaulted cellar storerooms of the 12th-century l'abbaye Saint-Julien at 16 rue Nationale (☎ **02-47-61-07-93**). Interesting displays are grouped by themes such as mythology, archaeology, religion, social rites, brotherhoods, and winemaking occupations. The museum is open June 15 to September 15 daily 9 a.m. to 12:30 p.m. and 2 to 6 p.m. and September 16 to June 14 Wednesday to Monday 9 a.m. to noon and 2 to 6 p.m. Admission is 2.60€ ($3.10) for adults and 2€ ($2.40) for students and seniors.

- ✔ **Musée du Compagnonnage,** 8 rue Nationale, highlights local artisans' guild associations (☎ **02-47-61-07-93**). The museum, which displays documents, paintings, tools, and masterpieces of stone and carpentry, is devoted to the journeymen who travel France after trade apprenticeships. Mid-September to mid-June, the museum is open Wednesday to Monday 9 a.m. to noon and 2 to 6 p.m.; late June to early September, hours are daily 9 a.m. to 12:30 p.m. and 2 to 6 p.m. Admission is 4.20€ ($5.05) for adults and 2.60€ ($3.10) for students and seniors, free for children 12.

- ✔ You can't help but notice the beautiful Renaissance residence that houses the **Musée Archeologique de l'Hôtel Gouin** (25 rue du Commerce; ☎ **02-47-66-22-32**). Inside are archaeological displays of every period of Tours history, from prehistoric and Gallo-Roman times through the medieval and Renaissance periods to the 18th century. The museum is open daily: January 2 to March 31 and October to December 31 9:30 a.m. to 12:30 p.m. and 2 to 5:30 p.m.; April 1 to September 30 daily 9:30 a.m. to 12:30 p.m. and 1:15 to 6:30 p.m. Admission is 4.50€ ($5.40) for adults and 3€ ($3.60) for students and children.

And on your left, Château de Chambord: Guided bus tours of the region

For 14€ to 45€ ($17 to $54), **Touraine Evasion** (☎ 06-07-39-13-31; www.tour evasion.com) offers trips by air-conditioned minibus to half a dozen of the nearby and most important châteaux, including Azay-le-Rideau, Chenonceau, Amboise, and Chambord. You can also rent the minibus and chauffeur and design your own route. The trips, available by reservation, depart from near the Tours tourist office or from your hotel.

Living It Up after Dark

Just follow the crowds to **"place Plume,"** where you can find densely packed cafes and bars, frequented especially by students. In summer, everyone sits outdoors in the square and then hits the post-11 p.m. club scene.

The best of the clubs is the cover-free **Le Louis XIV** (37 rue Briçonnet; ☎ 02-47-05-77-17), for cocktails and karaoke. Nearby **L'Excalibur** (35 rue Briçonnet; ☎ 02-47-64-76-78) offers the best disco scene (cover 10€/$12), but **Le Trois Orfevres** (6 rue des Orfevres; ☎ 02-47-64-02-73) is the place to go for live music (cover 8€ to 10€/$9.60 to $12). Another fun club is **Le Florida**, a 10€ ($12) disco at 40 Febrotte (☎ 02-47-20-65-52). Irish-pub fans can head to **Buck Mulligan's** (38–39 rue du Grand-Marché; ☎ 02-47-39-61-69).

Fast Facts

Country Code and City Code

The **country code** for France is **33**. The **city code** for towns in the Loire Valley region is usually **02**. To call from the United States, dial 011-33 plus the final nine digits of the number (dropping the initial zero). From within France, you dial all ten digits of the number.

Currency Exchange

Tours has money-changing facilities in the train station and at several nearby banks. For the best rate, go to major banks such as Bank of France or Crédit Lyonnais.

Emergencies

For **police,** call ☎ **17;** for the **fire department,** call ☎ **18.**

Hospitals

Hôpital Bretonneau (2 bd. Tonnele; ☎ 02-47-47-47-47) is just north of place de la Cathédrale.

Information

See "Getting Information and Getting Around," earlier in this chapter.

Internet Access

To check on or send e-mail messages, head to **Le Cyberspace Espace Internet** (27 rue Lavoisier; ☎ 02-47-20-89-69), which charges 4€ ($4.80) per hour and is open Monday to Saturday 9 a.m. to 7 p.m. and Monday to Saturday 9 a.m. to 12:30 p.m. and 1:30 to 7 p.m. If you want a Web pub, check out **Le Paradis Vert** (9 rue Michelet; ☎ 02-47-64-78-50), which has billiard tables in addition to computers and a full bar. It's open daily 10 a.m. to 2 a.m., and e-mail costs 14€ ($17) per hour.

Pharmacies

Several pharmacies are on rue Nationale near place Jean-Juarès; look for the green neon cross.

Post Office

The **main post office** is at 1 bd. Beranger (☎ 02-47-60-34-20).

Chapter 15

The Best of the Loire Valley Châteaux

In This Chapter

▶ Exploring the châteaux
▶ Learning about kings, queens, and mistresses
▶ Discovering medieval villages

*L*ying two hours southwest of Paris is the **Loire Valley,** a region famous for its crisp wines, pastoral countryside, and glorious castles. Besides Paris, the area offers the most historic sites, in the closest proximity to one another, in the whole of France. Among the countless châteaux in the Loire Valley are about 20 that are worthy of a visit; for this chapter, we've chosen the eight châteaux that are the most beautiful and interesting. Die-hard French history buffs can certainly visit more — or even all of them (for additional choices, see the sidebar "Other Loire Valley favorites" later in this chapter). For most people, four places will be sufficient before châteauxphobia (extreme fear of turrets and audio-guides) kicks in.

Because châteaux locations are so concentrated (about a dozen within a 976km/60-mile radius), you can easily visit four of them in a two-day trip. In high season, you may see plenty of bus-tour groups doing just that. The short distances also mean that biking enthusiasts can have fun pedaling from one town to the next. If you have the time, you may want to visit one château per day for three days, giving yourself the leisure to explore the towns and surrounding countryside, too.

If your time is limited to just one château, choose either **Chenonceau** (the most beautiful) or **Chambord** (the largest).

The cities of **Tours** (see Chapter 14) and **Orléans** (see the end of this chapter), 113km (70 miles) apart, serve as convenient boundaries to the district — to the west and east, respectively — and you'll enjoy spending a night in either of these lively centers.

What's Where? — The Loire Valley and Its Major Attractions

The Loire region is the "Valley of Kings," where a thousand years of French monarchs feasted and entertained, seduced and betrayed, and schemed and plotted. Major events of French history have occurred at these sites, from marriages to births to infidelities to murders. Each castle has a juicy story to tell, and all have tours (guided or self-guided with English audioguides) so that you can get the most from the experience.

The Loire Valley is crossed by half a dozen rivers, and the castles sit beside them, between them, high above them, and (in the case of Chenonceau) over them. The countryside is filled with medieval villages and small towns connected by uncrowded country roads. Although the castles are undoubtedly the stars of these towns, some towns (such as Amboise and Blois) are larger and provide other diversions, and some (such as Chenonceaux and Chambord) are tiny, without much to offer. The region is celebrated for its wines, and most restaurants have a good selection of local vintages on hand.

Southwest of Tours are the castles of **Azay-le-Rideau** (20km/13 miles from Tours), **Chinon** (48km/30 miles from Tours), and **Ussé** (34km/21 miles from Tours). Between Tours and Orléans are the castles of **Chenonceau** (26km/16 miles from Tours, 87km/54 miles from Orléans), **Amboise** (35km/22 miles from Tours, 77km/48 miles from Orléans), **Chaumont** (40km/25 miles from Tours, 72km/45 miles from Orléans), **Blois** (60km/37 miles from Tours, 53km/33 miles from Orléans), and **Chambord** (77km/48 miles from Tours, 18km/11 miles from Orléans). See the map, "The Loire Valley," for a visual reference.

Although you can get to almost all the châteaux by public transportation (with the exception of Ussé), the most efficient way to explore the region is by rental car. With a car, you can give a smaller sight a quick once-over in a couple of hours and spend half a day or longer exploring some of the more interesting towns and châteaux. If you want to drive from Paris, see Chapter 11 about where to rent a car; if you want to drive from Tours, see the rental information in Chapter 14. If you want to set out from Orléans, see the rental information near the end of this chapter.

Azay-le-Rideau: A Renaissance Masterpiece

The only attraction in the pretty little village of **Azay-le-Rideau** (with houses from the tenth century onward) is the castle, and it's one of the Loire Valley's most beautiful, nestled between two branches of a sleepy river. The château presents a dramatic sound-and-light show in summer. It takes about an hour to explore the village — a brochure, in French, with a map showing the route of a **self-guided walking tour** is available from the **tourist office** (place de l'Europe; ☎ 02-47-45-44-40). The tour

The Loire Valley

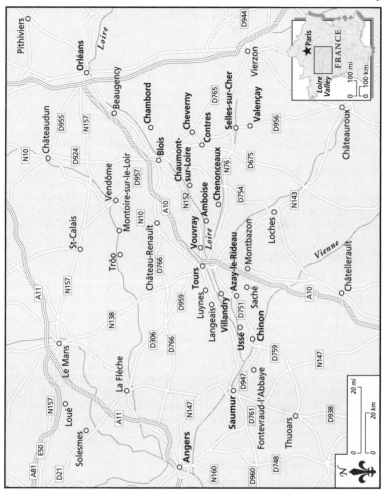

leads you past half-timbered medieval houses, an 11th-century church, and an ivy-covered mill along the slow-moving Indre River. July and August, the office is open Monday to Saturday 9 a.m. to 7 p.m. and Sunday 10 a.m. to 8 p.m.; May, June, and September, the hours are Monday to Saturday 9 to 1 p.m. and 2 to 6 p.m., Sunday 10 a.m. to 1 p.m. and 2 to 5 p.m.; October to April Monday to Saturday 9 a.m. to 1 p.m. and 2 to 6 p.m. Because Azay is only 21km (13 miles) from both Tours and Chinon, many people bike to this site.

Night markets take place in Azay-le-Rideau 5 p.m. to midnight on certain days in July and August. For dates, inquire at the tourist office above.

Vendors of food, crafts, and wine display their wares on the streets in the medieval section of town, and visitors mingle with villagers as they sample regional products and taste local wines.

Getting there

If you're **driving** from Tours, take D759 southwest, 21km (13 miles) to Azay-le-Rideau. You can catch a **bus** or **train** from Tours or Chinon (see "Chinon: Three Castles in One" later in this chapter). The train from Tours (three per day) takes 30 minutes and costs 4.50€ ($5.40); the bus takes 45 minutes and costs 4.50€ ($5.40). From Chinon to Azay, the train and bus take 20 minutes and cost 4€ ($4.80). For train and bus schedules, call ☎ 08-92-35-35-35 or 08-92-35-35-39 for English-speaking assistance.

Azay-le-Rideau is 261km (162 miles) from Paris, and the drive takes three to four hours. If driving from Paris, follow A10 to Tours and then D759 to Azay-le-Rideau. You can take an express train from Paris to Tours and change to a local train or bus that travels to Azay-le-Rideau. The trip from Paris to Tours takes about one hour and costs 35.80€ ($43).

Getting around

Everything you want to see in Azay-le-Rideau is within walking distance of the center. The bus stop is across from the tourist office, which is next door to the town's most historic hotel. Several other hotels and restaurants are within a few blocks. The castle is a three-minute stroll from the tourist office.

Be forewarned that the Azay **train station** (☎ 02-47-45-37-93) is a 25-minute walk (2.5km/1.6 miles) from the center of town, and there's no taxi service. Head to **Le Provost** (13 rue Carnot; ☎ 02-47-45-40-94) for bike rentals, which cost 9€ ($11) for half a day and 11€ ($13) for a full day. During July and August, it's open daily 9 a.m. to noon and 2 to 7 p.m.; September to June, hours are Tuesday to Saturday 9 a.m. to noon and 2 to 7 p.m.

Spending the night

If you're looking for ultra-upscale country house experience, reserve a room at the **Château d'Artigny,** along D17 (☎ 02-47-34-30-30; Fax: 02-47-34-30-39; www.artigny.com), near Azay-le-Rideau in the hamlet of Mont-bazon. The castle was built in the early 1900s for perfume/cosmetic king François Coty and now offers 65 gorgeous rooms (155€–395€/$186–$474) and serves superb food.

Best Western Hôtel Val De Loire
$ Azay-le-Rideau

This hotel is the town's most modern accommodation, and although it's short on charm, it offers all manner of amenities (such as hair dryers, safes, and minibars) in the 27 generic but comfortable rooms. An elevator takes you to the higher floors. The hotel is on the main road into town and only a few minutes' walk from the castle, so rooms in the front are noisy. English is spoken.

50–52 rue Nationale. ☎ *02-47-45-28-29. Fax: 02-47-45-91-19.* www.bestwestern. com/fr/hotelvaldeloire. *Parking: free. Rack rates: 54€–69€ ($65–$83) double. Breakfast: 8€ ($9.60). Closed Nov 10–Mar 20. AE, DC, MC, V.*

Hôtel de Biencourt
$ Azay-le-Rideau

An inexpensive option in the old part of town close to the castle, the Biencourt features 17 simple but comfortable rooms that will suit budget travelers. Innkeeper Cedric Marioton's 18th-century hotel is on a semi-pedestrian street in the medieval section of town, so it's very quiet.

7 rue Balzac. ☎ *02-47-45-20-75. Fax: 02-47-45-91-73.* www.hotelbiencourt.com. *Private parking is not available. Rack rates: 37€–52€ ($44–$62) double. Breakfast: 7€ ($8.40). Closed late Nov–Mar 15, and 1st week in July. AE, MC, V.*

Le Grand Monarque
$–$$ Azay-le-Rideau

Although this is the town's most historic and best-located hotel (next to the tourist office and across from the bus stop, with the castle a three-minute walk away), the rooms and the greeting are somewhat somber, and the building doesn't have an elevator. The 26 rooms and 2 suites are fairly spacious; the modern bathrooms include hair dryers. The annex rooms out back are quiet, while the front rooms on the main road are noisier. The inn's good restaurant, with the same name as the hotel, serves creatively prepared local fare (see "Dining locally" next).

3 place de la République. ☎ *02-47-45-40-08. Fax: 02-47-45-46-25.* www.legrand monarque.com. *Parking: 8€ ($9.60). Rack rates: 55€–150€ ($66–$180) double; 160€ ($192) suite. Breakfast: 8€ ($9.60). Closed Dec. AE, MC, V.*

Dining locally

L'Aigle d'Or
$$–$$$ Azay-le-Rideau   TOURAINE

Ghislaine and Jean-Luc Fevre operate L'Aigle d'Or, the best restaurant in town, serving traditional gourmet cuisine with fish dishes as a specialty. The inviting dining room on the village's main street is decorated with antiques, and in summer, dining is available in the garden. Favorite dishes include the house foie gras and various preparations of lobster. Expect formal service with lots of courses — they do it up here.

10 av. Adelaide-Riche. ☎ *02-47-45-24-58. Reservations recommended. Main courses: 13€–20€ ($16–$24); prix fixe: 18€–42€ ($22–$50) at lunch; children's menu: 10€ ($12). V. Open: Thurs–Tues noon to 2 p.m. and 7:30–9 p.m. Closed Sun nights year-round and Tues nights in low season.*

Le Grand Monarque
$$$ Azay-le-Rideau   TOURAINE

This hotel restaurant caters its menus to the best seasonal products. The restaurant has two dining rooms; the nicer one with a stone hearth is on the left as you enter the building. Summer dining is available in a large court-yard. Your meal may begin with a caviar *amuse bouche* (pre-appetizer), and then move on to *marbre d'aile de raie aux pommes vertes* (a very tasty ray prepared with green apples) and the grilled fish called *filet de dorade royale*. The food is flavorful but not heavy, and the desserts are exceptional.

3 place de la République (in the hotel). ☎ *02-47-45-40-08. Reservations required. Main courses: 17€–29€ ($20–$35); prix fixe: 27€–50€ ($32–$60); children's menu: 12€ ($14). AE, MC, V. Open: Daily noon to 2 p.m. and 7:30–9 p.m.*

Seeing the castle

Nestled on an island between two branches of the slow-moving Indre River, **Château d'Azay-le-Rideau,** in the center of town a few blocks from the tourist office (☎ 02-47-45-42-04; www.monum.fr), is a Renaissance masterpiece. Unlike some of the other châteaux, Azay was built and occupied by nobles rather than royalty, so it's less a fortress than a grand home. The castle was begun around 1515 by Gilles Berthelot, François I's finance minister, in part to display his social ascension. When Berthelot eventually fell out of favor, François seized the castle but allowed it to remain empty. In the late 18th century, Charles de Biencourt, a liberal-minded aristocrat, bought the property and restored it to its former glory. At the beginning of the 20th century, the French government purchased the property from an impoverished marquis, the last of the Biencourts.

Before entering, circle the château to admire its perfect proportions. Highlights are the **Grand Staircase** and the Biencourt **drawing room,** decorated in 19th-century style. Among many interesting artworks in the castle is a copy of the painting ***Bathing Lady,*** a seminude portrait believed to be of Diane de Poitiers, the mistress of Henri II.

A leisurely visit to the castle and grounds will take about 1½ hours. The castle offers no tours in English, but audioguides (4€/$4.80) and free brochures are available in English. Admission is 6€ ($7.20) for adults and 4.10€ ($4.90) for young people 18 to 25; free for children younger than 18. The castle is open daily (except January 1, May 1, and December 25): April, May, June, and September 9:30 a.m. to 6 p.m.; July and August 9:30 a.m. to 7 p.m.; October 9:30 a.m. to 5:30 p.m.; and November to March 9:30 a.m. to 12:30 p.m. and 2 to 5:30 p.m. The last entrance is 45 minutes before closing.

Between May and September, the château is the venue for a sound-and-light display, **Les Imaginaires,** where the romantic majesty of the castle's history is emphasized and celebrated. Performances begin, depending on a complicated schedule of seasonal changes, between 9:30 and 10:30 p.m., last for two hours, and make frequent references to the glories, ghosts, and deceptions of the *ancien régime*. During July and August, performances take place nightly; during May, June, and September, they're staged only Friday through Saturday. Tickets to the event cost 9€ ($11) for adults and 5€ ($6) for young people 12 to 25; children younger than 12 are free. Tickets for the castle and the nighttime performance cost 12€ ($14) for adults, 7€ ($8.40) ages 18 to 25, and 5€ ($6) ages 12 to 17; free for children younger than 18.

Chinon: Three Castles in One

The small town of **Chinon** is home to one of the oldest châteaux in France and boasts a good number of medium-priced hotels and restaurants, and a restored medieval quarter. A number of interesting sights are within biking distance of the town (such as the Château d'Ussé), so this area is a good base. Chinon's château, perched on a bluff high above the town, is actually the ruins of three fortresses. Although the château is mainly ruins, it offers plenty to see, so you need to allow a couple of hours to explore the site.

You can best appreciate the beauty of Chinon by viewing it from across the river Vienne, where you can see how the castle ruins rise above the town. Another great view is from high up on the castle ramparts, where you can look out over the town rooftops (all pointed spires like in a fairytale village) and just beyond the town to the acres of vineyards where workers harvest grapes for the famous red Chinon wine (you can try this wine at any of the area cafes or vineyards).

Chinon's medieval quarter has cobblestone streets and well-restored half-timbered buildings. If you wander around, you may happen on **rue de la Lamproie** and the 16th-century house where Chinon's most famous son, humanist writer François Rabelais, was reared. On **rue Voltaire,** a sign explains that Joan of Arc arrived in Chinon on March 6, 1429. Joan is honored in town by various plaques, a small museum (on the castle grounds), and a waxworks representation of that famous moment in history. The **tourist office** is at place Hossheim (☎ 02-47-93-17-85; www.chinon.com). May to September, it's open daily 10 a.m. to 7 p.m.; October to April, hours are Monday to Saturday 10 a.m. to noon and 2 to 6 p.m. You can find the usual brochures, and the staff will help you map your bike route or direct you to the best restaurants.

Getting there

Because Chinon's train station handles only slow local trains, the fastest way to get to Chinon from Paris is to take the speedy TGV (6 to 11 times daily from Paris's Gare Montparnasse) to Tours (see Chapter 14) and then another train from the Tours station to Chinon. Trains linking Tours and Chinon depart at the rate of 10 per day, taking 45 minutes and costing 7.50€ ($9). For information and reservations, call ☎ 08-92-35-35-35.

The train station is 0.8km (a half-mile) walk from town, so you may want to take a taxi.

If you're **driving** from Tours, take D759 southwest for 48.3km (30 miles); the trip takes about 40 minutes. To drive the 283km (176 miles) from Paris, which requires about three to four hours, follow A10 to Tours and then D759 southwest to Chinon.

Getting around

Exploring Chinon on foot is easy, including the old section of town on the far east side. You'll find a number of places to see that are not far from town if you have a rented car or bike. The place to rent bikes is the **Hôtel Agnès Sorel,** located beside the river on the far east end of town (4 quai Pasteur; ☎ 02-47-93-04-37), open daily 7:30 a.m. to noon and 2 to 8 p.m. Bike rental is 8€ ($9.60) for a half day and 15€ ($18) for a full day. You need to remind the pleasant staff here to give you a lock and a helmet. The route out of Chinon is very steep, and you may have to walk your bike for the first 15 minutes. It's about an hour bike ride (14.5km/9 miles) to Ussé, passing several other châteaux, attractive villages, and wine-tasting opportunities.

Spending the night

Best Western Hôtel de France
$–$$ Chinon

The handsomest hotel in Chinon, this centrally located 16th-century residence has been a hotel since the Revolution; today it offers 30 individually decorated rooms with modern amenities. Some units preserve the historic charm of the place, with stone walls and tapestries, and many open onto balconies with château views. The hotel has an inner courtyard planted with citrus trees. Au Chapeau Rouge, the hotel's restaurant with outdoor and indoor seating, is recommended under "Dining locally." English is spoken.

47–49 place du Général-de-Gaulle. ☎ *02-47-93-33-91. Fax: 02-47-98-37-03.* www. bestwestern.com/fr. *Parking: free. Rack rates: 70€–100€ ($84–$120) double; 180€ ($216) suite. Breakfast: 10€ ($12). Closed mid- to late Nov and mid-Feb to early Mar. AE, DC, MC, V.*

Hostellerie Gargantua
$ Chinon

This special place is the best hotel in town, named after the writer Rabelais's fictional giant, and occupying the 15th-century Palais de Baillage. The hotel is loaded with atmosphere, and the staff assures a pleasant stay. The spiral stone staircase leads to eight individually decorated, large rooms with antique appointments; some have canopied beds, oriental rugs, and beamed ceilings. The hotel has an excellent restaurant by the same name (see "Dining locally").

73 rue Voltaire. ☎ **02-47-93-04-71.** *Fax: 02-47-93-08-02.* www.hostellerie gargantua.com. *Parking: free. Rack rates: 50€–95€ ($60–$114) double. Closed early to mid-Jan and early to mid-Dec. MC, V.*

Hôtel Diderot
$ Chinon

This charming 27-room inn lies just off place Jeanne d'Arc. The hotel occupies an ivy-covered, partly 18th-century home boasting comfortable rooms — some are simple and small; others larger, with charming touches such as antique beds. Rooms on the rue Diderot side are noisy, so ask for one facing the quiet courtyard. In the common areas, you'll find half-timbered ceilings, a winding 18th-century staircase, and a 15th-century chimney — but no elevator. Also on the grounds are a renovated building, with more modern rooms, and a one-room cottage. At breakfast, the English-speaking staff serves homemade jams such as clementine and pumpkin.

4 rue Buffon. ☎ **02-47-93-18-87.** *Fax: 02-47-93-37-10.* www.hoteldiderot.com. *Parking: free in courtyard. Rack rates: 51€–71€ ($61–$85) double. Breakfast: 6.50€ ($7.80). AE, DC, MC, V.*

Le Plantagenet
$ Chinon

This 33-room hotel is a budget option (no elevator) on place Jeanne d'Arc, where the bus lets you off on the edge of the town's commercial district. (The square also is the site of a large Thursday-morning market.) Some rooms are very small, but they're comfortable and attractive, with bold wallpaper and reproduction furniture. Expect major improvements under the new owners. Breakfast is served in a separate small building behind the hotel. The staff is cheerful and English-speaking.

12–14 place Jeanne d'Arc. ☎ **02-47-93-36-92.** *Fax: 02-47-98-48-92. Parking: 5€ ($6). Rack rates: 46€–65€ ($55–$78) double. MC, V.*

Dining locally

You'll find rows of cafes and restaurants along **rue Rabelais,** but some of the best restaurants are at the far east end of town, in the medieval district.

Au Chapeau Rouge
$$$ Chinon   TOURAINE

This pleasant popular restaurant, with outdoor tables in an attractive square, is in the Best Western Hôtel de France (see "Spending the night"). Inside, the formal dining area consists of several rooms separated by high arches. The cuisine is traditional, emphasizing local products, and the most requested dishes are the terrine of duck foie gras and the *dos de sandre au beurre blanc* (perch with white-butter sauce). Another favorite is the *blanquette de veau* (veal in white sauce) prepared with wild mush-rooms. For dessert, try the version of baked Alaska called *l'omelette Norvegienne*. Menus are available in English.

49 place du Général-de-Gaulle (in the Best Western Hôtel de France). ☎ *02-47-93-33-91. Reservations recommended. Main courses: 19€–28€ ($23–$34); prix fixe: 25€–54€ ($30–$65). AE, DC, MC, V. Open: Tues–Sun noon to 2 p.m., Tues–Sat 7:30–9:30 p.m.*

Au Plaisir Gourmand
$$$ Chinon TOURAINE

This restaurant is the best in Chinon. It's where Jean-Claude Ribollet pro-duces his famous cuisine, which is served formally. The 17th-century house is located at the far east end of town, just off the busy main street, and isolated by a flower-filled courtyard. The restaurant is quite small, so you'll have to make reservations; it's also expensive, but worth every euro. The menu may include creative options such as *cassolette de queues d'écrévisses tiedes à la nage* (tails of crayfish casserole) and *aiguilettes de canard au miel et poivre rose* (slices of duck with honey and red pepper), or simple items cooked to perfection, such as *sandre au beurre blanc* (pick-erel fish with white-butter sauce). For dessert, try the pear with cassis-and-almond ice cream.

Quai Charles VII. ☎ *02-47-93-20-48. Reservations required far in advance. Main courses: 19€–26€ ($23–$31); tasting menu: 39€ and 59€ ($47 and $71). AE, V. Open: Wed–Sun noon to 1:30 p.m.; Tues–Sat 7:30–9 p.m. Closed mid-Feb to mid-Mar.*

Hostellerie Gargantua
$$ Chinon TOURAINE

Some may call the setup a little corny — waitresses wear medieval wench outfits on weekends — but the food is excellent at this charming restau-rant that's part of a very fine inn (see "Spending the night"). Although the inside is set up like a modern version of a medieval banquet hall, you may prefer the outside seating in summer, where you can view the castle ruins. The gimmick is that ancient recipes are used to create the dishes. The menu is full of classics such as local *sandre* (perch) prepared with Chinon wine and duckling with dried pears. The service is efficient and professional.

73 rue Voltaire (in the hotel). ☎ *02-47-93-04-71. Reservations recommended. Main courses: 13€–21€ ($16–$25); prix fixe: 23€–29€ ($28–$35). MC, V. Open: Daily noon to 2 p.m. and 7:30–9:30 p.m.; closed Wed and Thurs in off season.*

La Maison Rouge
$$ Chinon TOURAINE

Not to be confused with Au Chapeau Rouge (see earlier in this section), this atmospheric bistro is where locals go for a good, reasonably priced meal. The large menu reads like a catalog of favorite French foods, including *magret de canard* (duckling) in a green peppercorn sauce and andouilette (locally made sausages) with a tangy mustard sauce. If you're adventurous, you'll have an authentic meal here, surrounded by locals. Be forewarned: It can get a little rowdy when customers start drinking out of the wine casks.

38 rue Voltaire. ☎ *02-47-98-43-65. Reservations not necessary. Main courses: 6.50€–15€ ($7.80–$18); prix fixe: 12€–20€ ($14–$24). MC, V. Open: Apr–Oct Thurs–Mon noon to 2 p.m. and 7–9:30 p.m. and Tues 7–9:30 p.m.; Nov–Mar Thurs–Sat noon to 2 p.m. and 7–9:30 p.m., Sun noon to 2 p.m. and Tues 7 p.m.–9:30 p.m.*

L'Oceanic
$$ Chinon FRENCH

This restaurant, owned and operated by Marie-Paule and Patrick Descoubes, specializes in seafood; the fish dishes are indeed fresh and delicious. Carnivores can order the steak. Specialties change every day based on what's fresh, seasonal, and good at the marketplace. The restaurant is on main rue Rabelais, with a pleasing aqua-toned interior and cafe tables behind a turquoise balustrade. It fills up with mix of locals and visitors because it offers good value and attention to every detail.

13 rue Rabelais. ☎ *02-47-93-44-55. Reservations not necessary. Main courses: 18€–28€ ($22–$34). AE, MC, V. Open: Tues–Sun noon to 2 p.m.; Tues–Sat 7:30–9:30 p.m.*

Seeing the castle and more

Getting to the **Château de Chinon** (☎ 02-47-93-13-45) is a steep walk. Actually the ruins of three castles going back to the Middle Ages, this site is definitely worth seeing. From 1427 to 1450, Charles VII lived here almost continually, and Chinon briefly became his capital city and the most important castle in France. But the most famous event to occur here was in 1429, when a peasant girl named Joan arrived at the castle and inspired Charles to drive the English out of France.

Château du Milieu, at the center of the site, includes the reconstructed **royal apartments,** with tapestries, antique furniture, illuminated manuscripts, and a waxworks tableau of the fateful meeting between Joan of Arc and Charles VII. Courtiers tried to test Joan by asking her to pick the disguised Charles out of the crowd. When she chose correctly, Charles was so impressed that he agreed to attempt to recapture his kingdom from the invading English. As presented here, Joan's choice doesn't appear too miraculous: Dopey-looking Charles is the one in the purple tunic and the pointiest shoes. The actual place of the meeting, the **Main Hall,** is a roofless ruin next to the restored building.

At the far western end of the site is what's left of the **Château de Coudray:** several towers and dungeons, including the cylindrical **Tour de Coudray,** one of the best-preserved examples of a keep in France. **Donjon de Coudray** is where members of the order of Templars were imprisoned in 1308. The Templars were a wealthy community of military monks — yes, you read that right — founded to protect Christian realms. You can visit the dungeon if you don't mind going down about five flights of steps into the moldy depths of a cellar.

At the entrance to the site, the clock tower contains the **Joan of Arc museum** — three floors and seven small rooms of Joan collectibles, such as postcards, dinner plates, and posters. It's a bit scattershot but still mildly interesting. All that remains of **Château de St-Georges,** built in the 12th century, are ruins near the entrance to the site. After touring the buildings and towers, you may enjoy the view over the steeply pitched slate roofs in town to the vineyards beyond.

Allow yourself an hour to see the site and wander the grounds. Admission to the site is 6€ ($7.20) for adults and 4.50€ ($5.40) for children 7 to 18. The château has no audioguides, but tours are given in English at 9:45 a.m., 11:25 a.m., 2:25 p.m., 3:50 p.m., and 5:15 p.m. Tour times may change, so you'll need to call the castle at ☎ 02-47-93-13-45 to confirm. The château is open daily (except January 1 and December 25): April to September 9 a.m. to 7 p.m., October to March 9:30 a.m. to 5 p.m.

In town, the musty **Musée du Vieux Chinon** (44 rue Haute St-Maurice; ☎ 02-47-93-18-12) has rather extensive and interesting collections detailing the history of Chinon. The museum is housed in a 15th-century building containing the Salle des Etats-Générale, the grand room where the Estates General met in 1428. In this second-floor room, you can pay homage to Chinon's favorite son, François Rabelais, at his 1833 portrait by Delacroix, which was restored by the Louvre. On the first floor, chained leopards face off on the **cape of St. Mexme,** part of a 12th-century silk fabric that's the largest textile from this period in France. The top floor displays the work of *compagnonnage* (master craftsmen) from the town. On view are decorative parts of two porcelain heating units from the end of the *ancien régime.* Explanatory brochures, written in English, are available at the entrance. Admission is 2.30€ ($2.75) for adults and 1.50€ ($1.80) for children. Mid-April to mid-September, the museum is open daily but only from 4 to 6 p.m. (more hours available with appointment).

Nearby, between Chinon and Ussé, is the 15th-century **Château de la Grille** (☎ 02-47-93-01-95), a 50-hectare (125-acre) winery owned by the Gosset family, who have been winemakers for 14 generations. Free tastings of the special Chinon wine are offered in July and August Monday to Saturday 9 a.m. to noon and 2 to 6:30 p.m., and September to June Monday to Saturday 9 a.m. to noon and 1:30 to 6 p.m. English is spoken here.

Living it up after dark

La Licorne (15 rue Rabelais; ☎ 02-47-93-94-94) is a large brasserie and English pub where everyone hangs out. A quarter-size of Chinon wine goes for 3.50€ ($4.20), which you can sample with all the typical cafe fare served here.

Ussé: Fit for Sleeping Beauty

The tiny village of **Ussé,** near the intersection of the rivers Indre and Loire, is home to the privately owned château that was supposedly the inspiration for the story of *Sleeping Beauty,* written by Charles Perrault (rumor has it that he stayed here in the 17th century). The French call the castle, with its glistening white stone and soaring turrets and towers, *Château de la Belle au Bois Dormant* (Castle of the Beauty of the Sleeping Woods). You can easily picture beautiful ladies and brave lords strolling through the long halls and monumental stairways. While Ussé itself is a blink-and-you-miss-it kind of place, the château is worth a visit, particularly for children, who may enjoy the waxworks reconstruction of the *Sleeping Beauty* story that's set up in a tower.

Getting there

If you're **driving,** take D7 southwest from Tours, following it for about 30 minutes. From Chinon, follow the signs north out of town. Ussé is about a five- to ten-minute drive from Chinon. If you're coming from Paris, take A10 to Tours and then D7 to Ussé (about a three-hour drive). Ussé is a flat and easy 14.5km (9-mile) **bike** ride from Chinon; the tourist office in Chinon can give you a map and brochures of the interesting sights you can see along the way and nearby.

Spending the night and dining locally

You can grab lunch or a snack at the cafe **Le Bois Dormant** (open daily 10 a.m. to 5:30 p.m.), which has outside tables under shade trees, across the street from the castle on D7. (For dinner options, check out "Chinon: Three Castles in One," earlier in this chapter.)

Le Clos d'Ussé
$ Ussé

This lodging is the only option in the tiny village. You'll have more fun staying in neighboring Chinon, but if you must find a place to stay in Ussé, this hotel provides acceptable accommodations. The three rooms are very simple but clean and comfortable, with cheerful patterned curtains and pastel-colored walls. If you speak French, you may enjoy learning about the history of the castle from the kind proprietors.

Across the street from the château on D7, Rigny-Ussé. ☎ *02-47-95-55-47. Rack rates: 45€–55€ ($54–$66) double. Breakfast: 6€ ($7.20). DC, MC, V.*

Seeing the castle

The privately owned **Château d'Ussé** (☎ **02-47-95-54-05**) is set on a hill overlooking the River Indre. The Blacas family has lived here since the 19th century, occupying the left wing. Work began on the castle in 1455 on the foundations of an 11th-century fortress, but the castle today reflects its 16th-century conversion into a country château for gentry.

You can see Gothic (15th century), Renaissance (16th century), and classical (17th century) architectural influences. The grounds are beautifully landscaped, with formal 17th-century **gardens** designed by Le Nôtre, who created the gardens at Versailles. Among other century-old trees is a majestic cedar of Lebanon that was a gift in 1808 from writer Châteaubriand, a friend of the castle owner.

Other Loire Valley favorites

If you have extra time and are looking for another intriguing castle or two to visit in the area, consider these:

✔ **Château d'Angers:** Lying 56.3km (35 miles) from Tours, this moated ninth-century castle contains the famous Apocalypse Tapestries, masterpieces from the Middle Ages. The series of 77 panels, illustrating the book of St. John, stretches 102m (335 feet). You also find prison cells, ramparts, a chapel, and royal apartments to visit. Call ☎ 02-41-36-31-94 for information. The château is open daily from 9:30 a.m. to 6:30 p.m., charging adults 5.45€ ($6.55) and children 3.50€ ($4.20).

✔ **Château de Châteaudun:** Lying 129km (80 miles) from Tours, this castle is a mix of medieval and Renaissance architecture, with towering chimneys and dormers. Inside you'll find two carved staircases, tapestries, and a Sainte-Chapelle with robed statues. Call ☎ 02-37-94-02-90 for information. Hours are daily from 10 a.m. to 12:30 p.m. and 2 to 5 p.m., costing adults 6.10€ ($7.30) and children 4.10€ ($4.90), free for children younger than 18.

✔ **Château de Cheverny:** About 61km (38 miles) from Tours, this 17th-century castle, owned by a descendant of the original owner, is decorated in classic Louis XIII style, with antiques, tapestries, and *objets d'art*. The stone stairway, with carved fruit and flowers, is a standout. Call ☎ 02-54-79-96-29 for information. The château is open daily: January to February and November to December from 9:30 a.m. to noon and 2:15 to 5 p.m.; March and October from 9:30 a.m. to noon and 2:15 to 5:30 p.m.; April to June and September from 9:15 a.m. to 6:15 p.m.; and July and August from 9:15 a.m. to 6:45 p.m. Admission is 5.90€ ($7.10) for adults, 2.80€ ($3.35) for children 7 to 14, free for children 6 and younger.

✔ **Château de Loches:** About 40km (25 miles) from Tours, this castle, actually a walled citadel, is notable for its connection to Agnès Sorel, the first official mistress of a French king (Charles VII). Her remains are entombed in the west wing, and a copy of a painting, showing her as a fetching Virgin Mary, hangs in the royal apartments, along with other artworks and tapestries. Call ☎ 02-47-59-01-32 for information. The château is open April to September from 9 a.m. to 7 p.m. (closes at 5 p.m. October–March). Admission is 5€ ($6) for adults or 3.50€ ($4.20) for teenagers, free for children younger than 12.

✔ **Château de Langeais:** About 26km (16 miles) from Tours, this medieval fortress, built in 1465, has sumptuous period decor that includes fine tapestries. Call ☎ 02-47-96-72-60 for information. The château is open April to September daily from 9:30 a.m. to 6:30 p.m., and October to March daily 10 a.m. to 5:30 p.m., costing adults 6.50€ ($7.80) or children 4€ ($4.80).

Use these handy Post-It® Flags to mark your favorite pages.

✔ **Château de Saumur:** 67 km (42 miles) from Tours, this fortress overlooks the Loire. A museum is devoted to the history of the horse. Call ☎ **02-41-40-24-40** for information. The château is open Wednesday to Monday from 10 a.m. to 1 p.m. and 2 to 6 p.m. (closes at sunset October–March), charging 2€ ($2.40) for admission.

✔ **Château de Valençay:** Lying at a point 66km (41 miles) from Tours, this grandiose Renaissance château is adorned with domes, chimneys, and turrets. Inside, the private apartments are decorated in the Empire style, with a little Louis XV and Louis XVI (think Versailles) thrown in for good measure. Call ☎ **02-54-00-10-66** for information. The castle is open April to June and September to October daily 9:30 a.m. to 6 p.m., July and August daily 9:30 a.m. to 7:30 p.m., and November to March, Saturday and Sunday 2 to 5 p.m. Admission is 8.50€ ($10) for adults or 4.50€ ($5.40) for children.

✔ **Château de Villandry:** About 18km (11 miles) from Tours, this privately owned site is famous for its extensive 16th-century Renaissance gardens, mosaics of flowers organized by symbolic meanings, and vegetables of the period. The three levels of gardens include a top level of water gardens with pools and waterfalls. Call ☎ **02-47-50-02-09** for information. The château is open daily from 9 a.m. to between 5:30 and 6:30 p.m., depending on a complicated seasonal schedule. Admission is 7.50€ ($9) for adults or 5€ ($6) for children. To visit the gardens costs adults 5€ ($6) or children 3.50€ ($4.20).

Though the castle has no audioguide, brochures in English are available at the beginning of the tour. A French guide (three to five guided tours are offered per day) starts the tour at the small 1528 **chapel,** which has a pretty Renaissance porch with 12 carved apostles. The stone used in the chapel is from the region and retains its sparkling white color without restoration. Among the exterior's decorative elements are two gargoyles. Inside the chapel are ribbed vaulting and 16th-century carved wood choir stalls and a collection of Luca della Robbia ceramics from Florence. The **écurie,** close to the chapel entrance, is a garage-type building holding six antique vehicles, including a dog chariot, a 1920s horse-drawn car, and a 19th-century wicker carriage. Behind the chapel, **caves** used to store wine are set up with wax figures in a basic and somewhat humorous explanation of winemaking at the castle.

The guide leads you through half a dozen castle rooms fully decorated with interesting antiques. More than other Loire Valley châteaux, Ussé feels "lived in," as the owners have restored period details such as the 18th-century silks on the walls and 17th-century oak parquet floors. Most of the original 18th-century furniture was made for the château. You'll also find collections owned by the resident marquis de Blacas, including weaponry and oriental objects from the Far East, brought home by Comte Stanislas de Blacas. Mannequins in several of the rooms display items from the family's extensive antique clothing collection.

After the tour, you can climb the **round tower** on your own to see the elaborately set up waxworks of the *Sleeping Beauty* story, featuring the Wicked Fairy, as well as rooms displaying 19th-century children's toys and games. In the **Orangerie,** located on the grounds, is an artisan crafts shop selling unique gifts such as woven scarves and jewelry.

The castle is open daily: February to April, 10:30 a.m. to noon and 2 to 5 p.m.; May to September 9:30 a.m. to 6:30 p.m.; October to mid-November 10 a.m. to noon and 2 to 5 p.m. (closed mid-November to January). Admission is 9.80€ ($12) for adults and 3€ ($3.60) for children 8 to 16 years of age.

Chenonceau: Château des Dames

The small village of **Chenonceaux** consists of about half a dozen hotels, a few restaurants, a couple of shops, and the most beautiful castle in the Loire Valley, the Château de Chenonceau (note that the town's name ends with an *x* but the château's doesn't). You won't soon forget your first image of this grand edifice, with its graceful arches creating a covered bridge over the pastoral Cher River. After spending a couple of hours exploring the castle and gardens, you can wander a few blocks to your hotel and enjoy the serenity of Chenonceaux after the tour buses have left. Better yet, wander back to the castle for the nighttime sound-and-light show, which takes place daily in summer (see "Seeing the castle" later in this section for details). The **tourist office** is at 1 rue Bretonneau (☎ 02-47-23-94-45). Mid-April to October, it's open daily 10 a.m. to noon and 2 to 7 p.m.; November to early April, hours are Monday to Saturday 10 a.m. to noon and 2 to 6 p.m. and Sunday 2 to 6 p.m.

Getting there

Four **trains** per day and a couple of buses travel from Tours to Chenonceaux. The train trip from Tours takes 30 minutes and costs 5.30€ ($6.35) each way. For information and reservations, call ☎ 08-92-35-35-35. The train stop is located a block from the center of the village, next to the château entrance. Buses traveling between Tours and Chenonceaux cost 5.30€ ($6.35) and take an hour.

If you're **driving** from Paris, follow A10 past Blois, then D31 south past Amboise to N76 east, which leads to Chenonceaux. The drive from Paris to Chenonceaux takes about 2½ hours. From Tours, take N76 east to Chenonceaux. The drive from Tours to Chenonceaux takes about half an hour.

Getting around

A **taxi/minibus service** (☎ 02-54-78-07-65; Fax: 02-54-78-32-80; E-mail: taxiradioblois@wanadoo.fr) takes you from the Blois train station to either the two castles at Chambord and Cheverny (23€–32€/$28–$38) or the three castles at Chaumont, Amboise, and Chenonceaux (45€–65€/$54–$78).

Spending the night and dining locally

Hostellerie de la Renaudière
$ Chenonceaux

This elegant 18th-century house, high above the road, an eight-minute walk from the château, is an informal 15-room family hotel (no elevator) that has been cheaply, if lovingly, restored. Its landscaped grounds contain a pool and plastic playground equipment. The comfortable rooms come with hair dryers, mini-refrigerators, and bowls of fruit; some have views of the castle grounds. Train tracks are located across the road, so you may hear night trains if you have a room in front. The restaurant, with seating outside or in a glass-enclosed porch, highlights regional dishes and ancient recipes such as St-Maure *frais au chou vert*, a kind of coleslaw using green cabbage, and a special rabbit preparation with a heavy white sauce called *rable de lapin à la Tourangelle*. We've also enjoyed the boozy strawberry soup. The wine list concentrates on Loire Valley vintages. English is spoken.

24 rue du Docteur-Bretonneau. ☎ *02-47-23-90-04. Fax: 02-47-23-90-51. E-mail:* ger-hotel@club-internet.fr. *Rack rates: 47€–77€ ($56–$92) double; 185€ ($222) apartment. Breakfast: 5€ ($6). Closed mid-Nov to Feb 5. DC, MC, V.*

La Roseraie
$ Chenonceaux

This 17-room hotel, with beautifully landscaped grounds and rose gardens, is the best place to stay in Chenonceaux. The handsome old inn, a five-minute walk from the castle, drips with ivy and period charm. Friendly innkeepers Laurent and Sophie Fiorito have outfitted the rooms in French country style, with special windows that mean quiet nights even though you're on the town's main road. The cozy beamed restaurant serves three meals a day in the dining room or on the terrace beside the heated pool. You can rent bikes here for 15€ ($18) per day.

7 rue du Docteur-Bretonneau. ☎ *02-47-23-90-09. Fax: 02-47-23-91-59.* www.charmingroseraie.com. *Rack rates: 49€–95€ ($59–$114) double; 72€–90€ ($86–$108) family room for 4; 170€ ($204) apartment. Breakfast: 8€ ($9.60). MC, V.*

Seeing the castle

The "château des dames," the 16th-century **Château de Chenonceau** (☎ **02-47-23-90-07;** www.chenonceau.com), is the Loire Valley's most beautiful castle, set on graceful arches above the River Cher. Because this is everybody's favorite, it's always very crowded, but even with 30 buses full of tourists swarming around, it's still a magical place. You enter by walking down a long tree-lined path passing though a grand entrance framed by sphinxes and then down another long path lined by orange trees. In front of the castle are two lush **formal gardens,** one commissioned by Henri II's queen, Catherine de' Medici, and the other by her rival and Henri's mistress, Diane de Poitiers.

About a dozen castle rooms are open, all decorated with elaborately painted beams, period antiques, and an extensive collection of Flemish tapestries. Downstairs, you can visit the kitchens and pantry. In other rooms, you'll see a number of fine paintings, including *Virgin with Child* by Murillo and *Archimedes* by Zurburan, and works thought to be by Rubens, Van Dyck, and Poussin. You'll even find a dour portrait of Catherine de' Medici, who brought her Italian influence to the architecture of the castle. Originally, Henri II gave Chenonceau to the enchanting Diane, 20 years his senior; but after the king's death in a 1559 jousting tournament, Catherine forced her husband's "favorite" to move to the less desirable Chaumont (see the next section).

The castle contains Diane's bedroom, an alluring portrait of her as Diana the Huntress, and a case containing a copy of her signature. After ousting Diane, Catherine moved into Chenonceau and brought workmen from Italy to embellish it with Renaissance style. The château's signature **Gallery,** with its dramatic arches over the river, was built at this time; in Catherine's day, it was used as a ballroom, but today it's sometimes used to display the works of contemporary artists.

The **Galerie des Dames,** a waxworks museum, is in the former royal stables on the castle grounds. The exhibits feature the women who lived at Chenonceau, with special attention to fabrics and costumes. Also on the grounds are a **cafe,** a **restaurant,** a 16th-century **farm** with a tiny duck pond, a **playground,** and a **flower shop,** where you can buy one of the special rosebushes grown in the gardens. The castle property also features 40 hectares (98 acres) of **grapevines** that are handpicked. You can buy the wine produced from these grapes at a **wine shop** on site.

To avoid the scores of tour buses, try visiting the castle very late in the day, very early in the day, or at lunchtime.

Allow a couple of hours to see the château and wander the glorious gardens. The château is open March to September 16, daily 9 a.m. to 7 p.m.; closing hours vary from 4:30 to 6 p.m. during the rest of the year. Admission is 8€ ($9.60) for adults, 6.50€ ($7.80) for children 7 to 18 and for students up to age 27. The waxworks museum costs an additional 1.50€ ($1.80). July and August, a sound-and-light show called **Les Dames de Chenonceau** is presented nightly 9:30 to 11 p.m., costing 5€ ($6). The castle is illuminated, and music, singing, and historic commentary are broadcast over loudspeakers.

Chaumont: Exile of Diane de Poitiers

High above the Loire, with sweeping views of the countryside, **Chaumont** is one of Europe's greatest castles. However, the tiny village really has nothing but the château, so you'll probably want to hit this one as a half-day stop on the way to Amboise (to the west) or Blois (to the east). Built as a fortress in the Middle Ages, the castle was reinvented as an aristocrats' manor house in the 19th century, and the interiors reflect this use. In between, it witnessed a lot of history, including the banishment of Diane de Poitiers, the mistress of Henri II. Henri's wife, Catherine de' Medici, forced Diane to move out of Chenonceau (see the previous section) and into Chaumont after Henri's death in 1559. The most unique part of this site is the luxurious stables.

The **tourist office** is on rue du Maréchal-Leclerc (☎ **02-54-20-91-73**), open daily 9:30 a.m. to 7:30 p.m.

Getting there

If you're **driving,** follow A10 from Blois or D751 from Amboise (about 20 minutes from either). From Paris, take A10 to Blois, and continue for another 24km (15 miles) until you see signs for Chaumont. It's about 2½ hours from Paris by car. You have to park in the village and walk quite a distance up a tree-lined hill to the château.

Seven daily **trains** travel from Tours or Blois to Onzain, about 2.5km (1½ miles) north of the château, located on the other side of the Loire. You have to walk from the train station to the château. For information and reservations, call ☎ **08-92-35-35-35.** Trip time from Blois to Chaumont is 15 minutes, costing 3.50€ ($4.20) one way; trip time from Tours is 45 minutes, a one-way fare going for 8.50€ ($10).

Getting around

A **taxi/minibus service** (☎ **02-54-78-07-65;** Fax: 02-54-78-32-80; E-mail: taxiradioblois@wanadoo.fr) takes you from the Blois train station to either the two castles of Chambord and Cheverny (23€–33€/$28–$40) or the three castles of Chaumont, Amboise, and Chenonceaux (45€–65€/ $54–$78).

Spending the night and dining locally

Hostellerie du Château
$ Chaumont

This 15-room renovated half-timbered hotel, one of few lodging options in tiny Chaumont, is across from the château entrance. The hotel is on the bank of the Loire, and some rooms open onto river views. The pool is surrounded by terraces, where dinner is served in season.

2 rue du Maréchal Delatre-de-Tassigny. ☎ *02-54-20-98-04. Fax: 02-54-20-97-98.* www.
hostellerie-du-chateau.com. *Rack rates: 58€–75€ ($70–$90) double.
Breakfast: 8.90€ ($11). Closed Feb. MC, V.*

Seeing the castle

Château de Chaumont (☎ 02-54-51-26-26) is a delightful residence set
high above the Loire. Its clear strategic position, with views to the east
and west, betrays its original use as a fortress stronghold constructed
at the end of the Middle Ages. The original building was burned to the
ground, and construction on the present château, with its battlements
and turrets, began in 1465 and ended in the 16th century.

This château's most famous occupant was Diane de Poitiers, beautiful
mistress to Henri II. When Henri II died, his powerful and embittered
wife, Catherine de' Medici, forced Diane to give up the exquisite Château
de Chenonceau in exchange for exile at Chaumont, a lesser residence.

During the 18th and 19th centuries, various aristocrats used the château
as a private residence; it maintains that air today. Most notably, Princesse
Marie-Charlotte de Broglie, the heiress to the fortune of the Say (a huge
sugar importer), supervised extensive restorations to the château in 1875
with her husband, Prince Amedée de Broglie. Marie-Charlotte, one of two
daughters of an extremely wealthy sugar importer, first bought the castle
and then married the prince. She commissioned the architect to turn it
into a luxurious home. But the life of splendor caught up with her, and
after the prince died, she lost her fortune in the stock market crash of
1929. The French government bought the castle in 1938. In the center of
the library is a display case containing notable **terra-cotta medallions**
by potter Jean-Baptiste Nini, who lived at Chaumont from 1772 to 1786.
These medallions depict famous guests of the castle, including Benjamin
Franklin, and royalty of the period, such as Louis XV, Louis XVI, and
Marie Antoinette. The **Ruggieri Chamber** is where Catherine de' Medici's
royal astrologer, Cosimo Ruggieri, stayed; a sinister portrait of him is
near the door. The Broglies commissioned the elaborate **stables** on the
property, which were equipped with the latest equine amenities. Prince
and Princesse de Broglie were also responsible for laying out Chaumont's
elaborate park. At one time covering more than 2,400 hectares (about
6,000 acres), the park now encompasses 21 hectares (52 acres) on the
plateau surrounding the castle.

Allow yourself an hour to see the castle and stables. The château is open
daily (except January 1, May 1, November 1 and 11, and December 25):
April to September 9:30 a.m. to 6 p.m. and October to March 10 a.m. to
4:30 p.m. Admission is 6.10€ ($7.30) for adults and 4.10€ ($4.90) for students; free for children younger than 18. Brochures, written in English,
are available for self-guided tours.

From mid-June to late October at the château, the annual **Festival
International des Jardins** presents the best of contemporary garden

designers and attracts visitors from all across France. Admission is 8.50€ ($10) for adults and 3.50€ ($4.20) for children 8 to 12. For more information, call ☎ 02-54-20-99-22.

Blois: Château of Royalty

Blois is a good-sized town with wide shop-lined boulevards and winding medieval streets to explore. Lording over the town is the château, one of the primary residences of royalty in the Loire and the location of pivotal historic events. The **tourist office** is next to the château at 23 Place du Chaeau (☎ 02-54-90-41-41; Fax: 02-54-90-41-49; www.loiredeschateaux. com). It's open Monday 10 a.m. to noon and 2 to 6 p.m.; Tuesday to Saturday 9 a.m. to 12:30 p.m. and 2 to 6 p.m.; and Sunday and holidays 9:30 a.m. to 12:30 p.m. A light-board with a map, found next to the office, gives information on lodging if you're having trouble finding a place to stay.

Getting there

Six **trains** per day travel from Paris and pass through Orléans on their way to the Blois train station on avenue Jean-Laigret. The trip from Paris takes two hours and costs 21.50€ ($26). The trip from Orléans to Blois takes an hour and costs 8.80€ ($11). Five trains make the 30-minute trip from Tours, costing 8.50€ ($10) each way. Trains from Amboise take 20 minutes and cost 3.90€ ($4.70). For schedules and reservations, call ☎ 08-92-35-35-35. The **bus** station, across from the train station on avenue Victor-Hugo, services Chambord, among other nearby villages.

If you're **driving** from Tours or Orléans, follow N152 east or the speedy A10 west; it takes about 45 minutes to an hour from Tours or Orléans. From Paris, it's about a two-hour drive along A10 to Blois.

Getting around

The castle of Blois occupies a high position on a ridge in the center of town, overlooking the town and the river. Walking up to the castle is easy from anywhere in town.

Your rental options are cars or bikes. **Ecoto** (43 av. Chateaudun; ☎ 02-54-56-83-33) is a car-rental agency about a kilometer from the train station. If you want to rent bikes in Blois to travel to neighboring castles, **Cycles LeBlond** (44 levée des Tuilleries; ☎ 02-54-74-30-13) is open daily 9 a.m. to 9 p.m. (closed October 29 to November 6 and December 24 to January 2). The rental rates (per day) are 6€ to 12.50€ ($7.20–$15) for adults and 5€ ($6) for children.

The **bus** company (☎ 02-54-58-55-44) runs tours of Blois, Chambord, and Cheverny. From June to early September, tours depart from the train station in Blois at 9:10 a.m. and 1:20 p.m. and return about four hours later. The tours cost 10€ ($12) for adults and 8€ ($9.60) for children. You can buy tickets at the Blois tourist office. In addition, a **taxi/minibus service** (☎ 02-54-78-07-65; Fax: 02-54-78-32-80; E-mail: taxiradioblois@ wanadoo.fr) takes you from the Blois train station to the two castles of Chambord and Cheverny (23€–33€/$28–$40) or to the three castles of Chaumont, Amboise, and Chenonceaux (45€–65€/$54–$78).

Taxi Jean-Louis (20 rue Porte-Chartraine; ☎ 02-54-74-00-40) transports you to Chambord and Cheverny for 61€ ($73) on weekdays or 70€ ($84) on weekends and holidays or to Chenonceau, Amboise, and Chaumont for 26€ ($31) per hour.

You can take a 25-minute **horse-and-buggy ride** through the old town of Blois at a cost of 5€ ($6) for adults and 4€ ($4.80) for children 2 to 12. During May, June, and September, the carriage departs from place du Château on weekends and holidays 2 to 6 p.m.; July and August, it leaves daily 11 a.m. to 7 p.m. For more details, call the tourist office at ☎ 02-54-90-41-41.

Spending the night

Hôtel Anne de Bretagne
$ Blois

This 28-room hotel, very close to the castle and the train station, is a good budget option. The rooms are simple and small, but they're brightened by colorful patterned bedspreads. Although it's just the basics here, you'll find that the staff is particularly sunny. The hotel is on a busy road, but it's set back from the street. Nevertheless, request a room in the back.

31 av. Jean-Laigret. ☎ *02-54-78-05-38. Fax: 02-54-74-37-79. Free parking. Rack rates: 49€–58€ ($59–$70) double. Breakfast: 5.80€ ($6.95). Closed Jan. MC, V.*

Hôtel de France et Guise
$ Blois

This 50-room hotel boasts the best location in town, across the boulevard from the castle. Some rooms have views of the castle, which looks especially dramatic when lit at night. Alas, the lovely reception area, with its oriental rugs and antiques, is soured by the dour greeting of the proprietress. This is a city hotel on a busy road, so you'll hear cars at night and in the morning. The rooms come in a variety of sizes, from cozy to spacious, and the detailing befits the age of the hotel; some have elegant ceiling moldings and marble fireplaces. Be aware that room No. 1 is brightened all night by the hotel's neon sign. Breakfast is served in a room that has a gilded ceiling and attractive murals of nearby châteaux.

3 rue Gallois. ☎ *02-54-78-00-53. Fax: 02-54-78-29-45. E-mail:* hoteldefranceet guise@free.fr. *Rack rates: 44€–72€ ($53–$86) double. Breakfast: 6€ ($7.20). Closed Nov–Mar. MC, V.*

Ibis Blois Centre
$ Blois

Although it occupies an 18th-century town house, this 56-room chain hotel is fully modern inside, with all the usual amenities, including cable TVs. The hotel is conveniently located near the château. The rooms are clean, comfortable, and relatively spacious.

3 rue Porte-Cote. ☎ *02-54-74-01-17. Fax: 02-54-74-85-69.* www.accorhotels.com. *Parking: 5€ ($6) in the château lot. Rack rates: 65€ ($78) double. Breakfast: 6€ ($7.20). AE, DC, MC, V.*

Mercure Centre
$$ Blois

This thoroughly modern 96-room chain hotel, a concrete box on the far east end of town beside the river, is a 20-minute scenic walk from the château. The spacious rooms have amenities such as air-conditioning, hair dryers, and minibars. You can also find a bar, restaurant, pool with Jacuzzi, and fitness center.

28 quai St-Jean. ☎ *02-54-56-66-66. Fax: 02-54-56-67-00.* www.accorhotels.com. *Rack rates: 105€–114€ ($126–$137) double. Breakfast: 10.50€ ($13). AE, DC, MC, V.*

Dining locally

On the square next to the château are several cafes and tearooms serving the usual fare. You may find more interesting choices on the winding streets in the old section of town near the Eglise de St-Nicolas. Check out **rue Foulerie,** in the working-class east end of town, for ethnic food restaurants, including Moroccan cuisine.

Au Rendezvous des Pêcheurs
$$ Blois TOURAINE

Get ready for a delightful evening at this seafood restaurant, down a narrow winding road on the far west end of town. Chef/owner Christophe Cosme greets you at the door, takes your order, and bids you adieu at the end of your meal. That service and consideration would be enough to bring us back, but it's the outstanding, creative food that makes this place most memorable. Order the market menu, for which the chef uses the freshest products to concoct superb dishes. Two highlights are the *flan d'écrévisses* (freshwater crayfish tart with Vouvray wine) and the pairing of *dos de cabillau* (cooked codfish) with sausage and black olives. Although the specialty is seafood, meat eaters will find a few choices on the menu.

27 rue du Foix. ☎ *02-54-74-67-48. Reservations necessary. Main courses: 25€–37€ ($30–$44); prix fixe: 26€–74€ ($31–$89). AE, MC, V. Open: Tues–Sun 12:30–2 p.m. and 7–10 p.m. Closed first week in Jan and three weeks in Aug.*

Les Banquettes Rouge
$$ Blois TOURAINE

This little hole in the wall is on one of the atmospheric winding streets in the town's old section. The brightly lit interior, with color splashes on the walls and vibrant paintings, beckons passersby to join the hip young atmosphere. You can't go wrong with the simple, well-priced cuisine and friendly service. Favorites such as foie gras, *pot au feu* (braised beef simmered with vegetables), and fresh sole are summer standards, and in fall you'll find several fresh game dishes.

16 rue des Trois-Marchands. ☎ *02-54-78-74-92. Reservations not necessary. 13.50€ ($16) at lunch, 19.50€–37.50€ ($23–$45) at dinner. MC, V. Open: Tues–Sat noon to 2 p.m. and 7–10 p.m.*

Le Triboulet
$$ Blois TOURAINE

This casual restaurant, in the courtyard in front of the château, is a good option for a light meal before or after exploring the castle. Le Triboulet offers a nice selection of freshly made salads with meat and fish, oysters, and omelets with mushrooms, in addition to lots of dessert crêpes and ice cream. Most of the seating is outside in the château courtyard under bright awnings, although a few tables are inside.

18 place du Château. ☎ *02-54-74-11-23. Reservations not necessary. Main courses: 12€–16.50€ ($14–$20). MC, V. Open: Tues–Sat noon to 3:30 p.m. and 7–9:30 p.m. Open daily in summer. Closed Feb.*

L'Orangerie
$$$ Blois TOURAINE

This restaurant, next to the château and entered through a large gated formal courtyard, is the fanciest option in Blois, yet suitable for families. While seated in the floral-themed dining room, you'll be served a gourmet-level cuisine along the lines of filet mignon with truffles, a medley of *langoustines* and *noix St-Jacques* (shellfish and nuts in cream sauce), and zander (a whitefish) with fresh herbs. The intriguing dessert menu includes unusual homemade concoctions such as *fondant chaud chocolat et pistache* (melted chocolate and pistachio with crème fraiche).

1 av. Jean-Laigret. ☎ *02-54-78-05-36. Reservations required. Main courses: 25€–35€ ($30–$42); prix fixe: 29€–65€ ($35–$78); children's menu: 14€ ($17). MC, V. Open: Thurs–Tues 12:10–1:45 p.m. and 7:15–9:15 p.m. Closed Sun night and sometimes Tues night, mid-Feb to mid-Mar.*

Louis XII Brasserie
$ Blois CAFE

This restaurant, set at the foot of the château in front of the lively market, is a popular hangout for student types and others. It serves the usual fare of salads, omelets, crêpes, desserts, and ice cream. Children will enjoy sitting in this lively square, where the market spreads out on Saturdays.

1 rue St-Martin. ☎ *02-54-78-13-81. Main courses: 4€–9€ ($4.80–$11). AE, DC, MC. Open: Tues–Sat noon to 3 p.m. and 7–10 p.m. Closed Oct 15–Nov 15.*

Seeing the castle and town

Murder, mayhem, and intrigue — it all took place at the **Château de Blois** (☎ 02-54-90-33-32), which 400 years of royalty called home. You'll have plenty to see here, including the history of French architecture from the Middle Ages to the 17th century. The château, constructed in the tenth century, is made up of four stylistically distinct wings joined by a large courtyard.

Located in the château is the medieval **Salle des Etats-Généraux,** a 13th-century Gothic construction containing a grand conference room and a lapidary museum with original carvings and sculptures from the castle. **Aile de Louis XII** was built from 1498 to 1503 in the Flamboyant Gothic style; a fine arts museum is in the former royal apartments located in this wing. For fans of the grotesque: Don't miss the portrait **L'Hirsutism** of Antoinetta Gonsalvus; this young girl was the victim of a horrible hereditary disease that causes long hair to grow on the face. You can also find a fine collection of ironwork and a display of keys and locks.

Architectural historians call the **Aile de François I,** built from 1515 to 1524, a French Renaissance masterpiece, particularly for its exterior spiral staircase tower. François I was a king of extravagant tastes; he had the immense Château de Chambord (see later in this chapter) built to prove the supremacy of the monarchy. This wing at Blois contains apartments once lived in by François; his daughter-in-law, Catherine de' Medici (wife of Henri II); and his grandson, Henri III. Catherine's study contains hidden cabinets where she stored her poisons. The third floor contains the room where the infamous murder of the duc de Guise took place in 1588. Henri III, who wanted to prevent a coup attempt by the powerful duke, planned the murder. A whole room is devoted to paintings of the dastardly deed, and it's explained in detail in a brochure. **Galerie Gaston d'Orléans,** built from 1635 to 1637, is a tour de force of French classical architecture designed by François Mansart. Gaston d'Orléans was Louis XIII's brother and a powerful member of the court of Louis XIII.

Allow a couple of hours for your visit. The château is open daily (except December 25 and January 1): October 2 to April 2 9 a.m. to 12:30 p.m. and 2 to 5:30 p.m.; April 3 to October 3 9 a.m. to 6 p.m. Last admittance is at 5 p.m. Admission is 6.50€ ($7.80) for adults, 4.50€ ($5.40) for students 12 to 17, and 2€ ($2.40) for children 6 to 11. Brochures, written in English, are available for a self-guided tour. Parking is available on avenue Jean-Laigret across from the tourist office.

From late April to mid-September (except July 13), a **sound-and-light show** takes place nightly 10 to 10:30 p.m. at Château de Blois; the show is presented in English on Wednesday in May, June, and September. The show costs 9.50€ ($11) for adults and 6€ ($7.20) for children 6 to 20. For more information, call ☎ **02-54-78-72-76.**

In the town of Blois, **Cathédrale St-Louis,** built from the 12th to the 17th centuries in a predominantly Gothic style, is a handsome church with a stormy history. It's the fifth church built on the site; the others were destroyed by one disaster after another. In 1678, a hurricane left the building in ruins. Underground, the 11th-century Carolingian crypt St-Solenne is worth seeing — it was built to house the tomb of the saint, and enlarged several times to accommodate the numerous pilgrims who wanted to visit the site. As a result, it's one of France's largest medieval crypts. The cathedral is open daily 7:30 a.m. to 6 p.m., and admission is free.

Also worth a visit is the 12th-century **Eglise St-Nicolas** on rue St-Laumen in the medieval section of town, where you can see modern stained-glass windows in an ancient edifice. The old windows were destroyed during bombing in 1940. The brochure tactfully says that "this modern lighting plan is a subject open to discussion." We bet it caused quite a bit of discussion, but the windows are quite glorious, forming Cubist-type patterns along the stone walls. The church is open daily 7:30 a.m. to 6 p.m., and admission is free.

Shopping

You'll actually find some good shopping opportunities in Blois, particularly on **rue St-Martin** and **rue du Commerce.** The best toy store is **Du Coté du Bois** (19 rue Porte Côté; ☎ **02-54-56-84-83**), which specializes in wooden toys and puppets. Antiques buffs should try **Langlois Tapisseries** (1 rue de la Voûte du Château; ☎ **02-54-78-04-43**). Chocoholics flock to **Jeff de Bruges** (77 rue du Commerce; ☎ **02-54-74-26-44**) and **Max Vauché** (50 rue du Commerce; ☎ **02-54-78-23-55**), who elevate chocolate making to a fine art. On Saturday mornings, a **food market** is open on rue St-Lubin, lining several blocks in the center of town at the foot of the château.

Living it up after dark

The town's cybercafe is **L'Etoile Tex** (7 rue du Bourg-Neuf; ☎ **02-54-78-46-93**), which serves Mexican and Italian food. Other fun bars include **Au Bureau** (1 rue du Chant des Oiseaux; ☎ **02-54-56-81-81**), an old-fashioned pub; and **Pub Riverside** (3 rue Henri-Drussy; ☎ **02-54-78-33-79**), which specializes in beers and whiskeys. The nearest disco (10km/6.2 miles from Blois) is **Le Charleston** on Route de Nozieux (☎ **02-54-20-61-06**).

Amboise: A Fortified Château and Leonardo's Mansion

One of the most charming towns in the Loire Valley is **Amboise,** with a stately fortified château perched above the village and antique cobblestone streets made just for strolling. This town is also the town where Leonardo da Vinci spent his last years; you can visit his manor house, which remains pretty much as he left it when he died here in 1519. The **tourist office** (7 quai du Général-de-Gaulle; ☎ 02-47-57-09-28) has a good walking-tour map and can help you plan day trips to nearby sites. During July and August, the office is open daily 9 a.m. to 8 p.m.; September to June, hours are Monday to Saturday 10 a.m. to 1 p.m. and 2 to 6 p.m. and Sunday 10 a.m. to noon.

Getting there

Amboise is centrally located between Tours and Blois, with 14 **trains** per day making the trip from each town, taking about 20 minutes and costing about 4.50€ ($5.40). Trains also arrive in Amboise from Paris's Gare d'Austerlitz, taking 2½ hours and costing 25€ ($30). For schedules and information, call ☎ 08-92-35-35-35. Six **buses** travel daily from Tours to Amboise, taking 30 minutes and costing 3.15€ ($3.80). Call ☎ 02-47-47-17-18 for more information.

The **driving** route to Amboise from Tours or Orléans is N152 east or west, respectively; the trip takes about 45 minutes from either town. From Paris, it's a two-hour drive, taking A10 to the exit for Château-Renault and then D31 to Amboise.

Getting around

You can rent bikes by the day or the week at **Loca Cycle** (2 bis rue Jean-Jacques-Rousseau; ☎ 02-47-57-00-28), open daily 9 a.m. to 12:30 p.m. and 2 to 7 p.m. Rentals cost 11€ ($13) for half a day and 14€ ($17) for a full day. A **taxi/minibus service** (☎ 02-54-78-07-65; Fax: 02-54-78-32-80; E-mail: taxiradioblois@wanadoo.fr) takes you from the Blois train station to the two castles at Chambord and Cheverny (23€–33€/$28–$40) or to the three castles at Chaumont, Amboise, and Chenonceaux (45€–65€/$54–$78).

It's much cheaper to use a **minibus** service (☎ 06-82-00-64-51), as taxis charge by the hour. Minibuses charge flat rates as follows: From the Blois railway station to the two castles at Chambord or Cheverny, the minibus costs 31€ ($37); or from the railway station at Blois to the three castles (Chaumont, Amboise, and Chenonceau), the rate is 41€ ($49).

Spending the night

Le Choiseul
$$–$$$$ **Amboise**

The 32-room Le Choiseul (the area's premier hotel) occupies three 18th-century buildings joined by Italian-style gardens. In addition to rooms in the main building, known as the Hermit's House, five private apartments can be found in the Duke's House and Apothecary's House. The spacious rooms are elegantly decorated with oriental rugs, chandeliers, and antiques; most have comfortable seating areas. Alongside the heated outdoor pool is a raised terrace surrounded by gardens. The fine restaurant, with views of the Loire River, serves regional and seasonal specialties such as perch and Touraine chicken. The château is behind and above the hotel, though the entrance is a ten-minute walk down the road.

36 quai Charles-Guinot. ☎ *02-47-30-45-45. Fax: 02-47-30-46-10.* www.le-choiseul. com. *Rack rates: 180€–335€ ($216–$402) double; buffet breakfast 21€ ($25). Closed Dec 20 to Feb 6. AE, DC, MC, V.*

Dining locally

Brasserie de l'Hôtel de Ville
$$ **Amboise** **TOURAINE**

This casual brasserie with an English-speaking staff offers a convivial atmosphere in the village center near the Eglise St-Florentin. It specializes in local products, grilled meats, and fish. Families tend to fill the tables in the front of the restaurant, attracted by the wide range of affordable main courses on the menu. The convenient location means visitors tend to wander in for a late lunch after touring the sites, but unlike some of the other eateries in this part of town, you'll find good value for the euro here.

1–3 rue François-1er. ☎ *02-47-57-26-30. Reservations not necessary. Main courses: 12.50€–17.10€ ($15–$21); prix fixe 15.90€–18.90€ ($19–$23) lunch, 22.60€–29.60€ ($27–$36) dinner. MC, V. Open: Daily noon to 3 p.m. and 7–10 p.m.*

Seeing the castle and Leonardo's home

Six successive kings of France, from Charles VII to Henri II, lived at and modified the glorious **Château d'Amboise** (☎ 02-47-57-00-98; www. chateau-amboise.com), set on a rock high above the town. Perhaps the most influential was François I, who befriended master artist Leonardo da Vinci and set him up domestically just down the road at Le Clos Lucé. (An underground tunnel united the two residences so that the king could visit his court's genius, and vice versa, without mixing with the common people.) As originally built, the heavily fortified castle was a massive tower of stone evoking the Dark Ages, but it fell victim to successive attacks over hundreds of years. In the 15th century, French kings brought Renaissance improvements and embellishments, and renovations in the 16th century created a castle five times bigger than what exists today. But 400 years of battles and neglect left it a shadow of its former glory, and it was used mainly as a jail. France's last king, Louis-Philippe, presided over much the same edifice we see today.

The castle has been the setting for a host of historic events, including the rather undignified death of Charles VIII, who in 1498 fatally hit his head on a low doorway. His widow, Anne de Bretagne, didn't miss a beat — she married his successor, Louis XII, the following year. Then came the Amboise Conspiracy in 1560, when Protestants stormed the castle in the name of reform. Leaders of the movement were hanged or beheaded within the château walls. And the St. Bartholomew's Day Massacre in 1572 involved more bloody violence toward Protestants.

A brochure, written in English, assists you in a self-guided tour of the castle, where you'll wander through 11 rooms filled with an impressive collection of armor, tapestries (don't miss the tributes to Alexander the Great), paintings (note the portraits of Louis XIII and Henri IV), and antique furniture. The third floor features rooms with Restoration and First Empire antiques from the time Louis-Philippe spent at the château. You can find a portrait of Louis-Philippe in the music room. After wandering through the castle, head to the far northwest corner of the grounds near the entrance ramp to check out the beautiful Flamboyant Gothic **Chapelle de St-Hubert,** built in 1496, where Leonardo da Vinci is alleged to have been buried.

Allow yourself at least an hour to see Amboise. The château is open daily (except December 25 and January 1): January 2 to January 31 9 a.m. to noon and 2 to 4:45 p.m.; February 1 to March 15 9 a.m. to noon and 1:30 to 5:30 p.m.; March 16 to March 31 9 a.m. to 6 p.m.; April to June 30 9 a.m. to 6:30 p.m.; July 1 to August 31 9 a.m. to 7 p.m.; September 1 to November 1 9 a.m. to 6 p.m.; November 2 to November 15 9 a.m. to 5:30 p.m.; and November 16 to December 31 9 a.m. to noon and 2 to 4:45 p.m. Admission is 7.50€ ($9) for adults, 6.50€ ($7.80) for students, and 4.20€ ($5.05) for children 7 to 14. From late July to early September, a **sound-and-light show** is held on Wednesdays and Saturdays beginning at dusk and lasting 1½ hours. Admission is 13€ to 16€ ($16–$19) for adults and 7€ to 16€ ($8.40–$19) for children.

Leonardo da Vinci lived out his final four years about a kilometer from the castle at **Le Clos Lucé** (☎ 02-47-57-00-73; E-mail: closluce@wanadoo. fr), a brick-and-stone mansion given to him by François I. He died at the house on May 2, 1519. The house contains Leonardo's fine Louis XV furniture, including the bed where he drew his last breath. The basement is the attraction's highlight: 40 models based on Leonardo's drawings of airplanes, helicopters, parachutes, tanks, and other machines of war. You can sit in the Italian Renaissance rose garden behind the house and sip tea at the cafe. The house is open daily (except December 25 and January 1): January 10 a.m. to 5 p.m.; February to March 9 a.m. to 6 p.m.; April to June 9 a.m. to 7 p.m.; July to August 9 a.m. to 8 p.m.; September to October 9 a.m. to 7 p.m.; and November to December 9 a.m. to 6 p.m.

Admission is 11€ ($13) for adults, 9€ ($11) for students, and 6.50€ ($7.80) for children 6 to 15. It's a ten-minute walk from the castle to Le Clos Lucé.

If you're in the middle of your châteaux exploration and you're trying to keep all those turrets and towers straight, give yourself a refresher course at the **Parc Mini Châteaux** (route de Chenonceaux, Amboise; ☎ 02-47-23-44-44), which features 43 maquettes (small models) of Loire Valley châteaux built at ⅕th scale and surrounded by 4,000 bonzai. Admission is 12€ ($14) for adults, 8€ ($9.60) for children 4 to 14, and 8€ ($9.60) for students. The attraction is open daily: April 3 to July 16 10 a.m. to 7 p.m.; July 17 to August 21 10 a.m. to 8 p.m.; August 22 to August 31 10 a.m. to 7 p.m.; September 1 to September 30 10:30 a.m. to 7 p.m.; and October 10:30 a.m. to 6 p.m. (closed Nov–Mar). The park is located 4km (2½ miles) south of the castle of Amboise.

Chambord: The Loire's Largest Château

Most people's jaws drop when they first see the château at **Chambord,** a fantastic jumble of soaring turrets and belfries, graceful arches, and dormers. And that's just what François I wanted: the most impressive château ever built. Allow yourself plenty of time to explore the interior, with its refined Renaissance spaces, which are in stark contrast to its colossal opulent façade. The pièce de résistance is the monumental double staircase, with a design helped along by Leonardo da Vinci. Next to the castle you won't find anything but a hotel/restaurant and a few little tourist shops. Chambord also claims Europe's largest enclosed forest, stretching for more than 5,200 hectares (13,000 acres). This castle is our pick for best château — if you can visit only one. April to September, the small **tourist office** (place St-Michel; ☎ 02-54-33-39-16) is open mid-April to October daily 9:30 a.m. to 7 p.m.

Getting there

Buses (☎ 02-54-58-55-44) make the circuit from Chambord to Blois (20km/12.4 miles) three times a day. The trip takes 45 minutes and costs 3.65€ ($4.40).

If you're **driving** from Paris, follow A10 south to Orléans and then D951 southwest from Orléans (about two hours). From Blois, take D951 east (about 15 minutes). If you're driving from Orléans, take D951 southwest (about 35 minutes) and follow the signs to Chambord.

Getting around

The castle is just about the only thing of interest in the tiny village of Chambord. The village's only hotel/restaurant is a former outbuilding of the castle and is just a hop, skip, and a jump from the castle entrance.

The **bus** company (☎ 02-54-90-41-41) gives tours of Blois, Chambord, and Cheverny, with buses departing from the train station in Blois. From

June to early September, tours depart daily at 9:10 a.m. and 1:20 p.m., and return four hours later. The cost is 10€ for adults and 8€ for children. You can buy tickets at the Blois tourist office.

A **taxi/minibus service** (☎ 02-54-78-07-65; Fax: 02-54-78-32-80) takes you from the Blois train station to the two castles at Chambord and Cheverny (23€–33€/$28–$40) or to the three castles at Chaumont, Amboise, and Chenonceaux (45€–65€/$54–$78).

Spending the night and dining locally

Hôtel du Grand-St-Michel
$ Chambord

This 38-room hotel, a former royal dog kennel, is the only lodging in town. The area is renowned as a hunting park, and the St-Michel is decorated with some taxidermy, mostly stag heads. The rooms, some with château views, are quite spacious; even the smallest attic rooms are comfortable and cheery. The bathrooms have above-average space and modern fixtures. Before falling asleep, look out your window at the castle, sparkling with delicate white lights; in the morning, watch the sun rise over the castle. The hotel restaurant is quite good, and in fine weather, meals are served on the terrace facing the château. The parking lot holds only about five cars, but you can also park in the nearby château lot.

Place St-Michel. ☎ *02-54-20-31-31. Fax: 02-54-20-36-40. Parking: free. Rack rates: 52€–79€ ($62–$95) double. Breakfast: 6€ ($7.20). MC, V.*

Seeing the castle

Château de Chambord (☎ 02-54-50-40-00; www.monum.fr) is the region's largest and most elaborate castle (with 440 rooms, 365 chimneys, and 84 stairways). François I, the last of the kings from the Age of Chivalry, built it. After a decisive military battle, François was crowned king in 1515; he believed the best way to show the power of the monarchy was through extravagance, so his castles overflowed with riches and courtiers (more than 1,800 at Chambord). Constructed between 1519 and 1545, Chambord was François's hunting lodge, a kind of country house used for sporting activities of all kinds — including amorous pursuits. Some of the château's most innovative elements came from the king's pal, Leonardo da Vinci (see the preceding section on Amboise), and you'll see the innovative Italian's ideas reflected in the castle's symmetry, in its domes, and particularly in the double spirals used in its famous central staircase.

The castle's interior offers much to explore, including a luminous **chapel,** designed partly by Jules Hardouin-Mansart. You first enter the **keep,** where you'll see the famous double spiral "corkscrew" staircase, a masterpiece of the French Renaissance — one person can descend and another ascend, and they won't ever meet. Three levels of **royal apartments** are filled with important paintings, tapestries, sculpture, and furniture that are original to the residence. The third floor contains a **museum of hunting and animal art,** which plays up Chambord's history as a hunting lodge. Finally, you may want to climb up to the **roof** to see elements of the audacious architecture up close and to catch the panoramic views of the canals and forests of Chambord.

Long after François made Chambord his dream house, other powerful and rich men upheld its traditions. In the early 18th century, Stanislas Leszczynski, king of Poland, lived there. After him, well-connected Maurice de Saxe owned the residence for a couple of years. Saxe was chummy with Louis V and managed to receive items from Versailles (various paintings and a marble fireplace) as gifts to decorate the château. France eventually bought the property for 11 million francs and still plays host to official hunts for wild boar on the grounds. In 1983, the property was designated a World Heritage site.

You'll have fun exploring the site, so allow yourself at least a couple of hours to do so. The château is open daily (except January 1, May 1, and December 25) 9 a.m. to 6:30 p.m. (last entrance at 5:45 p.m.). Admission is 7€ ($8.40) for adults and 4.50€ ($5.40) for anyone age 18 to 25. The audioguide costs 4€ ($4.80), and brochures, written in English, are available. You can rent bikes and boats, next to the castle, to explore the grounds and waterways.

Les Ecuries du Maréchal de Saxe, an equestrian spectacle, takes place on Saturdays and Sundays (May, June, and September at 11:45 a.m. and 4 p.m. and July and August at 11:45 a.m. and 4:30 p.m.). It costs 7.50€ ($9) for adults, 5€ ($6) for children younger than 12.

Orléans: Saved by Joan of Arc

Orléans, sitting beside the mighty Loire River, is one of the oldest cities in France. French kings established their dynasties in Orléans in the Middle Ages before deciding to make Paris their capital. Royals in the 15th and 16th centuries were particularly fond of the Loire Valley, because it was only two days' ride on horseback from Paris. The city has also had its share of misfortune through the ages. Attila the Hun came to Orléans to make mischief in 451. Although that siege was unsuccessful, many more were to come. The city's heroine is the Maid of Orléans, Joan of Arc, who saved it from a seven-month siege by the English on May 8, 1429, a major turning point in the Hundred Years' War. Several sites are devoted to Joan, and the city commemorates her bravery annually at the Jeanne d'Arc Festival on May 7 and 8.

The **primary tourist office** is at 2 place de l'Etape (☎ 02-38-24-05-05; E-mail: infos@tourisme-orleans.com). The office is open Tuesday to Saturday 9:30 a.m. to 1 p.m. and 2 to 6 p.m.

Getting there

The one-way **train** fare from Paris's Gare d'Austerlitz is 15.70€ ($19), and the trip can be as short as an hour nonstop or as long as 1¾ hours with many stops. Another 12 trains per day travel from Tours, taking about 1½ hours and costing 15€ ($18). For information and reservations, call ☎ 08-92-35-35-35.

Don't get off the train one stop too soon at Les Aubrais Orléans — it's the suburban stop about 11.3km (7 miles) from the city.

If you're **driving,** the trip takes about 1½ hours from Paris on A10. From Tours, head east on A10 for about 1½ hours.

Getting around

You can rent a car near the train station at **Avis** (91 Ave. Andre Desseaux; ☎ 02-38-62-27-04). **Ecoto** has an office nearby at 19 av. de Paris (☎ 02-38-77-92-92). The **Hertz** office (248 Bis Faubourg Bannier; ☎ 08-25-86-18-61) is several miles from the train station and the center of town, so you'll have to take a cab to get here. For a cab, call **Taxi d'Orléans** at ☎ 02-38-53-11-11. To help get your bearings, see the nearby "Orléans" map.

Spending the night

Hôtel d'Arc
$ Orléans

A stately 1902 building, this 35-room hotel is the best choice in the town center, located a stone's throw from the train station. Régine and Alain Guilgaut provide the finest in hospitality. The attractive lobby boasts an antique elevator. The recently renovated rooms are generic in decor but are very comfortable, and most are spacious. All have minibars, and some open onto balconies.

See map p. 284. 37 rue de la République. ☎ *02-38-53-10-94. Fax: 02-38-81-77-47.* www.hoteldarc.fr. *Rack rates: 74€–89€ ($89–$107) double. Breakfast: 9€ ($11). AE, DC, MC, V.*

Hôtel de l'Abeille
$$ Orléans

This 31-room hotel near the train station is a little worn at the seams, but it has a lot of style, from the lobby with a terra-cotta Joan of Arc statue and Art Deco posters to the individually decorated rooms. The same family has run it since 1919. Most rooms are recently renovated, and some have French balconies fronting this busy section of town (those in the back are much quieter). Even the tiny units may have an added touch like a marble fireplace. Beware of the steep staircase (there's no elevator).

Orléans

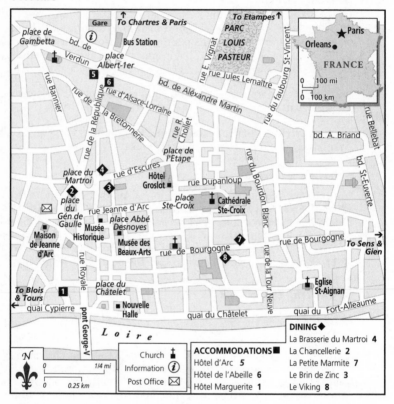

See map p. 284. 64 rue Alsace-Lorraine (at the corner of rue de la République).
☎ **02-38-53-54-87.** *Fax: 02-38-62-65-84. E-mail:* hotel-de-labeille@wanadoo.fr.
Rack rates: 52€–69€ ($62–$83) double. Breakfast: 6.50€ ($7.80). AE, DC, MC, V.

Hôtel Marguerite
$ Orléans

This 25-room hotel is a budget option, and if everything is booked in town, as often happens, it probably has a place for you. Some rooms have shared bathrooms in the hallways, but they're spacious and clean. Most of the accommodations on the second and third floors are more commodious than the simpler rooms on the first floor, and those on the upper floors open onto city views. The hotel's location on the market square isn't bad — it's fairly quiet. The owner is gracious.

See map p. 284. 14 place du Vieux-Marché. ☎ **02-38-53-74-32.** *Fax: 02-38-53-31-56. E-mail:* hotel.marguerite@wanadoo.fr. *Rack rates: 47€–57€ ($56–$68) double. Breakfast: 5€ ($6). MC, V.*

Dining locally

La Brasserie du Martroi
$$ Orléans ORLÉANAIS

This brasserie is located on the first floor of a grand building on place du Martroi. A specialty of the house is the pork pâté *rustique* with Armagnac; it also serves a very good guacamole of tuna (don't ask, just eat). Popular main courses are zucchini caviar and grilled trout, with exceptional profiteroles for dessert. The chef's signature dish is a filet of beef in a peppercorn sauce. The restaurant also offers an after-10:30 p.m. menu.

See map p. 284. 12 place du Martroi. ☎ 02-38-42-78-18. Reservations recommended. Main courses: 7.50€–17€ ($9–$20). AE, MC, V. Open: Daily noon to 2 p.m. and 7:30–10:30 p.m., Sun noon to 2 p.m.

La Chancellerie
$$$ Orléans ORLÉANAIS

This popular place run by Bernard Lefevre is a brasserie/restaurant, one of the city's best. As you enter the restaurant, you may notice the fresh fish and shellfish on ice displayed outside (oysters are indeed a specialty). For good value, check out the daily special. You may begin your elegant repast with smoked salmon with a homemade mayonnaise studded with capers and go on from there to order a superb roast duckling with wild mushrooms, or tender, well-flavored beef in a wine sauce. The brasserie fare includes omelets and steak tartare. You can dine out on the square or at marble-topped tables inside.

See map p. 284. 95 rue Royale (place du Martroi). ☎ 02-38-53-57-54. Reservations recommended. Main courses: 21€–28€ ($25–$34); children's menu: 7.80€ ($9.35). AE, MC, V. Open: Mon–Sat noon to midnight, Sun noon to 2:30 p.m..

La Petite Marmite
$$ Orléans ORLÉANAIS

Traditional cuisine rules at this little cafe on bustling rue de Bourgogne. The signature dishes are *coq au vin* (chicken stewed in red wine), *canard du maison* (roasted duck with cognac), and *lapin Lyonnais* (rabbit garnished with onions). For dessert, everyone orders *tarte tatin,* a caramelized apple pie that's a specialty of the region.

See map p. 284. 178 rue de Bourgogne. ☎ 02-38-54-23-83. Internet: www.lapetite marmite.net. Reservations recommended. Main courses: 11€–22€ ($13–$26); prix fixe: 20€–32€ ($24–$38). AE, MC, V. Open: Mon–Fri 7–10:30 p.m.; Sat–Sun noon to 2 p.m. and 7–10:30 p.m.

Le Brin de Zinc
$$ Orléans ORLÉANAIS

Mussels are a specialty here, and the extensive selection of mussels dishes are priced from 11€ to 12.50€ ($13–$15). The house mussels dish has lardons, mushrooms, onions, white wine, and crème fraiche. Besides vegetarian choices, you can find bistro specialties such as duck confit. Outdoor seating is available, but the inside, with stone walls, feels very cozy.

See map p. 284. 62 rue Ste-Catherine. ☎ *02-38-53-38-77. Reservations recommended. Main courses: 12€–18€ ($14–$22); prix fixe: 13.50€–25€ ($16–$30). V. Open: Daily noon to 3 p.m. and 6 p.m.–midnight.*

Le Viking
$–$$ Orléans   ORLÉANAIS

If you're looking for a simple place to have crêpes, look no further. This popular crêperie, with a beamed medieval atmosphere, has a good 17.90€ ($22) prix fixe menu and tasty food. The restaurant also has more elaborate and expensive fare, including a lovely duck dish with foie gras.

See map p. 284. 233 rue de Borgogne. ☎ *02-38-53-12-21. Reservations recommended. Main courses: 12.90€–19€ ($16–$23) prix fixe: 17.90€–33.90€ ($22–$41). AE, V. Open: Tues–Sat noon to 2 p.m. and 7–11 p.m. Closed Sun–Mon.*

Exploring the town

Orléans is an easily navigated metropolis with several Romanesque churches and a score of Renaissance buildings. The city's train station is located in a modern shopping mall. When you exit the shopping mall, you can look down the impressive **rue de la République,** a wide boulevard (laid out with cable-car tracks in the 18th century) that leads down to the Loire River. Walk a few blocks down rue de la République to **place du Martroi,** where you'll find a large 1855 statue of Joan of Arc (her exploits are carved in bas-relief on the statue base). Beyond place du Martroi, rue de la République becomes **rue Royale,** which has many fine shops. Most of the city's interesting sites and museums are on the left side of rue de la République/rue Royale if you're facing the river.

Cathédrale Ste-Croix (place Ste-Croix; ☎ 02-38-77-87-50) was built between 1607 to 1829 in a neo-Gothic style. Look for the 17th-century organ and early 18th-century woodwork (some by Mansart) in the chancel. You'll need a guide to visit the crypt, which contains a treasury with enamels, artifacts from Byzantine era. The church is open daily 9:15 a.m. to 5 p.m., and admission is free. Across the street is the **Musée des Beaux-Arts** (1 rue Fernand-Rabier; ☎ 02-38-79-21-55), with five stories of 16th- to 19th-century French, Dutch, and Flemish works, plus a very fine 20th-century art collection in the basement. The museum also has a Velasquez painting, ***Apostle St. Thomas.*** The fine arts museum is open Tuesday to Saturday 9:30 a.m. to 12:15 p.m. and 1:30 to 5:45 p.m., Sunday 2 to 6 p.m. (closed January 1, May 1, November 1, and December 25), and admission is 3€ ($3.60) for adults and 1.50€ ($1.80) for students, free for children younger than 12.

Around the corner from the fine arts museum is the Renaissance **Hôtel Groslot,** the former city hall on place de l'Etape just north of the cathedral. Built in 1550, the structure has been considerably altered through the years and is now used for receptions and weddings. The interior decoration is known as "Gothic Troubadour" style (try throwing that phrase around at a cocktail party). In November 1560, François II, the 17-year-old king of France, died in this mansion after suffering a "fainting fit" during vespers at the nearby Eglise St-Aignan. Admission is free, and the house is open Sunday to Friday 10 a.m. to noon and 2 to 6 p.m. and Saturday 4:30 to 6 p.m. You can also stroll through the harmonious and romantic gardens, where there are fragments of a 15th-century chapel.

After visiting the Groslot, you can backtrack to the cathedral square and walk down rue Jeanne-d'Arc, across rue Royale, to see a small museum dedicated to Orléans's favorite mademoiselle. **Maison de Jeanne-d'Arc** (3 place de Gaulle; ☎ 02-38-52-99-89) is a 20th-century reproduction of the 15th-century house where Joan of Arc, the liberator and patron of Orléans, stayed during her local heroics. The original house was much modified and then destroyed by bombing in 1940. The first floor has temporary exhibitions, and the second and third floors contain Joan-related models and memorabilia. The house is open Tuesday to Sunday: May to October 10 a.m. to 12:15 p.m. and 1:30 to 6 p.m. and November to April 1:30 to 6 p.m. Admission is 2€ ($2.40) for adults, free for children.

You may gain a better appreciation of Orléans with a self-guided tour of some of the city's historic sites and gardens. At the tourist office, pick up a brochure in English called the **Orléans Architectural and Historical Trail.** Two of the 43 sites on the trail — Louis Pasteur Park on rue Jules-Lemaitre and the gardens of the Vieille Intendance at the corner of rue Alsace-Lorraine and rue des Hugenots — are great places that you may not stumble across if you wandered around without guidance.

Shopping for local treasures

One of the city's main industries, from the Middle Ages to well into the 21st century, is vinegar making. You can buy some of the famous Orléans vinegar north of Orléans at **Vinaigre Martin Pouret** (236 Faubourg Bannier in Fleury-les-Aubrais; ☎ 02-38-88-78-49). Carrying on his family's business founded in 1797, M. Pouret, owner of Vinaigre Martin Pourret, is the only person left carrying on the slow, traditional vinegar-making method in the region. You can do a wine tasting at the **Cave de Marc & Sebastien** (7 place du Chatelet; ☎ 02-38-62-94-11), which is located just north of the Loire, west of rue Royale.

Living it up after dark

Everyone feels at home at the **Havana Café**, 28 place du Châtelet (☎ 02-38-52-16-00), which is packed most nights and stays open later than most clubs (until 3 a.m. nightly). **Bel Air,** 44 rue du Poirier, a block south of rue de Bourgogne (☎ 02-38-77-08-06), is a hip cocktail bar near the Halles Châtelet, the old market building. Nearby is **George V,** alongside the Halles Châtelet (☎ 02-38-53-08-79), with a DJ and small dance floor (8€/$9.60 cover). **Paxton's Head** (264 rue de Bourgogne; ☎ 02-38-81-23-29) has live jazz on Saturday nights. To check your e-mail while you sip a café, **Médiathèque,** place Gambetta (☎ 02-38-65-45-45), offers a trio of free computers with Internet access. In July and August, it's open Tuesday and Friday 1 to 7 p.m. and Wednesday, Thursday, and Saturday 1 to 6 p.m. Off-season hours are Tuesday and Friday 11 a.m. to 7 p.m., Wednesday 10 a.m. to 6 p.m., Thursday 2 to 8 p.m., and Saturday 11 a.m. to 6 p.m.

Part V
Normandy and Brittany

The 5th Wave   By Rich Tennant

"Welcome to the Hotel de Notre-Dame. If there's
anything else I can do for you, please don't
hesitate to ring."

In this part . . .

Touring Normandy and Brittany on France's west coast is a way to see some quintessential French countryside, charming towns, and famous sights. In Chapter 16, we cover the highlights of Normandy: rolling green hills, farmland, half-timbered houses, medieval churches, and even the D-Day beaches where 135,000 brave troops from the United States, Canada, and Great Britain managed against all odds to charge ashore and save Europe from the Nazis. It's a dramatic story that's told and retold in small and large monuments and museums along the coastline. Perhaps the most moving site is the 70 hectares (173 acres) of simple white crosses at the Normandy American cemetery near Omaha Beach. Nearby you can see the renowned Bayeaux Tapestry, the medieval scroll telling the story of when William the Conqueror of Normandy invaded England and was crowned king. One of France's most famous sights is also in Normandy: Mont-St-Michel, an abbey built on a rock just off the coast, has been a pilgrimage site for more than a thousand years.

When French people talk of going to the shore, they often mean the rugged coast of Brittany on the Atlantic Ocean. In Chapter 17, we explore this fiercely proud, independent region, which has its own language, and folk customs and costumes. A region of fishermen and artisans, Brittany is a place to eat oysters, buy Quimper pottery, and appreciate the traditions of a distinct community. Also in Brittany are France's largest prehistoric rock formations, hundreds of huge stones aligned like obedient soldiers in Carnac, which also is a seaside resort.

Chapter 16

Normandy

In This Chapter

▶ Following the footsteps of Joan of Arc in Rouen
▶ Deciphering the medieval Bayeux Tapestry
▶ Paying homage at the D-day beaches of World War II
▶ Climbing Mont-St-Michel to see one of Europe's great marvels

*O*ne of France's most appealing regions, Normandy is less than two hours from Paris by car or train (see the "Normandy" map). The capital is charming **Rouen,** where half-timbered houses and ancient churches line pedestrian streets paved with cobblestone. This was also the final resting place of France's favorite teenager, Joan of Arc, who was burned at the stake here by the English; her ashes were thrown in the Seine. In the town of **Bayeux,** you can find the famous tapestry that tells the story of how France came to rule England for a brief time in the 11th century. Nearby are the **D-day beaches,** where on June 6, 1944, about 135,000 soldiers from England, the United States, and Canada landed in preparation for the seminal battle of World War II. The ensuing Battle of Normandy, of course, led to the liberation of Europe from the Nazis. Normandy also boasts one of France's most popular attractions, the abbey at **Mont-St-Michel.** Known for years by pilgrims journeying to the site as *La Merveille* (The Marvel), the abbey is set high on a rock just off the coast of Normandy.

Rouen: Capital of Normandy

Rouen, the ancient capital of Normandy, has been rebuilt after suffering extensive bombing during World War II. But even if some of the half-timbered houses are "merely the mock," this remains a charming town with offbeat museums and historic sites. The lively center is filled with pedestrian streets lined with shops and restaurants. The 14th-century **Gros Horloge** is a big clock set in a Renaissance gateway that straddles the main pedestrian thoroughfare. Nearby is the **Cathédrale Notre-Dame,** which impressionist artist Claude Monet painted many times. The cathedral and the impressive Gothic churches of **St-Maclou** and **St-Ouen** form a triangle of spires that dominate the town. In the ancient **market square,** a modern church was built in memory of Joan of Arc; its clever design incorporates a market, a monument to St. Joan, and the ruins of a church that stood on the site but was destroyed during World War II.

Getting there

Trains leave hourly from Paris's Gare St-Lazare for Rouen's **Gare SNCF** at place Bernard-Tissot at the end of rue Jeanne-d'Arc. The trip takes from 70 minutes to 1¾ hours and costs 18€ ($22). For train information, call ☎ 08-92-35-35-39 or 08-92-35-35-35. **Gare Routière** (bus station) is at 25 rue des Charrettes. **CNA buses** (☎ 08-25-07-60-27) travel from Rouen to the Abbaye de Jumièges (see "Exploring the town" later in this chapter). The trip takes 45 minutes and costs around 5€ ($6).

Aéroport de Rouen is in Boos, 10km (6.2 miles) southeast of Rouen (☎ 02-35-79-41-00). No direct flights are scheduled from Paris to the Rouen airport, although you can get direct flights from Marseille, Nice, and Bordeaux. To get to the center of the city from the airport, you need to take a **taxi,** costing about 25€ to 30€ ($30–$36).

If you're **driving** from Paris, take A13 west for 133km (83.6 miles). The trip from Paris to Rouen is 1½ hours.

Getting around and getting information

If you want to rent a car, try **Avis** at the Gare SNCF (place Bernard-Tissot; ☎ 02-35-88-60-94) next to the info counter; it's open daily 8:15 a.m. to 12:15 p.m. and 2 to 6:30 p.m. Avis's main booking number is ☎ 08-02-05-05-05. **Hertz** is across the street at 130 rue Jeanne-d'Arc (☎ 02-35-70-70-71) and is open daily 9 a.m. to noon and 2 to 6 p.m. You can rent a bike at **Cycle Latour,** 11 rue Lorraine-Alsace (☎ 02-35-71-52-69), for 12€ ($14) per half day or 20€ ($24) for a whole day. For a **taxi,** call ☎ 02-35-88-50-50.

The **tourist office** is at 25 place de la Cathédrale (☎ 02-32-08-32-40; Fax: 02-32-08-32-44; www.rouen.fr). Housed in a magnificent Renaissance building across from the cathedral, this office offers hotel booking, money exchange (no commission), and guided two-hour walking tours (6€/$7.20). To check on or send e-mail, head to **Place Net** (37 rue de la République; ☎ 02-32-76-02-22), open Monday 2 to 8 p.m. and Tuesday to Saturday noon to 8 p.m.

Spending the night

Find these hotel options (and restaurants and attractions) in the nearby map, "Rouen."

Hôtel de Bordeaux
$ Rouen

The friendly staff and scenic views from the upper-floor rooms in this modern hotel go a long way toward making up for the generic smallish accommodations and depressing façade of this cinder-block building across from the Seine. Most of the 48 rooms have access to communal balconies that wrap around the building; some open onto views of the rooftops and Gothic spires and the greenish Seine.

Normandy

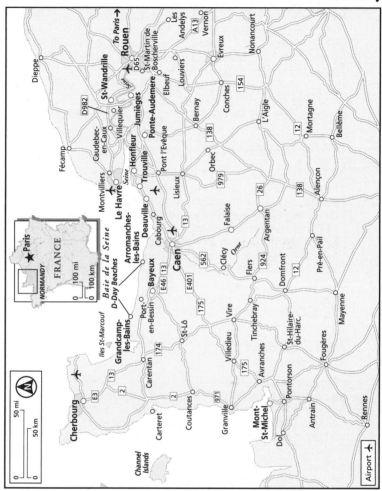

See map p. 295. 9 place de la République. ☎ *02-35-71-93-58*. Fax: 02-35-71-92-15. Parking: 7€ ($8.40). Rack rates: 54€–63€ ($65–$76) double. Breakfast 6.50€ ($7.80). AE, DC, MC, V.

Hôtel de Dieppe
$–$$ Rouen

Across from the train station, this reasonably priced Best Western is one of Rouen's best lodging options. It's on a busy road, so request a room on an upper floor in the rear. Some rooms are small, but all have modern décor and are comfortable. The attached restaurant, Les Quatre Saisons, is the pride and joy of the Guéret family, who have been running it and the hotel for five generations. The chef's favorites are *sole Michel à la arête* (sole prepared on the bone in the chef's style) and *caneton Rouennais à la presse "Félix Faure" préparé devant le client par un maître canardier* (pressed duckling prepared tableside). For dessert, nothing is finer than *soufflé du Président* (apple soufflé).

See map p. 295. Place Bernard-Tissot. ☎ *800-528-1234 in the U.S. and Canada, or 02-35-71-96-00. Fax: 02-35-89-65-21.* www.bestwestern.com. *Parking: 5€ ($6). Rack rates: 90€–102.50€ ($108–$123) double. Breakfast: 9€ ($11). AE, DC, MC, V.*

Hôtel de la Cathédrale
$ Rouen

The Cathédrale, an 18th-century house tucked into a narrow pedestrian side street paved with cobblestone, really feels like old Rouen; this is definitely the most charming medium-priced hotel in town. The hotel, located in an area that's quiet at night, is built around a beautiful interior courtyard filled with flowers and surrounded by half-timbered façades. (The courtyard serves as a tearoom in good weather.) The 26 cheerful rooms, painted in bright colors, are comfortable, although some are small.

See map p. 295. 12 rue St-Romain. ☎ *02-35-71-57-95. Fax: 02-35-70-15-54.* www.hotel-de-la-cathedrale.fr. *Parking: 5€ ($6). Rack rates: 59€–85€ ($71–$102) double. Breakfast: 7.50€ ($9). AE, MC, V.*

Hôtel le Cardinal
$$ Rouen

This hotel is for sound sleepers or those who want to admire the beautiful cathedral all night: It's on the cathedral square, and most rooms overlook the ornate façade, which is brightly lit at night. But be aware that the cathedral bell chimes every 15 minutes (and more jubilantly on the hour), and the square is noisy with late-night cafes on the first floor of the hotel building. The 18 rooms are fairly spacious, comfortable, and decorated in a plain contemporary style. The staff can be rather brusk, and parking is somewhat of a problem in this busy area.

See map p. 295. 1 place de la Cathédrale. ☎ *02-35-70-24-42. Fax: 02-35-89-75-14. E-mail:* hotelcardinal.rouen@wanadoo.fr. *Parking: 5€ ($6). Rack rates: 54€–66€ ($65–$79) double. Breakfast: 6.80€ ($8.15). Closed mid-Dec to early Jan. MC, V.*

Dining locally

Dishes you'll find frequently on Rouen menus include duck paté, Normandy sole, pressed Rouen duck, Rouen sheep's foot, local cheese, apple tart, and apple soufflés. To drink, locals favor bottled cider and Calvados apple brandy. One of Rouen's best restaurants is **Les Quatre Saisons** at the Hôtel de Dieppe (see the preceding section).

Rouen

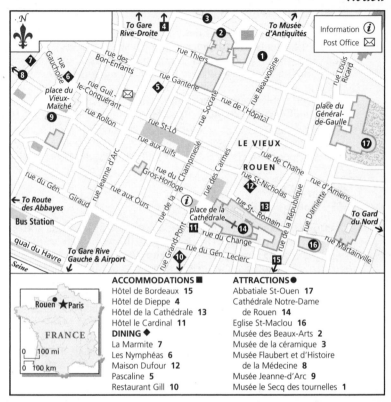

↑ To Gare Rive-Droite **4**

↗ To Musée d'Antiquités

Information ⓘ
Post Office ✉

rue des Bon-Enfants

rue Thiers

rue Gauchoise **7**
8
6

rue Ganterle

rue Beauvoisine

rue Louis Ricard

place du Vieux-Marché

rue Guil.-le-Conquérant ✉ **5**

rue de l'Hôpital

place du Général-de-Gaulle

rue Rollon

rue St-Lô

rue Socrate

9

rue aux Juifs

LE VIEUX

17

rue du Gén. Giraud

rue Gros-Horloge

rue du Champmesle

rue des Carmes

ROUEN

rue de Chaîne

rue St-Nicholas

rue d'Amiens

← To Route des Abbayes

Bus Station

rue Jeanne d'Arc

rue aux Ours

rue de la

ⓘ

place de la Cathédrale

12

rue St-Romain

13

rue de la République

rue Damiette

To Gard du Nord

quai du Havre

To Gare Rive Gauche & Airport

rue Grand-Pont

11

10

rue du Change **14**

rue du Gén. Leclerc

15

16

rue Martainville

Seine

FRANCE

Rouen ● ★ Paris

0   100 mi
0   100 km

ACCOMMODATIONS ■	ATTRACTIONS ●
Hôtel de Bordeaux **15**	Abbatiale St-Ouen **17**
Hôtel de Dieppe **4**	Cathédrale Notre-Dame
Hôtel de la Cathédrale **13**	de Rouen **14**
Hôtel le Cardinal **11**	Eglise St-Maclou **16**
DINING ◆	Musée des Beaux-Arts **2**
La Marmite **7**	Musée de la céramique **3**
Les Nymphéas **6**	Musée Flaubert et d'Histoire
Maison Dufour **12**	de la Médecine **8**
Pascaline **5**	Musée Jeanne-d'Arc **9**
Restaurant Gill **10**	Musée le Secq des tournelles **1**

La Marmite
$$$ Rouen FRENCH

This romantic fine dining restaurant is tucked into a side street just north of the *Vieille Marché* (old market) square. Elegant service and beautifully presented plates of traditional foods combine to assure a delightful meal. The menu includes regional specialties such as *foie gras de canard* (duck foie gras), *marmite de pomme* (apple casserole), and *camembert rôti* (roasted camembert). The wine list offers a range of affordable options.

See map p. 295. 3 rue Florence. ☎ *02-35-71-75-55. Reservations recommended. Main courses: 19€–25€ ($23–$30); prix fixe: 22€–48€ ($26–$58). AE, MC, V. Open: Wed–Sun noon to 2:30 p.m.; Tues–Sat 7:30–9:30 p.m.*

Les Nymphéas
$$$$ Rouen FRENCH

Set in an ancient half-timbered house near Vieille Marché, Les Nymphéas is one of Rouen's top restaurants, decorated with stylish contemporary flair. Chef Patrice Kukurudz prefers combinations of subtle flavors. His signature dishes are *foie gras chaud de canard au vinaigre de cidre* (hot duck foie gras with cider vinegar), *civet de homard au Sauternes* (lobster stew with sweet white wine), and *soufflé chaud aux pommes et Calvados* (hot apple soufflé with Calvados). In summer, lunch is served on a terrace.

See map p. 295. 7–9 rue de la Pie. ☎ 02-35-89-26-69. Reservations required. Main courses: 23€–50€ ($28–$60); prix fixe: 27€–63€ ($32–$76). AE, DC, MC, V. Open: Tues–Sat noon to 2 p.m.; Tues–Sat 7:30–9:30 p.m. Closed late Aug to mid-Sept.

Maison Dufour
$$$ Rouen FRENCH

Occupying a restored half-timbered corner building, this softly lit restaurant feels snug and cozy. The decor is rustic, with stone walls, beamed ceilings, hanging copper pots, and intimate rooms off the main room. The service is exceptional under the stern eye of Mme. Dufour, whose family has run the restaurant since 1904. The food is high quality, especially at these reasonable prices. Besides the usual Normandy favorites, the restaurant features *moules de Bouchots à la crème* (mussels in cream sauce) and *sole frit, citron et persil* (sole fried with lemon and parsley). The perfect dessert is the *soufflé au Calvados.*

See map p. 295. 67 bis rue St-Nicholas. ☎ 02-35-71-90-62. Reservations required. Main courses: 13€–20€ ($16–$24); prix fixe: 25€–38€ ($30–$46). AE, MC, V. Open: Tues–Sun noon to 2 p.m.; Tues–Sat 7:30–9:30 p.m.

Pascaline
$$ Rouen FRENCH

This informal bistro often is filled with regulars, a tradition dating from its opening in 1880. The decor hasn't changed much since then. The least expensive prix fixe menus are some of the best values in town. The best items on the menu are seafood, such as a *pavé* of monkfish with a roughly textured mustard sauce, or a savory *pot-au-feu* maison, *navarin* of monkfish, or a *cassoulet toulousain.* Don't come for a refined cuisine — instead, you can expect hearty and time-tested old favorites. On Thursday night, you can catch live jazz from a swing band.

See map p. 295. 5 rue de la Poterne. ☎ 02-35-89-67-44. Reservations recommended. Main courses: 9.90€–13.95€ ($12–$17); prix fixe: 12.95€–21.70€ ($16–$26). AE, MC, V. Open: Daily noon to 2 p.m. and 7:30–11:30 p.m.

Sampling the region's cuisine

Traveling through Normandy, you see the sleepy-eyed cows that produce some of this region's renowned dairy products: cream, milk, and cheeses. Of the many special cheeses from Normandy, Camembert is the most famous, but Livarot and Pont-l'Evêque also are from here. When food is prepared *à la normande,* it usually means the meat or seafood is cooked with cream, cider, or Calvados. Befitting Normandy's coastal location, menus often include Norman sole, Courseulles and Isigny oysters, Grandcamp scallops, and Honfleur prawns and cockles. Special meats to look for are Vallée d'Auge chicken, andouillé sausage from Vire, and Isigny lamb. The region also is known for apples, so local cider, the apple-based aperitif called *pommeau,* and Calvados (an apple brandy) are venerated drinks. For dessert, an apple tart is the perfect ending to any meal.

Restaurant Gill
$$$$ Rouen   FRENCH

In a sleek modern dining room on the busy road beside the Seine, Gill is Rouen's top restaurant, enjoying two Michelin stars. Expect to pace yourself during an elaborate multicourse meal. Delightful specialties of chef Gilles Tournadre are *salade de queues de langoustines poëlées, chutney de tomate et poivron rouge* (salad of pan-fried prawn with tomato–and–red-pepper chutney), *dos de cabillaud rôti, pommes et onion rouge* (roasted cod with apples and red onions), *pigeon à la Rouennaise avec sa raviole de foie gras* (guinea fowl with foie gras ravioli), and, for dessert, *millefeuille de minute* (pastry of the moment) or the traditional *soufflé au Calvados.*

See map p. 295. 9 quai de la Bourse. ☎ *02-35-71-16-14. Reservations required far in advance. Main courses: 28€–35€ ($34–$42); prix fixe: 58€–80€ ($70–$96). AE, DC, MC, V. Open: Tues–Sat noon to 2:30 p.m. and 7:30–10 p.m. Closed 2 weeks in mid-Apr, 3 weeks in Aug.*

Exploring the town

The *petit train* (little train) (☎ 02-32-18-40-21) runs 40-minute tours through the city, leaving daily from in front of the tourist office (25 place de la Cathédrale), at 10 and 11 a.m., noon, 2, 3, 4, and 5 p.m. It costs 4.90€ ($5.90) adults, 2.30€ ($2.75) children.

Rouen is fairly compact — it'll take you about 20 minutes to walk from one end of the old center to the other. **Rue Jeanne-d'Arc** is the main thoroughfare, leading from the train station to the center. Not far from the station are some of Rouen's top museums:

✔ **Musée des Beaux-Arts** (square Verdrei; ☎ 02-35-71-28-40; www.rouen-musees.com) contains a fine collection of paintings, drawings, and sculptures from the Middle Ages to the 20th century, including works by Caravaggio, Velasquez, Delacroix, Géricault (born in Rouen), Monet *(Rouen Cathedral in Gray Weather),* and Helen Frankenthaler. Impressionist paintings are particularly well represented. The museum is open Wednesday to Monday 10 a.m. to 6 p.m. Admission is 3€ ($3.60) for adults and 1.75€ ($2.10) for students and children.

✔ The entertaining **Musée le Secq des tournelles** (2 rue Jacques-Villon; ☎ **02-35-88-42-92;** www.rouen-musees.com) displays the greatest European collection of ironworks, including signs, tools, and keys and locks from the 3rd to the 19th centuries. The collection — housed in the former Eglise St-Laurent — was donated to the city by one collector in 1920. The museum is open Wednesday to Monday 10 a.m. to 1 p.m. and 2 to 6 p.m. Admission is 2.30€ ($2.75) for adults and 1.55€ ($1.85) for students. Children younger than 16 are admitted free.

✔ Walking south down rue Jeanne-d'Arc from the train station, you'll first come to an interesting little museum that specializes in the most famous craft of the region: *faïence.* **Musée de la céramique** (1 rue de Faucon; ☎ **02-35-07-31-74;** www.rouen-musees.com) is dedicated to Rouen *faïence* and ceramics from the 16th to the 18th centuries, when Rouen was a major pottery center. The collection is housed in an elegant mansion, Hôtel d'Hocqueville, and is open Wednesday to Monday 10 a.m. to 1 p.m. and 2 to 6 p.m. Admission is 2.30€ ($2.75) for adults and 1.55€ ($1.85) for students. Free for children younger than 18.

Down rue Jeanne-d'Arc and right on the main street of the pedestrian shopping district, **rue de Gros Horloge,** you can admire its many half-timbered buildings on your way to **place du Vieux-Marché,** the market square surrounded by cafes and restaurants. The ancient church on the square (Eglise St-Vincent) was destroyed during World War II bombing and replaced in 1979 with a remarkable modern building that's a church **(Eglise Ste-Jeanne-d'Arc),** a market with food shops, and a monument to Joan of Arc. The building's north side features a large cross on the site of the stake where Joan was burned to death for alleged heresy. The church boasts many echoes of the sea, including scalelike roof tiles in slate and copper, fish-shaped windows, and a wooden boat-shaped ceiling. The 16th-century stained-glass windows from the former church were saved and installed in the new church.

Devotees of Joan of Arc flock to the **Musée Jeanne-d'Arc,** located in a cellar off the central square (33 place du Vieux-Marché; ☎ **02-35-88-02-70;** www.jeanne-darc.com), just steps from the spot where she was burned alive at the stake on May 30, 1431. This musty place is filled with cheesy waxworks, but it's hard not to be moved by Joan's story. With a recorded commentary in English, the museum is open daily: May to September 9 a.m. to 7 p.m. and October to April 10 a.m. to noon and 2 to 6 p.m. Admission is 4€ ($4.80) for adults and 2€ ($2.40) for children and students.

Why all the half-timbered houses?

Those old buildings you see with visible wood framing filled in by masonry are half-timbered houses. Of the approximately 1,000 half-timbered houses (from the 14th to the 19th centuries) in Rouen's center, about 200 have been restored since World War II bombings. This style of building was popular because builders didn't have access to much stone, the most common building material, but they had access to plenty of oak in surrounding forests. After the war, the city used extensive records to restore buildings, and builders researched ancient construction methods to be as authentic as possible.

Continue west along rue de Crosne, which turns into avenue Gustave-Flaubert. Several more blocks (a 15-minute walk from place du Vieille-Marché) take you to a museum devoted to author Gustave Flaubert. **Musée Flaubert et d'Histoire de la Médecine,** in the Hôtel-Dieu at 51 rue de Lecat (☎ 02-35-15-59-95), displays souvenirs of the *Madame Bovary* author and Rouen native. In December 1821, Flaubert was born in this hospital, where his father was the resident surgeon. The museum features the tools of Flaubert's father, including medical and surgical instruments, documents, and hospital furnishings. Admission is 2.20€ ($2.65) for adults and 1.50€ ($1.80) students and children. The museum is open Tuesday to Saturday 10 a.m. to noon and 2 to 6 p.m. Closed the second and fourth Saturdays of every month.

On the other end of rue de Gros Horloge is the famous **Cathédrale Notre-Dame** (place de la Cathédrale; for information, call the tourist office at ☎ 02-32-08-32-40). Its complex asymmetrical façade just barely escaped total destruction during World War II bombing. The Flamboyant Gothic tower (with flamelike shapes) on the left is known as Tour de Beurre and contains a carillon of 55 bells. Legend has it that the money for the tower came from wealthy residents willing to pay for the privilege of eating butter during Lent. Added in the 19th century, the Tour Lanterne contains a spire made of cast iron and copper. It's the tallest in France. Impressionist Claude Monet painted the harmonious west façade countless times in inclement weather. Inside is stained glass from the 13th to the 16th centuries and the Renaissance tombs of Cardinals d'Amboise and Louis de Brézé. The church is open Monday to Saturday 8 a.m. to 7 p.m. and Sunday 8 a.m. to 6 p.m. Guided visits to the crypt (built in A.D. 1000 and containing a well that's nine centuries old) and the 14th-century Chapel of the Virgin (which has a medieval nativity painting and numerous magnificent tombs) take place June to August daily at 4 p.m. and September to May Saturday and Sunday at 3 p.m.

Behind the cathedral is the Flamboyant Gothic **Eglise St-Maclou** (☎ 02-35-71-71-72). The unusually elaborate entrance, with five porches containing five doors, is covered with Renaissance carvings. The church was badly damaged by a World War II bomb; photos inside detail the destruction. It's open Monday to Saturday 10 a.m. to noon and 2 to 6 p.m. and Sundays 3 to 5 p.m. (closed January 1, May 1, July 14, and November 11). East of the cathedral, **Abbatiale St-Ouen** (once part of a major Benedictine Abbey) was built from the 14th to the 16th centuries and is one of France's most beautiful churches. It's notable for its unity of the Flamboyant Gothic style, a refined architecture that incorporates lots of light. Inside are 18th-century wrought-iron choir gates and a superb 1630 organ with more than 3,000 pipes (renovated in the 19th century). St-Ouen is where Joan of Arc was sentenced to life imprisonment, though that sentence was later altered to death. Mid-March to October, the church is open Wednesday to Monday 10 a.m. to 12:30 p.m. and 2 to 6 p.m.; November to mid-December and late January to mid-March, hours are Wednesday, Saturday, and Sunday 10 a.m. to 12:30 p.m. and 2 to 4:30 p.m. For more information on the Abbatiale St-Ouen, call the tourist office at ☎ 02-32-08-32-40.

Mont-St-Michel (see "Mont-St-Michel: Medieval Marvel" later in this chapter) isn't the only famous abbey in these parts, but the others draw far fewer visitors. **Route des Abbayes,** a 140-km (87-mile) driving route that roughly follows the Seine, passes half a dozen abbeys. The two most interesting are less than 65km (40 miles) from Rouen. Leave Rouen west on D982 and then south on D65 to reach the first abbey.

✔ Many say France's most beautiful ruin is **Abbaye de Jumièges** (☎ 02-35-37-24-02), 11th-century remains surrounded by ancient yew trees. The Romanesque nave and two pillars, along with 16th-century chapels and stained glass, are all that's left from the Eglise St-Valentin. The abbey is open daily (except January 1, May 1, November 1, November 11, and December 25): late April to mid-September 9:30 a.m. to 6:30 p.m. and late September to mid-April 9:30 a.m. to 1 p.m. and 2:30 to 5:30 p.m. (last ticket sales are half an hour before closing). Admission is 4.60€ ($5.50) for adults and 3.10€ ($3.70) for anyone 18 to 25.

✔ Another 16km (10 miles) down D982 is the **Abbaye St-Wandrille de Fontenelle** (☎ 02-35-96-23-11), built in the 13th and 14th centuries. The Gothic cloisters from the 14th to the 16th centuries are the highlights. Guided tours are given on Saturdays at 3:30 p.m. and Sundays and holidays at 11:30 a.m. and 3:30 p.m. Gregorian chant services take place on Sundays at 10 a.m. and weekdays at 9:45 a.m. Admission is 3.50€ ($4.20).

Shopping for local treasures

A **food-and-produce market** is open at place St-Marc on Tuesday, Friday, and Saturday 8 a.m. to 6:30 p.m. On Sundays 8 a.m. to 1:30 p.m., place St-Marc becomes a **flea market**. At place du Vieux-Marché, you find a **food market** Tuesday to Sunday 6 a.m. to 1:30 p.m. Place des Emmurées plays host to a **food market** on Tuesdays and Saturdays and a **flea market** on Thursdays 8 a.m. to 6:30 p.m.

Rouen has long been famous for its *faïence* (painted pottery); many of its shops and antiques stores sell fine pieces. Be aware that antique *faïence* is expensive, but contemporary versions are affordable and abundant. For antiques, check out **rue St-Romain, rue Damiette,** and **rue Eau-de-Robec,** an area that plays host to an antiques fair on the first Saturday of every month. **Michel Carpentier,** (26 rue St-Romain; ☎ 02-35-88-77-47) sells high-quality contemporary *faïence* made in his shop.

Living it up after dark

Most of Rouen's nightlife is centered around place du Vieux-Marché. **Le Scottish** (26 Bis quai Gaston Boulet; ☎ 02-35-71-58-37) has live jazz and no cover. A popular beer pub is **La Taverne St-Amand** (11 rue St-Amand; ☎ 02-35-88-51-34). You can find highbrow entertainment at **Théâtre des Arts** (7 rue du Docter Rambert; ☎ 02-35-98-50-98), with classical music concerts, opera, and ballet. For plays, check out the **Théâtre des Deux Rives** (48 rue Louis-Ricard; ☎ 02-35-70-22-82).

The brochure *Cette Semaine à Rouen,* available free from the tourist office, lists all current events.

Bayeux and the Famous Tapestry

The town of **Bayeux** is famous for displaying the tapestry that tells how the French conquered England in 1066. With a story line like that, you know this display will be impressive — and indeed it is. But Bayeux is a pleasant place to stay, with a number of fine hotels and restaurants and handsome cobblestone streets for strolling. At fewer than 20km (12 miles) from D-day beaches, the town is a good base for tours.

The first weekend in July is **Fêtes Médiévales,** a lively two-day affair with costumed entertainers, parades, large markets, and late-night partying. The streets in the center of town are blocked off to cars during the festival.

Getting there

Trains traveling from Paris's Gare St-Lazare to Bayeux take 2½ hours and cost 29.50€ ($35). Six to twelve trains make the journey each day, and most stop in Caen, where you may have to change trains. Twelve trains per day travel from Caen to Bayeux, with the trip taking 20 minutes and costing 5.20€ ($6.25). The Bayeux **train station,** at place de la Gare, is about a 15-minute walk from the center of town. For train reservations and information, call **SNCF** at ☎ 08-93-35-35-39 or 08-92-35-35-35.

To **drive** from Paris to Bayeux, take A13 to Caen and E46 west to Bayeux. It's about a three-hour trip.

Exploring other Normandy favorites

If you have some additional time, check out these interesting spots:

✔ **Caen:** This mostly modern city, 103km (64 miles) from Rouen, serves as a convenient transportation hub and is the capital of Lower Normandy. The bustling city is about a 15-minute drive from the D-day beaches. The World War II Mémorial de Caen, at esplanade Dwight-Eisenhower, is the region's most impressive. The city also has a pair of noteworthy medieval abbeys: Abbaye aux Dames on place de la Reine-Mathilde and Abbaye aux Hommes on esplanade Jean-Marie-Louvel.

✔ **Deauville:** A stylish seaside resort since the mid-19th century, Deauville, 71km (44 miles) from Rouen, sports a number of diversions, including casinos, golf courses, polo grounds, and racetracks for wealthy vacationers. The sandy beach, lined by a wooden boardwalk, can be quite crowded in summer. Those looking for chic accommodations may want to contact Normandy Barrière (38 rue Jean-Mermoz; ☎ 02-31-98-66-22; Fax: 02-31-98-66-23; www.lucienbarriere.com), with rack rates at 215€ to 462€ ($258–$554) double.

✔ **Etretat:** This seaside village, 87km (54 miles) from Rouen, is the site of the unusual cliffs that Monet painted many times. The wide pebbly beach is accessed via a long concrete boardwalk. You can walk along the grassy tops of the cliffs and explore the tiny 19th-century Chapelle Notre-Dame de la Garde on top of the cliff on the east side of the beach. Etretat is an idyllic place to eat crêpes or *moules frites* (mussels and french fries) at one of its beach cafes.

✔ **Honfleur:** You'll be completely charmed by this fishing village at the mouth of the Seine, 66km (41 miles) from Rouen. Sit at a cafe by the harbor, take a spin on the carousel, catch a boat ride, or visit the historic house museums. You'll find a host of fine shops and art galleries on the streets near the port.

✔ **Pont de Normandie:** Drive across the spectacular cable bridge Pont de Normandie (5€/$6), which connects Le Havre to Honfleur across the Seine estuary. The bridge, completed in 1995, is 856m (936 yds.) long.

Getting around and getting information

For a **taxi,** call ☎ 02-31-92-92-40. The **tourist office** is at pont St-Jean (☎ 02-31-51-28-28; Fax: 02-31-51-28-29; www.bayeux-tourism.com), open January to March and November to December Monday to Saturday 9:30 a.m. to 12:30 p.m. and 2 to 6 p.m.; April to May and September to October daily 9:30 a.m. to 12:30 p.m. and 2 to 6 p.m.; and June to August Monday to Saturday 9 a.m. to 7 p.m. and Sunday 9 a.m. to 1 p.m. and 2 to 6 p.m.

Spending the night

Hôtel Churchill-Clarine
$–$$ **Bayeux**

The Churchill, in a handsome 19th-century stone building, claims an ideal location on the main street, a cobblestone pedestrian way lined with shops and restaurants. The property is well run and recently has undergone extensive renovations. The 32 rooms offer a cheerful decor along with some antiques and large windows, some of which overlook the majestic cathedral. In the center of the hotel is a flower-filled, glassed-in courtyard — the site of a restaurant serving breakfast and dinner.

14 rue St-Jean. ☎ *02-31-21-31-80. Fax: 02-31-21-41-66.* www.hotel-churchill. com. *Parking: free. Rack rates: 75€–145€ ($90–$174) double. Breakfast: 7.50€ ($9). Closed Dec to mid-Feb. MC, V.*

Hôtel d'Argouges
$–$$ **Bayeux**

The elegant exterior and lobby of this 18th-century mansion don't exactly jibe with the dowdy décor, small size of most rooms, and lack of an elevator. But if you're willing to pay more (and reserve far ahead), you can get one of the handsome suites. The hotel is in a fine location, facing central place St-Patrice. All 28 rooms have minibars; rooms in the back are quiet and look out on pretty gardens, but units in the front, though set back from the street by a courtyard, can be noisy. The staff is English-speaking and helpful, and the continental breakfast is particularly good.

21 rue St-Patrice. ☎ *02-31-92-88-86. Fax: 02-31-92-69-16. E-mail:* dargouges@ aol.com. *Parking: 2€ ($2.40). Rack rates: 67€–116€ ($80–$139) double; 162€–240€ ($194–$288) suite. Breakfast: 8€ ($9.60). AE, MC, V.*

Le Lion d'Or
$$ **Bayeux**

Bayeux's best hotel is on the town's main pedestrian street in a 17th-century stone coaching inn. This has been the top place to stay in town for more than 70 years, so make reservations far in advance. The 25 individually decorated rooms possess a charm that comes from attention to detail. All rooms have minibars. Half board is required here, meaning you must pay for lunch or dinner at the hotel restaurant, which serves traditional Norman cuisine.

71 rue St-Jean. ☎ *02-31-92-06-90. Fax: 02-31-22-15-64.* www.liondor-bayeux. fr. *Parking: 4€ ($4.80). Rack rates: 103€–184€ ($124–$221) double. Half board: 76€–117€ ($91–$140) per person. Closed Dec 22 to Jan 24. AE, DC, MC, V.*

Dining locally

L'Amaryllis
$$ Bayeux NORMAN

The unusual aspect (for France) of this quaint restaurant is that the entire front room, with several booths and large picture windows facing the street, is a no-smoking area. The service is very efficient, and the restaurant caters not only to locals, who appreciate the quality food, but also to visitors, who can order from an English menu. Depending on availability, the restaurant has local meats and fresh fish, such as Honfleur prawns and salt meadow Isigny lamb. The wine list offers many reasonably priced options, plus several good vintages by the glass.

32 rue St-Patrice. ☎ *02-31-22-47-94. Reservations accepted. Main courses: 15€–25€ ($18–$30); prix fixe: 15€–32€ ($18–$38). MC, V. Open: Tues–Sat noon to 2 p.m. and 7–9:30 p.m.; Sun noon to 2 p.m. Closed mid-Dec to Jan.*

Le Petit Normand
$$ Bayeux NORMAN

This simple restaurant, offering good value for home-cooked hearty meals, is near the cathedral in an ancient building. Traditional Norman food washed down with cider is the way to go here. The chef wisely recommends duck foie gras to start, followed by tripe cooked in Caen style or Vallé d'Auge chicken (free range). You can find a good selection of savory Normandy cheeses here, too.

35 rue Larcher. ☎ *02-31-22-88-66. Reservations accepted. Main courses: 10€–14€ ($12–$17); prie fixe: 9.50€–24.50€ ($11–$29). MC, V. Open: Daily noon to 2:45 p.m. and 6:45–10 p.m. Closed Dec and Jan.*

Le Pommier
$–$$ Bayeux FRENCH

One of the most appealing restaurants in Bayeux's historic zone occupies an antique building whose three dining rooms contain ceiling beams, stone ceiling vaults, and exposed masonry. The venue is devotedly Norman, with cuisine that reflects the region's long tradition of baking with apples (the restaurant's name translates as "the apple tree") and limited amounts of cream. Sauces are served on the side, and the health-conscious staff is proud of the way their dishes "aren't drowned in gravies and sauces." Menu items evolve with the seasons and the availability of ingredients, but you usually can usually expect dishes such as foie gras of duckling prepared house-style, rabbit stew braised in cider, and a platter that contains two kinds of fish served with chitterling sausage with a sauce made from cream and drippings from the chitterlings.

38 rue des Cuisiniers. ☎ *02-31-21-52-10. Reservations recommended. Main courses: 10.50€–16.50€ ($13–$20); prix fixe lunch: 10.50€ ($13), prix fixe dinner: 13.50€–22.50€ ($16–$27). AE, MC, V. Open: Apr–Oct daily noon to 2 p.m. and 7–9:30 p.m.; Nov–Mar Thurs–Mon noon to 2 p.m. and 7–9:30 p.m.*

Exploring the town

Bayeux is compact and easy to walk. The main road through the center is the pedestrian **rue St-Jean**. The tapestry and several smaller museums are south of rue St-Jean, as is the 11th-century **Cathédrale Notre-Dame** (rue du Bienvenu; ☎ 02-31-92-01-85). The cathedral was consecrated in 1077 but partially destroyed in 1105. Romanesque towers from the original church rise on the western side. The central tower is from the 15th century, and the nave is a fine example of Norman Romanesque style. Rich in sculpture, the 13th-century choir, a perfect example of Norman Gothic style, has Renaissance stalls. The crypt was built in the 11th century and then sealed, its existence unknown until 1412. Admission is free; the cathedral is open daily from 9 a.m. to 6 p.m. (until 7 p.m. in July and August).

The 11th-century **Tapisserie de Bayeux** is displayed in the **Centre Guillaume le Conquérant** (rue de Nesmond; ☎ 02-31-51-25-50). The 58 panels of the Bayeux Tapestry (actually an embroidery in wool on a background of linen), measuring 70m (230 ft.) long and 50cm (20 in.) high, tell the story of the Norman Conquest — when William the Conqueror invaded England, resulting in the Battle of Hastings on October 14, 1066 — and William's being crowned king of England. Born Billy the Bastard, William rose from ignoble beginnings to rule England, along with Normandy, until his death in 1087. The story involves the hapless Prince Harold, a Saxon earl, who tried to crown himself king of England against the wishes of the previous ruler, Edward the Confessor, who had promised the throne to William. It's believed that the tapestry was commissioned in 1077 by William's half-brother Odon, the bishop of Bayeux, for display in his cathedral.

The tapestry's survival is a story in itself. The first historical mention of the tapestry was in 1476, when it was said that the canons of the Bayeux Cathedral would unroll it every year for display. The tapestry may have been stolen during the French Revolution in 1789. In 1792, a local man was using it as a tarp to hold down the belongings in his cart. A lawyer, sensing the value of the piece, traded some rope for the tapestry, saving it from certain destruction. Thankfully, the tapestry eventually ended up back in the hands of town authorities.

After viewing much preliminary material to the tapestry (including a full copy with play-by-play translation, interpretation, and analysis), you'll get to see the real thing, behind thick glass in a dark tunnel-like room. Everything has English translations — an audioguide is available in English, and a 14-minute film is shown in English and French. Admission is 7.40€ ($8.90) for adults and 3€ ($3.60) for children and students. Open daily 9 a.m. to 6:30 p.m.

Southwest of the cathedral, at the **Musée Mémorial de la Bataille de Normandie 1944** (boulevard Fabian-Ware; ☎ 02-31-51-46-90), Bayeux commemorates its role as the first French town liberated from the Nazis. The startlingly modern building looks like a UFO bunker and uses soldier waxworks, weapons, military equipment, and memorabilia to outline all aspects of Operation Overlord (the code name for the invasion of Europe) and the Battle of Normandy, the decisive military operation of World War II. Admission is 5.50€ ($6.60) for adults and 2.60€ ($3.10) for children and students. The museum is open daily: May to mid-September 9:30 a.m. to 6:30 p.m., and late September to April 10 a.m. to 12:30 p.m. and 2 to 6 p.m.

The D-day Beaches

Some of World War II's most dramatic events took place on the coast of Normandy. On June 6, 1944, code-named **D-day,** the Allied troops invaded Normandy and put in motion the liberation of the European continent from the Nazis. More than 100,000 soldiers were killed in the ensuing battles. Today not many reminders are left on the beaches of these dramatic events besides some German bunkers. However, small museums and memorials are placed all along the coast, explaining in detail each critical event and battle.

Off the coast of Arromanches, you can see the remains of an artificial harbor that was constructed by the allies and code-named Mulberry Harbor. And, of course, the cemeteries with their acres of white crosses remind us of the heavy cost of freedom. The Battle of Normandy continued until August 21. Soon Paris was liberated, and a year later, when Allied troops entered Berlin, Germany surrendered.

Getting there

If you're **driving** from Paris to the D-day beaches, take A13 to Caen and E46 to Bayeux and then go north on D6 to the coastal road D514; the trip takes about three hours. Following coastal D514 takes you past the relevant D-day sites. You can also drive **Voie de la Liberté,** which follows the path of General Eisenhower and his troops as they liberated one village after another, from Utah Beach all the way to Belgium.

Bus Verts du Calvados (☎ 08-10-02-14-214) runs buses that travel to many of the villages along the coast. **Carte Liberté,** a day pass allowing unlimited travel on the buses, costs 17€ ($20). From July to September 1, bus No. 75 runs a tour that leaves from Caen's Gare Routière (bus station) at 9:30 a.m. and travels to Arromanches (the Musée du Debarquement, artificial harbor, and 360-degree film), Omaha Beach (the American Cemetery), and Pointe du Hoc (the place of the daring feat by Lt. Col. James Rudder's American Rangers, who took this German strongpoint on June 6), returning to Caen at 5:50 p.m.

Getting around and getting information

To rent a car, head to **Lefebvre Car Rental** (boulevard d'Eindhoven, Bayeux; ☎ 02-31-95-05-96). To hire a bike, go to **Cycles 14** (14 bd. Winston-Churchill, Bayeux; ☎ 02-31-92-27-75); bikes cost 7€ ($8.40) for half a day and 14€ ($17) for a full day. Although distances are short, bikers need to be aware that travel along the D-day beaches coastal route is a hilly and windy trek.

If you don't have access to a car, the best way to see the D-day beaches is by tour. **Normandy Tours,** at the Hôtel de la Gare in Bayeux (☎ 02-31-92-10-70), runs tours (in English) to Arromanches, Omaha Beach, the American Military Cemetery, and Pointe du Hoc for 35€ ($42) per person. **D-Day Tours,** 52 Route de Port (☎ 02-31-51-70-52), picks you up at your Bayeux hotel for English-speaking tours of the D-day beaches. A half-day trip costs 45€ ($54) for adults and 40€ ($48) for students, and a full-day trip goes for 65€ ($78) for adults and 55€ ($66) for students.

The tourist offices in Bayeux and Caen have information about visiting the beaches. The **Caen tourist office** is on place St-Pierre (☎ 02-31-27-14-14). July and August, the office is open Monday to Saturday 9 a.m. to 7 p.m. and Sunday 10 a.m. to 1 p.m. and 2 to 5 p.m., and September to June its hours are Monday to Saturday 9:30 a.m. to 1 p.m. and 2 to 6 p.m. and Sunday 10 a.m. to 1 p.m. The **Bayeux tourist office** is on pont St-Jean (☎ 02-31-51-28-28; Fax: 02-31-51-28-29; www.bayeux-tourism.com). You can pick up a brochure called _The D-Day Landings and the Battle of Normandy_ at all local tourist offices.

Exploring the beaches

The beaches' code names, from west to east, are **Utah** and **Omaha** (where the Americans landed), **Juno** (where the Canadians landed), and **Gold** and **Sword** (where the British landed). **Ste-Mère-Eglise,** the first village liberated, has installed on the roof of the church a model of a U.S. paratrooper who became entangled in the steeple. The village's museum, which honors the paratroopers, is the **Musée des Troopes Aéroportées** (14 rue Eisenhower; ☎ 02-33-41-41-35). It's open daily April 1 to September 30 9 a.m. to 6:45 p.m. and October to March 9:30 a.m. to noon and 2 to 6 p.m. (closed Dec and Jan). Admission is 5€ ($6) for adults and 2€ ($2.40) for students. The **American Cemetery** (☎ 02-31-51-62-00), with 9,000 headstones (white crosses and stars of David), is located near Omaha Beach at **Colleville-sur-Mer.** The cemetery is open daily year-round from 9 a.m. to 5 p.m.

The most impressive contemporary D-day museum/monument is the **Mémorial pour la Paix,** at esplanade Dwight-D.-Eisenhower in Caen (☎ 02-31-06-06-44; www.memorial-caen.fr). This comprehensive museum explains the major battles and explores themes, such as German Fascism, the French Resistance, and French collaboration. The museum is open daily (except the first half of Jan and Dec 25): July and August 9 a.m. to 8 p.m., late February to June and September and October 9 a.m. to 7 p.m., and November to mid-February 9 a.m. to 6 p.m. Last entrance is an hour before closing. Admission is 18€ ($22) for adults, 16€ ($19) for children. June to September, the museum runs tours (in English) of the beaches: The four-hour Montgomery Tour, which covers Gold, Juno, and Sword, leaves at 9 a.m. and 2 p.m. and costs 45€ ($54); the six-hour Eisenhower Tour of Omaha and Utah beaches leaves at 9 a.m. and costs 75€ ($90).

In the village of Ste-Marie du Mont, near Utah Beach, the **American Commemorative Monument** and the **Musée du Debarquement d'Utah-Beach** (☎ 02-33-71-53-35) trace the American landing at Utah. April to September, hours are daily 9:30 a.m. to 7 p.m.; and October to March, hours are Saturday and Sunday 10 a.m. to 5:30 p.m. Admission is 4.80€ ($5.75) for adults and 2€ ($2.40) for students. In Arromanches, near Gold Beach, **Musée du Debarquement** (☎ 02-31-22-34-31) explains the use of **Mulberry,** the allies' concrete artificial harbor. From the museum windows, you can see the harbor, which the British constructed off the coast. From May to August, hours are daily from 9 a.m. to 6:30 p.m. In April, hours are daily from 9 a.m. to 12:30 p.m. and 2 to 6 p.m.; in March and October, daily 9:30 a.m. to 12:30 p.m. and 2 to 5:30 p.m.; and in November and February, daily 10 a.m. to 12:30 p.m. and 2 to 5 p.m. Admission is 6€ ($7.20) for adults and 4€ ($4.80) for children and students. Nearby, the **Arromanches 360 Cinéma** (chemin du Calvaire; ☎ 02-31-22-30-30; www.arromanches360.com) projects, on a circle of screens, an 18-minute film about the Allied landings called *Le Prix de la Liberté (The Price of Freedom)*. The cinema presents films daily from 10 a.m. to 5 p.m. Admission is 4€ ($4.80) for adults and 3.50€ ($4.20) for children ages 10 to 18 and students.

Mont-St-Michel: Medieval Marvel

One of France's most popular attractions, the medieval abbey of **Mont-St-Michel** rises 79m (260 ft.) from the primordial quicksands of the bay, just off the coast of Normandy. A causeway allows the steady stream of visitors to walk to the village, which doesn't allow cars. A steep road leads past souvenir shops and restaurants to the abbey, with its flower-filled cloister and soaring chapel perched close to heaven at the top of the rock. Despite all the visitors and hype, this site is awe-inspiring. Mont-St-Michel is also famous for having the highest tides of continental Europe. The tides can rise as high as 15m (50 ft.) in a few hours; at its fastest, it's said to be the speed of a galloping horse.

Getting there

From Paris's Gare Montparnasse, fast **TGVs** run frequently to Rennes in Brittany (two hours; 39.60€/$48). For reservations and information, call **SNCF** at ☎ 08-92-35-35-39 or 08-92-35-35-35. You can then take a bus (75 minutes) to Mont-St-Michel. For bus information, call **Les Courriers Bretons** at ☎ 02-99-19-70-80. The nearest train station (slow trains only) is at **Pontorson,** 9km (5.6 miles) from Mont-St-Michel; a connecting bus (5.50€/$6.60) makes the ten-minute trip to the abbey.

Driving is the most convenient way to get to Mont-St-Michel. From Paris, take A13 to Caen and then N175 southwest to Pontorson and D976 to Mont-St-Michel (4½ hours). From Rouen, drive to Caen on A13 and follow directions from Paris. From Bayeux and the D-day beaches, head briefly southeast to Caen on E46 and then southwest to Mont-St-Michel. Try to park (2.50€/$3) as close as possible to the abbey, because you have a long walk ahead of you. Be aware that the spaces just below the abbey entrance are covered by water at high tide. Announcements warn motorists to move their cars in time.

Crowds gather in the **North Tower** of the abbey after the last tour of the day to watch the tide creep and then rush in. The fastest tides take place during the equinoxes in March and September.

 Seeing 75 tour buses parked in the lots at Mont-St-Michel isn't unusual. To avoid the crowds, arrive late in the day. Visitors staying overnight on the Mont are allowed to park in the best spots, closest to the entrance, and they have the additional luxury of visiting the abbey after all the others have left. In summer, the last regular tour of the abbey is at 5 p.m., and nighttime visits start at 6 p.m. Avoid Mont-St-Michel in August, when crowds are at their worst.

Getting information

The **Mont-St-Michel tourist office** is on the left as you enter the fortified gate of the Mont (☎ **02-33-60-14-30;** Fax: 02-33-60-06-75; www.ot-mont saintmichel.com). From late June to mid-September, the office is open Monday to Saturday 9 a.m. to 7 p.m. and Sunday 9 a.m. to noon and 2 to 6 p.m.; late September to mid-June, hours are daily 9 a.m. to 12:30 p.m. and 2 to 6 p.m. Check with the office for the times of English-language tours of the abbey. Next to the Mont-St-Michel tourist office are public toilets and a fountain where you'll see lines of hearty pilgrims washing thick gray mud off of their legs.

Spending the night

Hôtel du Mouton Blanc
$ Mont-St-Michel

The 15 rooms at this medieval hotel/restaurant about halfway up Grande Rue are just average; some are small, dark, and a little depressing. And there's no elevator. But the prices are good, and the restaurant is a charming place, serving some of the best food on the Mont, with views of the bay. Popular fare at the restaurant is a variety of seafood, including mussels from the bay and lobster in a creamy casserole.

Grande Rue. ☎ *02-33-60-14-08. Fax: 02-33-60-05-62. Rack rates: 64€ ($77) double. Half board: 52€–65€ ($62–$78). Breakfast: 7.50€ ($9). AE, MC, V.*

Les Terrasses Poulard
$–$$$ **Mont-St-Michel**

Several flights of steep stone steps lead up to this hotel, and there's no elevator, so if you have a lot of baggage, you may have difficulty getting to the entrance, though the English-speaking staff is most helpful. The 30 rooms, all with minibars, range from inviting to depressing. If you're willing to pay a lot more and reserve ahead, you can get a spacious room with a fireplace, sculpted moldings, and bay views. If you're traveling with children, ask for one of the larger rooms — reasonable prices and units with thick walls make this a good choice for families. Guests are served breakfast at the hotel's restaurant, a little farther up Grande Rue. Alas, tables for breakfast guests are grouped far from windows with a panoramic view. At lunch and dinner, the restaurant serves average fare with a view. The specialties are *moules frites* (mussels and french fries), grilled seafood, crêpes, and *galettes* (buckwheat pancakes).

Grande Rue. ☎ *02-33-89-02-02. Fax: 02-33-60-37-31.* www.terrasses-poulard.com. *Rack rates: 60€–280€ ($72–$336) double. Half board: 84€–129€ ($101–$155). Breakfast: 9€ ($11). AE, MC, V.*

Dining locally

Crêperie La Sirène
$ **Mont-St-Michel**   **CRÊPES**

The restaurants on Mont-St-Michel tend to be overpriced, so it's a relief to find this unassuming crêperie with friendly service, good food, and reasonable prices. The second-floor dining room, with a beamed ceiling and stone walls, offers views of the bustling Grande Rue teaming with visitors. You have a large choice of crêpes filled with vegetables and meat, as well as freshly made salads. For dessert, succumb to the banana crêpe smothered in chocolate sauce.

Grande Rue. ☎ *02-33-60-08-60. Reservations not accepted. Crêpes: 6.90€–8€ ($8.30–$9.60). AE, MC, V. Open: Daily noon to 2:30 p.m. and 6–9:30 p.m.*

La Mère Poulard
$$$ **Mont-St-Michel**   **NORMAN**

Is La Mère Poulard a tourist trap best avoided or a restaurant serving the best omelets in the world? Because it's nearly impossible to get a reservation, most people think the latter. At any rate, this restaurant is certainly the most expensive and most famous on Mont-St-Michel, located in the busiest square, right at the entrance into town. The omelets, made in long-handled copper skillets and served by women in Norman costume, are indeed fluffy and delectable. The menu also features *agneau du pré salé* (lamb raised on the adjacent salt marshes) and seafood from the bay.

Grand Rue. ☎ *02-33-60-14-01. Reservations necessary at least 3 days in advance. Main courses: 25€–35€ ($30–$42); prix fixe: 35€–65€ ($42–$78). AE, DC, MC, V. Open: Daily 11:30 a.m. to 2:30 p.m. and 6:45–10 p.m.*

Exploring the abbey

You can see the famous silhouette of **Mont-St-Michel** (☎ 02-33-89-80-00; www.monum.fr) from miles away, and many visitors cherish their first glimpse of *La Merveille* (The Wonder). After walking across the cause-way, you enter the island of Mont-St-Michel (see the "Mont-St-Michel" map) through the **Porte Bavole,** built in 1590, and follow **Grande Rue,** a steep and narrow pedestrian street up to the abbey. As you pass through the gate, on your left is the **Corps de Guard des Bourgeois,** a 15th-century building that now houses the tourist office.

A seemingly endless series of steep stone steps lead up to Mont-St-Michel, so you need to be well rested and in good shape to make the trek. This attraction is definitely not for travelers with disabilities.

If you think Mont-St-Michel is crowded now, you should've seen it in 5000 B.C., when the dramatic pointed rock just off the coast was a pagan place of worship. The site was first consecrated in A.D. 708 and dedi-cated to the archangel Michael, who's considered the protector of faith and the one who weighs the souls. His job of weighing the souls made Michael one influential archangel, explaining why pilgrims risked their lives walking through the patches of quicksand in the bay, braving the deadly tides, through thick fog and heavy rains, to visit the abbey.

Building and rebuilding the abbey (after several collapses) took about 500 years, so the site combines architectural styles from the Middle Ages to the 16th century. Construction began in the eighth century, when Aubert, a bishop of Avranches, claimed the archangel told him to build a monastery here. In 966, Richard, duc de Normandy, agreed to construct a Benedictine monastery over a set of crypts built at the peak of the rock, but it partially burned down in 1203. Later that century, Philippe Auguste of France made a donation that enabled the work to begin on the abbey's Gothic section, the part of the complex known to countless pilgrims as La Merveille. The two three-story buildings, crowned by the cloister and the refectory, are a marvel. In the 14th cen-tury, during the Hundred Years' War, fortifications were built to protect the abbey during a 30-year siege. The fortifications came in handy during World War II, when the Mont was the only part of France that didn't fall to the Germans. In the 15th century, a Flamboyant Gothic chancel was built for the abbey church. The abbey was used as a prison during the French Revolution and was finally turned over to France's Historic Monuments department in 1874. The steeple, spire, and bronze statue of the archangel were added in 1897. On the abbey's 1,000th anniversary in 1966, a monastic community moved back into it; a Benedictine Mass is celebrated daily at 12:15 p.m.

Among the highlights of the site is the 13th-century **cloister,** with its deli-cate zigzagging granite columns. The **center courtyard** has been planted with a medieval herb garden. Also interesting is the 13th-century **réfrec-toire,** a large dining room with Romanesque and Gothic elements, where 30 monks would eat daily in silence. While exploring the abbey, you can

Mont-St-Michel

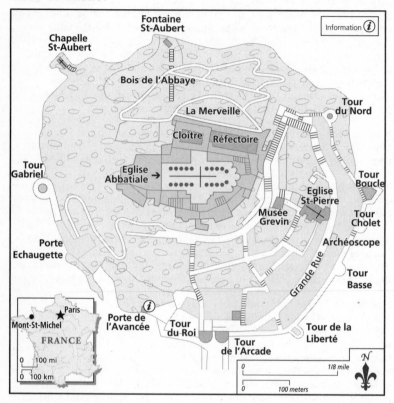

occasionally get a glimpse of the actual rock, which is green with lichens. Don't miss the huge 19th-century **treadmill** that was manned by six prisoners and used to bring supplies up to the site. Admission to the abbey is 7€ ($8.40) for adults and 4.50€ ($5.40) for ages 18 to 25. It's open daily (except January 1, May 1, and December 25): May to mid-September 9 a.m. to 7 p.m. and late September to April 9:30 a.m. to 6 p.m. Most days in summer, hour-long tours are given (in English) at 10 and 11 a.m. and 3 p.m. The tour is included with the price of admission.

Musée Maritime (Grande Rue; ☎ 02-33-89-02-05) bills itself as a Science and Environment Center and actually contains some interesting informa-tion about Mont-St-Michel Bay and the work being undertaken to pre-vent it from silting up. A major engineering project will tear down the causeway and turn Mont-St-Michel back into an island, reachable by bridge. The museum is the best of the ancillary attractions on the Mont. Admission is 7€ ($8.40) for adults and 4.50€ ($5.40) for children younger than 10. May through October, it's open daily 9:30 a.m. to 6 p.m.;

November to April, hours are Tuesday to Sunday 9 a.m. to 7 p.m. You can skip the waxworks museum and the 15-minute French film hosted by the archangel.

Mont-St-Michel is a sore subject in Brittany, and you're better off not bringing it up if you plan on visiting that region (see Chapter 17). Ancient Bretons coined the verse, "The River in its folly gave the Mont to Normandy," referring to the fact that the Selune River changed beds in A.D. 933, making Mont-St-Michel fall within the boundary of Normandy instead of Brittany. Bretons still are peeved about it.

Chapter 17

Brittany

● ●

In This Chapter

▶ Exploring Nantes, Brittany's ancient capital

▶ Finding the best places to buy Quimper pottery

▶ Marveling at the ancient rock formations of Carnac

● ●

The rugged coast of **Brittany** (see the "Brittany" map) is lined with seaside resorts and windswept cliffs overlooking the Atlantic. Brittany is a proud region with its own culture and traditions. More than 200,000 people speak the Breton language, which is more similar to Welsh than to French. Thanks to hearty Breton fishermen, you find excellent seafood in the region, particularly Belon oysters, which are world famous. Brittany also is home to hand-painted Quimper pottery, which features bright colors and simple patterns and is made in the small town of Quimper, near Brittany's west coast. Brittany's earliest residents were Neolithic tribes who left their megaliths behind. You can see these ancient stone formations in Carnac. The Celts first arrived in the sixth century B.C., and Brittany's separate identity evolved from those tribes from the British Isles. The region didn't become part of France until 1532 — it has been fiercely guarding its independence ever since.

Bretons love it when you acknowledge their language, which is closer to Welsh than it is to French. Here are three common words:

✔ **Hello:** *brav an amzer* (brahv ahn *ahmzer*)

✔ **Goodbye:** *kenavo* (*cay*-nah-voh)

✔ **Thank you:** *trugarez* (*true*-gahr-ez)

Nantes: Brittany's Ancient Capital

With a half million residents, **Nantes,** the former capital of Brittany, is a handsome and bustling town at the intersection of three rivers: the Loire, the Erdre, and the Sèvre. Though officially part of the Loire region, Nantes has always been historically linked to Brittany. The town gained a place in history books with the 1598 Edict of Nantes, in which Henri IV granted religious freedom to France's Protestant minority (however, Louis XIV revoked the edict in 1685). The huge château where the edict

Brittany

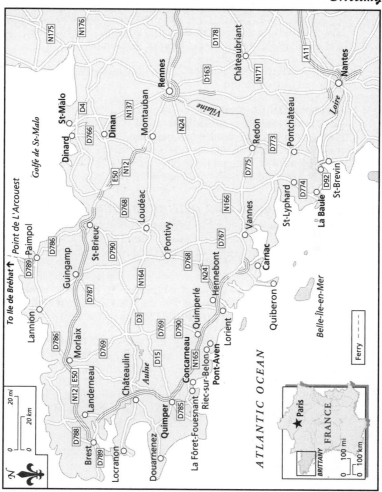

was signed **(Château des Ducs de Bretagne)** still occupies a central place in the city. Nantes today is a lively college town with about 30,000 students, offering plenty to see and do, including excellent shopping and hopping nightlife, and it's a fine first stop on the way to exploring the region.

Getting there

The **TGV (fast train)** from Paris's Gare Montparnasse takes about 2¼ hours to get to Nantes and costs 50.10€ ($60). Beware of slow trains that can take up to 5½ hours. For information, call ☎ **08-92-35-35-39** or

08-92-35-35-35. Nantes's **Gare SNCF** (train station) is at 27 bd. de Stalingrad, a five-minute walk from the town center. Trains from Nantes to Quimper (only two or three per day) take 2¾ to 4 hours (depending on how many stops the train makes) and cost 29.50€ ($35). See "Quimper and Its Hand-Painted Pottery" later in this chapter.

If you're **driving,** take A11 for 385km (239 miles) west of Paris. The trip takes about four hours.

Aéroport Nantes-Atlantique is 12km (7.5 miles) southeast of town (☎ 02-40-84-80-00), and **Air France** (☎ 02-98-94-30-30) offers daily flights from Paris. A shuttle bus between the airport and the Nantes train station takes 25 minutes and costs 6€ ($7.20). If you take a taxi from the airport, it costs from 20€ to 25€ ($24–$30), the ride lasting about 15 minutes.

Getting around and getting information

Nantes has an extensive bus system, in addition to a metro and tram system, but all the major sights, restaurants, and hotels are within walking distance of the center of town. The tourist office offers public transportation maps and schedules.

If you want to rent a car, note that **Budget, Hertz,** and **Europcar** have offices inside the train station. You can also find a taxi stand at the station. Call **Allô Taxi** at ☎ 02-40-69-22-22 to order a cab.

The **tourist office,** 3 Cour Olivier de Clisson (☎ 02-40-20-60-00; Fax: 02-40-89-11-99; www.nantes-tourisme.com), is open daily 10 a.m. to 6 p.m. The office changes money on days when banks are closed and organizes walking tours of the city (6€/$7.20 for adults and 3€/$3.60 for students and children). An **annex** at the château is open Tuesday to Sunday 10 a.m. to 1 p.m. and 2 to 6 p.m. To check or send e-mail, head to **Cyberhouse Café** (8 quai de Versailles; ☎ 02-40-12-11-84), open daily 2 p.m. to 2 a.m.; it serves drinks.

Spending the night

You can spot the hotel, restaurant, and attractions listed in the following sections in the nearby "Nantes" map.

Hôtel de France
$–$$ Nantes

This beautiful 18th-century hotel, on a pedestrian street lined with the city's best shops, is full of character and charm. In fact, it's classified a historic monument. All 74 rooms recently were renovated and contain soundproof windows; many are decorated with ornate Louis XV and Louis XVI antiques, and some are large with high ceilings. The hotel boasts a piano bar and a restaurant called L'Opéra, which serves regional specialties. The staff is friendly, and most speak English.

Nantes

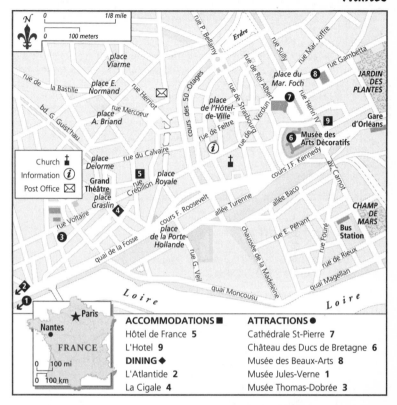

ACCOMMODATIONS ■	ATTRACTIONS ●
Hôtel de France **5**	Cathédrale St-Pierre **7**
L'Hotel **9**	Château des Ducs de Bretagne **6**
DINING ◆	Musée des Beaux-Arts **8**
L'Atlantide **2**	Musée Jules-Verne **1**
La Cigale **4**	Musée Thomas-Dobrée **3**

See map p. 317. 24 rue Crébillion. ☎ *02-40-73-57-91. Fax: 02-40-69-75-75. Parking: free. Rack rates: 74€–108€ ($89–$130) double. Breakfast: 10€ ($12). AE, MC, V.*

L'Hotel
$ Nantes

Within sight of the château and the cathedral, this 31-room hotel is, for the price, a perfect base in Nantes. Built in the 1980s, the place is neat and modern but maintains an inviting atmosphere. Guest rooms were renovated in 2003 and boast firm beds, rich colors, and contemporary furnishings. Some units have private balconies overlooking the château, while others open onto a garden and terrace. Each neatly tiled bathroom has a tub or shower. You'll find a paneled sitting area with couches and chairs next to the reception desk and a softly lit breakfast room with terrace views.

See map p. 317. 6 rue Henri-IV. ☎ *02-40-29-30-31. Fax: 02-40-29-00-95.* www.nanteshotel.com. *Parking: 6€ ($7.20). Rack rates: 68€–74€ ($82–$89) double. AE, MC, V.*

Sampling the region's cuisine

Besides oysters, lobsters, scallops, and other fresh fish, Bretons love to eat *gallettes,* buckwheat pancakes rolled around vegetables, cheese, meat, or fish. The *galette complète* contains ham, cheese, and egg. The perfect drink to accompany *galettes* is local cider. Cornouaille cider from the Cornouaille region in Brittany is the highest quality. A *bolées* is a traditional large mug of cider. Breton beer also is a popular beverage in the region. The best-known brands are Coreff from Morlaix, Lancelot barley beer, and Telenn Du buckwheat beer. The most basic ingredient in Breton cooking is salted butter. Breton cows graze on the lush fields and marshes near the Atlantic Ocean, which gives the butter an innate saltiness. For dessert, try the *far Breton,* a prune tart with the consistency of a sturdy custard. You can find the famous Brittany butter cookies with the brand name Traou Mad in stores throughout the region.

Dining locally

L'Atlantide
$$$ Nantes   FRENCH

Nantes's best restaurant, L'Atlantide, is an ultramodern glass-enclosed dining room on the fourth floor of an office building, with panoramic Loire views. Chef Jean Yves Guého prides himself on his menu's reflection of the seasons and the best market produce. Highlights are the starter of *oursin au petite coquillage* (sea urchin) and the main course of *tronçon de turbot rôti aux rattes et coques du croisic* (thick slices of turbot fish roasted with potatoes and cockles). The best dessert is *the petit banane rôti leger* (banana lightly roasted). The wine list is exemplary.

See map p. 317. 16 quai Ernest-Renaud. ☎ *02-40-73-23-23. Reservations required. Main courses: 30€–45€ ($36–$54); prix fixe: 31€–95€ ($37–$114). AE, V. Open: Mon–Fri noon to 2:30 p.m.; Mon–Sat 8–10 p.m. Closed the first 4 weeks of Aug and Dec 23–27.*

La Cigale
$$ Nantes   FRENCH

At this gorgeous 1895 Art Nouveau brasserie, the dining rooms boast elaborately painted, towering ceilings, multicolored tile arches, stained glass, and huge gilt-framed mirrors. Try to get one of the booths, and settle in for a fun evening. This place is great place for sampling Brittany's famous oysters — you can get a platter with six different kinds. Chef Gilles Renault changes the menu daily, but he always offers good-tasting seasonal soups, such as the *soupe crémeuse de potiron aux coques* (creamy pumpkin soup with cockles) in fall. One of the classic brasserie dishes is the *magret de canard rôti au miel, pommes sautées persillées* (roasted duck with honey and sautéed apples). The star among the homemade desserts is the Black Forest cake.

See map p. 317. 4 place Graslin. ☎ *02-51-84-94-94. Reservations recommended. Main courses: 10€–15€ ($12–$18); prix fixe: 22€ ($26). MC, V. Open: Daily 7:30– 12:30 a.m.*

Exploring the city

The **Nantes Decouvertes,** good for one (14€/$17), two (24€/$29), or three (30€/$36) days, gives you admission to all the major museums and free access to all the bus and metro lines. The pass is available at the tourist office on place du Commerce. For info, call ☎ **02-40-20-60-00.**

Occupying the symbolic center of the city is the **Château des Ducs de Bretagne** (4 place Marc-Elder; ☎ 02-51-17-49-00), where the Edict of Nantes was signed in 1598. François II, duc de Bretagne, built the château in 1466, and his daughter, Anne de Bretagne, was born here in 1477. Protected by a moat and thick fortified walls, the château is an imposing edifice. Through the years, it has served as a prison, and its most famous prisoner was Gilles de Retz, known more infamously as Bluebeard, the 15th-century mass murderer. You're free to walk around or picnic on the grounds, and usually a temporary exhibit is on display at the museum inside the walls. The museum is open daily 10 a.m. to noon and 2 to 6 p.m.; admission is free.

Just north of the castle, past a large public park, is the grand 15th-century Flamboyant Gothic **Cathédrale St-Pierre** (place St-Pierre; ☎ 02-40-47-84-64). Inside is the ornate Renaissance tomb of François II, duc de Bretagne, who ruled from 1458 to 1488. From the cathedral square, you can stroll down Nantes's best shopping streets to the commercial center. Take **rue de Verdun** to **rue de la Marne** to **rue d'Orléans** to **place Royale.** Continue on **rue Crébillon** to **place Graslin,** with its magnificent **Grand Théâtre.** Along the way, walk through the beautiful 19th-century shopping arcade **passage Pommeraye.** Heading toward the Loire River brings you to **place du Commerce,** with its lively cafe scene.

One block east of the cathedral in a *belle-époque* building, the impressive **Musée des Beaux-Arts** (10 rue Georges-Clemenceau; ☎ 02-51-17-45-00) contains sculptures and paintings from the 12th through 19th centuries Among the highlights are *Nymphéas* by Monet, *Madame de Senonnes* by Ingres, and *Le Joueur de Vielle* by Georges de la Tour. The most bizarre work is an 1887 statue of a gorilla carrying off a damsel. The museum is open Wednesday to Monday 10 a.m. to 6 p.m. Admission is 3.10€ ($3.70) for adults and 1.50€ ($1.80) for students and children; entrance to the museum is free on Sunday.

If you walk two blocks east, you can visit one of France's most beautiful botanical gardens, **Jardin des Plantes.** The northern entrance to the park is close to the Musée des Beaux-Arts, and the southern border is across from the train station. Admission is free, and it's open daily 8 a.m. to 8 p.m.

On the west end of town, two blocks from place Graslin, is the **Musée Thomas-Dobrée** (18 rue Voltaire; ☎ 02-40-71-03-50), housed in a 15th-century palace. The museum displays a collection of Roman antiquities, medieval paintings, and Renaissance decor. It's open Tuesday to Sunday 1:30 to 5:30 p.m., with an admission of 3€ ($3.60) for adults and 1.50€ ($1.80) for students and children. Walking south to the Loire River and another half-mile west takes you to the **Musée Jules-Verne** (3 rue de l'Hermitage; ☎ 02-40-69-72-52), with documents relating to the life of the 19th-century author, born in Nantes, who wrote *20,000 Leagues Under the Sea* and other classics. The museum is open Wednesday to Monday 10 a.m. to noon and 2 to 6 p.m. Admission is 1.50€ ($1.80) for adults and free for children.

Shopping for local treasures

One of France's most beautiful shopping plazas is the enclosed early 1900s tri-level **passage Pommeraye** at rue Crébillon and place Royale, decorated with statuary, gilded columns, gas lamps, and elaborate moldings. The Pommeraye is open daily 8 a.m. to 8 p.m. Nearby are the wide pedestrian shopping streets: **rue de la Marne, rue d'Orléans,** and **rue Crébillon.** The market is held at the **Marché de Talensac** and at **place du Bouffay,** Tuesdays to Saturdays 9 a.m. to 1 p.m.

Living it up after dark

You find many bars on **place du Bouffay** and on the ancient streets near the château, including **Buck Mulligan's** (12 rue de Château; ☎ 02-40-20-02-72). A great piano bar with a dance floor and occasional jazz concerts is **Le Tie Break,** 1 rue des Peties-Ecuries (☎ 02-40-47-77-00). The disco scene reigns at **L'Evasion** (3 rue de l'Emery; ☎ 02-40-47-99-84). Check out what's happening in the free brochure, *Le Mois Nantais,* from the tourist office.

Quimper and Its Hand-Painted Pottery

Set in a valley where the Odet and Steir rivers meet, the traditional town of **Quimper** (pronounced cam-*pair*) is the capital of the Cornouaille area of Brittany. Quimper's claim to fame is its brightly colored hand-painted pottery, which has been made here since the 17th century. Quimper is also the oldest Breton city — it was settled between A.D. 400 and 700. The medieval section of town, west of the cathedral, is a maze of cobblestone pedestrian streets lined with pricey boutiques.

Quimper is a fairly quiet town. A lively time to visit is during the week-long **Festival de Cornouaille** in late July. You'll need to book your hotel way in advance, because the festival is one of Brittany's largest events, celebrating music, dance, and storytelling. For details, call the tourist office at ☎ 02-98-53-04-05.

Getting there

TGVs from Paris's Gare Montparnasse make the trip to Quimper in 4½ hours and cost 68€ ($82). Four trains per day travel from Nantes, taking 2¾ to 4 hours (depending on how many stops the train makes) and costing 29.50€ ($35). For train information call ☎ **08-92-35-35-39** or 08-92-35-35-35. Quimper's **Gare SNCF** (train station) is on avenue de la Gare, 1km (0.6 miles) east of the town center.

Quimper is 570km (354.2 miles) from Paris, and the trip takes five to six hours. If you're **driving,** follow A11 to A81 west to Rennes. From Rennes, take E50 west to Montauban and continue west on N164 to Châteaulin and then south on N165 to Quimper. Driving from Rennes to Quimper takes two to three hours.

Getting around and getting information

To rent a car, try the **Hertz** branch across from the train station (19 av. de la Gare; ☎ **02-98-53-12-34**). Nearby are **Europcar** (16 av. de la Libération; ☎ **02-98-90-00-68**) and **ADA** (33 av. de la Libèration; ☎ **02-98-52-25-25**). An **Avis** office is inside the train station (☎ **02-98-90-31-34**). To order a **taxi,** call ☎ **02-98-90-21-21.**

The **tourist office** is on place de la Résistance (☎ **02-98-53-04-05;** Fax: 02-98-53-31-33; www.quimper-tourisme.com. April to June and September, it's open Monday to Saturday 9:30 a.m. to 12:30 p.m. and 1:30 to 6:30 p.m.; during July and August, hours are Monday to Saturday 10 a.m. to 7 p.m.; and from October to March it's open Monday to Saturday 9 a.m. to 12:30 p.m. and 1:30 to 6 p.m.

Spending the night

A fancy option about 13km (8 miles) north of Quimper is the **Manoir du Stang** in La Forêt-Fouesnant, off N783 (☎ **02-98-56-97-37**). May to September, this 16th-century manor rents 24 rooms, decorated with antiques, for 99€ to 140€ ($119–$168) double. Credit cards aren't accepted.

Hôtel Gradlon

$ Quimper

This 19th-century hotel is the best place to stay within the town center. It's on a side street with a new annex in the back (no elevator in either building). In the center of the hotel is a pretty rose garden with the glass-enclosed breakfast room beside it. The 22 rooms are individually decorated with stylish touches, such as Breton posters on the walls, and are regularly redecorated and updated. One of the best rooms is off the garden, with a separate entrance. The reasonable prices, central location, and relatively spacious rooms make this hotel popular for families.

30 rue de Brest. ☎ *02-98-95-04-39. Fax: 02-98-95-61-25. Parking: 8€ ($9.60). Rack rates: 66€–99€ ($79–$119) double; 140€ ($168) suite. Breakfast: 10.50€ ($13). Closed Dec 20–Jan 20. AE, DC, MC, V.*

Hôtel Oceania
$ Quimper

This rather bland member of an international chain has emerged as the top choice in town. It stands in a garden about a mile southwest of the town center. Follow the signs to route Pont-l'Abbé. Built in the 1980s with comfortable, standardized bedrooms, it boasts a Breton slate roof and is ideal for motoring families (the pool is a magnet in summer). Each room has lots of space, a writing desk, and a midsize bathroom with tub and shower. On site are a good restaurant and bar if you don't want to go into Quimper at night.

2 rue du Poher, pont de Poulguinan. ☎ *02-98-90-46-26. Fax: 02-98-53-01-96. Parking: free. Rack rates: 99€ ($119) double. Up to two children 16 and younger stay free in parents' room. Breakfast: 10€ ($12). AE, DC, MC, V.*

Dining locally

At **Pointe du Raz,** the westernmost point of France (take D784 west from Quimper), you can have a grilled lobster dinner at the **L'Etrave** (place de l'Eglise, Cléden-Cap-Sizun; ☎ **02-98-70-66-87**).

For an excellent breakfast or snack, head for **Pâtisserie Boule de Neige/Larnicol** (14 rue des Boucheries; ☎ **02-98-95-88-22**), whose display case is filled with pastries that are works of art. The restaurant has seating in the rear and in the garden courtyard.

L'Ambroisie
$$$ Quimper   BRETON

This attractive restaurant near the cathedral gets the best reviews in town — and they are deserved. The dining room is certainly lovely, with large paintings of Breton scenes. Chef Guyon prides himself on a "light and sophisticated" touch, and the menu is filled with intriguing Breton dishes with a contemporary twist — such as *blé noir* (crab rolled in buckwheat crêpes), *sauté de langoustines aux artichauts* (sautéed prawns and artichokes), and *filet St-Pierre* (John Dory fish). They serve smooth chocolate desserts here and, in summer, *fraises de Plougastel* (local strawberries).

49 rue Elie-Fréron. ☎ *02-98-95-00-02. Reservations recommended. Main courses: 24€–30€ ($29–$36); prix fixe: 21€–60€ ($25–$72); children's menu: 12€ ($14). MC, V. Open: Tues–Sun noon to 1:30 p.m. and 7:30–9 p.m. Closed the last week in June.*

Rive Gauche
$–$$ Quimper   BRETON

On lively rue Ste-Catherine, Rive Gauche stands out for its excellent prices matched with good food. The décor is hip and modern, and the waitstaff has a sense of fun and a hint of attitude. Many of the products used in the dishes come from local farms, and fishermen bring in fresh oysters. Many Bretons wisely start their meal with a dozen oysters served on seaweed and accompanied by a vinegar sauce. As a main course, we recommend thin slices of salmon served in a light cream sauce. If you want to go really local, order *andouilette des eleveurs d'armor* (a special local sausage), prepared with a cider sauce.

9 rue Ste-Catherine. ☎ *02-98-90-06-15. Reservations recommended. Main courses: 10€–13.50€ ($12–$16); prix fixe: 16€–27.50€ ($19–$33). MC, V. Open: Mon–Sat 12:30–2:30 p.m. and 7:30–10:30 p.m.*

Exploring the town

Cathédrale St-Corentin (place St-Corentin; ☎ 02-98-95-06-19) sits at the center of town. A stone equestrian statue of King Gradlon (legendary founder of Quimper) is set between the two 76m (250-ft.) spires. Built between the 13th and 15th centuries, the cathedral has recently undergone extensive renovations of its stonework, paintings, and 15th-century stained-glass windows. Admission is free, and the church is open daily 9 a.m. to 6 p.m. To the west, you find a maze of pedestrian streets with some of the best shopping in Brittany. Cross the river on one of the tiny pedestrian bridges to reach the tourist office. Another five minutes by foot brings you to *faïence* heaven, with the museum, tours, and shops devoted to this colorful local pottery.

For a good introduction to the Breton way of life, the **Musée des Beaux-Arts** (40 place St-Corentin; ☎ 02-98-95-45-20) has a large collection of paintings of the Brittany countryside and genre scenes of the Breton people. The museum also has a fine collection of paintings from the 16th through 20th centuries, including works by Rubens, Boucher, Fragonard, and Corot. A room is devoted to the Pont-Aven school, made famous by Gauguin; another room is devoted to Max Jacob, born in Quimper. July and August, the museum is open Wednesday to Monday 10 a.m. to 7 p.m.; September to June, hours are Wednesday to Monday 10 a.m. to noon and 2 to 6 p.m. Admission is 4€ ($4.80) for adults and 2.50€ ($3) for students and children.

Musée de la Faïence (14 rue Jean-Baptiste Bousquet; ☎ 02-98-90-12-72) displays a fun collection of the city's signature pottery. The museum is open from mid-April to October 19, Monday to Saturday 10 a.m. to 6 p.m. Admission is 4€ ($4.80) adults, 3.20€ ($3.85) students, and 2.30€ ($2.75) children.

Shopping for local treasures

If you're looking to immerse yourself in the world of Quimper pottery, you can take a factory tour, see the museum, and spend time in shops devoted to this local craft.

The main factory/*faïence* store is **HB Henriot** (16 rue Haute; ☎ 02-98-90-09-36). All year, 30-minute guided visits in English (3€/$3.60 for adults and 1.50€/$1.80 for children) take place Monday to Thursday 9:15 to 11:15 a.m. and 1:30 to 4:15 p.m., and Friday 9 to 11:30 a.m. and 1:30 to 4:15 p.m. After the tour, you can visit the factory store with the largest selection of Quimper pottery in town.

Other Brittany favorites

In addition to the major destinations discussed in this chapter, Brittany offers a few other worthy stops that are not so far off the beaten path.

✔ **Belle Ile:** This rustic island lies 15km (9 miles) off the southern coast of Brittany and is reachable by a 45-minute ferry (23€/$28 for adults, 13.87€/$17 for children, 105.34€/$126 for cars round trip). The island is the place to try **thallasotherapy,** a seawater therapy popular at coastal resorts. Treatments lasting two to four hours cost 35€ to 85€ ($42–$102). The island's top place to try a treatment and spend the night is the **Castel Clara.** This hotel (☎ **02-97-31-84-21;** Fax: 02-97-31-51-69; www.castel-clara.com), a Relais & Châteaux establishment overlooking the sea, has 26 rooms and half board costing 139€ ($167) per person for a double. The restaurant is very expensive and has an excellent reputation. The hotel is closed from late November to March 1. Next door is the less expensive **Manoir de Goulphar** (☎ **02-97-31-80-10;** Fax: 02-97-31-80-05; www.manoir-de-goulphar.fr), with rooms from 84€ to 186€ ($101–$223) for a double; half board is 146€ to 243€ ($175–$298).

✔ **Presqu'île de Crozon:** A drive around the Crozon Peninsula (58km/36 miles from Quimper, 261km/162 miles from Nantes) on Brittany's west coast offers wild and quintessential Brittany landscapes and seascapes. You'll find jagged cliffs at Chèvre, an ancient stone church at Rocamadour, grottoes at Morgat, and prehistoric stone alignments at Camaret.

✔ **Pont-Aven:** Fans of painter Paul Gauguin will want to visit this pretty little village, 32km (20 miles) from Quimper and 174km (108 miles) from Nantes. Stone houses and mills along the river Aven make a colorful scene. The small **Musée de l'Ecole de Pont-Aven** (☎ **02-98-06-14-43**) displays a couple of Gauguin prints, paintings by less well-known artists of the time, and many photos of the artists' colony that formed in the late 19th and early 20th centuries. Artistic types still are drawn to this village, whose streets are lined with galleries. Pont-Aven also is home to the cookie company **Traou Mad,** which makes the famous Brittany butter cookies.

✔ **St-Malo:** This walled town is on the northern coast of Brittany, 171km (106 miles) from Nantes. The charming town, with its pricey boutiques and lively cobblestone streets, is popular with day-trippers and tour buses. You can walk all the way around the town's ramparts and sunbathe on the brown-sand beaches below. Children in particular enjoy frolicking in the shallow warm waters surrounding St-Malo.

Other good shops for Breton wares are **Bed Keltiek** (2 rue de Roi Gradlon; ☎ **02-98-95-42-82**), which sells pottery, jewelry, and books; and located next door, **François Le Villec** (4 rue de Roi Gradlon; ☎ **02-98-95-31-54**), which offers traditional *faïence.* **Heoligou** (16 rue du Parc; ☎ **02-98-95-13-29**) has Brittany sweaters and other clothing. The **food market** is open at Halles St-François on rue Astor, Monday to Saturday 7 a.m. to 8 p.m. and Sunday 9 a.m. to 1 p.m.

Living it up after dark

Check out **rue St-Catherine** for a good sampling of bars. **Le Coffee Shop** (26 rue de Frout, behind the cathedral; ☎ 02-98-95-43-30) is a popular gay spot. **St. Andrews Pub** (11 place Stivel; ☎ 02-98-53-34-49) attracts an English-speaking crowd that enjoys the 45 kinds of beer available here. **Café des Arts** (on the corner of rue St-Catherine and bd. Dupleix; ☎ 02-98-90-32-06) is a nightclub with a huge drink menu and no cover.

Carnac and Its Prehistoric Stones

Carnac boasts France's biggest prehistoric site, where thousands of huge stones stand sentinel over miles of rolling fields near the seaside. The site has three major groupings, all within a mile of one another: Alignements du Ménec, Alignements de Kermario, and Alignements de Kerlescan. Estimated to be from 4500 to 2000 B.C., the stones predate Stonehenge and even the Egyptian pyramids. Carnac also is a popular seaside resort; most visitors combine sun and fun with rock-gazing.

Carnac is very quiet from October to May, making it the best time to wander around the ancient rocks without the distraction of crowds.

Getting there

The best way to get to Carnac is by **driving.** From Quimper, take N165 east to Auray and then D768 south to Carnac. Driving the 486km (302 miles) from Paris to Carnac takes about five hours. Follow A11 southwest from Paris to Le Mans and then A81 west to Rennes. From Rennes, take N24 and then N166 southwest to Vannes. Drive west on E60 to Auray and south on D768 to Carnac.

The nearest **TGV (fast train)** station is in Auray, 14km (8.7 miles) from Carnac. Trips from Paris's Gare Montparnasse to Auray by train take 3½ hours and cost 62€ ($74). From Auray, you can catch a bus costing 4€ ($4.80) and taking 30 minutes to Carnac. You can also take a taxi to Carnac, which takes 20 minutes and costs about 20€ ($24). In summer, you can board a train from Auray to Plouharnel, located 4km from Carnac. From Plouharnel, seven buses per day make the five-minute trip from Plouharnel to Carnac in summer only for 1.10€ ($1.30). Taxis at the Plouharnel train station will take you to Carnac center in five minutes for about 9€ ($11). For train information, call ☎ 08-92-35-35-35 or 08-92-35-35-39.

Getting around and getting information

You can rent bikes at **Le Randonneur** (20 av. des Druides, Carnac Plage; ☎ 02-97-52-02-55), open April to September daily 9 a.m. to 7 p.m. The cost is 8€ ($9.60) per half day and 10€ ($12) per full day.

The **tourist office** at 74 av. des Druides (☎ **02-97-52-13-52;** www.carnac.fr) is open July and August Tuesday to Friday 9 a.m. to 1 p.m. and 2 to 7 p.m.; Monday and Saturday 9 a.m. to 7 p.m. and Sunday 10 a.m. to 1 p.m. and 3 to 7 p.m. September to June, it is open Monday to Saturday 9 a.m. to noon and 2 to 6 p.m.

Spending the night

Hôtel Celtique
$-$$ Carnac Plage

This modern Best Western, a block from the beach, has 56 mostly spacious, comfortable rooms (some with balconies offering beach views). From the brightly lit lobby to the handsome bar, the amenities at this well-run hotel include a heated pool, hot tub, sauna, fitness room, and a large commons room with a billiard table — plenty of activities to spoil your kids. The restaurant, An Daol, serves excellent Breton specialties with an emphasis on seafood.

17 av. de Kermario or 82 av. des Druides. ☎ *02-97-52-14-15. Fax: 02-97-52-71-10.* www.hotel-celtique.com. *Parking: free. Rack rates: 67€–140€ ($80–$168) double. Breakfast: 9€–11€ ($11–$13). AE, MC, V.*

Hôtel le Diana
$$-$$$ Carnac Plage

Across from the main beach, this modern hotel is Carnac's top lodging. Most of the 31 individually decorated, comfortable rooms open onto balconies and ocean views. The restaurant overlooking the beach specializes in seafood. A large heated pool and sauna are adjacent to the popular hotel bar.

21 bd. de la Plage. ☎ *02-97-52-05-38. Fax: 02-97-52-87-91.* www.lediana.com. *Parking: free. Rack rates: 120€–230€ ($144–$276) double; 300€–400€ ($360–$480) suite. Breakfast: 15€ ($18). Half board: 210€–320€ ($252–$384) for two. Closed late Oct to mid-Apr. AE, DC, MC, V.*

Dining locally

Auberge le Ratelier
$-$$$ Carnac Ville   BRETON

This ancient ivy-covered inn, in a cul-de-sac close to the town center, is a warm rustic setting serving delicious Breton cuisine, highlighted by fresh local fish. Your meal may begin with *gaspacho de langoustines au basilic* (gazpacho with prawns and basil). As a main course, try *filet de dorade à la citronnelle, pommes de terre écrasées à l'huile d'olive* (dorade fish with lemongrass, served with potatoes with olive oil). For dessert, order *nougat glacé au miel et rosace de fraises* (candied-fruit ice cream with honey and strawberries). The inn also offers eight small, simple rooms upstairs at 38€ to 55€ ($46–$66) for a double.

4 chemin Douët. ☎ *02-97-52-05-04. Reservations necessary. Main courses: 12€–24€ ($14–$29); prix fixe: 17€–40€ ($20–$48). AE, MC, V. Open: Daily noon to 2:30 p.m. and 7:30–9:30 p.m. Oct to Apr closed Tues and Wed.*

Exploring the town and the mysterious stones

Carnac is divided into two sections: **Carnac Plage** is the beachfront resort with modern hotels lining the coast, and about 2.4km (1½ miles) inland is **Carnac Ville,** with shops, restaurants, and several nightclubs. The prehistoric rock formations are on the north side of the city, a few miles from the beach. A Celtic burial chamber dating from 5000 B.C., the **Tumulus St-Michel,** is on rue de Tumulus, less than a mile (1.5 km) east from Carnac Ville. Built above the chamber is a 16th-century church. The chamber is closed indefinitely for excavations.

While the purpose of the **Alignements de Carnac** (☎ **02-97-52-89-99**) remains a mystery, they can be dated to Neolithic times. Over thousands of years, villagers have used the rocks as a quarry, so it's impossible to know what the original formation was. What's visible now are rows of about 2,000 standing stones, some as high as 18m (60 ft.) and weighing many tons. The most common hypotheses about the stones are that they marked burial sites, charted the course of the moon and planets, or were part of a religious ritual. Legend has it that the rocks represent a Roman army turned to stone.

The three major sites from west to east are the **Alignements du Ménec, Alignements de Kermario,** and **Alignements de Kerlescan.** At Ménec, the site that's on route des Alignements to the west of rue des Korrigans, most of the 1,100 stones are less than 1m (3.2 ft) high. About a mile east on route des Alignements is the Kermario site, with about 1,000 stones in 10 lines; this site has a viewing platform. About half a mile farther is Kerlescan, with 555 stones in 13 lines.

Because of the sheer number of visitors trampling and damaging the site, the area is fenced off, and access is restricted. October to April, admission is free, and visitors can walk through the site. But May to September, admission is limited to 25 people at a time (180 per day maximum), and 90-minute tours cost 4€ ($4.80). The **visitor center** at the Alignements de Kermario is open daily 9 a.m. to 6 p.m. To reach the center from the direction of Carnac, take a right off rue des Korrigans onto route des Kerlescan.

Musée de Préhistoire (10 place de la Chapelle; ☎ **02-97-52-22-04**) displays interpretations of the alignments and Paleolithic and Neolithic artifacts dating back to 450,000 B.C. It also offers a helpful English-language brochure. Late June to mid-September, the museum is open daily 10 a.m. to 6:30 p.m.; late September to mid-June, hours are Wednesday to Monday 10 a.m. to noon and 1:30 to 7 p.m. Admission is 5€ ($6) for adults and 2.50€ ($3) for students.

Living it up after dark

Les Chandelles (avenue de l'Atlantique; ☎ 02-97-52-90-98) is the most popular disco in these parts, with a 9.10€ ($11) cover. Nearby, the **Whiskey Club** (8 av. des Druides; ☎ 02-97-52-10-52) has live music and dancing. At **Le Petit Bedon** (106 av. des Druides; ☎ 02-97-52-11-62), a 30-something crowd dances to oldies.

Part VI
Provence and the Riviera

The 5th Wave   By Rich Tennant

@RICHTENNANT

"I'M PRETTY SURE YOU'RE SUPPOSED TO JUST SMELL THE CORK."

In this part . . .

Provence and the French Riviera are sun-kissed regions in the southeast corner of France, where the air is perfumed by lavender and fresh herbs and the countryside is dotted with olive groves and vineyards that you may remember seeing in van Gogh and Cézanne paintings. In Chapter 18, we explore the top towns of Provence — Arles, Aix-en-Provence, Avignon, and St-Rémy-de-Provence — and show you how to stay safe in wild Marseille. This is France's most written-about region; its warm, dry weather and scenic countryside offer an idyllic vacation. You'll come across ancient Roman ruins, medieval towns, and sophisticated cities. The region's food and wines are famous, and you're sure to enjoy some of your most memorable meals here, enlivened by the colorful Provençal herbs and olive oil.

Beginning with Chapter 19, we move along to where the coastline meets the warm Mediterranean near the border of Italy — the part of Provence known as the magical French Riviera, also called the *Côte d'Azur*. With many beaches, charming hill towns, hot nightlife, stunning art museums, glamorous casinos, and seaside boardwalks, the Riviera is a festive playground where artists such as Picasso, Matisse, Léger, and Renoir chose to work and live, and the region's museums are full of their colorful canvases.

In Chapter 20, we take you to Nice, the region's largest city, and the tiny principality of Monaco, where Grace Kelly once reigned at the side of Prince Rainier III. Now, gamblers head here to try their luck at its famous casino, and visitors go to see the royal palace. Chapter 20 also covers the small but chic towns of Beaulieu and St-Jean-Cap-Ferrat.

Chapter 21 offers a stop for fun and sun in St-Tropez and for the frenetic nightlife of Cannes. The beautiful ports of St-Tropez and Antibes are a contrast to the hill towns of Biot, Vence, and St-Paul-de-Vence.

Chapter 18

The Best of Provence

*P*rovence, with its ancient towns, verdant countryside, and mild climate, is one of the most popular regions of France for visitors (see the "Provence" map). Whether idling away sunbaked afternoons in picturesque cafes and shops or seeking out major attractions such as the grand Palais des Papes in Avignon or the impressive Roman ruins of Glanum in St-Rémy, your time in Provence is bound to be among the most memorable of your trip. This region has long been popular with artists, and you can follow the footsteps of van Gogh in Arles and St-Rémy or seek out the favorite landscapes of Cézanne in and around Aix-en-Provence. Aix is one of France's most beautiful cities, where 18th-century mansions of golden-colored stone line cours Mirabeau, a magnificent boulevard, and sculpted fountains gurgle around seemingly every corner.

The fastest TGV train service to France's south coast made its debut in June 2001: from Paris to Avignon in 2 hours and 38 minutes, Paris to Marseille in 3 hours, and Paris to Aix in 3 hours.

Avignon and the Palais des Papes

The walled city of **Avignon,** capital of Christianity in the 14th century and home of the regal Palais des Papes, is a good base from which to tour the region. Because of its strategic site in the Rhône Valley, the city became a Roman outpost and major stop on trading routes. It rose to prominence until reaching its pinnacle in the 14th century. Instability in Rome made Pope Clement V move to France, and for the next 65 years, Avignon became the papal seat and capital of the Christian world. Seven French popes ruled over Christendom from the Palais des Papes, and the city's diplomatic, artistic, and commercial life prospered. Then, during the Great Schism (1376–1417), French cardinals decided to make trouble by continuing to elect French popes even after the papacy had returned to Rome. Soon all was sorted out, and Rome was back on top.

The period of prosperity forever changed Avignon, which, with its sumptuous mansions, grand squares, and towering palace, retains a look of pride and strength. But Avignon also has a resolutely modern side. In fact, the city is most famous today for its summer arts festival, which has helped turn Avignon into a year-round cutting-edge arts community.

Avignon was named a European City of Culture in 2000 (along with eight other cities). Because of that designation, the city tackled a number of projects that post-2000 visitors can enjoy: a new Museum of Contemporary Art that houses works from the 1960s to the present (see "Exploring the town and environs" later in this chapter), a walking path along the former boat-towing path on Ile de la Barthelasse, a riverboat shuttle to Ile de la Barthelasse, the renovation of place Pie, and improvements to the train station.

Festival d'Avignon (☎ **04-90-27-66-50;** www.festival-avignon.com) is one of France's premier arts festivals — officials claim it's the world's biggest theater festival — and the events at this festival aren't as expensive as those at the arts festival in nearby Aix-en-Provence. Created in 1947, the Festival d'Avignon features performances of theater, music, and dance, typically during the last three weeks in July.

Getting there

Trains arrive at Avignon's **Gare SNCF** on boulevard St-Roch, just outside the old city ramparts and a ten-minute walk from most hotels and the center of town. If you have a lot of luggage, a taxi stand is in front of the train station. If you're traveling from Paris, TGVs depart from Paris's Gare de Lyon. New trains and tracks have cut the trip time to Avignon from 3 hours and 20 minutes to 2 hours and 38 minutes. One-way trips from Paris to Avignon cost 86.10€ ($103) in second class and 118€ ($142) in first class. From Avignon, frequent trains travel to Marseille (70 minutes, 15.90€/$19) and Arles (30 minutes, 5.80€/$6.95). For train reservations and information, call ☎ **08-92-35-35-39** or check the Web site at www.sncf.com.

Avignon is infamous for attracting pickpockets and thieves. Keep a close eye on your bags, particularly at the train and bus stations.

Aéroport Avignon-Caumont (☎ **04-90-81-51-51**) is 8km (5 miles) southeast of Avignon, with hour-long direct flights from Paris's Orly Airport. To get from the airport to town, a taxi costs 15€ to 20€ ($18 to $24), depending on traffic. At the airport, you can find rental car offices for Hertz, Europcar, Avis, Budget, and National Citer.

Avignon's seedy **Gare Routière** (bus station) is on boulevard St-Michel, next to the train station (☎ **04-90-82-07-35**). The information desk is open Monday to Friday 8 a.m. to noon and 1:30 to 6 p.m., and Saturday 9 a.m. to noon. Buses connect to Aix (one hour, 15€/$18), Arles (1 hour, 8.40€/$10), and Pont du Gard (45 minutes, 5.90€/$7.10).

Provence

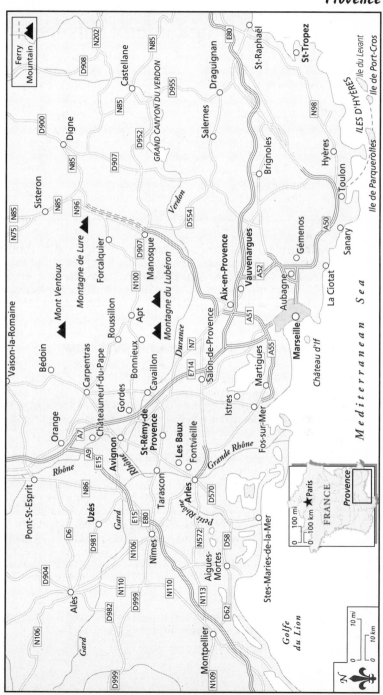

Sampling the region's cuisine

Avignon is capital of the Côtes du Rhône region, in which fine wines have been culti-vated for 2,000 years. The famous *grand crus* (top wines) are Châteauneuf-du-Pape, Gigondas, Vacqueyras, Lirac, Tavel, and Côtes du Rhône.

Regional food specialties include *friandise composée de chocolat fin, sucre et liqueur d'origan* (petit fours of chocolate, sugar, and liqueur), *fruits confits d'Apt* (fruit pre-served in sugar, a specialty of Apt), *berlingots de Carpentas* (soft candy, a specialty of Carpentras), *riz et sel de Camargue* (rice and salt from the Camargue region), *nougat de Sault* (nougat from Sault), and *calissons d'Aix* (almond-paste candy from Aix). Other food specialties include olive oil pressed in the village of Les Baux, *miel de Ventaux* (honey from Ventaux), olives, *ail* (garlic), *fromage de chèvre* (goat cheese), *pastis* (anise-flavored liqueur), *fougasse* (flavored bread), and of course *herbes de Provence*.

If you're **driving** from Paris, take A6 south to Lyon and A7 south to Avignon. Avignon is 683km (425 miles) south of Paris. From Nice, Marseille, or Lyon, follow A8 and A7 to Avignon. Orange is 30km (19 miles) away from Avignon, St-Rémy 20km (12 miles), Les Baux 25km (16 miles), Arles 35km (22 miles), Aix 60km (37 miles), and Marseille 99km (62 miles).

Getting around and getting information

Walking from one end of the walled city of Avignon to the other (see the "Avignon" map) is easy. Many hotels, restaurants, and historic sites, including the famous Palais des Papes, are clustered in the center of the city. However, you need to use some sort of public transportation or a car to get to the nearby walled suburb of Villeneuve-lez-Avignon, a lovely medieval village with several interesting historic sites.

To reach the walled suburb of Villeneuve-lez-Avignon (about ten min-utes), catch a No. 10 or 11 **bus** (Villeneuve puis Les Angles) from the main post office or the porte de l'Oulle on the west side of the city (Sundays and holidays it's the No. 10D bus). Buses run every 20 minutes (less frequently on Sunday) 7 a.m. to 8 p.m. and cost 7.50€ ($9). The 100-seat **Bateau Bus** (☎ 04-90-85-62-25) goes from Avignon to Ile de la Barthelasse and then to Villeneuve six times per day in July and August (1¼-hour round-trip). Tickets are 7.50€ ($9) for adults (6.76€/$8.10 with the tourist pass called Avignon Passion — see "Getting to know Avignon" later in this section for details) and 4€ ($4.80) for children younger than 12 (3.60€/$4.30 with pass).

Pick up city bus information and tickets across from the train station at the **Tourelle Porte de la République** (☎ 04-32-74-18-32).

You can rent a car at **Hertz** (816 rue Aulaniere; ☎ **04-90-89-23-60**). To hire a bike, try **Holiday Bikes,** next to the tourist office on cours Jean-Jaurès (☎ **04-32-76-25-88**), or **Cycles Peugeot** (80 rue Guillaume-Puy; ☎ **04-90-86-32-49**). Rentals are 12.96€ ($16) for a full day. For a **taxi,** call ☎ **04-90-82-20-20.**

A free **riverboat shuttle** takes visitors from Avignon to Ile de la Barthelasse, the island in the middle of the Rhône River. May to October, **Mireio** (☎ **04-90-85-62-25**) runs the ten-minute shuttle daily from the harbor on the east side of pont St-Bénezet, also known as the pont d'Avignon. The shuttle runs nonstop 10:30 a.m. to 7:50 p.m. in the middle of summer and less frequently in the shoulder seasons. After you reach the island, you can walk on an impressive walking trail along the river called the promenade du Chemin des Berges, which has panoramic views of Avignon.

The **Avignon tourist office** is at 41 cours Jean-Jaurès (☎ **04-32-74-32-74;** Fax: 04-90-82-95-03; www.ot-avignon.fr). April to October, it's open Monday to Saturday 9 a.m. to 5 p.m.; November to March, hours are Monday to Friday 9 a.m. to 6 p.m. and Saturday 9 a.m. to 5 p.m. During the July arts festival, hours are Monday to Saturday 9 a.m. to 7 p.m. Guides from the office lead tours of the city.

Villeneuve-lez-Avignon tourist office is at place Charles-David (☎ **04-90-25-61-33;** Fax: 04-90-25-91-55; www.villeneuvelezavignon.fr). July hours are Monday to Friday 9:30 a.m. to 7 p.m. and Saturday and Sunday 9:30 a.m. to 1 p.m. and 2:30 to 7 p.m.; August hours are daily 9 a.m. to 12:30 p.m. and 2 to 6 p.m.; and September to June hours are Monday to Saturday 9 a.m. to 12:30 p.m. and 2 to 6 p.m. To check or send e-mail, go to **Webzone,** 3 rue St-Jean le Vieux (☎ **04-32-76-29-47**), at Place Pie. Charges are 2.50€ ($3) for half an hour, and hours are Monday to Saturday 9 a.m. to midnight, Sunday noon to 8 p.m.

Spending the night

During the festival, hotel rooms are scarce. In addition to the locations reviewed in this section, here are a few more good medium-priced choices: **Citotel de Garlande** (20 rue Galante; ☎ **04-90-80-08-85**), **Hôtel Blauvac** (11 rue de la Bancasse; ☎ **04-90-86-34-11**), and **Hôtel Médiéval** (15 rue Petite Saunerie; ☎ **04-90-86-11-06**).

Hôtel Clarion Cloître Saint Louis
$$ Avignon

One of Avignon's best hotels, this is a pleasing combination of modern and antique styles. Located just inside the south city walls (close to the train station), the hotel was built as a Jesuit school in 1589 and became a military hospital during the Revolution. The lobby ceiling is constructed of ancient vaulting, and the furniture is black and sleek. The 80 spacious rooms and suites are decorated in a contemporary style and come with minibars, safes, and hair dryers. Their large windows overlook the cloister courtyard or the hotel gardens. The big modern wing, with tinted windows, looks like a Manhattan office tower; rooms in this wing have balconies. On top of the modern wing are a pool and sun deck, open from May to September. The restaurant serves all meals under the ancient cloister vaults or in the garden.

See map p. 337. 20 rue du Portail-Boquier. ☎ *04-90-27-55-55. Fax: 04-90-82-24-01.* www.cloitre-saint-louis.com. *Parking: 10€ ($12). Rack rates: 110€–155€ ($132–$186) double; 220€–315€ ($264–$378) suite. Breakfast: 15€ ($18). AE, MC, V.*

Hôtel d'Angleterre
$ Avignon

This 39-room hotel is a little far from the action, in the southwest corner of the city, not far from the train station and tourist office. The standard contemporary rooms are comfortable and well maintained — if on the small and plain side. The building, built around 1929 in the Art Deco style, has four floors. A tasty continental breakfast is served next to the lobby. The English-speaking staff will cheerfully recommend a restaurant or describe an attraction.

See map p. 337. 29 bd. Raspail. ☎ *04-90-86-34-31. Fax: 04-90-86-86-74. Free parking. Rack rates: 52€–78€ ($62–$94) double. Breakfast: 7€ ($8.40). Closed Dec 20–Jan 20. MC, V.*

Hôtel de l'Horloge
$–$$ Avignon

Just off place de l'Horloge and close to the Palais des Papes, this handsome 67-room hotel is part of a large French chain. The classical 19th-century facade belies the unabashedly modern guest room décor. The high-ceiling accommodations come with minibars and hair dryers; the more expensive ones open onto terraces overlooking the square. Because the hotel is located in a busy area, the rooms facing the street have soundproof windows. A continental breakfast buffet is served on the glassed-in veranda.

See map p. 337. 1–3 rue Félicien-David. ☎ *04-90-16-42-00. Fax: 04-90-82-17-32. E-mail:* hotelhorlage@wanadoo.fr. *Parking: 8€ ($9.60). Rack rates: 80€–160€ ($96–$192) double. Breakfast: 12€ ($14). AE, MC, V.*

Hôtel de la Mirande
$$$–$$$$ Avignon

The beautiful Mirande, occupying a Renaissance palace near the Palais des Papes, is the top lodging choice, if you have a few euros to spend. Each of the 20 rooms is individually decorated in grand style; a famous Paris decorator had unlimited resources to search out the most exceptional antiques, oriental rugs, handmade wallpapers, and damask curtains. The hotel has a highly regarded restaurant, as well as a cooking school. The inner courtyard, a secret garden, is lush with plants and sculpture.

Avignon

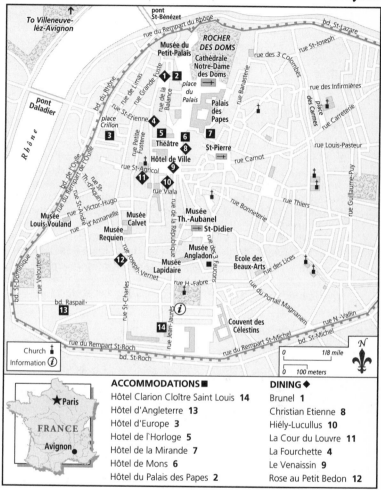

ACCOMMODATIONS ■
Hôtel Clarion Cloître Saint Louis **14**
Hôtel d'Angleterre **13**
Hôtel d'Europe **3**
Hotel de l'Horloge **5**
Hôtel de la Mirande **7**
Hôtel de Mons **6**
Hôtel du Palais des Papes **2**

DINING ◆
Brunel **1**
Christian Etienne **8**
Hiély-Lucullus **10**
La Cour du Louvre **11**
La Fourchette **4**
Le Venaissin **9**
Rose au Petit Bedon **12**

See map p. 337. 4 place de la Mirande. ☎ *04-90-85-93-93. Fax: 04-90-86-26-85.* www.la-mirande.fr. *Parking: 18€ ($22). Rack rates: 280€–340€ ($336–$408) double; 570€–640€ ($684–$768) suite. Breakfast: 26€ ($31). AE, MC, V.*

Hôtel de Mons
$ Avignon

On a quiet street off place de l'Horloge, this family-run hotel, with its 11 simple and odd-shaped rooms, is the best of Avignon's inexpensive lodgings. An atmospheric 13th-century chapel has been converted into a rough-around-the-edges hotel that nevertheless possesses a homelike charm. The real treat is the ancient building with its vaulted ceiling and old stone staircase that winds up to the beamed rooms. Breakfast is served in a vaulted nook off the lobby.

See map p. 337. 5 rue du Mons. ☎ *04-90-82-57-16. Fax: 04-90-85-19-15.* www.hotel demons.com. *Rack rates: 55€–65€ ($66–$78) double. Breakfast: 7€ ($8.40). AE, DC, MC, V.*

Hôtel d'Europe
$$–$$$$ **Avignon**

The Europe caters to patrons that appreciate overstated elegance. Built in 1580, the mansion of the marquis de Graveson has been a hotel since 1799. Guests have included Napoléon, Châteaubriand, Victor Hugo, Tennessee Williams, Salvador Dalí, and Picasso. The 44 spacious rooms feature antiques, oriental rugs, chaises, and chandeliers, and boast marble fireplaces, paneled walls and doors, and classical moldings. The top-floor suites open onto balconies: two with views of the Palais des Papes, one with a river vista. La Vieille Fontaine restaurant is decorated with tapestries. In summer, meals are served on the terrace near a fountain.

See map p. 337. 12 place Crillon. ☎ *04-90-14-76-76. Fax: 04-90-14-76-71.* www. hotel-d-europe.fr. *Parking: 15€ ($18). Rack rates: 129€–410€ ($155–$492) double; 616€–698€ ($739–$838) suite. Breakfast: 23€ ($28). AE, DC, MC, V.*

Hôtel du Palais des Papes
$–$$ **Avignon**

Considering the location and amenities, this hotel is a great deal in Avignon. For those who like to be in the heart of the city, the location couldn't be better — across the square from the Palais des Papes. (Keep in mind, however, that it's a half-mile walk from the train station.) The 25 rooms are charming and stylish, with antique fixtures and stone walls. Some have a view of the Palais des Papes, which is particularly magnificent at night. Breakfast can be served in the room. The hotel also has a reasonably priced Provençal restaurant.

See map p. 337. 1 rue Gérard-Philippe. ☎ *04-90-86-04-13. Fax: 04-90-27-91-17.* www.hotel-avignon.com. *Parking: 9€ ($11). Rack rates: 85€–115€ ($102–$138) double, 130€ ($156) suite. Breakfast: 5€ ($6). MC, V.*

Dining locally

For inexpensive ethnic food, head to **rue des Teinturiers.** You'll find Cuban cuisine at **Cubanito Café** (51 rue Carnot; ☎ 04-90-27-90-59), open Tuesday to Friday 8 a.m. to 1:30 a.m. and Saturday and Sunday 5 p.m. to 1:30 a.m. (during the festival in July open daily 8 a.m. to 1:30 a.m.). For Spanish cuisine, try **Tapalocas** (15 rue Galante; ☎ 04-90-82-56-84), open daily noon to 1 a.m. For a quick inexpensive meal, try one of the many cafes on **place de l'Horloge,** which stay open from about 9 a.m. to 11 p.m. You find great wine bars in Avignon, including the **Cave de Bancass**

(25 rue Bancass; ☎ 04-90-86-97-02), open Tuesday to Saturday noon to 2 p.m. and Thursday to Saturday 7:30 to 11 p.m., and **Caveau du Théâtre Le Chevalier Thierry Piedoie** (rue des Trois Faucons; ☎ 04-90-86-51-53), open daily 7 to 9:30 p.m.

Brunel
$$–$$$ Avignon PROVENÇAL

This flower-filled, air-conditioned restaurant is in the heart of Avignon. Managed by the Brunel family, it offers such delectable specialties as warm pâté of duckling and breast of duckling with apples. The chef prepares a superb plate of wild-mushroom–stuffed ravioli with roasted foie gras. The grilled John Dory is accompanied by artichoke hearts, and even the lowly pigs' feet emerge with a sublime taste. The excellent desserts are prepared fresh daily. Feel free to order house wines by the carafe.

See map p. 337. 46 rue de la Balance. ☎ *04-90-85-24-83. Reservations required. Main courses: 9.50€–18€ ($11–$22); prix fixe: 30€ ($36). MC, V. Open: Mon–Sat noon to 2 p.m. and 7:45–10 p.m.*

Christian Etienne
$$–$$$$ Avignon PROVENÇAL

This is dining at its most opulent. About half the tables are out on a narrow street near the Palais des Papes, but the atmospheric frescoed interior of this 12th-century building is almost worth the (very steep) price. Daring chef Christian Etienne specializes in tomatoes, truffles, and fish: He bases entire menus on tomatoes in summer, creates wonderous truffle-studded concoctions in winter, and prepares fresh fish with imagination. A typical first course is *bouillon de lentilles aux saucisses de couenne* (lentil-and-sausage soup). Main dishes include *tronçon de baudroie poêlé au vin rouge des Côtes du Rhône, poire aux épices* (monkfish slices panfried with red wine and spiced pear) and *caille farcie d'une brunoise de céleri, ragoût de muscat aux lardons* (celery-stuffed quail with bacon ragout). A homemade ice cream or sorbet with an unusual flavor is the perfect way to round out a rich meal.

See map p. 337. 10 rue de Mons. ☎ *04-90-86-16-50. Reservations recommended. Main courses: 20€–38€ ($24–$46); prix fixe: 30€–95€ ($36–$114). AE, DC, MC, V. Open: Tues–Sat noon to 1:15 p.m. and 7:30–9:15 p.m. Open daily with same hours in July.*

Hiély-Lucullus
$$–$$$ Avignon FRENCH

Before the arrival of Christian Etienne, this Relais Gourmand reigned supreme in Avignon. The chef here is Laurent Blondin, who trained under Paul Bocuse, France's most celebrated chef. The restaurant is decorated in Belle Epoque style, most elegant. We enjoyed the chef's veal chops for two, cooked with bacon and served in their own juice with a medley of mixed fresh vegetables. Locals often order the filet of bull with a red wine sauce and a skewer of vegetables. The dish is said to make a man out of you, even if you're a woman. For dessert, how about a tomato ice cream with Asian spices?

See map p. 337. 5 rue de la République. ☎ *04-90-86-17-07. Reservations required. Lunch fixed-price menu 22€ ($26). Dinner fixed-price menu 28€–45€ ($34–$54). AE, MC, V. Open: daily noon to 2 p.m. and 7–10 p.m. Closed 1 week in Feb, 1 week in June.*

La Cour du Louvre
$$ Avignon   MEDITERRANEAN

This lovely restaurant is set in a secluded courtyard in the center of town, but you can also dine inside, where the modern décor blends with the ancient building. The cuisine is Mediterranean with Italian influences. For the first course, try the excellent antipasta, a sampling of succulent meats and vegetables, or the *légumes grillés à la mozzarella* (grilled vegetables with mozzarella). As a main dish, look no further than the homemade pastas, served Provençal style with understated sauces containing herbs from the region. The hip waitstaff, looking for a chuckle, is likely to take your order with a Cockney accent.

See map p. 337. 23 rue St-Agricol. ☎ *04-90-27-12-66. Reservations recommended. Main courses: 9.80€–32€ ($12–$38); prix fixe: 14.50€–29€ ($17–$35) lunch, 29€ ($35) dinner. MC, V. Open: Tues–Sat noon to 2:30 p.m.; Tues–Sat 7:30–10 p.m.*

La Fourchette
$–$$ Avignon   PROVENÇAL

Long a favorite with locals, this intimate restaurant fills up early, so reservations are a must. What attracts people are the relatively low prices for the high-quality cuisine. Basically, this is updated bistro fare prepared with finesse. The big difference here is that more choices are on the prix-fixe menu than at most restaurants, and the dishes are quite elaborate for the price. A good first-course choice is the *sardines marinées à la coriandre* (sardines marinated in coriander); for a main course, look for the special *agneau grillé au romarin* (grilled lamb with rosemary).

See map p. 337. 17 rue Racine. ☎ *04-90-85-20-93. Reservations necessary. Main courses lunch: 23€–25€ ($28–$30); 28€ ($34) at dinner. MC, V. Open: Mon–Fri 12:15–1:45 p.m. and 7:15–9:45 p.m.*

Le Venaissin
$–$$ Avignon   PROVENÇAL

Of the many terrace restaurants and cafes on place de l'Horloge, this one fills up first. That's because it has the most varied menu and the lowest prices. The square is beautiful, particularly at night, when the city hall's *beaux-arts* facade is lit up and the nearby carousel spins to calliope tunes. Expect faster-than-usual service, tables crammed so tightly you're likely to compare dishes with your neighbors, and English menus and English-speaking waiters. A popular appetizer is the *salade mistral,* a chef-concocted mélange that includes melon, crab, and avocado. As a main course, the *loup au safran, courgette provençal* (seabass with saffron and eggplant Provençal style) and *éstouffade de noix de joue de boeuf à la provençal riz pilaf* (beef stew Provençal style with rice pilaf) are standouts. For dessert, try the *crème caramel* or *compote de pêche à la menthe fraîche* (peach compote with fresh mint). Kids will enjoy popular choices such as *steak frites* (steak with french fries).

See map p. 337. Place de l'Horloge. ☎ 04-90-86-20-99. Reservations accepted. Main courses: 7.50€–18€ ($9–$22); prix fixe: 11.50€ and 14.50€ ($14 and $17); children's menu 5.50€ ($6.60). MC, V. Open: Daily 11:30 a.m.–11 p.m.

Rose au Petit Bedon
$$–$$$ Avignon   PROVENÇAL

From the outside, this looks like a small nothing-special restaurant; but when tables fill up by 7:30 p.m., you know something wonderful is happening in the kitchen. It has two floors, so you need to inquire even when it looks full (better yet, make a reservation). The décor is understated elegance lit by romantic candles. The menu, with English translations, highlights seafood. Your best bet is the "catch of the day," usually prepared with Provençal herbs in a light sauce. The presentation of this dish is always artistic, with the chef creating patterns from the colors and textures of fresh vegetables and sauces.

See map p. 337. 70 rue Joseph-Vernet. ☎ 04-90-82-33-98. Reservations recommended. Prix fixe: 28€ and 35€ ($34–$42). AE, MC, V. Open: Tues–Sun noon to 2:30 p.m.; Mon–Sat 7:30–9:30 p.m. Closed Aug 15–31.

Exploring the town and environs

Avignon itself has a host of intriguing sights, including one of France's biggest attractions, the Palais des Papes. Nearby is Villeneuve-lez-Avignon, a medieval walled city where the wealthy cardinals affiliated with the Pope's Palace had their homes.

Getting to know Avignon

The main road through the city center, **cours Jean-Jaurès,** becomes **rue de la République** and leads from the train station outside the city's 14th-century ramparts to the **Palais des Papes** about a half-mile away. In summer, musicians and other entertainers perform on the cobblestone squares, particularly **place du Palais** (in front of the Palais des Papes). Next to the palace is the 12th-century **Cathédrale Notre-Dame des Doms.** From the back exit of the cathedral, you find the **promenade du Rocher des Doms,** a lovely garden with views of Villeneuve-lez-Avignon across the river. Just south of place du Palais is **place de l'Horloge** (a handsome square with outdoor cafes), the imposing **Hôtel de Ville** (which houses town offices), and the *beaux-arts* **Opéra d'Avignon.** In the area west of here, you can patronize exclusive stores such as **Christian Lacroix** and **Hermès,** along with excellent houseware, pottery, and antiques stores. Avignon also has good bargain-clothing and gift shops, particularly in the funky area of **rue de la Bonneterie** near Les Halles. Farther east is **rue des Teinturiers,** where many of the city's ethnic restaurants, bars, and nightclubs are located.

Just 3km (2 miles) west of the city, across the Rhône River, is **Villeneuve-lez-Avignon,** a walled suburb of Avignon (where the court of the pope and the cardinals lived). The best way to reach Villeneuve is to drive across the Rhône (and Ile de la Barthelasse) on pont Edouard-Daladier and head north. Several interesting sights are here, including one of the biggest Carthusian monasteries in Europe.

At the first attraction you visit (or at the tourist office), pick up a special free pass called **Avignon Passion.** You pay full price for the first site and then you get reduced rates on all the other attractions and tours.

From April to October, three-hour **guided walking tours of Avignon** leave Tuesday and Thursday at 10 a.m. from the tourist office (41 cours Jean-Jaurés; ☎ 04-32-74-32-72). The tours cost 10€ ($12), or 7€ ($8.40) with an Avignon Passion pass. During July and August, two-hour **guided tours of Villeneuve-lez-Avignon** leave Tuesday and Thursday at 5 p.m. from the tourist office and cost 4.50€ ($5.40), or 3.50€ ($4.20) with an Avignon Passion pass.

From mid-March to mid-October, the **tourist train** (☎ 04-90-82-64-44) takes in the old city, with main roads and famous monuments, and lesser-known roads that lead to more remote parts of the ancient city. It departs every 35 minutes daily (10 a.m.–7:30 p.m.) from place du Palais and costs 7€ ($8.40), or 5.50€ ($6.60) with an Avignon Passion pass. The train travels one of two routes: through the old town or through the Rocher des Doms gardens.

Visiting Palais des Papes and other Avignon sites

The world's most important Gothic palace, **Palais des Papes** (place du Palais; ☎ 04-90-27-50-73; www.palais-des-papes.com), is certainly monumental. It's one of the most visited historic sites in France. In the 14th century, popes ruled Christendom from this palace and caused a crisis in the Catholic Church, as Avignon and Rome competed for dominance. Rome won, but Avignon got to keep the palace, though Rome owned the site until the French Revolution. Allow at least an hour to see everything (you have 25 rooms to visit), and special exhibits are often set up (for example, during the July arts festival, the Grande Chapelle is used for an art show). Of the many sections of the palace (see the nearby map, "Palais des Papes"), the standouts are the **Chapelle St-Jean,** on the ground floor, with beautiful 14th-century frescoes; the **pope's bedroom** *(chambre à coucher),* on the first floor, decorated with murals of birds and foliage; and the adjacent **Studium,** also known as the Stag Room, which is a pope's study with frescoes of hunting scenes. Take a look at the large central courtyard known as the **Grande Cour** or the **Cour d'Honneur,** where plays are performed during the Avignon Festival. The palace doesn't have much décor, because the townspeople stripped the decadent interiors during the Revolution. So you mainly get

Palais des Papes

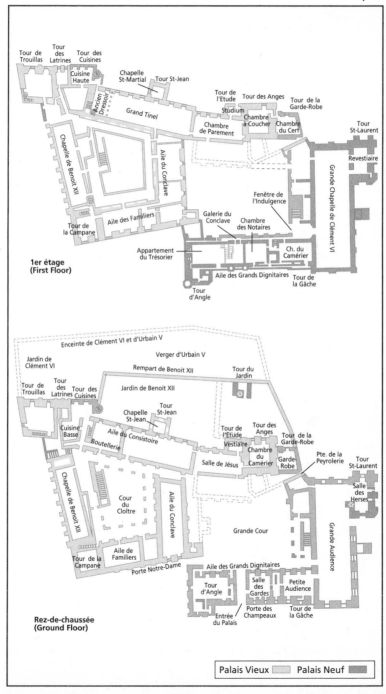

1er étage (First Floor)

Tour de Trouillas
Tour des Latrines
Tour des Cuisines
Cuisine Haute
Chapelle St-Martial
Tour St-Jean
Tour de l'Etude
Tour des Anges
Tour de la Garde-Robe
Ancien Dressoir
Grand Tinel
Studium
Chambre à Coucher
Chambre du Cerf
Tour St-Laurent
Chambre de Parement
Revestiaire
Aile du Conclave
Chapelle de Benoît XII
Grande Chapelle de Clément VI
Fenêtre de l'Indulgence
Tour de la Campane
Aile des Familiers
Galerie du Conclave
Chambre des Notaires
Appartement du Trésorier
Ch. du Camérier
Aile des Grands Dignitaires
Tour de la Gâche
Tour d'Angle

Rez-de-chaussée (Ground Floor)

Enceinte de Clément VI et d'Urbain V
Verger d'Urbain V
Jardin de Clément VI
Rempart de Benoît XII
Tour du Jardin
Tour de Trouillas
Tour des Latrines
Tour des Cuisines
Jardin de Benoît XII
Cuisine Basse
Chapelle St-Jean
Tour St-Jean
Aile du Consistoire
Tour de l'Étude
Tour des Anges
Tour de la Garde-Robe
Boutellerie
Vestiaire
Chambre du Camérier
Garde-Robe
Pte. de la Peyrolerie
Tour St-Laurent
Salle de Jésus
Salle des Herses
Chapelle de Benoît XII
Cour du Cloître
Aile du Conclave
Grande Cour
Grande Audience
Tour de la Campane
Aile de Familiers
Porte Notre-Dame
Aile des Grands Dignitaires
Tour d'Angle
Salle des Gardes
Petite Audience
Entrée du Palais
Porte des Champeaux
Tour de la Gâche

Palais Vieux ☐   Palais Neuf ■

to see large-scale spaces and frescoes while hearing about the exploits that took place here. Visits are by free guided tour or self-guided tour using an audioguide; the audioguide is your best bet as the tour guide tends to hurry you through. Although the audioguide doesn't dwell on scandalous papal activities, it does include plenty of tidbits. Admission is 9.50€ ($11) for adults and 7.50€ ($9) for students and children. Combined admission for the palace and pont St-Bénezet is 11.50€ ($14) for adults and 9€ ($11) for students and children. The palace is open daily July to September 9 a.m. to 8 p.m., April to June and October 9 a.m. to 7 p.m., and November to March 9:30 a.m. to 5:45 p.m. Admittance is not allowed an hour before closing.

Located in the 14th-century Palais des Archevêques, next to the Palais des Papes, is Avignon's best art museum, **Musée du Petit Palace** (place du Palais; ☎ **04-90-86-44-58**). This huge collection of medieval and Renaissance paintings focuses on Italian paintings from the 13th through the 16th centuries, Roman and Gothic sculpture from Avignon, and paintings of the school of Avignon from the 14th through 16th centuries. A highlight is Botticelli's *Virgin and Child.* The palace windows offer scenic views of Villeneuve-lez-Avignon across the river. The museum is open Wednesday to Monday (except Jan 1, May 1, July 14, Nov 1, and Dec 25) June through September 10 a.m. to 1 p.m. and 2 to 6 p.m. and October to May 9:30 a.m. to 1 p.m. and 2 to 5:30 p.m. Admission is 6€ ($7.20), or 3€ ($3.60) with the Avignon Passion pass.

Musée Angladon (5 rue Laboureur; ☎ **04-90-82-29-03**; www.angladon. com) features a small collection of minor Impressionist paintings by major painters. It's worth a look for fans of the genre and for those who enjoy seeing works in situ — that is, in the grand mansion of collector Jacques Doucet, the flamboyant Parisian fashion designer. Artists repre-sented include Degas, Daumier, Manet, Sisley, van Gogh, Cézanne, Picasso, and Modigliani (usually one painting apiece). Most of these works are on the ground floor. On the second floor are 18th-century–style salons with antique furniture and artworks from various periods. It's open Wednesday to Sunday 1 to 6 p.m., and admission is 6€ ($7.20) for adults and 4€ ($4.80) with the Avignon Passion pass and for students and children.

Musée Calvet (65 rue Joseph-Vernet; ☎ **04-90-86-33-84**) is Avignon's fine arts museum set in a magnificent 18th-century mansion. It displays a broad collection of paintings and sculptures from the 15th through the 20th centuries, and *faïences* (pieces of hand-painted pottery from the region), silverware, and bronzes. The modern art room has works by Soutine, Manet, Sisley, and Camille Claudel. Admission is 6€ ($7.20), or 3€ ($3.60) with the Avignon Passion pass. It's open Wednesday to Monday 10 a.m. to 1 p.m. and 2 to 6 p.m. In the 17th-century baroque chapel of the College of Jesuits is Avignon's archaeological museum, the **Musée Lapidaire** (27 rue de la République; ☎ **04-90-85-75-38**). The exquisite antique sculpture collection includes Egyptian, Etruscan, Greek, Roman, and Gallo–Roman works, plus antique vases, bronzes, and glassware. Admission is 2€ ($2.40), or 1€ ($1.20) with the Avignon Passion pass. It's open Wednesday to Monday 10 a.m. to 1 p.m. and 2 to 6 p.m. The town's decorative arts museum, **Musée Louis-Vouland** (17 rue Victor-Hugo; ☎ 04-90-86-03-79; www.vouland.com), features a superb collection of 17th- and 18th-century works, including tapestries and *faïences*, and has a beautiful garden. Admission is 4€ ($4.80), or 2.50€ ($3) with the Avignon Passion pass. The museum is open May to October Tuesday to Saturday 10 a.m. to noon and 2 to 6 p.m., and Sunday 2 to 6 p.m.; November to April it's open Tuesday to Sunday 2 to 6 p.m.

Medieval people had a funny saying about the **pont St-Bénezet** (rue Ferruce; ☎ 04-90-27-51-16; www.palais-des-papes.com): When crossing the bridge, you'd always meet two monks, two donkeys, and two prostitutes. The saying offers a glimpse into the medieval world, a heady mix of the sacred and the profane. Legend and lore whirl around this 12th-century bridge that leads to nowhere, with a Romanesque chapel perched over the raging river. Because of constant flooding by the mighty Rhône, the bridge was destroyed many times during the Middle Ages and finally abandoned in the 17th century. It's said that Louis XIV was the last to cross the bridge. What's left are just 4 of the bridge's original 22 arches that stretched across the river, once leading conveniently to Villeneuve-lez-Avignon. The bridge was built because of the insistence of the shepherd Bénezet, who allegedly received word from on high that a bridge should be constructed here. Locals laughed until the scrawny shepherd suddenly turned into Charles Atlas and started lifting boulders over to the riverside. The bridge's Chapelle de St-Nicolas is dedicated to the patron saint of bargemen: Bargemen have long plied the river's banks. The little museum below the bridge contains photos of paintings and engravings that have to do with the history of the bridge and what it looked like in the 18th and 19th centuries. An entertaining audioguide recounts the bridge's history. Admission is 4€ ($4.80) for adults (3€/ $3.60 with the Avignon Passion pass) and 3.30€ ($3.95) for students and children. It's open daily: May to September 9:30 a.m. to 7 p.m., July 9 a.m. to 9 p.m., August to September 9 a.m. to 8 p.m., April to June and October 9 a.m. to 7 p.m., and November to March 9:30 a.m. to 5:45 p.m. Admittance is not allowed a half-hour before closing.

The **Collection Lambert at the Musée d'Art Contemporain** (5 rue Violette; ☎ 04-90-16-56-20; www.collectionlambert.com) features art from the 1960s to the present. The museum is in a former private mansion, the Hôtel de Caumont, in the center of Avignon, and the 400 works on display had been in storage for 20 years. The collection includes minimal art, conceptual art, photography, and video, with the work of artists such as Brice Marden, Carl Andre, Anselm Kiefer, Cy Twombly, Andres Serrano, and Nan Golden. Admission is 5.50€ ($6.60) for adults and 4€ ($4.80) with the Avignon Passion pass and for students and children 4€ and 2€ ($4.80 and $2.40) with pass. The museum is open Tuesday to Sunday 11 a.m. to 6 p.m.

Beyond Avignon

Try the famous Châteauneuf-du-Pape wine at the **Musée des Outils de Vignerons** (avenue Bienheureux-Pierre-de-Luxembourg; ☎ **04-90-83-70-07**). It's open daily 9 a.m. to noon and 2 to 6 p.m. for a visit and "free and tutored tasting" of the Laurent-Charles Brotte and Père Anselme cuvée. Of course, you can also buy wine here. You can catch a bus from Avignon to Châteauneuf-du-Pape or drive 13km (8 miles) north on A9.

One of Provence's top sights is a great Roman aqueduct, **pont du Gard** (☎ **04-66-37-51-12**), about 20km (12 miles) from Avignon and 23km (14 miles) northeast of Nîmes, with its triple row of arches spanning the Gard River. You can walk across the aqueduct, built in 19 B.C., and around a nearby arboretum. Bring a picnic and a bottle of wine, or you can find restaurants nearby. Parking is free. The visitor centers on either side of the bridge show films. The center on the east side, called **Le Portal,** also has children's activities and an exhibit about the bridge. From Avignon, exit the city from the southwest on the pont de l'Europe on A9 and head toward Nîmes. Take N100 to N86, and cross the Gard River. Follow D981 north to the parking area for the pont du Gard. Several buses depart Avignon each day and arrive at a stop that's about a ten-minute walk from the pont du Gard (90 minutes, 5€/$6).

Seeing Villeneuve-lez-Avignon

Only 3km (2 miles) from Avignon, this suburb is a long walk or a quick bike ride across the river. You can also take a city bus (see "Getting around and getting information" earlier in this chapter) or a taxi.

Founded in the 14th century by Innocent VI (the fifth pope of Avignon), **Chartreuse du Val de Bénédiction** (60 rue de la République; ☎ **04-90-15-24-24**) is one of the biggest Carthusian monasteries in Europe, housing a church, three cloisters (typically public areas with arches, columns, and artifacts), a chapel full of frescoes, gardens, and 40 monk cells. You're free to walk around and take in the atmosphere without tour guides. Don't miss Pope Innocent VI's Gothic tomb inside the church. The monastery is the location of the Centre National des Ecritures du Spectacle and provides a lodging retreat for writers. Admission is 6.10€ ($7.30) for adults, 4.10€ ($4.90) with the Avignon Passion pass, and 3.50€ ($4.20) for children. It's open daily: April to September 9 a.m. to 6 p.m. and October to March 9:30 a.m. to 5:30 p.m.

The 14th-century Gothic **Fort St-André** (Mont Andaon; ☎ **04-90-25-45-35**) was built to protect the city of Villeneuve and show the popes in Avignon a little French muscle. The fort, ordained by Phillippe le Bel, once sheltered a tenth-century abbey but now displays pretty gardens with a grand view of the Rhône Valley and Avignon. Admission is 4.60€ ($5.50) for adults, 3.10€ ($3.70) with the Avignon Passion pass and 3.10€ ($3.70) for children. It's open daily: April to September 10 a.m. to 1 p.m. and 2 to 6 p.m. and October to March 10 a.m. to 1 p.m. and 2 to 5 p.m.

When the pont St-Bénezet stretched all the way across the Rhône River, **Tour Philippe le Bel** (rue Montée-de-la-Tour; ☎ 04-32-70-08-57) stood at the base of the bridge, marking the entrance to the Gothic town of Villeneuve. The guardians of the citadel effectively controlled access to the bridge for all those approaching Avignon from the north in the 14th century. Climb the steep spiral staircase for the best view of Avignon and the Rhône Valley. Admission is 1.60€ ($1.90) for adults and 1€ ($1.20) with the Avignon Passion pass and for students and children. It's open Tuesday to Sunday (except February) 10 a.m. to 12:30 p.m. and 3 to 6 p.m.

Shopping for local treasures

Most markets in Avignon are open 7 a.m. to 1 p.m. The big covered market is **Les Halles** on place Pie, open Tuesday to Sunday. Smaller **food markets** are on rue du Rempart St-Michel on Saturdays and Sundays, and on place Crillon on Fridays. The **flower market** is on place des Carmes on Saturdays, and it becomes a **flea market** on Sundays. A more upscale **antiques market** fills up rue des Teinturiers all day on Saturdays.

Living it up after dark

Avignon sports a lively nightlife, with the young and restless strolling up and down **rue de la République** deciding where to make a night of it. Try the **Auberge de Cassagne** (450 allée de Cassagne; ☎ 04-90-31-04-18) and **Brasserie Le Cintra** (44 cours Jean-Jaurès; ☎ 04-90-82-29-80; www. le-cintra.com). The **Red Zone** (27 rue Carnot; ☎ 04-90-27-02-44) offers live concerts featuring rock, country, and jazz. **Le Woolloomooloo** (16 rue des Teinturiers; ☎ 04-90-85-28-44) is a funky place featuring "food of the world" and live music with no cover.

St-Rémy-de-Provence and Its Roman Ruins

At the foot of the Alpilles mountains, ancient **St-Rémy-de-Provence** retains a *soupçon* (a tiny bit) of the small-town flavor of Provence that some of the more touristy towns have lost. The downside is that you won't find much to see or do, and it's difficult to get here by public transportation (the town has no train station). The main attraction is just outside town: The **Ruines de Glanum** — extraordinary Roman ruins that are still being excavated — include finds dating to the first millennium B.C. Famous residents of St-Rémy have included French astrologer Michel de Nostredame (better known as Nostradamus), whose enigmatic predictions have been a source of debate for centuries. Dutch artist Vincent van Gogh checked into a mental hospital in St-Rémy in 1889 and painted some of his most famous works here. St-Rémy has become a destination for shopping for the home, with many antiques and interior decorating stores.

An idyllic time to visit St-Rémy is during the **Fête de la Transhumance.** On Whit Monday (around June 11), shepherds from the surrounding area march their flocks into town, arriving around 10:30 a.m., and drive them twice around the center for about two hours. On August 15, **Carreto Ramado,** 50 horses pull an enormous cart loaded with local produce into town. Around that same date, the **Feria Provençale de St-Rémy** features bullfights in which the bull isn't killed.

Getting there

Buses arrive at and depart from St-Rémy's place de la République, near the large fountain just outside the old town center on the west side. Buses to and from Avignon take 40 minutes and cost 4.90€ ($5.90) (☎ 04-90-92-05-22). From Avignon, you can get bus or train connections to most other major Provence towns. The nearest **train** station is **Avignon Gare.** For information, call ☎ 08-92-35-35-39.

The nearest airport is the **Aéroport Avignon-Caumont** (☎ 04-90-81-51-15), which is 18km (11 miles) from St-Rémy. **Aéroport Nîmes-Garons** (☎ 04-66-70-49-49) is 40km (25 miles) away, and the **Aéroport Marseille-Provence** (☎ 04-42-14-14-14) is 85km (53 miles) away. With no buses from these airports to St-Rémy, you'll need to rent a car if you arrive by air. All three airports have rental car offices for Hertz, Avis, Europcar, National Citer, and Budget.

St-Rémy is 705km (438 miles) from Paris and 18km (11 miles) from Avignon. To **drive** from Paris, follow the directions to Avignon; then take D571 to St-Rémy. From the direction of Nice, follow A8 to A7 and the signs to St-Rémy. From the direction of Nîmes and Arles, take A9 to St-Rémy. St Rémy is centrally located in Provence. Aix is 50km (31 miles) from St-Rémy, Marseille 90km (56 miles), Avignon 21km (13 miles), Les Baux 10km (6 miles), and Arles 22km (14 miles).

Getting around and getting information

Abrivado (Zone Activites La Gare, 6 Traverse Meicocouliers; ☎ 04-90-92-06-34) is the location for Budget and National rental cars. You can rent mountain bikes at **Ferri** (35 av. de la Libération; ☎ 04-90-92-10-88), where the prices are 9€ to 12€ ($11–$14) for half a day and 15€ to 18€ ($18–$22) for a full day. For a cab, call **Taxi E. Grimauld** at ☎ 06-09-31-50-38 or **Dalgon Taxi** at ☎ 06-09-52-71-54.

The **tourist office** is on place Jean-Jaurès (☎ 04-90-92-05-22; Fax: 04-90-92-38-52; www.saintremy-de-provence.com). Late June to mid-September, it's open Monday to Friday 9 a.m. to noon and 2 to 7 p.m., and Saturday and Sunday 10 a.m. to 12:30 p.m. The office also has a wide range of brochures, including self-guided tours of locations where van Gogh painted. Ask about walking tours (in English) of the town center. You can send e-mail at **Compo Secretariat Services** (6 bis bd. Marceau; ☎ 04-90-92-48-11), open Monday to Friday 9 a.m. to noon and 2 to 6 p.m.

Spending the night

Just outside the medieval walls of Les Baux (a pedestrian-only hilltop village 13km/8 miles from St-Rémy) is a fancy Relais & Châteaux hotel, **L'Oustau de Beaumanière** (☎ **04-90-54-33-07**; Fax: 04-90-54-40-46), known for serving some of the best food in the region. Don't be fooled by the bland exterior — the rooms are opulent, renting for 260€ to 305€ ($312–$366) double and 425€ to 475€ ($510–$570) apartment.

For the location of other lodging described in this section, check out the "St-Rémy-de-Provence" map.

Château de Roussan
$ St-Rémy (west of town)

Set in a large landscaped park with sculpture gardens and fountains, this quirky manse, about a mile from St-Rémy, is for those who want to pay bargain rates to stay in a château with an amusing down-on-its-luck quality. The elegant neoclassical facade belies the neglected interior, and the atmosphere is casual to the extreme. The upside is that the toys belong to a cute family of black labs; a family of cats lives on the second floor. The 21 rooms are decorated with an unusual combination of interesting antiques and flea market finds, and the housekeeping is somewhat hit and miss. The common room has a billiards table, piano, and many board games. You can rent bikes for 16€ ($19) per day. The restaurant serves average, if pricey, fare.

See map p. 351. Route de Tarascon. ☎ *04-90-92-11-63. Fax: 04-90-92-50-59.* www. chateau-de-roussan.com. *Rack rates: 73€–99.50€ ($88–$119) double. Breakfast: 9€ ($11) in restaurant or room. Half board: 35€ ($42). AE, MC, V.*

Hostellerie du Vallon de Valrugues
$$–$$$$ St-Rémy (east of town)

An exquisite hotel east of the old town, Vallon de Valrugues is one of the region's top choices, featuring a blend of modernity and tradition on a large estate. The 34 spacious rooms and 18 grand apartments offer mountain views (Alpilles, Lubéron, and Mont Ventoux), deluxe amenities such as bathrobes and fine toiletries, safes, and minibars; 11 rooms contain Jacuzzis. The prestige suite has its own pool. Also on site are a large heated pool, a driving range and putting green, a sauna, a billiards table, and a children's garden. The restaurant — one of the best in town — specializes in Provençal fare.

See map p. 351. Chemin de Canto Cigalo. ☎ *04-90-92-04-40. Fax: 04-90-92-44-01.* www.vallondevalrugues.com. *Rack rates: 150€–260€ ($180–$312) double; 990€ ($1,188) suite; 370€–510€ ($444–$612) apartment.. Breakfast: 23€ ($28); half board: 90€ ($108). AE, MC, V. Closed Feb.*

Hôtel Château des Alpilles
$$–$$$ St-Rémy (west of town)

The Bon family has renovated this 19th-century bourgeois mansion, restoring it to its former grandeur. A private 4-hectare (10-acre) park, with 300-year-old trees, surrounds the hotel. Spacious and decorated with antiques, the 22 units, including six suites and an apartment, are spread among the castle, the 19th-century farmhouse, and La Chapel (a recent addition). Hotel amenities include a pool, two tennis courts, a bar, a sauna, and massages on request. The dining room features gourmet Provençal cooking; lunch is served next to the pool in summer. The agreeable staff speaks English.

See map p. 351. D31, Ancienne Route du Grès. ☎ **04-90-92-03-33.** *Fax: 04-90-92-45-17.* www.chateaualpilles.com. *Rack rates: 170€–240€ ($204–$288) double; 245€–370€ ($294–$444) suite; 245€–370€ ($294–$444) apt. Breakfast: 17€ ($20). AE, DC, MC, V. Closed mid-Nov–mid-Feb.*

Hôtel les Ateliers de l'Image
$$–$$$$ St-Rémy

Near the tourist office and a short walk from the old town's center, this hip hotel with a photography theme includes an art gallery, a photo lab, and a photo shop. The owners converted the old St-Rémy music hall into a very contemporary hotel with 32 rooms. Although it's on a busy street, this hotel is set back from the road down a narrow alley and is surprisingly tranquil. In the front terrace, you find a small heated pool. The glass-fronted lobby is all about light and space, with soaring ceilings and lots of glass. The rooms are simple, modern, and stylish, with personal fax machines, modem sockets, and hair dryers; some open onto mountain views. There's a billiards table, a bar, and bike rentals. The English-speaking staff is friendly and will pick you up at the Avignon train station or airport.

See map p. 351. 36 Blvd. Victor Hugo. ☎ **04-90-92-51-50.** *Fax: 04-90-92-43-52.* www.hotelphoto.com. *Rack rates: 150€–500€ ($180–$600) double. Breakfast is included. AE, MC, V.*

La Maison du Village
$$ St-Rémy

Our favorite nest in the *über*-Provençal town is this meticulously restored 18th-century townhouse in the center of St-Rémy. Warm and welcoming, each of the five units is a suite with a big sitting area and a luxurious bathroom. They're decorated in soft colors, with tasteful fabrics and wrought-iron beds. The old-fashioned, free-standing bathtubs are large enough for a romantic duo. On request, the innkeepers serve organic meals in the family-style dining room or the little "secret garden" out back. Drinks are served and soft music plays in the communal lounge.

See map p. 351. 10 rue du Mai 1945. ☎ **04-32-60-68-20.** *Fax 04-32-60-68-21.* www.lamaisonduvillage.com. *Parking: 7€ ($8.40). Rack rates: 190€ ($228) double. Breakfast: 12€ ($14). AE, DC, MC, V.*

St-Rémy-de-Provence

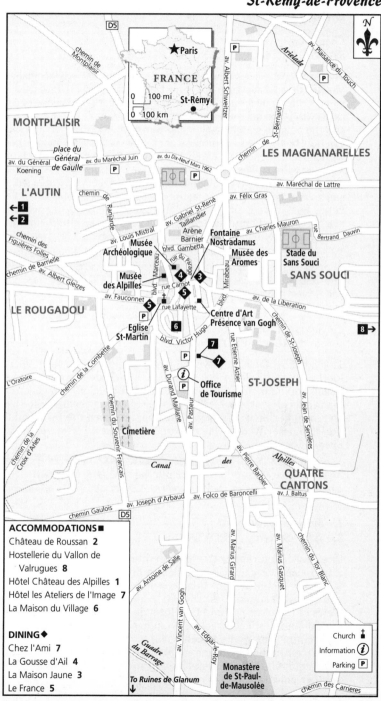

★Paris

FRANCE

St-Rémy

0   100 mi
0   100 km

MONTPLAISIR

chemin de Montplaisir

D5

av. Albert Schweitzer

Ariélade

av. Plaisance du Touch

P

P

LES MAGNANARELLES

chemin de St-Bernard

place du Général de Gaulle

av. du Général Koening

av. du Maréchal Juin

av. du Dix-Neuf Mars 1962

P

P

P

av. Maréchal de Lattre

L'AUTIN

chemin de Ranjarde

←**1**
←**2**

chemin des Figuières Folles

chemin de Barrielle

av. Albert Gleizes

av. Gabriel St-René Taillandier

av. Félix Gras

av. Charles Mauron

rue Bertrand Dauvin

av. Louis Mistral

Arène Barnier

Fontaine Nostradamus

Musée des Aromes

Stade du Sans Souci

SANS SOUCI

Musée Archéologique

blvd. Gambetta

rue du Parage

4 **3**

Musée des Alpilles

blvd. Marceau

rue Carnot

5

av. Fauconnet

rue Lafayette

blvd. Mirabeau

av. de la Liberation

LE ROUGADOU

P

Eglise St-Martin

6

Centre d'Art Présence van Gogh

chemin de St-Joseph

8→

L'Oratoire

chemin de la Combette

blvd. Victor Hugo

7

rue Etienne Astier

7

i

P

Office de Tourisme

av. Durand Maillane

ST-JOSEPH

av. Jean de Servières

Cimetière

chemin du Souvenir Français

chemin de la Croix d'Arles

Canal

des

av. Pasteur

av. Pierre Barbier

Alpilles

QUATRE CANTONS

av. J. Baltus

chemin Gaulois

D5

av. Joseph d'Arbaud

av. Folco de Baroncelli

av. Marius Girard

av. Marius Gasquet

chemin du Tor Blanc

ACCOMMODATIONS ■
Château de Roussan **2**
Hostellerie du Vallon de
    Valrugues **8**
Hôtel Château des Alpilles **1**
Hôtel les Ateliers de l'Image **7**
La Maison du Village **6**

DINING ◆
Chez l'Ami **7**
La Gousse d'Ail **4**
La Maison Jaune **3**
Le France **5**

av. Antoine de Salle

av. Vincent van Gogh

av. Edgar-le-Roy

Guadre du Barrage

To Ruines de Glanum
↓

Monastère de St-Paul-de-Mausolée

chemin des Carrieres

Church ✝
Information *i*
Parking P

Dining locally

Chez l'Ami
$$–$$$ St-Rémy   FRANCO-JAPANESE

Thanks to this place's minimalist décor and unusual hybrid cuisine, you may imagine that you've been suddenly transported back to Paris, except for the view of the Alpilles, the olive trees, and the nearby presence of a swimming pool within the surrounding park. The chairs are red, the walls are white, and the cuisine mingles Asian and European food with a nonchalance that can only be the result of months of creative planning. You may begin a meal with *giozan,* Japanese ravioli stuffed with crayfish, or a block of foie gras studded with truffles. Main courses include tournedos Rossini (filet layered with foie gras), ravioli stuffed with lobster and served with a sake and herb sauce, and calamari that's artfully shaped into replicas of miniature pine cones and served with risotto flavored with algae and squid ink. A wide selection of sushi and sashimi also is offered. Despite the implications of trendiness and high fashion, the dress code here is very relaxed.

See map p. 351. In the Hôtel les Ateliers de l'Image, 36 bd. Victor Hugo. ☎ *04-90-92-51-50. Reservations recommended. Main courses: 22€–38€ ($26–$46); prie fixe: 22€–69€ ($26–$83) lunch, 69€ ($83) dinner. AE, DC, MC, V. Open: Daily noon to 2 p.m. and 7–9 p.m. Closed Jan–Feb.*

La Gousse d'Ail
$–$$$ St-Rémy   PROVENÇAL

This small restaurant, a typical family-run place, serves delectable fresh food at reasonable prices. Specialties include *escargot à la provençal* (snails served with garlic and herbs from the region) and vegetarian dishes featuring colorful vegetables from the market, prepared with light sauces and local herbs. On Tuesday, the chef prepares the restaurant's famous bouillabaisse; Wednesdays feature live jazz all evening. The waitstaff speaks English.

See map p. 351. 6 Bd. Marceau. ☎ *04-90-92-16-87. Reservations recommended. Main courses: 15€–20€ ($18–$24); prix fixe: 15€ ($18) lunch, 30€–35€ ($36–$42) dinner. AE, MC, V. Open: Fri–Wed noon to 2:30 p.m. and 7–10 p.m. Closed Nov–Mar.*

La Maison Jaune
$$–$$$$ St-Rémy   PROVENÇAL

The best restaurant in the town center, La Maison Jaune serves memorable meals every time. It occupies an 18th-century building, and the décor is spare yet stylish, with huge casement windows providing lots of light and views. In summer, diners like to sit on the shady terrace and take in views of the old town and the Hôtel de Sade, which houses the archaeological museum. The specialties of chef François Perraud include *anchois frais marinés* (marinated anchovies), *semoule de blé épicés* (spiced wheat pasta), and a hearty *soupe de poisson* (fish soup). For dessert, try the *fraises et granité au safran et citron* (strawberries and saffron-and-lemon sherbet). English is spoken.

See map p. 351. 15 rue Carnot. ☎ *04-90-92-56-14. Reservations necessary. Prix fixe: 30€–55€ ($36–$66). MC, V. Open: Daily noon to 1:30 p.m. and 7:30–9:30 p.m. Closed Sun night and Mon in Jan and Feb.*

Le France
$–$$ St-Rémy   PROVENÇAL

This pretty little restaurant, an institution among locals, features fine Provençal cooking in an intimate atmosphere. This place offers a good opportunity to try some local specialties that you're not likely to find anywhere else, including *pieds et paquets* (literally, "feet and packages," a dish of lamb tripe and feet cooked in white-wine sauce). They make a hearty Camargue bull stew here, in addition to bouillabaise and bourride, two types of fish stew.

See map p. 351. 2 av. Fauçonnet. ☎ *04-90-92-11-56. Reservations recommended. Main courses: 7.50€–16€ ($9–$19); prix fixe: 13.50€–29.50€ ($16–$35). MC, V. Open: Tues–Sun noon to 2 p.m. and 6:45–10 p.m. Closed Nov–Mar.*

Exploring the town

St-Rémy **walking tours** (☎ 04-90-92-05-22) leave the tourist office at place Jean-Jaurès Fridays at 10 a.m.; with a minimum of 10 people, the tours last 1½ hours and cost 6.40€ ($7.70) for adults and 3.65€ ($4.40) or ages 12 to 18 and students. **Van Gogh tours** (☎ 04-90-92-05-22) departs the tourist office every Tuesday, Thursday, and Saturday at 10 a.m. and last 1½ hours; the cost is 6.40€ ($7.70) for adults and 3.65€ ($4.40) for ages 12 to 18 and students. The cost of the Van Gogh tour includes reduced admission to the Centre d'Art Présence Van Gogh and St-Paul de Mausolée (see later in this section). Guides take you to the locations painted by van Gogh in the St-Rémy area. You can arrange your own **self-guided tour** of locations painted by van Gogh by picking up a brochure with map from the tourist office.

One of southern France's major classical sites, the **Ruines de Glanum** (avenue Van Gogh; ☎ 04-90-92-23-79) is about a mile south of St-Rémy. The earliest findings from the ruins date to the Iron Age, during the first millennium B.C., when a fortified settlement likely occupied this site. Later the Celts arrived, and the ruins eventually came under Greek influence, turning Glanum into a religious and commercial center. It later fell under Roman rule, which explains the characteristic thermal baths, villas, basilica, and temples. Wander through the ruins of the first-century Roman town, complete with a main street and house foundations. Ongoing excavations began in 1921. Archaeologists believe the site is actually about six or seven times the size of what has been uncovered so far. Many of the findings from Glanum are displayed at the Musée Archéologique (see later in this section). The site is open daily (except January 1, May 1, November 1 and 11, and December 25) April through September 9 a.m. to 7 p.m. and October to March 9 a.m. to noon and 2 to 5 p.m. Admission is 6€ ($7.20) for adults and 4€ ($4.80) for ages 12 to 25; combined admission for Glanum and the Musée Archéologique is 7€ ($8.40).

Other Provence favorites

If you have the time and the interest, you can extend your exploration of Provence with the following sites:

✔ **Apt:** Centrally located in the hilly Lubéron region (54km/33 miles from Avignon), Apt is worth a visit particularly for its Saturday market, which features itinerant musicians in addition to the usual fresh produce, cheeses, and meats from the region. The town's 11th-century cathedral is famous for a relic known as the veil of St. Anne. The nearby Parc Naturel Régional du Lubéron is well suited for hiking and biking.

✔ **Cavaillon:** Home of famous melons, Cavaillon (21km/13 miles from Avignon) is an ancient town that's now an important farming area. Neolithic remains have been found on St-Jacques hill, which overlooks the town and provides panoramic views of the Lubéron region. The two Roman arches that sit on place François-Tourvel represent the Roman roots of the town.

✔ **Châteauneuf-du-Pape:** Grapes for one of the most famous wines of France are grown around the medieval village of Châteauneuf-du-Pape (13km/8 miles from Avignon), which was the summer home of the popes of Avignon. You can see the ruins of the 14th-century Château des Papes, from where you can find panoramic views of the valley. You can taste the famous wine at Père Anselme's cellar and Musée des Outils de Vignerons.

✔ **Grand Canyon du Verdon:** The gorges of the Ardèche in the Rhône Valley (40km/25 miles from Avignon), known as the Grand Canyon of France, is nature at its wildest and most beautiful — 289m (950-ft.) canyons dotted with grottoes and caves. The scenic D290 runs along the rim of the canyon, with spectacular views and plenty of places to park near well-marked footpaths. The north part of the canyon is less touristy than the southern section.

✔ **Les Baux:** Most people take a day-trip to Les Baux (13km/8 miles from Avignon), a pedestrian-only village perched on the white rocks of the Alpilles and capped by castle ruins. You can visit 13th-century castle ruins; troubadour concerts are played in the church at the top of the hill in July and August.

✔ **Orange:** Take in an outdoor concert, perhaps Pavarotti, at the impressive Roman **Théâtre Antique.** For ticket information, call ☎ **04-90-34-24-24.** Mid-July to mid-August, a theater, music, and dance festival is held here. Nearby is a Relais & Châteaux property, **Château de Rochegude** (☎ **04-75-97-21-10;** www.chateau derochegude.com), with tennis courts, a pool, and a gourmet restaurant. Orange is 26km (16 miles) from Avignon.

✔ **Roussillon and Bonnieux:** These two quaint hilltop villages (both about 40km/25 miles from Avignon) are quintessential Provence. Roussillon is well known for the ochre-colored rock surrounding the area, which boasts 17 shades from golden yellow to bright red. Bonnieux still has parts of its ancient ramparts surrounding the town. Both villages offer extraordinary views of the countryside. Near Bonnieux is a well-preserved Roman bridge called the pont Julien, with three arches spanning the Calavon River.

✔ **Tarascon:** This town on an island in the center of the Rhône River (23km/14 miles from Avignon) is worth a visit to see the most impressive Gothic castle in Provence, the 15th-century **Château de Tarascon.** Sitting on the edge of the river, the heavily fortified structure has a medieval apothecary, a collection of tapestries, and a Provençal garden. From the terrace are sweeping views of the surrounding countryside. Tarascon's most famous legend concerns a sea monster that was tamed by St. Martha. The town celebrates an annual festival in honor of the legend on the last weekend in June.

✔ **Toulon:** This bustling town (68km/42 miles from Marseille) is the headquarters of a French naval base. Hills topped with forts surround a large pretty harbor. Near the harbor are traditional markets and the **Cathédrale Ste-Marie-Majeure,** built in the Romanesque style in the 12th century. Two interesting museums are the **Musée de la Marine,** with figureheads and ship models, and the **Musée de Toulon,** with artworks from the 16th century to the present, including a good collection of Provençal and Italian paintings.

✔ **Uzès:** The center of this medieval village (38km/24 miles from Avignon) is the 13th-century castle called **Duché,** with apartments decorated in a Renaissance style. Nearby is the unique **Tour Fenestrelle,** a 42m (138-ft.) round tower with six levels of windows that used to be part of an early Romanesque cathedral. Seventeenth-century playwright Jean Racine lived here for a short time, and the village and countryside influenced him.

Musée Archéologique (rue du Parage; ☎ 04-90-92-64-04), located in the Hôtel de Sade — a beautiful 15th-century town house that belonged to the Sades, an old Provençal family — displays sculptures and objects found at Glanum (see earlier in this section), including pottery, coins, and jewelry. The museum is open year-round Tuesday to Sunday (except January 1, May 1, November 1 and 11, and December 25) 11 a.m. to 5 p.m. Admission is 3€ ($3.60); combined admission for Glanum and the Musée Archéologique is 7€ ($8.40).

Monastère de St-Paul-de-Mausolée (av. Edgar-le-Roy off av. Van Gogh; ☎ 04-90-92-77-00) is the 12th-century monastery where van Gogh checked himself in for mental health reasons from May 1889 to May 1890. He loved the place and painted prolifically there, completing more than 150 paintings, including his famous *Starry Night.* The ancient building still serves as a psychiatric hospital, but you can walk around the chapel and cloisters. It's open daily 9:30 a.m. to 6:30 p.m. Admission is 3.40€ ($4.10) for adults and 2.40€ ($2.90) for students and children.

Occupying a beautiful old mansion, **Centre d'Art Présence van Gogh** (8 rue Estrine; ☎ 04-90-92-34-72) is a small art museum that hosts three or four exhibits per year. The permanent collection is diverse, with works from ancient Egypt and Rome, and paintings from the 17th through 19th centuries. A room devoted to van Gogh has reproductions of some of the works he painted in the region. A few contemporary artists also are represented in the museum. A French film about the artist Poussin is shown a few times daily. Late March to December, it's open Tuesday to Sunday 10:30 a.m. to 12:30 p.m. and 2:30 to 6:30 p.m. Admission is 3.50€ ($4.20) for adults and 2.50€ ($3) for children.

 If you're looking for more Roman ruins, you can check out **Les Antiques,** the name given to two ancient sculptured monuments marking the southern entrance to St-Rémy on avenue Van Gogh across from the entrance to Glanum. **Mausolée des Jules** is a funerary monument from 30 to 20 B.C. and the triumphal arch next to it, the **Arc de Triomphe,** is from around 20 B.C.

Shopping for local treasures

St-Rémy is a center of home decorating, with many antiques shops and fabric stores on the boulevards surrounding the old town and on the old town's narrow streets. You can find a couple of good antiques stores on the outskirts of town: **Au Broc de St-Ouen** (route d'Avignon; ☎ 04-90-73-41-99) has several dealers, and **Portes Anciennes** (route d'Avignon; ☎ 06-09-51-72-62; www.portesanciennes.com) sells a good selection of antiques and flea-market finds.

Pierre Leron-Lesure has devoted his life to making what he calls *sylvistructures* (sculptures from juniper-tree trunks). You can see these unique sculptures in the workshop, on the marble spiral staircase, and in the garden of the **Chimères du Bois** — a gallery in an ancient mansion on rue de Parage across from the archaeological museum (☎ 04-90-92-02-28). Open by appointment only.

St-Rémy is known for having great **markets.** On Wednesday mornings on the streets of the old town, vendors spread out their wares, including spices, olives, fabrics, and crafts. On Saturday morning, a small market is open near the Eglise St-Martin on boulevard Marceau.

Arles: Following in the Steps of van Gogh

Boasting Roman ruins, medieval churches, 18th-century mansions, and tributes to 19th-century artist Vincent van Gogh, **Arles** is rich with history. Its strategic position on the Rhône has long made it popular. Greeks first settled in the area around the sixth century B.C. In the first century B.C., Julius Caesar gave the city prominence in his empire after the citizens of Arles assisted the Romans in their capture of Marseille. It experienced a Golden Age when it was known as *Rome of the Gauls.*

In the early years of Christianity, Arles became a great religious center, but invasions throughout the Middle Ages ravaged the town. It was revived in the 12th century, and you can see a number of impressive Romanesque buildings from that period, including Eglise St-Trophime, which once was a cathedral. In the 17th and 18th centuries, noblemen built mansions in the city center; the mansions surrounding place du

Forum are now elegant hotels. Today, Arles is most famous for being one of the final homes of Impressionist painter Vincent van Gogh. Fans of the tormented artist will find many reminders of him.

Getting there

Trains leave from Paris's Gare de Lyon and arrive at Arles's **Gare SNCF** (avenue Paulin-Talabot), a short walk from the town center. One high-speed direct TGV travels from Paris to Arles each day (4½ hours, 97.40€/ $117 for first class and 88.60€/$106 for second). For other trains, you must change in Avignon. Hourly connections travel between Arles and Avignon (15 minutes, 10.90€/$13) for first class and 7.10€/$8.50 for second), Marseille (one hour, 17.80€/$21 for first class and 11.90€/$14 for second), and Aix-en-Provence (1¾ hours, change in Marseille, 23.50€/ $28 for first class and 15.80€/$19 for second). For rail schedules and information, call ☎ **08-92-35-35-39** (www.sncf.com).

Aéroport International de Nîmes-Garons (☎ **04-66-70-49-49**) is 25km (16 miles) northwest of Arles (five flights per day arrive from Paris). The bus company **Société Ceyte Tourisme Méditerranée (CTM)** runs buses between Arles and the airport. Buses arrive at, and leave from, boulevard Clemenceau near the tourist office (see "Getting around and getting information," later in this chapter). **Aéroport International Marseille/ Provence** is 70km (44 miles) from Arles. From here, you need to rent a car to drive to Arles. The major rental car companies — Hertz, Avis, Europcar, National Citer, and Budget — can all be found at the Marseille Airport.

Arles's **Gare Routière** (bus station) is in front of the train station. For information, call ☎ **04-90-49-38-01.** Arles is on one end of a bus line to Marseille, with stops including Aix-en-Provence (1¾ hours, 12€/$14). Bus service to Avignon also is available (45 minutes, 7.50€/$9). For details, call the **CAT** at ☎ **04-90-93-74-90.**

If you're **driving,** note that D570 and N113 and A54 (between A9 and A7) lead to Arles. From Avignon, take A7 to A54 to N113. Driving time from Avignon to Arles is about 25 minutes. Driving from Paris to Arles takes about seven hours. Arles is 740km (450 miles) from Paris and 35km (22 miles) from Avignon.

Getting around and getting information

All of the major sites in Arles are within walking distance from the center of town. The only site that's inconvenient to walk to is the Musée de l'Arles Antiques (about 15 minutes away); it's an awkward walk past major roadways (with sidewalks).

For a rental car, try **Avis** (avenue Paulin-Talabot; ☎ **04-90-96-82-42**), **Hertz** (boulevard Victor-Hugo; ☎ **04-90-96-75-23**), or **Europcar** (boulevard Victor-Hugo; ☎ **04-90-93-23-24**). You can rent bikes at **Peugeot**

(15 rue du Pont; ☎ **04-90-96-03-77**) for 10€ ($12) per half day and 15€ ($18) per day. For a cab, call **Arles Taxi** at ☎ **04-90-49-69-59** or 04-90-93-31-16.

The **tourist office** is on boulevard des Lices (☎ **04-90-18-41-20**; www. arles.org). April to September, it's open daily 9 a.m. to 7:45 p.m.; October to March hours are Monday to Saturday 9 a.m. to 4:45 p.m. and Sunday 10:30 a.m. to 2:15 p.m. A **small annex** is open at the train station Monday to Saturday 9 a.m. to 1 p.m. The tourist offices can book accommodations for a small fee, and they change money. If you want to check or send e-mail, head to **Point Web** (10 rue du 4 Septembre; ☎ **04-90-18-91-54**), open Monday to Saturday 8:30 a.m. to 7:30 p.m. No food or beverages are served.

Spending the night

You can locate the hotels and restaurants reviewed in the upcoming sections in the "Arles" map.

Hôtel Calendal
$ Arles

Mme Cécile Lespinasse-Jacquemin runs this attractive hotel — the best medium-priced lodging in Arles. Built in the 17th century, the Calendal is centrally located, near the Roman Arènes and next to the Roman Theater. The English-speaking staff lays out the breakfast buffet in the large shady courtyard, which also operates as a tearoom serving light meals. The cheerful reception area includes a fax machine and a computer on which you can check e-mail. The 38 recently renovated rooms are cozy, with Provençal-style décor; some have terraces with seating areas. The front rooms open onto views over the ruins, while the rooms overlooking the garden courtyard offer a quiet setting.

See map p. 359. 5 rue porte de Laure. ☎ *04-90-96-11-89. Fax: 04-90-96-05-84.* www. lecalendal.com. *Parking: 10€ ($12). Rack rates: 45€–99€ ($54–$119) double. Breakfast: 7€ ($8.40). AE, DC, MC, V.*

Hôtel d'Arlatan
$–$$ Arles

The Arlatan, the ancient town house of the comtes d'Arlatan de Beaumont, perfectly combines the antique with the modern. Built in the 15th century and accessible from a narrow alley, this hotel near place du Forum is loaded with charm. Tasteful antique furnishings decorate the public areas and guest rooms. Huge windows ensure that the 47 individually decorated rooms and apartments are filled with light; views are of the roofs of the old city, the garden, or the terrace. In the courtyard is a garden patio where breakfast is served in good weather. Archaeologists found a first-century Roman drain and statue plinth while digging under the hotel. Both items are available for you to admire.

Arles

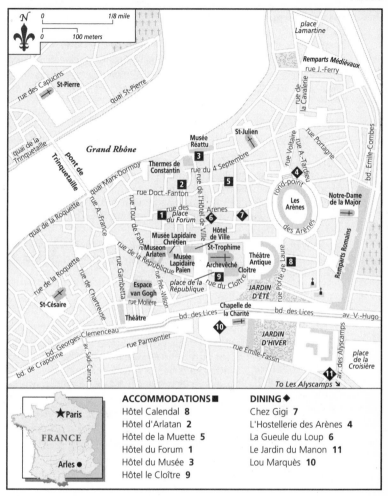

N

0   1/8 mile
0   100 meters

place Lamartine

Remparts Médiévaux
rue J.-Ferry

rue des Capucins
St-Pierre
quai St-Pierre

rue de la Cavalerie

quai de la Trinquetaille
Grand Rhône

pont de Trinquetaille

Musée Réattu
St-Julien

rue Voltaire
rue A.-Tardieu
rue Portagne
bd. Emile-Combes

Thermes de Constantin
rue du 4 Septembre

3

rue Marx-Dormoy

2

rue Doct.-Fanton

5

rond-point

4

Les Arènes

Notre-Dame de la Major

quai de la Roquette
rue A.-France

rue Tour de Fabre

rue des place du Forum
Arenes

1   **6**   **7**

des Arènes

Remparts Romains

Musée Lapidaire Chrétien
Hôtel de Ville

Museon Arlaten
Musée Lapidaire Paien
St-Trophime
Archevêché
Cloître
Théâtre Antique

8

rue de la République
rue Gambetta
rue des Prés-Wilson

9

place de la République
rue du Cloître

rue Porte de Laure

Espace van Gogh
rue Molière
St-Césaire

JARDIN D'ÉTÉ

rue de la Roquette
rue de Chartreuse

Théâtre
bd. des Lices

Chapelle de la Charité
bd. des Lices
av. V.-Hugo

10

bd. Georges-Clemenceau
av. Sadi-Carnot
rue Parmentier

JARDIN D'HIVER

av. des Alyscamps

place de la Croisière

bd. de Craponne
rue Emile-Fassin

11

To Les Alyscamps ↘

FRANCE
★ Paris
Arles ●

ACCOMMODATIONS ■
Hôtel Calendal **8**
Hôtel d'Arlatan **2**
Hôtel de la Muette **5**
Hôtel du Forum **1**
Hôtel du Musée **3**
Hôtel le Cloître **9**

DINING ◆
Chez Gigi **7**
L'Hostellerie des Arènes **4**
La Gueule du Loup **6**
Le Jardin du Manon **11**
Lou Marquès **10**

See map p. 359. 26 rue Sauvage. ☎ *04-90-93-56-66. Fax: 04-90-49-68-45.* www.hotel-arlatan.fr. *Parking: 11€–12.50€ ($13–$15). Rack rates: 97€–153€ ($116–$184) double; 177€–243€ ($212–$292) suite. Breakfast: 10.50€ ($13). AE, MC, V.*

Hôtel de la Muette
$ Arles

The pleasant staff and good location make the Muette a solid bargain in the medieval section of town, a few minutes' walk from the Arènes. This ancient hotel has sections built in the 12th and the 15th centuries. Access to the rooms is up a steep, narrow, winding stone stairway. The 18 rooms are on the small side, but they're brightened by Provençal fabrics on the bedspreads and curtains. Fans help to alleviate the summer heat. Breakfast is served on the terrace in front of the hotel.

See map p. 359. 15 rue des Suisses. ☎ *04-90-96-15-39. Fax: 04-90-49-73-16.* www. hotel-muette.com. *Parking: 7€ ($8.40) in public garage across from the hotel. Rack rates: 54€–65€ ($65–$78) double. Breakfast: 6€ ($7.20). AE, DC, MC, V.*

Hôtel du Forum
$–$$ Arles

Although this is one of Arles's most elegant hotels (right on the central square), the reasonable rates make it a great value. The 38 spacious and attractive rooms are decorated with antiques and luxurious fabrics. The windows are soundproof, but if you like it extra quiet, request a room in the rear. The commons rooms are comfortable. The hotel also has a bar and a heated pool.

See map p. 359. 10 place du Forum. ☎ *04-90-93-48-95. Fax: 04-90-93-90-00.* www. hotelduforum.com. *Parking: 8€ ($9.60). Rack rates: 70€–125€ ($84–$150) double. Breakfast: 8€ ($9.60). AE, DC, MC, V.*

Hôtel du Musée
$ Arles

You'll love the atmosphere of this hotel located in a 16th-century mansion on a tranquil street across from the Musée Réattu. The quiet location guarantees a good night's sleep, and the 28 rooms feature Provençal décor and comfortable beds. Breakfast is served on the garden patio behind the building.

See map p. 359. 11 rue du Grand Prieuré. ☎ *04-90-93-88-88. Fax: 04-90-49-98-15.* www.hoteldumusee.com.fr. *Parking: 7€ ($8.40). Rack rates: 48€–78€ ($58–$94) double. Breakfast: 7€ ($8.40). AE, DC, MC, V. Closed Jan–mid-Feb.*

Hôtel le Cloître
$ Arles

A welcoming English-speaking couple runs this cozy hotel. It's difficult to find — tucked away on a steep side street between the Roman Theater and a medieval cloister. One side of the hotel is held up by 13th-century vaults from the adjacent cloister. The rooms in the back of the hotel have views of the cloister garden, while the other units offer views of the Romanesque Eglise St-Trophime. The 30 accommodations boast antique details such as beamed ceilings and stone walls.

See map p. 359. 16 rue du Cloître. ☎ *04-90-96-29-50. Fax: 04-90-96-02-88.* www.hotel cloitre.com. *Rack rates: 45€–65€ ($54–$78) double. Breakfast: 5.75€ ($6.90). AE, MC, V. Parking 5€ ($6). Closed Nov 1–mid-Mar.*

Dining locally

If you're looking for a light meal, head to **place du Forum,** where you can find several cafes with tables spilling into the square (including the cafe made famous by van Gogh in his *Café at Night, Place du Forum*).

Chez Gigi
$ **Arles** PROVENÇAL

A few steps from the Arènes, this popular neighborhood restaurant offers home-cooking at reasonable prices. The setting is casual, with families of several generations squeezed next to young dating couples. The menu is heavy on regional specialties, using Provençal herbs, and prepared with care. Noteworthy dishes are the *soupe des poissons* (fish soup served with crusty breads and cheese) and the authentic *dorade provençal* (an ocean fish grilled with Provençal herbs). You can sample a lovely *crème brûlée* for dessert.

See map p. 359. 49 rue des Arènes. ☎ *04-90-96-68-59. Reservations recommended. Main courses: 8.50€–14.50€ ($10–$17). MC, V. Open: Tues–Sun 7–11 p.m.*

La Gueule du Loup
$$ **Arles** FRENCH/PROVENÇAL

Named after its founder, who, according to local legend, grew to resemble a wolf as he aged, this cozy, well-managed restaurant occupies a stone-fronted antique house in the historic core of Arles, near the ancient Roman arena. Today it's owned by members of the Allard family, who prepare serious gourmet-style French food that's more elaborate than the cuisine at many competitors. The best examples include hearty filet of bull braised in red wine, monkfish in saffron sauce, roasted cod with green and sweet red peppers in saffron sauce, and superb duckling cooked in duck fat and served with flap mushrooms. Reservations are important — the cozy room seats only 30.

See map p. 359. 39 rue des Arènes. ☎ *04-90-96-96-69. Reservations recommended. Main courses: 12€–22€ ($14–$26); prie fixe: 26€ ($31). MC, V. Easter–Oct Tues–Sat noon to 2:30 p.m., Mon–Sat 7–9:30 p.m., Nov–Easter noon to 2:30 p.m. and 7–9:30 p.m.*

Le Jardin du Manon
$–$$$ **Arles** PROVENÇAL

A short walk from the old town center, this traditional restaurant with garden seating provides solid fine dining in an attractive setting filled with locals. The menu features Provençal specialties served with the freshest ingredients. The best main course is the *millefeuille de brousse et tomate confit basilic* (pastry of goat's cheese and tomato-basil confit). As a meat dish, the chef recommends *suprême de poulet farci à la tapenade, roti à la broche* (guinea fowl breast stuffed with olive paste and spit roasted). For dessert, try the special *croustade de poire amande* (pear-and-almond pastry).

See map p. 359. 14 av. des Alyscamps. ☎ *04-90-93-38-68. Reservations not necessary. Main courses: 14€–22€ ($17–$26); prix fixe: 19€–40€ ($23–$48). AE, MC, V. Open: Thurs–Tues noon to 1:45 p.m. and 7–9:45 p.m. Closed Feb.*

L'Hostellerie des Arènes
$–$$ Arles PROVENÇAL

Here you can dine alfresco across from the majestic Roman Amphitheater. The simple Provençal fare is served by friendly English-speaking waiters, and the prices are low considering the quality. Locals know about the good value here, so the small restaurant frequently needs to turn diners away as the night wears on. Recommended are the *salade Arlesienne,* with salmon, pinenuts, cucumbers, and olives, and the *superbe bouillabaisse,* fish-and-shellfish stew. The dishes are presented with a flourish and sides like ratatouille. For dessert, try the *crème caramel.*

See map p. 359. 62 rue du Refuge. ☎ *04-90-96-13-05. Reservations not necessary. Main courses: 10€–17.50€ ($12–$21); prix fixe: 14.50€–17.50€ ($17–$21). MC, V. Open: Wed–Mon noon to 2 p.m. and 7–9 p.m.*

Lou Marquès
$$$–$$$$ Arles PROVENÇAL

Lou Marquès, part of a Relais & Châteaux hotel, has the highest reputation in town for its quality cuisine. Seating is in the formal dining room or on the terrace. The cuisine features creative twists on Provençal specialties. A first course could be *queues de langoustine en salade vinaigrette d'agrumes et basilic* (crustacean and a salad with citrus-and-basil vinaigrette) or *risotto de homard aux truffes* (lobster risotto with truffles). As a main course, try *pavé de loup en barigoule d'artichaut et à la sauge* (a thick slice of wolf fish with sage-stuffed artichokes) or *filet mignon de veau et ragoût fin de cèpes et salsifis* (veal with a stew of mushrooms and oyster plant). For dessert, you can't go wrong with *biscuit glacé au miel de lavande* (a small cake glazed with lavender honey).

See map p. 359. At the Hôtel Jules-César, 9 bd. des Lices. ☎ *04-90-52-52-52.* www. hotel-julescesar.fr. *Reservations recommended. Main courses: 30€–90€ ($36–$108); prix fixe: 20€–27€ ($24–$32) lunch, 37€–75€ ($44–$90) dinner. AE, DC, MC, V. Open: Daily noon to 1:30 p.m. and 7:30–9:30 p.m. Closed Nov–Dec.*

Exploring the town

The historic center of Arles is **place de la République,** with a monumental obelisk towering over a fountain. Facing the fountain are the ornate 17th-century **Hôtel de Ville,** the town hall, and the Romanesque **Eglise St-Trophime.** A block east are the first-century ruins of the **Théâtre Antique** and, close by, the even more impressive first-century **Amphithéâtre** (also called the **Arènes**), where bullfights are held. All that remains of the old Roman forum in **place du Forum** are a couple of columns (part of the Hôtel Nord-Pinus), but the area is now a pretty square filled with cafes and surrounded by deluxe hotels.

In search of van Gogh

In February 1888, Dutch artist Vincent van Gogh (1853–1890) took the train to Arles to escape dreary Paris. Although he arrived to find snow and ice, he decided to stay. That fall, his friend and fellow artist Paul Gauguin visited, but the two had a terrible falling out, and Gauguin left. A drunken van Gogh then cut off his own left earlobe and presented it to a prostitute at a nearby brothel. The townspeople were concerned about this "lunatic from the North," so van Gogh allowed himself to be hospitalized at the Hôtel Dieu in Arles. He continued to paint prolifically but soon transferred to a rest home in St-Rémy. In July 1890, van Gogh attempted suicide and died two days later. However, during those 18 months in Arles, he produced more than 200 paintings and more than 100 drawings and watercolors, including some of his most famous works *(The Yellow House, The Bedroom at Arles, Vincent's Chair, The Night Café,* and *Café at Night, Place du Forum).* He also wrote hundreds of letters.

Though you won't find any van Gogh paintings in Arles, fans of the artist enjoy seeing some of the sites he painted and some of the tributes to him. A statue of the artist with one ear is in the **Jardin d'Eté,** just south of the Théâtre Antique. The Hôtel Dieu where van Gogh was institutionalized is now a cultural center called the **Espace Van Gogh** (place Félix-Rey; ☎ **04-90-49-39-39**). In this center, you can admire the flower-filled cloister he painted. The building also houses a library and an art gallery and shows free films. Admission is free to the Espace Van Gogh, which is open Tuesday 12:30 to 7 p.m., Wednesday and Saturday 10 a.m. to 12:30 p.m. and 2 to 5 p.m., and Friday 12:30 to 6 p.m. True van Gogh fans should visit **Les Alyscamps,** the Roman cemetery that the artist painted several times. The **cafe** made famous in the painting *Café at Night* is in the southeast corner of place du Forum. Perhaps the most rewarding site for van Gogh buffs is the **Fondation Van Gogh** next to the Arènes, displaying homages to van Gogh by artists such as David Hockney, Jasper Johns, and Roy Lichtenstein (see later in the chapter for more details).

Easter to October, the **Petit Train d'Arles** (☎ **04-93-41-31-09**) tours the town in 35 minutes at a cost of 6€ ($7.20) for adults and 4€ ($4.80) for children ages 3 to 10. The train leaves from the Arènes entrance daily 10 a.m. to noon and 2 to 7 p.m.

If you plan to see a lot of sights, you can save money by purchasing a special ticket at the first museum you visit or at the tourist office. The **Villet Global** pass (13.50€/$16 for adults, 12€/$14 for students and children younger than 18) gets you into the Amphithéâtre, Théâtre Antique, Cryptoportique, Thermes de Constantin, St-Trophime, Les Alyscamps, Musée Reattu, Musée de l'Arles Antique, and Musée Arlatan.

Many of the sights in Arles (Amphithéâtre, Théâtre Antique, Thermes de Constantin, Cryptoportique, St-Trophime, Les Alyscamps, and Musée Réattu) follow these daily hours: December to January 10 a.m. to noon and 2 to 4:30 p.m., February 10 a.m. to noon and 2 to 5 p.m., March 9 a.m. to 12:30 p.m. and 2 to 5:30 p.m., April to mid-June and late September

9 a.m. to 12:30 p.m. and 2 to 7 p.m., late June to mid-September 9 a.m to 7 p.m., October 10 a.m. to 12:30 p.m. and 2 to 5:30 p.m., and November 10 a.m. to 12:30 p.m. and 2 to 5 p.m. These sights also share the same admission: 4€ ($4.80) for adults and 3€ ($3.60) for students and children under 18.

The A.D. 80 **Amphithéâtre (Arènes)** (rond-pont des Arènes; ☎ 04-90-49-36-86) is Arles's most dramatic Roman ruin. The space was used in Roman times for brutal gladiator-type sporting events (using wild animals). In the Middle Ages, the Arènes became a fortress and later a squatters' camp. Though the steps and seats have been ravaged by time, the theater, built for 20,000 spectators, can still hold about half of its original capacity. Today, the city uses the space to host the Arles version of a bullfight (which is not bloody like the Spanish version) during Les Dix Jours du Toro from mid- to late April and the Fêtes d'Arles in early July and mid- to late September. (Occasionally, Spanish-style bullfights take place during these festivals. If you don't want to see the occasional Spanish-style bullfights where the bull is killed, avoid events with the description "*mise-à-mort.*") The most popular bullfighting event in Arles is more of a pageant-type spectacle in which bulls raised in the nearby Camargue region are taunted but not harmed. In this event, called a *cocarde,* the bull is outfitted with colorful ribbons tied to its horns, and the *razeteurs* are the men in the ring who try to remove the ribbons. For details on the events held here, call ☎ 04-90-96-03-70. See earlier in this section for hours and admission.

Fans of van Gogh and contemporary art may enjoy the **Fondation Van Gogh** (24 bis rond-pont des Arènes; ☎ 04-90-49-94-04; www.fondation vangogh-arles.org). The homages to van Gogh are conceived in paintings, sculptures, photos, mixed media, letters, and musical scores — all loaded with van Gogh colors and motifs, such as ragged shoes, cane chairs, sunflowers, cypresses, and ears. Artists represented include Alex Katz, Francis Bacon, Larry Rivers, David Hockney, Jasper Johns, Robert Motherwell, and Roy Lichtenstein. The works contemplate his sorrow and solitude and pay tribute to his energy and his vision's intensity. English translations are available throughout. The museum is open daily late March to November 10:30 a.m. to 8 p.m. and December to mid-March 11 a.m. to 5 p.m. Admission is 7€ ($8.40) for adults and 5€ ($6) for students and children.

When the **Théâtre Antique** (rue de la Calade; ☎ 04-90-49-36-25) was built in the first century B.C., it could hold 10,000 spectators. Alas, all that remains are lots of ancient rubble and two sad-looking Corinthian columns nicknamed the *Deux Veuves* (two widows). For hundreds of years, beginning in the fifth century, the theater was used as a rock quarry, helping to build churches, homes, and fortifications. But the space is now back to its original use as an open-air theater: July brings a performing-arts festival and a costume festival called the Festival of the Queen of Arles. See earlier in this section for hours and admission.

Built from the 12th through the 14th centuries, **Eglise et le Cloitre St-Trophime** (place de la République; ☎ 04-90-49-36-36), with its elaborately carved facade, is one of the most beautiful Romanesque churches in Provence. A famous Last Judgment image is sculpted above the imposing brick-red doors. The most beautiful part of the church is the cloister, with evocative stone carvings and two Romanesque and two Gothic galleries. See earlier in this section for hours and admission.

The entire family may enjoy the comprehensive **Museon Arlaten** (29 rue de la République; ☎ 04-90-93-58-11), a museum of Provençal culture (the name is in the Provençal language) founded in 1896 by Nobel Prize–winner Frédéric Mistral. The large museum, staffed by costumed docents, contains clothing, furniture, toys, ironworks, guns, farm equipment, photos, paintings, pottery, musical instruments, and model ships. Seek out the two 19th-century iron bikes *(velocipedes)* or the thrones for Napoléon III and his empress, Eugénie (circa 1860). The Dodekatheion, the ruins and statuary of a Roman temple, are in the central courtyard. The museum is open daily (except January 1, May 1, November 1, and December 25) June through August 9:30 a.m. to 1 p.m. and 2 to 6:30 p.m.; April, May, and September Tuesday to Sunday 9:30 a.m. to 12:30 p.m. and 2 to 6 p.m.; and October through March Tuesday to Sunday 9:30 a.m. to 12:30 p.m. and 2 to 5 p.m. Admission is 4€ ($4.80) for adults and 3€ ($3.60) for students and children younger than 18.

You have a long, dusty walk on major roadways and past a skateboard park to get to the **Musée de l'Arles Antiques** (avenue de la 1ère Division Française Libre; ☎ 04-90-18-88-88), located about half a mile from town, but it's well worth it. This modern air-conditioned museum contains the extraordinary archaeological finds of Arles from prehistory to the sixth century, with a large collection of sculptures, sarcophagi (elaborate tombs), and amphores (double-handled jars), in addition to scaled models of all of Arles's Roman monuments, including the extraordinary circus (currently being excavated next door) where chariot races were held. Catwalks hover over ancient mosaics so that you can see them in their entirety. The museum is open daily (except January 1, May 1, November 1, and December 25): April to October 9 a.m. to 7 p.m. and November 2 to March 10 a.m. to 5 p.m. Admission is 5.50€ ($6.60) for adults and 4€ ($4.80) for students and children younger than 18.

Les Alyscamps (avenue des Alyscamps; ☎ 04-90-93-27-53), an ancient necropolis, is really a unique site and well worth the ten-minute walk southeast of the city center. The area has been an inspiration to many artists, including van Gogh, who described Les Alyscamps in a letter to his brother, Theo; the text is reproduced at the site. Van Gogh and Gauguin both painted Les Alyscamps several times. Alyscamps was used as both a Roman burial site and an early Christian cemetery from the 4th through 12th centuries. By the Middle Ages, 17 churches were here; now all that remains are the ruins of one Romanesque chapel — St-Honorat. During the Renaissance, royals, nobles, and even monks were in the habit of giving away the most beautifully sculpted sarcophogi as gifts, so only the plainest of stone coffins line this sacred path. See earlier in this section for hours and admission.

In the 15th-century priory of St. Gilles (Knights of Malta), you can find the **Musée Réattu** (10 rue du Grand-Prieuré; ☎ 04-90-96-37-68), which features the paintings of local artist Jacques Réattu, drawings by Picasso, and a collection of 16th-century Flemish tapestries. The museum also houses Henri Rousseau drawings of the region (including images of the Arles arena), a collection of paintings by 19th- and 20th-century artists, and temporary exhibits of photography. See earlier in this section for hours and admission.

If you haven't had your fill of Roman ruins, here are two more: the **Thermes de Constantin** and the **Cryptoportique.** The Thermes de Constantin (rue Dominique-Maïsto next to the Rhône River) are the ruins of a huge bathhouse and are all that remains of the Emperor Constantine's fourth-century palace. The Cryptoportique (next to the Arlaten Museum) are double underground galleries in the shape of a U dating from 30 to 20 B.C. See earlier in this section for hours and admission.

Shopping for local treasures

A colorful **market** takes place Wednesdays 7:30 a.m. to 12:30 p.m. on boulevard Emile-Combes and Saturdays 7:30 a.m. to 12:30 p.m. on boulevard des Lices. For Provençal fabrics and gifts, head to **Les Olivades** (2 rue Jean-Jaurès; ☎ 04-90-96-22-17), and **Souleiado** (4 bd. des Lices; ☎ 04-90-96-37-55).

Aix-en-Provence and the Cours Mirabeau

Writers and artists drawn to **Aix-en-Provence** have long heralded this exquisite place, calling it the "Queen of Sweet Provence" and the "Athens of Southern France." This cosmopolitan city, founded in 122 B.C., is distinguished by its sculptured fountains, its golden-hued mansions, its regal cours Mirabeau, and the winding streets of the old town. Its cafes are packed with students, and its markets overflow with colorful produce. These qualities are quintessentially Aix (pronounced simply as "ex"). It's a town rich with discoveries — every corner you turn, you see an intriguing shop, a new restaurant, and a gurgling fountain. Aix's favorite painter is Paul Cézanne, who loved to paint the countryside around Aix and whose last studio is just outside town.

Aix is also a major university town (the Université Aix-Marseille, founded in the 15th century) and home to the famous **Festival d'Aix-en-Provence** (☎ 04-42-17-34-00; www.festival-aix.com), a deluxe fête in July, featuring classical music, opera, and ballet. Ancillary festivals and many street musicians fill the town from late June to early August, so summer is a fun time here. Because Aix doesn't have the "must see" sights of some other towns, you can relax into Provence time here and spend a day or two wandering this lovely town that seems kissed by the sun.

Getting there

Two viable railway stations service Aix: the older, somewhat outmoded station (Aix-Centre-Ville) in the heart of town, and a newer one, specifically designed for the TGV trains, in Vitroll, about 14km (9 miles) to the west. Know in advance that if you're coming from relatively long distances, including Paris, you'll almost invariably arrive at Vitroll, from which a bus — marked simply "Société Comett" — departs every 20 minutes for the short ride, priced at 3.60€ ($4.30) each way, to the center of Aix. Most trains arriving at Aix-Centre-Ville originate in other nearby towns of Provence, including Marseille. Most of the TGV trains from Paris travel directly from the Gare de Lyon to Aix, making a stop, but no change of equipment, in Avignon. Other (non-TGV) trains from Paris may or may not make several stops en route, including, among others, in Marseille. Transit time from Paris, depending on the route and the train, takes between three and five hours, and costs around 86€ ($103) each way.

Gare Routière (bus station), on avenue de l'Europe, is the place to catch buses to Marseille (40 minutes, 4.30€/$5.15), Arles (1 hour and 50 minutes, 11.50€/$14), Vitroll (20 minutes, 5.10€/$6.10), and Avignon (1 hour, 13€/$16). For information, call ☎ **04-42-91-26-80.** The office is open year-round Monday to Saturday 7:30 a.m. to 7:30 p.m. and Sunday 7:30 a.m. to noon and 1:30 to 6 p.m.

If **driving** to Aix from Avignon or other points north, take A7 south to RN7 and follow it into town. From Marseille or other points to the south, follow A51 north into town.

Getting around and getting information

Aix is a great town for strolling, so be sure to give yourself some free time. Of special interest are the medieval walkways, such as **passage Agard** off the east end of the cours Mirabeau.

You can rent a car at **National Citer** (42 av. Victor Hugo; ☎ **04-42-93-07-85**), **Budget** (16 av. des Belges; ☎ **04-42-38-37-36**), and **Avis** (11 cours Gambetta; ☎ **04-42-21-64-16**). For a bike rental, try **Cycles Zammit** (27 rue Mignet; ☎ **04-42-23-19-53**), where rentals cost 12.20€ ($15) per day. For a taxi, call **Taxi Radio** at ☎ **04-42-27-71-11.**

The **tourist office** (2 place du Général-de-Gaulle; ☎ **04-42-16-11-61;** Fax: 04-42-16-11-62; www.aixenprovencetourism.com) is open Monday to Saturday 8:30 a.m. to 7 p.m. and Sunday and holidays 10 a.m. to 1 p.m. and 2 to 6 p.m. To check on or send e-mail, head to **Hub Lot Cybercafe** (15–27 rue Paul-Bert; ☎ **04-42-21-37-31**), which also serves cafe fare. It's open daily 9 a.m. to 11 p.m.

Spending the night

Hotel and restaurant listings in these two sections are shown in the nearby "Aix-en-Provence" map.

Grand Hôtel Nègre Coste
$–$$ Cours Mirabeau

Staying at this grand 18th-century hotel on the cours Mirabeau puts you in the center of the action, but the soundproof windows mean you don't have to stay up all night — unless you want to. Nègre Coste has long been an important address and has played host to some important guests, including royalty and celebrities. The formal public rooms include the Provençal Salon and Salon Louis XV, in addition to a gleaming bar. All 37 spacious guest rooms are furnished with antiques and boast a historic flavor, with touches such as beamed ceilings and attractive moldings. Rooms look out on the busy and beautiful central boulevard or the narrow streets of the old town.

See map p. 369. 33 cours Mirabeau. ☎ **04-42-27-74-22.** *Fax: 04-42-26-80-93.* www. hotelnegrecoste.com. *Parking: 10€ ($12). Rack rates: 70€–140€ ($84–$168) double. Breakfast: 8€ ($9.60). AE, DC, MC, V.*

Hôtel Cardinal
$ Mazarin

Natalie Bernard has owned this 18th-century townhouse for years, and every year she renovates and restores several of the 29 units (23 rooms, 6 suites). The restored rooms tend to be more exactingly decorated, but all of the units, with fireplaces and cozy sitting areas, have a certain bohemian charm and are larger than those in comparable hotels. The suites contain kitchenettes. The Cardinal, across from the house where writer M. F. K. Fisher lived in the 1950s, has been an address for writers and artists for decades. The windows give you a view of this pretty residential area, where the aristocracy of Aix built their mansions. Just a few blocks away is the cours Mirabeau.

See map p. 369. 24 rue Cardinale. ☎ **04-42-38-32-30.** *Fax: 04-42-26-39-05. Rack rates: 65€ ($78) double; 80€–100€ ($96–$120) suite. Breakfast: 8€ ($9.60). MC, V.*

Hôtel des Augustins
$–$$$ Vieil Aix

Because of its historic atmosphere (it occupies a 15th-century convent that once hosted Martin Luther), central location, and sound management, this hotel is a pricey favorite in Aix. It has been a hotel since 1892, although it was fully restored in 1984. The careful restoration kept many historic details, such as the stone walls and vaulting, stained glass, and wood paneling. The 29 rooms are spacious and soundproof — crucial for this busy part of town — and come with minibars; some have Jacuzzis and terraces. The décor is Provençal, with colorful bedspreads, curtains, and wallpapers. The hotel offers views of the rooftops of Aix and the famous cours Mirabeau.

See map p. 369. 3 rue de la Masse (at the corner of cours Mirabeau). ☎ **04-42-27-28-59.** *Fax: 04-42-26-74-87.* www.hotel-augustins.com. *Rack rates: 95€–230€ ($114–$276) double. Breakfast: 8€ ($9.60). MC, V.*

Aix-en-Provence

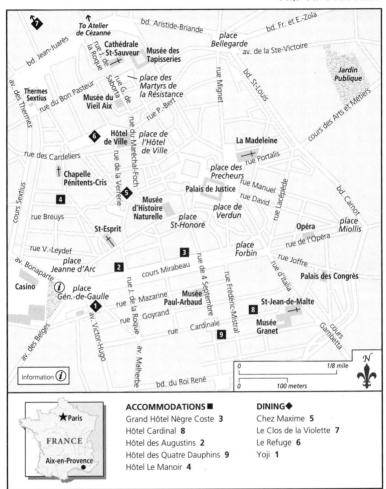

ACCOMMODATIONS ■
Grand Hôtel Nègre Coste **3**
Hôtel Cardinal **8**
Hôtel des Augustins **2**
Hôtel des Quatre Dauphins **9**
Hôtel Le Manoir **4**

DINING◆
Chez Maxime **5**
Le Clos de la Violette **7**
Le Refuge **6**
Yoji **1**

Hôtel des Quatre Dauphins
$ **Mazarin**

A charming small hotel in the quiet residential Mazarin district, Quatre
Dauphins is a solid choice. This hotel is named after one of Aix's most
memorable fountains, located nearby, which has water cascading from the
mouths of four finely carved dolphins. Set on a quiet street, the hotel is a
short walk from the train station and cours Mirabeau (the main boulevard). The 13 rooms, some on the small side, are decorated in a contemporary style with Provençal fabrics; all have minibars.

See map p. 369. 54 rue Roux-Alphéran. ☎ 04-42-38-16-39. Fax: 04-42-38-60-19. Rack rates: 60€–78€ ($72–$94) double. Breakfast: 9€ ($11). MC, V.

Hôtel Le Manoir
$ Vieil Aix

This hotel is a real value considering you're staying in a 14th-century cloister on a quiet street in the heart of the old town, near rue Tanneurs — a street lined with a large number of inexpensive restaurants. The 40 rooms are attractive and decorated with contemporary or antique furniture. The rooms have high ceilings (some with beams); ancient vaulting is evident throughout the hotel. Most accommodations look out on the quiet interior garden courtyard. The staff is exceedingly friendly.

See map p. 369. 8 rue d'Entrecasteaux. ☎ 04-42-26-27-20. Fax: 04-42-27-17-97. www.hotelmanoir.com. Free parking. Rack rates: 54€–82€ ($65–$98) double. Breakfast: 7€ ($8.40). AE, DC, MC, V.

Dining locally

Aix is a great restaurant town, with lots of ethnic choices — along with the typical mouth-watering Provençal cuisine. On **place Ramus** in the old town, you can find Cuban, Thai, Japanese, Senegalese, and Chinese restaurants. Other good restaurant streets are **rue de la Verrerie** and **rue des Tanneurs.** Aix is also an idyllic town for cafe-lingering. The king of all cafes is **Les Deux Garçons** (53 cours Mirabeau; ☎ 04-42-26-00-51). You can sit outside and people-watch along the avenue, but don't forget to check out the *beaux-arts* interior of this classic establishment.

Chez Maxime
$–$$ Vieil Aix PROVENÇAL

This long-running hit with locals and visitors alike is set on bustling place Ramus. Most people sit on the square, but the inside is attractive and cozy — especially the tables by the front windows. This restaurant specializes in meats, thickly sliced and prepared with Provençal herbs. A popular main course is *terrine de légumes rôti au provençal* (a vegetable terrine that comes with tapenade, an olive paste that's a regional specialty). The best main courses are the *pavé d'agneau aux herbes provençal* (lamb with fresh herbs) and *pavé de boeuf à la fondue de foie gras et au cêpes* (beef served with foie gras and white mushrooms). For dessert, look no further than the *parfait glacé au fruit confit* (ice cream parfait with fruit).

See map p. 369. 12 place Ramus (a couple blocks north of cours Mirabeau). ☎ 04-42-26-28-51. Reservations recommended. Main courses: 9.70€ ($12); prix fixe: 14.90€ ($18) lunch, 29€ ($35) dinner. AE, MC, V. Open: Tues–Sat noon to 2 p.m.; Mon–Sat 7–10 p.m. Closed mid- to late Jan.

Le Clos de la Violette
$$$$ **Northern Aix   PROVENÇAL**

This restaurant, located on the northern edge of town, is Aix's best. To get here from the center of town, you can take a long walk or a short taxi ride. In this cozy yet elegant setting, you can sample innovative cuisine. The menu changes depending on the season and best market fare. Two of the chef's favorites are the *queues de langoustines rôti ravioli fourré au corail* (roast langoustine tails with ravioli stuffed with shellfish eggsack) and *carré d'agneau rôti en croûte au chevre frais et champignons* (roast rack of lamb with a pastry of goat cheese and mushrooms). For dessert, you may choose a platter of cookies such as the *gros calissons d'Aix* (large almond-paste cookies) or *biscuit friable aux noisettes et brousse battue à la vanille, aux longs copeaux de chocolat* (vanilla-nut cookies with chocolate shavings). The complete wine list boasts unusual and special selections from exclusive small wineries in the region.

See map p. 369. 10 av. de la Violette. ☎ *04-42-23-30-71. Reservations necessary. Main courses: 42€–61€ ($50–$73); prix fixe: 54€ ($65) lunch, 120€ ($144) tasting menu. AE, MC, V. Open: April–Oct Mon 7:30–9:30 p.m., Tues–Sat noon to 1:30 p.m. and 7:30–9:30 p.m.; Nov–Mar Tues–Sat noon to 1:30 p.m. and 7:30–9:30 p.m. Closed late Dec–early Jan, Feb, and early Aug.*

Le Refuge
$–$$ **Vieil Aix   SMOKED MEAT AND FISH**

Although Le Refuge is a specialized place, if you like smoked salmon and/or smoked duck, you'll be in heaven. Most of the seating is on hip place des Cardeurs, and the setting inside the tiny restaurant is après-ski, with snowshoes hanging on the wood-paneled walls. As the cheerful waiter explained to me, "We are in a mountain cabin." Whatever. The menu is very limited, but what they do, they do well. You choose from prix fixe menus that include salad, main course, dessert, and a glass of wine. Basically, you have a choice among salmon, lobster, and duck, mostly smoked. The duck also comes barbecued, and there's homemade foie gras, too. The meals are served with fries, salad, creamy homemade coleslaw, and a cup of hot mulled wine. Jazz and blues play on the tape box, and the atmosphere is very relaxed and fun.

See map p. 369. 13 place des Cardeurs. ☎ *04-42-96-17-23. Reservations recommended. Main courses: 15€–30€ ($18–$36). MC, V. Open: Tues–Sat noon to 2 p.m. and 7:30–11:30 p.m;, July–Aug daily 7:30-11:30 p.m.*

Yoji
$$–$$$ **south of Cours Mirabeau   JAPANESE**

Yoji is the best Japanese restaurant in Aix — an excellent alternative for those looking to escape from French cuisine for a night. Although the restaurant is on busy avenue Victor-Hugo, the dining room has a calm aura, with a sleek décor and low lighting. It serves authentic Japanese and Korean cuisines, including enticing combinations of sushi and sashimi that are reasonably priced.

See map p. 369. 7 av. Victor-Hugo. ☎ 04-42-38-48-76. Reservations recommended. Main courses: 17€–25€ ($20–$30); prix fixe: 20€–33€ ($24–$40). AE, MC, V. Open: Tues–Sun noon to 2 p.m. and 7–11 p.m.

Exploring the town

The recently renovated **cours Mirabeau,** a gorgeous wide boulevard lined with lush 150-year-old plane trees, is the main intersection of town. Cafes, shops, and hotels line the north side of the street, while 18th-century mansions stand on the south side. The boulevard is bookended by two huge fountains. The 1860 **Fontaine de la Rotonde,** on the west end of the street, has statues representing Justice (facing cours Mirabeau), Agriculture (facing Marseille), and Fine Arts (facing Avignon). On the east end of the street, the 19th-century **Fontaine du Roi René** shows the medieval King René (who brought the Muscat grape to Provence) with a bunch of grapes in his hand. Also on the cours Mirabeau are the 1691 **Fontaine des Neuf Canons,** displaying nine cannons, and the 1734 **Fontaine d'Eau Chaude,** said to be fed by thermal sources.

The neighborhood south of the cours Mirabeau is the **quartier Mazarin,** designed in the 17th century with streets in a grid pattern. It's where the aristocracy of Aix lived. Walk down rue 4 Septembre to see **place des Quatre Dauphins,** with its whimsical dolphin fountain. On the way, you pass the **Musée Paul-Arbaud,** displaying *faïence.* A left at the fountain down rue Cardinale brings you to the **Eglise St-Jean-de-Malte,** a fortified 12th-century Gothic church, and the **Musée Granet,** with works by Cézanne and other artists upstairs, and Roman excavations, including mosaics and statuary, in the basement. North of cours Mirabeau is **Vieil Aix,** the old town, with its maze of semipedestrian streets and large squares. Take spooky passage Agard at the east end of cours Mirabeau to reach the 19th-century **Palais de Justice** on **place de Verdun,** where the flea market is held three times a week. Two blocks north and one block west is the 18th-century **Ancienne Halle aux Grains** (the old Corn Exchange, now a post office) on **place Richelme,** where a fruit-and-vegetable market is open every morning on the square. Two blocks up rue Gaston de la Saporta is the **Musée du Vieil Aix,** displaying a history of the town. **Place de l'Archevêché** is where you find the 17th-century **Palais de l'Archevêché,** a grand residence where the prestigious music festival called Festival International d'Art Lyrique (☎ 04-42-17-34-00; www.festival-aix.com) is held every year in July. On the first floor of the palace is a **Musée des Tapisseries** displaying beautiful tapestries. Just beyond is the **Cathédrale St-Sauveur,** unique because it contains architectural styles from the 5th through 17th centuries.

The tourist office runs a **free two-hour walking tour** (in English) of the city from July to October on Wednesdays at 10 a.m. and on Sundays and public holidays at 9:30 a.m. for 8€ ($9.60). From May to October, walking tours of Aix are on Saturdays at 10 a.m. Theme tours of Aix (literature, architecture, Cézanne, Zola, fountains, history) are given on other days depending on the time of year. Check with the tourist office at ☎ 04-42-16-11-61. The office also organizes full-day and half-day tours of the region costing 26€ to 48€ ($31–$58). Among the tours are Lavender Roads, Marseille, Les Baux and St-Rémy, Arles, and Cassis and its deep rocky inlets.

If you want to follow in the footsteps of painter Paul Cézanne, who was born and who died in Aix, walk along the **Circuit de Cézanne;** the sidewalk markers bearing his name begin at the tourist office. The walk highlights the places Cézanne used to frequent, the school where he studied, images he painted, and the shop where his father worked. The tourist office has a free accompanying brochure called "In the Footsteps of Paul Cézanne." Another choice is driving or walking the **route de Cézanne** along D17 (Route de Tholonet), which leaves Aix from the southeast and travels for about 6km (4 miles) toward Mont St-Victoire (Cézanne's favorite peak). The route shows images that Cézanne painted and places where he used to set up his easel.

Paul Cézanne was an artists' artist. At the **Atelier de Cézanne** (9 av. Paul-Cézanne; ☎ 04-42-21-06-53), about a mile north of town, you're likely to encounter artists making the pilgrimage to see the painter's milieu, motifs, and the views of the countryside he painted continuously. Cézanne's last studio was built on a hill outside Aix, in 1901, in full view of Mont St-Victoire — one of his favorite subjects. In 1906, Cézanne died of pleurisy contracted while painting outdoors. The studio is set up as though Cézanne had just stepped out — with paints, a glass of wine, and a pipe perched near an easel. It's a place to "witness the unfolding of his sensations," according to the curator of the space. The studio is open daily (except January 1, May 1, and December 25): April through September 10 a.m. to noon and 2:30 to 6 p.m., July to August 10 a.m. to 6 p.m., and October to March 10 a.m. to noon and 2 to 5 p.m. Admission is 5.50€ ($6.60) for adults and 2€ ($2.40) for students and children. To get here, take the No. 1 bus, leaving from La Rotonde (place Général-de-Gaulle) in Aix every 20 minutes, to stop Cézanne.

Located on the first floor of the grand Archbishop's Palace, **Musée des Tapisseries** (28 place des Martyrs de la Résistance; ☎ 04-42-23-09-91) contains a rich collection of textiles from the 17th and 18th centuries. Highlights are "The Grotesque," a 17th-century theatrical series depicting musicians, dancers, and animals, and "The History of Don Quixote," a series of ten works showing scenes from the Cervantes story. The contemporary art section displays colorful abstract and figurative tapestries by living artists. It's open Wednesday to Monday 10 a.m. to 12:30 p.m. and 1:30 to 5 p.m. (closed January 1, May 1, and December 25). Admission is 2€ ($2.40) for adults and free for students and children.

Set in the 18th-century Hôtel d'Estienne de St-Jean, the **Musée du Vieil Aix** (17 rue Gaston-Saporta; ☎ 04-42-21-43-55) displays a mildly interesting collection of ephemera relating to Aix, including early maps and a large collection of *santons* — the folklore doll figures popular in Provence. It's open Tuesday to Sunday April through September 10 a.m. to noon and 2:30 to 6 p.m. and October through March 10 a.m. to noon and 2 to 5 p.m. Admission is 4€ ($4.80) for adults and 2.50€ ($3) for students and children.

Many people head to the **Musée Granet** (place St-Jean-de-Malte; ☎ 04-42-38-14-70), which occupies a 17th-century Knights of Malta palace, to see the only Cézanne works in town. After renovations, the museum is scheduled to reopen in 2006. The museum also has an interesting collection of 18th- and 19th-century paintings, including works by Van Dyck, David, Delacroix, and Ingres, and many paintings by its namesake, the academic Provençal painter François Marius Granet. In the basement is perhaps the most interesting part of the museum: archaeological finds from the area, including glorious Roman statues and mosaics. It's open Wednesday to Monday 10 a.m. to noon and 2 to 6 p.m. (closed January 1; May 1, 8, and 21; July 14; August 15; November 1 and 11; and December 25 and 31). Admission is 2€ ($2.40) for adults and free for students and children up to age 5.

Fans of *faïence,* locally made hand-painted pottery, should head to the quartier Mazarin to check out the **Musée Paul-Arbaud** (2 rue du 4 Septembre; ☎ 04-42-38-38-95). This 18th-century mansion houses an interesting collection of Provençal earthenware, paintings, illuminated manuscripts, and other rare books. The museum is open Monday to Saturday 2 to 5 p.m. (closed January). Admission is 3€ ($3.60) for adults and 1.50€ ($1.80) for students and children.

Shopping for local treasures

Aix offers the best markets in the region. Place Richelme is filled with a **fruit-and-vegetable market** every morning, the place to buy the exquisite products of Provence, such as olives, lavender, local cheeses, and fresh produce. A **flower market** is at place des Prêcheurs on Sunday mornings, and on Tuesday, Thursday, and Saturday mornings at place de l'Hôtel-de-Ville. The **fish market** is open mornings on rue des Marseillais.

La Cure Gourmande (16 rue Vauvemarques; ☎ 04-42-21-26-48) stocks the classic Provence sweets, such as *provençaux biscuits* (Provence cookies), *artisanaux chocolats* (handmade chocolates), *calissons d'Aix* (almond-paste cookies), *caramels à l'ancienne* (old-fashioned caramels), and *confiseries traditionelles* (traditional sweets). Another excellent candy shop is **Calissons du Roy René** (rue Clemenceau; ☎ 04-42-26-67-86), specializing in *calissons* — those yummy almond-paste sweets. **La Blanche Boutique** (4 rue Gibelin; ☎ 04-42-21-34-82) is a beautiful gift shop selling handmade baskets and good things to put in them. And **Papiers Plumes** (8 rue Papassaudi; ☎ 04-42-27-74-56) is a stationery shop selling papers, pens, and stylish notebooks.

Living it up after dark

A student town, Aix is lively at night. You may see roving groups of young people looking for the nearest hot spot. **Forum des Cardeurs,** a bustling square in the center of Old Aix, has a high concentration of bars attracting students and 30-somethings. **Le Scat** (11 rue de la Verrerie; ☎ 04-42-23-00-23) is a good jazz club with a 12€ ($14) cover. Also, the dance club **Le Mistral** (3 rue Mistral; ☎ **04-42-38-16-49**) imposes a 16€ ($19) cover. Musicians entertain strollers on summer evenings — look for them on the cours Mirabeau and place d'Albertas west of the Palais de Justice in the old town.

Marseille: Crime and Bouillabaisse

Most people steer clear of **Marseille** because of its reputation as a seething haven of iniquity. Alas, this city's bad reputation, which has existed for at least 2,000 years, is highly deserved. Visitors tend to be those looking for drugs and/or sex, or young people into adventure-type tourism — where they go to dangerous places and look for trouble. They'll probably find it in Marseille, its streets crawling with shady characters. It's all a shame, really, because some interesting historic sites are here.

If you're determined to brave Marseille, you need to be on guard at all times. Tourism literature claims that Marseille (like Naples in Italy) is experiencing a renaissance and has improved much over the last few years. To some extent, this is true, but keep your guard up.

Marseille is both an ancient city and a thoroughly modern one — a cosmopolitan center and a huge metropolis of a million residents. The city's center is the Vieux Port, the old port claimed by Greek sailors in 600 B.C. Romans took over in 49 B.C. Staunchly independent, Marseille didn't become a part of France until 1660. The Black Plague in 1770 decimated the population, but by 1792, residents rose to prominence when they marched into Paris singing what's now called *La Marseillaise* (the French national anthem). Today, Marseille is looking boldly into the future while planning the celebration of its 26th centennial.

Marseille is a town of intriguing religious **pilgrimage festivals.** Here are the major dates and locations: February 2 at St-Victor, June 18 at Sacré-Coeur, August 15 at Notre-Dame de la Garde, and September 8 at Notre-Dame de Galine. Pastoral festivals take place from the end of December to the end of January.

Getting there

The grand **Gare St-Charles** train station (place Victor-Hugo; ☎ **08-92-35-35-39;** www.sncf.com) is at the top of a huge stone staircase. If you have a lot of luggage, it's best to take a cab to your hotel. The information and ticket windows are on the lower level of the station. Ten to 12 fast TGVs travel from Paris to Marseille each day, costing 70.80€ to 119.20€ ($85–$143). Trip time from Paris (Gare de Lyon) to Marseille is three hours. Hourly trains to Nice take 2½ hours and cost 25.90€ ($31). Trains also go to Avignon (40 minutes, 23.20€/$28) and Aix (30 minutes, 6.10€/$7.30).

If you're walking from the train station, go down the huge staircase and walk straight on boulevard d'Athènes to the McDonald's. Then take a right onto La Canebière, which leads to the old port, the location of the largest concentration of hotels, restaurants, and shops, as well as the tourist office. It's a ten-minute walk.

Aéroport Marseille-Provence (☎ **04-42-14-14-14;** www.marseille. aeroport.fr), is 28km (17.4 miles) northwest of the city. A shuttle bus (8.50€/$10) between the airport and the Gare St-Charles departs every 20 minutes daily from 6 a.m. to 10 p.m. (later if there are late flights). You can buy tickets at the ticket office in the airport between terminals 1 and 2. For information, call ☎ **04-42-14-31-27.** The shuttle bus leaves the Gare St-Charles for the airport every 20 minutes daily 5:30 a.m. to 9:50 p.m.

Gare des Autocars (bus station) is on place Victor-Hugo (☎ **04-91-08-16-40**). The station has frequent buses to Aix (40 minutes, 5.50€/$6.60), Arles (3 hours, 15€/$18), Avignon (1 hour, 14.50€/$17), Cannes (2½ hours, 20€/$24), and Nice (3 hours, 24€/$29).

If you're **driving** from Paris, follow A6 south to Lyon, then continue south along A7 to Marseille. The drive takes about 7 hours. From towns in Provence, take A7 south to Marseille.

Don't plan on bringing a car to Marseille; it'll likely be broken into or stolen. Your best bet is to take the train into town and rely on public transportation.

Getting around and getting information

This town is one where you feel practically obligated to rely on the **tourist train** (see "Exploring the city" later in this section) because walking around Marseille isn't that safe, and the attractions are quite spread out. You can also take local **buses** and **subways.** Information and maps for the public transportation system are available at **Espace Info** (6 rue des Fabres; ☎ **04-91-91-92-10**). Tickets for the bus and subway system, available at the tourist office, are 1.60€ ($1.90); day passes are 4.50€ ($5.40).

Two rental-car agencies near the train station are **Europcar** (7 bd. Maurice-Bourdet; ☎ **04-91-50-12-76**) and **Thrifty** (8 bd. Voltaire; ☎ **04-91-95-00-00**). For a cab, call **Radio Marseille Taxi** at ☎ **04-91-02-20-20, Taxi Blanc Bleu** at ☎ **04-91-51-50-00,** or **Radio Taxi France** at ☎ **04-91-05-80-80.**

The **tourist office** is at 4 La Canebière (☎ **04-91-13-89-00;** Fax: 04-91-13-89-20; www.marseille-tourisme.com). It's open year-round Monday to Saturday 9 a.m. to 7 p.m. and Sunday and holidays 10 a.m. to 7 p.m. This large office has a souvenir shop, runs guided tours, and sells bus and metro passes. A **small annex** is at the Gare St-Charles (on the left as you exit the station), which is open Monday to Friday 10 a.m. to 5 p.m. To check on or send e-mail, head to **Info Web Café** (1 quai de Rive-Neuve; ☎ 04-91-33-74-98), a hip café/bar on the north side of the old port. Info Web Café is open Monday to Saturday 8:30 a.m. to 10 p.m. and Sunday 2:30 to 7:30 p.m.

Spending the night

The hotel and restaurant reviews here are mapped in the nearby "Marseille" map.

Hôtel Kyriad
$ Old Port

The least expensive of the many standard hotels on the old port, the Kyriad formerly was part of the Climat franchise, so the rooms still have a chain-hotel quality. The location is good — on the border of the old port and the historic center of Marseille. The 49 rooms have radios and hair dryers, and the hotel also has a bar.

See map p. 379. 6 rue Beauvau. ☎ *04-91-33-02-33. Fax: 04-91-33-21-34. E-mail:* kyriad.vieux-port@wanadoo.fr. *Rack rates: 68€–74€ ($82–$89) double. Breakfast: 7€ ($8.40). AE, MC, V.*

Hôtel Petit Nice
$$–$$$$ 7e Arrondissement

This Relais & Châteaux member is the top lodging choice. The Passédat family has turned two Greek villas on the coast into a luxurious destination and an oasis of tranquility in hectic Marseille. The 13 light and airy rooms are all individually decorated in a modern style with deluxe amenities. The hotel has a large pool and a terrace where meals are served in good weather. Gérald Passédat runs the kitchen — the best in Marseille — and serves specialties from the region. Diners have views of the coast.

See map p. 379. Anse de Maldormé, Corniche J.-F. Kennedy. ☎ *04-91-59-25-92. Fax: 04-91-59-28-08.* www.petitnice-passedat.com. *Free parking. Rack rates: 275€–510€ ($330–$612) double; 510€–810€ ($612–$972) suite. Breakfast: 25€ ($30). AE, DC, MC, V.*

Mercure Beauvau Vieux-Port
$$–$$$$ Old Port

This classic hotel, part of the Mercure chain, has undergone a renovation to restore some of its former grandeur. Most of the 73 rooms open onto port views, and some contain balconies. All have large windows that let in lots of light and air. The lobby is attractively decorated with antiques and oriental rugs.

See map p. 379. 4 rue Beauvau. ☎ *04-91-54-91-00. Fax: 04-91-54-15-76. E-mail:* H1293@accor-hotels.com. *Rack rates: 132€–400€ ($158–$480) double. Breakfast: 15€ ($18). AE, MC, V.*

New Hotel Vieux-Port
$$ Old Port

Part of the New Hotel chain, this high-rise has 42 rooms — most with ter-
races overlooking the old port. The terraces are shared by several rooms.
The room décor is uninspired and generic, with stucco walls and maybe a
tired print or tourist poster; some units are quite large, with high ceilings.
All accommodations have minibars and hair dryers. The hotel is in a busy
part of town, but the soundproof windows make the rooms fairly quiet.
A large buffet breakfast is served in the breakfast room (with port views).

See map p. 379. 3 bis rue Reine-Elisabeth. ☎ *04-91-99-23-23. Fax: 04-91-90-76-24.*
www.new-hotel.com. *Rack rates: 125€–165€ ($150–$198) double. Breakfast: 11€
($13). AE, DC, MC, V.*

Dining locally

Marseille is the birthplace of bouillabaisse. The city's pride in this clas-
sic fish stew has necessitated the bouillabaisse contract — a guarantee
of quality and authenticity that many chefs who make the soup have
signed. The other famous dish here is *pieds et paquets* (literally, "feet
and packages"). To make this dish, small squares of lamb stomach are
rolled into packets; garnished with bacon, garlic, and parsley with lamb
"trotters" (feet); and cooked in a sauce of white wine and tomatoes.

Le Miramar
$$$–$$$$ Old Port   PROVENÇAL

This restaurant is the best in Marseille. Le Miramar is set on the north side
of the old port, with views of the hilltop Notre-Dame de la Garde. Prepare
for a hearty meal, especially if you order the restaurant's special *bouilla-
baisse,* which comes in two courses and is exquisitely prepared with fresh
herbs and fish. The restaurant also has succulent lobster preparations,
including the *fricassée de homard* (lobster stewed Provençal-style with
fresh herbs).

See map p. 379. 12 quai du Port. ☎ *04-91-91-10-40. Reservations necessary. Main
courses: 31€–48€ ($37–$58); bouillabaisse 50€ ($60). AE, DC, MC, V. Open: Tues–Sat
noon to 2:30 p.m. and 7–9:30 p.m.*

Les Mets de Provence, Maurice Brun
$$$–$$$$ Old Port   PROVENÇAL

At this family-run dining spot, a meal is still an event that takes up the
better part of the day — the entire day, if digestion is included — so don't
plan on rushing if you come here. The basic five-course menu includes
a platter of grilled fish prepared Provençal style, as well as a serving of
chicken or other meat with seasonal vegetables, a cheese course, and
dessert.

See map p. 379. 18 quai de Rive-Neuve, 2nd floor. ☎ *04-91-33-35-38. Reservations
necessary. Prix fixe: 36€ ($43) lunch, 52€ ($62) dinner. MC, V. Open: Tues–Fri noon
to 1 p.m.; Mon–Sat 8–10 p.m. Closed Aug 10–24.*

Marseille

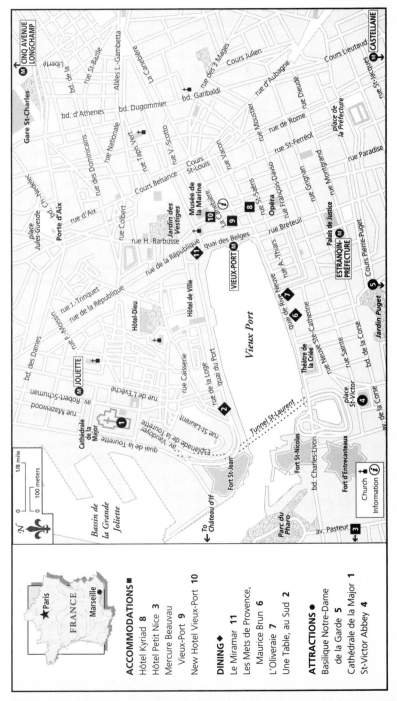

ACCOMMODATIONS ■
Hôtel Kyriad **8**
Hôtel Petit Nice **3**
Mercure Beauvau
Vieux-Port **9**
New Hotel Vieux-Port **10**

DINING ◆
Le Miramar **11**
Les Mets de Provence,
Maurice Brun **6**
L'Oliveraie **7**
Une Table, au Sud **2**

ATTRACTIONS ●
Basilique Notre-Dame
de la Garde **5**
Cathédrale de la Major **1**
St-Victor Abbey **4**

L'Oliveraie
$$ Old Port PROVENÇAL

You can expect a warm welcome here. The waitstaff is happy to recommend or explain dishes. L'Oliveraie is a busy place, and the atmosphere can be somewhat frantic, but diners usually enjoy sitting by the window and watching the strollers on the busy square. All the specialties of the region are offered, and so is bistro fare. Good choices are any of the regional fish dishes like baked cod or grilled red mullet, served with market fresh vegetables and herbs. The reasonably priced wine list features wines of the region.

See map p. 379. 10 place aux Huiles. ☎ *04-91-33-34-41. Reservations recommended. Prix fixe: 17€ ($20) lunch, 24€ ($29) dinner. MC, V. Open: Mon–Fri noon to 2:30 p.m.; Mon–Sat 7:30–11 p.m.*

Une Table, au Sud
$$–$$$ Marseille PROVENÇAL

Some of the most creative cuisine in Marseille is served one floor above street level, within a south-facing, hypermodern dining room whose windows encompass views of the Old Port. You'll recognize the historically important 19th-century building in which it's located because of the sculpted lion heads that embellish its façade. Lionel Levy *(chef de cuisine)* and his wife, Florence *(maître d'hotel),* are the creative forces here, serving cuisine that changes daily according to the ingredients available at the local markets. The best menu items include rack of Provençal lamb stuffed with white beans and a confit of lemons; mullet served with a saffron and herb risotto; and a succulent version of roasted squab whose juices are flavored with arabica coffee. Your meal may begin with an octopus artfully layered with grilled fennel and Nyon olives. Desserts may include, depending on the mood of the chef, a pineapple *dacquoise* served with vanilla-flavored whipped cream.

See map p. 379. 1 quai du Port. ☎ *04-91-90-63-53. Reservations recommended. Main courses: 22€ ($26); prix fixe: 39€–78€ ($47–$94). AE, MC, V. Open: Tues–Sat noon to 1:30 p.m. and 7:30–10 p.m. Closed Aug.*

Exploring the city

Like Paris, Marseille is divided into arrondissements (Marseille has 16). **La Canebière,** nicknamed Can o' Beer by World War II GIs, is the main intersection, leading to the old port with its many hotels and restaurants. Just east of the old port is the huge covered shopping mall **Centre Bourse.** The streets a block in from the port on the port's south side are lined with restaurants with outdoor terraces. The old quarter, called **Panier,** is on the north side of the port.

Petit Train de la Bonne Mère (tourist train) makes two circuits around town. January to November, train No. 1 makes a 50-minute round-trip to Notre-Dame de la Garde via the old port and the St-Victor Abbey. Easter through October, train No. 2 makes a 40-minute round-trip of old Marseille via the cathedral, Vieille Charité, and the Quartier du Panier. The trains depart from quai des Belges and cost 5€ ($6) for adults and 3€ ($3.60) for children for one trip, or 10€ ($12) for adults and 6€ ($7.20) for children for both trips. For details, call ☎ 04-91-40-17-75.

The tourist office can arrange a **taxi tour** that ranges from 1½ to 4 hours (32€–85€/$38–$102). A taxi tour is a great way for three adults, or two adults and two children, to see the major sights. The tourist office distributes **"Le Fil de l'Histoire"** ("The Red Line of History"), which includes a map and self-guided tour brochure for the Panier district, Marseille's colorful old quarter. Markers have been placed throughout the district for you to follow as you walk.

Exercise caution in Marseille, and follow these safety tips: Stay near the old port; travel in groups of at least two if possible; avoid deserted streets; avoid the Panier district at night; and take taxis to tourist destinations.

Just 4.8km (3 miles) from the port of Marseille, the small rocky island of If (pronounced *eef*) contains an imposing fortress prison, the **Château d'If** (☎ 04-91-55-50-09). François I built this fortress off the coast in 1524. The fortress became a prison soon after it was built. The prison has harbored many unfortunate souls — many jailed on political and religious grounds. Château d'If has become especially famous for the fictional prisoner, the Count of Monte Cristo, from the novel by Alexandre Dumas. Depending on the weather, the château is open daily (except Jan 1 and Dec 25) 9 a.m. to 5 p.m. Admission is 10€ ($12) for adults and 5€ ($6) for children. You can get to the château by taking a 20-minute boat ride that departs from the quai des Belges. Round-trip fare is 10€ ($12).

The basilica **Notre-Dame de la Garde** (☎ 04-91-13-40-80) was constructed on the highest point in the city in 1853. With its strategic location, the site always has been a lookout post, fortification, and place of worship all rolled into one. It's also a popular pilgrimage site. The church is Romanesque Byzantine style, with domes; multicolored stripes of stone; and lots of gilding, marble, and mosaics. The lower church features the vaulted crypts; the upper church houses the sanctuary. You can find panoramic views of the city from the garden in front of the church. It's open daily: May to October 7 a.m. to 9 p.m. and November to April 7 a.m. to 7 p.m. Admission is free. Café Lo Vive is on the premises for snacks. To get to Notre-Dame de la Garde, take bus No. 60 or the tourist train (see earlier in this section), or walk through the Jardin de la Colonne at the top of the cours Pierre-Puget (about a half-hour walk).

Shopping for local treasures

Here's a sampling of the best markets in Marseille (unless indicated, they're open Monday to Saturday): The **Capucins Market** on place des Capucins is open daily 8 a.m. to 7 p.m. This market has fruit, herbs, fish, and food products. **Quai des Belges** is a fish market on the old port, open daily 8 a.m. to 1 p.m. **Allées de Meilhan on La Canebière** is where you can find flowers on Tuesday and Saturday 8 a.m. to 1 p.m.; it has vendors selling *santons* daily from the last Sunday in November to December 31 8 a.m. to 7 p.m. On **cours Julien** near Notre-Dame du Mont, you'll find a market with fruits, vegetables, and other foods.

Marseille is the place to buy *santons* — clay Nativity figurines that are popular throughout Provence. The elaborately decorated figurines, many of which are villagers outfitted for the common trades and professions of the Middle Ages, are highly collectible. You'll find countless stores along **La Canebière** selling these colorful dolls. Another good santon store is **Ateliers Marcel Carbonel,** 47 rue Neuve-Sainte-Catherine (☎ **04-91-54-26-58**), near the old port. You can also find a famous soap made in Marseille, which is stamped with the city's name. The soap is sold in all the city's large department stores, in the **Centre Bourse,** or at **La Savonnerie du Sérial** (50 bd. Anatole de la Forge; ☎ **04-91-98-28-25**).

Living it up after dark

A good late-night cafe/bar near the old port is **Pêle Mêle** (8 Place Aux Huiles; ☎ **04-91-54-85-26**). For cabaret performances, there's **Le Chocolat Théâtre** (59 cours Julien; ☎ **04-91-42-19-29**). Call for hours and information about performances and prices. A popular and reasonably safe disco is **Café de la Plage** in Escale Borély, a mall on avenue Mendès-France (☎ **04-91-71-21-76**).

Chapter 19

Introducing the Riviera

- -

In This Chapter

▶ Discovering the Riviera's major destinations
▶ Getting to the French Riviera
▶ Finding other Riviera gems

- -

*B*esides Paris, France's most popular draw for visitors is the **French Riviera,** known as *Côte d'Azur.* And it's no wonder. Sophisticated resorts lined along the Azure Coast boast top-notch amenities and cultural activities, and miles of warm-water beaches beckon sun worshipers of all ages. In fact, these chic seaside towns and charming hillside villages have been attracting sunbathers, socialites, and artists for more than a century. Artists have left their legacy in the many top-notch museums focusing on 20th-century works and featuring artists such as Picasso, Matisse, Léger, Chagall, and Renoir. With so much to see and do on the Riviera, you can easily spend two weeks here — and we set out to provide you the basics in the next two chapters.

For the Eastern Riviera, you can base in Nice, making day trips to nearby attractions, including hilltowns such as St-Paul-de-Vence or even the Principality of Monaco. The easiest way to do this is rent a car that you can drive from village to village along the coast or explore hilltown to hilltown in the hinterlands.

For exploring the Western Riviera, the best bases are the resorts of **Cannes** or **St-Tropez.** The drawback, however, is that neither resort is centrally located; St-Tropez lies in the far western corner of the Riviera, and Cannes is in the east. St-Tropez is almost a destination unto itself. Anchor here to enjoy its hedonistic lifestyle. If touring is part of your plan, then base in Cannes. From Cannes, you can visit offshore islands, St-Paul-de-Vence or Venice, or the port of Antibes of Picasso fame.

What's Where: The French Riviera and Its Major Attractions

The Riviera occupies the southeast corner of the country, near where France meets the border of Italy. This section offers you just a brief taste of what you find in this region, which is shown in the nearby map, "The French Riviera."

- ✔ **Nice:** The Riviera's capital city, Nice also is the gateway to the Riviera. Most transportation to this area makes its way through Nice. A multifaced seaside city, Nice is a good choice if you're looking for a base location from which to explore the Eastern Riviera. Nice is a premier destination for art aficionados, with nearly 20 galleries and museums. See Chapter 20.

- ✔ **Cannes:** To the west of Nice, Cannes also is a place to avoid during its famous annual Film Festival. Visit the flamboyant Cannes at other times of the year, however, for shopping, sun-worshipping, strutting your stuff, and exploring the city's historic *Le Suquet* (Old Town). See Chapter 21.

- ✔ **Monaco:** East of Nice, this glamorous principality occupies a small slice of mountainous coastline close to the Italian border. A tiny country, actually, it may be best known for cars (the Monaco Grand Prix takes place in May) and casinos and for a "once-upon-a-time" princess named Grace. See Chapter 20.

- ✔ **St-Tropez:** The most famous village on the Riviera, this beach and sun mecca is for anyone in search of the hectic heart and sassy soul of this region. See Chapter 21.

- ✔ **Beaulieu:** Nestled into a coastal inlet between Nice and Monaco, this village is a *luxe* beach resort with some welcoming lodging alternatives to some of the busier destinations. See Chapter 20.

- ✔ **St-Jean-Cap-Ferrat:** An exclusive peninsula south of Beaulieu that's really a small fishing port, St-Jean-Cap-Ferrat is the home of the grandest of the grand hotels in the Riviera: Grand Hôtel du Cap-Ferrat. See Chapter 20.

- ✔ **Antibes:** A lively town between Nice and Cannes, Antibes is a yachting base, with two major summer events: Les Voiles d'Antibes in June and the Antibes Cup in July. South of Antibes at the tip of a peninsula is **Cap d'Antibes,** an exclusive beach area with private estates and fancy hotels. See Chapter 21.

- ✔ **Biot:** Famous for crafts such as glass-blowing and pottery, this tiny inland village west of Nice also features a museum devoted to the cubist Ferdinand Léger. See Chapter 21.

- ✔ **Vence:** This circular cobblestone village is best known for the Chapelle du Rosaire, designed in 1949 by Henri Matisse. See Chapter 21.

> ✔ **St-Paul-de-Vence:** A pedestrian-only village built on a steep rock, this village is much more touristy than its neighbor Vence, but worth a stop if for nothing else than the Fondation Maeght, one of the best modern art museums in France. See Chapter 21.

Getting there

To get to the Riviera, you can catch one of the frequent daily flights from Paris to Marseille (see Chapter 18) or Nice (see Chapter 20), or hop on one of the fast TGV trains leaving several times daily from Paris's Gare de Lyon to Marseille (3½ hours), to Cannes (5¾ hours — requires a change in Toulon), and to Nice (6¼ hours — requires a change in Toulon).

 You also can reach the region through Marseille, renting a car after arriving by air from Paris or by train from Paris's Gare de Lyon. In fact, since 2001, the fastest train yet, the TGV train, zooms from Paris to Marseille in only 3½ hours. Getting from Marseille to Nice (190km/118 miles) will take you about 3 hours, depending on traffic. See Chapter 18 for details about getting to Marseille.

Pokey regional trains run along the coast from Marseille all the way to Italy, making stops at St-Raphaël (where you can take boats to St-Tropez in season), Cannes, Antibes, Biot (the train station is about 8km/5 miles from the village), Nice, Beaulieu, and Monaco, and a dozen other towns. For details on getting to each town on the Riviera, see the individual town sections in Chapters 20 and 21.

 When taking trains and buses on the Riviera, sit on the right side if you're going east and on the left side if you're heading west to better take in the panoramic coastal view.

Sampling the region's cuisine: French meets Italian

The Riviera's cuisine is certainly one of the high points of a visit. Here you can dine on classic French fare prepared in the light and flavorful Provençal manner, with liberal use of olives and olive oil. You can also find authentic Italian cuisine — you can't go wrong by making a beeline to any restaurant advertising *pate fraîche* (fresh home-made pasta).

As befits such a sophisticated region, many towns on the Riviera boast a range of good ethnic restaurants, including Asian and African cuisines. And it's no coincidence that the birthplace of the thong offers the best selection of vegetarian restaurants in France. The region's proximity to the Mediterranean means fish always is on the menu: Plan to feast on steamy fish stews like *bourride* and bouillabaisse, sauces such as *tapenade* (olive paste) and *aïoli* (a garlic mayonnaise), and lots of freshly caught fish and shellfish.

The French Riviera

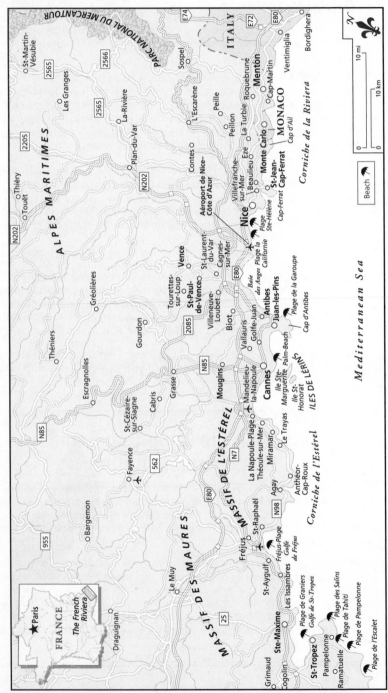

PARC NATIONAL DU MERCANTOUR

ITALY

E74

E72

E80

St-Martin-Vésubie

2565

2566

Sospel

Les Granges

2565

La-Rivière

L'Escarène

Ventimiglia

Bordighera

2205

Plan-du-Var

Peille

Peillon

La Turbie

Roquebrune

Menton

Cap-Martin

N202

Contes

Èze

MONACO

Cap d'Ail

Thiéry

Touët

Aéroport de Nice–
Côte d'Azur

Villefranche-
sur-Mer

Beaulieu

St-Hélène

Monte Carlo

St-Jean–
Cap-Ferrat

Corniche de la Riviera

A L P E S   M A R I T I M E S

N202

Nice

Cap-Ferrat **Cap-Ferrat**

Plage
Ste-Californie

Plage la
Californie

Vence

St-Laurent-
du-Var

Cagnes-
sur-Mer

E80

Plage
des Anges Plage la

Baie
des Anges

Mediterranean Sea

Gréolières

Tourettes-
sur-Loup

St-Paul-
de-Vence

Villeneuve-
Loubet

Biot

Antibes

Juan-les-Pins

Plage de la Garoupe

Théniers

Gourdon

2085

Vallauris

Golfe-Juan

Cap d'Antibes

Escragnolles

Grasse

N85

Mougins

Mandelieu-
la-Napoule

Cannes

Ile Ste-
Marguerite Palm-Beach

Plage de
l'Antibes

St-Cézaire-
sur-Siagne

Cabris

Ile St-
Honorat

ILES DE LÉRINS

ILES DE LÉRINS

M A S S I F   D E   L ' E S T É R E L

N7

La Napoule-Plage
Théoule-sur-Mer

Le Trayas

Fayence

562

Miramar

Anthéor-
Cap-Roux

Corniche de l'Estérel

Bargemon

E80

Agay

955

St-Raphaël

N98

Fréjus

Fréjus-Plage
Golfe
de Fréjus

Le Muy

St-Aygulf

Les Issambres

Plage de Graniers
Golfe de St-Tropez

M A S S I F   D E S   M A U R E S

25

Draguignan

FRANCE

★ Paris

The French
Riviera

Ste-Maxime

St-Tropez

Plage des Salins
Plage de Tahiti

Pampelonne

Grimaud

Cogolin

Ramatuelle

Plage de Pampelonne

Plage de l'Escalet

N

10 mi

10 km

Beach

Getting information

To help you find Web sites for hotels, restaurants, and other businesses along the Riviera, check out www.cote.azur.fr.

 The **Carte Musées Côte d'Azur** gives you free access to 62 museums, monuments, and gardens in the region. A three-day pass (to be used over three consecutive days) costs 17€ ($20), and a seven-day pass (to be used over seven consecutive days) costs 27€ ($32). You can purchase the passes at any participating sight and at individual tourist offices. For more information and details on which sights offer the pass, call any museum or tourist office.

Searching for Some Other Riviera Gems

 If you happen to have some extra time and a deep interest in this region, the Riviera has more intriguing places you can visit:

- ✔ **Grasse:** This town, 23km (14.5 miles) from Antibes, is called the "Perfumed Balcony of the Riviera" for good reason: It's the center of the region's perfume business. Three factories are open for tours (**Molinard, Gallard,** and **Fragonard,** named after painter François Fragonard, who was born in Grasse), and 70 others operate in town. An old city surrounded by ramparts, Grasse is a bustling place, with 45,000 residents and a 12th-century cathedral boasting a painting by Rubens.

- ✔ **La Napoule-Plage:** This secluded resort (8km/5 miles from Cannes) has a beige sandy beach. Also here is the **Musée Henry Clews** (☎ 04-93-49-95-05), with collections and works of an eccentric American sculptor who died in 1937.

- ✔ **Mougins:** The hilltop medieval village of Mougins, the longtime home of Picasso, contains one of the Riviera's most famous restaurants, **Le Moulin de Mougins** (☎ 04-93-75-78-24) — reserve far in advance. A photography museum at the top of the hill features candid photos of Picasso.

- ✔ **Roquebrune and Cap-Martin:** These two resorts, one a hilltown and one shoreside, are close to the border of Italy. Roquebrune is 26km (16 miles) east of Cannes, and Cap-Martin is 24km (15 miles) east of Nice. Roquebrune is accessed by the Grande Corniche, the mountain road that runs along the eastern part of the French Riviera. It's a charming village where cobblestone streets are lined with boutiques, gift shops, and galleries. You also find the **Château de Roquebrune** (☎ 04-93-35-07-22), a tenth-century castle that houses a museum. Cap-Martin once was popular with celebrities, royalty, and politicians, and still attracts a wealthy crowd. The beach is rocky but scenic. A walking path here, **Promenade Le Corbusier,** named after the architect who used to come to the resort, is one of the finest on the Riviera for coastal views.

✔ **Menton:** Very close to the border of Italy, Menton (8km/5 miles from Monaco) enjoys more sunshine than any other town on the Riviera. Menton has pretty — though very crowded — beaches, and the old town close to the shore is charming with cobbled winding streets and intriguing boutiques. **Musée Jean-Cocteau** (☎ 04-93-57-72-30) features works and memorabilia of the artist. Menton is particularly popular with retirees, who have apartments in many of the large residential hotels lining the shore.

Chapter 20

Nice, Monaco, and Beyond

● ●

In This Chapter

▶ Experiencing the art scene in Nice

▶ Finding a bit of France that isn't really in France: The Principality of Monaco

▶ Discovering the villas of Beaulieu and St-Jean-Cap-Ferrat

● ●

*T*his chapter covers the area of the French Riviera that extends 35km (22 miles) west from the border with Italy to Nice. We start with Nice, the Riviera's largest city, because it serves as kind of a gateway to the region. If you're traveling to the Riviera via almost any kind of public transportation, you'll go through Nice. And with the exception of St-Tropez (about 100km/62 miles from Nice), every Riviera destination discussed in this book is within a 35km (22-mile) radius of Nice.

Although you'll find plenty to see and do in Nice, we suggest a few other regions to visit, including the opulent Monaco, actually a tiny country surrounded by French countryside and the Mediterranean Sea, and two small but luxurious resort villages in between Nice and Monaco: Beaulieu and St-Jean-Cap-Ferrat.

Nice: A Study in Contrasts

The seaside city of **Nice** (the Riviera's largest) is at once sophisticated and giddy, regal and honky-tonk, and dignified and disorderly. With a population of 485,000, Nice is large enough to offer many contrasting elements. You may be struck by the grace of the city, its buildings decorated with filigreed wrought-iron balconies and multicolored shutters, and by its boisterous energy. The promenade des Anglais, along the crescent-shaped Baie des Anges, is the Riviera's most beautiful beachfront boardwalk. The Old Town, a maze of winding narrow streets crowded with vendors, is the heart of a city that cherishes its uniqueness. Street names in the Old Town are written in French and Nissart. Nissart is not a dialect but a real language that is closer to Italian than it is to French. Because Nice still holds tight to its traditions and history of independence, elderly Niçoise still speak the language, and some young people learn it in school.

A Nice history

Nice didn't actually become a part of France until 1860, when a treaty between France's Napoleon III and Italy's Victor Emmanuel sited it distinctly within France. The city's history stretches back to the fourth century B.C., when the Greeks settled on the Colline du Château (known as just Le Château). In 100 B.C., Romans built a town called Cemenelum on the hill of Cimiez. Barbarians and Saracens subjected the town to six centuries of invasions until the counts of Provence resettled the Colline du Château in A.D. 500. In the 14th century, the Niçoise agreed to be under the sovereignty of Italy's House of Savoy. But between 1691 and 1731, and 1792 and 1814, Nice fell briefly under French rule. In 1704, Louis XIV, annoyed with the Niçoise because they wanted their independence from France, destroyed all buildings on the Castle Hill. Finally, in 1860, Napoléon III and King Victor Emmanuel II of Sardinia signed the Treaty of Turin, which made Nice a part of France again and paved the way for it to become a popular winter resort during the early 1900s — and what is now the capital of tourism on the French Riviera.

You'll find many interesting sights in Nice. With 19 galleries and museums, Nice is a city of art. One of the country's foremost modern art museums, Musée d'Art Modern et d'Art Contemporain, occupies a dramatic contemporary building in the center of town. The city has museums devoted to Henri Matisse (who lived in Nice for many years and is buried here) and Marc Chagall, in addition to the Museum of Fine Arts (in a building formerly owned by Russian aristocrats); the Museum of Naïve Art; a museum of decorative art (the Musée d'Art et d'Histoire Palais Masséna); and the Palais Lascaris, with baroque art.

Getting there

Nice is a major transportation hub and a convenient base from which to explore the region. **Aéroport International Nice Côte d'Azur** (☎ **08-20-42-33-33;** www.nice.aeroport.fr) is France's second-busiest airport, with up to 45 planes per day flying from Paris to Nice and a flight from New York to Nice five days a week. The airport, with two terminals, is 7km (4 miles) from the city center. Terminal 1 is used for international flights. For information about public transportation and to summon a taxi to any point within Nice, call ☎ **08-20-42-33-33.** A taxi to the city center takes 20 minutes and costs 25€ to 30€ ($30–$36). Buses leave the airport every 30 minutes for the town center, the SNCF train station, and the **Gare Routière** (municipal bus station); each bus costs 3.50€ ($4.20) and takes 30 minutes.

From Paris's Gare de Lyon, the rapid **TGV train** takes 6½ hours to get to Nice's **Gare SNCF** and affords panoramic views along the coast — particularly from Cannes to Nice. Two trains run per day from October to May, three per day from June to September. The train from Paris costs

70€ ($84). The slow trains that travel along the coast of the Riviera stop in Nice, so you'll find frequent service to Cannes, Monaco, and Antibes, among others places. For train information, call ☎ **08-92-35-35-39.** Trains arrive in the center of the modern part of the city on av. Thiers.

Gare Routière de Nice (bus station) is at promenade de Paillon (☎ **04-93-85-61-81**). Buses are a cheap and practical way to visit nearby villages and towns. For instance, a one-way trip by bus to Monte Carlo is only 3.80€ ($4.55); a bus ticket to Cannes is 5.90€ ($7.10).

If you're **driving** to Nice, you can get there via A8; the Route Napoléon; or the national highway 7, 98, or 202. Nice is 931km (579 miles) from Paris and 190km (118 miles) from Marseille. Driving from Paris to Nice takes about ten hours. The trip from Marseille to Nice takes about three hours, depending on traffic.

Getting around and getting information

You don't need a car in Nice, as the Old Town and many attractions are within walking distance (see the nearby "Nice" map). City buses are a convenient way to see the museums in Cimiez, a suburb of Nice. The bus company is **Agence SUNBUS** (10 av. Félix-Faure; ☎ **04-93-13-53-13**), open Monday to Friday 7:15 a.m. to 8:30 p.m. and Saturday 7:15 a.m. to 6 p.m. You can pick up route maps in the office. Tickets, which you can buy on the buses, cost 4€ ($4.80) for unlimited rides all day. A single ride goes for 1.30€ ($1.55). With the **Sun Pass,** you can travel freely on all regular bus lines in Nice and the hills of Cimiez for one day (4€/$4.80), five days (13€/$16), or seven days (17€/$20).

You can rent a car at the airport and at other city locations. **Avis** is at the airport (☎ **04-93-21-36-33** Terminal 1 or 04-93-21-42-80 Terminal 2) or at the SNCF train station (☎ **04-93-87-90-11**). You can also find **Budget** at the airport (☎ **04-93-21-36-50** Terminal 1 or 04-93-21-42-51 Terminal 2) and across the street from the SNCF train station at 23 rue de Belgique (☎ **04-93-16-24-16**). **Hertz** is represented in Nice by an affiliate known as Nicea Location Rent, with headquarters at 12 rue de Belgique (☎ **04-93-21-36-72**); a branch office directly within the railway station at 9 av. Thiers (☎ **04-97-03-01-20**); and with additional branches at the Nice airport (☎ **04-93-21-42-72**).

You can rent a bike at **JML** (34 av. Auber; ☎ **04-93-16-07-00**) or **Nicea Location Rent** (12 rue de Belgique; ☎ **04-93-82-42-71**).

The main **taxi stands** are located at esplanade Masséna, promenade des Anglais, place Garibaldi, rue Hôtel des Postes, the SNCF train station, Nice's airport, and Acropolis, which also is known as the Palais des Congrès and is located a half-mile north of the center of town. To summon a cab, call **Central Taxi Riviéra** at ☎ **04-93-13-78-78.** (Prepare to pay a higher rate from 7 p.m. to 7 a.m.)

The **main tourist office** is at 5 promenade des Anglais (☎ 08-92-70-74-07; www.nicetourisme.com). During July and August, the tourist office is open Monday to Saturday 8 a.m. to 8 p.m. and Sunday 9 a.m. to 7 p.m., and from September through June hours are daily 9 a.m. to 6 p.m. The bureau has **branch offices** at the airport in Terminal 1 that are open daily 8 a.m. to 10 p.m. and at the train station on av. Thiers with the same hours as the main office. To check on or send e-mail, head to **Panini Web** (25 bis promenade des Anglais; ☎ 04-93-88-72-75), which maintains eight Internet-connected computers, fax machines, and a scanner, and serves an assortment of sandwiches and drinks. It's open Monday to Friday from 9 a.m. to 11 p.m. and Saturday and Sunday 9 a.m. to 11 p.m.

Spending the night

Hôtel du Petit Palais
$–$$ North of Center

Formerly the home of French actor/writer Sacha Guitry, this Belle Epoque property boasts 25 rooms. The hotel is set high in a residential district, about a five-minute drive up from the center of town and within walking distance of the Chagall Museum. The interior retains its elegant details, including sculpted ceiling moldings and paneled walls. The commons rooms and guest rooms are furnished with antiques; some units open onto terraces and distant sea views. An attractive garden is on the property.

See map p. 393. 17 av. Emile-Bieckert. ☎ *04-93-62-19-11. Fax: 04-93-62-53-60.* www. hotel-petit-palais.com. *Parking: 10€ ($12). Rack rates: 76€–144€ ($91–$173) double. Breakfast: 10€ ($12). AE, DC, MC, V.*

Hôtel Ambassador
$$ Center

With a prestigious location overlooking central place Masséna, the 45-room Ambassador occupies a beautiful *beaux-arts* building. It offers all the modern amenities you'd expect. The rooms are spacious and comfortable, and many have balconies with views of the plaza and the beaches along the promenade des Anglais. The English-speaking staff is efficient and friendly. Although no restaurant is on site, plenty of places to dine are nearby.

See map p. 393. 8 av. de Suède. ☎ *04-93-87-90-19. Fax: 04-93-82-14-90.* www. holidaycityeurope.com/ambassador-nice. *No on-site parking. Rack rates: 106€–160€ ($127–$192) double. Breakfast: 11€ ($13). Closed Nov–Jan. AE, DC, MC, V.*

Hôtel Brice
$$ Center

This Mediterranean-style hotel, part of the Tulip chain, claims an ideal location, a few blocks from the beaches and a short walk to the Old Town, and features a memorable garden with a fountain and statuary. In the

Nice

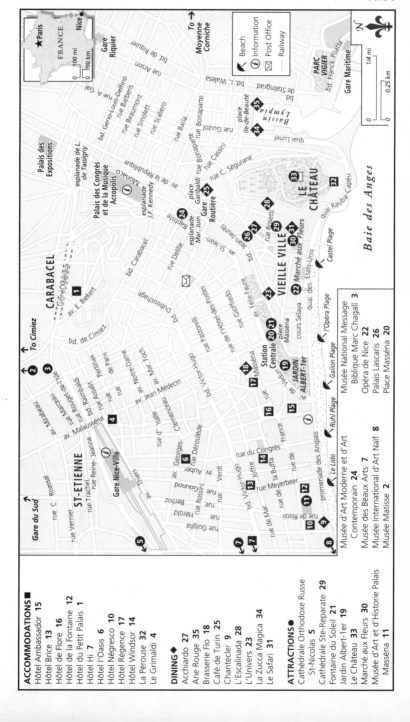

ACCOMMODATIONS ■
Hôtel Ambassador **15**
Hôtel Brice **13**
Hôtel de Flore **16**
Hôtel de la Fontaine **12**
Hôtel du Petit Palais **1**
Hôtel Hi **7**
Hôtel l'Oasis **6**
Hôtel Négresco **10**
Hôtel Régence **17**
Hôtel Windsor **14**
La Pérouse **32**
Le Grimaldi **4**

DINING ◆
Acchiardo **27**
Ane Rouge **35**
Brasserie Flo **18**
Café de Turin **25**
Chantecler **9**
L'Escalinada **28**
L'Univers **23**
La Zucca Magica **34**
Le Safari **31**

ATTRACTIONS ●
Cathédrale Orthodoxe Russe
  St-Nicolas **5**
Cathédrale Ste-Reparate **29**
Fontaine du Soleil **21**
Jardin Albert-1er **19**
Le Château **33**
Marché aux Fleurs **30**
Musée d'Art et d'Historie Palais
  Masséna **11**
Musée d'Art Moderne et d'Art
  Contemporain **24**
Musée des Beaux Arts **7**
Musée International d'Art Naïf **8**
Musée Matisse **2**
Musée National Message
  Biblique Marc Chagall **3**
Opéra de Nice **22**
Palais Lascaris **26**
Place Masséna **20**

colonial-style sitting room, the hotel staff is available to answer questions or help with special requests. Many of the 58 rooms are filled with light, and those looking out over the garden are the most desirable. All rooms have the usual amenities; some contain French balconies with intricate wrought-iron work. The hotel offers a reasonably priced restaurant, in addition to a sauna, gym, and solarium.

See map p. 393. 44 rue Maréchal-Joffre. ☎ *04-93-88-14-44. Fax: 04-93-87-38-54.* www.nice-hotel-brice.com. *Parking: 14€ ($17). Rack rates: 115€–135€ ($138–$162) double. Breakfast: 9€ ($11). AE, MC, V.*

Hôtel de Flore
$$ Center

A location in a pedestrian area and standard rooms are what you get at this 64-room Best Western in the center of the modern part of Nice, a block from the promenade des Anglais. The rooms are compact but comfortable, each renovated in 2002 in Provençal style, and special windows keep out the city noise. Although the rooms are somewhat generic, they have comfortable beds and furnishings. The staff is friendly and efficient, and speaks English.

See map p. 393. 2 rue Maccarani. ☎ *04-92-14-40-20. Fax: 04-92-14-40-21.* www.hoteldeflore-nice.fr. *No on-site parking. Rack rates: 89€–144€ ($107–$173) double, 175€–205€ ($210–$246) suite. Breakfast: 10€ ($12). AE, DC, MC, V.*

Hôtel de la Fontaine
$–$$ Center

A block from the deluxe Négresco and the promenade des Anglais, this hotel, renovated in the late 1990s, rises above the competition by virtue of its friendly and attentive management. The 29 rooms are standard but comfortable, with attention paid to details such as better-than-average sheets and towels. In summer, breakfast is served in the garden courtyard beside the attractive fountain.

See map p. 393. 49 rue de France. ☎ *04-93-88-30-38. Fax: 04-93-88-98-11.* www.hotel-fontaine.com. *No on-site parking. Rack rates: 82€–120€ ($98–$144) double. Breakfast: 9€ ($11). AE, DC, MC, V.*

Hôtel Hi
$$–$$$$ West of Center

An architectural and decorative statement, this 38-room hotel occupies a former boardinghouse. Spearheaded by Matali Crasset, a former colleague of Philippe Starck, a team of architects and engineers created one of the most aggressively avant-garde hotels in the south of France. The angular seven-story hotel opened in 2003. Each of the nine high-tech room concepts is different. They range from hospital white-on-white, to birchwood veneer and acid green, to cool violet and gray. As an example of the unconventional layouts of the rooms, consider the bathtubs, which may be tucked behind a screen of potted plants or elevated to a position of theatrical prominence. Electronic gizmos include state-of-the-art CD systems. The Japanese word "hi" describes the black mottling on the back of an ornamental carp, which traditionally is associated with good luck. Hi's special feature is a rooftop swimming pool.

See map p. 393. 3 av. des Fleurs. ☎ **04-97-07-26-26.** *Fax 04-97-07-26-27.* www.hi-hotel.net. *Parking: 20€ ($24). Rack rates: 175€–500€ ($210–$600) double. Breakfast 28€ ($34). AE, DC, MC, V.*

Hôtel l'Oasis
$–$$ Center

This small hotel, built around 1900, is in a calm and quiet area about halfway between the train station and the beach. It is indeed an oasis, set in a lush garden and boasting an outdoor pool. The 38 rooms are small, but they're clean and comfortable, and the rates are reasonable. Ask about the hotel's most famous guests: Chekhov and Lenin apparently stayed here during the Belle Époque era, when, because of its large community of expatriate Russians, Nice was called "Moscow-by-the-Sea."

See map p. 393. 23 rue Gounod. ☎ *04-93-88-12-29. Fax: 04-93-16-14-40. Parking: 8€ ($9.60). Rack rates: 85€–105€ ($102–$126) double. Breakfast: 6€ ($7.20). AE, MC, V.*

Hôtel Négresco
$$$–$$$$ Center

Built in 1912, Nice's most famous hotel, with its pink dome, sits majestically on the promenade des Anglais. The 150 posh rooms are individually decorated with museum-quality furniture and artwork, and many have balconies facing the sea. Each floor features rooms in a different style, from Louis XV to Empire to Napoléon III. The Salon Royal, with its glass dome, is where you have a drink before dining at the acclaimed Chantecler (see "Dining locally," later in this chapter). The beautiful brasserie La Rotonde is for less expensive dining.

See map p. 393. 37 promenade des Anglais. ☎ *04-93-16-64-00. Fax: 04-93-88-35-68.* www.hotel-negresco-nice.com. *Free parking. Rack rates: 235€–510€ ($282–$612) double; 602€–1,500€ ($722–$1,800) suite. Breakfast: 28€ ($34). AE, DC, MC, V.*

Hôtel Régence
$ Center

Régence is situated on one of the busiest pedestrian streets in the modern part of Nice but within easy walking distance of the Old Town and beaches. The central location means street life goes on outside your window until the wee hours, with a major strolling scene, street performers, and musicians. Fortunately, the 60 rooms, which are small but immaculate, have soundproof windows. Breakfast is served in a sunny room or on a small terrace. In the lobby, you can find a huge binder with extensive sightseeing information in English.

See map p. 393. 21 rue Masséna. ☎ *04-93-87-75-08. Fax: 04-93-82-41-31.* www.hotel regence.com. *Parking: 10€ ($12). Rack rates: 60€–80€ ($72–$96) double. Breakfast: 6€ ($7.20). AE, DC, MC, V.*

Hôtel Windsor
$–$$ Center

This transformed 19th-century hotel near the promenade des Anglais is a celebration of contemporary art. Local and nationally recognized artists decorated the 57 rooms with murals, paintings, and sculptures, and the result is sometimes ravishing, sometimes startling, but always unique. One room is decorated with works by Henri Olivier, who makes "living still-lifes," and another features the conceptual poetry of Lawrence Wiener (his poem about dreams is written in bright colors on the wall above the bed). Breakfast is served in the attractive dining room or the exotic garden. The fitness area offers a sauna and massage room. You can enjoy swimming in the pool, surrounded by tropical plants and listening to piped-in bird songs. The hotel has a very fine restaurant and an attractive bar with live piano music some nights.

See map p. 393. 11 rue Dalpozzo. ☎ *04-93-88-59-35. Fax: 04-93-88-94-57.* www.hotel windsornice.com. *Parking: 10€ ($12). Rack rates: 75€–155€ ($90–$186) double. Breakfast: 10€ ($12). AE, MC, V.*

La Pérouse
$$–$$$$ near Castle Hill

The classy La Pérouse, originally built in the 1930s and completely renovated in 1999, is one of Nice's top hotels, with a special location on the side of the Colline du Château, overlooking the sea. The rooms, each decorated in the Provençal style, have sweeping views of the coastline and the Old Town. The 62 low-ceilinged rooms are decorated luxuriously with the Mediterranean in mind, with blue and green florals predominating. The hotel has a heated pool in the garden and a Jacuzzi. The restaurant is open for lunch and dinner from mid-May to mid-September only.

See map p. 393. 11 quai Rauba-Capeu. ☎ *04-93-62-34-63. Fax: 04-93-62-59-41.* www. hotel-la-perouse.com. *Parking: 18€ ($22). Rack rates: 150€–405€ ($180–$486) double, 600€–800€ ($720–$960) suite. Breakfast: 17€ ($20). AE, DC, MC, V.*

Le Grimaldi
$–$$ Center

This recently renovated, 46-room hotel is housed in two interconnected buildings, each with Art Deco facades from the 1930s. An excellent value in a convenient central location, it lies about halfway between the railway station and the beach. Its rooms are individually decorated with modern panache, using brightly colored *Souleïado* (Provençal) fabrics. The four types of rooms (standard, classic, superior, and junior suite) all have big windows, with some opening onto French balconies, and are bathed in light. You can choose between a breakfast buffet served in the sleek breakfast room or an American breakfast brought by room service. You need to book early for this one; it's become a hip place to stay.

See map p. 393. 15 rue Grimaldi. ☎ *04-93-16-00-24. Fax: 04-93-87-00-24.* www.le-grimaldi.com. *Parking: 16€ ($19). Rack rates: 90€–185€ ($108–$222) double; 190€–230€ ($228–$276) suite. Breakfast: 15€ ($18). AE, DC, MC, V.*

Dining locally

The Niçoise pride themselves on their cuisine, which features a number of unique specialties. *Socca* is a steaming crêpe made of chickpeas that's sold from street vendors in the heart of the Old Town. *Pissaladière* (onion tart) and *les petite farcis* (stuffed vegetables) are favorite appetizers. *Beignets de fleurs de courgettes* are fried zucchini flowers, and *tarte de blettes* is a tart garnished with Swiss chard. Visitors have a hard time ordering *merda de can,* which translates literally as dog excrement, but it's actually very delicious gnocchi with spinach. Small local olives, *poutine* (fried little fish), and preserved fruits are also specialties of Nice. Last, but not least, is the famous *salade niçoise,* made with tuna, potatoes, tomatoes, olives, anchovies, green beans, and capers.

Acchiardo

$ Vieille Ville   NIÇOISE

This restaurant, established in 1927 by the grandmother of the kindly owner, is where you can find one of the cheapest good meals in town. It's a small, unpretentious place in the Old Town that attracts locals and visitors alike. Patrons tend to wander in after perusing the inexpensive menu. Specialties are fish soup, homemade ravioli, *les petis farcis niçoises* (a medley of stuffed vegetables), minestrone, and fresh pastas. Your best bet is the copious proportioned *plat du jour,* which is bound to be a hearty traditional dish.

See map p. 393. 38 rue Droite. ☎ *04-93-85-51-16. Reservations recommended. Main courses: 11€–12.50€ ($13–$15) each. No credit cards. Open: Mon–Fri noon to 1:30 p.m.; Mon–Fri 7–10 p.m. Closed Aug.*

Ane Rouge

$$–$$$$ Nice   PROVENÇAL/SEAFOOD

Facing the old port and occupying an antique building whose owners have carefully retained its ceiling beams and stone walls, Ane Rouge is one of the city's best-known seafood restaurants. In the two modern dining rooms noteworthy for their coziness, you can enjoy traditional and well-prepared specialties such as bouillabaisse, bourride, filet of John Dory with roulades of stuffed lettuce leaves, mussels stuffed with breadcrumbs and herbs, and salmon in wine sauce with spinach. Service is correct and commendable.

See map p. 393. 7 quai des Deux-Emmanuels. ☎ *04-93-89-49-63. Reservations required. Main courses: 30€–55€ ($36–$66); prix fixe: 46€–64€ ($55–$77) dinner. AE, DC, MC, V. Open: Fri–Tues noon to 2 p.m. and Thurs–Tues 8–10:30 p.m. Closed 2 weeks in Feb.*

Brasserie Flo
$–$$ Center NIÇOISE

Across from the Galeries Lafayette department store and near place
Masséna, Flo has a convenient central location. The hip brasserie is set in
a converted 19th-century theater, meaning it positively drips with atmosphere, with the highlight being the soaring frescoed ceilings. With something to appeal to every family member, the menu offers typical brasserie
fare such as fresh shellfish, grilled fish, or excellent soups.

See map p. 393. 2–4 rue de Sacha-Guitry. ☎ *04-93-13-38-38. Reservations recommended. Main courses: 12€–30€ ($14–$36); prix fixe: 29.90€ ($36); children's menu:
12.50€ ($15). AE, DC, MC, V. Open: Daily noon to 2:30 p.m. and 7 p.m. to midnight.*

Café de Turin
$$ Center NIÇOISE

The Turin, a bustling brasserie on place Garibaldi, is known for a menu
that includes virtually no meat, lots of fish, and some of the best shellfish
in Nice. Its solid reputation has borne the test of time, and since 1908,
locals and visitors have come here for towering seafood platters with oys-
ters, clams, shrimp, and other shellfish. Although this place is popular for
before-dinner drinks or apéritifs, it's never easy to find a table.

See map p. 393. 5 place Garibaldi. ☎ *04-93-62-66-29. Reservations recommended.
Main courses: 16.80€–25€ ($20–$30). AE, DC, MC, V. Open: Daily 8 a.m.–11 p.m.*

Chantecler
$$$–$$$$ Center NIÇOISE

For the best and perhaps most expensive meal in Nice, head to the exqui-
site Chantecler. The setting is palatial — the ornately carved wood panel-
ing was purchased from a château, as were many of the antiques. Chef
Bruno Turbo uses top-quality ingredients such as black truffles, foie gras,
giant prawns, and lobster to create enchanting dishes. Many of the culi-
nary specialties here are presented as *tapas,* delicate morsels bursting
with flavor. The menu changes according to the freshest produce and
meats, but a first-course highlight is *pommes de terre nouvelles poêlées,
anchois marinés et brochette de suppions* (pan-fried new potatoes, mari-
nated anchovies, and skewered cuttlefish), and a main-course highlight is
épigrammes d'agneau de lait (breaded, braised, and grilled lamb).
Sommelier Patrick Millereau can help you select the perfect wine, though
you may have trouble finding one for a reasonable price.

See map p. 393. At the Hôtel Négresco, 37 promenade des Anglais. ☎ *04-93-16-64-00.
Reservations required far in advance. Main courses: 45€–60€ ($54–$72); prix fixe:
45€–55€ ($54–$66) lunch, 90€–130€ ($108–$156) dinner. AE, DC, MC, V. Open: Daily
12:30–2 p.m. and 8–10 p.m. Closed Jan to Feb 7.*

La Zucca Magica
$–$$ Port VEGETARIAN/ITALIAN

The chef at this popular harborside restaurant is hailed as the best Italian chef in Nice. That this honor should go to a vegetarian restaurant is the most startling part of the news. Chef Marco, who opened his restaurant in 1997 after cooking for many years in Rome, certainly has a fine pedigree — he's a relative of Luciano Pavarotti. He serves refined cuisine at reasonable prices, using recipes from Italy's Piedmont region, updated without meat or fish. The pink-and-green decor puts you in the mood for the creative cuisine. You'll have to trust Marco, though, because everyone is served the same meal. You can count on savory cuisine using lots of herbs, Italian cheeses, beans, and pasta. Lasagna is a specialty.

See map p. 393. 4 bis quai Papacino. ☎ *04-93-56-25-27. Reservations recommended. Prix fixe: 17€ ($20) lunch, 27€ ($32) dinner. No credit cards. Open: Tues–Sat 12:30–2:30 p.m. and 7:30–10 p.m.*

Le Safari
$–$$ Vieille Ville NIÇOISE

Arrive at Le Safari before 9 p.m. if you don't want to wait for a table. The crowds flock to this restaurant at the far east end of cours Saleya because the prices are reasonable, and the food is good. The waiters must train like Olympic athletes, the way they speed around the huge terrace. The restaurant also has seating inside, but you won't be able to enjoy the free entertainment from traveling musicians, who tend to pause to play some tunes in front. The menu emphasizes pastas and grilled fish. The Niçoise *merda de can* (gnocchi with spinach) is a specialty, and so is beef stew. The staff speaks English, and English menus are available.

See map p. 393. 1 cours Saleya. ☎ *04-93-80-18-44. Reservations recommended. Main courses: 18€–24€ ($22–$29); prix fixe: 28€ ($34). AE, MC, V. Open: Daily noon to 6 p.m. and 7–11 p.m.*

L'Escalinada
$–$$ Vieille Ville NIÇOISE

The terrace tables on this bustling street corner fill up first, because this is a prime people-watching section of the Old Town. This tiny restaurant, with its cheerful English-speaking staff, serves excellent specialties such as *pissaladière* and a variety of pastas. But the real standout is the home-made gnocchi, a melt-in-your-mouth version of potato dumplings, which come heaped on a steaming platter, deep-fried zucchini, and Niçoise-style tripe. The authentic food is served in generous portions.

See map p. 393. 22 rue Pairolière. ☎ *04-93-62-11-71. Reservations recommended. Main courses: 4.50€–20€ ($5.40–$24); prix fixe: 22€ ($26). No credit cards. Open: Daily noon to 2:30 p.m. and 7:30–10:30 p.m. Closed Nov 15–Dec 15.*

Did you hear the cannon?

Listen for a cannon shot from the Colline du Château every day at noon. Why? Well, in the late 19th century, the Englishman Lord Coventry retired from the army and came to live in Nice. He had an absent-minded wife, so he built a cannon on Castle Hill and fired it every day to remind her to prepare lunch for him.

L'Univers
$–$$$$ Vieille Ville   NIÇOISE

A fine restaurant on the border of old Nice, the dining room's decor is deceptively simple, considering the complex tastes being devised in the kitchen. Wrought-iron chairs surround glass-topped tables in the center of the room, but you'll want one of the tables on the perimeter — they're better for watching the gourmets of Nice come and go. The most famous dish here is the red mullet with asparagus. Other good choices are the summer special, fried calamari and *morue fraîche aux artichauts* (fresh cod with artichokes). The restaurant offers a succulent strawberry tart for dessert.

See map p. 393. 54 bd. Jean-Jaurès. ☎ *04-93-62-32-22. Reservations necessary. Main courses: 18€–50€ ($22–$60); prix fixe: 20€–68€ ($24–$82) lunch, 42€–68€ ($50–$82) dinner. AE, DC, MC, V. Open: Tues–Fri 12:30–2 p.m.; Mon–Sat 7:30–10 p.m.*

Exploring Nice

Nice is divided into two distinct parts. The **modern area** in the center of the city and to the west of the Old Town boasts the famous **promenade des Anglais,** hands-down the Riviera's best beach boardwalk. Hotels in a wide range of price categories line the promenade. **Vieille Ville,** on the east side, is home to Old Town, a magical place with winding ancient streets leading to charming cafes, markets, and unique shops. You can always find a lively street life here. While passing colorful markets, you may see a hurdy-gurdy player or other street performers along cours Saleya. Between the Old Town and the harbor is the **Colline du Château,** also known as just Le Château. This hill no longer has a castle, but it does offer a panoramic view over the bay. An elevator takes you to the top, or you can ride the tourist train to the top.

Within the core of central Nice, you find two different tourist trains, each painted in cheerful colors and each rolling on rubber tires through the city's historic core. The less comprehensive of the two is *Le Petit Train Touristique de Nice* (☎ 06-16-39-53-51), which travels around the Old Town as far as the panoramic summit of Castle Hill, taking 40 minutes and costing 6€ ($7.20). A more comprehensive option is offered by the *Bus-Le Grand Tour* (☎ 08-92-70-74-07). Priced at 17€ ($20) per person, its tours last an hour and include a greater number of sights. Both trains depart from the esplanade Albert 1er, across from the Hotel Méridien, allow children younger than 6 to ride free with their guardians, and operate daily as follows: July and August 9:30 a.m. to 6:50 p.m., April through June and September 9:30 a.m. to 6:50 p.m., and October through March 10 a.m. to 5 p.m.

On a hill north of town is the suburb of **Cimiez,** which also has a rich historical record, as is evident from the **Roman ruins.** Next to the ruins is the famous **Musée Matisse,** the most popular museum in Nice.

Nice's wild **Carnaval** takes place the last two weeks in February and features parades, concerts, balls, fireworks, and general merriment. The Mardi Gras Parade goes from place Masséna down av. Jean-Médecin, and the flower processions are on promenade des Anglais. The other big annual event is the **Festival du Jazz,** which takes place in July under the olive trees of the Cimiez Gardens and in the nearby Roman Arenas, on three stages simultaneously. For the event, the city plays host to more than 200 musicians from around the world. Call the tourist office for details.

Beware of pickpockets in Nice, particularly near the train station and in the Old Town.

Walking around Nice

If you want to follow your own walking tour, begin on **promenade des Anglais,** which was the grand idea of a vacationing Englishman who saw many beggars here after the harsh winter of 1820–21 and set them to work building the boardwalk. The promenade follows the Baie des Anges along 15 pebbly private beaches, which are crowded with restaurants and concessions. On the other side of the boulevard, grand seaview hotels line the road; check out one of the Riviera's top hotels, the Négresco, with its whimsical pink dome. In the evening, jazz, salsa, swing, and classical musicians perform along the promenade.

Then it's on to **Vieille Ville,** where the streets are lined with cafes, bars, and shops. Begin on **cours Saleya,** which, depending on the hour and day, is filled with a market of vegetables, flowers, or antiques. On the north side of the street is the **Chapelle de la Miséricorde,** a small 18th-century church with a jewel box of an interior.

Farther up cours Saleya, take a left on rue de la Poissonerie. Near the tops of buildings throughout the Old Town are interesting architectural flourishes, such as multicolored murals, stucco friezes, and *trompe l'oeil.* For instance, on a building on the right side of rue de la Poissonerie is a 1584 fresco of Adam and Eve. Nearby is a lintel from the Middle Ages inscribed with the name of the family that lived in the house. Soon you reach the **Eglise Ste-Rita de l'Annonciation** (open daily 7:30 a.m. to 6:30 p.m.), built in the Middle Ages but "baroquialized" in the 18th century. This popular church is devoted to St. Rita, the patron saint of desperate causes. It's the most visited chapel in the Old Town and one of the oldest churches in Nice.

Take a left on rue de la Préfecture to reach the early-17th-century **Palais de la Préfecture,** formerly the residence of the governors and princes of Savoy. Now it contains the office of the president of the General Council and the prefect of the Alpes-Maritimes region. Retrace your steps back on rue de la Préfecture to rue Droite, an ancient street used in medieval times to cross the Old Town from one city gate to the other. Turn left onto rue Droite and look for the **Eglise St-Jacques Le Majeur ou du Gésu.** After the Jesuits built this church in 1650, many wealthy families constructed palatial homes nearby. The beautiful church facade was used as a model for baroque churches throughout the region. The church is infrequently open, so seeing the facade will have to suffice.

Rue de Gésu, across from the church, leads to **place Rosetti,** which is the largest square in Old Town thanks to Monsieur Rosetti, a local who gave money to destroy all the buildings in front of the cathedral in order to improve the view from the cathedral steps. Rue Rossetti off the square leads again to rue Droite. Take a left onto rue Droite to see the **Palais Lascaris,** a museum of decorative arts (see later in this section for details). A cannonball embedded in the corner building near the Palais Lescaris is from a 1543 siege of the town. Follow rue Droite to rue St-François and **place St-François,** where a fish market is open on Tuesday to Sunday mornings.

Beyond the square is rue Pairoliere ("cauldron"), "the belly" of Nice, lined with food shops such as *charcuteries* (pork butchers) and *boucheries* (butchers). A shortcut on tiny rue du Choeur leads to place St-Augustin, with the **Eglise St-Martin et St-Augustin,** a baroque church with a fine *Pietà* attributed to Ludovic Brea (a famous Niçoise artist of the Middle Ages). Rue Sincaire runs to rue Catherine-Ségurane, which leads to the **harbor;** the **flea market;** and a **monument to Catherine Ségurane,** Nice's most beloved heroine. This washerwoman became famous during a 1543 siege of Nice by the Turks. She climbed to the top of the ramparts that surrounded the town back then, pulled up her dress, and mooned the advancing Turks, thus allegedly slowing down the enemy (and/or boosting the morale of the Niçoise).

Seeing the top sights in Nice and Cimiez

You can get a **Passe-Musées** for museums in Nice or for the region. A one-week pass for all Nice museums is 6€ ($7.20), and a one-week pass for all regional museums in Cote d'Azur is 27€ ($32).

In the Old Town, a fine art collection is housed in the **Palais Lascaris** (15 rue Droite; ☎ 04-93-62-72-40), a 17th-century Genoese-style palace with a grand central staircase and baroque staterooms. The palace was the home of the Lascaris-Ventimiglia family, which in 1648 combined four houses to make the residence. The family sold the palace in 1802, and it became a rabbit warren of squalid apartments until the city of Nice came to the rescue in 1942, purchasing the building and restoring it. On display are 17th- and 18th-century objects, including Flemish tapestries, *faïence* (colored pottery) vases, and displays of crafts such as weaving and pottery making. Year-round, it's open Wednesday to Monday 10 a.m. to 6 p.m. Admission is free.

Built from 1650 to 1680, the baroque **Cathédrale Ste-Reparate,** in the heart of the Old Town (place Rossetti; ☎ 04-93-62-34-40), is devoted to the patron saint of Nice, St. Reparate. Legend has it that her body was put on a barge out to sea, arriving back in the bay escorted by angels and doves (thus the name of Nice's bay, *Baie des Anges,* or Bay of Angels). The church's 12 chapels, which belonged to wealthy families and corporations, are decorated in rich stucco and marble. The bell tower was added in the 18th century. The cathedral also has the designation "basilica," meaning a very important cathedral that hosted cardinals and bishops. It's open daily 7:30 a.m. to noon and 2 to 6 p.m. Admission is free. Tuesday afternoons from 2 to 5 p.m., a staff person leads free guided tours of the cathedral, following a vague, unstructured schedule that usually requires an advance telephone call and which is most willingly configured for groups of six participants or more.

Built in 1990, the enormous and daring **Musée d'Art Moderne et d'Art Contemporain** (Promenade des Arts; ☎ 04-93-62-61-62; www.mamac-nice.org) is highly entertaining as it follows the history of European and American avant-garde painting, starting in the 1960s. Quite a bit of space is devoted to the works of Yves Klein, a Niçois who made a big splash in the 1960s with his famous blue paintings and his happenings. The museum also has a large collection of American pop art, with works by Warhol, Rauschenberg, and Lichtenstein. It's open Tuesday to Sunday 10 a.m. to 6 p.m.; it's closed January 1, Easter Sunday, May 1, and December 25. Admission is 4€ ($4.80) adults, 2.50€ ($3) students. Children younger than 18 free.

The beautiful **Musée Matisse** (164 av. des Arènes de Cimiez; ☎ 04-93-81-08-08; www.musee-matisse-nice.org), situated in an Italianate villa high above Nice, houses a wonderful collection of monographs, drawings, and engravings by Matisse, in addition to personal items of the artist, including sculptures, paintings he cherished, furniture and vases that appear in his paintings, and even a huge kouros (an ancient Greek statue) he owned. The museum also owns Matisse's first painting, a dour 1890 still life, and one of his last gouaches from 1953. Matisse lived in Nice from 1917 until his death in 1954 and is buried in the cemetery nearby. To get to the museum, take the No. 15, 17, 20, or 22 bus to Cimiez, and get off at the Arènes stop. The museum is open year round Wednesday to Monday 10 a.m. to 6 p.m. It's closed January 1, May 1, and December 25. Admission is 4€ ($4.80) for adults; 2.50€ ($3) for students; children younger than 18 free.

Nice even has Roman ruins. Next to the Musée Matisse in Cimiez is the ancient **Baths of Cemenelum,** founded in 14 B.C. by Augustus. Admission is 4€ ($4.80) adults, 2.50€ ($3) students, children younger than 18 free. To find out more, visit the **Musée Archéologique de Nice-Cimiez,** at 160 rue des Arènes on the western boundary of the ruins (☎ 04-93-81-59-57). The collections range from the Metal Ages (1100 B.C.) to the Middle Ages and include ceramics, glass, coins, jewelry, and sculptures. Hours and admission for both are the same as for the nearby Musée Matisse.

While in Cimiez, you can peer into the **Monastère de Cimiez** (place du Monastère; ☎ 04-93-81-00-04). The convent embraces a church that owns three of the most important works from the primitive painting school of Nice by the Bréa brothers. See the carved and gilded wooden main altarpiece. In a restored part of the convent where some Franciscan friars still live, **Musée Franciscain** is decorated with 17th-century frescoes. Some 350 documents and works of art from the 15th through 18th centuries are displayed, and a monk's cell has been recreated in all its severe simplicity. The gardens offer a panoramic views of Nice and the Baie des Anges. Matisse and Dufy are buried in the cemetery. Admission is free; the museum is open Monday to Saturday from 10 a.m. to noon and 3 to 6 p.m., the church daily from 9 a.m. to 6 p.m.

While living in nearby Vence between 1960 and 1966, artist Marc Chagall worked on his Bible paintings. His paintings form the core of the collection at the **Musée National Message Biblique Marc Chagall,** on av. du Docteur-Menard, at the corner of bd. de Cimiez (☎ 04-93-53-87-20). The museum's collection, which is the largest public Chagall collection, spans the artist's life with works from the 1930s to his death in 1985 — paintings, drawings, engravings, mosaics, glass windows, and tapestries. The stark modern building that houses the works is set in a park in Cimiez, about a five-minute drive or short bus ride (No. 15) north of the center of Nice. The museum is open year-round Wednesday through Monday 10 a.m. to 6 p.m. Admission is 6.70€ ($8.05) adults, 5.20€ ($6.25) for students, children younger than 18 free. Entrance is free on the first Sunday of every month.

Nice's **Musée des Beaux-Arts** (33 av. des Baumettes; ☎ 04-92-15-28-28; www.museebeauxarts-nice.org) is housed in an early-1900s Italianate mansion on the west side of town, the former residence of the Ukrainian Princess Kotchubey. The fine-arts museum covers the 17th century to early 20th century, with a collection of more than 6,000 works. The 17th-century section includes Italian paintings and Dutch landscapes. The late-19th- and early-20th-century collection features works by Dufy, Van Dongen, Monet, Degas, and Renoir. The large sculpture gallery presents works by Rodin and others. The museum is open Tuesday to Sunday 10 a.m. to 6 p.m.; guided tours in English are Fridays at 3 p.m. for 3€ ($3.60) per person. Admission is 4€ ($4.80) adults; 2.50€ ($3) students; children younger than 18 free.

A donation by art critic Anatole Jakovsky enabled the **Musée International d'Art Naïf** (av. de Fabron, at the corner of av. Val Marie; ☎ 04-93-71-78-33; Bus: Nos. 9, 10) to open in the early 1980s in the attractive Château Ste-Hélène. The collection of 700 paintings, drawings, and sculptures on display traces the history of naïve painting from the 18th century to the present. The museum is open Wednesday to Monday 10 a.m.

to 6 p.m. Admission is 4€ ($4.80) for adults, 2.50€ ($3) students; children younger than 18 free.

In the late 19th century, the Russian aristocracy began wintering on the Riviera and transformed Nice in the process. You can't miss the soaring ornate onion domes at the top of the **Cathédrale Orthodoxe Russe St-Nicolas,** on av. Nicolas II off bd. du Tzarévitch (☎ **04-93-96-88-02**). Built from 1902 to 1912, this magnificent church houses a large collection of icons, elaborate woodwork, and frescoes. The cathedral is open daily May to September 9 a.m. to noon and 2:30 to 6 p.m. and October to April 9:30 a.m. to noon and 2:30 to 5:30 p.m. Entrance costs 2.50€ ($3) for adults, 2€ ($2.40) for students. It's free for children younger than 12.

Shopping

Nice's famous flower market, **Marché aux Fleurs,** takes place on cours Saleya, the Old Town's pedestrian street, Tuesday to Saturday 6 a.m. to 5:30 p.m. and Sunday 6 a.m. to 1 p.m. You can find a **fruit-and-vegetable market** on the eastern side of cours Saleya Tuesday to Saturday 6 a.m. to 5:30 p.m. and Sunday 6 a.m. to 1 p.m. The antiques and flea market, **Marché à la Brocante,** is open on cours Saleya Mondays 8 a.m. to 6 p.m. The flea market, **Marché aux Puces,** is at place Robilante (on the port) Tuesday to Saturday 10 a.m. to 6 p.m. And the fish market, **Marché aux Poissons,** is open on place St-François Tuesday to Sunday 6 a.m. to 1 p.m. The stretch of **rue Pairolière** to rue du Marché has shops specializing in cheeses, olives, fruits and vegetables, and herbs and spices.

Special items to look for in Nice include **glassware** from Biot, **pottery** from Vallauris, **perfumes** from Grasse, *faïence* from Moustier, **wine** from nearby Bellet, and *fougasse à la fleur d'oranger* (local bread made with orange blossoms).

You'll find the best olive oil at the **Maison de l'Olive** (18 rue Pairolière; ☎ **04-93-80-01-61**) and the most enticing candied fruit at the **Confiserie Florian du Vieux Nice** (14 quai Papacino; ☎ **04-93-55-43-50**). The **Caves Caprioglio** (16 rue de la Préfecture; ☎ **04-93-85-71-36**) is the oldest wine store (established 1910) in Nice and one of the oldest in France, selling wines from around the world.

For Provençal gifts, souvenirs, textiles, and pottery, head to **La Maïoun** (1 rue du Marché; ☎ **04-93-13-05-75**). At **Le Chandelier** (7 rue de la Boucherie; ☎ **04-93-85-85-19**) and **Les Olivades** (8 av. de Verdun; ☎ **04-93-88-75-50**), you can browse through a great collection of Provençal fabrics in Riviera colors and motifs.

If you're looking for arts and crafts, visit **Atelier Contre-Jour** (3 rue du Pont Vieux; ☎ **04-93-80-20-50**) for handcrafts in painted wood, painted furniture, picture frames of painted wood, and silk lampshades. Plat Jérôme (34 rue Centrale; ☎ **04-93-62-17-09**) offers varnished pottery. Many **artists' studios/galleries** are located on side streets near the cathedral in the Old Town.

Living it up after dark

Nice offers some of the best nightlife on the Riviera. You can go to the opera, hang out in an Irish pub, party at a disco, or wander along the promenade des Anglais, where itinerant musicians jam 'til the wee hours. For happenings about town, check out the free guides *Le Mois à Nice* and *L'Exés* and also *La Semaine des Spectacles* and *L'Officiel des Loisirs Côte d'Azur* (all are available at newsstands).

For highbrow entertainment, attend the **Opéra de Nice** (4 rue St-François-de-Paule; ☎ 04-92-17-40-00), an early-1900s palace designed by Charles Garner, architect of Paris's Opéra Garnier. Opéra de Nice presents a full repertoire of opera and concerts, with tickets ranging from 10€ to 60€ ($12–$72). On the other end of the scale are the 10 p.m. Vegas-style shows on Fridays and Saturdays at the **Casino Ruhl** (1 promenade des Anglais; ☎ 04-93-87-95-87). The casino is open for slot-machine gambling 10 a.m. to 5 a.m.; the more formal gaming rooms are open 8 p.m. to 5 a.m. Entrance to the formal rooms is 10€ to 13€ ($12–$16). If you play the slot machines, you don't need a passport, but for the formal gaming rooms, you do. Men are not required to wear a jacket and tie, but sneakers are frowned upon.

Nice has many bars in the Old Town where Americans will feel right at home, including the **Scarlett O'Hara Irish Pub,** located on the corner of rue Rosetti and rue Droite ☎ 04-93-80-43-22; **Wayne's** (15 rue de la Préfecture; ☎ 04-93-13-46-99); and **William's Pub** (4 rue Centrale; ☎ 04-93-62-99-63), which has live music. If you'd rather hang out with French people, try **La Civette,** a popular spot for apéritifs (29 rue de la Préfecture; ☎ 04-93-62-35-51).

Nice also has a big gay scene — the most popular club is **Blue Boy** (9 rue Spinetta; ☎ 04-93-44-68-24). One of Nice's most in-vogue nightspots is **Le Klub** (6 rue Halévy; ☎ 04-93-16-27-56), where gays, straights, and hipsters of indeterminate gender and sexual preferences congregate, dish, dance, flirt, and brouhaha.

Monaco: Big Money on "The Rock"

Visitors flock to the principality of **Monaco** to ogle the ultrarich gamblers, watch the changing of the guard at the Grimaldi Palace, and stroll through the exotic gardens. Looking for a quaint little place on a sliver of coast near the border of Italy, most people are struck by the overdevelopment — particularly the densely packed skyscrapers. This tiny country, with 40,000 residents and 150 hectares (371 acres — the size of a small town), is built into the side of a steep ridge. The roads and streets are in vertical layers that are difficult to navigate, so elevators take people from one level to the next. But most people don't bother to use them — they drive. Monaco and its Monégasques absolutely adore the automobile (the famous Grand Prix in late May or early June is the year's biggest event). The town is crisscrossed by fast roads with no sidewalks or very narrow ones. If you don't have a car, the best way to get around is by bus.

Besides cars, the other thing worshiped in Monaco is money. The Monégasques don't pay income tax, and the whole principality, with its wall-to-wall condominium towers and casino culture, seems obsessed with lucre — filthy or otherwise. Two-thirds of its hotel rooms are contained within government-rated four-star deluxe hotels, so Monaco has always been a destination for the rich and famous.

You can find pockets of beauty here and a number of interesting sights. Orange trees line rue Grimaldi, the main road through the region's center, and you can catch a glimpse of the yacht-filled harbor from almost anywhere in Monaco. The Old Town surrounding the palace has narrow cobblestone streets and charming restaurants and shops. The parks and gardens of the principality, especially the Jardin St-Martin with views out to sea, are spectacular. And if you're willing to scrub up and plop down a 14€ ($17) cover charge, you can wander around the famed Monte Carlo Casino, with its gilded columns and frescoed ceilings, or have a drink at the terrace bar in the Hôtel Hermitage with breathtaking views.

The Grimaldi family, originally from Genoa, acquired the lordship of Monaco in 1308, and since then, the title Prince de Monaco has been bestowed on the heirs. Prince Rainier III is the current head of the family — you probably know that in 1956 he married American actress Grace Kelly, who died in a car crash here in 1982. The European tabloid press follows closely the exploits of Rainier and Grace's three children: Albert, Caroline, and Stephanie. Many visitors go to Monaco's cathedral (4 rue Colonel Bellando de Castro; ☎ 93-30-87-70) to pay homage at Princess Grace's burial site. Monaco has a heavy police presence, and rowdiness isn't tolerated in the principality. You can assume that most men you see riding scooters in Monaco are police. The benefit of that, of course, is that Monaco is the safest place in Europe. Lots of security forces are around to protect everyone's money, and the streets are safe at all hours. Children take buses alone. It's also one of the cleanest places in Europe, and you'll rarely see litter on the ground.

Monaco's telephone numbers have eight digits, as opposed to France's numbers with ten digits. When calling Monaco from France, dial ☎ 00-377 plus the eight-digit number. To dial Monaco from the United States, dial ☎ 011-377 plus the eight-digit number. To call a number in France from Monaco, dial ☎ 00-33 plus the last nine digits of the number.

Getting there

With no border formalities, Monaco is easy to get to by car, bus, or train, with frequent **train** service (every half-hour) to and from Cannes, Nice, Antibes, and Menton. Trips from Nice to Monaco cost 3.10€ ($3.70) and take 25 to 30 minutes. From Paris, at least two trains per day depart from Gare de Lyon, each requiring between 6 and 6¾ hours one way, and sometimes requiring a change of equipment and a brief stopover in Nice. One-way fares cost around 102€ ($122) per person. For train schedules, call ☎ **93-10-60-01** in Monaco or 08-92-35-35-35 in France.

Monaco's enormous train station has three exits on three levels, and if you don't know which exit to use, you may have trouble finding your hotel. Monaco is a confusing place to navigate, so you may want to pick up a free map at the station's tourist office (open Monday to Saturday 9 a.m. to 7 p.m.). Arriving at the Monaco train station after 9 p.m. is like arriving on Wall Street after 9 p.m. — it's desolate, and there's not a soul on the street. On the bright side, Monaco restaurants serve dinner late, so you can usually get a full meal at least until 11 p.m.

Monaco has frequent **bus** service (every 15 minutes) to Nice, Beaulieu, and Menton on line No. 100 of the French bus company Rapides Côte d'Azur (☎ **04-93-85-64-44**). The trip from Nice to Monaco by bus takes half an hour and costs 3.80€ ($4.55) round trip or one way (your choice). The times and prices are the same to Menton. The easiest place to catch a bus is in front of the gardens that face the Casino, but it also stops in front of the port (on bd. Albert-1er at the Stade Nautique stop) and at several other spots around town.

If you're **driving** from Nice to Monaco, take N7 northeast. The 12-mile (19 km) drive takes about 35 minutes because of heavy traffic; Cannes to Monaco requires about 55 minutes. If driving from Paris, follow A6 to Lyon. In Lyon, take A7 south to Aix-en-Provence and A8 to Monaco.

Getting around and getting information

The best way to get around Monaco (see the nearby "Monaco" map) is by **bus,** and you can buy bus cards, which cost 1.30€ ($1.60) per ride, directly on the bus. Stops are set up every few blocks on the main streets in town, including bd. Albert-1er, av. St-Martin in Monaco Ville, and bd. des Moulins in Monte Carlo. Buses go to the major tourist sights; the front of the bus shows the destination.

For a taxi, call ☎ **93-15-01-01.** Taxi stands are in front of the Casino on av. de Monte-Carlo, at place des Moulins in Monte Carlo; at the Port de Monaco on av. Président J. F. Kennedy; and in front of the Poste de Monte-Carlo on av. Henry-Dunant. A **Hertz** car-rental office is at 27 bd. Albert-1er (☎ **93-50-79-60**), and an **Avis** office at 9 av. d'Ostende (☎ **93-30-17-53**).

The **Corniches** are the three major scenic coastal highways of the Riviera stretching from Nice to Menton and passing around Monaco. The lower road is called the **Corniche Inférieure;** the middle road is the **Moyenne Corniche,** which runs through the mountains; and the **Grande Corniche** is the highest road over the top of the mountains bordering the Riviera.

Monaco

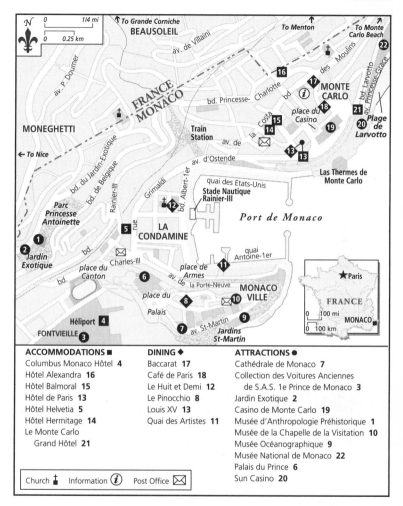

0 — 1/4 mi
0 — 0.25 km

N

To Grande Corniche
BEAUSOLEIL

To Menton

To Monte Carlo Beach

av. de Villaini

des Moulins

bd. Princesse-Charlotte

Charlotte

bd.

(i) **MONTE CARLO**

FRANCE MONACO

av. P. Doumer

MONEGHETTI

← To Nice

Train Station

av. de

place du Casino

bd. Larvotto

av. Princesse-Grace

Plage de Larvotto

bd. du Jardin-Exotique
bd. de Belgique
Rainier-III

av. d'Ostende

Las Thermes de Monte Carlo

Parc Princesse Antoinette

quai des Etats-Unis

Stade Nautique Rainier-III

Port de Monaco

Grimaldi

bd. Albert-1er

rue

LA CONDAMINE

quai Antoine-1er

bd.

place du Canton

Charles-III

Jardin Exotique

place de Armes

av. de la Porte-Neuve

MONACO VILLE

★Paris

FRANCE

MONACO

place du Palais

Héliport

FONTVIEILLE

av. St-Martin

Jardins St-Martin

0 — 100 mi
0 — 100 km

ACCOMMODATIONS ■	DINING ◆	ATTRACTIONS ●
Columbus Monaco Hôtel 4	Baccarat 17	Cathédrale de Monaco 7
Hôtel Alexandra 16	Café de Paris 18	Collection des Voitures Anciennes
Hôtel Balmoral 15	Le Huit et Demi 12	de S.A.S. 1e Prince de Monaco 3
Hôtel de Paris 13	Le Pinocchio 8	Jardin Exotique 2
Hôtel Helvetia 5	Louis XV 13	Casino de Monte Carlo 19
Hôtel Hermitage 14	Quai des Artistes 11	Musée d'Anthropologie Préhistorique 1
Le Monte Carlo		Musée de la Chapelle de la Visitation 10
Grand Hôtel 21		Musée Océanographique 9
		Musée National de Monaco 22
		Palais du Prince 6
Church ✝ Information *(i)* Post Office ✉		Sun Casino 20

If you're driving around Monaco, be *very careful* on the wicked curves of the corniches. The changing of the palace guard (La Releve de la Garde del Palais des Grimaldi) takes place at 11:55 a.m., which creates a major traffic jam in Monaco between 10:30 and 11:30 a.m. If you're driving in or around Monaco during that time, you'll have major delays.

The **tourist office** is at 2A bd. des Moulins, Monte Carlo (☎ 92-16-61-66), and is open Monday to Saturday 9 a.m. to 7 p.m., Sunday 10 a.m. to noon.

Spending the night

Columbus Monaco Hotel
$$$–$$$$ Fontvieille

In the modern Fontvieille sector of Monaco is a stylish and contemporary 181-unit hotel. This hotel is the harbinger of a hotel chain launched by Scotsman Ken McCulloch. McCulloch is called the "champion of high style at low prices." He says he believes that low prices don't have to mean low-brow. Facing Princess Grace's former rose garden and the sea, this first-class hotel is open year-round. Bedrooms are done in what McCulloch calls "Hybrid Hip," evocative of both Miami and London at the same time. Among the disadvantages, the pool is shared with residents of the condo complex in which the hotel is situated. But as a grace note, guests are carried in a boat shuttle to a tranquil sandy beach nearby. The on-site brasserie serves a fabulous antipasto buffet along with savory pastas and pizzas; and the bar, **Downstairs,** is lively with lounge music. A hip crowd of locals and visitors are attracted to it, including Prince Albert.

See map p. 409. 23 av. des Papalins. ☎ *92-05-90-00. Fax: 92-05-91-67.* www.columbushotels.com. *Parking: 23€ ($28). Rack rates: 240€–330€ ($288–$396) double, 330€–900€ ($396–$1,080) suite. AE, MC, V.*

Hôtel Alexandra
$$ Monte Carlo

Close to the casino, the early-1900s Alexandra has an idyllic corner location. The friendly reception makes you feel right at home. A recent renovation cleaned up the beautiful facade and spruced up the 56 rooms, which are spacious and comfortable, although some are dark. They include modern modular wall units forming desks and closets and extras such as soundproof windows, minibars, and hairdryers. The rooms with French balconies open onto street views. The continental breakfast is served only in the rooms.

See map p. 409. 33 bd. Princesse-Charlotte. ☎ *93-50-63-13. Fax: 92-16-06-48. E-mail:* hotel-alexandra@monaco377.com. *Parking: 7€ ($8.40). Rack rates: 110€–140€ ($132–$168) double. Breakfast: 13€ ($16). AE, DC, MC, V.*

Hôtel Balmoral
$$ Monte Carlo

One of the great deals on the Côte d'Azur, the 66-room Balmoral is a few blocks from the casino; it's beside the Hermitage on a promontory, so you have the same view as those paying three times the rate next door. Many rooms have French balconies, where you can enjoy a perfect sunrise over the sea. Breakfast is served in a rather depressing basement room, but it is a pretty good buffet, with cheeses, meats, and pâtés in addition to the usual fare. The large patio and garden overlooking the harbor are perfect for strolling or sitting. The restaurant is open for lunch and dinner.

See map p. 409. 12 av. de la Costa. ☎ *93-50-62-37. Fax: 93-15-08-69.* www.hotel-balmoral.mc. *Parking: 8€ ($9.60). Rack rates: 110€–200€ ($132–$240) double; 150€–300€ ($180–$360) suite. Breakfast: 15€ ($18). AE, DC, MC, V.*

Hôtel de Paris
$$$$ Monte Carlo

One of Europe's grandest hotels, Hotel de Paris, built in 1864, sits beside the famous casino on Monte Carlo's central square. The elaborate facade is a *beaux-arts* wonder surpassed only by the gilded lobby with marble columns, classical statuary, crystal chandeliers, and frescoes. The 191 high-ceilinged accommodations are individually decorated with antiques and stylish accessories, and many have balconies. The hotel features four restaurants: Alain Ducasse's Louis XV, the Grill, the Restaurant Salle Empire, and the Côté Jardin. Le Bar Américain is a sophisticated piano bar. The hotel is connected to Thermes Marins, an ultramodern seawater therapy spa. The hotel also offers an indoor pool, saunas, and a fitness center. Guests are given a gold card allowing free access to the casino and the Monte Carlo Beach Club, with its private pool and beach. The card also offers a 50 percent discount at the Monte Carlo Country Club, with 23 tennis courts and the Golf Club.

See map p. 409. Place du Casino. ☎ *92-16-30-00. Fax: 92-16-38-50.* www.montecarloresort.com. *Parking: 25€ ($30). Rack rates: 385€–750€ ($462–$900) double; 690€–7,630€ ($828–$9,156) suite. Breakfast: 30€–35€ ($36–$42). AE, DC, MC, V.*

Hôtel Helvetia
$ La Condamine

Hôtel Helvetia is the best inexpensive hotel in Monaco, with a good location just steps from rue Princesse-Caroline, a four-block-long cafe-lined pedestrian street leading to the port. The hotel also is only a short walk from place d'Armes, where Monaco's outdoor food market is open Saturday mornings. Of its 25 rooms, 19 have private baths. For breakfast in the pleasant street-front dining room, you can choose from a continental or full breakfast, both with homemade jam.

See map p. 409. 1 bis rue Grimaldi. ☎ *93-30-21-71. Fax: 92-16-70-51. E-mail:* hotel-helvetia@monte-carlo.mc. *Rack rates: 55€–72€ ($66–$86) double without bathroom, 75€–95€ ($90–$114) double with bathroom. AE, MC, V.*

Hôtel Hermitage
$$$$ Monte Carlo

Second only to the Hôtel de Paris (see earlier in this section), the Hermitage is a glistening *beaux-arts* palace, with a location high on the precipice. Like the Paris, the Hermitage is owned by the Société des Bains de Mer, an organization founded in 1863 to develop Monte Carlo. The facade, facing the port and the sea, has an Italian-style loggia and vaulting with ceiling frescoes. Inside is a Winter Garden, built by Gustave Eiffel, with a Tiffany-type stained-glass dome. The lovely 280 rooms, including 20 suites, are decorated in period decor in the central part or in a cheerful contemporary style in the newer wings. Many of the rooms have balconies with wicker furniture. You have access to the attached seawater therapy spa (also attached to the Paris), with a large pool. The restaurant and bar Le Vistamar opens onto a beautiful terrace that is the best place to have a drink in Monaco. Guests are given a gold card allowing free access to the casino and the Monte Carlo Beach Club, with its private pool and beach. The card also offers a 50 percent discount at the Monte Carlo Country Club, with 23 tennis courts and the Golf Club.

See map p. 409. Square Beaumarchais. ☎ *92-16-40-00. Fax: 92-16-38-52.* www. montecarloresort.com. *Parking: 25€ ($30). Rack rates: 355€–490€ ($426–$588) double; from 1,680€ ($2,016) suite. Breakfast: Continental breakfast 26€ ($31); buffet breakfast 30€ ($36). AE, MC, V.*

Le Monte Carlo Grand Hôtel
$$$–$$$$ Monte Carlo

In a feat of daring engineering and questionable aesthetics, the 619-room Grand was built over the water at the edge of Monte Carlo. To fit six floors of rooms, the ceilings are on the low side, particularly in the lobby, so the impression of grandness is limited. Nevertheless, this is a top-notch hotel with a down-to-earth quality and a friendly staff. A country French decor and a liberal use of wicker brighten up the rooms, many of which have balconies overlooking the sea. The hotel contains two restaurants: l'Argentine, serving Italian food, grilled steaks, and seafood; and Le Pistou, an upscale Provençal restaurant. On the premises also are the Sun Casino; a patisserie; a cafe; a fitness center; and, on the rooftop, a heated fresh-water pool.

See map p. 409. 12 av. des Spélugues. ☎ *93-50-65-00. Fax: 93-30-01-57.* www.monte carlograndhotel.com. *Parking: 20€ ($24). Rack rates: 245€–485€ ($294–$582) double; 560€–1,750€ ($672–$2,100) suite. Breakfast: Continental breakfast 22€ ($26); English breakfast 30€ ($36). AE, DC, MC, V.*

Dining locally

The national dish of Monaco is *stocafi,* a heavy stockfish dish prepared with olive oil, onions, tomatoes, white wine, potatoes, black olives, and cognac. *Pissaladière* is a pizza with onions, and *barbagiuan* is a stuffed dumpling with rice, squash, leeks, eggs, and cheese. *Beignet de fleur de courgettes* are batter-fried zucchinis stuffed with veal and cheese. And a special Monaco aperitif is *pastis Casanis,* a local brand of pastis, which is an anise-flavored liqueur.

Baccarat
$–$$$$ Monte Carlo   ITALIAN

Established late in 2002 as one of Monaco's most upscale and elegant restaurants, Baccarat is a sedate testimonial to the flavors and presentations of Italy, with a special emphasis on Sicily, birthplace of owner and chef Carmelo Gulletta. In a vaguely Art Deco ambience with high-backed cardinal-red chairs, a not particularly riveting view over the street, and off-white walls lined with the avant-garde paintings of Monégasque painter Clérissy, you'll enjoy a cuisine that the owners say is more Italian, and less Monégasques, than anything else in Monaco. The dining room is supervised by Guletta's France-born, English-speaking wife, Patricia. The antipasto selection is the best in the principality, ranging from steamed asparagus with hollandaise to an Andalusian gazpacho. The chefs turn out risottos as good as any found in Italy, along with Monaco's most enticing pastas, especially a savory spaghetti with baby clams. Fish dishes such as sole meunière are generally better than the meat and poultry offerings.

See map p. 409. 4 bd. des Moullins. ☎ *93-50-66-92. Reservations recommended. Main courses: 15€–45€ ($18–$54). AE, MC, V. Open: Sun–Fri noon to 2:30 p.m.; daily 7–10:30 p.m.*

Café de Paris
$–$$$ Monte Carlo   FRENCH

Its *plats du jour* are well prepared, and its location, the plaza adjacent to the casino and the Hôtel de Paris, provides you with a front-row view of the comings and goings of the nerve center of Monte Carlo. But to our tastes, this 1985 re-creation of old-time Monaco is a bit too theme-ish, a bit too enraptured with the devil-may-care glamour of early-1900s Monte Carlo. Despite that, Café de Paris continues to draw patrons who appreciate the razzmatazz and all the glass and chrome. Menu items change frequently, and local office workers appreciate the platters, because they can be served and consumed relatively quickly, with dishes such as fresh grilled sea bass and steak tartare with matchstick *frites*. Adjacent to the restaurant, you'll find (and hear) a jangling collection of slot machines and a cliché-riddled cluster of boutiques selling expensively casual resort wear and souvenirs.

See map p. 409. Place du Casino. ☎ *92-16-20-20. Reservations recommended. Main courses: 20€–52€ ($24–$62). AE, DC, MC, V. Breakfast daily for 17€–24€ ($20–$29). Open: Daily 7 a.m.–1 a.m.*

Le Huit et Demi
$–$$ La Condamine   ITALIAN/MONÉGASQUE

This authentic restaurant, just off pedestrian rue Princesse-Caroline, is named after the seminal Fellini movie *8½* and the patrons usually include several large tables of Italians. The movie theme extends to the interior walls, which are painted with names of classic movies. Most of the seating is outside, where you can sit on director's chairs under brightly colored umbrellas and enjoy a cool breeze blowing off the port. Skip the fish dishes, and stick with the specialty: homemade pasta. The restaurant also serves good pizza priced at 11€ ($13), made the Italian way with thin crust, easy on the tomato sauce, and lots of garlic.

See map p. 409. 4 rue Langlé. ☎ *93-50-97-02. Reservations recommended. Main courses: 11€–25€ ($13–$30). AE, DC, MC, V. Open: Mon–Fri noon to 2:30 p.m. and Mon–Sat 7–11 p.m.*

Le Pinocchio
$–$$ Monaco Ville   ITALIAN

This restaurant near the palace has been serving hearty Italian home cooking since 1973. The owner, Enzo, displays a certain *sang-froid,* not to say crankiness, but he means well. The restaurant has tables outside, under awnings, on the narrow street; inside seating is cozy, with tables forming two long rows along the walls. The specialties of the chef (whose ingredients are the freshest) are risotto, ravioli Pinocchio (homemade and stuffed with meat), and spaghetti with shrimp.

See map p. 409. 30 rue Comte-Félix-Gastaldi. ☎ *93-30-96-20. Reservations recommended. Main courses: 12€–19€ ($14–$23). MC, V. Open: Daily noon to 2 p.m. and 7:30–10:30 p.m. (closed for lunch on Sun). Closed mid-Dec to mid-Jan.*

Louis XV
$$$$ Monte Carlo   PROVENÇAL/TUSCAN

This golden palace is one of the best restaurants in the world. The restaurant offers haute cuisine in a resplendent if imposing setting, and that means astronomical prices. Chef Alain Ducasse, who has his hand in many other restaurants in Paris, London, New York, and Japan, is the maestro behind the operation. He calls the cuisine "southern flavors and Mediterranean cuisine." You can choose from two menus at every meal or order à la carte: The more expensive menu, "Pour les Gourmets," offers meat and fish choices, and the "Jardin de Provence" is closer to a vegetarian menu. The menus change seasonally to reflect the freshest ingredients. A typically delectable first course is *légumes des jardins de Provence mijotés à la truffe noire rapée* (garden vegetables of Provence simmered with grated black truffles). For a main course, the chef recommends *poitrine de pigeonneau, foie gras de canard et pommes de terre au jus d'abats* (breast of pigeon with duck foie gras and potatoes with a broth of organ meats). A justifiably famous dessert is *frais des bois, sorbet au mascarpone* (wild strawberries with mascarpone sorbet).

See map p. 409. At the Hôtel de Paris, Place du Casino. ☎ *92-16-30-01. Reservations recommended. Jacket and tie required for men. Main courses: 60€–96€ ($72–$115); prix fixe: 150€–180€ ($180–$216). AE, MC, V. Open: Thurs–Mon 12:15–1:45 p.m. and 8–9:45 p.m. Also open Wed at lunch during July and Aug.*

Quai des Artistes
$$ La Condamine   BRASSERIE

Artists and creative types hang out at this Parisian-style bar/brasserie/ restaurant on the west side of the harbor. Not surprisingly, the restaurant offers lots of outdoor seating, so you can watch the yachts come and go.

The inside is sleek and stylish, with a long inviting bar. Standouts include the special preparation of *suprême poulet fermier* (tender breast of farm-raised chicken roasted with lemon verbena and crisp young leeks) and the carpaccio of tuna Japanese style, served with eggplant caviar. For dessert, try the homemade sorbets, with raspberry being the most popular.

See map p. 409. 4 quai Antoine-1er. ☎ *97-97-97-77. Reservations recommended. Main courses: 19€–28€ ($23–$34); prix fixe: 21€ ($25) lunch only. AE, DC, MC, V. Open: Daily noon to 2:30 p.m. and 7:30–11:30 p.m.*

Exploring the principality

Monaco has five sections. **Monaco Ville** is the charming Old Town up on "The Rock," to the west of the harbor. Here you find the palace (where the changing of the guard takes place), the Oceanographic Museum and Aquarium, the cathedral, the St-Martin Garden, and lots of shops and restaurants. **Monte Carlo,** to the east of the harbor, is home to the famous casino; fancy shops; and luxury hotels such as the Paris, the Hermitage, and the Monte Carlo Grand. West of Old Town, **Fontvieille** is an industrial suburb that was created by filling in a marshy area. Monaco's car museum is located in this neighborhood. **La Condamine,** the center of Monaco in front of the Port d'Hercule, boasts lots of shops and restaurants, and some inexpensive hotels. **Larvotto,** on the far east end of the principality, has a good stretch of public beach called Plage du Larvotto and the Grimaldi Forum, where conferences and events took placed.

 With commentary in English, the red-and-white tourist train **Azur Express** (☎ 92-05-64-38) winds through the Old Town and travels to Monte Carlo in 30 minutes round trip. The train arrives at and departs from the Musée Océanographique in Monaco Ville every half-hour daily 10:30 a.m. to 6 p.m. The fare is 6€ ($7.20).

Monaco's royal palace

Palais du Prince (place du Palais; ☎ 93-25-18-31), where an aging Prince Rainier lives, has a defensive appearance, betraying its beginnings as a 13th-century fortress. In the 15th century, the Grimaldis transformed it into a royal palace, and in the late 16th century, they hired Italian artists to decorate the property (the courtyard and interior still bear this heavy Italian Renaissance influence). A guide leads you on a half-hour tour through a dozen finely furnished rooms, including the throne room. You can see marble floors and stairways, 16th-century frescoes, paneled walls, and even a hall of mirrors (a smaller version of the one at Versailles). The large official portrait of the present-day Grimaldis is in one of the last rooms on the tour: Albert wears a tennis sweater, while Caroline and Stephanie are in ballgowns; the painting within the painting is a larger-than-life portrait of Princess Grace, looking supernaturally serene. These days just father and son (Prince Rainier and Albert) occupy the palace, and Caroline and Stephanie make their homes elsewhere. In season, you may find long lines here daily.

The best time to visit is early or late in the day, and the worst time to visit is after the changing of the guard, when crowds are at their peak. Crowds form early for the 11:55 a.m. changing of the guard in front of the palace, which lasts less than 10 minutes. For a good view, arrive at least 20 minutes before the event.

In another wing of the palace, **Musée des Souvenirs Napoléoniens et Archives** (☎ 93-25-18-31) is a small museum containing some interesting Napoléon materials, such as the hat he wore on Elba (the site of Napoléon's first exile), a piece of mahogany from his coffin, and his death mask in bronze. An entertaining description by Napoléon of the harrowing birth of his son also can be seen. While his second wife, Marie-Louise, endured 26 hours of hard labor, she shouted at Napoléon, "You want to sacrifice me for the sake of my son?" The museum also features exhibits about the history of Monaco. Most exhibits have English translations.

Admission to the palace is 6€ ($7.20) for adults, 3€ ($3.60) ages 8 to 14, and free for those under 7. Admission to the museum is 4€ ($4.80) adults, 2€ ($2.40) children 8 to 14, and free for children under 8. The palace is open June to September daily 9:30 a.m. to 6 p.m.; October daily 10 a.m. to 5 p.m.; closed otherwise. The museum is open June to September daily 9:30 a.m. to 6 p.m., and December to May 10:30 a.m. to 12:30 p.m. and 2 to 5 p.m. English-speaking tours are available.

Museums and other sights

Built on the edge of a cliff overlooking the sea, **Musée Océanographique** (av. St-Martin; ☎ 93-15-36-00; www.oceano.mc) occupies a beautiful *beaux-arts* building and includes one of Europe's largest aquariums. Prince Rainier I, great-grandfather of the present ruler, built this museum in 1910 to house his extensive collections from sea travels and explorations. The aquarium has 3,000 fish, including many rare species and a coral reef from the Red Sea. Don't miss the elegant polka-dot grouper named after Grace Kelly *(merou de Grace Kelly)*, the aquarium's oldest fish (a fierce moray eel caught off Antibes in 1968), or the decisive Napoléon fish. The whale room shelters whaling boats and skeletons of their victims. One skeleton is from a fin whale that washed up on the Italian coast some months after the prince harpooned him in 1896. Other interesting exhibits are the "first submarine," a tortoise-shaped vessel built by American David Bushnell and used during the American Revolution. The museum also shows fun 19th-century films of the research ship *Princesse Alice* and its crew (the prince is the one in the straw boater and walrus mustache). The exotic fish and the incredible history displays are sure to keep every member of your family entertained. The museum is open daily (except the Sunday of the Grand Prix race) April through September 9 a.m. to 7:30 p.m. and October through March 10 a.m. to 6 p.m. Admission is 11€ ($13) for adults and 6€ ($7.20) for children from 6 to 18 years old and students.

Two interesting attractions are on the side of a rocky cliff on the west end of Monaco: the **Jardin Exotique** and the **Musée d'Anthropologie Préhistorique de Monaco** (62 bd. du Jardin-Exotique; ☎ 93-15-29-80). In 1912, Prince Albert I created, in the Jardin Exotique, a strange world with thousands of blooming cacti, including rare species and giant cacti more than 100 years old. You wander over paths and bridges with panoramic views of Monaco and the sea. Among other unusual plants is the elephant-eared kalanchoe, with large velvety leaves used by mothers in Madagascar to carry their babies. Near the bottom of the gardens are caves reachable by 300 steps. You can visit the caves, filled with stalactites and stalagmites forming natural sculptures, by guided tour, on the hour daily 10 a.m. to 6 p.m. Also on the property is the Musée d'Anthropologie, with more collections of the intellectually curious Albert I. These anthropology exhibits prove that even Cro-Magnon man liked the Côte d'Azur. Apparently, archaeologists found prehistoric skeletons, including two people embracing, in the nearby caves, as well as cave paintings. The museum also houses taxidermy of bear, bison, and moose. Scientists discovered evidence that bears and panthers lived in the caves on the rocks. The garden and museum are open daily (except November 19 and December 25) mid-May to mid-September 9 a.m. to 7 p.m. and late September to early May 9 a.m. to 6 p.m.

Built in 1875, the **Cathédrale de Monaco** at 4 rue Colonel Bellando de Castro in Monaco-Ville (☎ 93-30-87-70) is where Princess Grace is buried. You can pay homage at her tomb, marked by an inscribed stone *(Gracia Patricia Principis Rainerii III)* and bushels of roses. The cathedral was built in 1875 in a part-Romanesque, part-Byzantine style.

The tiny **Musée de la Chapelle de la Visitation** (place de la Visitation; ☎ 93-50-07-00) contains the personal collection of Barbara Piasecka Johnson: 17th-century paintings, about 20 of them, including works by Rubens, Zubaran, and Ribera. The works are exhibited in a baroque style 17th-century chapel, a brightly lit room with marble floors and columns. The museum is open Tuesday to Sunday 10 a.m. to 4 p.m., and admission is 3€ ($3.60) adults, 1.50€ ($1.80) children ages 6 to 18.

Prince Rainier's antique car museum, **Collection des Voitures Anciennes de S.A.S Prince de Monaco** (Les Terrasses de Fontvieille; ☎ 92-05-28-56), contains about 105 shiny vehicles, including the 1956 Rolls-Royce Silver Cloud that Prince Rainier and Princess Grace rode on their wedding day. The museum is open daily 10 a.m. to 6 p.m. (except December 25). Admission is 6€ ($7.20) for adults and 3€ ($3.60) for children 8 to 14 and students.

Musée National de Monaco (17 av. Princesse-Grace; ☎ 93-30-91-26) displays a large collection of dolls and automatons made in Paris in the late 19th century. The dolls are presented in showcases with period furniture, chinaware, and other items of daily life. A dollhouse villa designed by Charles Garnier, the architect who designed the Paris and Monaco opera houses, also is displayed. The museum also plays host to temporary exhibitions that are sure to please kids of any age — one recent show featured Barbie dolls wearing dresses created by international designers. The museum is open daily (except January 1, May 1, November 19, and December 25) April through September 10 a.m. to 6:30 p.m. and October to Easter 10 a.m. to 12:15 p.m. and 2:30 to 6:30 p.m. Admission is 6€ ($7.20) for adults and 3.50€ ($4.20) for children 6 to 14 and students.

Shopping for local treasures

Monaco's **food market** takes place Saturdays 7 a.m. to 1 p.m. on place d'Armes (6 Le Marché de la Condamire) at the top of rue Grimaldi. A **flea market** is open Saturdays from 10 a.m. to 5 p.m. at the Port de Fontvieille. All the designer boutiques — including Cartier, Louis Vuitton, Yves St-Laurent, Chanel, and Gucci — are located in Monte Carlo in the rue des Beaux-Arts near the grand hotels. The best shopping street, with unique stores, in La Condamine is pedestrian **rue Princesse-Caroline,** starting at rue Grimaldi and stretching three blocks to the port.

The best of the small boutiques are **Sorasio Fleurs,** an elegant flower shop at 6 av. des Beaux-Arts in the Hôtel de Paris (☎ 93-30-71-01); **Boutique du Rocher,** at 1 av. de la Madone (☎ 93-30-91-17) and 11 rue Emile de Loth (☎ 93-30-33-99), the official store of the Princess Grace charitable foundation, selling art and handcrafts; and **Yves Delorme,** at Centre Commercial le Métropole (☎ 93-50-08-70), for luxurious housewares, linens, clothing, gift objects, and fashion.

Living it up after dark

Casino de Monte Carlo (place du Casino; ☎ 92-16-21-21) was once a very formal place (you may remember its cameo appearance in the *I Love Lucy* episode where Lucy wins a fortune here by accident). Today, busloads of disheveled visitors trip up the marble steps to play the one-armed bandits. But the casino does have more formal private rooms, where you won't find electronic gaming, and a jacket and tie are required after 9 p.m. for men. To enter the gaming rooms, you must be 21, present a passport or driver's license, and pay 10€ ($12) for the Salons Européens (opening at noon) or 20€ ($24) for the Salons Privés (opening at 3 p.m.). Salons Privés are extraordinary, with muraled walls and frescoed ceilings; it's actually worth going in and gawking. The casino's Les Monte Carlo Follies **Cabaret** (☎ 92-16-36-36), around the left side of the building, plays host to Vegas-style nightclub shows from mid-September to the end of June, Tuesday to Sunday 10 to 11:30 p.m. (admission is 40€ /$48 including a drink). Dinner plus the show costs 62€ ($74).

If you prefer more sophisticated entertainment, the place to see concerts, ballet, and opera is the **Opéra de Monte-Carlo,** a *beaux-arts* opera house that's also part of the casino building. For tickets and information, call Atrium du Casino at ☎ 92-16-22-99 or stop by the box office daily 10 a.m. to 5:30 p.m. Tickets run 35€ to 115€ ($42 to $138).

Fun bars in Monaco include **Sass Café** (11 av. Princesse-Grace; ☎ 93-25-52-00), which has a piano bar, and **Quai des Artistes** (4 quai Antoine-1er on the port; ☎ 97-97-97-77), attracting a young after-dinner crowd to the large bar area (see "Dining locally," earlier in this section).

Finally, for insight into the terribly fashionable, terribly blasé, and terribly jaded nocturnal pleasures of the Monégasques, consider dropping into **Jimmy'z,** in Le Sporting Monte Carolo, 26 av. Princesse-Grace (☎ 92-16-22-77). Acquired by Monaco's Société des Bains de Mer, it boasts metallic walls, dozens of potted plants, deep upholsteries, a decorative lagoon, and a roof that opens wide during warm weather for a view of the moon and stars. Entrance is free, but once you're inside, you'll be strongly encouraged to order a drink, or perhaps several, with whisky priced at 39€ ($47) each. It's open nightly from 10:30 p.m. to around 4 a.m. Between October and May, it's closed every Monday and Tuesday. Men are encouraged to wear jackets or at least long-sleeved shirts.

St-Jean-Cap-Ferrat and the Rothschild Villa

You may equate the name "Cap-Ferrat" with images of extreme opulence, but the village of **St-Jean-Cap-Ferrat** is really just a small touristy fishing port with a dozen reasonably priced restaurants bordering the harbor and a handful of little boutiques nearby. The real estate on this lush peninsula is among the Riviera's priciest. At the tip of the peninsula, 3km (2 miles) from the port, is one of the area's most expensive and luxurious hotels, Grand Hôtel du Cap-Ferrat. The Rothschild villa, on the highest and most central spot on the peninsula, is a fascinating museum that illustrates life in the Belle Epoque era and is surrounded by magnificent French gardens.

Getting there

The village of Cap-Ferrat is about a mile from the nearest train station at Beaulieu (see "Beaulieu and the Villa Kérylos," later in this chapter); it's a scenic walk along the bay. For train information, call ☎ 08-92-35-35-39 or 08-92-35-35-35. With no bus service available from the center of Beaulieu to the village of Cap-Ferrat, you need to take a **taxi** (11€/$13), if you don't have a car.

Nice is about 4km (6 miles) away, and **buses** frequently make the half-hour trip at a cost of 2€ ($2.40). The bus between Nice and Cap-Ferrat, the No. 111, runs from Monday to Saturday (not holidays). **Aéroport Nice Côte d'Azur** is 20 minutes (21km/13 miles) from Cap-Ferrat. You can rent a car from the airport or take a shuttle bus to the center of Nice and pick up a bus to Cap-Ferrat from the Nice bus station. Monaco is 16km (10 miles) away from Cap-Ferrat, while Cannes is 40km (26 miles) away. To drive to Cap-Ferrat from Nice, take N7 east.

Getting around and getting information

You really need a car for Cap-Ferrat — mainly to arrive and depart from the peninsula. Villa Ephrussi de Rothschild is technically within walking distance (about 20 minutes) from the village, but access is from a busy road with a narrow sidewalk and then up a long winding driveway with no sidewalk. If you stay at a hotel near the harbor, you can walk to restaurants and shopping, but the car still comes in handy to explore the peninsula by driving through the steep residential area, out to the Grand Hôtel. You can also take long walks along coastal paths on Cap-Ferrat. The **tourist office** is at 59 av. Denis-Séméria (☎ **04-93-76-08-90**; www.ville-saint-jean-cap-ferrat.fr). During July and August, the office is open daily 9 a.m. to 6 p.m.; September to June, hours are Monday to Saturday 9 a.m. to 5 p.m. The tourist office offers free trail maps for exploring the peninsula on foot.

Spending the night

Grand Hôtel du Cap-Ferrat
$$$–$$$$ St-Jean-Cap-Ferrat

One of the Riviera's grandest hotels is Grand Hotel du Cap-Ferrat. As reflected in its name and prices, they don't nickel and dime you here: admission to the pool is included. It's a mirror of heated salt water that seems to float just above the Mediterranean (pool admission is charged at the Eden Roc in Antibes; see Chapter 21). And the staff is quite friendly. All is palatial at the Grand, from the lobby, with its inlaid marble floor and soaring columns, to the 53 gorgeous rooms, many with terraces and sea views. The 5.6-hectare (14-acre) estate features floral garden paths. The restaurant is superb (see "Dining locally," later in this chapter), with dining outside on the sea-facing terrace or inside in the gilded dining room.

71 bd. du Général-de-Gaulle. ☎ *04-93-76-50-50. Fax: 04-93-76-50-76.* www.grand-hotel-cap-ferrat.com. *Free outdoor parking. Rack rates: 205€–1,075€ ($246–$1,290) double; 740€–2,525€ ($888–$3,030) suite. Ask about much-lower off-season (Mar, Apr, Nov, Dec) rates. Breakfast 25€ ($30). AE, MC, V. Closed Jan–Feb.*

Hôtel Belle Aurore
$–$$ St-Jean-Cap-Ferrat

The English-speaking staff is accommodating at this hotel (with no elevator), a pleasant seven-minute walk from town. Although the lobby and bar area are somewhat dreary, just outside is a good-sized pool surrounded by a large terrace, where breakast is served. The pool includes the whimsical touch of a tiny island with a tall palm tree in the middle. The 20 rooms are motel-style but comfortable, and many open onto terraces with views of the village and port. All units have extras such as safes and minibars.

49 av. Denis-Séméria. ☎ *04-93-76-24-24. Fax: 04-93-76-15-10. No on-site parking. Rack rates: 80€–180€ ($96–$216) double. Rates include breakfast. AE, DC, MC, V.*

Hôtel Brise Marine
$$ St-Jean-Cap-Ferrat

By virtue of its location in the Old Town, a few blocks up from the harbor, this is the best choice for a medium-priced hotel. The 17-room circa 1870 Brise Marine is a very attractive pale-yellow villa set high, with panoramic views of the Riviera coast all the way to Italy. It's also quite near Paloma Plage, one of the two public beaches. The high-ceilinged rooms are pretty and fresh, some with balconies; the eight rooms with views are more expensive. Breakfast is served in the large stone courtyard overlooking the sea. The same family has owned and operated the hotel since 1945.

58 av. Jean-Mermoz. ☎ *04-93-76-04-36. Fax: 04-93-76-11-49.* www.hotel-brise marine.com. *Parking: 10€ ($12). Rack rates: 130€–145€ ($156–$174) double. Breakfast: 11€ ($13). AE, DC, MC, V. Closed Nov–Jan.*

Hôtel Clair Logis
$–$$ St-Jean-Cap-Ferrat

This 16-room hotel is a lovely, very large early-20th-century villa with two outbuildings (one originally constructed as a garage). The location, high in the central part of the peninsula in a residential area, means you're somewhat isolated. The walk to town or the beaches is long, so access to a car is critical if you stay here. The rooms range in size: A modern 1970s-era annex has simple smaller rooms, and the pavilion has the largest rooms, such as Hibiscus, with a balcony and huge bath. The hotel is surrounded by a dense canopy of trees, so is has no water views.

12 av. Centrale. ☎ *04-93-76-51-81. Fax: 04-93-76-51-82.* www.hotel-clair-logis.fr. *Free parking. Rack rates: 90€–180€ ($108–$216) double. Breakfast: 13€ ($16). AE, MC, V.*

Hôtel La Voile d'Or
$$$–$$$$ St-Jean-Cap-Ferrat

La Voile d'Or is luxurious and down-to-earth — perhaps it's the sight of the gregarious owner, who has run the hotel for nearly 50 years, walking around in casual clothes and checking on the comfort of guests. Or it could be the dining room, which, though lovely, has a distinct beachy-ness. The 45 rooms, perched above the harbor, actually have more interesting views than those at the Grand Hôtel (see earlier in this section); they look out over the sweep of coastline from Beaulieu to Monaco. The rooms are the height of elegance and comfort — all have Florentine-inspired furniture, and most have French doors leading to terraces. You can easily walk to the village and portside restaurants. The hotel offers garden terraces for dining, in addition to a cheerful dining room with wraparound windows. The heated pool is above the harbor and sea, and a private beach is a short walk down the embankment.

7 av. Jean-Mermoz. ☎ *04-93-01-13-13. Fax: 04-93-76-11-17.* www.lavoiledor.fr. *Parking: 22€ ($26). Rack rates: 215€–815€ ($258–$978) double, 815€–1,525€ ($978–$1,830) suite. Rates include breakfast. AE, DC, MC, V. Closed Oct 15–Mar.*

Hôtel l'Oursin
$–$$ St-Jean-Cap-Ferrat

Originally built in 1925, this is an inexpensive hotel with a difference: The 14 stylish rooms are decorated with artwork, photography, and antiques. The three rooms on the highest floors feature harbor views. The rooms are small with stucco walls, but they do get lots of sunlight. The hotel also is well located in the heart of the village, across from the harbor, a five-minute walk from Paloma Plaza. All units have TVs, and seven are air-conditioned.

1 av. Denis-Séméria. ☎ *04-93-76-04-65. Fax: 04-93-76-12-55.* www.hoteloursin. com. *No on-site parking. Rack rates: 45€–120€ ($54–$144) double. Breakfast: 8€ ($9.60). AE, MC, V.*

Dining locally

Capitaine Cook
$$ St-Jean-Cap-Ferrat   PROVENÇAL/SEAFOOD

Next door to the fancy Hôtel La Voile d'Or (see "Spending the night," earlier in this section), a few blocks uphill from the center of the village, this restaurant specializes in seafood served in hearty portions. You get a panoramic view of the coast from the restaurant's terrace, and inside the decor is rugged-sea-shanty style. Oysters, served on the half shell or in several creative ways with sauces and herbs, are a specialty. Although roasted catch of the day is the mainstay, the filet mignon also is a succulent choice. The staff speaks English.

11 av. Jean-Mermoz. ☎ *04-93-76-02-66. Reservations not needed. Main courses: 14€–27€ ($17–$32); prix fixe: 22€–28€ ($26–$34). MC, V. Open: Fri–Tues noon to 2 p.m.; Thurs–Tues 7:30–10 p.m. Closed mid-Nov–Dec.*

Grand Hôtel du Cap-Ferrat
$$$–$$$$ St-Jean-Cap-Ferrat   PROVENÇAL

The restaurant here is extravagance defined, and the stellar service can't fail to impress. The restaurant offers seating outside on the garden terrace or inside in the lavishly decorated dining room. Chef Jean-Claude Guillon has a solid reputation, and you'll have to put yourself in his hands, because the menu detailing unusual ingredients and preparations is likely to leave even an expert translator perplexed. The famous lamb for two, *carré d'agneau des Alpes du sud rôti et gratinée au pistou* (rack of lamb from the Alps roasted and browned with basil-and-garlic sauce), is delectable, as are the *tournedos* of beef, layered with *foie gras façon Rossini*. Especially charming is a platter containing three separate salads, each concocted from some combination of freshwater crayfish and Canadian lobster.

71 bd. du Général-de-Gaulle. ☎ *04-93-76-50-50. Reservations required. Main courses: 50€–60€ ($60–$72); prix fixe: 73€–90€ ($88–$108). AE, MC, V. Open: Daily noon to 2 p.m. and 7:30–9:30 p.m. Closed Jan–Mar.*

Le Provençal
$$$–$$$$ St-Jean-Cap-Ferrat   PROVENÇAL

What distinguishes this restaurant, just up from the harbor in the village center, is that you get a very fancy meal in an elegant setting, with views of the harbor and coast. Le Provençal serves dishes that include *mille-feuille de caille en fouille de poireaux nouveaux, artichauts violets, fricassée de seiche* (puffed pastry with quail, new leeks, small artichokes, and braised squid), the main dish *épaule d'agneau confite miel et épices* (lamb shoulder with a confit of honey and spices), or *rouget rôti au cocofrais* (roasted red mullet with coconut). The dessert specialty is the rich *crème brûlée*.

2 av. Denis-Séméria. ☎ *04-93-76-03-97. Reservations required. Main courses: 43€–85€ ($52–$102); prix fixe: 72€–160€ ($86–$192). AE, MC, V. Open: May–Oct daily noon to 2:30 p.m. and 7:30–11 p.m.; Nov–Apr Fri–Sun noon to 2:30 p.m. and 7:30–11 p.m.*

Le Skipper
$$ St-Jean-Cap-Ferrat   PROVENÇAL

This harborside restaurant specializes in fish and features the chef's famous seafood soup with Parmesan rouille. The dense brown broth is accompanied by toasted bread roundlets that you spread with a very hot sauce and dunk into the soup. As a main course, two standouts are lasagna or sea scallops with chervil sauce. You also find an upscale version of surf and turf with basil sauce. But perhaps the most popular dish, and with good reason, is the mussels marinara (the key is in the rich broth). For dessert, try the excellent *citron tart meringue*. The menu has English translations. You'll dine in a mostly paneled dining room loaded with nautical memorabilia, and additional seating is available outside.

Port de St-Jean-Cap-Ferrat. ☎ *04-93-76-01-00. Reservations not needed. Main courses: 22€–34€ ($26–$41); prix fixe: 25€–37€ ($30–$44). AE, DC, MC, V. Open: Daily noon to 2 p.m. and 7–10:30 p.m.*

Le Sloop
$$ St-Jean-Cap-Ferrat   PROVENÇAL

Of the dozen or so restaurants next to the harbor, this one gets the most favorable reviews year after year. It's a favorite of many guidebooks and *Gourmet* magazine — so it tends to fill up first. The decor is yacht-club attractive, with blue-and-white chairs and awning, and the waiters are snappily dressed in black and white. Not surprisingly, fish is the thing here. The delightful *quenelle de sole* (sole dumpling) is often on the menu, as is the whole roasted turbot with mushroom sauce. For dessert, the restaurant features homemade ice cream.

Port de St-Jean-Cap-Ferrat. ☎ *04-93-01-48-63. Reservations recommended. Main courses: 18€–27€ ($22–$32); prix fixe: 27€ ($32). MC, V. Open: Thurs–Tues noon to 2 p.m. and 7–10:30 p.m. Closed mid-Nov to mid-Dec.*

Exploring the villa and beaches

Villa Ephrussi de Rothschild (rue Ephrussi de Rothschild; ☎ 04-93-01-33-09; www.villa-ephrussi.com) is one of the Riviera's most beautiful villas. In 1912, the highly eccentric Béatrice Ephrussi, baronne de Rothschild (1864–1934), built this pink-and-white Italianate mansion, with Italian Renaissance influences, at the peninsula's highest point and named it Ile de France after her favorite ship. Béatrice, born a Rothschild, was the daughter of a Banque de France director and wife of the wealthy banker Maurice Ephrussi. She discovered Cap-Ferrat in 1905 and bought about 7 hectares (18 acres) on which to build her dream villa. The project took 7 years, involving 20 to 40 architects. The baronne purchased exquisite antiques, memorabilia from the *ancient* regime, frescoes, and artwork from all around the world. Equally remarkable are the property's seven themed gardens: Spanish, Florentine, lapidary, Japanese, exotic, Provençal French, and the rose garden (which is at its best in May). Ironically, Béatrice, with homes in Paris and Monaco (her preferred home), never spent much time here. She left the villa, along with its collections, to the Académie des Beaux-Arts de l'Institut de France, which now runs the museum. You can have lunch or a snack in the tearoom, with views of the port of Villefranche, or on a terrace surrounded by the gardens. You can tour the downstairs with a brochure in English, but the upstairs rooms require a guide and cost an extra 2€ ($2.40). Mid-February through October, hours are daily from 10 a.m. to 6 p.m. (until 7 p.m. during July and Aug); November to mid-February, hours are Monday to Friday from 2 to 6 p.m. and Saturday and Sunday from 10 a.m. to 6 p.m. Admission is 8.50€ ($10) adults and 6.50€ ($7.80) students; children younger than 7 free. Guided tours of the second floor (in French) are given at 11:30 a.m. and 2:30, 3:30, and 4:30 p.m. and cost an extra 2€ ($2.40).

Take your kids to the **Grand Hôtel du Cap-Ferrat's pool** for the day, open daily 2:30 to 7 p.m. for outside guests. The daily rate is 60€ ($72) for adults and 45€ ($54) for children, while the half-day rate (charged after 2 p.m.) is 45€ ($54) for adults and 25€ ($30) for children. Day rates for cabanas, each with phone line, are 260€ ($312), with four lounge beds (which include mattresses); a small cabana is 130€ ($156) per day, with two beds; a massage is 110€ ($132), and a swimming lesson is 80€ ($96). **Club Dauphine** is the poolside restaurant.

It's difficult to actually see the sandy beaches of Cap-Ferrat, because almost every inch of sand is taken up by the beach chairs lined up by the beach concession. Nevertheless, these attractive warm-water beaches have views of the sweeping coastline and mountains. **Plage de Passable** (chemin de Passable; ☎ 04-93-76-06-17) is on the west side of the peninsula, less than a mile from the village. Concessions include a bar, a restaurant open for lunch and dinner, and an ice-cream stand. **Plage Paloma** (route de St-Hospice; ☎ 04-93-01-64-71) is in a pretty spot on the east side of the island just past the port (a five-minute walk from town), with views of the coastline and Beaulieu. Restaurants and concessions are beachside. Both beaches have free parking.

Beaulieu and the Villa Kérylos

Beaulieu, between Monaco (4km/6 miles east) and Nice (4km/6 miles west), is a small beach resort that features side-by-side Relais & Châteaux deluxe hotels. Although there's not much to do in Beaulieu besides enjoy the beautiful Mediterranean beaches, it has one sight worth a special trip: the *faux*-Greek Villa Kérylos. The Berlugans (people from Beaulieu) are a friendly crowd, so this is a nice place to base yourself for day trips to Monaco, Nice, and Cap-Ferrat.

Getting there

Beaulieu is a stop on the Riviera's main **train** line, which has frequent service to Nice and Monaco. The train station, **Gare SNCF,** is located at place Georges-Clémenceau in the center of town. For train information or reservations, call ☎ **08-92-35-35-39. Buses** traveling a coastal route to Nice stop in Beaulieu at the corner of bd. Maréchal-Leclerc and bd. Maréchal-Joffre. For bus information, call ☎ **04-93-85-64-44** or 04-97-00-07-00. The drive from Nice to Beaulieu takes about 30 minutes.

Getting around and getting information

You can walk from one end of Beaulieu to the other in about 15 minutes, but if you want a taxi, try the stand at place Georges-Clémenceau (☎ **04-93-01-03-46**). You can rent a car at **Avis** (3-5 Bd. Maréchal-Joffre; ☎ **04-93-01-62-54**) or **Hertz** (port de Plaisance; ☎ **04-93-01-62-30**).

The **tourist office** is on place Georges-Clémenceau (☎ **04-93-01-02-21**; Fax: 04-93-01-44-04; www.ot-beaulieu-sur-mer.fr). It's open daily July and August 9 a.m. to 12:30 p.m. and 2 to 7 p.m. (closed Sunday afternoon), and September through June Monday to Saturday 9 a.m. to 12:30 p.m. and 2 to 6 p.m. (until 5 p.m. on Saturday).

Spending the night

Hôtel Frisia
$–$$ Beaulieu

Americans feel right at home at the 35-room Frisia because owner Daniel Hoessly is American/Swiss. The hotel has a good location, across from the port and not far from Plage Petite Afrique, and 16 rooms have sea views. All rooms recently were renovated and include minibars and safes; the family units fit four people comfortably. A pool has been installed, and the top floor of the hotel has a solarium terrace with panoramic views. The bar is a comfortable place to chat with your friendly hosts and meet other guests.

2 bd. Eugène-Gauthier. ☎ *04-93-01-01-04.* Fax: 04-93-01-31-92. www.frisia-beaulieu.com. *Parking: 9€ ($11). Rack rates: 55€–115€ ($66–$138) double, 130€–195€ ($156–$234) suite. Breakfast: 9€ ($11). AE, DC, MC, V. Closed mid-Nov to mid-Dec.*

Hôtel Le Havre Bleu
$ Beaulieu

This whitewashed circa 1880s villa with bright-blue shutters (no elevator) is quite welcoming, but the neighborhood has a wrong-side-of-the-tracks quality. The 21 rooms are small and simple — modernized long ago with virtually none of the original architectural adornments — but very clean and dressed up with Provençal fabrics. The amenities are a little nicer here than at most government-rated two-star hotels (higher-quality towels and linens, Galimard soap). Breakfast is served in room or in a cheerful breakfast room. The staff is efficient though taxed.

29 bd. Maréchal-Joffre. ☎ *04-93-01-01-40. Fax: 04-93-01-29-92. Free parking. Rack rates: 53€–70€ ($64–$84) double. Breakfast: 7.50€ ($9). AE, MC, V.*

La Réserve de Beaulieu
$$–$$$$ Beaulieu

Of the two government-rated four-star hotels on the waterfront, La Réserve boasts the more renowned reputation mainly because of its restaurant, one of Les Grandes Tables du Monde (an organization of the world's top restaurants). The hotel is also a member of the prestigious Relais & Châteaux group. The Italianate rose-pink villa, built in 1881, contains sleek interiors with marble floors, gold damask curtains, and wrought-iron chandeliers. All 38 rooms and suites feature lush carpeting, antique furniture, and comfortable seating areas. Many have balconies, where you can enjoy breakfast with a sea view. Beautiful gardens lead to the heated seawater pool, which sits just above a private beach and port. A health club and spa also are on site.

5 bd du Général-Leclerc. ☎ *04-93-01-00-01. Fax: 04-93-01-28-99.* www.reserve beaulieu.com. *Free parking. Rack rates: 170€–1,000€ ($204–$1,200) double; 590€–2,630€ ($708–$3,156) suite. Breakfast: 28€ ($34). AE, DC, MC, V. Closed mid-Nov to Christmas.*

Le Métropole
$$–$$$$ Beaulieu

Built in the early 1900s to resemble an Italian palace, this government-rated four-star Relais & Châteaux hotel is on the beach and practically next door to La Réserve. The hotel's 35 rooms and 5 apartments are more modern and less grand than those of its neighbor. The rooms are attractive and quite spacious, decorated with Provençal fabrics, wicker, and over-stuffed couches. Many have French doors that lead to balconies overlooking the sea (though these rooms are twice the price). The pool is heated to 86°F year round. The restaurant, with a large terrace looking out over the sea, serves expensive Provençal cuisine.

15 bd. du Maréchal-Leclerc. ☎ *04-93-01-00-08. Fax: 04-93-01-18-51.* www.le-metropole.com. *Free parking. Rack rates: 170€–590€ ($204–$708) double; 460€–1,100€ ($552–$1,320) suite. Half board: 70€ ($84) per person. Breakfast: 23€ ($28). AE, DC, MC, V. Closed late Oct to late Dec.*

Dining locally

La Pignatelle
$–$$ Beaulieu PROVENÇAL

This restaurant is a favorite with locals, who appreciate the value of its well-priced and good food. You dine in a tasteful and pleasant yellow-and-white room, and in summer, seating is available on the terrace in the shady garden. The chef concentrates on simple, traditional preparations of fresh fish and vegetables, which may include a classic salade Niçoise; roasted sea bream with Provençal herbs; an elaborate "pyramid" composed of fresh raw vegetables, vinaigrette, and mozzarella cheese; or roasted rack of lamb with Provençal herbs.

10 rue de Quincenet. ☎ *04-93-01-03-37. Reservations recommended. Main courses: 13€–25€ ($16–$30); prix fixe: 12€–26.80€ ($14–$32). MC, V. Open: Thurs–Tues noon to 2 p.m. and 7–10 p.m. Closed Nov.*

La Réserve de Beaulieu
$$$$ Beaulieu PROVENÇAL

"The king of restaurants and the restaurant of kings," La Réserve is one of France's finest restaurants, serving haute cuisine in a spacious room with Mediterranean views. The walls are decorated with Aubusson tapestries and the ceiling with Italianate frescoes. Lovely first courses include *balico de petits rouget aux artichauts* (small red-leaf lettuce with artichokes) and *salade de homard aux pousses d'épinards et panisses au parmesan* (lobster salad with spinach-and-Parmesan pancake). Main courses to be savored are roasted rack of lamb from the Alps and *loup de Méditerranée au bellet rouge et poire épicée* (sea bass with spiced pear). The restaurant also offers a special foie gras dish: *foie gras d'oie en coque de sel et côtes de blettes a l'orgeat* (foie gras in a shell of salt and special Swiss chard). During summer, lunches are relatively informal.

5 bd. du Général-Leclerc. ☎ *04-93-01-00-01. Reservations required far in advance. Main courses: 49€–89€ ($59–$107); prix fixe: 95€–130€ ($114–$156). AE, DC, MC, V. Open: Daily noon to 2:30 p.m. and 8–10:30pm. June–Sept 7:30–10 p.m. Closed Nov 3–Dec 20.*

Les Agaves
$–$$$ Beaulieu PROVENÇAL

Les Agaves, in the 1900 Palais des Anglais, is the best restaurant in town if you don't want to break the bank at La Réserve. This bistro has received laudatory press for many years. The best surprise is that prices are quite reasonable for the creative cuisine. Chef/owner Jacky Lelu's specialties are homemade ravioli and grilled dishes; his ultimate ravioli dish is served with *cèpes* (white flap mushrooms) and truffles. The restaurant also offers an excellent *coquilles St-Jacques,* the classic scallop dish, and *filet de rascasse à la crème de truffe* (scorpion-fish with truffle sauce). English is spoken.

4 av. Maréchal-Foch. ☎ *04-93-01-13-12.* www.les-agaves.com. *Reservations recommended. Main courses: 27€–40€ ($32–$48); prix fixe: 32€ ($38). AE, MC, V. Open: Daily 7:30–10 p.m. Closed Nov 15-Dec 15.*

Exploring the villa and beaches

Théodore Reinach (1860–1928) created his dream house at the tip of a rocky promontory jutting into the sea and named it the **Villa Kérylos** (rue Gustave-Eiffel; ☎ 04-93-01-01-44; www.villa-kerylos.com). An archaeologist, man of letters, and scholar of ancient Greece, Reinach wanted his home to replicate a Greek villa from the second century B.C. So the house, built from 1902 to 1908, is a completely unique mingling of early-1900s techniques with ancient Greek sensibility; it's a fun and fascinating combination. Reinach wanted to eat, sleep, and party like the Greeks, so his dining room chairs are vertical chaise longues for reclining next to three-legged tables. His bed is framed by fluted columns, and his marble bathtub can fit ten men. The villa has mosaics, frescoes, and reproductions of artworks from Pompeii and ancient Greece. A gallery of antiquities is in the stone basement, which is surrounded by windows level with the sea. You can watch windsurfers while admiring copies of famous statues such as the *Venus de Milo* and the *Discus Thrower*. After touring the house, stroll through the garden, and have a bite to eat at the cafe. From February 3 to November 3, the villa is open daily 10 a.m. to 6 p.m.; July and August, hours are daily 10 a.m. to 7 p.m.; November 4 to February 2, hours are Monday to Friday 2 to 6 p.m., Saturday and Sunday 10 a.m. to 6 p.m. Admission is 8.50€ ($10) for adults and 6.50€ ($7.80) for students and children ages 7 through 18.

The two beaches with concessions are **Plage Petite Afrique** off promenade Pasteur (☎ 04-93-01-11-00) and **La Calanque** at Baie des Fourmis (☎ 04-93-01-45-00). These are attractive, if crowded, beaches. Plage Petite Afrique, the easternmost, is a crescent-shaped beach dotted with palm trees and lush vegetation.

Living it up after dark

At the Art Deco-style **Grand Casino de Beaulieu** (4 av. Fernand-Dunan; ☎ 04-93-76-48-00), jackets are encouraged for men, and tennis shoes are forbidden. Entrance fee is 11€ ($13). The slot machine section, where dress is more casual, is free to enter and doesn't require a passport. For the game rooms, you need a passport.

Chapter 21

The Western Riviera: From St-Tropez to Cannes

In This Chapter

▶ Hitting the beach in St-Tropez

▶ Mingling with the stars — or not — in Cannes

▶ Appreciating the craftswork of Biot

▶ Watching the yachts in Antibes

▶ Walking the cobblestone streets of Vence and St-Paul-de-Vence

*W*est of Nice, the French Riviera offers travelers seaside and inland opportunities, from the Mediterranean sands near Cannes, Cap d'Antibes, and St-Tropez to the quaint villages of Biot and Antibes to the pedestrian-only hamlets of Vence and St-Paul-de-Vence. This chapter explores the diversity of the western Riviera.

St-Tropez: Sun and Fun

Forget all the hype about topless bathing, hedonistic bar scenes, and preening celebrities — **St-Tropez** is hands down the Riviera's most charming town, a pastel-colored fishing village that happens to be one of the most glamorous spots on earth. Just don't come in July or August, when dense crowds make even a stroll in front of the yacht-filled harbor nearly impossible. Unlike other Riviera towns, St-Tropez has a perfectly preserved center — a colorful port unmarred by high-rise hotels and virtually unchanged for more than a century. (For evidence, visit the portside Impressionist museum L'Annonciade to see the early 20th-century images of St-Tropez.) Bustling cafes crowd the old port, and behind them, the winding village streets beckon with exclusive boutiques and romantic restaurants. All paths lead up to the citadel, a 16th-century fort perched at the top of the town.

The beaches of St-Tropez are a lively scene — an integral part of the Tropezienne experience. The most famous beaches are located several miles from town and lined with restaurants and clubs. **Pampelonne**

Beach, on the peninsula's southeast coast, is the most famous (or notorious) stretch of sand on the Riviera. After a day on the beach, it's time to gear up for a memorable dinner and a taste of St-Tropez after dark. The crowd is young and starts out late: Dinner is at 10 p.m., and bar hopping begins shortly thereafter. If you aren't into the bar scene, you may enjoy strolling along the old port or people-watching from one of the portside cafes.

Getting there

St-Tropez is difficult to get to without a car (no trains stop there) or even with a car. Plan on at least a half-day of travel to reach the resort. Summer traffic onto the peninsula can be bumper-to-bumper for miles.

The closest major bus-and-train hub is **St-Raphaël,** 38km (24 miles) east of St-Tropez. **Bus** fares from Cannes to St-Raphaël require a change at the agrarian hamlet of Le Trayas, take about 70 minutes of travel time, and cost 5.90€ ($7.10) each way. Continuing on by bus from St- Raphaël to St-Tropez costs an additional 3€ ($3.60). For information and schedules, call either **Raphaël Bus** at ☎ **04-94-83-87-63** or **Société Vanoise D'Autocars** at ☎ **04-94-95-95-16**.

St-Raphaël is on the main coastal **train** line for the Riviera. A train from Nice to St-Raphaël takes between 50 and 75 minutes and costs 9.70€ ($12); trains from Cannes to St-Raphaël take 22 minutes and cost 7.30€ ($8.75). Other nearby train stations are at Toulon (60km/37 miles) and Marseille (134km/83 miles). For train information, call ☎ **08-92-35-35-39** or 08-92-35-35-35.

Transports Maritimes Raphaëlois (☎ **04-94-95-17-46**) runs a **shuttle boat** service between St-Raphaël and St-Tropez. Boats run daily (July and August), taking 50 minutes and costing 11€ ($13) one-way. From April to June and in September and October, only two shuttle boats travel between St-Raphaël and St-Tropez each week. St-Tropez is about 20 minutes by boat from St-Maxime (14km/9 miles east of St-Tropez), and two companies make shuttle boat trips between them daily (in season): **Transports Maritimes** (☎ **04-94-96-51-00**), running from April to November 4, and **Les Bateaux Verts,** which run year-round (☎ **04-94-49-29-39**). Both charge 11€ ($13) for adults and 5.50€ ($6.60) for children ages 4 to 12.

The major **airports** (and distances) nearest St-Tropez are the **Aéroport Toulon-Hyères** (56km/35 miles), **Aéroport International de Nice Côte d'Azur** (91km/57 miles), **Aéroport International de Marseille-Provence** (115km/72 miles), and **Aéroport St-Tropez-La Môle** (15km/9 miles). La Môle, located to the northwest of St-Tropez is a relatively new landing strip, suitable only for small planes whose arrival and departure rituals may remind you of equivalent small-plane "puddle jumps" throughout the Caribbean. The airports have offices for all major **car-rental** agencies. A taxi from the Nice airport to St-Tropez costs a whopping average of 180€ ($216) each way for up to four passengers. The distance from the other airports to St-Tropez makes a rental car your best option.

A good time to visit St-Tropez is during the **Voiles de St-Tropez,** a week-long competition in late September and early October, when a flotilla of antique sailboats — some of them among the most photographed in the Mediterranean — sail furiously around an obstacle course defined by a network of carefully positioned buoys anchored offshore. For details, contact the tourist office or the **Société Nautique de St-Tropez** (☎ 04-94-97-30-54; www.snst.org).

Getting around and getting information

The area around St-Tropez is hilly, but you can bike to most of the beaches on the peninsula. A scooter is a good way to get to the beaches of Pampelonne, which are further away. You can rent bikes, scooters, and motorbikes at **Holiday Bikes** (14 av. du Général-Leclerc; ☎ 04-94-97-09-39); **Espace 83** (2 av. du Général-Leclerc; ☎ 04-94-55-80-00), scooters and motorbikes only; or **Location Mas** (3 rue Quaranta; ☎ 04-94-97-00-60). Rentals start at 12€ ($14) per day for bikes; motorbikes and scooters start at 34€ ($41) per day. These shops usually are open daily 9 a.m. to 7 p.m. from June to September. They don't close for a lunchtime break. You can rent a car, scooter, or bike at **Locazur,** located at 9 route des Plages, near the Plage de Bouillabaisse (☎ 04-94-97-57-85). Car rentals start at 65€ ($78) per day, scooters from 49€ ($59) per day.

About every half-hour daily 8 a.m. to 5 p.m. in summer, and mornings only during the off season (Oct through May), **beach shuttles,** costing 2€ ($2.40), leave from place des Lices to the beaches of Pampelonne and Salins. If you drive to the beaches, you'll have to pay around 3.50€ ($4.20) for parking. Bear in mind that taxi fees in St-Tropez are very high.

The **tourist office** is at quai Jean-Jaurès (☎ 04-94-97-45-21; www.ot-saint-tropez.com). It's open daily July and August 9:30 a.m. to 8 p.m., June and September 9:30 a.m. to 12:30 p.m. and 2 to 7 p.m., and October to May 9 a.m. to 12:30 p.m. and 2 to 6 p.m. You can pick up your e-mail and also enjoy a drink at **La Girafe,** 16 rue du Portail neuf (☎ 04-94-97-13-09), which boasts six computers, costing 2.50€ ($3) for 15 minutes. Only a two-minute walk from the tourist office, it is open daily from 10 a.m. to 3 a.m.

Spending the night

Most of the hotels and restaurants recommended here are located around the old port area (see the "St-Tropez" map).

Hôtel Byblos
$$$$ St-Tropez

This government-rated four-star hotel, a cluster of stucco buildings painted in cool Mediterranean colors and situated high above the village near the citadel, is the most exclusive in St-Tropez. The 96 rooms and suites are elegant, as you'd expect, decorated with antiques and statuary. The complex includes boutiques; restaurants; a bar; and the Caves du Roy disco, which attracts the elite of St-Tropez. The centerpiece of the garden courtyard is a large pool, where you may want to spend the day while the staff caters to your every whim. Major renovations to the hotel since 1998 have included a radical reconfiguration of each of the bedrooms.

See map p. 433. Av. Paul-Signac. ☎ *04-94-56-68-00. Fax: 04-94-56-68-01.* www. byblos.com. *Parking: 30€ ($36). Rack rates: 360€–470€ ($432–$564) double; 685€–1,700€ ($822–$2,040) suite. Breakfast: 32€ ($38). AE, DC, MC, V. Closed mid-Oct–mid-Apr.*

Hôtel de La Ponche
$$–$$$$ St-Tropez

Composed of four interconnected and luxuriously appointed fishermen's cottages, this is the smallest government-rated four-star hotel in St-Tropez, with 18 rooms. On a narrow winding street in the heart of historic St-Tropez, the rear overlooks the fishermen's port, and the simple cottages are imbued with an authentic charm. The pretty rooms sport designer linens and antique lamps, and many have large private balconies with sea views; others look out over the church tower and tiled roofs of the village. The hotel has five suites that are ideal for families and a popular restaurant on site with a large terrace overlooking the harbor. The Ponche is popular with Americans, who seem to prefer its understated elegance to the more ostentatious luxury at the Byblos. The hotel offers an unusual amenity for late sleepers: Breakfast is served until 3 p.m.

See map p. 433. 3 rue des Remparts (place du Revellin). ☎ *04-94-97-02-53. Fax: 04-94-97-78-61.* www.laponche.com. *Parking: 18€ ($22). Rack rates: 160€–385€ ($192–$462) double; 335€–505€ ($402–$606) suite. Breakfast: 19€ ($23). AE, MC, V. Closed mid-Nov to mid-Feb.*

Hôtel Ermitage
$–$$ St-Tropez

The most common comment about this hotel is that the 27 rooms are too small. Nevertheless, the English-speaking staff is welcoming; the prices are good; and the hotel, in business since the 1930s, is well situated at the top of the hill with views sweeping out over the village and the sea near the exclusive Byblos. Some rooms have views over the gardens and out to sea; others look toward the citadel, past a noisy road. All units are simple and well maintained; the larger ones light and airy, with arched windows looking out over rooftops to the sea. The hotel has an attractive garden, a pretty bar area with a stone fireplace, and a patio overlooking the harbor.

See map p. 433. Av. Paul-Signac. ☎ *04-94-97-52-33. Fax: 04-94-97-10-43. Free parking. Rack rates: 75€–181€ ($90–$217) double. Breakfast: 10€ ($12). MC, V.*

Hôtel La Bastide du Port
$$–$$$ St-Tropez

This 27-room hotel is located across from the bay, near the new port, within walking distance of Plage de Bouillabaisse and a five-minute stroll

St-Tropez

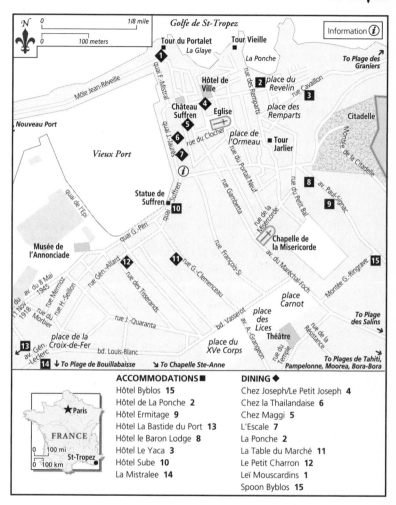

ACCOMMODATIONS ■	DINING ◆
Hôtel Byblos **15**	Chez Joseph/Le Petit Joseph **4**
Hôtel de La Ponche **2**	Chez la Thailandaise **6**
Hôtel Ermitage **9**	Chez Maggi **5**
Hôtel La Bastide du Port **13**	L'Escale **7**
Hôtel le Baron Lodge **8**	La Ponche **2**
Hôtel Le Yaca **3**	La Table du Marché **11**
Hôtel Sube **10**	Le Petit Charron **12**
La Mistralee **14**	Leï Mouscardins **1**
	Spoon Byblos **15**

from the center of town. Don't let the bland exterior fool you: The high-ceilinged rooms are cheerful, with tile floors, large windows, and wrought-iron chandeliers. The units in the front of the hotel face the harbor and have balconies with bay views. But despite soundproof windows, these rooms are definitely noisier, as the hotel is on the main road into town. The accommodations in the rear look onto the palm-tree-lined courtyard where breakfast is served in good weather.

See map p. 433. Port du Pilon. ☎ *04-94-97-87-95. Fax: 04-94-97-91-00.* www.bastide duport.com. *Free parking. Rack rates: 125€–180€ ($150–$216) double. Breakfast: 10€ ($12). AE, MC, V. Closed Dec–Feb.*

Hôtel le Baron Lodge
$–$$ St-Tropez

This 11-room hotel at the top of the hill near the entrance to the citadel gardens has an ultracool feeling about it. The building also houses a cafe; a restaurant serving Basque food; and a bar with an African-themed décor, including wooden sculptures and elephant paintings. The rooms are light and airy, though small, and some have French doors leading to tiny balconies. The location is good, with a number of little restaurants, shops, and galleries on the nearby old winding streets.

See map p. 433. 23 rue de l'Aioli. ☎ *04-94-97-06-57. Fax: 04-94-97-58-72.* www.hotel-le-baron.com. *Parking: 18€ ($22). Rack rates: 50€–100€ ($60–$120) double. Breakfast: 7€ ($8.40). MC, V.*

Hôtel Le Yaca
$$$–$$$$ St-Tropez

This quintessentially Mediterranean hotel, which is elegant yet cozy, has 28 rooms and suites in four adjoining historic houses, one of which was occupied by Colette in 1827. All rooms are individually decorated in a modern style, with touches such as marble fireplaces; some have terraces or balconies with water views; others overlook St-Tropez's winding streets or an interior courtyard dotted with flowers. The least expensive rooms are small but just as pretty as the expensive rooms. A fine Italian restaurant with terrace seating in summer is on site, and so is a good bar. Breakfast is served in the poolside garden in summer. The English-speaking management is extra-accommodating and professional.

See map p. 433. 1 bd. d'Aumale. ☎ *04-94-55-81-00. Fax: 04-94-97-58-50.* www.hotel-le-yaca.fr. *Parking: 20€ ($24). Rack rates: 255€–525€ ($306–$630) double; 505€–1,105€ ($606–$1,326) suite. Breakfast: 22€ ($26). AE, DC, MC, V. Closed early Oct to mid-Apr.*

Hôtel Sube
$$–$$$ St-Tropez

You can't get any more centrally located than this 28-room second-floor hotel on the old port behind the bronze statue of Vice-Admiral Pierre André de Suffren. The rooms are simple and small, with perfect harbor views. Dashing young sailors hang out in the nautical-themed bar, where the balcony has a panoramic bay view. Alas, you won't get a room here unless you book way ahead. And don't plan on getting to sleep until the wee hours; your fellow guests like to party.

See map p. 433. 15 quai Suffren (on the old port). ☎ *04-94-97-30-04. Fax: 04-94-54-89-08.* www.hotel-sube.com. *Rack rates: 125€–250€ ($150–$300) double. Breakfast: 10€ ($12). AE, MC, V.*

La Mistralee
$$–$$$$ St-Tropez

This ten-room hotel is one of the newest in St-Tropez, converted from a private manor into a luxury hotel in 2000. This 1850 villa is the former vacation home of Alexandre, a famous Parisian hairdresser born and reared in St-Tropez. His tastes ran to the baroque (the home is full of opulent details), from elaborate ceiling moldings to festive wall murals to gilded paneled walls. The rooms are spacious and decorated with unusual antiques. The grounds are inviting: You follow a series of red-ochre columns through a lush garden to a tiled pool with chaises under Japanese umbrellas. Thick pool towels are stacked in wicker baskets in the Roman villa-style pool house.

See map p. 433. 1 av. du Général-Leclerc (near place des Lices). ☎ *04-98-12-91-12. Fax: 04-94-43-48-43.* www.hotel-mistralee.com. *Free parking in courtyard. Rack rates: 190€–590€ ($228–$708) double; 370€–760€ ($444–$912) suite. Breakfast: 18€–25€ ($22–$30). AE, MC, V.*

Dining locally

Chez Joseph/Le Petit Joseph
$$–$$$$ St-Tropez **PROVENÇAL**

These side-by-side restaurants are serviced by the same kitchen, and the menus are quite similar. Le Petit Joseph is quieter and more romantic, with low beamed ceilings, an Asian decor, and cozy banquettes. Chez Joseph, where you sit with other patrons at long tables, tends to be completely booked and packed at 10 p.m. Both restaurants offer outdoor seating, but Le Petit has just a few tables; Chez features a large terrace. The traditional yet creatively presented cuisine emphasizes fish, and the menu changes often. For dessert, the *parfait léger* is a treat — vanilla custard with chocolate powder on a cherry crumble with a scoop of cherry-vanilla ice cream and fresh fruit.

See map p. 433. 1 place de l'Hôtel-de-Ville. ☎ *04-94-97-01-66. Reservations recommended at Chez Joseph. Main courses: 21€–48€ ($25–$58). AE, MC, V. Open: Daily noon to 2 p.m. and 7:30 to midnight.*

Chez la Thailandaise
$$$ St-Tropez **THAI**

For something a little different, try this atmospheric restaurant on the harbor. The entrance is flanked by little stone elephants, and the decor includes plenty of Asian touches, such as bamboo chairs. House specialties include sautéed duck with mushrooms and oyster sauce, chicken salad with fresh ginger, and fresh squid and prawns with Thai herbs and garlic. You also find the usual Thai dishes, such as crispy spring rolls and pad Thai. Dessert is a plate of exotic fruit.

See map p. 433. Quai Jean-Jaurès (on the old port). ☎ *04-94-97-88-22. Reservations recommended. Prix fixe: 40€ ($48). AE, MC, V. Open: Apr–Dec daily noon to 2 p.m. and 7–10:30 p.m.*

Chez Maggi
$$ St-Tropez PROVENÇAL/ITALIAN

St. Tropez's most flamboyant gay restaurant and bar also draws straight diners and drinkers. At least half its floor space is devoted to a bar, where patrons range in age from 20 to 60. Consequently, cruising at Chez Maggi, in the words of loyal patrons, is *très crazée* and seems to extend for blocks in every direction. Meals are served in an adjoining dining room. Menu items include chicken salad with ginger; goat-cheese salad; *petits farcis provençaux* (vegetables stuffed with minced meat and herbs); brochettes of sea bass with lemon sauce; and chicken curry with coconut milk, capers, and cucumbers.

See map p. 433. 7 rue Sibille. ☎ *04-94-97-16-12. Reservations recommended. Main courses: 16€–29€ ($19–$35); prie fixe: 32€ ($38). MC, V. Open: Daily 7 p.m. to midnight (bar open till 3 a.m.); closed Oct to mid-Mar.*

La Ponche
$$–$$$ St-Tropez PROVENÇAL

This stylish restaurant in the chichi Hôtel de La Ponche boasts exceptional food, service, and views — and it's actually not as expensive as it may seem. Located on the city's ancient ramparts next to an old stone city gate, it overlooks the sea and fishing port. Chef Christian Geay highlights summery dishes such as *salade de crustaces à la vinaigrette de truffes* (seafood salad with truffles) and *moules à la marinière* (mussels with red sauce). Filet de boeuf layered with foie gras is an enduring specialty. A favorite dessert is *nougat glace au coulis de framboise* (nougat ice cream, which has almonds and honey, with puréed strawberries).

See map p. 433. 3 rue des Ramparts (in the Hotel de La Ponche). ☎ *04-94-97-02-53. Reservations recommended. Main courses: 22€–38€ ($26–$46); prix fixe: 23€ ($28) lunch, 35€ ($42) dinner. AE, MC, V. Open: Mid-Feb to Nov daily noon to 2:30 p.m. and 7:30–11:30 p.m.*

La Table du Marché
$$$ St-Tropez PROVENÇAL/JAPANESE

This restaurant skillfully combines a Parisian-style bistro and tearoom, replete with red-velvet banquettes and mirrors. Chef Christophe Leroy displays the day's pastries in the window for those who drop in during the morning or afternoon for coffee or tea; then he transforms the site into a bustling restaurant during the lunch and dinner hours. Specialties include spit-roasted organic chicken served with a rich and flavorful gratin of macaroni and cheese, or pan-fried red snapper with flap mushrooms.

See map p. 433. 38 rue Georges-Clémenceau. ☎ *04-94-97-85-20. Reservations recommended. Main courses: 20€–30€ ($24–$36) bistro; prix fixe: 18€ ($22) bistro. AE, DC, MC, V. Open: Daily 8 a.m.–11 p.m.*

Leï Mouscardins
$$$$ St-Tropez PROVENÇAL

Chef Laurent Tarridec runs the fanciest and most expensive restaurant in town. It's set on the second floor of a port-side building, and all tables open onto harbor views. One prix fixe menu features an upscale version of a *bourride*, a fish soup that's a meal in itself, but slightly less lavish than a full fledged bouillabaisse. Other recommendable dishes are *grenouilles menunière* (frogs' legs) and *épaule de lapin* (rabbit), but preparations of fresh fish, locally caught, are the specialty. The Grand Marnier soufflé is a delight. In good weather, terrace seating is available.

See map p. 433. Tour du Portalet (on the old port). ☎ *04-94-97-29-00. Reservations required. Main courses: 36€–45€ ($43–$54); prix fixe: 67€ ($80) lunch, 67€–112€ ($80–$134) dinner. AE, DC, MC, V. Open: June–Sept daily noon to 2 p.m. and 7:30–10 p.m.; Oct–May Thurs–Mon noon to 2 p.m. and 7:30–9:30 p.m. Closed Nov–Feb.*

Le Petit Charron
$–$$ St-Tropez PROVENÇAL

Anne Violaine and Christian Benoit own this intimate, charming nautically decorated restaurant. The small menu is not so much limited as it is focused on a few items, each prepared perfectly. The fish soup and gazpacho with mussels and herbs are fine summer fare. The main courses always include freshly caught fish of the day, simply prepared, in addition to a scallop risotto with truffles. If you're looking for heartier fare, try the lamb, beef, or duck served with delicacies such as cèpe mushrooms and homemade gnocchi.

See map p. 433. 6 rue des Charrons. ☎ *04-94-97-73-78. Reservations recommended. Main courses: 18€–22€ ($22–$26). DC, MC. Open: Daily 7:30–9:30 p.m. Closed mid-Nov to Dec 1, Jan 15–30, Feb 15–28, and Aug 1–15.*

L'Escale
$$–$$$ St-Tropez PROVENÇAL

Fish lovers will be attracted by the sight of the live fish and lobsters in tanks at the entrance. Most of the seating at this large harborside restaurant is in a glass-enclosed terrace, so you can do some people-watching in any weather; however, the banquettes and wicker chairs are packed close together. Try one of the multitiered seafood plates — the three-tiered seafood plate (loaded with oysters, shrimp, clams, mussels, lobster, and more) is an excellent choice. It is priced at 50€ ($60) per person, and served to a minimum of only two diners at a time. You can get the famous *tarte tropezienne* here, made just down the street at Sénéquier. And for after your meal, the restaurant offers special coffees from New Guinea, Ethiopia, Guatemala, and Haiti.

See map p. 433. 9 quai Jean-Jaurès (on the port). ☎ *04-94-97-00-63. Reservations recommended. Main courses: 12€–29€ ($14–$35); prix fixe: 36€ ($43). AE, DC, MC, V. Open: Thurs–Tues noon to 2:30 p.m. and 7:30–10:30 p.m. Closed: Sun and Mon night, Nov–Feb.*

Spoon Byblos
$$$ St-Tropez FRENCH/INTERNATIONAL

The creation of Alain Ducasse, considered by some the world's greatest chef, Spoon originally was launched in Paris and since has opened locations from London to the Riviera. It serves the cuisine of many cultures, with produce mainly from the Mediterranean, but draws special inspiration from the food of Catalonia, Andalusia, and Morocco. The restaurant opens onto a circular bar made of blue-tinted glass and polished stainless steel. Entrees include shrimp and squid consommé with a hint of jasmine and orange, spicy king prawns on a skewer, delectable lamb couscous, or spit-roasted John Dory. Top off a meal with the chef's favorite cheesecake or a slice of neapolitan with the taste of strawberry, vanilla, and pistachio. The restaurant offers more than 300 wines from around the world.

See map p. 433. In the Hotel Byblos, av. Paul-Signac. ☎ 04-94-56-68-00. Reservations required. Main courses: 29€–38€ ($35–$46). AE, DC, MC, V. Open: June–Sept 8 p.m.–12:30 a.m., off-season daily 8–11 p.m.

Exploring the town and the beaches

After you walk around St-Tropez's old port, head to the beautiful small **L'Annonciade, Musée de St-Tropez** (place Grammont; ☎ 04-94-97-04-01) to find out how artists painted this port about 75 years ago. The museum is housed in a former chapel, an austere church built next to the port in 1568. The highlights among the colorful, cheerful collection of Impressionist and fauvist works are paintings by Derain, Seurat, Braque, Matisse, Signac, Bonnard, Utrillo, and Dufy. It's open Wednesday to Monday June through September 10 a.m. to noon and 3 to 7 p.m., and October through May 10 a.m. to noon and 2 to 6 p.m. (closed the month of November, January 1, May 1, and December 25). Admission is 5.50€ ($6.60) for adults and 3.50€ ($4.20) for children 4 to 15.

Walk past the old port and up quai Jean-Jaurès, and you soon come to the **Château Suffren,** built in 980. The building now houses an attractive art gallery with large plate-glass windows overlooking the port. Pass through place de l'Hôtel de Ville to rue de la Ponche and follow it for several blocks. Take a right on rue des Remparts, which turns into rue Aire du Chemin and eventually ends at rue Misericorde. Turn left and walk two blocks to reach the **Chapelle de la Miséricorde,** which has a brightly colored tiled roof.

Port Grimaud, 6km (4 miles) northwest of St-Tropez, is an attractive village made to look old, where stone houses sit beside canals and people moor their boats practically right outside their doors. The village has a number of fine shops and restaurants. You can get there by driving 5km (3 miles) west on A98 and one mile north on route 98.

In St-Tropez, and along most of the French Riviera, going to the *plage* (beach) means setting up camp at a concession location that provides beach chairs, umbrellas, snacks, a restaurant, a bar, and sometimes water sports. When you choose a beach, you're choosing a business to patronize for the day. The most popular St-Tropez beaches are Bouillabaisse, Graniers, Salins, Pampelonne, and Tahiti:

✔ **Bouillabaisse:** An easy walk from town, this beach offers **Golfe Azur** (☎ 04-94-97-07-38), a restaurant that specializes in grilled fish. A section of beach at Bouillabaisse, just west of town, has clean shallow waters, making it a good choice for kids. Parking costs 3.50€ ($4.20) per day.

✔ **Graniers:** This beach is one of the best for families and is within walking distance of town. There's free parking and **Les Graniers** (☎ 04-94-97-38-50), the main restaurant at the beach, is one of the better beach concessions. It serves the usual Provençal cuisine, lots of grilled fish, and *moules frites* (mussels and french fries). Its 22€ ($26) *plat du jour* is reasonably priced when compared to most restaurants.

✔ **Pampelonne:** Here you find about 35 businesses on a 4.8km (3-mile) stretch, located about 10km (6.2 miles) from St-Tropez. You need a car, bike, or scooter to get from town to the beach. Parking is about 3.50€ ($4.20) for the day. Famous hedonistic spots along Pampelonne include the cash-only club **La Voile Rouge** (☎ 04-94-79-84-34),** which features bawdy spring-break-style entertainment. Also thriving are **Le Club 55** (☎ 04-94-55-55-55) and **Nikki Beach** (no phone). **Plage des Jumeaux** (☎ 04-94-79-84-21) is another actively patronized beach spot but with a large percentage of families with young kids because it has playground equipment. **Marine Air Sports** (☎ 04-94-97-89-19) rents boats; **Team Water Sports** (☎ 04-94-79-82-41) rents Jet Skis, scooters, water-skiing equipment, and boats.

✔ **Salins:** Located just north of Pampelonne and 3km (2 miles) from St-Tropez, the popularity of this wide sandy beach is evident by how fast the parking lot fills up. Arrive early to get a good spot on the sand. Parking costs 3.50€ ($4.20). The most popular restaurant on Salins beach is **Leï Salins** (☎ 04-94-97-04-40).

✔ **Tahiti:** This wild spot permits topless, and even nude, sunbathing. Tahiti beach is 5km (3 miles) from St-Tropez, and parking costs about 3.50€ ($4.20). Known as the region's most decadent beach, Tahiti tends to attract a young crowd interested in cruising.

The gulf of St-Tropez is so beautiful that you may be tempted to take a **boat ride.** Captain Henri (☎ 06-84-07-41-87) has been offering harbor cruises on his classic 1936 gaff-rigged wooden sailboat *Thule* since 1993. The 60-minute cruise, with narration in English and other languages, costs 8€ ($9.60) for adults and 4€ ($4.80) for children younger than 10. From April to early October, tours leave daily at 11 a.m. and 6 p.m., cruising past oceanfront houses of celebrities such as George Michael, Arnold Schwarzenegger, and Sylvester Stallone. From your waterside perch, you float past the medieval ramparts surrounding old St-Tropez, and the beaches — Plage des Graniers and Plage de la Cannoubière included — many of which, at least in high season, are jam-packed with scantily clad sunbathers. If you'd like, you can help to haul the sails as the boat cruises around the gulf.

Shopping for local treasures

When strolling in St-Tropez, check out the **pedestrian alleys,** which are usually lined with exclusive shops. A rough guide: Shops on the harbor sell cheap sexy clothes, and shops a few blocks from the harbor feature expensive sexy clothes. **Hermès** (☎ 04-94-97-04-29) is tucked into an old building on rue de la Ponche. The best shoe store (selection and price) is **Les Sandales Tropeziennes** (Rondini) at 16 rue Georges Clémenceau, near place des Lices (☎ 04-94-97-19-55). You also find a number of good housewares stores, such as **HM France** (12 rue Georges Clémenceau; ☎ 04-94-97-84-37), a chain specializing in fine linens.

Jacqueline Thienot (10 rue Georges Clémenceau; ☎ 04-94-97-05-70), situated down a medieval-looking alley, is a very fine antiques shop whose proprietor speaks English. Perhaps the most surprising store in St-Tropez is **Le Jardin de Zita** (12 aire du Chemin; ☎ 04-94-97-37-44), a sort of high-class junk shop filled with odds and ends for decorating your bohemian yet stylish home. You can find a large selection of beautiful pottery at **Poterie Augier** (19 rue Georges Clémenceau; ☎ 04-94-97-12-55).

The **fish, vegetable, and flower market** is located down a tiled alley (Place aux Herbes) behind the tourist office. It operates daily 8 a.m. to noon in summer and Tuesday to Sunday 8 a.m. to noon in winter. On Tuesday and Saturday mornings on place des Lices, you can find an **outdoor market** with food, clothes, and *brocante* (flea-market finds).

Living it up after dark

St-Tropez is famous for its nightlife. From partying at bars and clubs to people-watching at cafes along the old port, there's something for everyone. The key words are *loud* and *late,* so take a disco nap and get ready to hit the town. In addition to the in-town venues, the beach clubs also stay rowdy until the wee hours (see "Exploring the town and the beaches," earlier in this chapter).

Live music adds to the merriment at the friendly **Kelly's Irish Pub** (quai F. Mistral; ☎ 04-94-54-89-11), which serves Guinness and Irish whiskey, among other beverages. **Papagayo** (in the Résidence du Port, next to the harbor; ☎ 04-94-97-76-70) is where the yachting crowd gathers for drinking, dining, meeting, and greeting. At the well-established and very visible Hôtel Sube, partyers practically hang off the balcony of the second-floor **Bar Sube** (15 quai Suffren; ☎ 04-94-97-30-04). Stop by cozy **Chez Palmyre** (2 rue du Petit Bal; ☎ 04-94-97-43-22) during its 7 to 9 p.m. happy hour for cocktails and tapas. **L'Esquinade Bar de Nuit** (3 rue du Four; ☎ 04-94-97-87-44) can be a lot of fun, if you don't mind the emphasis on the staff deciding who is hip and who might not be.

Intensely swank — a nighttime staple in St-Tropez for many years — is **Les Caves du Roy,** within the Hôtel Byblos (☎ 04-94-56-68-00), where the crowd is chic and a bit jaded, and where drinks, priced at around 20€ ($24) each, are far from cheap. **Le Pigionnier** (13 rue de la Ponche; ☎ 04-94-97-84-26) is a popular gay club, as is **Chez Nano** (17 rue Sybille; ☎ 04-94-97-72-59). **The VIP Room** (in the Résidence du Port; ☎ 04-94-97-14-70) is a bar and lounge next to the new port, and it attracts all ages. A central cafe on the old port, **Sénéquier** (quai Jean-Jaurès; ☎ 04-94-97-00-90) offers prime people-watching and serves famous desserts. **Café de Paris** (15 quai Suffren; ☎ 04-94-97-00-56) is a popular brasserie/ sushi bar beneath the Hôtel Sube. And **Café des Arts** (place des Lices; ☎ 04-94-97-17-29) is one of St-Tropez's most famous cafes.

Cannes: More Than Just the Film Festival

Cannes, famous for the annual International Film Festival, is the Riviera at its gaudiest and most banal — for some, that's reason enough to stop here. Overdevelopment has erased much of this seaside city's beauty, but it certainly has a fun quality, and offers unrivaled people-watching and excellent shopping. The famous La Croisette boardwalk along the beach is lined with "palaces," the government-rated four-star grand hotels that have long attracted the rich and famous.

Most visitors make a beeline for the Film Festival palace, a huge con-crete monstrosity set on the beach. During the festival in May, images of stars walking up the steps on the red carpet, surrounded by paparazzi, are projected around the world. The city also spreads out the famous carpet in July, August, and December, so visitors can pose for photos. Handprints of directors and actors line the square near the steps.

 We suggest that you avoid Cannes during the ten-day Film Festival in May. You can't attend any of the fabulous events, and the crush of media people is overwhelming. If you must visit during the festival, your best bet for celebrity spotting is to eat lunch or dinner at one of the beach restaurants owned by the grand hotels. The best time to visit Cannes, a city of 60,000 people, is April, May (not during the festival), June, September, and October. July and August are so crowded, it's difficult to find a square of sand or a cafe table.

Getting there

Cannes is a major Riviera hub, with frequent train and bus service. From Paris, the fast **TGV train** to Cannes takes about six hours and costs 98.70€ ($118). The Cannes **Gare SNCF** (train station) is on rue Jean-Jaurès (☎ 04-93-99-19-77). For train schedule information and reserva-tions, call ☎ 08-92-35-35-35 or 08-92-35-35-39.

The focal point for **bus** transits into, out of, and within Cannes is the **Gare Routière** (bus station), on place Bernard Cornut-Gentille. For infor-mation about municipal buses that operate within three miles (4.8 km) of the city limits, call ☎ 04-93-45-20-08; for information about buses coming in from farther away, call **Voyages Phocéens,** 5 square Mérimée (☎ 04-93-39-79-40).

Trans Côte d'Azur (☎ 04-92-98-71-30; www.trans-cote-azur.com) runs **boats** to and from Monaco (32€/$38 round-trip) between July and mid-September, and to and from St-Tropez (31€/$37 round-trip) between July and mid-October. They arrive and depart from Cannes's quai St-Pierre, at the port, near the terminus of the rue Maréchal-Joffre, close to the Hotel Sofitel. A competitor with roughly equivalent routes, schedules, and prices, is **Compagnie Esterel Chanteclair** (☎ 04-93-39-11-82).

The **Aéroport International de Nice Côte d'Azur** (☎ 08-20-42-33-33) is 27km (17 miles) from Cannes. **Rapides Côte d'Azur** (☎ 04-93-39-11-39) runs from the airport to Cannes for 12.70€ ($15) and takes 30 minutes. A taxi from the Nice airport to the center of Cannes takes half an hour and costs 60€ ($72).

Getting around and getting information

You don't need a car to get around Cannes; the city is quite compact (see the "Cannes" map). **Allo Taxi** (☎ 04-92-99-27-27) will drive you from one end of town to the other or make pickups at Nice's airport.

Cannes is a good base for exploring the region. It's 9km (6 miles) from Antibes, 25km (16 miles) from St-Paul-de-Vence, 32km (20 miles) from Nice, 50km (31 miles) from Monaco, and 79km (49 miles) from St-Tropez. To rent a car, try **Access Rent a Car** (5 rue Latour-Maubourg; ☎ 04-93-94-06-05) or **Alliance Location** (19 rue des Frèrers Pradignac; ☎ 04-93-38-62-62).

For bike and scooter rentals, call on **Cycles Daniel** (2 rue du Pont-Romain; ☎ 04-93-99-90-30), **Holiday Bikes** (32 Ave Maréchal Juin; ☎ 04-93-94-30-34), and **Locations Mistral** (4 rue Georges-Clemenceau; ☎ 04-93-99-25-25).

The **main tourist office** is in the Palais des Festivals (to the left of the famous steps on the ground floor) on bd. de la Croisette (☎ 04-93-39-24-53; www.cannes.fr), open daily 9 a.m. to 7 p.m., with a second office in the train station (☎ 04-93-99-19-77), open Monday to Saturday 9 a.m. to 7 p.m. To send or receive e-mail, or cruise the Web, spend some time at the **Snoozie** (15 square Mérimée; ☎ 04-93-68-19-21), where a battery of available computers connects you to the Internet for a fee of around 4€ ($4.80) per half hour.

Spending the night

Hotels do book up in Cannes. If you're having trouble getting a reservation, try **Cannes Réservations** (8 bd. d'Alsace; ☎ 04-93-99-99-00; Fax: 04-93-99-06-60; E-mail: sandla@canne-sreservations.com), open Monday to Saturday 9 a.m. to 6 p.m.

Cannes

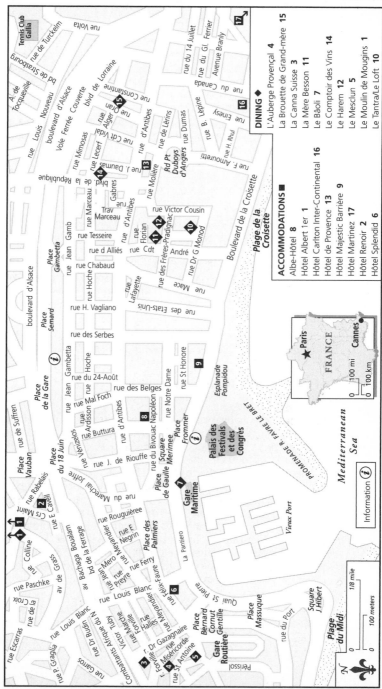

DINING ◆

L'Auberge Provençal **4**
La Brouette de Grand-mère **15**
La Canna Suisse **3**
La Mère Besson **11**
Le Bâoli **7**
Le Comptoir des Vins **14**
Le Harem **12**
Le Mesclun **5**
Le Moulin de Mougins **1**
Le Tantra/Le Loft **10**

ACCOMMODATIONS ■

Albe-Hôtel **8**
Hôtel Albert 1er **1**
Hôtel Carlton Inter-Continental **16**
Hôtel de Provence **13**
Hôtel Majestic Barrière **9**
Hôtel Martinez **17**
Hôtel Renoir **2**
Hôtel Splendid **6**

Albe-Hôtel
$ **Cannes**

This 24-room hotel is a budget alternative in Cannes. The location is good; it's situated opposite the main post office, close to place de Gaulle, and just a few short blocks from La Croisette (the waterfront boardwalk). The rooms are simple and small, but comfortable, and come with the usual stable of amenities. Owners Nelly and Marcel Moura are the somewhat jaded and harrassed owners.

See map p. 443. 31 rue Bivouac Napoléon. ☎ *04-97-06-21-21. Fax: 04-97-06-21-27.* www.albe-hotel.com. *Parking: 10€ ($12). Rack rates: 45€–80€ ($54–$96) double. Breakfast: 6€ ($7.20). MC, V.*

Hôtel Albert 1er
$ **Cannes**

Originally conceived as a private villa, the 11-room Albert 1er (*1er* is pronounced *premier*) is a good budget choice. The hotel is on the far side of the main highway into Cannes. Although it isn't an ideal location, it's convenient, a ten-minute walk directly uphill from the city's old port, and you won't find a better price for a decent room. Some third-floor rooms have distant water views of the old port, and all rooms have soundproof windows. The hotel also provides a bowl of fruit in the rooms (which is unusual for a two-star hotel).

See map p. 443. 68 av. de Grasse. ☎ *04-93-39-24-04. Fax: 04-93-38-83-75. Free parking. Rack rates: 60€-65€ ($72–$78) double. Breakfast: 6€ ($7.20). AE, MC, V.*

Hôtel Carlton Inter-Continental
$$$$ **Cannes**

One of the famous palace hotels on the waterfront (its two shapely domes make it an unmistakable landmark), the Carlton has long been popular with Americans. The grand entrance and the lobby, with its marble columns and frescoed ceiling, wowed the upper classes in 1912, when the hotel opened, and continue to do so. The 338 rooms and suites are as luxurious as any on the Riviera, and a number have balconies with sea views; the 12-room imperial suite boasts its own elevator and butler. In high season, the hotel maintains three separate restaurants: La Brasserie; a more upscale restaurant called La Côte; and a beachfront snack bar, La Plage, open only for lunch. In winter, only La Brasserie is open. The hotel also has a hot tub and a health club. The beach across from the hotel is rather narrow and composed of gravel and small, water-worn pebbles, but it's often the place for celebrity sightings.

See map p. 443. 58 bd. de la Croisette. ☎ *04-93-06-40-06. Fax: 04-93-06-40-25.* www.cannes.intercontinental.com. *Parking: 30€ ($36). Rack rates: 280€– 620€ ($336–$744) double; 790€-2,680€ ($948–$3,216) suite. Breakfast: 32€ ($38). AE, DC, MC, V.*

Hôtel de Provence
$ Cannes

Located behind a private garden, this 30-room hotel is a good choice if you're looking for a relatively inexpensive hotel. The location isn't bad either: It's in a relatively quiet neighborhood, only a few blocks from La Croisette. The hotel has a homelike feel to it — in the public rooms and in the guest rooms. Accommodations are decorated simply, but with attention to detail, and include safes. All doubles open onto terraces that offer views of the garden, with its century-old palm trees.

See map p. 443. 9 rue Molière. ☎ *04-93-38-44-35. Fax: 04-93-39-63-14.* www.hotel-de-provence.com. *Parking: 13€ ($16). Rack rates: 79€–99€ ($95–$119) double. Breakfast: 7.50€ ($9). AE, MC, V. Closed mid-Nov to mid-Dec.*

Hôtel Majestic Barrière
$$$$ Cannes

Its bright-white undulating facade distinguishes the Majestic from the other grand hotels along La Croisette. The hotel also boasts a classically inspired lobby with immense Greek-style statues, a casino, and a garden courtyard. In 2002, each of the 305 rooms and suites underwent renovations. The hotel's beach is known for its water-sports program, with instructors and rentals available. The hotel also boasts a pool, health club, and tennis court. The fancy restaurant, La Villa des Lys, has a hot young chef, Bruno Oger, who has received a number of accolades. In 2002, a branch of a luxurious and upscale brasserie restaurant in Paris (Fouquet's) opened on site, adding touches of Belle Epoque glamour and a dining venue that manages to be both elegant and relaxed.

See map p. 443. 10 bd. de la Croisette. ☎ *04-92-98-77-00. Fax: 04-93-38-97-90.* www.lucienbarriere.com. *Parking: 33€ ($40). Rack rates: 250€–870€ ($300–$1,044) double, 1,035€–3,600€ ($1,242–$4,320) suite. Breakfast: 24€ ($29). Closed mid-Nov to Dec. AE, DC, MC, V.*

Hôtel Martinez
$$$–$$$$ Cannes

The largest of the grand palaces along La Croisette, this 413-room Art Deco 1930s hotel is also the site of Cannes's most famous deluxe restaurant, La Palme d'Or. But because the Martinez has become popular with group tours and conventions, it feels less elegant than the other hotels along La Croisette, even though it offers the same deluxe room amenities, such as high-quality linens and marble baths. The hotel also has a pool, a hot tub, and tennis courts.

See map p. 443. 73 bd. de la Croisette. ☎ *04-92-98-73-00. Fax: 04-93-39-67-82.* www.hotel-martinez.com. *Parking: 27€ ($32). Rack rates: 230€–420€ ($276–$504) double, from 800€ ($960) suite. Breakfast: 26€ ($31). AE, DC, MC, V.*

Hôtel Renoir
$–$$ **Cannes**

Originally conceived as a private villa and transformed into a hotel in the early 1990s, this stylish 27-room hotel is a good medium-priced choice, offering big hotel amenities. The rooms are cheerfully decorated in Provençal style, with colorful bedspreads and painted furniture. Although the hotel is a three-minute walk from the public beach, Plage Publique du Festival (Festival Beach), it has a private beach, and south-facing units on the upper floors have distant water views. But ask for a room facing north, because the south accommodations face a busy highway (although they do have double soundproof windows to temper the noise). Each room has a kitchenette.

See map p. 443. 7 rue Edith-Cavell. ☎ *04-92-99-62-62. Fax: 04-92-99-62-82.* www. hotel-renoir-cannes.com. *Parking: 12€ ($14) day. Rack rates: 82€–149€ ($98–$179) double, 89€–243€ ($107–$292) suite. Breakfast: 12€ ($14). AE, MC, V.*

Hôtel Splendid
$–$$ **Cannes**

The Splendid is for people who want a grand water-view hotel but don't want to splurge on the famous palace hotels blocks away. Originally built in 1871 as a private home, it has been transformed into a hotel and enlarged in several different stages to the point where today it contains 62 rooms. It has an excellent location, just a block from the Palais des Festivals. The pretty Belle Epoque facade gives you a good idea of the rooms, which are beautifully decorated and full of luxurious touches. Considering the location and amenities, this is good-value lodging for Cannes, particularly as many of the units open onto water views. The hotel is next to place de Gaulle, one of the busiest squares in Cannes, but rooms have soundproof windows, so it's quiet. The hotel has no parking on site, no restaurant, and no pool.

See map p. 443. 4 rue Félix-Faure (across from the port). ☎ *04-97-06-22-22. Fax: 04-93-99-55-02.* www.splendid-hotel-cannes.fr. *Rack rates: 95€–110€ ($114–$132) double, 180€–230€ ($216–$276) suite. Breakfast: 17€ ($20). AE, MC, V.*

Dining locally

Cannes's small romantic restaurants are clustered in Le Suquet, the Old Town. In fact, on rue St-Antoine (the Old Town's main street), about 70 percent of the businesses are restaurants. The top luxury restaurants can be found in the grand hotels along La Croisette.

La Brouette de Grand-mère
$$ **Cannes**   **PROVENÇAL**

Locals love this old-fashioned restaurant (the name means "grandmother's wheelbarrow") that serves homelike, traditional food. The restaurant is very small, and you must make reservations. The only option is a set menu. It may seem expensive, but it's actually a real bargain because wine and an apéritif (premeal drink) are included. The few seats on the outdoor terrace fill up first. The menu is loaded with regional dishes that include *pot-au-feu;* roasted quail in cream; chicken stew cooked slowly in beer and herbs; grilled beefsteaks; and *andouillettes,* the earthy specialty of the mountainous region of central France, made from pork intestines (a.k.a. chitterlings).

See map p. 443. 9 bis rue d'Oran (off rue d'Antibes). ☎ 04-93-39-12-10. Reservations necessary. Prix fixe: 33€ ($40). MC, V. Open: Mon–Sat 7:30–11 p.m. Closed Nov to mid-Dec.

La Canna Suisse
$–$$ Cannes   SWISS

Two sisters own this small-scale 1970s restaurant in Old Town, decked out like a Swiss chalet and specializing in the cheese-based cuisine of the Swiss Alps. Because its cuisine is so closely geared to cold-weather dining, the restaurant wisely opts to close during the crush of Cannes' midsummer tourist season, although doing a landmark business in autumn, winter, and early spring. The menu features only two kinds of fondue — a traditional version concocted from six kinds of cheese and served in a bubbling pot with chunks of bread on skewers, plus another that adds either morels or cèpes (flap mushrooms) to the blend, depending on your wishes. The only other dining options here include *raclette* and *tartiflette* (an age-old recipe that combines boiled potatoes with fatback, onions, cream, herbs, and Reblochon cheese). A long list of (mostly white) French and Swiss wines usually taste wonderful when served with any of these ultratraditional dishes.

See map p. 443. 23 rue Forville (Le Suquet). ☎ 04-93-99-01-27. Reservations recommended. Main courses: 15€–22€ ($18–$26). AE, MC, V. Open: Mon–Sat 7:30–10:30 p.m. Closed: June to mid-Aug.

La Mère Besson
$$ Cannes   PROVENÇAL

The candlelit tables under the awning at La Mère Besson, located on a quiet street just a few blocks up from La Croisette, are among the best places to dine in Cannes. This classic restaurant has been dishing out homecooking to families since the 1930s. The daily specials here are like a course in Provençal cuisine, featuring *osso bucco* (veal braised with tomatoes) and *lapereau farci aux herbes de Provence* (baked rabbit stuffed with meat and Provençal herbs), and shoulder of Provençal lamb studded with garlic cloves and herbs and slowly roasted in its own juice.

See map p. 443. 13 rue des Frères-Pradignac. ☎ 04-93-39-59-24. Reservations necessary. Main courses: 13€–35€ ($16–$42); prix fixe: 27€–32€ ($32–$38). AE, MC, V. Open: Mon–Sat 7:30–10 p.m.

L'Auberge Provençal
$$–$$$ Cannes   PROVENÇAL

The oldest restaurant in town, L'Auberge Provençal, opened in Le Suquet in 1860 and has been serving traditional regional dishes ever since. The 25€ ($30) menu, which has six main dish choices, is a good value. Although the cooking can be inconsistent, several dishes are always good, including bouillabaisse (the rich fish stew); *filet de boeuf aux foie gras;* and *carré d'agneau de Sisteron* (rack of lamb), a regional specialty. For dessert, try *le petit crêpe flambé à la liqueur d'orange* (a flaming crêpe with orange liqueur). A terrace provides outdoor seating in summer.

See map p. 443. 10 rue St-Antoine. ☎ *04-92-99-27-17. Reservations accepted. Main courses: 18€–42€ ($22–$50); prix fixe: 25€ ($30). AE, DC, MC, V. Open: Daily noon to 2:30 p.m. and 7–11:30 p.m.*

Le Bâoli
$$–$$$$ Cannes   FRENCH/JAPANESE

One of the ultimate hip joints in Cannes occupies a waterfront site outfitted like a temple garden in Thailand, complete with lavishly carved doorways, potted and in-ground palms, and hints of the Spice Trade scattered artfully in out-of-the-way corners. ("Le Bâoli" derives from a well in Indonesia with reputed mystical powers.) The restaurant has room, either indoors or on a terrace overlooking the twinkling lights of La Croisette, for up to 350 diners at a time, and plenty of room after the end of the dinner service for a dance club venue (midnight to 4 a.m.; no cover) where at least some of the clients may dance frenetically, in scantily clad giddiness, on the tables. Menu items include Japanese-inspired teppanyaki dishes prepared tableside by a samurai-style chef. The French dishes include tartare of tuna spread on toasts, crisp ravioli stuffed with shrimp, lobster in citrus sauce with a confit of tomatoes, filet of sea wolf with fennel, and a particularly elegant version of macaroni that's "perfumed" with an essence of lobster. Vegetarians appreciate the availability of such dishes as risotto with green asparagus, broccoli, and fava beans.

See map p. 443. Port Canto, bd. de la Croisette. ☎ *04-93-43-03-43. Reservations recommended. Main courses: 18€–72€ ($22–$86). AE, MC, V. Open: Daily 8 p.m. to midnight. Closed Nov–Apr.*

Le Comptoir des Vins
$–$$ Cannes   PROVENÇAL

This wine bar/restaurant in an atmospheric cellar is a favorite hangout for oenophiles and a lively scene on most nights. Every day, a changing array of about ten France-derived wines are sold by the glass, always including a champagne and a sweet dessert wine; about 250 wines are sold by the bottle. Menu items focus on hearty, savory, and flavorful food that makes the wine taste even better. These include fresh pastas, *blanquettes de veau,* a variety of *estouffades* (slow-cooked cuts of meat, sometimes known in

Provence as a daube); and platters of marinated salmon, pâtés, terrines, and cheeses.

See map p. 443. 13 bd. de la République. ☎ *04-93-68-13-26. Reservations not needed. Main courses: 12.50€–18.50€ ($15–$22); prix fixe: 22.50€ ($27). MC, V. Open: Mon–Sat noon to 2 p.m. and 7:30–10 p.m.*

Le Harem
$$–$$$$ Cannes MOROCCAN/MEDITERRANEAN

Set in the heart of Cannes, midway between rue d'Antibes and La Croisette, this is the hippest, most popular, and most sought-after Moroccan restaurant in Cannes, as proven by the bevy of soccer, pop music, and cinema stars who have visited it since its opening in May 2002. It contains a trio of dining rooms, each lavishly outfitted, *à la marocaine,* with chastened brass coffeepots, tribal carpets from the Sub-Saharan Desert, geometrically carved panels, and leatherwork. If you opt for a meal here, don't expect just another ethnic restaurant, as this one contains a well-defined postmodern twist, both in its decor and in its cuisine. The menu acknowledges the cuisines of Morocco, Tunisia, Algeria, Spain, and Italy. There are at least a half-dozen *tagines* (clay pots in which chicken, lamb, fish, and vegetables are spiced, slow-cooked, and made savory) and at least three different versions of couscous (such as a traditional version with only lamb; a *royale* version containing merguez sausage, chicken, lamb, and beef; and a super-deluxe seafood version, priced at 70€ per person, that's loaded with lobster and shellfish). Other dishes, not deriving from North Africa, include tuna fried with Iberian cured ham in the Basque style, a salad of chickpeas with coriander and mint, and an Andalusia-inspired tomato-based gazpacho.

See map p. 443. 15 rue des Frères Pradignac. ☎ *04-93-39-62-70. Reservations recommended. Main courses: 22€–70€ ($26–$84). AE, DC, MC, V. Open: Daily 8 p.m. to midnight.*

Le Mesclun
$$$ Cannes PROVENÇAL

A set menu is the only option for dining here, but the price is so reasonable, and the choice so varied, that the place is genuinely popular not only with locals but also with out-of-towners. The well-crafted three-course menu is described in English and French, with a choice (that changes every two weeks) of eight starters and eight main courses. Possibilities include a terrine of foie gras of duckling, served with a sweet-and-sour onion jam; herb-infused rack of lamb; scallops served with mashed potatoes, garlic, and parsley; and fried John Dory with tomatoes and aromatic herbs. The venue is a paneled dining room within Old Town, amid a color scheme of terra cottas and ochres inspired by Provence.

See map p. 443. 16 rue St-Antoine. ☎ *04-93-99-45-19. Reservations accepted. Prix fixe: 35€ ($42). AE, MC, V. Open: Thurs–Tues 7:30–11 p.m. Closed mid-Nov to Dec.*

Le Moulin de Mougins
$$$–$$$$ Mougins   FRENCH

The new chef here has a big toque to fill. In 2004, Alain Llorca took over the celebrated inn, until recently the kingdom of Roger Vergé, a *maître cuisinier de France* and one of the country's top three chefs. After seven years as chef of the fabled Négresco Hotel in Nice, Llorca was just the man to succeed Vergé. He employs market-fresh ingredients in his "cuisine of the sun," a reference to Provence's light-drenched countryside. If our first meal at this former 16th-century olive mill is any indication of Llorca's talent, he's going far to retain Vergé's most loyal clients. Roast flank of beef, in red wine and its own juices, was a delectable choice. Provençal lamb came with oranges *en confit,* fresh spinach, and a fondant of carrots. And roasted turbot with braised celeriac and flap mushrooms deserves an award. Llorca's brother, Jean-Michel, is the extraordinarily talented pastry chef.

See map p. 443. Av. Notre-Dame de Vie, Mougins (4 miles from Cannes). ☎ *04-93-75-78-24. Reservations required. Main courses: 43€–120€ ($52–$144); prix fixe: 48€–150€ ($58–$180) lunch, 98€–150€ ($118–$180) dinner. AE, DC, MC, V. Open: Tues–Sun noon to 2 p.m. and 7:30–10 p.m.*

Le Tantra/Le Loft
$$–$$$ Cannes   FRENCH/ASIAN

An enduring favorite on the city's dine-and-then-dance circuit, this duplex-designed restaurant and disco is on a side street that runs directly into La Croisette. On the street level, you find a Tao-inspired dining room, artfully simple and outfitted in a way that, if it wasn't filled with chattering and gossiping diners, might inspire a meditation or a yoga class. Menu items focus on a French adaptation of Asian cuisine, with lots of sushi; tempura that includes a succulent combination of deep-fried banana slices, zucchini flowers, shrimp, and lobster; a Japanese-style steak of Kobe beef marinated in teriyaki, soy, and garlic; and deep-fried noodles dotted with chunks of shrimp and lobster. The 9 p.m. seating is relatively calm, but the 11 p.m. seating is more linked to the disco madness upstairs. Here, until 4 a.m. (no cover), in a venue lined with plush, scarlet sofas and exposed stone, you witness the gyrations and mating games of a scantily clad crowd of all kinds of hipsters from across the wide, wide range of social types inhabiting (or visiting) Cannes.

See map p. 443. 13 rue du Dr. Monod. ☎ *04-93-39-40-39. Reservations strongly recommended. Main courses: 18€–38€ ($22–$46). AE, DC, MC, V. Open: Daily seatings at 9 and 11 p.m.*

Exploring the town and the beaches

One of the best ways to get your initial bearings in Cannes (and to get an idea of the difference between the city's new and old neighborhoods) is to climb aboard one of the white-sided **Petits Trains Touristiques de Cannes.** Diesel-powered, and rolling on rubber tires through the streets of the city, the trains operate year round (except November) every day from 9:30 a.m. to between 7 and 11 p.m., depending on the season. Two itineraries are offered:

✔ For views of glittery modern Cannes, board the train at a designated spot in front of either of the town's two casinos for rides along La Croisette and its side streets.

✔ For a ride through the relatively narrow streets of Vieux Cannes (Le Suquet), board the train at a clearly designated site along La Croisette on its seaward side, immediately opposite the Hôtel Majestic Barrière.

Both tours depart every hour, and each lasts between 30 and 40 minutes, depending on traffic, and costs between 5€ and 6€ ($6 and $7.20) for adults and 2.50€ and 3€ ($3 and $3.60) for children younger than 10, depending on the tour. (The tour of Vieux Cannes is the less expensive of the two.) A combination ticket granting access on both tours (which can be enjoyed on separate days, if you prefer) goes for 8€ ($9.60) for adults and 5€ ($6) for children younger than 10. For details, call ☎ 06-14-09-49-39.

You may want to explore Cannes on your own and not on a formal walking tour. You get the best feel for the city by exploring the narrow streets of **Le Suquet** (the Old Town), which most evokes the walled town turned fishing village that rose up here in the Middle Ages. Just past the small restaurants and boutiques on rue St-Antoine, you can climb the ancient steps to a square where you find the impressive **Musée de la Castre** (☎ 04-93-38-55-26), housed in a 12th-century former priest dormitory. The museum contains collections donated by 19th-century explorers and ethnographers, with a focus on Mediterranean and eastern archaeology and indigenous art. The museum's Eskimo art collection is growing. An interactive exhibit of musical instruments from around the world enables you to hear the sounds of the instruments. On the second floor is a collection of paintings by artists from Cannes and the region. In the painting *Le Suquet au coucher du soleil, vu du Nord,* which shows Cannes in 1864, the sky is the only thing that still looks the same. The museum is open Tuesday to Sunday as follows: October to March 10 a.m. to 1 p.m. and 2 to 5 p.m.; April, May, and September, 10 a.m. to 1 p.m. and 2 to 6 p.m.; June to August 10 a.m. to 1 p.m. and 3 to 7 p.m. Admission costs 3€ ($3.60) for adults. Entrance is free for students and for persons younger than 18. From the ramparts surrounding the museum, you have a panoramic view over the city, the old harbor, and the sea. Even in high season, you may be the only one enjoying this peaceful and romantic place — everyone else will likely be at the beach.

After exploring Le Suquet, you can check out one of Cannes's famous markets. **Marché Forville** on rue Meynadier (near to Le Suquet, just off rue St-Antoine) is the largest fruit, vegetable, fish, and cheese (and to a lesser extent, meat) market in Cannes. Keep walking east on the pedestrian-only rue Meynadier, where you'll find some of the best shops, everything from bargain clothing stores to fancy food stores. Afterward, you can walk south a few blocks to the **old port,** where luxury yachts tie up next to local fishing boats. Next to the old port is the **Palais des Festivals,** which houses the tourist office (just left of the grand steps) and is the venue for the Film Festival events. When the Film Festival isn't in session, it serves as a conference hall year round. Now you're on **La Croisette,** Cannes's boardwalk, officially known as bd. de la Croisette, which stretches 3km (2 miles) and is lined with grand hotels. Feel free to wander into a lobby, plop down on a plush wing chair, and watch the local comings and goings.

Cannes has more than 30 public and private beaches, and most are a combination of sand with pebbles. But going to the beach in Cannes isn't a back-to-nature experience. In fact, you can't really see the sand because the beach chairs cover almost every square inch of it. An important part of the beach scene here involves posing and checking out the poseurs. Entrance to one of the private beaches requires payment of an entrance fee, which entitles you to the use of a parasol and a mattress and/or lounge chair. A full day's use, with wide variance depending on the facilities and the degree of exclusivity of the beach, costs from 15€ ($18) to as much as 44€ ($53), usually with a 40 percent discount if you arrive after 2 p.m. Private beaches almost always have at least one food-and-drink concession and, at the fancier ones, a full-fledged restaurant. Some of the best-established private beaches are the ones associated with the town's palace hotels. They include the **Carlton** (☎ 04-93-06-40-06), **Majestic Barrière** (☎ 04-92-98-77-00), **Martinez** (☎ 04-92-98-73-00), and **Noga Hilton** (☎ 04-92-99-70-00). The private beaches of other hotels charge a little less for half-day and full-day rates at the beach. The beach restaurants associated with the palace hotels usually have a dish of the day on a set-price lunch menu that's not too expensive (25€/$30). The palace hotel beaches also have the best watersports concessions.

For a free public beach with lifeguards, head to **Plage de Midi** (☎ 04-93-39-92-74), on the west side of the old port. The beach also has a restaurant with reasonable rates serving lunch, dinner, and snacks.

Shopping for local treasures

Most stores in Cannes are open Monday to Saturday 10 a.m. to 7:30 p.m. in summer (in winter, 10 a.m. to 6:30 or 7 p.m.).

Cannes is famous for its food, flower, and flea markets, open in various squares all across town. The biggest market is the **Marché Forville,** just a few steps east of the Vieux Cannes or Le Suquet and a few blocks north of the old port. This colorful market features produce and fish in a block-long covered building. Restaurateurs and other gourmands come from all over the region to buy fish here from the fishwives selling their husbands' catch of the day. It's open Tuesday to Sunday 7 a.m. to 12:30 p.m. On Mondays, a flea market takes over the space (October to June 8 a.m. to 6 p.m. and July to September 3 to 6 p.m.).

From July to September, a flower market is open daily at the **Allées de la Liberté** 7 a.m. to 1 p.m.; October to June, the hours are Tuesday to Sunday 7 a.m. to 1 p.m. Several markets specializing in clothes are open on Saturdays 8 a.m. to 12:30 p.m. at **place Gambetta, place du Commandant Maria,** and **place de Cannes la Bocca.** Flea markets are held in these locations on Thursdays 8 a.m. to 6 p.m.

The pedestrian **rue Meynadier** has the best selection of specialty food shops. **Ernest Traiteur** (52 rue Meynadier, at the corner of rue Louis-Blanc; ☎ 04-93-06-23-00) is a famous pâtisserie specializing in cakes and deli that handles Film Festival receptions; the prepared foods are expensive but good. **Ceneri** (22 rue Meynadier; ☎ 04-93-39-63-68) is a famous third-generation cheesemaker that sells to the region's most famous restaurants.

The town's best candymaker is **Maiffret** (31 rue d'Antibes; ☎ 04-93-39-08-29), making bonbons since 1885. The chocolate laboratory on the second floor is open to visitors Tuesday to Friday 2 to 3 p.m. The other top chocolatier is **Bruno** (13 rue Hoch; ☎ 04-93-39-26-63), which also makes enticing *gelée de fruits.*

The wine store **La Cave de Forville** (3 place du Marché Forville; ☎ 04-93-39-45-09) carries, among other fine vintages, *La Vendage des Moines* (Monks' Vintage), the wine made by monks on the nearby island of St-Honorat. **Cannelle,** in the Galerie Grey-d'Albion (32 rue des Serbes; ☎ 04-93-38-72-79), adjacent to the Hotel Grey d'Albion, is a deluxe specialty grocery store that's similar to Fauchon in Paris. It doubles as a *salon du thé,* serving delectable teacakes at noon on the terrace Monday to Saturday from 9 a.m. to 7 p.m.

If you are shopping for clothing, **rue Meynadier** is known for its inexpensive shops, while **rue d'Antibes** has middle-range prices. The high-end designer shops (including Chanel, Dior, and Saint-Laurent) are on or near **La Croissette.**

Living it up after dark

Public perception of Cannes is invariably associated with permissiveness, filmmakers celebrating filmmaking, and gambling. If gambling is your thing, a couple of world-class casinos are in Cannes, each loaded with addicts, mere voyeurs, and everyone else in between.

 ✔ **Casino Croisette,** in the Palais des Festivals (1 jetée Albert-Edouard; ☎ 04-92-98-78-00), is the better established of the two. It's run by the Lucien Barrière group and a well-respected fixture in town since the 1950s.

 ✔ **Palm Beach Casino,** place F.D. Roosevelt (pointe de la Croisette; ☎ 04-97-06-36-90) lies on the southeast edge of La Croisette. Originally inaugurated in 1933, and rebuilt in 2002 by the Partouche group, it features three restaurants, an Art Deco decor, and a format that's glossier, newer, and a bit hungrier (and trying harder) for new business.

Both casinos maintain slot machines that operate daily from 10 to 5 a.m. and suites of rooms devoted to *les grands jeux* (blackjack, roulette, and *chemin de fer*) that are open nightly from 8 p.m. to 5 a.m. Both charge 10€ ($12) for access to *les grands jeux,* where presentation of a passport or an identity card is required.

In the cellar of the Hotel Grey d'Albion is the long-term nightlife staple, the disco **Jane's** (38 rue des Serbes; ☎ 04-92-99-79-79). It isn't considered ultrahip or even particularly cutting edge, but you can have a lot of fun here, merely because of the exoticism of the diverse crowd of occasionally single people. Cover is between 10€ and 13€ ($12–$16), depending on the night of the week, and women are admitted free every Friday and Saturday before midnight. At the Casino Croisette is the nightclub **Jimmy's de Régine** (☎ 04-92-98-78-78), with a 12€ to 18€ ($14–$22) cover.

Le Love Disco (50 bd. de la Croisette; ☎ 04-92-99-70-00) is outfitted in tones of red and set in the cellar of the Noga Hilton Hotel. This disco was inaugurated in the summer of 2002 as a trial run by a hotel that's noted for its appeal to Hollywood cinematic types. Expect a roster of music that includes love themes as defined by Jamaican Soca, Dominican merengue, and the Summer of Love as interpreted by Lovemasters Jimi Hendrix and Jim Morrison. It's open every night from around 11:30 p.m. until dawn, but only from June through September. The entrance charge of 20€ ($24) includes the first drink.

Zanzibar (85 rue Félix-Faure; ☎ 04-93-39-30-75) is not only a gay bar, but a gay bar with a past, both scandalous and literary. Established in 1885 as a mainstream bar and cafe, it experienced a shift in its clientele around 1925, when it evolved into something more distinctly lavender. Since then, it has welcomed most of the seminal figures in the history of the French gay movement, including Jean Cocteau; Jean Genêt; and Jacques Charron, one of the premier actors in the Comédie Française during the late 1950s and 1960s. Expect a one-room venue layered with maritime (nonerotic) frescoes and a mostly male clientele of virtually every physical and sexual persuasion. It's open daily year-round from 6 p.m. until dawn. Entrance is free; beer costs 5€ ($6).

Biot and the Léger Museum

In the tiny hilltop village of **Biot,** craftspeople specializing in pottery and glassmaking ply their ancient trades. Romans first settled the village in 154 B.C. In the Middle Ages, the Black Plague wiped out the population of Biot, and 50 families resettled it in 1470. Many current residents of the village are descendents of these early settlers.

Because Biot is so small and offers just one hotel in the Old Town, many people make this destination a half-day trip from Cannes or Nice. A walk from one end of the village to the other takes about ten minutes. The renowned Musée Fernand Léger is located 3km (2 miles) from the village, with signs that direct you to it.

At Biot's pottery and glass-blowing studios, you can watch the pieces being made. Most of the artisan studios are on the highway on your way to the village, so a car is helpful here. Because Biot is set on a hill, walkers have to trudge up very steep steps to get to town. Although the old village itself is pedestrian only, a parking lot is at the top of the hill near the village center.

Getting there

Biot is 8km (5 miles) inland from Antibes, 9km (6 miles) from Cagnes (2€/$2.40 by bus), 15km (9 miles) from both Nice and Cannes. If **driving,** take N7 east from Antibes or west from Nice.

The Biot **train** station lies on the main coastal rail route, though the actual village is inland. Biot has frequent service each way from Nice (30 minutes, 3.50€/$4.20) and Antibes (15 minutes, 1.30€/$1.55). For rail information and schedules, call the railway station in Nice directly (☎ 04-97-03-80-80), and if they don't answer (and sometimes they won't), try ☎ 08-92-35-35-39 or 08-92-35-35-35. The Biot train station is located about 8km (5 miles) from the actual hilltop village of Biot. Between the station and the village is an unattractive highway with no sidewalks — not a pleasant walk. Bus service from the railway station to the heart of the village of Biot is via line 10A; the fare is 1.10€ ($1.30) per person, each way, for the five-minute ride.

Buses depart every 20 to 90 minutes, depending on the season and the day of the week, with the least frequent service occurring Sunday in midwinter. **La Sociéte Sillages** (☎ 04-92-30-96-38) runs buses between Biot and Antibes; trips take 20 minutes and cost 1.10€ ($1.30). Monday to Saturday, ten buses leave hourly 7:20 a.m. to 6 p.m.; Sunday and holidays, seven buses per day depart from 8 a.m. to 6 p.m. Buses leave from place Guynemer, the square at the entrance to town near the post office. Buses also stop at Musée Fernand Léger and La Verrerie de Biot (glass-blowing studio).

Getting around and getting information

The local taxi service is **Central de Taxis** (☎ 08-20-90-69-60).

The **tourist office** is located at 46 rue St-Sebastien (☎ 04-93-65-78-00; www.biot-coteazur.com). From September through June, the office is open Monday to Friday 9 a.m. to noon and 2 to 6 p.m. and Saturday and Sunday 2 to 6 p.m.; July and August, hours are Monday to Friday 10 a.m. to 7 p.m. and Saturday and Sunday 2:30 to 7 p.m.

Spending the night

Domaine du Jas de Biot
$$–$$$ Biot

This government-rated three-star hotel, a Spanish-style complex offering 19 rooms with terraces, is along a dusty highway about half a mile downhill from the entrance to the Old Town. It's conveniently situated about halfway between the old city and the Léger museum — within walking distance from each. The rooms are modern and good-sized, with lots of sunlight, but this hotel is not a lot of fun, and the staff could be far more welcoming. The hotel also has a pool and bar.

625 route de la Mer. ☎ *04-93-65-50-50.* Fax: 04-93-65-02-01. www.domainedu jas.com. *Rack rates: 100€–235€ ($120–$282) double. Breakfast: 11€ ($13). AE, MC, V. Closed Nov–Mar.*

Hôtel des Arcades
$ Biot

Under the medieval arches on the village's main square, this 12-room hotel, built in 1480, is the only lodging in the Old Town. With an ambience "*très* Greenwich Village," according to the owners, it serves as a hotel, bistro, tobacconist, art gallery, and a hangout for locals. Alas, it's tough to get a room here because it's the only game in town and fills up fast. To reach the rooms in this ancient stone house, you climb a curving tiled stairway; the stairway's walls are covered with original abstract art. The rooms, which vary in size, are cheerfully decorated in a simple and artsy style (a tapestry may be used to cover the bath area) and have views over the rooftops. Some rooms open onto terraces or small balconies. The bistro is known for excellent homecooking. The Brothier family has run the hotel for half a century.

16 place des Arcades. ☎ *04-93-65-01-04.* Fax: 04-93-65-01-05. *Rack rates: 50€–90€ ($60–$108) double. Breakfast: 7€ ($8.40). AE, DC, MC, V.*

Dining locally

In addition to the more formal locations listed below, **Crêperie du Vieux Village,** an atmospheric hole in the wall, located near place des Arcades at the top of the village (2 rue St-Sébastien; ☎ **04-93-65-72-73**), offers the option of a cheap crêpe meal, with an extensive selection of main course and dessert crêpes.

Café de la Poste
$$ Biot   PROVENÇAL

Biot's classic cafe, where visitors mingle with artists and locals, was founded in 1885, and the decor is retro, with antiques in the cozy dining room. The cafe dishes out authentic recipes from the old country, including *pot au feu grand-mère* (beef and vegetable stew), *tête de veau* (calf's heads), a stew of wild boar, and rabbit with olives, in addition to a large selection of salads. The children's menu features hamburgers, french fries, and ice cream. Sitting on the large shaded terrace on the village's main street allows you to monitor all the goings-on. In season, the cafe features live jazz at rare intervals and only in summer in the evenings.

24 rue St-Sébastien. ☎ *04-93-65-19-32. Reservations not needed. Main courses: 10.50€–23€ ($13–$28); children's menu: 8€ ($9.60). MC, V. Open: Tues–Sun noon to 3 p.m. and 7–10 p.m. Closed Nov.*

Le Restaurant Galerie des Arcades
$$ Biot PROVENÇAL/NIÇOISE

The only hotel in town (see "Spending the night," earlier in this chapter) is also the best place to eat dinner. People travel for miles for this home-cooked Niçoise cuisine prepared by Mimi Brothier, a former model for Picasso. Patrons sit family style on long banquet tables. Specialities include quintessential dishes such as *blettes* and *courgettes* (swiss chard and zucchini), *salade niçoise* (salad with tuna and potatoes), veal tenderloin, *soupe au pistou* (garlic soup), *bourride* (fish soup), and *ravioli tout nu* (homemade). The wines here are chosen by a special *oenologue* (wine expert).

16 place des Arcades. ☎ *04-93-65-01-04. Reservations not needed. Main courses: 14€–16€ ($17–$19); prix fixe: 32€ ($38). AE. Open: Tues–Sun noon to 2 p.m.; Tues–Sat 7:30–9:30 p.m. Closed mid-Nov to mid-Dec.*

Les Terraillers
$$–$$$$ Biot PROVENÇAL

The best and most expensive restaurant in town, Les Terraillers is located down the hill from the medieval center in a 16th-century building that used to be a pottery studio. The dining room is decorated with antiques and majestic bouquets, and outdoor dining on the garden terrace is offered in season. Chantal and Pierre Fulci have been running this restaurant for more than 20 years. Chef Jacques Claude is an expert at assembling unique and flavorful combinations. For instance, his *courgettes fleurs* (zucchini flowers) are served with truffle butter, and his ravioli is made with foie gras. The fresh fish may be roasted and served on spaghetti. For dessert, try the light and fluffy *coco Suzette* (coconut crêpe). The wine cellar is extensive.

11 route du Chemin-Neuf. ☎ *04-93-65-01-59. Reservations recommended. Main courses: 32€–35€ ($38–$42); prix fixe: 30€–60€ ($36–$72) lunch, 42€–60€ ($50–$72) dinner. MC, V. Open: June–Sept Fri–Wed noon to 2 p.m., daily 7–10 p.m.; Oct–May Fri–Tues noon to 2 p.m. and 7–10 p.m. Closed Nov.*

Exploring the village and the Léger museum

In the center of the village is **place des Arcades,** located at the top of the hill. The arches around the square date from the 13th and 14th centuries. Also in this square are the 16th-century gates to the city and remains of medieval ramparts. At the far end is the 15th-century **Eglise de Biot.**

The tradition of glassmaking in Biot began only in 1956, when ceramic engineer Eloi Monod opened the **Verrerie du Biot** glass studio and museum (chemin des Combes; ☎ **04-93-65-03-00;** www.verrerie biot.com), which still is the largest and oldest glass studio in town. Admission is free. Open May through September Monday to Saturday 9:30 a.m. to 8 p.m., Sundays and holidays 10 a.m. to 1 p.m. and 3 to 7:30 p.m.; October through April Monday to Saturday 9:30 a.m. to 6 p.m., Sundays and holidays 10:30 a.m. to 1 p.m. and 2:30 to 7 p.m.

Since Monad opened his studio, eight glass artists have opened their own galleries, including **Jean Claude Novaro** at place des Arcades (☎ **04-93-65-60-23**), and **Jean-Michel Operto** at Silice Creation (173 chemin des Combes; ☎ **04-93-65-10-25**). Each artist offers his own take on the contemporary stylings of glass, and it's fascinating to watch them, lit by flaming ovens, as they create the glassware.

For centuries, Biot has been associated with pottery — mainly large earthenware amphora containers called Biot jars. You'll find them at **La Poterie Provençale** (1689 route de la Mer; ☎ **04-93-65-63-30**).

Closed for renovations until 2006, **Musée National Fernand-Léger,** located at chemin du Val de Pome, on the eastern edge of town (☎ **04-92-91-50-30**), houses an impressive collection devoted to the beloved Cubist; people who aren't familiar with Léger's vibrant works are in for a treat. The building is an immense contemporary structure built after Léger's death and designed especially to highlight his *oeuvre.* Huge colorful mosaics, stained-glass windows, and giant metal sculptures decorate the exterior. Inside, the building's large spaces give ample room for Léger's monumental paintings, drawings, ceramics, and tapestries executed between 1905 and 1955. This is exciting, life-affirming work. A French film about Léger runs hourly, and a brochure in English is available. The ground floor plays host to changing exhibits. The museum is open Wednesday to Monday as follows: July through September, 10:30 a.m. to 6 p.m.; October through June 10 a.m. to 12:30 p.m. and 2 to 5:30 p.m. Entrance to the permanent collections costs 5€ ($6) for adults, and entrance to temporary exhibitions costs an additional 6.20€ ($7.45) for adults. Students and persons younger than 18 receive discounts of about 40 percent, and children younger than 6 enter free. Entrance is free for everyone the first Sunday of every month.

Antibes and Cap d'Antibes

The town of **Antibes** manages to blend its ancient past and jazzy present in an appealing way. Antibes has a historic center of pedestrian streets ringed by a newer section of town, attractively laid out with smart shops and handsome squares, including place Général-de-Gaulle, where you can find the tourist office. As the unofficial capital of the yacht industry, Antibes is full of young people — mainly Brits, Americans, Australians, and Kiwis (New Zealanders) — looking to be crewmembers on yachts and giving the town an anglicized feel. This youthful populace also distinguishes Antibes from some of the other Mediterranean towns that are popular with retirees. The town's two big yachting events are **Les Voiles d'Antibes** in June and the **Antibes Cup** in July. The **Jazz Festival,** which takes place for three weeks in July, is one of the more famous in France.

Antibes is actually one of the region's most ancient cities, founded by Greek seafarers around 400 B.C. as a convenient stopover between Corsica and Marseille. The original city was called Antipolis ("opposite") because it was opposite Corsica. The region became a Roman province, and Antipolis was again an important stop along a trade route. When Nice and Cannes were only villages, the people of Antipolis erected temples, public baths, aqueducts, a triumphal arch, and large fortifications. In the 11th century, the name of the city was changed to Antibes.

The old port of Antibes, with its ancient ramparts, is next to the new Port Vauban, where most of the colossal yachts are moored. Antibes is quite lively in season, and those wandering around town may be treated to impromptu entertainment, such as a Dixieland jazz band playing on place Nationale. **Cap d'Antibes** (the tip of the peninsula) is an isolated residential area, with private estates and fancy hotels, located about 5km (3 miles) uphill from town. Crowded sandy beaches are near town, but the Garoupe beaches, 3km (2 miles) from town toward the tip of the peninsula, are the preferred spot for sunbathing or strolling along the beachfront pedestrian path.

Getting there

Antibes is 11km (7 miles) east of Cannes and 21km (13 miles) west of Nice. The bus station, Gare Routière, is centrally located on place Guynemer (☎ **04-93-34-37-60**). It takes about 30 minutes (3.80€) by **bus** from Cannes or Nice. The train station, Gare SNCF, is at place Pierre-Semard north in the Old Town. **Trains,** running every half-hour to and from Cannes, take 10 minutes and cost 4.10€ ($4.90); trains that run every half-hour to and from Nice take 20 minutes and cost 2.90€ ($3.50). For information and reservations, call ☎ **08-92-35-35-39.**

If you're **driving** from Nice, take N98 west for about 15 minutes; from Cannes, it's an even quicker trip, about 10 minutes east on A8.

Aéroport de Nice Côte d'Azur (☎ **08-20-42-33-33**) is 23km (14 miles) from Antibes. For information on flights, call ☎ **08-36-69-55-55.** A bus ("Tam Zoo") to town costs 7.50€ ($9) and takes 40 minutes. A taxi takes about half an hour and costs 70€ to 80€ ($84–$96).

Getting around and getting information

Frequent local **bus service No. 2A** (☎ **04-93-34-37-60**) loops all the way out to the tip of the peninsula and back to town, costing 1.50€ ($1.80) per ride. You can pick up the bus at Gare Routière (bus station), or along bd. Albert-1er, where several stops are marked along the wide sidewalk. The bus takes about 20 minutes to travel from the bus station to the Eden Roc hotel at the tip of the peninsula.

For a cab, call **Allo Taxi Antibes** at ☎ **04-93-67-67-67.** To rent a car, try **Avis** (32 bd. Albert-1er; ☎ **04-93-34-65-15**), **Budget** (40 bd. Albert-1er; ☎ **04-93-34-36-84**), or **Europcar** (2 bd. Foch; ☎ **04-93-34-79-79**). For bike or scooter rental, head to **Scoot Azur** (43 bd. Wilson; ☎ **04-93-67-45-25**) or **Auto Moto Location JML** (93 bd. Wilson; ☎ **04-92-93-05-06**). Bikes rent for 14€ ($17) per day and scooters for 21€ ($25) per day.

The **tourist office** is at 11 place Général-de-Gaulle (☎ **04-92-90-53-00;** www.antibes-juanlespins.com). During July and August, the tourist office is open daily 9 a.m. to 7 p.m.; January through June and September through December, hours are Monday to Friday 9 a.m. to 12:30 p.m. and 1:30 to 6 p.m., and Saturday 9 a.m. to noon and 2 to 6 p.m. To check on or send e-mail, head to the **Workstation Cyber Café** (1 av. St-Roch; ☎ **04-92-90-49-39**), open Monday to Friday 9 a.m. to 7 p.m. and Saturday 10 a.m. to 6 p.m. The cafe serves coffee.

Spending the night

Auberge Provençale
$ Antibes

This family-run inn, located on the Old Town's busy place Nationale, has seven very basic rooms at bargain prices. The centrally located hotel and restaurant (popular and reasonably priced; see "Dining locally," later in this chapter) is about a two-minute walk from the port and beaches. This area stays loud late at night, as late diners mingle with bar hoppers. The inn does not employ the most refined staff — so be duly warned.

61 Place Nationale. ☎ *04-93-34-13-24. Fax: 04-93-34-89-88. Free parking. Rack rates: 60€–80€ ($72–$96) double. MC, V. Breakfast: 6€ ($7.20).*

Hôtel Castel Garoupe
$$ Antibes

Set on a parcel of land that's unusually large (about two acres) for over-crowded Antibes, this circa-1968 hotel resembles a privately owned Provençal *mas* (private farmhouse) set amid a luxuriant garden of parasol pines and trailing bougainvillea. Bedrooms are average in size, 24 of them with private verandas, all of them with wall-to-wall carpeting, white walls, and tile-sheathed bathrooms, each with tub and shower combinations. The hotel offers a swimming pool, tennis court, and even a ping-pong room — great for the kids. It's only 54m (60 yds.) from the sea, across the busy coastal highway (bd. de la Garoupe), and has a particularly charming staff. The in-house restaurant serves breakfast and snacks (never formal dinners) all day until 10 p.m.

959 bd. de la Garoupe. ☎ *04-93-61-36-51. Fax: 04-93-67-74-88.* www.castel-garoupe.com. *Free parking. Rack rates: 117€–150€ ($140–$180) double; 139€–168€ ($167–$202) studio for two. AE, MC, V. Closed early Nov to mid-Mar. Breakfast: 9€ ($11).*

Hôtel du Cap-Eden-Roc
$$$$ Cap d'Antibes

Legendary for the glamour of its setting and its clientele, this Second Empire hotel, opened in 1870, is surrounded by masses of gardens. It's like a country estate, with spacious public rooms, marble fireplaces, paneling, chandeliers, and upholstered armchairs. The guest rooms are among the most sumptuous on the Riviera, with deluxe beds. Bathrooms are spacious with brass fittings and tub and shower combinations. Even though the guests snoozing by the pool, which was blasted out of the cliffside at enormous expense, may appear artfully undraped during the day, evenings here are upscale, with lots of emphasis on clothing and style. The world-famous Pavillon Eden Roc, near a rock garden apart from the hotel, has a panoramic sea view. Venetian chandeliers, Louis XV chairs, and elegant draperies add to the drama. Lunch is served on an outer terrace, under umbrellas and an arbor.

Bd. Kennedy. ☎ *04-93-61-39-01. Fax: 04-93-67-76-04.* www.edenroc-hotel.fr. *Free parking. Rack rates: 360€–559€ ($432–$671) double; 810€–1,200€ ($972–$1,440) suite. Breakfast: 25€ ($30). No credit cards; personal checks must be accompanied by a letter from your bank vouching for the amount. Closed mid-Oct to Apr.*

Hôtel Mas Djoliba
$$ Antibes

Named after a tributary of the Niger River in the 1920s by a doctor, fresh upon his return from a research trip to Africa, this pretty 13-room hotel is located in a kind of nowheresville (a steep residential area on the edge of town); it isn't too far from the beach, with about a 10-minute walk to the historic center. *Mas* means *farmhouse*, but this hotel, surrounded by lush foliage, feels more like a private villa. Some of the charming rooms offer distant sea views, and one has a balcony; all rooms are relatively spacious. The top-floor two-bedroom suite can sleep five people and has a terrace and sea view. Families seem particularly at home at Djoliba, with the heated pool supplying hours of distraction for kids. The staff is particularly friendly. Between mid-May and the end of September, the hotel requires halfboard.

29 av. de Provence. ☎ *04-93-34-02-48. Fax: 04-93-34-05-81.* www.hotel-djoliba.com. *Free parking. Rack rates: Mid-May to Sept 140€–180€ ($168–$216) double, 210€–240€ ($252–$288) suite, includes half board; off-season 80€–120€ ($96–$144) double, 130€–180€ ($156–$216) suite. Breakfast: 10€ ($12). DC, MC, V. Closed Nov–Jan.*

Hôtel Royal
$–$$ Antibes

This 40-room waterfront hotel, with its own private beach, has been owned and operated by the Duhart family since 1950. Many of the modern motel-style rooms have French balconies or terraces, and almost all open onto sea views. The hotel has two eating spots: Le Dauphin, a restaurant in a glass-enclosed wing; and Restaurant Royal Beach, a more casual cafe for lunch only, on the hotel's beach. From July through September, half-board rates (two meals at the hotel) are obligatory.

16 bd. Maréchal-Leclerc. ☎ *04-93-34-03-09. Fax: 04-93-34-23-31.* www.hotel royal-antibes.com. *Parking: 8€ ($9.60). Rack rates: July to Sept 166€–191€ ($199–$229) double, includes half board; off-season 90€–110€ ($108–$132) double. Breakfast: 11€ ($13). AE, DC, MC, V. Closed Nov–Dec.*

Le Relais du Postillon
$ Antibes

This former coaching inn, originally built 150 years ago where stage coaches picked up and dropped off weary travelers, is a rarity in Antibes: a medium-priced hotel centrally located in the old city, with an excellent restaurant. Though the sheets and towels are very thin, the 16 rooms are pretty, with attractive bedding and curtains, and some have terraces facing the square. The rooms are definitely a good value, though they vary con-siderably in size. For instance, the room called *Malte* is a large and well-decorated room on the top floor with a balcony overlooking the square, while *La Valette* and *Berlin* are both small but charming rooms facing the rear of the building. Newest of the lot is *Capri*. Cozy and a bit cramped, it sits on the ground floor and has its own expansive terrace.

8 rue Championnet (across from the Parc de la Poste; ☎ *04-93-34-20-77. Fax: 04-93-34-61-24.* www.relaisdupostillon.com. *Rack rates: 44€–82€ ($53–$98) double. Breakfast: 7€ ($8.40). MC, V.*

Dining locally

L'Armoise
$$–$$$ Antibes   PROVENÇAL

This charming little restaurant is in a historic building near the market. The cuisine is classic Provençal with Italian influence, and one glance at the menu tells you that this is serious food. For example, a first course offering is *raviole de cèpes "maison" au beurre de truffes et aux pignons* (house ravioli with white flap mushrooms with truffle butter and pine nuts). Delectable main courses are the homemade *ravioli aux blettes sauce foie gras* (ravioli with swiss chard and foie gras), *noisettes d'agneau au parfum de truffes* (lamb chops with truffle oil), and *filet de boeuf au foie gras, sauce au jus de cèpes* (steak with foie gras and white mushroom sauce).

2 rue de la Touraque. ☎ *04-93-34-71-10. Reservations recommended. Main courses: 15€–20€ ($18–$24); prix fixe: 24€–43€ ($29–$52). DC, MC, V. Open: Tues–Sun 7:30–10 p.m.*

La Taverne du Saffranier
$–$$ Antibes   PROVENÇAL

One of the most appealing and solidly entrenched (established in the 1940s) bistros in town, this restaurant focuses on Provençal recipes and local ingredients. Even the staff has the kind of Provençal twang in their accents that people from northern France find endearing. This traditional brasserie with garden terrace seating is a dependable choice for a good-quality, reasonably priced meal. The service is friendly, gracious, and efficient. Provençal favorites are served, including bouillabaisse, and grilled fish is the focus of the menu. The restaurant offers a kid's menu.

Place Safranier. ☎ *04-93-34-80-50. Reservations not needed. Main courses: 23€–30€ ($28–$36); prix fixe: 16€ ($19) lunch only. No credit cards. Open: Tues–Sun noon to 2:15 p.m. and 7–10:30 p.m. Closed mid-Dec to mid-Jan.*

L'Auberge Provençale
$$ Antibes   PROVENÇAL

Solid, hearty, and traditional Provençal cuisine, including roast beef, bouillabaisse, and grilled fish, are the specialties at this family-owned restaurant on the always-animated place Nationale, where you'll usually find strolling entertainment from passers-by. Most diners head straight back to the restaurant's large garden courtyard, where tables are set up under brightly colored umbrellas. The food can be creative (for example, breast of guinea fowl with vanilla sauce), but fresh fish and grilled meats dominate.

61 place Nationale. ☎ *04-93-34-13-24. Reservations not needed. Main courses: 17€–30€ ($20–$36). MC, V. Open: Daily noon to 1:30 p.m. and 7–9:30 p.m.*

Le Brulot
$$ Antibes   PROVENÇAL

On a tiny Old Town street lined with restaurants, this sometimes very animated spot stands out for good food and value. The moment you walk into the intimate dining room, you smell the *raison d'être* of the place: wood-grilled fish. The menu features catch of the day prepared on the grill with a variety of sauces and herbs. The most popular dish, other than fish, is the filet of duck. The restaurant also offers outside seating on a busy pedestrian street.

3 rue Frédéric-Isnard. ☎ *04-93-34-17-76. Reservations not needed. Main courses: 17€–22€ ($20–$26); prix fixe: 18€–25€ ($22–$30). AE, MC, V. Open: Thurs–Sun noon to 2 p.m. and daily 7:30–10 p.m. Closed 2 weeks in Jan and early to mid-Aug.*

Le Jardin
$–$$ Antibes PROVENÇAL

A relative newcomer to Antibes' restaurant scene, and set within a thick-walled historic home in the heart of Antibes' oldest neighborhood, this restaurant boasts well-prepared food and a decor composed of bright colors (especially dark tangerine and yellow) and iron chairs. The best menu items include *rougets à la Niçoise* (red mullet), stuffed and deep-fried vegetables, and a zesty supreme of duck in orange-flavored honey sauce. Deep-fried zucchini flowers are a favorite here.

5 rue Sade. ☎ 04-93-34-64-74. Reservations recommended. Main courses: 15€–25€ ($18–$30); prix fixe: 15€–29€ ($18–$35). Open: Daily 7–11 p.m.

Le Relais du Postillon
$$ Antibes PROVENÇAL

Expect excellent food, creatively prepared and stylishly presented, at this small restaurant in the hotel of the same name (see "Spending the night," earlier in this chapter) off rue de la République. The menu changes daily as the masterful chef improvises, but what arrives on your plate inevitably consists of beautiful colors, shapes, and textures. Standbys are *foie gras de canard* (duck foie gras), *risotto de langonstines* (rice with cream sauce and crayfish), filet of sea bass with balsamic vinegar, and lobster salad. *Panache de la mer* is a combination of seafood prepared in a variety of ways, including dumplings and tarts. The lunch menu is limited, usually with a choice of one or two main courses, so check the chalkboard out front before sitting down. The restaurant has half a dozen tables outside on the square; inside is a romantically lit cozy dining room fronted by a long bar.

8 rue Championnet (across from the post office park). ☎ 04-93-34-20-77. Reservations preferred. Main courses: 24€–27€ ($29–$32). MC, V. Open: Tues–Sun 7:30–10 p.m. Closed Nov.

Restaurant Albert-1er
$–$$$ Antibes PROVENÇAL

This 1950s-era brasserie, just across the boulevard from the beach, a setting that appeals to families, is known for having extremely fresh fish that's served in a dining room lavishly decorated with framed photographs of the stars and celebrities who have dined here. It specializes in oysters and other shellfish, as well as superb versions of, among others, paella and turbot or grouper and sauterne sauce. In summer, everyone — including extended families with their children — sits on one of three different terraces, each with a view of the beach.

46 bd. Albert-1er. ☎ 04-93-34-33-54. Reservations accepted. Main courses: 15€–28€ ($18–$34); prix fixe: 30€ ($36). MC, V. Open: Thurs–Tues noon to 2:15 p.m. and 7–10:30 p.m. Closed mid-Nov to mid-Dec.

Restaurant de Bacon
$$–$$$$ Cap d'Antibes   PROVENÇAL

This is Antibes' most deluxe restaurant, with a reputation for attracting the rich and famous that goes back to the 1950s. The dining room and shaded terrace offer views of the sweeping coast and sandy beaches. The menu is dependent each day on what's the freshest and best fish available. The creative preparations may be *fricassée de rougets* (braised red mullet in red wine sauce) or *chapon en papillote* (chicken — young rooster, actually — baked in parchment). But the restaurant prides itself on its preparation of that regional specialty, boullabaisse — and it works; we think it's the best on the entire Riviera. For dessert, a selection of fresh tarts and other delicacies always are available.

Bd. de Bacon. ☎ 04-93-61-50-02. Reservations necessary. Main courses: 16€–110€ ($19–$132); prix fixe: 45€–75€ ($54–$90). AE, MC, V. Open: Wed–Sun noon to 2 p.m., Tues–Sun 8–10 p.m. Closed Nov–Jan.

Exploring the town and the beaches

The peninsula containing the towns of Antibes on the east, Juan-les-Pins on the west, and Cap-d'Antibes at the tip is just east of Nice. The coastline, with sandy beaches and rocky embankments, is 24km (15 miles) long.

Antibes has an easy layout. From central **place Général-de-Gaulle,** rue de la République (a pedestrian street) leads to the **Old Town,** with its cobblestone pedestrian streets, and ends at **place Nationale,** the liveliest square in the Old Town. Rue Sade, on the south side of place Nationale, a street loaded with restaurants, leads to **Cours Massena,** which is set up for several blocks with a covered market. One block south is the **Château Grimaldi,** housing the Musée Picasso and the Cathédrale d'Antibes (see later in this section for details on both). Just beyond the ramparts of Château Grimaldi is the **old port,** crowded with pleasure yachts. To get to Cap d'Antibes at the tip of the peninsula, you need to drive or take a city bus. Several bus stops are along bd. Albert-1er, stretching from place Général-de-Gaulle to the beach. Antibes's **Provençale Market,** with food and flowers, is open in the covered market building on Cours Massena daily, except Monday, 6 a.m. to 1 p.m. In the afternoon, crafts are displayed in the market building. A good **flea market** is open every Thursday and Saturday 8 a.m. to 5 p.m. on place Audiberti.

Le Petit Train d'Antibes (☎ 06-03-35-61-35) runs frequent half-hour tours of Antibes and Juan-le-Pins. In Antibes, the train leaves from place de la Poste and passes by the pedestrian streets, Provençal market, Old Town, port Vauban, and ramparts. Tickets are 6.50€ ($7.80) for adults and 3.50€ ($4.20) for children 3 to 10. The train operates between March and October only, originating from a well-marked spot on the Cours Massena and rumbling down, among others, rue de la République. During July and August, it operates daily from 10 a.m. to 11 p.m.; from March through June and during September and October, it runs daily from 10 a.m. to noon and from 2 to 6 p.m.

You can also tour Antibes on foot as part of a guided tour. **Gérard Lavayssière** (☎ 04-93-34-56-82) organizes two-hour walking tours of the town's historic core if he has a minimum of eight participants. Tours cost 7.50€ ($9) per person and originate every Monday at 5:30 p.m. on the sidewalk in front of the tourist office and every Tuesday at 9:30 a.m. in front of the Musée d'Archéologie. Reservations are important.

In the old stone Château Grimaldi, sitting high on a bluff overlooking the sea, **Musée Picasso** (place Mariéjol; ☎ 04-92-90-54-20) is one of Riviera's loveliest museums. Prolific artist Pablo Picasso spent the fall of 1946 painting at the villa, which was owned by the town; in gratitude he donated to Antibes the 181 works he completed there, as well as ceramics and sculpture. The museum, which frequently plays hosts to themed exhibits of modern and contemporary art, has a large collection of works by 20th-century artists. The sculpture garden opens onto a terrace with a panoramic view. The museum is open Tuesday to Sunday as follows: June through September 10 a.m. to 6 p.m.; October through May 10 a.m. to noon and 2 to 6 p.m. Admission costs 6€ ($7.20) for adults, 3€ ($3.60) for students and persons 18 to 26. Children younger than 18 enter free.

Cathédrale d'Antibes, on place Mariéjol (☎ 04-93-34-06-29), is one of the Riviera's most beautiful cathedrals — it's a baroque church with a graceful facade that boasts stripes of burnt orange and yellow. The cathedral was built on the site of a Roman temple dedicated to Diana. Inside, you find a 12th-century Roman choir, an 18th-century baroque nave, and the famous Brea altarpiece painted in 1515. It's open daily 9 a.m. to 6 p.m., and admission is free.

The imposing **Musée d'Archéologie,** on Bastion St-André, just southwest of the Picasso Museum (☎ 04-93-34-00-39), contains an impressive collection of antiquities found in Antibes and in shipwrecks nearby (some dating back to 1200 B.C.). This museum tends to put on "fun" exhibits, such as images on ceramics of Dionysus (Greek god of wine) from the sixth to third centuries B.C. It's open Tuesday to Sunday June through September 10 a.m. to 6 p.m. (Fridays till 10 p.m.), and October through May 10 a.m. to noon and 2 to 6 p.m. Guided visits are given on Friday at 3 p.m. Admission is 3€ ($3.60), 1.50€ ($1.80) for students, children younger than 18 free.

At Cap d'Antibes, next to the Hôtel du Cap-Eden-Roc and surrounded by a 5-hectare (12-acre) park, **Musée Naval et Napoléonien** (av. Kennedy; ☎ 04-93-61-45-32) contains Napoleonic memorabilia and is worth the trip for military history buffs. The museum also has a fine collection of model ships, paintings, and marine objects. Year round, the museum is open Tuesday to Saturday from 9:30 a.m. to noon and 2:15 to 6 p.m. and Saturday from 9:30 a.m. to noon. Admission is 3€ ($3.60) adults, 1.50€ ($1.80) students and children younger than 18 are free.

Marineland, on route de Biot (RN7), just east of Antibes center (☎ 04-93-33-49-49), is Europe's largest marine zoological park and is home to killer whales, dolphins, sea lions, seals, penguins, sharks, and aquariums of exotic fish. You can watch the frequent feeding of seals and sea lions. It's open year round daily 10 a.m. to 5 p.m., but the last admission is at 4 p.m. Admission is 32€ ($38) for adults and 23€ ($28) for children ages 3 to 12.

Antibes has some of the best beaches on the Riviera, in terms of sand and cleanliness. The entire peninsula with Antibes and Juan les Pins has 25km (16 miles) of coastline and 48 beaches. The ones at the Cap are the prettiest and have the best sand. **Plage de la Salis** is located just south of town, within walking distance. On the eastern neck of the cape are the **Plages de la Garoupe,** which are the peninsula's nicest beaches, a long stretch of 3km (2 miles). All beaches have concessions with chairs and umbrellas to rent, and variety of water sports. And a restaurant is always nearby, serving snacks and full meals.

Living it up after dark

You find much more nightlife in nearby Juan-les-Pins, a suburb of Antibes reachable in a few minutes by car, but Antibes does have its share of good bars, especially on **bd. d'Aguillon** near the port. The **Hop Store** (38 bd. d'Aguillon; ☎ 04-93-34-15-33) is a good Irish pub. **La Siesta** (route du Bord de Mer; ☎ 04-93-33-31-31) is a disco, piano bar, casino, and restaurant that's open Friday and Saturday only from September through May (daily in July and August).

Vence and the Matisse Chapel

Most visitors come to **Vence** to see a masterpiece by Matisse — the Chapelle du Rosaire, the Dominican chapel he designed in the hills just outside the town center. But the town itself is a suitable stop for lunch and a stroll. Vence, with a population of 15,000, has a pedestrian-only medieval center surrounded by ramparts. Along the Old Town's narrow cobblestone streets are cafes, galleries, and small shops. Vence is much less touristy than neighboring St-Paul-de-Vence (see later in this chapter), but it offers its own understated charms.

Getting there

Buses travel frequently between Nice and Vence, and the one-hour (24km/15-mile) trip costs 4.70€ ($5.65). Buses arrive and depart from place du Grand Jardin, near the tourist office. For bus schedules, call **Bus S.A.P. (Societe Automobile de Provence)** at ☎ 04-93-58-37-60. Vence has no train station, but the nearest train station is in Cagnes-sur-Mer about 7km (5 miles) away. From there, you can take an S.A.P. bus (see earlier for number).

To **drive** from Nice to Vence, take N7 west to Cagnes-sur-Mer and then D236 north to Vence.

Getting around

The local bus service for Vence is **Ste. T.A.V.L.** (☎ 04-93-42-40-79). You can order a taxi by calling ☎ 04-93-58-11-14 or by going to the taxi stand on place du Grand Jardin.

To rent a car, try **Europcar** (26 bd. Maréchal Foch; ☎ 04-93-34-79-79) or **Budget** (av. Rhin et Danube; ☎ 04-93-58-04-04). You can rent bikes at **Vence Motos** (av. Henri-Isnard; ☎ 04-93-58-56-00). Rentals cost 10€ ($12) for a half day and 17€ ($20) for a full day.

The **tourist office** is at 8 place du Grand Jardin (☎ 04-93-58-06-38). It's open June through September Monday to Saturday 9 a.m. to 7 p.m., Sunday 9 a.m. to 1 p.m., and October through May Monday to Saturday 9 a.m. to 5 p.m. To check on or send e-mail, go to **Net Space 06,** 32 av. Henri Isnard (☎ 04-93-24-01-00), open Monday to Friday 9:30 a.m. to 12:30 p.m. and 2 to 6 p.m.

Spending the night

Le Château St-Martin
$$$–$$$$ Vence

Vence's most deluxe dining/lodging option, Le Château St-Martin also is one of the region's top options. The hotel features 40 rooms and suites in the main house, and 5 villa-like cottages (Bastides) on the sprawling 14-hectare (35-acre) property, with a pool and two tennis courts. Paths run through the landscaped property, set in the hills with distant views to the sea. The spacious rooms are decorated in an elegant style. At the acclaimed restaurant La Commanderie, chef Phillippe Guerin turns out poetic inspirations that include *mignon de veau mariné au gingembre et miel de Provence, fricassée de légumes et soja* (veal marinated with ginger and Provençal honey with fricasée of vegetables and soybeans).

Av. des Templiers (3km/1.9 miles north from the center of Vence, about a 20-minute drive from Nice's airport). ☎ *04-93-58-02-02. Fax: 04-93-24-08-91.* www.chateau-st-martin.com. *Free parking. Rack rates: 260€–830€ ($312–$996) double; 650€–1,550€ ($780–$1,860) suite. Breakfast: 23€ ($28). AE, DC, MC, V. Closed Nov to mid-Feb.*

Hôtel Le Provence
$ Vence

To reach Margaretha and Francis Sobata's simple 16-room hotel, you pass through a garden courtyard filled with roses and climbing bougainvillea — and that's perhaps the most memorable thing about this unassuming place. Originally built as a villa, it was transformed into a hotel in the 1950s. The hotel is situated in a fine location, across from the circular ramparts to the Old Town. The Sobatas, a young friendly couple who speak English, purchased the property and have slowly renovated each room in progression. The rooms vary from quite small to medium size; some rooms have private balconies, and most offer views of the garden or the village rooftops and the distant sea.

9 av. Marcellin-Maurel. ☎ *04-93-58-04-21. Fax: 04-93-58-35-62. Free parking. Rack rates: 42€–72€ ($50–$86) double. Breakfast: 6€ ($7.20). MC, V.*

Dining locally

Auberge des Seigneurs
$–$$$ Vence   PROVENÇAL

At this rustic 17th-century hotel/restaurant, once a part of the nearby Château de Villenueve, the dining room features beamed walls and ceilings, a long central table, and a huge fireplace where chicken, lamb, and hams are roasted on spits. The combination of atmosphere and reasonable prices is popular with visitors. The decorative theme of the restaurant was inspired by the reign of François 1er (1515–47), France's quintessential Renaissance-era monarch. In addition to the roasted chicken (which takes an hour to be roasted) and ham, the limited menu also features fish such as sea wolf and bream. Meals are brought to the table and served family-style from large platters. The service is friendly, if harried, and a shaggy dog (Monsieur Tim) sometimes greets guests. An acoustic guitarist provides entertainment on some nights. The hotel has six simple rooms renting at 66€ to 71€ ($79–$85) double. Breakfast costs 8€ ($9.60) extra per person.

Place du Frene. ☎ *04-93-58-04-24. Reservations recommended. Main courses: 16€–25€ ($19–$30); prix fixe: 29€–40€ ($35–$48). AE, DC, MC, V. Open: Fri–Sun 12:30 to 2 p.m.; Tues–Sun 7:30–9:30 p.m. Closed Nov to mid-Mar.*

Jacques Maximin
$$$–$$$$ Vence   PROVENÇAL

This much-lauded restaurant, with its star chef, has been a destination of gourmands for a quarter of a century. Settle into the luxurious dining room for dishes such as *filet de loup rôti à la niçoise* (roasted sea bass niçoise style) and *canard entier du lauragais rôti à l'ail, sauce poivrade* (whole duck roasted with garlic and a peppery wine sauce). Other specialties include roasted baby pigeon (thighs and wings) served with wild mushrooms; a salad of warm scallops and truffles, served with potatoes and an Andalusian-style tomato-flavored cream sauce; and several different preparations of lobster. The setting is an early 20th-century manor house, loaded with fine art that's set within an extensive private park and garden.

689 Chemin de la Gaude (about 3km/1.9 miles from Vence along route Cagnes-sur-Mer). ☎ *04-93-58-90-75. Reservations necessary. Main courses: 35€–38€ ($42–$46); prix fixe: 50€ ($60) dinner. AE, MC, V. Open: Wed–Sun 12:30–1:30 p.m.; Tues–Sun 7:30–10 p.m.*

La Farigoule
$$–$$$ Vence   PROVENÇAL

The best restaurant in the village center, La Farigoule nevertheless is small and fills up fast. The dining room is cheerful and cozy, with bright pastel and colored fabrics decorating the tables and windows. In summer, the restaurant offers seating on the interior courtyard. English menus are available. The most requested dish is a special *aïoli provençale*. You can also order a zesty poached octopus in pepper-and-lemon broth as an appetizer. Main course specialties include sea bass with lemon-and-tomato marmalade, tournedos of tuna with shellfish sauce and stuffed peppers, sea scallops with artichoke hearts, and La Farigoule's famous *tarte fine au caviar de cèpes* (mushroom pie). Another very special dish can be found in the cheese course: *millefeuille de pain d'épices au roquefort* (puff pastry of spiced bread with roquefort cheese).

15 rue Henri-Isnard. ☎ *04-93-58-01-27. Reservations necessary. Prix fixe: 20€–35€ ($24–$42) lunch; 35€–45€ ($42–$54) dinner. MC, V. Open: Thurs–Mon noon to 2 p.m. and 7:30–10 p.m.*

Exploring the town

Place du Peyra, inside the ramparts, contains the **Vieille Fontaine,** a huge urn-shaped fountain, and a tenth-century cathedral decorated with a Chagall mosaic on the left as you enter. Near the town's west gate, the 15th-century **Château Villeneuve** (place du Frene; ☎ 04-93-24-24-23) houses a private modern art museum; the permanent collection includes works by Matisse, Dufy, Dubuffet, and Chagall. It's open Tuesday to Sunday 10 a.m. to 12:30 and 2 to 6 p.m. Admission is 5€ ($6) adults, 2.50€ ($3) for students with I.D. and children 12 to 18, free for children younger than 12.

In 1947, at age 77, Henri Matisse agreed to create a Dominican chapel in the hills near Vence. Two years later, after hundreds of preparatory drawings and many sleepless nights, Matisse had designed one of his most unusual works, the **Chapelle du Rosaire,** 466 av. Henri-Matisse (route de Saint-Jeannet), 1.5km (1 mile) east from the center of town (☎ 04-93-58-03-26). On the building's completion, he said, "I want those entering my chapel to feel themselves purified and lightened of their burdens." The building is owned today by a community of nuns, the Dominican Sisters of the Rosary *(les Dominicaines du Rosaire)*, who live in the community nearby. It is somewhat of a pilgrimage site for thousands of Matisse-ophiles, who visit the chapel in different seasons and times of day to see the changes sunlight makes on the stained-glass reflections. Matisse designed every aspect of the building — not only the stained glass and tiles, but also elements such as the altar and the priests' vestments. When driving or walking toward the building from Vence, you first notice the 12m (40-ft.) wrought-iron cross on a low-lying, unassuming whitewashed building. Inside, down a flight of stairs, the chapel is a luminous space with bright stained-glass windows and black-and-white-tiled walls, with three minimalist tile designs: a powerfully executed Stations of the Cross, an immense Madonna and Child, and a portrait of a faceless St. Dominic (to the right of the altar). Outside the chapel, an exhibit area, **L'Espace Matisse,** displays Matisse's drawings and samples of vestments in bright colors and starbursts designed by the artist. A brochure is available in English. Admission to the chapel is 2.50€ ($3) for adults, 1€ ($1.20) for children younger than 16. From December through September, the chapel is open Tuesday and Thursday 10 to 11:30 a.m. and 2 to 5:30 p.m. and Monday, Wednesday, and Saturday 2 to 5:30 p.m. (closed October and November). Sunday Mass starts at 10 a.m. and is followed by a visit at 10:45 a.m.

Living it up after dark

The most popular bars and cafes are clustered around the main squares of the village. **Le Clémenceau** (☎ **04-93-58-24-70**) is a cafe on place Clémenceau; **Henry's Bar** tends to have patrons spilling out onto place de Peyra; and **La Régence** is always full on place du Grand Jardin.

St-Paul-de-Vence and the Fondation Maeght

St-Paul-de-Vence, one of the most beautiful villages in France, is a small pedestrian-only medieval burg built into a steep hill, with dozens of art galleries lining the cobblestone streets. St-Paul-de-Vence is popular with visitors making a day trip of strolling the narrow, steep streets and walking around the ramparts of this fortified town. After the day-trippers leave, the village is peaceful in the evenings.

St-Paul's history can be traced back to the sixth century B.C., when a fortified enclosure was built here. The site came under Roman rule in 154 B.C. and prospered as a key stop on an east–west trading route. The castle on the top of the hill was built in the 12th century, as was the Romanesque church nearby. In the 15th and 16th centuries, the village became prosperous as a provincial capital and took on the look it retains today. In the 20th century, celebrities discovered St-Paul, and artists, writers, and filmmakers flocked to the village. Expensive hotels and restaurants soon followed. A short walk from the entrance to the village is the Fondation Maeght, one of the best modern art museums in France.

Getting there

The best way to get to St-Paul is to **drive.** From Nice, take A8 to Cagnes-sur-Mer and then follow the signs and the route de la Colle (RD 436) to St-Paul-de-Vence. The drive from Nice takes about 35 to 40 minutes.

The nearest **bus** stop is located on the route de Vence, ½km (¼ mile) from the town ramparts. Buses leave frequently from Nice (31km/19 miles from St-Paul) and the neighboring town of Cagnes-sur-Mer (6km/4 miles from St-Paul). The bus from Nice (No. 400 or No. 410) costs 4.20€ ($5.05), and the bus from Cagnes-sur-Mer costs 2.10€ ($2.50). Call the bus company **Cie SAP** (☎ 04-93-58-37-60) for the schedule. The closest **train** station is in Cagnes-sur-Mer, 6km (4 miles) away. The train from Nice to Cagnes-sur-Mer takes about 7 minutes and costs 3.70€ ($4.45). For train schedules, call ☎ 08-92-35-35-35.

Getting around and getting information

St-Paul is small and easy to walk through. No cars are allowed within the ramparts, except for people who have reservations at one of the hotels. If you have a reservation, you can drive in and park at your hotel. The town has two local cab companies: **Taxi Gilbert** at ☎ 06-85-57-13-10 and **Taxi Jean-Luc** at ☎ 06-08-26-11-72.

The **tourist office** is at 2 rue Grande (☎ 04-93-32-86-95; Fax: 04-93-32-60-27; www.saintpaulweb.net). The office is open daily October through May 10 a.m. to 6 p.m. and June through September 10 a.m. to 7 p.m. To send or check on e-mail, stop at **St-Paul Web** (4 rue de l'Etoile; ☎ 04-93-32-07-80). It's open daily 10 a.m. to 7 p.m.

Spending the night

Hostellerie les Remparts
$ St-Paul-de-Vence

How unexpected to find an affordable hotel in St-Paul. After all the day-trippers have left, you can wander the romantic streets in peace and make your way to this medieval house, located in the center of the village, for a candlelit dinner and quiet slumber. The rooms are on the small side, but they're unique, with arches, stone walls, paintings, and antiques. Each room has a view of the village or the valley below, and some have floor-to-ceiling windows. The restaurant, with a terrace and noted for its quick, simple food, offers reasonably priced Provençal cuisine.

72 rue Grande. ☎ *and fax **04-93-32-09-88**.* www.stpaulweb.com/remparts. *Free parking. Rack rates: 39€–80€ ($47–$96) double. Breakfast: 7€ ($8.40). MC, V.*

Hôtel le Hameau
$–$$$ St.-Paul-de-Vence

This former farmhouse, built in the 1700s, about a kilometer (half-mile) north from St-Paul, is a pleasant place to stay, with views of the village. The rooms are attractive — some have tiled floors and beamed ceilings, and all contain antiques. The large garden has jasmine, honeysuckle, and a greenhouse-inspired orangerie. The hotel also has a large pool with a Jacuzzi. Breakfast, in your room or on the terrace, includes homemade orange marmelade. When artist Marc Chagall visited St-Paul, he stayed here.

528 route de la Colle. ☎ ***04-93-32-80-24**. Fax: 04-93-32-55-75.* www.le-hameau.com. *Free parking. Rack rates: 94€–159€ ($113–$191) double; 159€ ($191) suite. Breakfast: 12.50€ ($15). MC, V.*

Hôtel le St-Paul
$$–$$$ St-Paul

This Relais & Châteaux location, occupying a 16th-century house in the heart of the village, offers St-Paul's most deluxe accommodations within the ramparts. The 19 rooms and suites are grandly decorated with antiques and the finest fabrics. The hotel has a fine Provençal restaurant, with three dining rooms and a terrace, where you're surrounded by flowering window boxes and centuries-old village buildings. Set menus cost 45€ to 82€ ($54 to $98) at lunch and 65€ to 82€ ($78–$98) at dinner. It's open daily for lunch and dinner.

86 rue Grande. ☎ *04-93-32-65-25. Fax: 04-93-32-52-94.* www.lesaintpaul.com. *Free parking. Rack rates: 170€–300€ ($204–$360) double; 270€–560€ ($324–$672) suite. Breakfast: 20€ ($24). AE, DC, MC, V.*

Le Mas d'Artigny
$$ St-Paul

About 2km (1¼ miles) south from St-Paul, and constructed in 1973 to emulate a solidly built large-scale Provençale *mas* (farmhouse), this exquisite 85-room hotel is set among acres of pine groves. All rooms have balconies with distant sea views, and the hotel has 25 luxury suites. Amenities include a heated pool, tennis courts, mountain bikes, a golf driving range, billiards, a fitness jogging course, and a small gym. The expensive restaurant features the cuisine of chef Francis Scordel, who won the Toque d'Or (golden chef's hat) in 1999, an annual award presented by the National Academy of Cuisine.

Route de la Colle. ☎ *04-93-32-84-54. Fax: 04-93-32-95-36.* www.mas-artigny.com. *Free parking. Rack rates: 120€–150€ ($144–$180) double; 360€–990€ ($432–$1,188) suite. Breakfast: 25€ ($30). AE, DC, MC, V.*

Dining locally

La Colombe d'Or
$–$$$ St-Paul-de-Vence PROVENÇAL

This world-famous hotel/restaurant has been host to the rich and famous for decades. But over the years, the Golden Dove has become a bit of a tourist trap, with its food not measuring up to the high prices. Expect to find the most typical Provençal cuisine, with first courses such as foie gras and main courses such as roasted monkfish with herbs and Sisteron lamb. The most memorable aspect of the meal is the remarkable art collection on the walls of the public rooms, with works by Matisse, Braque, Léger, and Calder, among others. The hotel also has 26 expensive rooms and suites (265€/$318 for a double; 320€/$384 for a suite), with access to a heated pool and sauna.

Place de Gaulle. ☎ *04-93-32-80-02. Reservations necessary. Main courses: 17€–28€ ($20–$34). AE, DC, MC, V. Open: Daily noon to 2 p.m. and 7:30–10 p.m. Closed Nov–Dec.*

Exploring the town

Musée d'Histoire Locale (place de l'Eglise; ☎ 04-93-32-41-13), celebrates the events that shaped St-Paul-de-Vence and the region around it
with artifacts and dozens of photographs showcasing life here around
1910. On site are several wax figures representing the celebrities who
made the town their temporary home, including French actors Yves
Montand, Lino Ventura, Jean-Paul Belmondo, and Simone Signoret.
Except for an annual holiday during two weeks in November, it's open
daily from 10 a.m. to 12:30 p.m. and 1:30 to 5:30 p.m. The entrance price
is 3€ ($3.60) for adults, 2€ ($2.40) for students and persons 6 to 16.
Entrance is free for children younger than 6.

The privately owned **Fondation Maeght,** located just outside the town
walls (☎ 04-93-32-81-63; www.fondation-maeght.com), is dedicated to
modern art. The building itself is a striking contemporary art statement;
the grounds and building exterior display monumental sculptures,
ceramics, and stained glass by artists such as Giacometti, Miró, and
Chagall. Although it owns an important collection of works (by artists
such as Bonnard, Braque, Calder, Chagall, Giacometti, Matisse, and
Miró), the museum is usually filled with special exhibits drawn from
public and private collections. This museum is large, so you may need to
allow yourself a couple of hours to go through it. It's open daily October
through June 10 a.m. to 12:30 p.m. and 2:30 to 6 p.m. and July through
September 10 a.m. to 7 p.m. Admission is 11€ ($13) for adults and 9€
($11) for children ages 10 to 25. Children younger than 10 are admitted
free.

Shopping for local treasures

The village streets are chock-full of expensive boutiques and galleries.
Some top galleries include **Atelier/Boutique Christian Choisy** (5 rue de
la Tour/Ramparts Ouest; ☎ 04-93-32-01-80) and **Galerie Lilo Marti** (à la
Placette; ☎ 04-93-32-91-22). Jewelry lovers will want to check out
Nicola's Tahitian Pearl (47 rue Grande; ☎ 04-93-32-67-05).

Climb down some steep steps to a 14th-century wine cellar to visit **La
Petite Cave de St-Paul** (7 rue de l'Etoile; ☎ 04-93-32-59-54), which
stocks an excellent selection of regional wine. Among the shop's most
prized wines are bottles from Le Mas Bernard, the winery owned by
Fondation Maeght, which owns only 3 hectares (7 acres) of vineyards
west of St-Paul. The wine from Le Mas Bernard is very good and unavail-
able in the United States because of the small production.

Part VII
The Part of Tens

The 5th Wave   By Rich Tennant

"Here's something. It's a language school that will teach you to speak French for $500, or for $200 they'll just give you an accent."

In this part . . .

This part, a standard of *For Dummies* books, offers you some info on French foods and gifts so that your trip is easier and more fun. The fabulous food is one of the best things about France: You shouldn't leave the country without trying some of its specialties. In Chapter 22, we list the foods you simply will want to try while in the gourmet capital of the world. In Chapter 23, we list ten special gift ideas for those jealous friends and family members that you left behind.

Cuisses de Grenouilles (cweess duh gre-noo-yuh)

Frogs' legs do taste a little like chicken, but they're more delicate and salty. You'll find the best examples of this classic French dish in the Loire Valley.

Pâté de Foie Gras (pat-ay duh fwoh grah)

A staple of every fancy restaurant in France is goose liver pâté, which is often *à la maison* (homemade) and *poêlé* (pan-fried). Rich and creamy, with dense flavor and a delicate texture, *pâté de foie gras* is a quintessential French food.

Truffes (troof)

France's most expensive food, delectable *truffes* are a rare kind of black fungus (like mushrooms) that need to be dug out of the ground by special dogs or pigs trained for the task of locating them. Truffle season is November to March. Truffles appearing on any dish *(aux truffes)* up the price of the meal by 25 or more euros ($30). Look for them particularly on omelets and pasta.

Chariot de Fromage (chair-ree-aht duh frwoh-mazh)

Ah, the chariot of cheese: brie, camembert, roquefort, chèvre, gruyère, and so on. At the best restaurants, the selection of cheeses is so enormous, it must be wheeled to you on a trolley. When the waiter brings it over, ask which are the best cheeses of the region *("Les fromages de la region?")*, and choose which ones you want by pointing to several. The waiter will serve them, and you can eat them with a knife and fork.

Tarte Tartin, Soupe de Fraises, Ile Flotant, Crème Brûlée, Mousse au Chocolat (tart tah-tihn, soup duh frez, eel flo-tahnt, krem bruh-lay, moose oh shawk-oh-lah)

Apple tart, boozy strawberry soup, floating island (meringue with a custard sauce), custard topped with caramel, chocolate mousse . . . and the list goes on. Having dessert in a French restaurant is reason enough to visit the country. *C'était bon!*

Chapter 23

The Art of the Souvenir: Ten Gifts to Buy in France

In This Chapter

▶ Buying the perfect gift

▶ Bringing home a taste of France

▶ Finding the best crafts

Many people come to France specifically to shop (you know who you are), but this list is more for travelers who, in the midst of exploring this most special country, want to bring home a gift or two for those less fortunate. These gift givers often need a bit of direction, so here are ten perfect gifts that whisper "France."

 If you're a serious shopper, you may want to buy a copy of *Born to Shop Paris* or *Born to Shop France,* by Suzy Gershman (both published by Wiley).

Scarves in Paris

The first thing you notice about Parisian women is that they're very stylish. The second thing you notice is that they all wear scarves. So buy a few for yourself or your significant other. And while you're at it, buy them for all your female friends and family. They come in all price ranges — from the priciest at Hermès to the best bargains at street vendors. And they're easy to pack. While searching for the perfect scarves, you may want to pick up a few neckties for the men on your list, assuming your male acquaintances still wear them. Once again, a wide range of prices and styles is available, from vibrant silk Hermès ties to whimsical Tour Eiffel–patterned ties available at street vendors near — where else? — the Tour Eiffel.

Stationery in Paris

Although the art of the snail-mail letter is fading fast, you still can find exquisite papers and stationery sets in Paris's fine shops, including the big department stores such as La Samaritaine, Au Printemps, Au Bon Marché, and Galeries Lafayette. You'll find the most original selections at boutiques on the Left Bank and the least expensive selection in the student area of St-Germain.

Quimper Pottery in Brittany

Quimper pottery has been a famous collectible for antiques buffs for many years. You can buy contemporary examples of the hand-painted craft at several shops in the town of Quimper, including the premier maker, H. B. Henriot, which also offers factory tours.

Fishermen's Sweaters in Brittany

After a day or two on the blustery coast of Brittany, you may be looking to buy one of those bulky fishermen's sweaters. The most common types have blue-and-white or red-and-white horizontal stripes. The best brands are St. James and Tricommer. These rugged sweaters will last a lifetime.

Santons in Provence

Made of clay or wood, *santons* often are hand-painted and highly individualistic renderings of ordinary townspeople and their professions and of saints and nativity cast members. These highly popular collectible figurines are available throughout Provence and the Riviera.

Fabrics in Provence

Nothing says "Provence" like those brightly colored cotton fabrics sold all across the south of France. You'll see the Souléiado brand and store name in most towns in Provence and the Riviera. Though the style is imitated heavily, the designs were originated in the 18th and 19th centuries. They make great tablecloths and napkins, as well as dresses and purses. You can find them at discount prices at markets in Provence and at department stores in Paris.

Perfume in Grasse

The town of Grasse on the Riviera is the perfume-making capital of France. After touring one of the three factories open to tourists — Molinard, Galimard, and Fragonard — you can sign up for a class to make your own perfume or buy some of the specially packaged wares. In Paris, head to rue de Rivoli across from the Louvre for the best perfume shops, including those offering discounts. You can find all the top names here, in addition to some boutique French perfume not easily found in the United States.

Lingerie on the Riviera

It's no surprise that the Riviera offers the best lingerie shops anywhere. You can buy a wide range of top-of-the-line teddies, nightgowns, and underwear for relatively good prices. Swimsuits *(maillot de bain)* also are fun to shop for here, and you'll find a variety of daring styles. Because the French practically invented sex appeal and spare no expense to achieve it, expect to splurge.

Handmade Glass Objects in Biot

The tiny hilltop village of Biot, located between Cannes and Nice on the Riviera, is France's capital of glass. You can watch about a dozen top artisans blowing and sculpting exquisite glass objects in its many studios and galleries. Among the names to look for are Novaro, Saba, and Pierini. Most of Biot's galleries will pack and ship their wares internationally.

Cider and Calvados in Normandy

The apple orchards throughout Normandy's rolling green landscape are known for producing the exceptional fruits Normans use for a variety of beverages. They traditionally drink with their meals a light, refreshingly fizzy cider instead of wine. Bringing a bottle of this cider home will immediately transport you back to the region's half-timbered houses. And after a meal, Normans enjoy Calvados, a fiery brandy served with or in coffee. It takes 12 to 15 years to bring this famous liqueur to term.

Appendix

Quick Concierge

Fast Facts

American Express

American Express's Paris office (11 rue Scribe, 9e; ☎ 01-47-77-79-28; Métro: Opéra, Chausée-d'Antin, or Havre-Caumartin; RER: Auber) is the largest American Express office in France, and the place where lesser branches of American Express sometimes refer their problems. It maintains a travel agency and facilities for resolving problems with stolen or over-their-limit American Express cards, open Monday to Saturday 9 a.m. to 6:30 p.m. Also on-site is a currency exchange, mail deposit and pickup, and traveler's check service, open Monday to Friday 9 a.m. to 6:30 p.m. and Saturday 9 a.m. to 5:30 p.m.

The Nice office (11 promenade des Anglais; ☎ 04-93-16-53-53) is open as a travel agency Monday to Friday 9 a.m. to noon and 2 to 6 p.m., and as a currency exchange office Monday to Saturday 9 a.m. to 7 p.m., and Sunday 10 a.m. to 12:30 p.m. and 1 to 5:30 p.m.

The Monaco office (35 bd. Princesse Charlotte; ☎ 93-25-74-45) is open for currency exchange, traveler's checks, and credit-card issues Monday to Friday 9 a.m. to 5 p.m.

Banks or currency exchange offices in other cities throughout France act as semi-autonomous representatives of American Express, performing limited functions related mostly to traveler's checks and currency exchange. The tourist office in any French town will be able to direct you to such an office, if it exists, or to an equivalent bank, travel agent, or currency exchange office.

ATM Locators

ATMs are widely available throughout the country. For a list of ATMs that accept MasterCard or Visa, ask your bank or go to www.visa.com or www.mastercard.com.

Business Hours

In Paris, the *grands magasins* (department stores) are generally open Monday to Saturday 9:30 a.m. to 7 p.m.; **smaller shops** may close for lunch and reopen at 2 p.m., but this schedule is rarer than it used to be. Many stores stay open until 7 p.m. in summer; others close on Monday, especially in the morning. Large **offices** remain open all day, although some close for lunch. Throughout the country, **banks** are normally open weekdays 9 a.m. to noon and 1 or 1:30 to 4:30 p.m. Some banks also open on Saturday morning. Some currency-exchange booths are open very long hours (see "Currency Exchange"). In the rest of the country, most stores are open 9:30 a.m. to noon and 2 to 6 p.m., with later hours in summer.

Credit Cards

Visa, MasterCard, American Express, and Diners Club are all accepted throughout the country, but the most commonly accepted are Visa and MasterCard. See also "Lost Property."

Currency Exchange

Banks and *bureaux de change* (exchange offices) almost always offer better exchange rates than hotels, restaurants, shops, and even **American Express** offices, which you should use only in emergencies. You'll find exchange offices in central commercial areas of all towns and cities in France.

Customs

Non-EU nationals can bring the following items into France duty-free: 200 cigarettes or 100 cigarillos or 50 cigars or 250 grams of smoking tobacco; 2 liters of wine and 1 liter of alcohol more than 38.80 proof; 50 grams of perfume, one-quarter liter of toilet water; 500 grams of coffee, and 100 grams of tea. Travelers ages 15 and older can also bring in 230€ ($276) in other goods; for those 14 and younger, the limit is 115€ ($138). **EU citizens** may bring any amount of goods into France, as long as it's for their personal use and not for resale.

Returning **U.S. citizens** who've been away for 48 hours or more are allowed to bring back, once every 30 days, $800 worth of merchandise duty-free. You'll be charged a flat rate of 10% duty on the next $1,000 worth of purchases; on gifts, the duty-free limit is $100. You cannot bring fresh food-stuffs into the United States; tinned foods, however, are allowed.

Citizens of the U.K. who are **returning from a European Union country** have no limit on what can be brought back, as long as the items are for personal use (this includes gifts), and the necessary duty and tax has been paid. Guidance levels are set at 3,200 cigarettes, 200 cigars, 3 kg smoking tobacco, 10 liters of spirits, 90 liters of wine, and 110 liters of beer.

Canada allows a $750 exemption (which can be used only once a year), and you're allowed to bring back the following items duty-free: 200 cigarettes, 1.5 liters of wine or 1.14 liters of liquor, and 50 cigars. In addition, you may mail gifts to Canada from abroad at the rate of C$60 a day, provided they're unsolicited and don't contain alcohol or tobacco or advertising matter. Write on the package "Unsolicited gift, under $60 value." All valuables should be declared on the Y-38 form before departure from Canada, including serial numbers of valuables you already own, such as expensive foreign cameras.

The duty-free allowance in **Australia** is A$400 or, for those younger than 18, A$200. Personal property mailed back from France needs to be marked "Australian goods returned" to avoid payment of duty. Upon returning to Australia, citizens can bring in 250 cigarettes or 250 grams of loose tobacco, and 1,125 ml of alcohol. If you're returning with valuable goods you already own, such as foreign-made cameras, you need to file form B263.

The duty-free allowance for **New Zealand** is NZ$700. Citizens older than 17 can bring in 200 cigarettes or 50 cigars or 250 grams of tobacco (or a mixture of all three if their combined weight doesn't exceed 250 grams), plus 4.5 liters of wine or beer or 1.125 liters of liquor.

Dentists

Call your consulate and ask the duty officer to recommend a dentist. For dental emergencies in Paris, call **SOS Dentaire** (☎ 01-43-37-51-00) daily 9 a.m. to midnight. If you're not in Paris, go to the nearest hospital, which will have a dentist on duty or know how to reach one.

Doctors

Call your consulate and ask the duty officer to recommend a doctor. In Paris, call **SOS Médecins** (☎ 01-47-07-77-77), a

24-hour service. If you are not in Paris, go to the local hospital or ask at the police station for the number of a doctor who speaks English. *Remember:* You need to have your health insurance card with you unless you want to pay cash for the services.

Drugstores

Marked with green crosses, pharmacies are often upscale affairs that sell toiletries in addition to prescription drugs and over-the-counter remedies. If you're shopping for products other than drugs, it's almost always cheaper to buy them elsewhere, such as a *supermarché* (supermarket).

Electricity

The French electrical system runs on 220 volts. Adapters to convert the voltage and fit sockets are cheaper at home than in Paris. Many hotels have two-pin (in some cases, three-pin) sockets for electric razors. It's a good idea to ask at your hotel before plugging in any electrical appliance.

Embassies/Consulates

If you have a passport, immigration, legal, or other problem, contact your consulate. Call before you go: They often keep strange hours and observe both French and home-country holidays. Each of the following is in Paris: **Australia,** 4 rue Jean-Rey, 15e (☎ 01-40-59-33-00; Métro: Bir-Hakeim); **Canada,** 35 av. Montaigne, 8e (☎ 01-44-43-29-00; Métro: Franklin-D.-Roosevelt or Alma-Marceau); **New Zealand,** 7 ter rue Léonard-da-Vinci, 16e (☎ 01-45-00-24-11, ext. 280 from 9 a.m. to 1 p.m.; Métro: Victor-Hugo); **United KIngdom,** 35 rue Faubourg St-Honoré, 8e (☎ 01-44-51-31-00; Métro: Madeleine); **United States,** 2 ave. Gabriel, 1er (☎ 01-43-12-22-22; Métro: Concorde).

Emergencies

Call ☎ **17** for the **police.** To report a **fire,** dial ☎ **18.** For an **ambulance,** call ☎ **15,** or call ☎ 01-45-78-74-52 for **SAMU** (Service d'Aide Médicale d'Urgence). In Paris, for help in English, call **SOS Help** (☎ 01-46-21-46-46) between 3 and 11 p.m. The main police station (9 bd. du Palais, 4e; ☎ 01-53-71-53-73; Métro: Cité) is open 24 hours.

Information

Before you go, contact the **French Government Tourist Office** at 444 Madison Ave., 16th floor, New York, NY 10022-6903 (☎ 212-838-7800; Fax: 212-838-7855; www.francetourism.com). Of the many locations in Paris, try the **Office de Tourisme de Paris** at Carrousel du Louvre, Place de la Pyramide Inversée 99, Ruede Rivoli, 1e (☎ 08-92-68-30-00 at .34€ [40¢] per minute). Each town in France has its own tourist office, which are listed in the appropriate chapters of this book.

Internet Access

To surf the Net or check your e-mail, open an account at a free e-mail provider, such as Hotmail (www.hotmail.com) or Yahoo! Mail (http://mail.yahoo.com), and all you need to check e-mail while you travel is a Web connection, available at Net cafes in almost every town in France. Check with the local tourist office for locations. After logging on, just point the browser to your e-mail provider, enter your username and password, and you have access to your mail. In addition, you can open up an e-mail account for reasonable fees at many post offices in larger towns in France, because they offer computers for e-mail and Internet access.

Laundry and Dry Cleaning

To find a laundry, ask at your hotel or consult the Yellow Pages under *Laveries pour particuliers.* Take as many 1, 2, or 3€ coins as you can. Washing and drying 6kg (13.25 lbs.) costs about 6€ ($7.20). Dry cleaning is *nettoyage à sec;* look for shop signs with the word *pressing.*

Liquor Laws

Supermarkets, grocery stores, and cafes sell alcoholic beverages. The legal drinking age is 16. Persons younger than 16 can be served an alcoholic drink in a bar or restaurant if accompanied by a parent or legal guardian. Wine and liquor are sold every day of the year. *Be warned:* France is very strict about drunk-driving laws. If convicted, you face a stiff fine and a possible prison term of two months to two years.

Lost Property

Lost property (*objets trouvés*) offices are in most big cities; ask the tourist office for the location. In Paris, the central office is **Objets Trouvés** (36 rue des Morillons, 15e; ☎ 08-21-00-25-25; Métro: Convention), at the corner of rue de Dantzig. The office is open Monday, Wednesday, and Friday 8:30 a.m. to 5 p.m. and Tuesday and Thursday 8:30 a.m. to 8 p.m.

If you lose your **Visa** card, call ☎ 08-36-69-08-80; for **MasterCard,** call ☎ 01-45-67-53-53. To report lost **American Express** cards, call ☎ 01-47-77-72-00.

Luggage Storage/Lockers

Most Paris hotels store luggage for free, a good idea if you plan to return to Paris after a tour of the provinces. Also try the *consignes,* the luggage offices at large railway stations. Otherwise, you have to lug your luggage with you — pack light.

Mail

Every substantial town in France has at least one post office. Large post offices tend to be open Monday to Friday 8 a.m. to 7 p.m., and Saturday 8 a.m. to noon; small post offices may have shorter hours. Paris's main post office is at 52 rue du Louvre, 75001 Paris (☎ 01-40-28-76-00; Métro: Louvre-Rivoli). A complete roster of its services is available at the hours noted above, but it remains open 24 hours a day for a limited roster of services that include buying stamps; weighing and depositing letters and packages; and handling urgent mail, telegrams, and telephone calls. It stores *Poste Restante* mail sent to you in care of the post office until you pick it up; be prepared to show your passport and pay .45€ (55¢) for each letter you receive. If you don't want to use Poste Restante, you can receive mail in care of **American Express.** Holders of American Express cards or traveler's checks get this service free; others have to pay a fee.

Airmail letters and postcards of less than 20 grams (about ¾ of an ounce) cost .90€ ($1.10) for destinations in North America, .46€ (55¢) for anywhere within Europe, and .79€ (95¢) for Australia and New Zealand.

Maps

Maps of Paris, printed by the department stores, are usually available for free at hotels. The maps are good if you're visiting Paris for only a few days and hitting the major attractions. But if you plan to really explore all the nooks and crannies of Paris, the best maps are those of the *Plan de Paris par Arrondissement,* pocket-sized books with maps and a street index, available at most bookstores. They're extremely practical, and prices start at around 8€ ($9.60). Free maps of other French cities, towns, and villages are available at local tourist offices.

Newspapers and Magazines

In major cities, newsstands carry the latest editions of the *International Herald Tribune* and the major London papers. *Time* and *Newsweek* are readily available. So is *USA Today*'s International edition. The weekly entertainment guide *Pariscope,* which comes out on Wednesday, has an English-language insert that gives you up-to-the-minute information on the latest cultural events. You can also get *The New York Times* in some of the bigger English-language bookstores.

Police

Dial ☎ **17** in emergencies.

Restrooms

You can find public restrooms at train stations, airports, tourist sites, and often tourist offices. Every cafe has a restroom, but it's supposed to be for customers only. The best plan is to ask to use the telephone; it's usually next to the *toilette*. For .30€ (35¢), you can use the street-side toilets, which are automatically flushed out and cleaned after every use. Some Métro stations have serviced restrooms; you're expected to tip the attendant .30€ (35¢).

Safety

France, particularly in the provinces, is safe. Exceptions are the heavily touristed areas of Provence and the Riviera, which tend to attract thieves, particularly at train and bus stations. Paris is a relatively safe city, and violent crime is rare. Your biggest risks are pickpockets and purse snatchers, so be particularly attentive on the Métro and on crowded buses, in museum lines, and around tourist attractions. Women need to be on guard in crowded tourist areas and on the Métro against overly friendly men who seem to have made a specialty out of bothering unsuspecting female tourists. Tricks include asking your name and nationality, then sticking like a burr to you for the rest of the day. They're usually more harassing than harmful, but if you're too nice, you may be stuck spending time with someone with whom you prefer not to. A simple "leave me alone" (*laissez-moi tranquille* ["lay-say-mwa tran-*keel*"]) usually works. Special mention should be made of Marseille, which is a rough-and-tumble town. The very high unemployment means that a large number of men seem to be loitering around looking for someone to rob. Watch your back.

Smoking

Restaurants are required to provide no-smoking sections, though you may sit next to the kitchen or restrooms. Even here, your neighbor may light up and defy you to say something about it. Large brasseries, expensive restaurants, and places accustomed to dealing with foreigners are likely to be the most accommodating.

Taxes

Watch out: You can get burned. As a member of the European Union, France routinely imposes a standard 19.6% value-added tax (VAT, in France known as the TVA) on many goods and services. The tax on merchandise applies to clothing, appliances, liquor, leather goods, shoes, furs, jewelry, perfume, cameras, and even caviar. You can get a refund — usually 13% — on certain goods and merchandise, but not on services. To get a refund, the minimum purchase is 182€ ($218) in the same store for nationals or residents of countries outside the European Union.

Telephone/Telex/Fax

Public phone booths take only telephone debit cards called *télécartes,* which can be bought at post offices and at *tabacs* (cafes and kiosks that sell tobacco products). You insert the card into the phone and make your call; the cost is automatically deducted from the "value" of the card recorded on its magnetized strip. The télécarte comes in 50- and 120-unit denominations, costing 7.45€ and 15€ ($8.95 and $18), respectively, and can be used only in a phone booth.

Cashiers will almost always try to sell you a card from France Télécom, the French phone company, but cards exist that give you more talk time for the same amount of money. Instead of inserting the card into a public phone, you dial a free number and tap in a code. The cards come with directions, some in English, and can be used from public and private phones, unlike France Télécom's card. Look for *tabacs* that have advertisements for Delta Multimedia or Kertel, or ask for a *télécarte international avec un code.*

To place **international calls from France,** dial 00, the country code (for the United States and Canada, 1; for Britain, 44; for Ireland, 353; for Australia, 61; for New Zealand, 64), the area or city code, and then the local number (for example, to call New York, you'd dial 00 + 1 + 212 + 000-0000). **To place a collect call to North America,** dial 00-33-11, and an English-speaking operator will assist you. Dial 0800-99-00-11 for an AT&T operator; MCI 0800-99-00-19; Sprint 0800-99-00-87.

To **call from France to anywhere else in France** (called *province*), always dial ten digits. The country is divided into five zones with prefixes of 01, 02, 03, 04, and 05; check a phone directory for the code of the city you're calling.

If you're **calling France from the United States,** dial the international prefix, 011; then the country code for France, 33; followed by two-digit city code and the eight-digit local number, but leave off the initial zero on the two-digit city code (for example, 011 + 33 + 1-0-00-00-00-00).

Avoid making phone calls from your hotel room; many hotels charge at least .30€ (35¢) for local calls, and the markup on international calls can be staggering.

You can send **telex** and **fax** messages at the main post office in any town, but it's often cheaper at your hotel or at a neighborhood printer or copy shop.

Time

Paris is six hours ahead of eastern standard time; noon in New York is 6 p.m. in France.

Tipping

Service is supposedly included at your hotel, but the custom is to tip the **bellhop** about 1€ ($1.20) per bag, more in expensive hotels. If you have a lot of luggage, tip a bit more. Don't tip housekeepers unless you do something that requires extra work. Tip a few euros if a reception staff member performs extra services.

Although your *addition* or *note* (restaurant bill) or *fiche* (cafe check) bear the words *service compris* (service charge included), always leave a small tip (5% is acceptable).

Taxi drivers appreciate a tip of at least .50€ (60¢). When the fare exceeds 15€ ($18), a 5% to 10% tip is appropriate. At the **theater and cinema,** tip .50€ (60¢) if an usher shows you to your seat. In **public toilets,** a fee is often posted. If not, the maintenance person expects a tip of .30€ (35¢), usually in a basket or plate at the entrance. **Porters** and **cloakroom attendants** are usually governed by set prices, which are displayed. If not, 1€ to 1.25€ ($1.20–$1.50) per suitcase, and .30€ to 1€ (35¢–$1.20) per coat is fine.

Trains

The telephone number for reservations on France's national railroads (SNCF) is ☎ 08-36-35-35-35, or to get an English-speaking operator ☎ 08-36-35-35-39 (.30€ [35¢] min.). The service is available within France every day from 7 a.m. to 10 p.m., and telephone wait times can be interminable. A more convenient, and less expensive, means of gathering railway schedules and fares, buying tickets, and reserving seats is the SNCF's Web site at www.sncf.com. *Remember:* Depending on the train, you'll validate your train ticket in the orange *composteur* (ticket validator) on the platform, or (in the cases of long-distance rides beyond the limits of greater Paris) have it validated manually by an onboard conductor.

Water

Tap water in France is perfectly safe, but if you're prone to stomach problems, you may prefer to drink bottled water.

Weather Updates

Call ☎ 08-36-70-12-34 (.30€/35¢ per min.) for France and abroad; ☎ 08-36-68-02-75 (.30€/35¢ per min.) for Paris and the Ile de France.

Toll-Free Numbers and Web Sites

Major airlines

Air Canada
☎ 888-247-2262 in the U.S.
☎ 01-44-50-20-20 in France
www.aircanada.ca

Air France
☎ 800-237-2747 in the U.S.
☎ 08-20-82-08-20 in France
www.airfrance.com

American Airlines
☎ 800-433-7300 in the U.S.
☎ 01-55-17-43-41 in France
www.aa.com

British Airways
☎ 800-247-9297 in the U.S.
☎ 08-25-82-54-00 in France
www.britishairways.com

Continental Airlines
☎ 800-525-0280 in the U.S.
☎ 01-42-99-09-09 in France
www.continental.com

Delta Air Lines
☎ 800-221-4141 in the U.S.
☎ 08-00-30-13-01 in France
www.delta.com

Iceland Air
☎ 800-223-5500 in the U.S.
☎ 01-44-51-60-51 in France
www.icelandair.com

Northwest/KLM
☎ 800-225-2525 in the U.S.
☎ 08-90-71-07-10 in France
www.nwa.com

United Airlines
☎ 800-241-6522 in the U.S.
☎ 08-10-72-72-72 in France
www.united.com

USAirways
☎ 800-428-4322 in the U.S.
☎ 08-10-63-22-22 in France
www.usairways.com

Car-rental agencies

Auto Europe
☎ 888-223-5555 in the U.S.
☎ 08-00-94-05-57 in France
www.autoeurope.com

Avis
☎ 800-230-4898 in the U.S.
☎ 08-20-05-05-05 in France
www.avis.com

Budget
☎ 800-472-3325 in the U.S.
☎ 01-49-75-56-00 in France
www.budget.com

Hertz
☎ 800-654-3131 in the U.S.
☎ 01-45-74-97-39 in France
www.hertz.com

Kemwel Holiday Auto (KHA)
☎ 800-678-0678
www.kemwel.com

National
☎ 800-CAR-RENT in the U.S.
☎ 01-44-38-61-61 in France
www.nationalcar.com

Getting More Information

The information sources in this section are the best of the lot. Dig in before you go, and you'll be well prepared for your trip.

Touring the tourist offices

For general information about France, contact an office of the **French Government Tourist Office** at one of the following addresses:

✔ **In the United States:** The **French Government Tourist Office,** 444 Madison Ave., 16th floor, New York, NY 10022-6903 (☎ **212-838-7800**; Fax: 212-838-7855; www.francetourism.com); 676 N. Michigan Ave., Chicago, IL 60611-2819 (☎ **310-271-6665;** Fax: 312-337-6339); or 9454 Wilshire Blvd., Suite 715, Beverly Hills, CA 90212-2967 (Fax: 310-276-2835).

✔ **In Canada: Maison de la France/French Government Tourist Office,** 1981 av. McGill College, Suite 490, Montréal PQ H3A 2W9 (☎ **514-876-9881;** Fax: 514-845-4868).

✔ **In the United Kingdom: Maison de la France/French Government Tourist Office,** 178 Piccadilly, London W1J 9AL (☎ **09068-244-123** (60p/min); Fax: 09068-244-123).

✔ **In Australia: French Tourist Bureau,** 25 Bligh St. Level 22, Sydney, NSW 2000 Australia (☎ **02-9231-5244;** Fax: 02-9221-8682).

✔ **In New Zealand:** You won't find a representative in New Zealand; contact the Australian representative.

✔ **In Paris: The Office de Tourisme et des Congrès de Paris,** Carrousel du Louvre, Place de la Pyramide (☎ **08-92-68-30-00** [.34€/.40¢ min]; Inversée 99, rue de Rivoli, 1e; Métro: Palais Royal).

Surfing the Web

You'll find a lot of excellent information about France on the Internet — restaurant reviews, concert schedules, subway maps, and more.

France

✔ **Avignon and Provence** (www.avignon-et-provence.com): Here you'll find restaurant reviews (many restaurants provide their menus), museum listings, ideas for outdoor activities, and plenty of history about the popes of Avignon, in addition to practical information for emergencies and classified ads.

✔ **Brittany Holiday Guide** (www.brittany-guide.com): Come here for thorough descriptions, with photos of places of interest, hotels and guest houses, transportation information (including roadwork), history, and an events calendar for the region.

✔ **France Way** (www.franceway.com): With many suggestions for your trip to France — especially Paris — this guide covers dining, lodging, and transportation. The detailed listings of restaurants in Paris don't appear to be paid ads.

✔ **French Government Tourist Office** (www.francetourism.com): Here you find information on planning your trip to France and practical tips, family activities, events, and accommodations.

✔ **French Tourism Board for Normandy** (www.normandy-tourism.org): This site has hotel descriptions, information on museums and attractions, and an interactive parks and gardens list with photos and information about the many gardens in the region.

✔ **Frommers.com** (www.frommers.com): Click here for travel tips, reviews, online booking, bulletin boards, travel bargains, and travel secrets for hundreds of destinations.

✔ **Giverny and Vernon** (www.giverny.org): Visitors to the region forever associated with Claude Monet will find loads of useful travel and transportation information. The site gives details on the area's castles, museums, and places of archaeological interest, as well as the artist's famous gardens.

✔ **Mappy** (www.mappy.fr): This handy site provides exact mileage, precise directions, toll prices, and time it takes to drive anywhere in France. You can print the maps or have them mailed to you.

✔ **Provence Touristic Guide** (www.provence.guideweb.com): Dig into the "Art & culture" section for pictures, exhibit descriptions, and contact information for museums. The site also has a directory of hotels and guest houses that includes photos, and the ability to take online reservations.

✔ **Riviera Côte d'Azur** (www.guideriviera.com): On this site, excursions and outdoor activities around the Côte d'Azur are arranged by season. Take a photo tour to see where you can go hiking or four-wheeling. Find out where you can get a Carte Musée Côte d'Azur; the pass is good at 62 museums on the Riviera.

✔ **SNCF (French Rail)** (www.sncf.com): The official Web site of the French railway system, this site sells seats online for trips through France. You can also find timetables and prices here.

✔ **Subway Navigator** (www.subwaynavigator.com): This site provides detailed subway maps for Paris and other French cities, plus 60 other cities around the world. You can select a city and enter your arrival and departure points, and then Subway Navigator will map out your route and estimate how long your trip will take.

Paris and environs

✔ **Aeroports de Paris** (www.adp.fr): This site provides transfer information into Paris, and lists terminals, maps, airlines, boutiques, hotels, restaurants, and accessibility information for travelers with disabilities.

✔ **Bonjour Paris** (www.bparis.com): Utilize this fun and interesting site chock full of information about the city. You'll find everything from cultural differences to shopping to restaurant reviews, all written from an American expatriate point of view.

✔ **Paris France Guide** (www.parisfranceguide.com): This site has plenty of useful information about Paris, with current nightlife, restaurant, music, theater, and events listings.

✔ **Paris Free Voice** (www.parisvoice.com or www.thinkparis.com): This is the online version of the free Paris monthly, *The Paris Voice*. It's hip and opinionated with many listings for performance art, music, and theater.

✔ **Paris Tourist Office** (www.paris-touristoffice.com): The official site of the Paris Tourist Office provides information on the year's events, museums, accommodations, nightlife, and restaurants.

✔ **RATP (Paris Urban Transit)** (www.ratp.fr): On this site, you can find subway and bus line maps, timetables, and information, in addition to routes and times for Noctambus, Paris's night buses that run after the Métro closes.

Hitting the books

Most bookstores have several shelves devoted entirely to Paris- and France-related titles. Here are a few other books that may be useful for your trip. All are published by Wiley.

✔ *Frommer's France,* updated every year, is an authoritative guide that covers the entire country.

✔ *Frommer's Irreverent Guide to Paris* is a fun guide for sophisticated travelers who want the basics without a lot of excess.

✔ *Frommer's Memorable Walks in Paris* is for those who want to explore the city in-depth and on foot, with easy directions and descriptions of important sights.

✔ *Frommer's Paris from $90 a Day* is for you if you want to visit Paris comfortably but don't want to spend a fortune doing it.

✔ *Frommer's Paris,* updated every year, covers everything you may want to know about the City of Light.

✔ *Frommer's Portable Paris* is the pocket-sized version of *Frommer's Paris.*

✔ *Frommer's Provence & the Riviera* takes you to the best offerings in the south of France.

✔ *Paris For Dummies* focuses on the City of Light in the easy-to-read *For Dummies* format.

Brushing Up on Basic French

Whether you just want to pick up the most basic words and phrases or you want to conduct yourself with (limited) sophistication at the dinner table, use the following six tables to improve your understanding of the French language.

Basics

English	*French*	*Pronunciation*
Yes/No	**Oui/Non**	wee/nohn
OK	**D'accord**	dah-*core*
Please	**S'il vous plaît**	seel voo *play*
Thank you	**Merci**	mair-*see*
You're welcome	**De rien**	duh ree-*ehn*
Hello (during the day)	**Bonjour**	bohn-*jhoor*
Good evening	**Bonsoir**	bohn-*swahr*
Goodbye	**Au revoir**	o ruh-*vwahr*
What's your name?	**Comment vous appellez-vous?**	kuh-mahn voo za-pell-ay-*voo?*
My name is	**Je m'appelle**	jhuh ma-*pell*
Happy to meet you	**Enchanté(e)**	ohn-shahn-*tay*
How are you?	**Comment allez-vous?**	kuh-mahn tahl-ay-*voo?*
Fine, thank you, and you?	**Trés bien, merci, et vous?**	tray bee-ehn, mair-*see*, ay *voo?*
So-so	**Comme ci, comme ça**	kum-*see,* kum-*sah*

English	French	Pronunciation
I'm sorry/ excuse me	**Pardon**	pahr-*dohn*
I'm so very sorry	**Désolé(e)**	day-zoh-*lay*

Getting around/Street smarts

English	French	Pronunciation
Do you speak English?	**Parlez-vous anglais?**	par-lay-voo ahn-*glay?*
I don't speak French	**Je ne parle pas français**	jhuh ne parl pah frahn-*say*
I don't understand	**Je ne comprends pas**	jhuh ne kohm-*prahn* pah
Could you speak	**Pouvez-vous parler**	Poo-*vay* voo par-lay
more loudly/ more slowly?	**plus fort/ plus lentement?**	ploo for/ ploo lan-te-*ment?*
Could you repeat that?	**Répetez, s'il vous plaît**	ray-pay-*tay*, seel voo *play*
Hold on (literally, don't leave)	**Ne quittez pas**	neh key-*tay* pah
What is it?	**Qu'est-ce que c'est?**	kess-kuh-*say?*
What time is it?	**Qu'elle heure est-il?**	kel uhr eh-*teel?*
What?	**Quoi?**	kwah?
How? or What did you say?	**Comment?**	kuh-*mahn?*
When?	**Quand?**	kahn?
Where is/are?	**Où est/sont?**	ooh-eh/sohn?
cashier	**la caisse**	lah *kess*
elevator	**l'ascenseur**	lah-sahn-*seuhr*
luggage storage	**consigne**	kohn-*seen*-yuh
telephone	**le téléphone**	luh tay-lay-*phone*
toilets	**les toilettes/ les WC**	lay twa-*lets*/ les vay-*say*
Who?	**Qui?**	kee?
Why?	**Pourquoi?**	poor-*kwah?*
here/there	**ici/là**	ee-*see*/lah
left/right	**à gauche/ à droite**	a goash/ a drwaht
straight ahead	**tout droit**	too drwah

English	*French*	*Pronunciation*
I'm American	**Je suis américain(e)**	jhe sweez a-may-ree-*kehn*
I'm Canadian	**Je suis canadien(ne)**	jhe sweez can-ah-dee-*en*
I'm British	**Je suis anglais(e)**	jhe sweez ahn-*glay (glaise)*
Fill the tank (of a car), please	**Le plein, s'il vous plaît**	luh plan, seel-voo-*play*
I'm going to	**Je vais à**	jhe vay ah
I want to get off at	**Je voudrais descendre à**	jhe voo-*dray* day-son-drah ah
airport	**l'aéroport**	lair-o-*por*
bank	**la banque**	lah bahnk
bridge	**Pont**	pohn
bus station	**la gare routière**	lah gar roo-tee-*air*
bus stop	**l'arrêt de bus**	lah-*ray* duh boohss
cathedral	**cathédrale**	ka-tay-*dral*
church	**église**	ay-*gleez*
entrance (to a building or a city)	**une porte**	ewn port
exit (from a building or a freeway)	**une sortie**	ewn sor-*tee*
ground floor	**rez-de-chausée**	ray-de-show-*say*
highway to	**la route pour**	la root por
hospital	**l'hôpital**	low-pee-*tahl*
museum	**le musée**	luh mew-*zay*
second floor	**premier étage**	prem-ee-*ehr* ay-*tajh*
store	**le magazin**	luh ma-ga-*zehn*
street	**Rue**	roo
subway	**le métro**	le may-tro
ticket office	**vente de billets**	vahnt duh bee-*yay*
by means of a bicycle	**en vélo/par bicyclette**	uh *vay*-low/par bee-see-*clet*
by means of a car	**en voiture**	ahn vwa-*toor*
dead end	**une impasse**	ewn am-*pass*

English	French	Pronunciation
no entry	**Sens interdit**	sehns ahn-ter-*dee*
no smoking	**défense de fumer**	day-*fahns* de fu-may
on foot	**à pied**	ah pee-*ay*
police	**la police**	lah po-*lees*
rented car	**voiture de location**	vwa-*toor* de low-ka-see *on*
slow down	**ralentir**	rah-lahn-*teer*
suburb	**banlieu, environs**	bahn-*liew,* en-veer-*ohn*

Necessities

English	French	Pronunciation
I'd like	**Je voudrais**	jhe voo-*dray*
driver's license	**permis de conduire**	per-*mee* duh con-*dweer*
gasoline	**du pétrol/de l'essence**	duh pay-*trol*/de lay-*sahns*
insurance	**les assurances**	lez ah-sur-*ahns*
key	**la clé (la clef)**	la clay
one-day pass	**ticket journalier**	tee-kay jhoor-nall-ee-*ay*
one-way ticket	**Aller simple**	ah-*lay sam*-pluh
room	**une chambre**	ewn *shahm*-bruh
round-trip ticket	**Aller-retour**	ah-*lay* re-*toor*
ticket	**un billet**	uh *bee*-yay
How much does it cost?	**C'est combien?/ Ça coûte combien?**	say comb-bee-*ehn?*/ sah coot comb-bee-*ehn?*
Do you take credit cards?	**Est-ce que vous acceptez les cartes de credit?**	es-kuh voo zak-sep-*tay* lay kart duh creh-*dee?*
I'd like to buy	**Je voudrais acheter**	jhe voo-dray ahsh-*tay*
aspirin	**des aspirines/ des aspros**	deyz ahs-peer-*een*/ deyz ahs-*proh*
cigarettes	**des cigarettes**	day see-ga-*ret*
condoms	**des préservatifs**	day pray-ser-va-*teef*
dictionary	**un dictionnaire**	uh deek-see-oh-*nare*
dress	**une robe**	ewn robe
envelopes	**des envelopes**	days ahn-veh-*lope*

English	French	Pronunciation
gift	**un cadeau**	uh kah-*doe*
handbag	**un sac**	uh sahk
hat	**un chapeau**	uh shah-*poh*
magazine	**une revue**	ewn reh-*vu*
map of the city	**un plan de ville**	unh plahn de *veel*
matches	**des allumettes**	dayz a-loo-*met*
necktie	**une cravate**	uh cra-*vaht*
newspaper	**un journal**	uh zhoor-*nahl*
phone card	**une carte téléphonique**	ewn cart tay-lay-fone-*eek*
postcard	**une carte postale**	ewn carte pos-*tahl*
road map	**une carte routière**	ewn cart roo-tee-*air*
shirt	**une chemise**	ewn che-*meez*
shoes	**des chaussures**	day show-*suhr*
skirt	**une jupe**	ewn jhoop
soap	**du savon**	dew sah-*vohn*
socks	**des chaussettes**	day show-*set*
stamp	**un timbre**	uh *tam*-bruh
trousers	**un pantalon**	uh pan-tah-*lohn*
writing paper	**du papier à lettres**	dew pap-pee-*ay* ah *let*-ruh

In your hotel

English	French	Pronunciation
Are taxes included?	**Est-ce que les taxes sont comprises?**	ess-keh lay taks son com-*preez?*
balcony	**un balcon**	uh bahl-cohn
bathtub	**une baignoire**	ewn bayn-*nwar*
for two occupants	**Pour deux personnes**	poor duh pair-*sunn*
Is breakfast included?	**Petit déjeuner inclus?**	peh-*tee* day-jheun-*ay* ehn-*klu?*
room	**une chambre**	ewn *shawm*-bruh
shower	**une douche**	ewn doosh
sink	**un lavabo**	uh la-va-*bow*
suite	**une suite**	ewn sweet
We're staying for . . . days	**On reste pour . . . jours**	ohn rest poor . . . jhoor

English	French	Pronunciation
with air-conditioning	**Avec climatization**	ah-*vek* clee-mah-tee-zah-sion
without	**Sans**	sahn
youth hostel	**une auberge de jeunesse**	oon oh-bayrjh duh jhe-*ness*

In the restaurant

English	French	Pronunciation
full (no seating available)	**complet**	cohm-*play*
I would like	**Je voudrais**	jhe voo-*dray*
to eat	**manger**	mahn-*jhay*
to order	**commander**	ko-mahn-*day*
Please give me	**Donnez-moi, s'il vous plaît**	doe-nay-*mwah*, seel voo play
an ashtray	**un cendrier**	uh sahn-dree-*ay*
a bottle of	**une bouteille de**	ewn boo-*tay* duh
a cup of	**une tasse de**	ewn tass duh
a glass of	**un verre de**	uh vair duh
a plate of breakfast	**une assiette de le petit-déjeuner**	ewn ass-ee-*et* duh luh puh-*tee* day-zhuh-*nay*
cocktail	**un aperitif**	uh ah-pay-ree-*teef*
check/bill	**l'addition/la note**	la-dee-see-*ohn*/la noat
dinner	**le dîner**	luh dee-*nay*
fork	**une fourchette**	ewn four-*shet*
knife	**un couteau**	uh koo-*toe*
napkin	**une serviette**	ewn sair-vee-*et*
platter of the day	**un plat du jour**	uh plah dew jhoor
spoon	**une cuillère**	ewn kwee-*air*
Cheers!	**A votre santé!**	ah vo-truh sahn-*tay*!
Can I buy you a drink?	**Puis-je vous acheter un verre?**	*pwee*-jhe voo *zahsh*-tay uh *vaihr*?
fixed-price menu	**un menu**	uh may-*new*
Is the tip/service included?	**Est-ce que le service est compris?**	ess-ke luh ser-*vees* eh com-*pree*?
Waiter!/Waitress!	**Monsieur!/Mademoiselle!**	mun-*syuh*/mad-mwa-*zel*

English	*French*	*Pronunciation*
wine list	**une carte des vins**	ewn cart day *van*
appetizer	**une entrée**	ewn en-*tray*
main course	**un plat principal**	uh plah pran-see-*pahl*
tip included	**service compris**	sehr-*vees* cohm-*pree*
drinks not included	**boissons non comprises**	bwa-*sons* no com-*pree*
It's good.	**C'était bon.**	set-*tey* bohn

Calendar

English	*French*	*Pronunciation*
Sunday	**dimanche**	dee-*mahnsh*
Monday	**lundi**	luhn-*dee*
Tuesday	**mardi**	mahr-*dee*
Wednesday	**mercredi**	mair-kruh-*dee*
Thursday	**jeudi**	jheu-*dee*
Friday	**vendredi**	vawn-druh-*dee*
Saturday	**samedi**	sahm-*dee*
yesterday	**Hier**	ee-*air*
today	**aujourd'hui**	o-jhord-*dwee*
this morning/ this afternoon	**ce matin/ cet après-midi**	suh ma-*tan*/ set ah-preh mee-*dee*
tonight	**ce soir**	suh *swahr*
tomorrow	**demain**	de-*man*

Index

Notes

BUSINESS, CAREERS & PERSONAL FINANCE

0-7645-5307-0   0-7645-5331-3 *†

Also available:
- Accounting For Dummies †
  0-7645-5314-3
- Business Plans Kit For Dummies †
  0-7645-5365-8
- Cover Letters For Dummies
  0-7645-5224-4
- Frugal Living For Dummies
  0-7645-5403-4
- Leadership For Dummies
  0-7645-5176-0
- Managing For Dummies
  0-7645-1771-6

- Marketing For Dummies
  0-7645-5600-2
- Personal Finance For Dummies *
  0-7645-2590-5
- Project Management
  For Dummies
  0-7645-5283-X
- Resumes For Dummies †
  0-7645-5471-9
- Selling For Dummies
  0-7645-5363-1
- Small Business Kit For Dummies *†
  0-7645-5093-4

HOME & BUSINESS COMPUTER BASICS

0-7645-4074-2   0-7645-3758-X

Also available:
- ACT! 6 For Dummies
  0-7645-2645-6
- iLife '04 All-in-One Desk Reference
  For Dummies
  0-7645-7347-0
- iPAQ For Dummies
  0-7645-6769-1
- Mac OS X Panther Timesaving
  Techniques For Dummies
  0-7645-5812-9
- Macs For Dummies
  0-7645-5656-8
- Microsoft Money 2004 For Dummies
  0-7645-4195-1

- Office 2003 All-in-One Desk
  Reference For Dummies
  0-7645-3883-7
- Outlook 2003 For Dummies
  0-7645-3759-8
- PCs For Dummies
  0-7645-4074-2
- TiVo For Dummies
  0-7645-6923-6
- Upgrading and Fixing PCs
  For Dummies
  0-7645-1665-5
- Windows XP Timesaving
  Techniques For Dummies
  0-7645-3748-2

FOOD, HOME, GARDEN, HOBBIES, MUSIC & PETS

0-7645-5295-3   0-7645-5232-5

Also available:
- Bass Guitar For Dummies
  0-7645-2487-9
- Diabetes Cookbook For Dummies
  0-7645-5230-9
- Gardening For Dummies *
  0-7645-5130-2
- Guitar For Dummies
  0-7645-5106-X
- Holiday Decorating For Dummies
  0-7645-2570-0
- Home Improvement All-in-One
  For Dummies
  0-7645-5680-0

- Knitting For Dummies
  0-7645-5395-X
- Piano For Dummies
  0-7645-5105-1
- Puppies For Dummies
  0-7645-5255-4
- Scrapbooking For Dummies
  0-7645-7208-3
- Senior Dogs For Dummies
  0-7645-5818-8
- Singing For Dummies
  0-7645-2475-5
- 30-Minute Meals For Dummies
  0-7645-2589-1

INTERNET & DIGITAL MEDIA

0-7645-1664-7   0-7645-6924-4

Also available:
- 2005 Online Shopping Directory
  For Dummies
  0-7645-7495-7
- CD & DVD Recording For Dummies
  0-7645-5956-7
- eBay For Dummies
  0-7645-5654-1
- Fighting Spam For Dummies
  0-7645-5965-6
- Genealogy Online For Dummies
  0-7645-5964-8
- Google For Dummies
  0-7645-4420-9

- Home Recording For Musicians
  For Dummies
  0-7645-1634-5
- The Internet For Dummies
  0-7645-4173-0
- iPod & iTunes For Dummies
  0-7645-7772-7
- Preventing Identity Theft
  For Dummies
  0-7645-7336-5
- Pro Tools All-in-One Desk
  Reference For Dummies
  0-7645-5714-9
- Roxio Easy Media Creator
  For Dummies
  0-7645-7131-1

SPORTS, FITNESS, PARENTING, RELIGION & SPIRITUALITY

0-7645-5146-9

0-7645-5418-2

Also available:

🖊Adoption For Dummies
0-7645-5488-3

🖊Basketball For Dummies
0-7645-5248-1

🖊The Bible For Dummies
0-7645-5296-1

🖊Buddhism For Dummies
0-7645-5359-3

🖊Catholicism For Dummies
0-7645-5391-7

🖊Hockey For Dummies
0-7645-5228-7

🖊Judaism For Dummies
0-7645-5299-6

🖊Martial Arts For Dummies
0-7645-5358-5

🖊Pilates For Dummies
0-7645-5397-6

🖊Religion For Dummies
0-7645-5264-3

🖊Teaching Kids to Read
For Dummies
0-7645-4043-2

🖊Weight Training For Dummies
0-7645-5168-X

🖊Yoga For Dummies
0-7645-5117-5

TRAVEL

0-7645-5438-7

0-7645-5453-0

Also available:

🖊Alaska For Dummies
0-7645-1761-9

🖊Arizona For Dummies
0-7645-6938-4

🖊Cancún and the Yucatán
For Dummies
0-7645-2437-2

🖊Cruise Vacations For Dummies
0-7645-6941-4

🖊Europe For Dummies
0-7645-5456-5

🖊Ireland For Dummies
0-7645-5455-7

🖊Las Vegas For Dummies
0-7645-5448-4

🖊London For Dummies
0-7645-4277-X

🖊New York City For Dummies
0-7645-6945-7

🖊Paris For Dummies
0-7645-5494-8

🖊RV Vacations For Dummies
0-7645-5443-3

🖊Walt Disney World & Orlando
For Dummies
0-7645-6943-0

GRAPHICS, DESIGN & WEB DEVELOPMENT

0-7645-4345-8

0-7645-5589-8

Also available:

🖊Adobe Acrobat 6 PDF
For Dummies
0-7645-3760-1

🖊Building a Web Site For Dummies
0-7645-7144-3

🖊Dreamweaver MX 2004
For Dummies
0-7645-4342-3

🖊FrontPage 2003 For Dummies
0-7645-3882-9

🖊HTML 4 For Dummies
0-7645-1995-6

🖊Illustrator CS For Dummies
0-7645-4084-X

🖊Macromedia Flash MX 2004
For Dummies
0-7645-4358-X

🖊Photoshop 7 All-in-One Desk
Reference For Dummies
0-7645-1667-1

🖊Photoshop CS Timesaving
Techniques For Dummies
0-7645-6782-9

🖊PHP 5 For Dummies
0-7645-4166-8

🖊PowerPoint 2003 For Dummies
0-7645-3908-6

🖊QuarkXPress 6 For Dummies
0-7645-2593-X

NETWORKING, SECURITY, PROGRAMMING & DATABASES

0-7645-6852-3

0-7645-5784-X

Also available:

🖊A+ Certification For Dummies
0-7645-4187-0

🖊Access 2003 All-in-One Desk
Reference For Dummies
0-7645-3988-4

🖊Beginning Programming
For Dummies
0-7645-4997-9

🖊C For Dummies
0-7645-7068-4

🖊Firewalls For Dummies
0-7645-4048-3

🖊Home Networking For Dummies
0-7645-42796

🖊Network Security For Dummies
0-7645-1679-5

🖊Networking For Dummies
0-7645-1677-9

🖊TCP/IP For Dummies
0-7645-1760-0

🖊VBA For Dummies
0-7645-3989-2

🖊Wireless All In-One Desk Reference
For Dummies
0-7645-7496-5

🖊Wireless Home Networking
For Dummies
0-7645-3910-8

7645-6820-5 *†   0-7645-2566-2

Also available:

- Alzheimer's For Dummies
  0-7645-3899-3
- Asthma For Dummies
  0-7645-4233-8
- Controlling Cholesterol For
  Dummies
  0-7645-5440-9
- Depression For Dummies
  0-7645-3900-0
- Dieting For Dummies
  0-7645-4149-8
- Fertility For Dummies
  0-7645-2549-2

- Fibromyalgia For Dummies
  0-7645-5441-7
- Improving Your Memory
  For Dummies
  0-7645-5435-2
- Pregnancy For Dummies †
  0-7645-4483-7
- Quitting Smoking For Dummies
  0-7645-2629-4
- Relationships For Dummies
  0-7645-5384-4
- Thyroid For Dummies
  0-7645-5385-2

DUCATION, HISTORY, REFERENCE & TEST PREPARATION

-7645-5194-9   0-7645-4186-2

Also available:

- Algebra For Dummies
  0-7645-5325-9
- British History For Dummies
  0-7645-7021-8
- Calculus For Dummies
  0-7645-2498-4
- English Grammar For Dummies
  0-7645-5322-4
- Forensics For Dummies
  0-7645-5580-4
- The GMAT For Dummies
  0-7645-5251-1
- Inglés Para Dummies
  0-7645-5427-1

- Italian For Dummies
  0-7645-5196-5
- Latin For Dummies
  0-7645-5431-X
- Lewis & Clark For Dummies
  0-7645-2545-X
- Research Papers For Dummies
  0-7645-5426-3
- The SAT I For Dummies
  0-7645-7193-1
- Science Fair Projects For Dummies
  0-7645-5460-3
- U.S. History For Dummies
  0-7645-5249-X

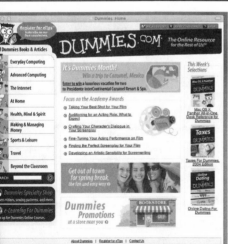

Get smart @ dummies.com®

- **Find a full list of Dummies titles**

- **Look into loads of FREE on-site articles**

- **Sign up for FREE eTips e-mailed to you weekly**

- **See what other products carry the Dummies name**

- **Shop directly from the Dummies bookstore**

- **Enter to win new prizes every month!**